A MIND OF
MY OWN

A MIND OF MY OWN

My Life with Robert Maxwell

ELISABETH MAXWELL

SIDGWICK & JACKSON
LONDON

First published 1994 by HarperCollins Publishers Inc, New York

First published in Great Britain by Sidgwick & Jackson
an imprint of Macmillan General Books
Cavaye Place London SW10 9PG
and Basingstoke

Associated companies throughout the world

ISBN 0 283 06251 7

1 3 5 7 9 8 6 4 2

A CIP catalogue record for this book is available
from the British Library

Printed by Mackays of Chatham PLC,
Chatham, Kent

To the four "White Knights" who saved me when I was hounded, homeless and greatly in debt, when no one else had the courage to do so.

To my sister, who has been endlessly generous with her time, money and medical skills.

To members of Bob's and my family and many old and new friends who helped me to survive financially or bought back some of my possessions at auction. To all those who have given me freely of their time, expertise and love and who continue to weave an invisible safety net around me, supporting me when I falter.

To all those whose friendship and support for my two beleaguered sons remain undiminished.

Finally, to all my beloved children, whose infinite love, tenderness, constant help and support have been my spur to fight another day, and another and another, till God grants me leave to retire.

ACKNOWLEDGMENTS

Soon after starting to write this book in May 1992, I realized that I had greatly underestimated the amount of work involved and that I would have to concentrate on my writing virtually to the exclusion of all other activities. My family and friends have encouraged me unstintingly and I would particularly like to thank my long-time friend Wendy Whitworth, who has been my closest collaborator and without whose constant support, coupled with excellent research and editing skills, I doubt I would have been able to complete the book. I also owe a debt of gratitutde to Robert Stewart, the distinguished American editor who helped me in the formulation of the initial publishing proposal.

Special thanks also go to all those who have been directly involved in publishing my book in England, America and France. In London, my literary agent, Hilary Rubenstein, has been an unfailing source of encouragement; it was largely thanks to him that I decided to write this book. He in turn introduced me to William Armstrong, my English publisher, in charge of Macmillan's Sidgwick and Jackson imprint. In New York, my literary agent, Owen Laster, of William Morris, kept up my morale when I despaired of finding an American publisher, and it also gives me pleasure to thank Rupert Murdoch, who "turned the tide" for me by reading the proposal himself and recommending the book to HarperCollins. I could not have wished for a more understanding, enthusiastic and supportive editor at Harper than Larry Ashmead, whose unfailing courtesy and experience have been a real source of support at every step of the publishing process. Last but not least, I wish to thank my French publisher, Bernard Fixot, Chairman of Robert Laffont-Fixot, for his early support, understanding and patience at a time when the sky was very dark indeed; he has proved a staunch friend.

I am indebted to countless people who allowed me to interview them and who answered my many queries, however abstruse, researching in their own archives and unraveling past mysteries for me; and to many other friends who have supported me in a multitude of ways through the last two years with infinite kindness and patience. I am particularly grateful to Jean Baddeley for relieving me of so much of my day-to-day correspondence and other administrative burdens, to Oping Aranar for looking after my physical and material well-being and doubling up as office clerk and to Robert Ord for countless hours of driving and endless fetching and carrying in his free time.

INTRODUCTION

Many people will wonder why I have written this book; some will condemn me for it, some will think I did it for my own aggrandizement; many who are prejudiced by what they have read in the newspapers or who only knew my husband in the last few years of his life will assume it is a hagiography and dismiss it as such. But I hope there will be a majority, still, who can approach the book with an open mind. Laurie Lee wrote that "Autobiography can be the laying to rest of ghosts as well as an ordering of the mind." I share his view that it is also a "celebration to praise the life I'd had and so preserve it, and to live again both the good and the bad."[1] This book is above all an exploration of the events of my life based on my memories, my archives, the diaries I kept and the thousands of letters I wrote or received from my parents, from Bob, the children and our many friends throughout my life. Much of the factual material of my book has been drawn from or checked against those original documents, although of course my interpretation of them may well differ from that of other observers.

I had always intended to write a book about my life alongside Bob, although originally it would have been written only for my family and close friends. Throughout my life, I collected thousands of papers and other items for my scrapbooks, which over the years have developed into a comprehensive personal archive. When, therefore, in the circumstances of 1991 I felt compelled to write my story for a wider audience, I had much of the necessary material at hand.

---

1. Laurie Lee, *I Can't Stay Long* (London: Penguin Books, 1947), p. 49.

These unique archives have enabled me to review many original documents and then write with authority and in detail on a wide range of subjects; through them, I was also able to ascertain the literally hundreds of incorrect facts that have already appeared in the various published biographies about Bob Maxwell.

One important motive for my writing the book was to try and set the record straight concerning several key areas of Bob's life and thereby enable readers to form their own opinion based on a fuller and more accurate account of events than has been provided hitherto. I also wanted to describe events from my own perspective in order to balance some of the more fantasy-inspired accounts that have appeared in the press and try to counter the dehumanizing tendencies evident in much of the comment about him since Bob's death. Living with Bob from 1945 to 1991 gave me a unique insight into his character, and I developed a detailed and personal knowledge of many aspects of his life. I refer not only to our family life, but to Bob's business ventures as well, from their beginnings in the postwar period until the early eighties when he entered his "tycoon" phase and spent more time on his own. I was at his side as he built up his publishing house Pergamon Press and was heavily involved in political work in his North Bucks constituency. In another important area, that of Bob's early life from 1923 to the end of the war, I was certain that I could contribute by far the most authoritative and accurate record so far, based on my earliest wartime memories of his own account of his youth and our contemporaneous correspondence, and subsequently on my own contacts with his family. I wanted to be able to provide a personal dimension to Bob's character, since obviously I can claim to have known this side better than anyone else. I knew what he cared most about, what his motives were, his anxieties and the pain he suffered.

No future assessment of Bob's life and career can possibly claim to be complete without some analysis of the human and intimate aspects of his character known only to close family members and long-standing friends and colleagues. Nowhere, to my knowledge, has there been a sufficiently comprehensive attempt to analyze Bob's psychological makeup and interpret his various and deepest motives. Such efforts as there have been are of limited scope and broadly hostile. Indeed, since his death, whenever two different motives could be ascribed to his actions, almost invariably the least favorable one was chosen to present him in the worst possible light, with little attempt to depict the multiple facets of a complex character. I can by no means claim to have filled this important lacuna completely, but I am certain that I have provided some useful material for future consideration of Bob's personality. In so doing, I have tried to write about him sympathetically, yet have not shrunk from revealing less attractive features of his private behavior.

It was not an easy decision to make public certain aspects of our private life, which in different circumstances would have been better left unsaid. In this dilemma, I was helped by one of my mentors, Roy Eckardt, who quoted Edward L. Galligant's words to me: "Artists cannot be choosers, they have to do the work that wants to be done by them, not the work that sensible people think they ought to do."[2] Faced with the wholly distorted picture that the public now has of Bob, I felt I had to publish intensely personal correspondence between us that, while revealing the many flaws in his character as I saw them, also depicts a passionate and intensely loving husband and father. His faults were by nature different from those ascribed to him by people who only knew him slightly or not at all. He was in the final analysis only a man, not the degenerate monster the press has invented.

It would not be possible to refute the myriad allegations made about Bob after his death, many prompted by malice or based on a desire to cash in on the public's thirst, fanned by the press, for scandalous "revelations." Such an approach would be tiresome and disruptive to the thread of my own story. The sheer complexity of Bob's life and business affairs already made my task difficult enough. My memories of close to fifty years of life with him were so rich and so numerous that "the pain of selection became a daily concern, and progress was marked by what was left out."[3] Thousands of hours of life together had to be compressed into a few pages, yet the reader has to be made aware of the passing of time and the excitement surrounding the events of our lives. As a guideline, I followed the advice of the French biographer Marguerite Yourcenar that one must be in a position to reveal every last detail, but refrain from doing so because many are unimportant.

The daunting complexity of Bob's life perhaps explains to a large extent the inconsistencies in the published biographies about him. I have learned from experience how difficult and time-consuming it is to piece together authoritative accounts of some of the major and controversial events of his life and frequently found it necessary to carry out

---

2. Roy Eckardt, *Collecting Myself* (Atlanta: Scholars Press, 1933), p. vii.

3. Laurie Lee, *I Can't Stay Long,* p. 51.

further research and to interview the protagonists concerned to confirm and put right errors in previous accounts that I knew or felt instinctively to be untrue. I hope in the end that my book will contribute a valuable quantum of new information to facilitate the understanding of certain key episodes—Bob's relationship with Ferdinand Springer, his early business ventures, the foundation and growth of Pergamon Press, the Leasco affair and the successes and failures of his political career—all of which to a greater or lesser degree I participated in. In the case of other milestone events in his business career, particularly in the last ten years of his life, I was far more remotely involved, if at all, frequently learning of major investments and acquistions after the fact. Although I may have added a useful dimension to these subjects, I make no claim to have understood everything perfectly, on the contrary. I am simply offering a version of events and the personalities who took part in them as seen through my eyes. There are many things that still puzzle me and I have not hesitated to say so.

For this reason, I consider my book part—and only part—of a long and unfolding process of elucidation, interpretation and understanding of the continuing controversy surrounding our family and Bob's business career. Given the historical backdrop of our respective lives, the story could only be a complex one. There was first the difference in our religious backgrounds and upbringing in such vastly different social milieux, the turbulence of the times in which we met and the fast-changing postwar years. Most important of all, there was the added complexity of the close entwinement of our family and business lives, in the midst of my trying to raise our family alongside a business that, at its height, employed some 30,000 people worldwide. Herein lay the real crux of my problem, for while writing my own autobiography, I was also of necessity writing Bob's biography; in fact, I have come to think of my work as a "dual biography." Although this made writing the book more complicated and the difficulties of selection and balance more acute, it is nevertheless true to the life we led together.

Yet I have called my book *A Mind of My Own*, focused on me and not on Bob, because one of the most important themes in the book is my own struggle to live beside such a dominating and demanding man without having important aspects of my own personality submerged in his. Although I realize that the majority of people will read my book for its stories and for the insights into Bob Maxwell's character, I hope that some will find encouragement in the account of my own survival and my gradually discovering greater confidence in my own abilities, as well as a deeper understanding of Bob's psychology. It will remain to my eternal regret that I did not understand earlier in our lives together the strength that Bob derived from his own Jewish tradition, without his being fully conscious of it himself, and the extent to which his religion could have helped him overcome some of his worst flaws of character. He seemed cast right from the beginning in the role of the Greek tragic hero, who is inevitably defeated in the end, since in Greek mythology, man cannot avoid the gods' anger or vengeance if he rebels against them in an attempt to alter his destiny. "Man is punished, executed by order of the gods. Once the verdict is given, man has no recourse, no future. Man's death, therefore, is never natural—it is always murder. In this view of history, man's future is paralyzed, petrified in the present. The first defeat is also the last."[4] Bob, however, never accepted defeat, he fought over and over again and triumphed against tremendous odds, but towards the end of his life, his "worship of power had resurrected the demon of power."[5] This obsession was to transform his life completely, dangerously stunting his appreciation of beauty and grandeur, the more humble joys of life, the warmth of family love, leading him to throw elementary caution to the wind and seek increasingly to discard all restrictions in his life. It was ultimately to lead to the total collapse of the business he had worked so hard to create, with ensuing untold consequences for his own family and friends and for colleagues, employees and their loved ones.

Writing *A Mind of My Own* represented a great challenge for me, not least because of the complexity of the task and the limitations imposed by the impending trial of my sons Ian and Kevin. I make no claims to have provided all the answers and can only echo Aneurin Bevan's telling comment, "This is my truth; what is yours?"[6]

---

4. Elie Wiesel, *Against Silence: The Voice and Vision of Elie Wiesel* (New York: Holocaust Library, 1985), p. 322.

5. John C. Merkle, *The Genesis of Faith: The Depth Psychology of Abraham Joshua Heschel* (New York: Macmillan Inc., 1985) p. 56.

6. Jennie Lee, *My Life with Nye* (London: Jonathan Cape, 1980), p. 22.

PROLOGUE

The sun was going down over Jerusalem, setting the horizon afire. On the Mount of Olives the crowd gathered around the tomb was silent. Even the swarm of journalists and photographers lining the top of the cemetery wall had momentarily abandoned their intrusive activity at the splendor of the spectacle.

Against the crimson streaked skies rose the massive ruins of the Second Temple surrounded by Herod's ancient walls. The golden dome of the great mosque shimmered in the sun's dying rays and the minarets and steeples of the old city stood out against the horizon, like lances decked with rich purple and gold-fringed banners, an unforgettable backdrop to the tragedy whose last scene was unfolding before us.

As the evening haze began to blur the landmarks of the walled city and the amphitheater of the surrounding hills of Judea vanished in the approaching night, the grave diggers, helped by men of the family, shoveled rapidly to cover the sealed grave with stony earth, which had to be completed, according to custom, before sunset. All eyes were riveted on the tomb and on the horizon at the same time; it was as if everyone was holding his breath in a curious moment of complete silence. Then, all of a sudden, a vibrant and tumultuous chorus shattered the frozen silence with a kyrie of pealing bells, the song of cantors and the call of countless muezzins. Overhead the sky became leaden, while a sudden gust of icy wind from the Kidron Valley carried the ancient liturgies on the air, uniting them in adoration of divinity. It was a pageant of *son et lumière,* which no one present would ever forget.

Shivering in the autumn wind that shot right through my hastily assembled funeral outfit, I cast a final glance at the place where I was leaving the man of my life for ever. He was at peace. We had traveled a long way through life together and now he had left me to face the world alone. Strengthened by the love and concern of my Israeli friends, who cleared a path for me through the bystanders gathered on that narrow terrace, I walked back to the only car allowed to enter the cemetery. It was going to take me back to the plane waiting at Jerusalem's Atarot Airport.

For a moment, I was completely lost, frightened, bewildered. I had so wanted to be strong for the children and for myself, but six days of high drama had taken their toll. I wished I could have been laid by Bob's side in that heavenly place of enduring peace.

I was brought back to reality sharply when two of my daughters joined me for the drive to the airport. As the car sped away, with the last camera flashes piercing the darkness, the moving words of Shimon Peres resounded in my ears: "He lost his breath in the vast sea, but not his soul. It will float above the waves as a marker to anyone believing that a man's life can be bigger than the cards he is dealt."

Yes, Bob would have been proud of such a breathtaking and dramatic funeral in the Holy City, dignified yet unexpectedly public, with so many of the Israeli government present to mourn one of their own, the prodigal son who had come home, the soldier who had defied the odds, the courageous friend of Israel, the loving husband and father, the survivor who had finally surrendered his life into the hands of his God and his body to the earth of Israel.

When we arrived at Atarot, there was yet more handshaking and more formal good-byes before I was able to board the plane. I welcomed the familiar, cool surroundings of the Gulf Stream jet; it was a real haven of peace. For the return journey to London, I had arranged to be accompanied only by my children. Very soon, the plane soared through the obscurity of night. For the first time since that fateful moment six days earlier when I learned that my husband was lost at sea, I was no longer on display, no longer on parade. My family and I were totally exhausted; we had all shared an enormous burden. But in the end, we had done our utmost for a man who would have expected no less.

After a brief exchange of final impressions, we all returned to our seats and to our own thoughts. I let my mind drift, unimpeded, into waves of daydreaming, slipping back unconsciously through the web of the past. All kinds of memories bombarded my mind, the most recent clamoring for my attention. I was not dozing. I was awake, but I was dreaming. Where was I? What was happening? Was all this drama I had just lived through real? What on earth was I doing in this plane without Bob? I felt certain that any minute now he might come and sit down opposite me and rest his legs on either side of my body, just as he always liked to do when we were traveling together. Had I really left him all alone on that sacred hillside?

Miraculously, I had succeeded in carrying out his last wishes, according to his will. Surely he would have approved of everything I had done. Tomorrow, he would say, "Thanks Betty, please forgive me for leaving you all alone to bury me in Israel and in the most difficult circumstances. But I knew you could and would do it. Now you have done it and I am proud of you; I am at peace and you should be content."

Yes, I was content that he was buried in Jerusalem, exactly where he wanted. All the rites of his own Jewish tradition had been observed; he was safe, he was surrounded by loving people who respected their dead; there was nothing more I could do for him.

It had all happened so quickly, and yet, when everything appeared to conspire against the successful completion of my task, the days had seemed so interminably long. Was it really only six days since my son Kevin had telephoned me that Tuesday morning?

"Mummy, I've got to break some dreadful news. I don't know how to tell you this. I'm so sorry . . . Dad is lost at sea."

"What do you mean, 'lost at sea'? How can Dad get lost? Are you trying to tell me he's drowned?"

"No, just that he's not on the boat, he's nowhere to be found."

"I don't believe it. It must be a joke. Have they looked everywhere?"

"Yes, they've searched the boat three times. All they can assume is that somehow or other he left the *Lady Ghislaine* and that he's possibly drowned. You'll have to fly out immediately to Tenerife and assist in any way you can. Dad just has to be found, dead or alive. I've got a plane waiting for you at Farnborough and I'm sending the helicopter to fetch you. One of the family will go with you. Mum, we love you, be strong for all of us."

I remember calling for Oping, my Filipino housekeeper who had been with me for over two decades, telling her there had been an accident and that I had to fly out to the boat immediately. Hurriedly I grabbed a bag and threw in a few clothes, all as somber as my own mood. As I left my bedroom, a sudden impulse made me pick up my Bible from my bedside. Then I rushed off with every conceivable scenario racing through my mind.

Minutes before my departure from Oxford, the *Daily Mirror*'s editor, Richard Stott, phoned me. He was offering his help and wanted to send some staff to accompany me: John Jackson, one of his most experienced journalists and a personal friend, together with a top photographer, Ken Lennox, whom Bob liked. Both men were apparently stunned by the news; they were sensitive and would help me cope with the world's press, who would undoubtedly harass me. It was a suggestion I readily accepted.

I recall little of those nightmare helicopter journeys, first to Maxwell House in London to see Kevin and Ian, and then, with my eldest son Philip, to Farnborough Airport. All I remember is my desperate attempt to remain rational and collected in spite of the gloom that pervaded my every thought. Philip was to travel with me to Tenerife since his fluent Spanish would be of infinite help, and Ian and Kevin had decided that it was better for them to stay at the helm in London to face the reaction of the business world when the news became public.

We flew in one of the company's jets, and as the plane roared off on its journey towards Spain's Canary Islands, the news of the search for Bob was tracked on the on-board radio, and the pilot relayed the information to me in his tactful and compassionate way. As I sat, numb and frozen, the echo of Kevin's last words haunted my thoughts: I had to find my husband—dead or alive.

When still in London, we had learned that a Mayday signal had gone out to all shipping in the vicinity of the *Lady Ghislaine* and that rescue planes and helicopters had left the Spanish mainland and were scouring the waters of the Atlantic Ocean for miles around. About three in the afternoon, Philip managed to make radio contact from our plane with the Madrid HQ of the Spanish Air-Sea Rescue Service. The latest news was that no body had yet been sighted, but the search would continue until sunset. To me that journey seemed interminable. All I could do was sit and wait, my heart heavy, my body tense, frustrated at my total inability to take any action whatsoever. I just prayed and racked my brain for a plausible explanation. Philip contacted Madrid again, this time to ensure that every possible resource had been deployed in the search. Then, at around six in the evening, when visibility was virtually zero and the search was close to being abandoned for the day, news came that a body had been spotted and would be picked up by helicopter. Half an hour later, we heard that the body recovered from the sea seemed to correspond to the description of the missing press magnate, but official identification would be required before it could be confirmed that it was my husband's.

At this point, we gave instructions to our pilot to seek to divert to Gando military air base on Las Palmas Island, since we had learned from the Air-Sea Rescue Service that they would take the body there. We were given permission and told they would wait until our plane had landed before transferring the body from the rescue helicopter to the airport buildings. I was still trying to absorb the initial shock. I was observing and reacting to events like a stranger, detached, almost as if all this was happening to someone else.

As I stepped from the plane, at about 8:30 P.M., a throng of photographers was already assembled. I walked briskly, an air force officer clearing a path for me through the crowd, and was ushered into the office of the major on duty, where I was also met by the British vice-consul for Las Palmas. Dazed and shaken, I let my eyes wander to the window and caught sight of a stretcher covered in white canvas being unloaded from a nearby helicopter and brought into the base. My heart lurched. My only thought was to follow the stretcher immediately. I blurted out my request but was politely told I would have to wait until the room was ready, whatever that meant. Soon the helicopter pilot, Captain Jesus Fernandez Vaca of the Spanish National Rescue Service, came personally to meet me and I asked him to tell me about the search. I desperately wanted to hear the truth from him. I wanted him to tell me in detail how he had found my husband's body and how he had managed to recover it from the sea. It still seemed so unreal. In his good English, he described everything he knew about the rescue mission; how they had searched for hours finding nothing, how they had been almost ready to give up for the day, when suddenly with the sun already very low on the horizon, he had spotted a body. He told me the exact condition of the body when he found it and its geographical location, and gave me his opinion that it had been in the water for about twelve hours. I remember asking him a few more questions about his own experience and discovering that he had been doing rescue operations for some twelve years; he had recovered literally hundreds of bodies from the sea. No one could dispute his expertise and, curiously, his honest and matter-of-fact way of answering my questions helped me to withstand the shock.

t half an hour later, a judge arrived; Philip and I were then
down a confined corridor to a room at the end. As we went
w a body covered with a white sheet stretched out on a nar-
able. Two doctors, a man and a woman wearing white coats,
were in attendance, standing near the body. The vice-consul, a police
officer and other officials were seated on chairs lined up along one
side of the room.

I braced myself, fearing from all I had heard about drowning
that the body would look bloated or mauled by sharks. I walked
slowly towards the head of the stretcher. The lady doctor lifted the
sheet, uncovering Bob's face and torso. It was him as he had been in
life; his jet-black hair was slightly discolored by the sun and the saltwater, his face at peace. Even in death he looked a most impressive
figure. His arms were resting alongside his body, but they were
slightly bent at the elbows and his fists were clenched, almost aggres-
sively. He seemed taller; his body was completely straight and his
whole bearing was one of extreme dignity, even defiance. His presence was commanding in death, just as it had been when he was
alive. There he was, lying dead and yet his imposing attitude moved
everyone in the room into silence. We were all stunned, and I felt
intimidated: the combined emotions of grief, shock, fear, sadness,
awe and perplexity that overshadowed us were almost too much to
bear.

I would dearly have liked to be alone for a moment with my
giant of a man, but this was not even suggested. Although I felt
embarrassed, I asked them to remove the sheet completely: I needed
to be sure that his body was whole and intact. I noticed nothing
abnormal, except for slight bleeding from the nose, which I was told
was usual in such circumstances of death. I touched his forehead and
tried to put my hand into his clenched fist. His hand felt almost soft,
and I remember finding it strange that rigor mortis had not set in.
His face, untouched by the pallor of death, still looked slightly
tanned, as it always had.

Also present were two pathologists—Dr. Carlos Lopez de
Lamela, who turned out to be the director of the Las Palmas Forensic Institute and Dr. Garcia Cohen. They and Dr. Maria Ramos were
later to carry out the autopsy, but at that point they asked me a few
straightforward questions about Bob's health and about the drugs he
used to take. Philip and I stayed there some twenty minutes, whis-
pering our impressions to each other, both equally struck by how
lifelike he seemed and how distinguished he looked in death.

Before I left, the doctors told me they believed he must have died of a heart attack, but his body would be needed for an official autopsy. When we asked how long it would take, we were told it would be a few days and that they personally would be doing it. "Do you require the presence of a British pathologist?" asked the Spanish doctors. We consulted, and I declined. At the time, this question seemed totally incongruous to me: what good would it do to fly in any doctors? Bob was dead, no one could bring him back to life. All I wanted was to bury him as soon as possible.

This, however, was not going to be as straightforward as I had hoped. Not only was an autopsy to be carried out but also some kind of inquest or inquiry by the Spanish authorities. A judge, who was present at the air base, then told us that we would be required to attend a hearing in Las Palmas the next day to answer questions and make statements.

Philip and I then prepared to leave the air base. Preceded by the officers and the two *Mirror* reporters who had rejoined us in the corridor, we faced the mass of photographers and journalists, which by this time had doubled in size. We eventually managed to fight our way through to our plane and took off immediately for Tenerife Airport on Gran Canaria Island. Fortunately, Julio Claverie, a local lawyer chosen for me by my friend Dr. Samuel Pisar, a well-known international lawyer, was there at Tenerife Airport to help us. He cleverly organized taxis to elude the pursuing reporters as we made our way to Los Cristianos harbor, where the *Lady Ghislaine* was now anchored.

Mercifully, our intended movements had not been divulged to the media, and we boarded the yacht without being besieged. As we went aboard, the captain and entire crew lined up, as was the custom when the owner arrived, offering their condolences as I passed by. Captain Rankin then introduced me to a police officer who was on board, before asking me which cabin I wished to use. Almost without thinking, I replied "Mine," meaning the owner's cabin. But the captain told me that this would not be possible; the police had apparently requested that nothing should be touched. Turning to the police officer, I inquired how long his investigation would last. I was dumbfounded to hear him reply that in fact he had already finished.

"Have you completely finished?"

"Yes."

"You've seen all you wish to see?"

"Yes."

"Then you have no objection to my using the cabin tonight?"

"None at all, but just one thing—you won't be able to use the safe because it's been sealed."

"Sealed? Why was it sealed?"

"Because it couldn't be opened."

"Why not, since the captain has the key?"

"The captain says he hasn't got a key."

"But the captains have always had the key. What's happened to it?"

"No, Mrs. Maxwell, I've never had the key."

I could not understand this. The captains have always had the safe key, so they could give it to charterers. I had a key as well, which was always kept on the boat with my costume jewelry. The stewards who cleaned the cabin knew perfectly well where to find it. And when the yacht was under charter, my own key, along with all my personal possessions, went into the hold and the captain gave the charterers the only remaining key. The system had always worked very well.

At this point, I went straight to the jewelry drawer in my dressing room, found the key and handed it to the police officer. But he refused to take it and said that the safe could not be opened unless his commanding officer, who had sealed it, was present. We agreed that it could be done the next morning.

The mystery of the key troubled me, especially the captain's response. I had not met Captain Rankin before. He was tall and rather stout, in uniform, but casually so, not giving the spruce naval appearance of previous captains, as one would expect on a luxury yacht like the *Lady Ghislaine*. Some of the crew gave me the same first impression. The boat did not seem quite "ship-shape" to me. It had, admittedly, been preparing for a long sail, but that was all the more reason to run a tight crew—and that did not appear to be fully the case. I felt that not enough attention had been paid to details of the kind Bob used to insist on, or which I did when I went on the boat. Perhaps I was hypersensitive in those incredibly difficult first moments on board, and above all I must recognize that the captain and the crew themselves were under great stress, too. During my few days on the *Lady Ghislaine,* my painful impression about the crew never quite left me. The captain did not know me, yet he immediately adopted a familiar way of talking about Bob, which I did not like at all because it didn't quite ring true, familiar as I was with Bob's loathing for intimate conversation. But I desperately needed his cooperation, so I tried hard not to pass judgment on first impressions, formed perhaps as a consequence of my own state of mind.

When the Spanish police officer had taken his leave, I asked the captain to sail the *Lady Ghislaine* out of the harbor so that we would at least be able to sleep in peace, away from the frantic attention of the world's press. I also remember asking to be left alone in the cabin for a moment, so that I could telephone London and talk to Ian and Kevin, then change into cooler clothes. I told the stewardesses that as soon as I was ready, I would like them to straighten out the cabin, put clean linen on the bed and in the bathrooms, hang my clothes up and follow normal procedure, just as if Mr. Maxwell were still alive.

Speaking to my sons in London, I was able to confirm what they already knew from the media, adding some details I thought they would like to hear from me, and I in turn wanted to hear from them that their sisters had all been told the news. We agreed that I would talk again to the captain and then speak to them later that night.

When I went into the cabin, it looked precisely as Bob would leave it at any time of the day or night: his swimming trunks, still damp, lay on the bathroom floor, his trousers in a heap on the carpet just where he had stepped out of them, a pair of undershorts a bit further away; sweatshirts were strewn on the settee, socks near the bed, orange peel on the floor, an empty glass on the bedside table. I noticed there was a nightshirt lying crumpled in a corner near the bed, but that, too, was perfectly normal. I knew that Bob would wake up several times during the night, get up, take a stroll or fetch a drink. Because he perspired a great deal, he would invariably change his clammy nightshirt for a freshly laundered one before getting back into bed. The entire scene before me looked so very familiar. I could hardly believe I wouldn't see him framed in the doorway any minute.

After freshening up in the mess of my own bathroom, which Bob used as well as his own because it was more spacious, I joined my guests to see them comfortably settled into their respective cabins. I then asked the captain to come and see me; I was longing to ask him a whole host of questions which perturbed me, but we only had a short talk because I was tired and knew that my companions were hungry. Nevertheless, at the very least, I had to know when the captain had discovered that Bob was missing, what he had done and what he thought had happened. But none of the explanations I hastily gathered that night eased my mind. I would talk to the captain at greater length the next morning. I had to be satisfied for the moment with his explanations.

At about ten o'clock that Tuesday evening, the fifth of November, we sat down to a frugal dinner with Philip, Ken and John going over the events of the day and starting to speculate as to what could possibly have happened. Both outsiders were very discreet, sympathetic, obviously moved and slightly uneasy in my presence since we had never met before. I did my best to put them at their ease, thanked them for having come and for whatever help they would be able to give me in the days that lay ahead.

Dinner was constantly interrupted by a stream of telephone calls. There were so many that I find it difficult to remember them all, but I distinctly recall the one from Samuel Pisar, who represented my husband in France. His words were comforting, supportive, yet he was the first person to sow doubts in my mind about Bob's death. Had I noticed anything abnormal on Bob's body or in talking to the captain and crew? Was it possible that he'd been murdered? My heart missed a beat. In a flash, I recalled all the death threats Bob had received over the years. My whole world was shaken to its core; from now on, reality gave way to high drama. Sam then told me about the local Spanish lawyer, Julio Claverie, whom he had located and who would come to visit me the next day; without such legal help, he said, I would have no hope of completing all the necessary procedures to allow me to take Bob's body out of Spanish territory, even less of flying it to Israel before the coming Sabbath. In any case, we would stay in close touch and I was to phone him at any hour of the day or night if there was any news. On his side, Sam would liaise with Israel. It was clear that if I did not obtain the necessary documentation to fly the body out in time, the funeral would be postponed until the following week. This was not only contrary to Jewish custom, but I really did not feel strong enough to endure ten days of morbid waiting. Sam assured me that he would alert Bob's lawyer in Israel, Yaakov Neeman, to put everything in motion for his funeral in Jerusalem; he would also find out what had to be done to comply with the rites of the Jewish religion and an Orthodox Jewish burial, as Bob had requested in his will.

I was so grateful to Sam. However well informed and knowledgeable we are about a religion other than our own, it is extremely difficult to understand fully the conventions of another tradition. We always lack the deep and instinctive knowledge that is acquired during childhood or by experience. I so wanted to respect every minute requirement, with all the precise attention to detail which Bob had always tried to inculcate in his family.

I finally went back to my cabin at about midnight. I lay in bed wide awake, trying to think what I should be doing, what Bob would have liked, what he would have expected me to do—"the guardian of his Jewish soul," he liked to call me. The more I thought about the mystery of his death, the less I could comprehend it. How could it have happened? I must admit that the idea that he might have committed suicide did cross my mind, but I could not take it seriously. It was just not in character. Bob was totally against suicide; he considered it the coward's way out and used to say it was against his religion! I remembered how fiercely we had argued over the double suicide of Arthur Koestler and his wife; how I had judged it to be immensely courageous, feeling that though I could never approve of such an act, I admired their bravery and the love that had prompted his wife, even though she was much younger than he, to take her own life. The thought kept nagging at me, but I could not think of anything I knew about Bob's life that would justify his dying by his own hand. If there had been any premeditation, I kept thinking, surely he would have left some sort of note for me, or for his children or for his lawyers.

It was very late, but sleep eluded me. This idea of a note totally obsessed me. I decided to search the cabin. I knew Bob's habits very well: all his life he had had special places where he would put his money or an important letter. Often it was absurdly obvious, like the pocket of his dressing gown, or his handkerchief drawer, or his pullover drawer, between the pages of a book or on the highest shelf in his cupboard. I knew all these little hiding places—so did his valet. They were almost a joke. So I started searching his dressing room, meticulously. I went through all his pockets, all his drawers, all the shelves. I looked under the mattress, in the pillowcases, in the bathroom, everywhere. I didn't just do it once, I did it three times. If Bob had planned his death, I was absolutely certain he would have left a note, at least for me.

Then I went next door to Bob's study; on the desk lay a heap of faxed newspaper articles, front pages and leaders from the major British and American newspapers. Beside it stood five black leather pilot cases, which he used as briefcases. Looking into my husband's papers was something I never did unless Bob specifically asked me to. All our lives together, I had respected his papers totally, as he had mine. I had never known him to pry in my desk and read a single letter, nor I in his. Our confidence in each other was partly based on this very simple mark of respect for each other's "private garden." I looked at every sheet of paper, every file, every envelope, bent only on discovering a note in Bob's own hand that might give me a clue. There was nothing, absolutely nothing to alleviate my pain. It was nearly five o'clock in the morning when I finally decided to give up and go to bed. I was worn out, bewildered, my mind was in a spin, but through sheer exhaustion, I ultimately fell asleep. Meantime the boat sailed through the night, away from Los Cristianos towards Santa Cruz, Tenerife.

It was already ten o'clock when I woke up on Wednesday morning. The yacht was anchored in Darcena, a little fishing village north of Santa Cruz. My first full day as Bob Maxwell's widow had begun. I had a bath, dressed and went up the internal staircase to the observation lounge, where I found my new friends having breakfast. Philip had woken up early and had started talking to some crew members before they had to leave to be questioned by the Spanish police leading the investigation, as was routine when a man was lost at sea. Whilst I was having breakfast, Señor Julio Hernandez Claverie, "my" new Spanish lawyer, arrived. He was simpatico enough, spoke good English and, thankfully, put me wise immediately as to what to expect from the Spanish authorities following such a catastrophe.

I listened to Señor Claverie's outline of events with a growing sense of foreboding. First of all, he would accompany both Philip and me later that morning to make declarations and be questioned by the judge on Las Palmas Island, in whose jurisdiction Bob's body then was. As for the autopsy, that would take a week. By then I had realized that if I were to have the slightest hope of burying my husband in Jerusalem, on the following Sunday, in accordance with Orthodox Jewish requirements and the wishes of the Israeli authorities, I would have to intervene forcefully, Maxwell style, and not leave the direction of operations to the Spaniards and their traditional *mañana*. Poor Señor Claverie then had to listen to my version of forthcoming events. I told him that my husband was Jewish, that his wish was to be buried in the Orthodox tradition in Jerusalem, that it had to happen at the latest next Sunday (that is, in four days' time), that no burial rites could take place on the Sabbath and that no body could be received in Israel after sunset on Friday. All of this meant my husband's body would have to be on board our plane on Thursday evening and we would have to leave the Canary Islands before midnight—only sixty hours away.

I watched as Señor Claverie's face, already sallow in complexion, turned literally ashen. "Missis Maxehwell," he said, "this is just impossible, but I shall try." On this he departed, after giving me various addresses and telephone numbers where I could reach him.

I remember vividly the telephone call I received early that Wednesday morning from the company's insurance brokers, telling me that pathologists acting for the insurance companies would arrive on Saturday. "But that will be too late," I told them, and I went on to outline the plans for the burial in Israel, emphasizing why they would have to come right away. The brokers said they would talk to the insurers and come back to me. That did not happen until Thursday morning, when they told me that the English pathologists chosen, Dr. West and his wife, were busy elsewhere and could travel to the Canaries only on Friday at the earliest. In any case, they told me, it didn't matter very much because Dr. West would prefer to carry out an autopsy in Tel Aviv, where the laboratories had better facilities. So the relevant Tel Aviv authorities were contacted for permission to conduct the autopsy in Israel on the Saturday after the Sabbath, which was eventually granted, after I had impressed on Yaakov Neeman how important Dr. West's examination would be. We learned later that the Wests and a team of Israeli pathologists worked all that Saturday evening and throughout the night. Later still, we were to see tangible proof in the videotape stolen from the laboratory and sold to the French magazine *Paris Match* that the collaboration had been friendly and that all facilities had been extended to Dr. West.

In time for 11 A.M. as planned, Philip and I were flown to Las Palmas and went to the office of Judge Gutierrez Ruiz, where we had to declare our relationship to the deceased, how long we had known him, what we knew of his lifestyle, of his health and how we thought he might have come to his end. We then returned to the *Lady Ghislaine*, with the promise that the death certificate would follow in due course. By the time we returned from our meeting with the judge, it was already fairly late in the afternoon.

Later that day, I had a further talk with the captain, asking him to describe in full detail everything he could remember that had happened since Bob boarded the *Lady Ghislaine* in Madeira the week before. As he did this, I asked him the myriad questions that were tormenting me: what mood had my husband been in; how was his health and had he shaken off his cold; what did he eat, what did he say; what had they talked about; where did they sail to; who phoned him last and when; what time and by whom was it first discovered he was missing; why did he wait so long to start the search, and so on. I questioned him about the crew, especially the engineer who was apparently the last person to see Bob alive, and the chef who claimed to have been up at 4:30 A.M. and then again at 6 A.M. How did the captain think Bob had died? Could he have slipped? Where from? I needed to find some truth in all of this. Yet, following this talk with the captain, I felt a sense of malaise that is difficult to describe or explain. Nothing was suspicious in his answers and yet Bob's death still made no sense to me.

Philip had determined to interview all members of the crew thoroughly, one by one, including the captain. He felt uneasy, just as I did, about what exactly had happened to his father.

It was the first time I had met this crew, many of whom had been recruited fairly recently in New York when the *Lady Ghislaine* was anchored in the Hudson River. I did not know any of them and this in itself was unusual: we had certainly never had a completely new team like this before.

The captain had not been planning to have guests on board; the yacht was scheduled to sail to the United States, and he had obviously started his preparations for the long haul across the Atlantic. He was concerned that his supplies were inadequate. This was, of course, the last thing on my mind, and I reassured him that anything good enough for the crew would be fine for me and my guests. The cook would simply need to buy fresh fruit, vegetables and local bread for our few days on board. He was also worried that his crew was short of a chief steward, who was on holiday, but as there were two stewardesses and a sailor acting as steward, I thought it was more than sufficient. I had already decided that the boat would provide us with the greatest safety and privacy while we were in Spain, and I made it clear that I was going to stay on board until I could fly to Israel with Mr. Maxwell's body.

Captain Rankin was concerned about his own immediate future. Would he still be sailing to New York as planned? I advised him that I thought it very unlikely and recommended he should return to his berth in Palma, Majorca, after our departure to await orders. He then asked me for money. We did a rough calculation of the amount of fuel required to sail to Majorca and the cost of looking after the crew for fifteen days, after which I told him he would have to take further orders from Marine Aviation Management International (MAMI) in London, who were responsible for both the yacht and the company's G4 and G2 jet planes. At this, I gave him £10,000 in cash, for which he signed a receipt. It was money belonging to

MAMI (handed to me by the pilot of the plane) and had been sent precisely to meet a situation of this kind, which necessitated a sudden change of plan.

A welcome diversion came with the arrival that evening of my youngest daughter, Ghislaine, after whom Bob had named the yacht. She traveled in the G2 with my favorite pilot, Captain Brian Hill, who had flown Bob constantly for the last few years. When they arrived, Brian came to see me immediately, offering me his condolences and telling me that Kevin had asked him to return to London first thing the next morning, taking with him all the business papers and documents his father might have had with him on the boat.

By Wednesday evening, all the passengers on board had established a routine of sorts. We met for meals at regular intervals and the conversation invariably returned to the subject of Bob, with Ken and John recounting a great many anecdotes I had never heard before. They were extraordinarily friendly, almost brotherly, and I found their stories both moving and amusing, depicting him as his colleagues at the *Mirror* saw him, which was of course a different angle for me. We were like a close-knit family engaged in a rather long wake. It wasn't Bob's body we were keeping watch over, but his spirit, present to such an extent that it haunted all our conversations. I never ventured on deck at all, since the press was buzzing on the quayside like flies, watching our every move. Every time I went on or off the yacht, the horde rushed to the side of the quay. Cameras whirred into action, flashes exploded and the journalists closed in on me, firing a barrage of questions in French, Spanish, English and German. I just walked past them, erect, my eyes fixed slightly above the horizon, a wan smile on my face, just as I had been taught to do so long ago, when my mother made me take a course in deportment in Paris. I never said a word.

At lunch that day, my two *Mirror* friends gently explained that it would be better at some point to give the press some definite news; it would keep them at bay and content, rather than hostile and avidly curious. I agreed, but found it difficult, as yet, to face them. We decided that Ghislaine, who speaks fluent Spanish, would deliver a prepared message after lunch, before we left for Tenerife. This she did with great poise and aplomb, striking exactly the right note, although visibly very moved herself.

As advised by John, Ghislaine also told the press that it was too early yet for me to make any statement, but that I would certainly speak to them before leaving Spain. She went on to tell the assembled journalists that we were pressing the authorities to give us permission to leave, taking Mr. Maxwell's body with us. At this stage, she could not say when we would go, or from which airport we would fly. We just did not know ourselves. She ended by thanking them for their courtesy and their understanding of our grief. Amongst all the nationalities present in that media jamboree, the Spanish press showed far greater sensitivity to me and my family than any other journalists I encountered then or since.

The *Lady Ghislaine*'s two satellite phones were our main lifeline to the world outside, coupled with the morning or evening visits of Señor Claverie. At times he brought or phoned with good news; at others, our hearts sank as it became increasingly clear that first the autopsy, or then the release of the body to the undertakers, or the actual undertaking work or the issue of all the legal certificates required, might not be finished on time.

When I woke up on Thursday morning, the seventh of November, I was starting to panic. Two days had already slipped by and I realized that it was going to be touch and go to get Bob's body out of Spain in time to fly it to Israel to comply with all the strictures of Jewish Orthodoxy. My only hope was to put pressure on Señor Claverie, so I phoned him to ensure that he really was moving heaven and earth to obtain the death certificate and exit permit. He assured me that he had been virtually "living" at the courts and that the body was now with the embalmers at the funeral parlor. I had absolutely no idea why embalmers had come into the act, especially as I knew that this was not permitted by Jewish religious laws, but I was told that because of the heat, the body had started to decompose and that it was necessary. During that day, I was also getting frantic phone calls from Israel, from friends of Bob's in high places, urging me to do the impossible to reach Israel before sunset the next day.

Ian and Kevin were preparing to fly out from England and were anxious to know how things were progressing. What was I doing? Would we reach Israel on time? We then had to overcome a new crisis: our plane was too small to take a coffin. Even an average-size one could not go through the door of the plane and make the right-angle turn into the central passenger section. To make doubly sure of the fact, I asked the funeral parlor to provide an empty coffin for a trial run, but they reported that that was an impossibility. I called Ian in London to tell him of the problem and it was decided that we would have to hire a plane specially adapted for this kind of transport. The pilot and MAMI then helped us to locate a suitable plane in Switzerland, which was able to come and pick us up in the Canaries and take us to Israel, providing we left Las Palmas not later than ten o'clock on Thursday evening. Israel being three hours ahead, we could make it comfortably before the Sabbath began—if we were able to keep to that schedule!

The day passed by with similar anxious moments and relentless demands from everyone, and the situation was exacerbated by the police on the Canary Islands, who had finally caught on to the fact that they were dealing with a famous personality and had become officious, to say the least. The funeral parlor got in touch with me, wanting to know Bob's height and weight and what kind of coffin I wanted to purchase. I remember thinking that it was rather late in the day to be asking for such crucial details, but I explained that only the simplest pine coffin available was needed, since it was for transport purposes only. In the Jewish religion, the body is buried wrapped in the deceased's tallith (prayer shawl), and then placed directly in the earth, so nothing out of the ordinary was necessary. The undertakers assured me they understood and that my wishes would be fully complied with.

I was constantly being asked to make decisions—either directly, on the telephone or through a third party. Bob sometimes used to tell me that at times he felt like a decision-making machine. He had no time to think, all he could do was say yes or no. It was my turn now to make the decisions, but I needed time to think; I could not risk making a mistake. One moment it was the Israeli lawyer on the line, giving me details of the site of the tomb and explaining that so many ministers and government officials wanted to attend Bob's funeral that they had decided to hold it on Sunday after the closing of the Knesset, about four o'clock in the afternoon, and was I agreeable? Another time, I had to decide from long distance about hotels in Jerusalem; who should go where and how many rooms we needed to book. Every single detail went through my hands, the number of vehicles required, which rabbi would say which prayer, the different places where the body would be at rest, who would keep watch over it, who would be there to receive it when the plane arrived. It was endless.

At the same time, calls poured in from Paris, from New York, from London and Oxford, from Bob's family, from mine, from his numerous friends and colleagues. Orders and counter-orders rained down on me. An interminable stream of messages was disgorged from the fax machine. I remember one in particular from our Paris lawyers, suggesting questions I should ask the captain and crew about Bob's last movements and his life on board. Our French lawyers were also worrying, quite rightly, as events would later prove, whether proper and serious investigations were being carried out by the judges and doctors. On a more mundane level, I realized that since I had left home very hurriedly, I had no suitable clothes with me; I had to try to focus at a distance on the question of funeral wear—and a very public funeral at that, to be held in the full glare of the media. One of the children would have to bring me something suitable; there was no time to do anything else.

Everyone at home and overseas was worrying about me; I was worrying desperately about Ian and Kevin, still so young and so inexperienced to shoulder the burden of such a legacy. Reliving those days of anguish, I wonder how on earth we managed to survive the ordeal. Had I had any inkling then of what the future held, I wonder if I would have had the strength to get through that week, let alone what was to follow.

Far from being a peaceful prelude to a comfortable, well-planned journey to Israel, those last hours in Tenerife were simply hair-raising. To make matters still more difficult, only that afternoon Julio Claverie had informed me that both Philip and I, and every member of the crew, would have to present ourselves before a second judge—Judge Oliva—in Granadilla, near Los Cristianos at the southern tip of Gran Canaria, at 5 P.M. This unexpected demand nearly upset what chances we had of leaving the islands for Israel on time. But it was a legal order from the Spanish investigating judge, which could not be countermanded.

So, at the appointed time, we duly left by taxi for Granadilla, with my now constant companions from the *Mirror* in tow. As we entered the court building, we were asked to wait and were left with the distinct impression that we might not even be seen that day! At this point, our lawyer, who had accompanied us, engaged in a long conversation with the judge to explain the urgency of the circumstances and the fact that the street outside was teeming with journalists and photographers. The judge, I was to learn, was enormously displeased to hear this and proceeded to have us taken from the court entrance through a subterranean maze of corridors to a small courtroom where we were again left waiting. Eventually, after a long and frustrating hour, Philip and I were led into the judge's office. Judge Isabel Oliva was a slip of a girl, in her early thirties, unusually attractive and smartly dressed, with blond hair and large hazel eyes. In her hand, she held our first depositions and, after offering her personal sympathy, she began by questioning me.

She seemed especially interested in the history of Bob's health. Had he been ill before this trip? What medicines did he use? Did I see any pills near his bedside or in his bathroom? Did he drink? She seemed to concentrate particularly on the fact that a nearly empty bottle of red Martini was found next to a full one in one of his bedroom cupboards, yet at the same time she told us that only traces of alcohol had been found in his stomach. All her questions were easy to answer. I knew that these bottles of Martini had been there for some years and had always wondered why they had not been removed. Bob hated Martini; in fact it was my drink—on the rare occasions when I indulged. Bob himself was not a heavy drinker. In the past he would have an occasional whiskey, but he would make it last for the duration of a cocktail party. He did like wine with his meals, but his favorite drink was champagne. Towards the end of his life, he rarely drank any alcohol other than champagne or perhaps a brandy with Perrier water or soda as a nightcap. Perrier was in fact his preferred drink, probably because he liked the fizziness and somehow or other it seemed to relieve his continual stomach pains.

Judge Oliva also wanted to hear about Bob's way of life, his habits on the boat, whether we thought there had been foul play, what in our view might have happened and whether we believed he could have committed suicide. She spoke and understood French, but her English was rather limited, so she mostly spoke Spanish and an interpreter relayed her words to us in English. This was not very satisfactory, so for most of the time, I spoke French and Philip spoke to her in Spanish. On learning that Bob was Jewish, she told us she was a Catholic; I then said I was a French Huguenot Protestant, Philip said he was an Anglican Protestant and with that our respective ecumenical religious positions were well defined!

Throughout her questioning, she was constantly stopping to write down her own summary of our depositions. At first she concentrated on me, then she turned to Philip, who, with his mania for precision, provoked yet more questions and an even more meticulous résumé.

After nearly two hours of questions, answers and summing up in long hand, the judge handed her effort over to be typed. When this was complete, we were asked to read and sign the documents. During my studies at Oxford University, I had painfully learned the art of précis, and I admired the judge's conciseness and interpretation of our answers. I signed readily, but Philip felt he wanted to amend his statement, adding details here, deleting them there. Devoured by scruples, he wanted absolute precision on every point and felt I had misrepresented his father's state of health. He insisted that it should be formally recorded that his father was in failing health. All of this delayed us even more.

Whilst the documents were being typed, we talked with Judge Oliva. By this time, I had discovered a certain number of disquieting factors about Bob's death. I myself no longer felt sure of anything, and I transmitted my uncertainty to the judge. She told us that she had received a first autopsy report in which the doctors had concluded that Bob died of natural causes, probably of a heart attack after having slipped on deck and fallen into the sea. The conclusion of the brilliant Spanish medical fraternity was that Bob had died because his heart had stopped beating.

Who was I, at this stage, to contradict the experts? I asked Judge Oliva when we might expect to get a death certificate, so that I could take Bob's body out of Spain. But she seemed completely unable to answer my question. Then an unknown man, who had remained seated in the background throughout the entire interview, rose and came towards us, saying that he was a lawyer working in this jurisdiction and with this judge. He assured us that if he were to get involved in our affairs, things would definitely progress more rapidly. I was rather taken aback at this, but the conversation took place with the judge looking benevolently on this offer of help.

As for our lawyer, Julio Claverie, he seemed to find it perfectly normal for another colleague to poach on his territory; he even encouraged me to use his services! In fact, the fellow was a genuine "friend of the court," but all I wanted to do was get on to Israel and leave Tenerife far behind.

In the end, we had to leave that God-forsaken place on the double when it was confirmed that if we did not board the plane to fly out of the islands within a few hours, we would definitely not be allowed by the Israeli authorities to land in Jerusalem. As it turned out, the Tenerife airport nearest the boat was about to close, and our plane had to be shifted to the more distant airport of Los Rodeos in the south of the island; from there we would have to fly to Las Palmas before boarding the Swiss charter aircraft that was to take us to Israel.

We first had to get back to the boat! We eventually arrived on the *Lady Ghislaine* at nine o'clock at night, exhausted and famished, and still not knowing if Bob's body would be released to us, or if we could physically get from the boat to Las Palmas or even if the Swiss plane would arrive on time.

Thankfully I heard from Julio that a death certificate had been issued, together with an exit visa for the body. Everything seemed at last to be on course. But at the same time, the funeral parlor manager-cum-embalmer returned to the attack. He had been working against the clock and against regulations, he claimed. True, he had at last been able to locate a coffin which was long enough, but the embalming was not finished and, one final point, he wanted to be paid before he let go of his charge. There were further heated discussions with the lawyers; I remember telling them we were not exactly "fly by nights" and asking them to guarantee the payment until I returned to England. Once home, I would settle the funeral parlor fees straight away. Upon which, the lawyer himself started worrying about his fees! I reminded him that he had been hired by Samuel Pisar, who was well known to the Spanish legal profession, and he should therefore turn to him for assurances that he would be paid. That did it.

The minutes were ticking away. On the yacht, we all packed our bags and then I gathered all my companions together to let them know the exact state of play. I was beginning to feel very pessimistic: I told them I was frantically trying to fly to Israel before the deadline, but that it was far from certain that we were going to make it. At that stage, John and Ken advised me to talk to the press. They were getting more and more agitated on the quayside, sensing that something was about to happen, probably tipped off by the Spanish authorities.

I agreed that this was a good idea, and John announced to the waiting journalists that we had received permission to leave Spain with Mr. Maxwell's body and that I would make an official announcement at the airport before leaving for Las Palmas and Israel. We did not know the exact departure time, but if all went according to plan, we should be leaving before midnight.

We prepared for our last meal on the *Lady Ghislaine*. In the tension of those final hours, I felt the need to have a last look around the boat. I stood at the place where Bob's life was thought to have ended, gazing at the open sea, questioning, wondering, perturbed. I went back through the sitting room to the observation lounge, and paused for a moment, memorizing the beauty of the room, its vast expanse extending the entire width of the yacht, with its uninterrupted and often breathtaking views from the semicircular windows. I touched the fabric of the upholstered settees beneath the windows, caressing the places where everyone loved to lounge, where Bob liked to entertain his guests. From there I went down to the great formal dining room, with its shimmering memories of stately dinners, then up an internal staircase to the study and finally back to Bob's cabin, where his last hours had been spent, and I tried to fathom the mystery of his death. I opened the various cupboards, the drawers on his side of the bed. I looked in the drinks cupboard and noticed that the gifts I had received from the *Lady Ghislaine*'s designer, Jon Bannenberg, and its Dutch builders, Amsells, on the day we had launched her in Holland, still lay where I had left them five years before. I recognized the beautiful set of sterling silver sugar castors, chased with a stylized flower design, and the china plates from the Nankin cargo. I remembered that I had always intended to have them specially displayed in the sitting room. I was tempted to take them with me but realized I would have to carry them on the trip to Israel and back to London. It was safer to leave these reminders of happy times on board; I would have them collected later. I also left behind all my personal clothes, costume jewelry and the usual toiletries that were normally kept on board, not to mention many other personal items—books, family photos and all Bob's clothes.

It did cross my mind at the time that I would be unlikely ever to sail again on this great yacht; I knew it was a luxury the boys would certainly not wish to maintain, nor could they afford it. But it never once occurred to me that I would have to beg an official receiver for permission to recover my own possessions!

Food was then served and we sat down for the last time in the observation lounge. John asked me to approve a statement he had written for me to give to the press. After eating, we polished and amended the piece and I added a few personal remarks. He also advised me how to answer or deflect the difficult questions that would certainly be asked. Above all, John and Ken gave me the confidence to face the world at large, a world which I had always shunned but which I knew would be seething with curiosity. But at that time, of course, I had no reason to believe their interest would be anything but sympathetic.

We lingered over dinner, waiting for the funeral director to release Bob's body, wondering whether we were actually going to make it to Israel in time. The deadline given to us by the pilot was already long past. I was getting more and more desperate; the phone never stopped ringing. Ian and Kevin, harassed by the press in England for information, had made public their father's wish to be buried in Israel, announcing that I would be flying directly from Spain and they would be leaving London for Jerusalem on Saturday. I prayed to God that somehow the impossible would happen. Suddenly the lawyer came in, huffing and puffing, to tell me that the funeral parlor had finally released the coffin, and it would be taken to the plane at two in the morning. I had to leave for the airport straight away. It was then 11 P.M.; the journey by car to the local airport would take an hour, then I would fly to Las Palmas to board the Swiss plane immediately and wait for the coffin to be loaded. Frantic telephone calls to the airport assured us that we could still just make Israel in time, providing we left by no later than 2 A.M.

The situation was no longer in my hands. I felt completely limp. After a hurried good-bye to the crew, I left the *Lady Ghislaine,* preceded by my friends from the *Mirror,* who were kindly dealing with the press. Philip was holding my arm on one side, Ghislaine on the other.

Remembering this moment of departure from the *Lady Ghislaine* reminds me of an incident which was quite spontaneous, and with hindsight not lacking in humor. As we left, I handed John a small black canvas bag, which I had been clutching everywhere I went. It was heavy and I thought it would not exactly enhance the photos being constantly taken by the press. Little did he realize how precious it was!

When Ghislaine had arrived on the boat, she had given me £30,000 in cash, which Kevin had asked her to bring. It was money destined to cover any potential costs incurred by the captain for the yacht. Ian and Kevin had no idea what arrangements had been made by their father with the captain as far as the yacht was concerned, and they wanted to preempt any refusal by the crew to do what was necessary to bring the yacht back to harbor, or anywhere else it had to be sent. All but the uninitiated will be well aware that in foreign waters, most yachting transactions take place in cash, whether it's a matter of fuel, harbor fees, food or crew's wages. Since I had already negotiated the *Lady Ghislaine*'s return to Palma for £10,000 and was not prepared to hand over any more money without definite orders from MAMI, I took this cash with me when I left the boat, knowing I would give it back to Kevin when I got back—which I did.

So at the time, I was carrying this £30,000 in cash, plus some of my own money that I had brought from Oxford, not to mention my passport and a host of other essential and precious life-savers, like credit cards of all descriptions—all in this insignificant-looking black bag, whose infinite capacity for extension and excellent security had made it my constant companion for the last five years.

As I handed it over to John, I remember saying, "Guard it with your life," and he assured me he would, for as long as was necessary. I wonder what he thought it contained?

At last we were leaving the *Lady Ghislaine,* on the first leg of our journey to Jerusalem. With an escort of police cars in front and behind, we set off for the airport, with a whole procession of press cars in hot pursuit. Once we had arrived, the police took over and I began to feel as if I were floating on air. All decisions had been taken from me and I now just followed instructions. It was such a relief to have the burden lifted. I was happy to let someone else take control. I was going through the motions of thinking, acting, speaking, while at the same time feeling slightly removed and disconnected from all that was happening around me. And this was to continue in the days ahead.

I was ushered into a large room, which had been specially prepared for my statement to the press. Mechanically, I found myself climbing on to a podium bristling with microphones, to face the barrage of journalists, photographers and television cameras. I was floodlit like a star and felt rather like an Edith Piaf double, standing there, a small figure in a black suit, fragile and all alone. I read my statement, a few questions were asked, which I answered as I had prepared. Then for endless minutes the photographers had a field day, with my diminutive person their sole target. The police took over again; I was taken out on the tarmac and boarded our plane immediately. It was well past 2 A.M. when we reached Las Palmas and went abourd the Challenger but there was no sight of the coffin.

We waited anxiously when, about 3 A.M., a huge hearse appeared, carrying the most gigantic mahogany coffin I have ever seen, complete with silver handles and decorations. I simply could not believe my eyes. With considerable difficulty, the coffin was hoisted into the rear of the plane, occupying all the available space there. I breathed a sigh of relief when the doors were finally closed. But still we could not leave. The manager of the funeral parlor had come aboard and was wasting more of my time, telling me in his unbearably unctuous manner that my husband was handsome, that he was sure he had not suffered and a whole string of such meaningless and inane platitudes. At long last he took his leave and we were free to depart. The plane door had only just been closed when the pilot began to head for the takeoff runway. Before we had time to catch our breath, we had made the most unbelievable vertical takeoff I have ever experienced in my life. Thrust with enormous force to the backs of our seats, we did not recover until we were fully airborne and the aircraft steady. Having come back to our senses, I have to admit that our reaction was to burst irreverently into the most uncontrollable laughter. We commented that Bob would have enjoyed it. This catapulting into space had left me uneasy about the flight ahead, but soon the pilot, framed in the cabin door, explained to us that he could not afford to lose a single second if we were going to make Jerusalem before sunset; and that was the reason for this rocketing takeoff. My respect for the Swiss went up a notch.

When the pilot had returned to the controls, I decided to open the inside rear door. I wanted to make sure that the coffin I had fought so hard to retrieve was still safely in place. Ghislaine and Philip went with me, and I watched as Ghislaine placed some flowers that she had been given at the airport on the coffin. Looking at that mighty, solid box in front of me, I simply could not comprehend its lavishness or its size. It was only many weeks later when I questioned the amount of the undertaker's bill that I was made aware that Bob had been laid in two coffins: one of lead, hermetically sealed with a glass lid to permit identification of the body as required by the Spanish law on repatriating bodies, and a second coffin made of mahogany, which looked to me like the most expensive one the funeral parlor could sell me.

Reassured that we still had Bob with us, we all settled down to a strange few hours in the curiously entrancing Mediterranean night skies. It was comforting to know that as soon as we left Spain our plane was picked up by Israeli flight controllers. I knew they were following our progress hour by hour and I felt strengthened all of a sudden by the thought that I was being protected—me and my precious cargo. The pilot told me he had never known that to happen before, but he was well pleased, sensing that it would overcome the usual questioning which starts whenever a plane enters Israeli airspace.

While we basked in that sense of reassurance, we suddenly heard three enormously loud bangs, rather like repeated knocking, coming from the rear of the plane. When we had recovered from our fright, we all looked at each other, feeling absolutely certain that Bob was trying to tell us something! I went back and opened the door again with great apprehension, fearing a similar apparition to that of the Commendatore in Mozart's *Don Giovanni*. But the coffin was still there, deathly still. As I was returning to my seat, slightly shaken, we heard another loud explosion, just like the detonation of a bomb, on the port side. It was quite alarming, and when we asked the pilot for an explanation, he did little to quell our fears. Somehow we still felt that Bob might be up to one of his tricks!

The plane journey seemed unending, but we were partially distracted by the splendor of the night skies and the sun in all its glory as we flew further east. At times, flight routine took over; unappetizing snacks appeared and disappeared, but none of us had any taste for food at this stage. We dozed; we recounted anecdotes; we tried to imagine what would happen when we landed; we wondered whether any members of our Israeli family would be there to meet us. I was exhausted, yet I felt elated. I had achieved the impossible: my husband would be buried in the land of Israel. Drowsiness overcame me. I had done what I had to do; he would be content.

As we entered Israeli airspace, we suddenly found our plane flanked on either side by two Israeli aircraft. We had now acquired a guard of honor! Our Swiss pilot was at first rather concerned, imagining that he was being pursued and would be forced to land. But after the customary challenge, when the Israelis were clearly satisfied that we were who we said we were, the pilot soon understood that the escort planes were friendly. Contrary to his earlier instructions, he was then told to fly directly to Jerusalem where rarely granted permission had been given for our plane to land. This was just as well, since the Sabbath was fast approaching and I was getting more and more anxious, knowing the inflexibility of Orthodox religious tradition.

We finally landed in Jerusalem at four in the afternoon of Friday. For a moment, I wondered what would happen next. I need not have worried for one second. It was as I had hoped; matters were now completely out of my hands. Far from being in torment, I simply felt enormous relief. My many years of research on the Jewish Holocaust and study of Jewish civilization and religion were standing me in good stead. Although I was unfamiliar with the details, I had a good idea of what an Orthodox burial would entail. For this reason, I could not help wondering how Bob's body was going to be released to the pathology department of the Tel Aviv Institute. What extraordinary subterfuge would they dream up? I knew for certain that the body was supposed to be watched over constantly and without interruption by Orthodox rabbis, praying for Bob's soul until his burial.

As soon as the engines stopped, the rear door of the plane was opened. Members of the Burial Society immediately came on board and covered the coffin with a tallith. It was then lowered from the plane, ready to be lifted into a hearse waiting nearby. While all this was happening, the solitary figure of Ghislaine walked down the plane steps to accompany the coffin as far as the hearse and wait until it was driven away. I myself had chosen to remain inside the plane with Philip until this stage was completed. When finally I descended the steps, Yaakov Neeman and a whole cohort of officials were there to meet me. I was ushered into a limousine with my children and Yaakov, and we then drove at full speed to the King David Hotel while my other companions made their way separately to the Laromme Hotel.

During that short drive to the hotel, Yaakov sketched out the ceremony planned for the following Sunday. He told me he had secured a wonderful plot on the Mount of Olives, the place he knew Bob wanted to be buried. Since Yaakov is very religious, he also made it clear he could only see me next on Saturday after sunset, but he would then give me all the details of what had been organized. In the meantime, he left me in the friendly care of Alisa Eshed, Bob's private assistant in Israel, who would deal with any problems. I knew her to be a lady of considerable talent, formerly private assistant to Shimon Peres, and she spoke perfect English. Above all, she was a tower of strength, despite her obvious personal grief at the loss of a man she had come to admire greatly.

At the King David Hotel, Yaakov had booked the presidential suite for me, the rooms which Bob always used to occupy when he was visiting Jerusalem. A further seven rooms had been reserved for our family. My *Mirror* companions and all our other friends coming directly from London were to stay at the Laromme. Ken and John had been very helpful all along and I invited them to join me at the King David later on. We would then devise a plan of action for handling the media, deciding which journalists I would see, which I would not; which ones I would give an interview to, and so on. For my part, I would pass on all I knew by then about the organization of the funeral.

A huge crowd of journalists was besieging the King David, thankfully kept at a healthy distance by the police. Walking into the suite, I was instantly struck by the familiarity of it all. Alisa had set up everything just as she used to for Bob: telephone lines, fax machines, a bar, baskets of fruit, soft drinks. And when you opened the French windows and stood on the balcony, the entire city of Jerusalem lay at your feet. It was breathtaking. Some years previously, Bob had stood on that very terrace, looking out towards the Mount of Olives. Turning to Yaakov, he had remarked, "What a wonderful place to be buried." And so it would be.

Within the suite, I decided to use the bedroom where Bob had always slept, with Ghislaine taking the room that had been "mine" whenever our trips to Israel coincided. Philip had a room along the same corridor, as did other members of the family. It was all so familiar, yet so very different. Police in civilian clothes with radio telephones stood guard around the clock; no one was allowed near me who had not been vetted as a bona fide visitor.

Alisa had prepared a complete schedule of events for my stay in Israel, just as she would automatically have done for Bob. Almost every single line, starting from 5 P.M. that day, contained the names of people who wanted to see me, which she had penciled in awaiting my instructions. Looking through this schedule with Alisa, I soon decided that I could only cope with meeting very close friends and relatives and anyone who was absolutely crucial to the organization of the funeral. I remember that one of the first callers was Teddy Kollek, the mayor of Jerusalem, who had been a good friend of Bob's for some years. We greatly admired him and his extraordinary achievements, both in the enhancement of the city of Jerusalem and in his contribution to its stable political climate. Later on, I was visited by Ehud Olmert, the then Minister of Health and also a close friend. I had got to know him well in 1990 on the March of the Living at Auschwitz, when I was given the honor of lighting a torch in memory of the Righteous Gentiles. We had marched arm in arm the two miles from the original Auschwitz death camp to Birkenau. I had been privileged to be supported on my left by Ehud and on my right by General Gurs of the Entebbe raid; further along our line were Elie Wiesel, Edmond Safra, Rabbi Lau and a host of other well-known Holocaust survivors, politicians and some ten thousand youngsters from all over the world, including my own daughter Ghislaine. Ehud's visit was a welcome reminder of that occasion, a comfort amongst suffering and the vacuum of loss.

By six o'clock, my *Mirror* friends had returned and we sat down with Alisa to organize a realistic timetable of interviews. I was grateful for their advice as to who to see and who to turn down, since I was faced with a seemingly endless list of requests and my time was limited. The rest of my family would be arriving the next day, Saturday, and I wanted to have time with them; we needed to be together to mourn in private and, not least, to gather our strength for the ordeal of the funeral in the public glare.

I ordered dinner in the suite and we continued our discussions over a hot consommé and cold buffet. All the time people were constantly coming in and out of the suite, having passed the police security checks at the entrance. They were bringing messages, newspapers, letters, condolences, flowers, fruit. We were plunged back into the atmosphere that had prevailed on the boat: my suite had become a hive of activity, with fax machines pouring out an endless stream of messages and, once again, we were besieged in our bastion by a clamoring outside world.

Suddenly, I felt totally weary and wanted to retire for the night. I was sure we should all get a good rest before facing another long day when emotions would certainly run high. My other children and their spouses would be arriving, along with Bob's sister and her family, and there were still so many important decisions to make and details to attend to.

Although the Sabbath is a day of rest for Israel, it certainly was not for me! On that Saturday, I still had to face the insatiable demands of the world's press. Ken and John had naturally advised me to give interviews to journalists from our own newspapers—those within the Mirror Group, our Israeli paper, *Maariv,* and *The European,* and I had agreed to this. So interviews were arranged with Mary Riddell of the *Mirror,* Peter Donnelly of *The European,* Gill Martin of the *Sunday Mirror* and with Israeli journalists.

It was such a great relief when my other children started to arrive: Kevin and Pandora, Ian and Laura, Anne, Philip's wife, Nilda, and his stepdaughter Marcela from London; Isabel and David from San Francisco; Helene and Michael, Bob's eldest sister's children from New York, close members of the family since they had been brought up with our own children. Later on, Bob's sister Sylvia arrived with her husband and three children. She was understandably very distressed: Bob had acted as father to her since the day he had found her and her sister Brana in a Displaced Persons camp in Germany after the war. We had looked after her every need from the age of fifteen until her marriage to Dr. Dennis Rosen. Friends were also starting to arrive from London, from Paris, from the United States. Naturally, they wanted to be with me and my children. It was so difficult that day to be all things to all people, trying to comfort all those who cried for a father, a brother, an uncle, a true friend, when my own heart was bleeding to death.

The arrival of Sam and Judith Pisar was a great solace. I had originally introduced Sam to Bob after the unforgettable impression he made on me when I went to ask him to address a conference I was chairing on the Holocaust in 1988. His famous book, *Of Blood and Hope,* in which he relates his experiences as a youngster in a Nazi death camp, had also touched me profoundly.[1] I remember

---

1. Samuel Pisar, *Of Blood and Hope* (New York: Little, Brown), 1980.

returning from Paris and saying to Bob that I had just met a man who had made the strongest impression on me since I had met him, Bob, all those years ago. I also remember his answer: "Then I must meet that man, too." Both men were deeply affected by that initial meeting, perhaps because they had both lost their families in similar circumstances. I knew that Sam would bring me strength, comfort and understanding. As for Judith, his extraordinary wife, if I had been able to cry on anyone's shoulder, it would certainly have been hers. Immensely perceptive and affectionate, highly intelligent, cultured and beautiful, she had trained herself to face the world with an incredible air of elegance and coolness. I admired her and we had in common the challenge of living with exceptional men.

In the midst of this highly charged atmosphere, one of the tasks still remaining was the writing of a speech in memory of Bob, to be given at the funeral by one of our sons. At the time, we were not absolutely sure that Philip would have the strength to carry it through; he was starting to suffer from delayed shock after having withstood the onslaught so bravely in Spain. At any rate we decided that, as the eldest son, he should give the speech, but that we would all contribute to help him write it. In the end, if the pressure was too much, Ian would take over the actual delivery.

I also had to stay in constant touch with my daughter Christine, who was in Paris, only days away from giving birth to her third child and unable to risk the journey to Jerusalem. She was distraught. Only one month before the death of her father, her home in the Oakland Hills of California had been completely razed to the ground in the disastrous fire that had claimed twenty-four lives and left five thousand people homeless. Christine, her husband, Roger, and their two little boys were all lucky to be alive. But everything they possessed had gone up in smoke.

At times, my vast sitting room in the King David looked rather like an Oriental bazaar: people came and went, some gathered in groups around the tables laden with sandwiches, fruit, cakes and soft drinks. Alisa reigned over the office area. Ken and John regularly brought in the latest newspapers, piles and piles of them, keeping us up to date with world reaction. Telephones rang constantly; the nearest person would pick up the receiver, then scurry down the corridors in search of Ian, Kevin, Isabel, Ghislaine or whoever was needed.

Others gathered on the balcony, reclining in deck chairs, their conversations animated while at the same time admiring the unbelievable scenery of the walled city and the surrounding hills. There were moments when you had no choice but to go into the bedrooms if you wanted to have a private word with someone. In the midst of all this hubbub, I was giving interviews, trying hard to concentrate on the questions being asked. Photographers would precede or follow the interviewers. I felt like an automaton. If I was asked for a photo, I posed; if a microphone was pushed in front of my mouth, I spoke. Above all, I was determined to remain calm. No fuss, no drama; there was enough real tragedy all around me and I am not prone to loud demonstrations of feeling and hysterical sobbing. Fifty years of living in England has left its mark on me; I am no longer the typical French southerner, as far as emotional display is concerned.

Saturday finally came to an end, and I was left alone with my family for a brief moment. We exchanged our news; we tried to fathom what could possibly have happened from the impressions and knowledge we had so far. We made plans for the return journey on Sunday, who would go where and with whom. Talking until exhaustion overcame us, we finally kissed each other good night. I fell asleep, pondering on the events of the next day, wondering how to face the very public burial of Robert Maxwell.

Sunday dawned; its mood was very different from the day before. People appeared dressed in mourning, more subdued, more considerate. I tried to occupy myself with practicalities. I had asked for a hairdresser to come and attend to my hair, a maid to press my suit, which Anne had brought with her. I had chosen a simple, black cashmere costume and a black veiled hat with a polka dot bow, which had seen better days at Ascot. I applied my own makeup, using more rouge than I usually do. All hint of color seemed to have drained from my face and a ghost stared back at me from the mirror.

Yaakov Neeman arrived as promised at about ten o'clock in the morning to talk to me about the funeral and let me know everything that had been arranged. He was so very kind, explaining why things were done that way, who would be saying which prayer, who would be giving which speech. I was happy to have left the organization of the ceremony completely in his capable hands. Ian had worked through the night on a first draft of the speech in memory of Bob, giving it to Philip at dawn before catching a few hours sleep himself. Philip then refashioned it, adding many moving words of his own. Our preparations were all but complete. I made only one request: for fifteen minutes, I wanted to be alone with Bob's body, with only my immediate family around me. I wanted nobody else. I needed this short moment of private grief. This had obviously not been part of the original plan, which had been worked out with clockwork precision, but eventually my request was granted.

At midday, we left in limousines from the King David Hotel, heading for the Hall of the Nation, where Bob's body was to lie in state for one hour, so that people could pay their last respects. I must admit that I was astounded when I discovered that Bob was being given a hero's send-off and given what amounted to a state funeral. Nothing had prepared me for the shock of the lavish ceremonial authorized by the government. At the time I was largely unaware of the extent of Bob's involvement in Israel's economic and foreign affairs. It was a mystery I only unraveled a year after his funeral, when I was able to discuss the matter with leading Israeli politicians and businessmen. Alerted by the media, people were lining the streets leading to the Hall of the Nation, a building of vast dimensions. Inside, a large balcony was already bursting with photographers and journalists. Since they were not allowed in the hall itself, all their photos had to be taken from above, although later it was clear that some unauthorized photos had also been taken at ground level. As we entered, I could see that the hall was already packed with people standing. We were then ushered into a room at the back of the hall, where Bob's body lay on a stretcher, covered with a tallith. At my request, everyone left the room, with the exception of two Orthodox rabbis who were totally engrossed in their prayers and incantations.

My children and I stood around the stretcher for a while. We were then joined by members of my children's families, Bob's sister and her husband and children, Helene and Michael Atkin, and Bob's former private assistant, Jean Baddeley, who for many years had been part of our extended family. We stayed there for the full fifteen minutes I had asked for, each one of us feeling the closeness of our family ties, yet alone with our memories, our grief, our apprehension for the future, our prayers for a man who had dominated our lives for so long.

After this short, peaceful moment of family love and togetherness, we felt stronger to cope with what lay ahead. We walked down the hall to find our allocated places on the east side of the building, opposite the balcony where the photographers immediately opened fire with their flashguns. Soon after, six pallbearers brought in the stretcher and Bob's body lay there, at a short distance from us, in the flickering light of four tall candles.

At this point, the crowd started to file past, slowly moving along the line shaking our hands. There was Kevin, then Ian, then me, Ghislaine, Isabel, Anne, Philip and Sylvia. Other members of our family formed the second row, while the third consisted of close friends, ministers and members of the Israeli government, headed by President Herzog and Prime Minister Yitzhak Shamir, Shimon Peres, the leader of the opposition, Ehud Olmert, Minister of Health, Moshe Ahrens, Minister of Defense, Ariel Sharon, former Minister of Defense and countless others. Then came more close friends who had traveled from far afield to be with us. For one long hour, this handshaking continued, right up to the start of the ceremony. Representatives from so many spheres of Bob's many-faceted life had gathered to pay tribute to him—scientists, authors, businessmen, bankers, politicians, journalists. There were also friends of mine who had made a great effort to travel that far to be near me. I was particularly touched that Lord Coggan, the former Archbishop of Canterbury and president of the Council of Christians and Jews, had undertaken this journey, tiring for a man of his age, coming not only as the Council representative but also as a personal friend. These marks of sympathy did help me a great deal at the time, especially knowing that for all our friends from Europe and America, it had meant great disruption of their schedules and a costly effort in time and money.

But there was also a sea of people who were quite unknown to me. Every now and then, I would recognize a face, but they were mostly complete strangers: people who had known Bob or admired him from afar; people who had read about him and had been moved by his efforts on behalf of Israel. Some told me they had escaped with him; some said they had fought the war with him; some said they came from the same village; some had been to school with him; some were distant relatives. A delegation of children from Chernobyl came to pay homage to the man who had helped them to travel to Israel for medical treatment for leukemia. I could never have envisaged such crowds of people wanting to be present; it was beyond anything I had ever experienced—moving, confusing, humbling and yet an immense source of pride. I could scarcely believe what was happening. But when the prescribed hour was over, this procession of well-wishers stopped and it was time for the religious ceremony to begin.

The service opened with prayers for the dead, but sadly, since it was in Hebrew, our family could not understand it. This was followed by the singing of a lament which moved me immensely with its touching poignancy.

Samuel Pisar then took the podium to say Kaddish, one of the most sacred traditions of the Jewish religion. Although I had never known him to be particularly religious, the emotion in his voice was palpable and understandable to all. His own family had been murdered by the Nazis when he was a little boy in Bialystok, Poland,

and he had never been able to say Kaddish for them. There had not been time, for Sam had soon found himself force-marched to Auschwitz, where he had acquired the dubious honor, at fourteen years of age, of being the youngest "working man" in the death camp. Similarly, Bob had not been able to say Kaddish for his own murdered loved ones. Since our sons Philip, Ian and Kevin are Christians and could not say the traditional prayers for their father, we and the Israeli authorities all felt that the person best able to do this in this hallowed place was Sam. Not being an Israeli, his articulation of the ancient text seemed a little strange to young Israeli ears, but it sounded very familiar to the older generation, who recognized his traditional Ashkenazic pronunciation. Its dramatic impact communicated itself to all the people assembled in the Hall of the Nation. There stood one of the best-known survivors of the Holocaust, saying Kaddish for another survivor and, we all felt, for his own murdered family and massacred people. The pathos of the situation overwhelmed all those who remembered the Holocaust and could grasp the force and significance of Sam's prayer that day.

The president of Israel, Chaim Herzog, Bob's friend of many years, then spoke. As he recalled in his speech, he had fought alongside Bob during the war when they were both in the British army. Since then, they had met again in recent years to work for the prosperity and peaceful future of Israel. His was a fine and powerful eulogy, so full of meaning for most of those assembled there:

He scaled the heights of human endeavor. Kings and princes waited on him. Many admired him. Many disliked him. But none was indifferent to him.

The words rang out in the silence of the hall. I was struck by the truth and honesty of his remarks, not least his closing words:

Few are the persons who stride across the stage of human experience and leave their mark. Robert Maxwell was one of them.

The moment had come for Philip to mount the podium. He was very nervous at first; he took his time, looking around him like a caged lion, before he voiced his first words. We, his family, were willing him with all our hearts not to break down under the strain. Mercifully, he did not. He carried it through, valiantly and with great dignity, delivering a splendid eulogy which his father would have been very proud to hear, ending with words which came from the depths of his broken heart:

Dear Dad, Soldier, Publisher and Patriot, Warrior and Globetrotter; father of nine children and grandfather of eight; newspaper proprietor and football club owner; speaker of nine languages; we salute you, we love you, we need you, we miss you, we cry for your presence and our very great loss.

For your courage in adversity, we salute you;
For your strength, for your success, we admire you;
For your love as a husband and father and uncle, we remember you;
For the example of your life, we give thanks.

Philip's words, the last to be spoken there that day, echoed in the vast hall and lingered long after he returned to his place. It was the pallbearers who broke the reverberating silence left by Philip's speech, as they came to lift the stretcher and carry it down the hall to the entrance porch. Family, friends and government officials followed them outside, where an immense crowd, too numerous to enter the hall, had gathered. Waiting there was the Chief Rabbi of Haifa, who had got to know Bob in the last year and had asked to perform the last rites. He was by tradition not allowed to enter a house containing a corpse, and so his prayers and eulogy resounded from outside the hall. We all listened as he began to speak:

We bring Robert Maxwell here today to his eternal rest in the Holy City of Jerusalem, at the end of a long and stormy journey, which made him a legend in his lifetime, to remain a mystery in his death.

He then went on to broach the difficult question of Bob's own Judaism, repeating in full that famous saying of Bob's, so many times ill-quoted:

I and my family were observant Jews. I still believe in God, the God of Israel. I do believe in the ethical lessons of Judaism. I love and admire my people's devotion to the study of Torah. I definitely see myself as a Jew. I was born as a Jew, and I shall die as a Jew, so help me God.

As the Chief Rabbi brought that part of the ceremony to a close, an incident occurred which I have never fully understood. Another rabbi stepped onto the rostrum the Chief Rabbi had just left and started to speak. Other rabbis then immediately tried to force him down, whereupon a tall, younger Lubavitch rabbi tried to protect the intruder (it transpired that he, too, was a Lubavitch rabbi). A slight scuffle ensued, the Lubavitch rabbi continued to speak but his words were drowned by loud protests and there was more jostling amongst the younger rabbis. Eventually, the stretcher was picked up and lifted into the hearse.

My family and I were then driven to the cemetery on the Mount of Olives. Once there, our car alone was allowed to approach close to the grave site while the other mourners had to make their way on foot. After a while, a vast crowd of people gathered around Bob's grave, encircling the deep hole in the ground, carefully shored up to allow the body to slide down into it from the front. The stretcher was brought near the grave. A mass of journalists and photographers overlooked us, standing on top of the huge retaining wall that surrounds that part of the cemetery.

Organized in a series of terraces, the cemetery stretches extensively over the Mount of Olives, where Jews have been buried for three thousand years. The narrow terrace Yaakov had chosen for Bob's tomb was nearest the top, at the base of the retaining wall, a truly privileged burial place. From the foot of the grave, I stood and stared at the most glorious panorama of the city of Jerusalem and I remembered the time-honored tradition: when the Messiah comes, the Jews buried on the Mount of Olives will be the first to be resurrected.

The sun was slowly setting as Shimon Peres and Ehud Olmert delivered the final words of eulogy and farewell. I was deeply moved by Shimon's words, which expressed not only the closeness of their friendship, but some vital truths about my husband:

Bob was a man who looked life in the eye and extracted the utmost from it. His spiritual strength was that of the Jewish people. He was a tireless defender of freedom of expression. He was different from other people and yet allowed others to be different from him. He is buried today as a Jew, on the Mount of Olives in Jerusalem. He is closing the circle of a life that knew want and plenty, danger and grandeur but never surrender and despair.

And with a touch of humor which Bob would have appreciated, Ehud Olmert's concluding words struck a memorable note:

Not so bad for a young Jewish boy from the shtetl! Indeed Bob, not bad at all!

Ehud had scarcely finished uttering these words when the grave diggers brought the stretcher to the opening of the tomb and one of them went down inside. Then, whilst four people held the tallith over the body and the opening of the tomb, they slid the body at an angle into the earth. The man inside then secured it in position, before emerging, by some means or other, leaving space for the corpse to slip, completely flat, into the grave. Slabs of Jerusalem stone were then immediately put in place to seal the tomb. At this point, members of the burial society started to shovel sand over the grave, inviting the men of the family nearby to help them since the sun was fast sinking beneath the horizon and everthing had to be finished before sunset. Friends started leaving, throwing earth or pebbles as they filed past the grave. I picked up a handful of sand and sprinkled it over the tomb whilst a small white board inscribed with Bob's Hebrew name was stuck in the earth marking his final resting place. The sun suddenly disappeared from view and night enveloped the sky.

If Bob had wanted to organize his own funeral, even he, an unquestionably superb organizer with an eye for both detail and pageantry, could not have thought of a more spectacular laying to rest in the place of his choice. Nor could he have ever dreamt of the role Nature would play in that unforgettable event. He would have been proud of the homage Israel had paid him. It would, in some way, have soothed the wound inflicted on him by the Nazis' murder of his family.

I had come full circle in my recollections of that memorable day. The aircraft engines suddenly changed tune, bringing me back to reality with a start. Our plane was directly over Heathrow and we would soon be back to the chill of a November night in England. It was less than a week since I left, but I had traveled years. I stepped from the plane, anonymous, no longer subjected to media intrusion since no advance notice of our arrival had been given. We got into the cars waiting for us, and very soon I was en route for my home in Oxford. At last I was off the world stage.

Leaning back and closing my eyes in the car, all I wanted was peace. Peace to reflect on my memories and rebuild a life without Bob.

1

What we chang'd
Was innocence for innocence; we knew not
The doctrine of ill-doing, nor dream'd
That any did.

SHAKESPEARE, THE WINTER'S TALE

How could my mother have cherished me,
Knowing that on the day of calamity,
He shall not be a shield on their threshold
Their fugitive son.

URI TZVI GREENBERG, UNGVAR

From the moment Bob walked into my life, he changed it irrevocably. In September 1944 I was working for the Paris Welcome Committee in the Place de la Madeleine under the supervision of its director, Madame Maloubier. It was an organization, rather along the lines of the Overseas League Club in London, whose aim was to welcome the droves of Allied officers requesting our services and introduce them into French homes, trying to match backgrounds as best one could in the short time available.

Imagine if you will two relatively small rooms, jampacked with officers and their would-be hosts, all clamoring for attention, absolutely besieging an overworked staff of four girls who were desperately trying to keep their cool amidst the uproar. Every day we were inundated by a noisy and impatient throng and barely had time to think as we arranged as many "pairings" as possible between battle-weary Allied servicemen and Parisians who wanted to entertain them.

One September morning, at the height of the usual hubbub, I

was called into Madame Maloubier's office. As I went in, I caught sight of a tall, sunburned British army sergeant. He was rather a wild-looking, mustachioed young man, dressed in battle gear with the most extraordinary leather boots laced right up to his knees, a pistol in a holster on his thigh and a black infantryman's beret set at an angle on his dark brown hair. She introduced him to me as Sergeant Ivan du Maurier, telling me he had been commissioned in the field and was in Paris waiting for his papers to come through. He had been sent by Lady Moore, friend of Brigadier Carthew-Yorstoun, commander of the British troops in Paris at the time. I was to do all I could to introduce him to people he wished to meet in Paris, starting right away. Brigadier Carthew had phoned her personally and she had promised to look after his protégé.

I left the room with the sergeant following close behind. When I reached my desk, I turned and for the first time looked into the eyes of du Maurier—or Robert Maxwell, as he would later be known—asking what I could do to help. He told me that he wanted to meet people who could tell him about the occupation of Paris and France, people who could describe what life had been like for the French in the last four years. I heard his words, but found myself distracted by his personality. I found it hard to concentrate on the matter at hand.

By chance, an intelligent young lawyer had been to visit us at the office just the day before—he was the very person to deal with Sergeant du Maurier. I phoned him immediately and arranged a rendezvous for the two men that evening. I was well pleased with myself with this arrangement and passed on to the next customer as Sergeant du Maurier walked out of the room. But I paused for a while before I plunged back into my work, finding it hard to put him out of my mind.

Sergeant du Maurier turned up again the next day. I can still see him now, framed in the doorway, gazing intently at me over the heads of the crowd, whilst I tried to carry on working. Every time I looked up, I saw him standing there. He did not move; he just watched me. After a while, he came to the desk and I asked him if anything had gone wrong. "No, no," he said, "it was all fine, but I would like to go out with you this evening."

I was well familiar with requests of that sort. At the end of those hectic days in the office, we would often be stuck with a couple of officers who had no partner or host family. Although we were absolutely worn out, we would agree to be taken out just because we felt so bad at abandoning lonely officers on the streets of Paris. It was almost impossible to refuse them when we knew they only had forty-eight hours' leave and had already spent an entire day sleeping off battle fatigue. All they wanted was a little human warmth and female companionship before they had to go back to the front. We would invariably go to a restaurant, then to the cinema or a show and finish up at one of the many officers' dances then held in Paris. Most of the time we had trouble staving off their amorous intentions, which really were an awful bore! So we always tried to go out in a foursome or three couples together. There was safety in numbers and we stood more chance of disentangling ourselves at a reasonably early hour of the morning, knowing that we had to start work at eight. It was always a difficult situation and doubly so in this instance because I knew that du Maurier was a protégé of a senior British officer. I explained that unfortunately I was not free that evening, perhaps another time.

He was back again at midday the next day, his tall silhouette again filling the doorway, his piercing eyes staring at me. I was rooted to the spot, transfixed. A strange sensation of warmth flooded through my body, then the blood seemed to drain from me, my legs felt like jelly and I fell with a thud on the chair, my head swimming, the room revolving around me. In a flash, du Maurier was there. Practically catching me in his arms, he escorted me to Madame Maloubier's office.

I slowly came around from my faint. As we were pondering why on earth I had passed out like that, with Madame Maloubier suggesting I was possibly coming down with the flu, du Maurier immediately took charge of the situation. "I know what's wrong with that girl," he said, "she's hungry." Upon which, he propelled me out of the office, half carrying me, towards the nearby Cancellier Hotel, which served as an NCO mess.

In those terrible days of food shortages, I was very slight and thin and perpetually hungry. I remember clearly being fed that day with sausages and beans on toast, and eating ravenously while he watched me kindly but with amazement. Some color had eventually returned to my cheeks when I looked up into the eyes of the man who had realized I was starving. He suggested that I should not go back to work that afternoon; instead we could sit quietly somewhere and talk. I let myself be persuaded by the pleasure of being with him and by my own curiosity to know more about this stranger who had had such a profound physical effect on me.

I did not feel like walking, so we stayed, cozily ensconced in a corner of the hotel lounge, talking endlessly. We talked about his life in England, about my life under the German occupation. We talked

about our families, about our childhood. Each of us came to discover the existence of a completely different milieu from the one of
our birth and upbringing. In the course of the following months and
years, I was to enter into a tradition, a civilization even, about which
I knew absolutely nothing. Just like Lewis Carroll's Alice when she
first plunged headlong into the black depths of the rabbit hole, I had
succeeded in finding the key which unlocked the door of a secret garden, and my natural curiosity tempted me to explore it. As for Bob,
he was experiencing a similar adventure. Like the peasant's son in
Hans Christian Andersen's tale, "The Traveling Companion," he was
setting out to conquer his princess and her kingdom, fully aware that
in order to win her heart, he would be repeatedly called upon to
endure great trials.

Although broadly familiar with the geography and history of
Central Europe, I had no notion of the complex mosaic of its peoples. For me Hungarians lived in Hungary, Romanians in Romania,
Ukrainians in Ukraine and Poles in Poland. As for Sub-Carpathian
Ruthenia, Bob's homeland, it sounded a bit like Ruritania; I wondered whether it really existed and would have been incapable of
finding it on a map. Perhaps when we studied the Great War of
1914, my history and geography teachers had told us about the different ethnic groups and the reasons behind the division of Europe
after the Treaty of Versailles in 1919, but the details had never really
penetrated my consciousness.

As I think back now to that unforgettable day in the Cancellier
Hotel, I can almost hear Bob asking me to tell him all about myself.
At first, I gave him the briefest of outlines, but he wanted to know
much more than that. I was not by nature inclined to confide in
strangers, but I soon found myself describing my life with a candor
which surprised me.

I remember very clearly the girl I was at twenty-three. According
to the standards of the time, I was well educated, but with a bookish
kind of culture which nowadays would appear old-fashioned. I was
extraordinarily innocent for my age and ignorant of almost everything
outside the realm of my personal experience. The moral standards
which had shaped my youth were certainly Protestant in origin—that
is, Puritan, middle class and fiercely centered on the family unit. Steering my life with this moral rudder, I had so far kept pretty much on
course and always managed to come into harbor safe and sound. Sitting with Sergeant du Maurier in that hotel, still protected from the
storms of life, I could look back calmly over the years of my youth,
plunging into my past as I tried to depict it for him.

I was born in 1921 in a small French village in the province of Dauphiné, the younger daughter of parents who themselves had met as a result of the vagaries of the 1914–18 war. My father, Paul Meynard, born in 1876, could easily have been my grandfather. He was a handsome man, renowned for his charm and exceptional gifts as a raconteur. He had exquisite manners and was permanently good-humored, even in his extreme old age. His great success with the ladies in his youth is hardly surprising when you picture him in Saumur, a crack officer and excellent horseman in the prestigious Cadre Noir Unit, impressive in his splendid uniform trimmed with astrakhan and famed for his lavish generosity. His Diederichs cousins, who themselves had a rather free and easy reputation, nicknamed him "Chic, Cheque and Shock." We heard tales of his love affairs with some of the great ladies of the Belle Epoque, including Liane de Pougy, and we have letters which the alleged Dutch spy Mata Hari, a dancer in Paris who moved in officer circles, wrote to him in her married name, Mrs. McLeod.

On the death of his mother, my father, like all his brothers and sisters, inherited a million in gold of the period but lost most of it gambling in the casino at Monte Carlo, and even managed to get himself into debt. As an officer at St. Cyr, then at the Cadre Noir, he had become friendly with the count of Bourbon Busset who led him into an extravagant life of luxury. But the count was decent enough to pay off all my father's gaming debts, on condition he would stop gambling. He made a solemn promise and never went near a gaming table again.

Beneath this rather eccentric and apparently frivolous exterior, there lay a great capacity for hard work, a lively and original mind and sound education. He had, admittedly, a daredevil side to his character, much in evidence in his time as a cavalry officer, when he regularly took first place in all the military racing events, or later still when he won the Croix de Guerre with bar and two stars for his repeated bravery in the face of the enemy. But he also had a more serious and reflective side to his nature. So, for instance, he refused to take his first communion at the age of sixteen, feeling unable to shoulder the moral commitment it entailed, and only did so for the first time on the occasion of my sister's own first communion.

My father came from a long line of Huguenots. Although he was descended from the kings of France through Robert d'Anjou, this illustrious side of the family had converted to Protestantism centuries before. On his mother's side, he was descended from de Percy, one of William the Conqueror's companions at arms, whose French descendants had all been Protestant since the time of Henri of Navarre, and from the de Vernejoul family, who had been Protestant since the Reformation. They had all suffered in the religious persecutions, but none more than the Meynards who had been at the forefront of the struggle and were all in turn tortured, sent to the galleys, imprisoned and deprived of their lands and possessions.

My mother was eight years younger than my father and came from a much humbler background; perhaps this was why she made such a great effort to preserve all the outdated traditions of my father's aristocratic family. She suffered from constant migraines, never went out, hated walking, sports and everything else she later did her best to instill in us to ensure we wouldn't become home birds like her. Beneath a frail exterior, however, lay a heart of steel. Colombe Pentel was a strong and courageous woman with a pronounced sense of duty. These were precisely the qualities she had demonstrated as a telephone supervisor during the Great War; when Arras was evacuated and occupied by the German army, she had remained alone at her post on two different occasions, in order to pass on information about enemy positions to army headquarters. These heroic actions, which could easily have led her straight to a firing squad had she been caught, earned her the Croix de Guerre with bar in 1917. My father, who fought in the Arras sector, had heard of her great courage and was eager to meet a woman clearly so different from all those he knew. Maman was not especially pretty, but she had charm and managed to dress with elegance, although she was not wealthy. She used to tell us that when Papa called to see her, loaded with presents, she was actually rather scared of him and tried at first to deter her highly assiduous suitor. But his persistence finally won the day and they were married in 1916.

Through her mother, Jeanne Daubigny, she was descended from a very Catholic family. My grandmother had been engaged to one of the Pope's Zouaves, who was killed by Garibaldi's troops as he defended the Supreme Pontiff. On her father's side, her Pentel ancestors had fought in the French Revolution in the armies of the young Republic. They were free thinkers and freemasons.

My father was the first Protestant my mother had ever met. His family was absolutely intransigent on the question of religion, and could not even contemplate the idea of having Catholic descendants. My mother was therefore unable to promise to bring up her children as Catholics and for this reason was excommunicated from the Catholic Church. At that time there was no trifling with canonical law! This was a great source of suffering for her for the next twenty years. Then in 1936, upon the intercession of a priest and first cousin who was in Rome completing seminary studies, Pope Pius XI lifted the excommunication, thus allowing her to return to the fold. Being a woman of her word with a great sense of duty, she helped my father to bring us up as good Protestants.

My parents' home was a large eighteenth-century bourgeois residence, typical of the region. It was the first house you came to as you approached the hamlet of La Grive along the main road from Lyon to Bourgoin in the department of Isère. The village itself, Saint Alban de Roche, was situated high on a ridge of rocky hills overlooking an ancient glacial valley. Topped with oak and chestnut trees, these escarpments plunged down in huge steps towards vast, hollowed-out quarries, whose whitish yellow rock had all been extracted to construct the buildings all around. The old Roman road that leveled out on the eastern side of the village must have given it its name, overlooking as it did the white—*alba*—road. For about a kilometer, the highway was lined with rather featureless shops and trades: wine merchants, grocers, the cobbler, the inn.

Two roads ran down parallel from this main road. At the entrance to the village, one led to a group of houses that in past centuries had been a coaching inn. It had once stood on the main road through the village when the old road, and the Roman road long before it, passed through lower down. The old manservant who took me to school would tell me stories of his own childhood, one of which I still remember well. He was playing one day with his friends near the old inn, digging and shoveling the earth as boys like to do, when to their horror—and delight—they unearthed a heap of ancient skulls. And the old men of the village had described in gory detail how in the eighteenth century the innkeepers would first fleece travelers, then murder them under cover of the Revolution. A row of workers' cottages lay along the other road leading off the highway, which descended steeply towards the Bourbre, the river that turned the hydraulic wheel of the big weaving factory built in 1827 by my great-great-grandfather, Samuel Debar, which my father now ran. He had inherited this family enterprise and had been persuaded by his siblings to carry on the business although by inclination he would have preferred to remain in the army.

Our house looked out on the main road; by the time I was a child, it had already been separated from a big walled orchard right next door to the highwaymen's inn, to which it had originally been joined. Right opposite, against that orchard wall, a very old fountain tirelessly tipped its waters into a basin of mossy stone.

This ancestral home was extremely comfortable. When Debar had bought it, the house consisted of only two stories and a basement of wine cellars. But his granddaughter, Eugénie Schloesing, my grandmother on the Meynard side whom I never knew, extended it by another complete floor, thereby going down in the family lore as a spendthrift.

I had such fun in that house. I knew its every nook and cranny. It had about twenty rooms in all, including ten bedrooms, several salons, offices, games and linen rooms and a wonderful attic of the kind that nowadays only features in books. The polished staircase went up in a fairly gentle slope, which allowed me and my sister Vonnic, some three years my senior, to invent a fabulous game. We would start from the second floor and literally bump down the stairs rolled up in a bedside rug. Down we would go at top speed, landing at the bottom in the entrance hall without too many bruises to show for it!

My oldest memories all center on Maman's drawing room. I used to spend hours playing in the cupboards with toys that had belonged to previous generations, which she would let me have to keep me quiet, although she rarely joined in my games. This room, with its French window opening on to a terrace, was my mother's domain; she had put her piano in there and used to supervise my music practice. It was an Erard piano, which had a history all its own. When the raids on Arras had torn my mother's flat apart, the piano had been stolen by the Jerries. Not without great risk to himself, my father had gone into the enemy trenches once the town had been recaptured and had somehow succeeded in bringing it back. The traces of its glorious past were still clearly visible in patches of shrapnel damage and the scuffs and kicks it had received from enemy jack boots.

I remember one day when Aunt Belle, one of my father's two sisters, came to visit, bringing with her my cousin Aliette, then a nine-month-old baby. She had put her to sleep on a blanket in a playpen outside on the terrace, and I can still recall staring at that little phenomenon from inside the house, my nose glued against the windowpane. The vast covered terrace was shielded from the road by a wisteria-covered wall and ran above two huge orangeries; it was bordered with deep cement tubs planted with shrubs, carnations, roses, lavender and other sweet-smelling plants and led eventually to the wood. The recollection of that little baby invading my play territory when I was only a very little girl must be one of my earliest memories, since my cousin is only two years younger than me. Two other very early incidents rival this one for first place, but these I can date with absolute precision.

On the morning of April 4, 1924, I was with Maman in her drawing room when one of the maids brought in a blue telegram. It was bad news; her father had died. She was very fond of him and I remember her standing by the fireplace and dissolving into tears, while at her feet, with all the insouciance of a child, I was busy playing with the tongs and poking the hearth. I had just had my third birthday.

That summer my parents went by car to the Pas de Calais to see my widowed grandmother and took us on holiday to Boulogne where my mother had once lived. We were taken to the beach most days, and since we were still in mourning, we wore dark purple swimsuits. Our parents would hire a tent for the day and settle down on the beach, looking on fondly as we built sand castles to our heart's content. One morning, armed with my little bucket and spade, I wandered off in search of adventure and got completely lost. I can still remember my panic when I couldn't find my parents amongst all those rows of identical tents. As I stood there sobbing, an Englishman luckily took pity on me and led me back safe and sound to my father and mother who were, I think, still happily oblivious of my disappearance.

When I think back over the first ten years of my life, I can still picture myself playing incessantly. My vivid imagination compensated for my lack of contact with other children and played an enormous part in all the games I invented and persuaded my older sister to join in. We had a big bedroom containing huge cupboards that we had turned into dolls houses, furnishing them with toys that had originally belonged to one of my father's sisters. I also loved playing school. I was the teacher, of course, and would line up all our dolls in front of a real schoolmaster's desk that Maman had given us, behind which she had set up a big blackboard. I used to make little exercise books, then I invented homework that I marked in red pen, giving stars to the dolls that had excelled. We also had a lovely games room, which we called the pink parlor from where, I recall, you could see Mont Blanc and the Alps on a clear day. In there, we each had a big store cupboard for our toys, and whenever a storm was brewing, we used to take refuge in those cupboards, crouching down to blot out the thunder and lightning. That playroom was our exclusive domain. There we used to read, practice the violin, do our homework and invent our dream worlds. That was where on Christmas Eve we would place our shoes beside the fireplace in the hope that Father Christmas would come along and fill them with presents.

And come he did on Christmas day, when a tall Christmas tree laden with tinsel, gold and silver baubles and multicolored candles transformed the appearance of the drawing room. The sight of that beautiful, glittering tree, when we were finally allowed into the room, will stay with me for ever as a moment of sheer magic. Father Christmas, dressed all in red with a flowing, curly white beard, would come to distribute our presents, after first asking us if we had been good little girls all through the year. As soon as he left the drawing room, I would wait impatiently for permission to leave the room, then rush into the entrance hall and press my nose against the glass panes of the front door, peering into the endless darkness, wondering where he had gone to and how he had disappeared so quickly without leaving any footsteps in the snow. One year, I discovered little pieces of curly white fluff on the staircase and I put two and two together. I was eight years old.

Once a year, my father would come home from the factory carrying a long cardboard box which we called "the coffin." It contained samples of all the silk fabrics currently being woven at the works—brightly colored shimmering silk, seersucker cloth in pastel shades, embossed velvet. Most of these samples were big enough to make dresses for us. When Maman had selected the fabrics she coveted for herself or for us, we would carry off the remaining treasures to the pink parlor, where we turned them into wonderful fancy dress costumes and makeshift frocks which we considered the height of fashion.

On another occasion, my father came home enormously proud of his acquisition of our first radio, an extraordinarily exciting event for the whole family. I can still picture it, an enormous object with a massive Bakelite loudspeaker, from which distant voices would come and go in "les fadings," those mysterious gremlins which seemed to swallow up sound! That was how we heard the voice of Charles Lindbergh, the American aviator who made the first nonstop solo flight across the Atlantic in 1927. Then in 1930, it was the turn of the Frenchmen Costes and Bellonte who made the first nonstop flight between Paris and New York. But entertainment generally in those days was more a question of using your own resources and your immediate surroundings.

One of our favorite pastimes was to explore the house. There were lots of rooms we were not allowed into as a rule, but those of course were the very ones that attracted us; foremost amongst them was Father's study. It was dark with a high ceiling, its walls lined with Louis XVI bookcases filled with my grandfather's collection of antiquarian books, and right in the middle stood two enormous desks, permanently piled high with correspondence, with drawers enticingly full of stationery that we had no hesitation in using. The telephone, Number 2 as I recall (Number 1 was our factory's), was one of those early contraptions you see now only in museums; I remember that I used to think it only brought us bad news.

As you went upstairs, the tables on the landings were laden with a plentiful supply of candlesticks and lamps, since power failures were frequent at a time when electricity was only just spreading to country districts. Long corridors led off these landings, along which the guest rooms were situated. A room was named either after the family member who most used it or by words describing its decor. So there was Aunt Daisy's room, Aunt Belle's, Uncle Jacques's, the black room, the rosewood room and so on. And if you peeped into the desk drawers in those spare rooms, you found a treasure trove of old notepaper, goose quills and gold powder used in the nineteenth century for drying ink on letters. In the rosewood room with its Second Empire wardrobes, a glass globe of the type fashionable in the Victorian era, stood on top of a chest of drawers; beneath its dome was a bonsai tree with stuffed exotic birds in all their richly colored plumage perching on its branches; in the dried moss at its base, you could see little Chinese statues, stuffed dwarf tortoises and big dried beetles. That particular heirloom came down to us from an "American uncle" who had gone to North Carolina as a minister, and we were certain that the birds were stuffed with nuggets of gold. It was an extraordinary ornament, but it really fired our imaginations, as did the portraits of our old aunts and great-grandmothers which hung in splendor around the house. We loved to play hide and seek in the spaces beside the beds, in the alcoves and behind the thick double curtains; we opened up the huge old wardrobes which were full of ancient paraphernalia—fabrics, blankets, furs and top hats.

The salon on the ground floor was an imposing, elegant room which opened onto the garden through four big French windows. It was furnished with Louis XVI sofas and easy chairs, inlaid console tables, chiffoniers and secretaires, a grand piano, which we were not allowed to play, and hung with huge paintings of snow-capped Alpine scenes and the portraits of our ancestors, the Debars and the Meynards.

Of course we also loved to make forays into the kitchen, dominated by its huge coal stove, vast sink and impressive rows of copper pots and pans. Beyond that very Victorian kitchen lay a whole series of pantries, laundry rooms and coal sheds. Alphonsine, a buxom local girl trained by my mother, reigned supreme down there; whenever we paid her a visit, she used to spoil us with little cakes fresh from the oven or with a taste of her latest jam, straight from the pots standing in rows on the table ready to be sealed with glycerine paper.

Another favorite place was the attic—what a horde of treasures lay hidden there! As soon as you opened the door, you were bombarded with the delicious smells of apples, quince paste and dried prunes stored there. That favored haunt of ours extended over two thirds of the area of the house, and half of it was taken up with huge heaps of furniture, shrouded in enormous white sheets, piled up as high as the ceiling. A whole wall was fitted with cupboards, and we never tired of exploring their contents, to the great annoyance of our mother who tried in vain to keep them all tidy. All the space not taken up by drying fruit, furniture and the huge wardrobes was filled with an incredible accumulation of bric-a-brac. There was everything you could possibly imagine: sabers, First Empire pistols, military helmets from bygone ages, wicker chairs, old portraits and ancient books galore. There were bristly pigskin trunks and big wicker work cases that had traveled all around the world, old leather, Phileas Fogg style, traveling bags, beach tents, Second Empire picture frames containing daguerreotypes or the first photos of our ancestors, old-fashioned scrapbooks and toys, a hunting horn. An entire past era unfolded before our eyes, but for us it was terribly present and a source of enormous delight.

Next door to the attic were the servants' quarters, but there was another room, furnished with tall wardrobes, which filled us with excitement; for those huge cupboards were crammed full of all the civil and military apparel of our ancestors from the age of Napoleon onwards, including all our grandmothers' gowns with crinolines, hoops and strapless bodices. Top hats, hoods and capelines, tail coats and boots, fans and reticules, absolutely nothing was missing from that two-hundred-year-old costume museum. Sometimes, when older cousins came to visit us, Maman would organize games of charades and amateur theatricals, and all that fascinating finery would come out of storage, diffusing an intoxicating smell of mothballs, which for me never fails to conjure up a vision of the house of my childhood.

From the earliest days of my infancy, I have indelible memories of Fanny, the old housekeeper who had been with our family for four generations. She used to take us for walks in the village; we would go to the cemetery, where we would put modest little bunches of wildflowers on the tomb of her husband, Petrus, who had once been my grandparents' manservant, but had long since died. I can still hear her now, telling us repeatedly as we gathered our flowers, "Pick them with nice long stalks, young ladies, nice long stalks." She also used to take us down to the quarries, where we loved to model little pots and dishes out of the local gray clay, leaving them to dry in the sun. When we got home, she taught us how to lay the table, showing us how to place the crystal finger bowls on the dessert plates and how to position the silver knives, forks and spoons to absolute perfection. Dear Fanny, she was upright and dignified, and carried herself like a queen; she had natural style. She used to read aloud to my refined great-grandmother, who had gone blind in her old age, and that contact further enhanced Fanny's innate sense of distinction. She had acquired a certain culture through these readings of a serious, religious, historical or moral nature, thereby completing her own necessarily inadequate education, the kind of schooling received by children from poor families who were sent to work at the age of twelve. We regularly used the familiar *tu* when we spoke to her, as did our father, and I remember we were surprised that she always responded more formally, using *vous*. "No, no, no," she would say, "you are my young mistresses. It's not proper for a servant to be familiar with his master or mistress." Dear, dear Fanny, how we loved you!

But the place we treasured above all others was the grounds surrounding our house. It was a lovely estate extending over some sixty acres, a huge rectangle enclosed on two sides by the roads leading up from the hamlet of La Grive to the medieval village of Saint Alban; and on the other two sides by the main road and the railway line which cut the property in two. As the village was built on a rocky outcrop, our property had a splendid and commanding view; on one side it overlooked the backyards and gardens of all the other houses, although rows of very tall trees and hedges, centuries old and very dense, separated it physically from them; and on the other side there was a copse of oak and box trees, high up on a steep cliff, above the railway track which separated the property from a magnificent orchard. The cliff itself sloped down towards an old quarry which had been turned into a lake.

To gain access to those woods with their myriad, mysterious crisscrossing paths, you either went along the terrace which ran at the height of the first floor of the house, above the orangery, or else you went up a little stone staircase hewn out of the cliff itself. Some five hundred yards away from the property, there was a really ancient building hollowed out of the rock, rather like a troglodyte dwelling, with a big stone wash house. In its outhouses there was an old goat cart which had been the pride and joy of my father and his brothers and sisters when they were children. If you followed around the foot of the cliff, you came across a tennis court, long since abandoned. The garden immediately around our home extended up to the main road on one side and on the other was bordered by stables and grooms' quarters. Maman had had a climbing frame built near the house on which we loved to clamber and balance. My sister liked the trapeze and the climbing rope; being younger, I preferred the knotted rope, the swing and the rope ladder.

One Christmas, when I was four years old, my parents gave me a tricycle and my sister a little bicycle. We were always on them, pedaling furiously on the path around the house. Later my sister had a proper bicycle and the little one was handed down to me, and we raced each other endlessly all around the property. We also loved climbing the trees. Up there in the spreading branches, we had our "town" and "country" residences, according to whether we chose a fir tree or a yew that day, or else we would swing on the pliable branches of the big boxwood trees.

When you went beyond the wall which virtually surrounded the garden, you first passed through an iron gate, and from there you entered the second realm of our childhood escapades. In one direction, there was a very old, enormous fountain, a huge building called the *four à chaux* (the lime oven), a level area for playing boules and a new tennis court which my parents had had built. In the other was a wooden summer house used as a changing cabin for the swimming pool built at the foot of the cliff. By the time we were children, it was no longer used as a swimming pool, but had been turned into a pond for ducks and geese.

From there the property went steeply down towards the railway track, and if you kept going, you came to a second iron gate leading to a real forbidden paradise. Two steep paths branched off from there: one went up into the pine woods overlooking the road, attracting us like a magnet, for that was the road to secret meetings with the village children; and the other descended abruptly towards the lake, the site of our most exciting and dangerous games, the furthest place away from the house. That was where one day my sister and I decided to build a dam of stones. Neither of us could swim, but the idea that we might drown had never even occurred to my mother, who did not seem to worry about our outdoor games. Home-loving as she was, she was firmly of the opinion that being outdoors was good for our health! The lake was teeming with fish because nobody ever went fishing there, and older cousins showed us how to fish using bent pins and pellets of bread or worms as bait. I distinctly recall going home with buckets so full of fish that we couldn't carry them and had to drag them behind us as far as the kitchen. I don't know if the cook was particularly happy with our catch, but we were absolutely jubilant.

My ancestors had virtually created the village of La Grive by financing the draining of the marshes of the river Bourbre in order to build a cotton mill in the vicinity, for which they brought in Italian laborers who were quickly assimilated amongst the native population. They had also built a hundred or so workers' houses, a school and an infirmary—unheard-of in 1827. The factory was then extended by the addition of first cotton, then silk weaving plants, and for a long time was the only source of income in the village. Both my great-grandfather and grandfather were cultured, upright and reserved. Like the factory's founder, Samuel Debar, they were driven by a deep sense of religion and social conscience; they commanded respect. The local people treated them rather like lords of the village and their social standing was vastly different from that of their workers.

We attended the local school where we were put right at the front of the class, separated from the other children by a wider space than normal—so they wouldn't pass on any lice! And the same applied to our coat hooks in the cloakroom. My mother taught me to read when I was four and I started school in October of that year, before my fifth birthday. Madame Villars, a good and dedicated school mistress endowed with a generous bust, took charge of the "little ones," while her husband, an outstanding teacher, taught the older children, preparing them to take their leaving certificate. Thanks to my mother who gave me work to do at home as well, I was very advanced in my schoolwork and was quite soon able to join Monsieur Villars's class.

Although the facade of the school building proclaimed GIRLS on one side and BOYS on the other, the teaching was in mixed classes. Each class had three divisions and the pupils worked more or less at their own pace, helped by committed and competent teachers who got good results despite the children's repeated absences when they were needed for work in the fields. Madame Villars taught us to read, to count, to draw and to sew. The big girls joined us for sewing lessons while the little boys did woodwork with Monsieur Villars. I can still see myself embroidering A's in cross-stitch on a piece of canvas prepared by the teacher, then trying my hand at running stitch and slip stitch with red thread on white cotton material, but there was no hiding my incompetence at needlework!

Mornings and afternoons were punctuated by playtime outside. The playground was divided in two: one side for the boys, the other for the girls. Most of our games involved dancing in a circle and singing, "La tour prend garde," "Nous n'irons plus au bois," "Le petit navire," and lots of other familiar songs. When it rained or snowed, we used to walk round and round in the covered area, in groups of four, our arms locked round one another's waists.

Our school was typical of all those built in France during the Third Republic. Opposite the classroom door, there was a teacher's rostrum, where the master or mistress sat. In the middle of the central aisle stood a black stove with its long black pipe wending its way to the exterior wall outside. There was a big blackboard on the wall behind the teacher's desk and another one propped on an easel which the teachers used for arithmetic or dictation or writing up the "moral of the day," like "Bien mal acquis ne profite jamais" (Ill-gotten goods seldom prosper) that we had to copy out in our best handwriting; it was the first thing we did each morning.

Opposite the teacher's desk, at the other end of the room, there was a glass-fronted cupboard which served as both bookcase and "museum," with all the school's treasures heaped up side by side: fossil shells, a stuffed bird, rock crystal and other local minerals. The cupboard also contained all the necessary equipment to do elementary physics and chemistry experiments, which the teacher indulged in once a month. I remember that we children loved them because their success, or more often their failure, created great suspense and a few minutes' lull when we didn't have to work. In full glory on top of the cupboard sat a plaster bust of Marianne wearing her Phrygian cap, the symbol of the Republic and our freedom. Between the teacher's desk and the treasure cupboard, stood four rows of double desks for the thirty to forty children in the class, each with its hinged lid, inkwell and pencil groove. On the windowsill stood a globe that rotated on its axis, which the teacher would take down occasionally and spin before our eyes, especially at the end of the year when he ventured to talk to us about the world beyond the confines of Europe.

School had its own particular rituals, by then more than a hundred years old, and school terms were interspersed by secular "cults," when my father, as the village mayor, and our teacher officiated, rather than the priest. In the autumn term, on the eleventh of November, we celebrated the armistice of the last war. It was the day when we honored "our" dead of the Great War. The entire school would walk to the War Memorial in Saint Alban, which was decorated specially with chrysanthemums. It was a familiar sight in most French towns: the bronze statue of a helmeted First World War soldier, brandishing the tricolor, eternally launching himself into the attack, thereby ensuring that France would never forget the sacrifice he had made.

Maman was always included amongst the official party. Wearing a severe black suit with the Croix de Guerre ribbon in her lapel and a matching velvet hat, she would stand near to my father and the town dignitaries. All the villagers gathered to hear the speeches that day; first came the mayor and then the teacher, who extolled the virtue of love of one's country. The war was still present in everyone's mind and parents' stories fostered the patriotic sentiment in their children. Then the war veterans, proudly displaying their medals, took the salute and all the men took off their hats when, at the appointed time, a young local recruit raised his trumpet to play the last post.

The other national holiday, towards the end of the summer term, was July 14, the revolutionary anniversary of the storming of the Bastille. Early in the morning, all the villagers decked out in their Sunday best, and all the schoolchildren would once again make their way to the War Memorial, preceded by the village band and drums, with the flag flying in the wind. On that day, we thought of the dead in terms of joy and the victory we owed them. We sang the *Marseillaise,* we laid wreaths trimmed with tricolor ribbons and then everyone went back down to school for prize-giving, which was held in the playground. My father was guest of honor while my mother sat beside him, presenting books to the prizewinners. On this occasion, she would be wearing a white suit with her medal once again proudly displayed on her lapel, and her outfit was completed with a broad-brimmed, brown straw hat bought by my father from one of the great Paris fashion houses.

My sister and I were regularly taken to school by a manservant, usually Drevet, and when it rained or snowed, he used to harness the horse and carriage so we wouldn't dirty our little brown lace-up boots. I absolutely hated those leather boots: my fondest dream was to have black clogs like all the other schoolchildren. With clogs on your feet you could make a marvelous clattering noise as you walked along. I thought they were so wonderful, those wooden-soled shoes made by Ugazzio, the village cobbler. I was never allowed to have any. Even our compulsory black smocks were different in cut from the other children's, and Maman used to cover our books and exercise books in blue glazed paper while all our other little friends had theirs done in ordinary brown. That really annoyed me and made me miserable. All I wanted was to be exactly like everybody else! One day I found two pence on the ground and begged Drevet to take me home via the grocer's; I had made up my mind to buy a sheet of brown paper to cover my exercise books, just like the other children's. I can't remember what Maman's reaction was to that little escapade! Kind old Drevet was very fond of "his little lady," as he called me. Sometimes, as we came back from school, he would stop for a moment at his own home where his wife would be expecting us with a huge heap of buns at the ready, made from delicious batter from a Lyons recipe. I don't know whether it was really the buns or the mere idea of flouting parental authority, but no cakes ever tasted as good as those!

On Sundays my father used to take us to see our cousins by marriage, the Diederichs family, who all lived in the village of Jallieu, not far from the nearest town, Bourgoin. Our family ties went back as far as my great-great-grandfather Samuel Debar who had become friendly with this local Protestant family originating from Alsace, manufacturers of weaving looms. The Diederichs were a large family; they were rich, elegant and much more "with it" than the Meynards. They gave dances and big dinner parties, and the church fête was always held in their garden. The boys drove sports cars, and the girls had their hair cut in a bob, wore makeup and dresses just above the knee and danced the Charleston. For me it was a first glimpse of a society that bore little resemblance to our own.

Maman would get us ready early in the morning and then we would set off by car with Papa, for the main object of that weekly outing was to take us to Sunday school, where we were taught the rudiments of our religion, while our father went to morning service. Once Sunday School was over, one of the teachers would take us back to the Diederichs' opulent-looking family home, which was quite close to the church. There we played with our cousins, who were much older than us, while we waited for Papa and the other adults to return. They usually brought Pastor Vinard back with them, and then everyone would settle down in the spacious drawing room to exchange family news before going back home.

Once a week after school, the Pastor used to come to La Grive to give us private lessons in religious education, which my mother attended as well, sitting quietly sewing in the background. Dear Maman, she was always so dignified and I never once heard her complain about being forced to abandon her own religion. My father's undying love for her must, however, have largely compensated her for her sacrifice. They never quarreled, although religious discussions were taboo since that was the only domain in which my father found it difficult to give way to her in his usual gentlemanly fashion. The rest of the week, we studied our Bible storybooks with Maman guiding our reading. All the stories had been specially adapted for children, and far from seeming off-putting, they nurtured me from the cradle.

As winter approached each year, the gypsies used to bring their circus to the village common. The caravans were still pulled by horses in those days and the animals were left to graze by the roadside, while the vehicles themselves were parked alongside the school wall. Of course, that gave us a ringside seat every morning to watch the progress of the festivities. My parents always took us to the show on the opening night and there it was that I first saw live wild animals: an elephant, lions, tigers, bears, monkeys. There were also performing dogs, led into the ring by clowns, acrobats and trapeze artists. Since then I've seen the great circuses of the world in Paris and London, but none has ever filled me with tingling ecstasy in the way that that little circus did when it passed through our village when I was a little girl.

Once or twice a year, my parents used to take us to Lyon to do some shopping and visit relatives. Maman spent most of her time in Galeries Lafayette, equipping us from head to foot for the coming year. We would get home late and exhausted, but overjoyed with all our lovely new things. Another great excursion was to go and spend New Year's Eve with our Aunt De Riaz. She was a great lady, my grandfather's favorite first cousin, and lived in a splendid mansion called La Jolivette, built on the banks of the Saône by the architect Soufflot. She treated us like princesses. Her dinners were sumptuous, and she was determined to leave us with marvelous memories of the days we spent with her. The presents she gave us were always exactly what we longed for and she invariably arranged the seating at table so that we were as far away as possible from our parents—so they couldn't scold us for bad behavior! She would have every single toy in that vast house brought downstairs for us to play with, and I can still picture the servants fussing over us, making sure we had everything we needed to have lots of fun. I remember there were rocking horses, tricycles, a delightful play house we could stand up in, with doors and windows that opened, skipping ropes, balls, hoops, board games, puzzles, picture books—it was sheer bliss. Her own children were much older than us, so we were well and truly spoiled by every-one.

In sharp contrast to those visits to our affluent cousins in Lyon, we would often go and see my mother's sister, aunt Hélène, who lived on a farm quite close to us. Maman had in fact been instrumental in bringing her to live there, after she and her husband had found themselves in financial straits. My father's deep love for my mother meant that he was also devoted to her immediate family; to please her, he would have done anything for them. She was very close to her two elder sisters, Hélène and Jeanne, and when they fell on hard times, my father found it perfectly natural to house them and pay for their children's education. After all, in his youth he had seen his father do exactly the same thing for members of his mother's family.

That was how he came to buy a sizable farm called La Savane, not too far from La Grive, for Aunt Hélène, where she and my uncle kept livestock and grew fruit on some hundred acres of land. First of all they had a large herd of cattle, then a flock of two hundred sheep and later on they switched to pig-rearing. I remember quite often being sent to stay at Aunt Hélène's on the pretext that I was sickly and needed fresh milk to build me up. I was never actually conscious of being delicate at all, but spent some wonderful days on the farm, joined by my sister in the holidays, or on Thursdays and Sundays when there was no school. My memories are dominated by the wholesome farm food which I can almost taste as I think about it: the rich butter my aunt would churn and spread generously on warm home-baked bread, excellent charcuterie from the pigs they bred and cured themselves, fresh eggs, farm roast chicken. But there were other untold delights: we would play in the haystacks all day long or climb on the carts full of straw after the harvest or feast on succulent ripe peaches. Sometimes we would take a picnic and go with my uncle to the fields, rocked along the stony tracks in a cart pulled by a tractor.

My uncle had been brought up on the land in his childhood but had moved to Paris when he was a teenager. He was not keen on being a farmer and missed city life, so ten years later they decided to return to Paris. My parents kept the farm, however, which they then let, retaining the farmhouse for their own use: a low, spacious, pleasant building, which they eventually sold towards the end of the last war.

Some of my other most vivid childhood memories center around our car journeys all over France. Our comings and goings were determined by the seasons, and my mother rather liked this bohemian side to our lives, simply because she was forced to wrench herself away from her home-loving instincts. My father, a former cavalry officer, had transferred his love of thoroughbred horses to motorized horsepower. He was one of the first to possess a driving license in the Rhône district and from 1900 onwards always had a car. I can still remember a very early De Dion, a Licorne and a Hotchkiss, but it was the Licorne which witnessed our most daring exploits. These adventures were sometimes dangerous and high-lighted the perfect union between my parents. My mother (not a lover of sports, to put it mildly) seemed to give free rein to a desire for something out of the ordinary which normally lay hidden beneath her acute sense of duty. When my father was at the wheel, the rather daredevil side of his character came to the fore, but it didn't seem to worry my mother in the slightest. She had such confidence in him that nothing flustered her. If occasionally she had to face potential danger, then she was right there in the front rank, just as she had been in the war.

As a very little girl, I had traveled right across France from north to south, since Maman came from the Pas de Calais and loved Brittany, while Papa, on his father's side, came from Provence and on his mother's, from the Lot et Garonne in the southwest; and of course we lived at the foot of the Alps. People traveling nowadays in the Alps would hardly believe what the roads were like then—one carriageway, with hairpin bends where you had to maneuver constantly in cars that didn't have very good steering. Sometimes you met a coach or another car which refused to give way, so you had to reverse at your peril until you came to a slightly wider part of the road. All the family would get out of the car and scream with fright when the car wheels got too close to the edge, a hair's breadth away from plunging down a steep precipice.

We frequently had punctures and generally arrived very late at night to stay with cousins whom we only saw on those travels. The servants, woken up to look after us, rushed about with lavender-scented sheets, making up beds in those old family houses, while we trotted about after them. The adults, meanwhile, pleased to see one another again, would busy themselves getting up to date with the latest family news. Once we were in bed, my sister and I would enjoy giving each other the creeps with ghost stories, and the shadows thrown on the walls by the paraffin lamps did nothing to quell our fears. We would set off again early next morning, loaded with food for glorious picnics on riverbanks, ready to embark on visits to medieval abbeys, fortified castles or prehistoric caves, most of which were still off the tourist track.

In our eyes, Provence was the land of magic par excellence. The area we used to visit is rather like the landscapes of Palestine: olive groves, rows of cypresses to protect the crops, bending before the relentless mistral, almond trees, little vineyards planted in terraces on the rocky slopes of the hills, low houses of white stone, bleached by the scorching sun beneath a cloudless sky, shepherds tending flocks of hungry-looking sheep, donkeys and carts, patiently waiting to transport their loads of pine branches, cut by old women clad in black.

When I was a child, my father and his brother and sisters owned an old family property called La Bourdille, in the village of Mérindol. The house still exists and its ancient square farmyard, silkworm rearing galleries and pigeon loft have recently attracted the attention of the Historical Preservation Society. We would regularly spend our Easter holidays there; my father was always delighted to see his sisters and younger brother and we were equally delighted to be able to play with our Arnal cousins again who were the same age as us. Part of the house dated back to the foundation of the village, but my great-grandfather, a graduate of the Ecole Polytechnique and government civil engineer, had considerably extended and modernized it in 1880, although it still retained an air of Protestant austerity.

We used to have enormous fun with our cousins, racing along till we were out of breath in a lilac grove, while on the terrace our parents sat happily chatting and drinking coffee. One of our favorite games was "Kings and Queens." First of all we would plait lilac flowers together to make the crowns. Then we constructed our "palace," a series of flowery arbors amongst the lilac shrubs. My sister, the oldest of our band, was always Queen, my cousin Olivier King and my other cousins and I shared the other roles, only too happy to be allowed to run around the grove and serve our royal masters.

I have enchanting memories of those holidays: visions of tea roses cascading down the century-old bower; huge clusters of wisteria clinging to the high wall; and behind the wall a row of very tall cypress trees, named by preceding generations after Charlemagne's valiant knights, seemed to stand sentinel. Borders of purple irises ran along the foot of the wall and the terrace. A pond with octagonal coping reflected the rare clouds in its blue-green waters, while little green frogs sat croaking on the lily pads in chorus with the shrill, insistent buzz of the cicadas and crickets.

Beyond the garden gate, you went through scrubland leading to a delightful grove of pines and the ruins of Les Bonins, our ancestors' first houses. They were built at the top of a rocky cliff which sloped steeply down towards the Durance Valley, concealing the natural wealth of La Bourdille and its plentiful spring named "La Bonne Fontaine" by our forebears, which watered the fertile fields lower down. Across all these years, I can still smell the fragrance of lilac in flower and the intoxicating scent of thyme and pine trees wafting on the breeze as if it were yesterday, and I can still see that mysterious velvet night sky which we would gaze at in awe as my father taught us to recognize the constellations.

On Easter day, before the fiery sun scorched the scrubland, we children would set off to hunt Easter eggs that the adults had hidden for us in the grove. When we came back with our treasure, the eggs were shared equally between the younger and older children, then everyone attended the Easter service at the village Protestant church, which had survived the persecutions. There, after a sermon befitting the occasion, we would sing hymns at the tops of our voices. When we came out of church, our parents stayed to chat with friends and relatives on the church square while the children went back down from the village, stopping at the bakers' shop to buy *fougaces,* delicious cakes made with oil, and warm bread, half of which would have disappeared by the time we got back to La Bourdille!

In the afternoon, the entire family would go together on a pilgrimage across the scrubland to the gorge of Régalon, where our ancestors had taken refuge from the relentless persecutions of Baron d'Oppède and the King's dragoons. We used to walk back to Mérindol along the top of the Lubéron hills as far as the old ruined castle, its remaining keep a relic of past fratricidal struggles between Catholics and those of "the so-called Reformed religion." From there there was a wonderful view over the entire Lubéron, the Durance Valley and the range of the Alpilles on the far horizon. As we went back down from the castle to La Bourdille, our father and aunts would point out single cypress trees, the only known tombs of some of our Meynard ancestors who had been denied burial in the cemetery because they were Protestants.

It was in Mérindol that my love of history was nurtured when, in the evenings, my father and his brother and sisters would recount tales of their childhood and stories that their own parents and grandparents had told them. Adults and children would gather around the log fire in the drawing room and listen enraptured to the well-loved family lore. My father had known Mathilde Debar, his grandmother, very well; she had gone to live with his family soon after she was widowed and stayed until her death in 1904 at the age of ninety-four, when my father was twenty-eight. She had been very close to her own father, Samuel Debar, and had vivid memories of all the stories he had told her about the French Revolution (he was then nine years old) and his several encounters with Napoleon I, when he formed part of the guard of honor for the Emperor's visit to Lyon in 1805. Samuel had also passed on anecdotes about his mother-in-law's aristocratic family, many of whom had been beheaded on the Place des Terreaux in Lyon. Mathilde herself remembered having curtsied to Napoleon when she was only four years old and recalled the many visits to their home of Maréchal Augereau, Duc de Castiglione, especially his cocked hat and sword, which he would leave in the entrance hall. She also had fond memories of Franz Liszt, who had given her piano lessons when she was in her teens.

Papa would tell us stories he had heard at his own father's knee about the life and career of his great-grandfather, Jean-Jacques Meynard, the Member of Parliament for Vaucluse and intimate friend of Louis Philippe. The King had given him an inscribed gold snuff box and had presented his wife, my great-great-grandmother, with a beautiful inlaid secretaire, which still stood in the drawing room in Mérindol. Jean-Jacques had also been appointed one of the King's personal representatives on the mission to St. Helena to bring Napoleon's ashes back to Paris.

On the wall of the drawing room, there was a portrait of our celebrated ancestor, Manon de Nérac, my father's great-great-grandmother, who had married a de Vernejoul and saved her husband from the guillotine. An aristocrat, he had been imprisoned in Bordeaux and was destined for the next tumbril. His wife had already moved heaven and earth to try to secure his release, but in vain, although she had managed to make contact with a young prison guard whose parents were farmers on her husband's estate. This young man told her that her husband's file lay on the Prison Governor's desk; if it was not removed that very night, his death warrant would be signed the next morning. By a stroke of luck, her guard happened to be on duty that night and arranged for her to be lowered down the chimney into the governor's office. There she would search for her husband's file and he would release her from the room when he came to relieve the guard. All went well and she was duly smuggled in, storm lamp in hand. But as she stood behind the desk thumbing through the pile of death warrants awaiting signature, a guard on the early shift knocked on the door and said, "You're working late tonight, sir." Petrified, she answered with an inarticulate grunt and carried on looking for her husband's file, which she soon found and lodged in her bosom. Glancing at the next file, she realized it was that of her husband's best friend, la Caussade, and, on impulse, she removed that one as well. At great risk to them both, the friendly guard then arrived to lead her out of the prison.

The tumbril made its journey to the guillotine next morning without Vernejoul or la Caussade, and since the following day was 9 Thermidor which marked the fall of Robespierre and the end of the Terror, they were saved. Our two families naturally remained friendly. Before his death in 1984, I would often visit Ferrand de la Caussade in his château in the Lot et Garonne. Never once did he fail to greet me without gallantly stooping to kiss my hand, hugging me close to his chest, saying, "My dear, dear Betty, if it were not for your brave ancestor, I would not be here with you today."

Of course, my imagination was fired by all these tales and I dreamt of emulating Manon de Nérac.

Nearer to us in time were my father's own adventures on his journey to Patagonia in 1904, where he had gone gold-prospecting for a French bank. His stories of that expedition fascinated us just as much as Jules Verne's. He chartered a boat in Lisbon and selected his crew, but they were hit by terrible storms and almost went down in the Straits of Magellan. The petrified sailors were also aggrieved at what they considered the scarcity of their rations. They mutinied and almost threw my father overboard! But he finally arrived safe and sound in Terra del Fuego, where of course he found no more than a few nuggets of gold here and there, nothing like the Eldorado his bank had been expecting. He would describe how, sleeping under canvas, he had woken one morning to find snakes curled up all over his bed and had been saved by the presence of mind of a native who lured them away with a bowl of goat's milk. He then continued his journey to Sao Paulo and Rio de Janeiro, recording all his adventures in a handwritten diary, which my own sons find enthralling.

On a less heroic note, my father would recount how he had traveled in the same railway carriage as the Empress Eugénie, wife of Napoleon III, and describe all the people of note he had met in Saumur during the Belle Epoque. When I used to tell these stories to my own children, they thought at first that I was making them all up. To them it all seemed so very long ago. But because my father, grandfather and great-grandfather had all married late and lived to a ripe old age, the generations stretched way back into history. Not everyone can boast a great-great-grandfather who was nine years old when the French Revolution broke out! Nor must one forget that some legendary historical figures like Eugénie de Montijo, Empress of the French, only died in 1920 at the age of ninety-four.

All that enchanted life was to come to a sudden end however. Following the Crash of 1929, my father's silk factory went into liquidation in March 1932 and my parents decided to leave La Grive and settle less grandly in Lyon. There my endlessly courageous mother opened a boarding house and small private school in a large villa, while my father desperately looked for work. The year before, my mother, determined to protect me from the looming threat of the family's impending ruin, had decided to send me to join my sister in England at a convent run by the Sisters of Compassion.

It was fairly common then for French girls aged about thirteen to be sent to school in Germany or England, either to boost their first foreign language or get them started on a second. Maman had chosen that particular convent school because she knew some of the nuns personally and had been so happy with them in her own schooldays. Along with numerous other teaching orders, the nuns had sought refuge in England after anticlerical laws were passed in France at the turn of the century.

Having found out that 183 of the 240 pupils were Protestants, my father raised no objection to our being sent there, and our grandfather, who had been so adamant about our religious upbringing, had by then died. My sister had settled happily there, writing back enthusiastic letters about her life in England, so Maman was not too worried about sending me, even at the tender age of ten. It was only going to be for a few months, until the end of the summer term, and after that she would review the situation.

So it was that shortly before my tenth birthday, I left by train with my father for Paris, where we stayed overnight with Aunt Daisy, my father's sister. The next day, we resumed our journey for Birmingham. I can still see my father, looking very English in his bowler hat, although neither he nor I spoke a word of the language.

We arrived late in the day at Acock's Green, where Papa deposited me at the convent. He spent the following day at the school, meeting the nuns and taking the opportunity to see my sister. That same evening, he left for France, and the next day I had my first day at school, not understanding a single word of what was said to me, nor able to utter a word that my playmates could understand.

But far from being distressed and disturbed by this upheaval in my life, I viewed it all as a tremendous adventure. I was following in the footsteps of the great travelers of my storybooks, excited at the prospect of the journey across France, over the English Channel and through the English countryside and delighted at the thought of having my father to myself for several days. Although I was going to be separated from my parents, I had little sense of insecurity then. I knew that once I arrived in Acock's Green, my sister would be there to help me. She already spoke English well, the nuns spoke French and there were a few other French girls in the school; anyway, I was only going for a few months until the summer holidays. I really can't remember feeling unduly anxious about it; on the contrary, it seemed rather like a long holiday and a welcome diversion from routine. Looking back on it now, I realize that my home life had, to a certain extent, prepared me for this separation. As was common in well-to-do families, I was used to being looked after by governesses and maids and Maman and Papa were rather more distant figures in my daily life. So I set off for England in the best of spirits, childishly unconcerned by my parents' underlying reasons for sending me away.

After spending five months in England, I went back to France with my sister in July. My indulgent parents, still trying desperately to protect us from their business problems, met us in Paris where they took us to the Colonial Exhibition. It made a strong impression on me and I remember to this day my "discovery" of Africa and Asia and my open-mouthed amazement at the life-size reconstruction of parts of the temple of Angkor Wat.

From there our parents took us by car to visit the battlefields of the last war and the big military cemeteries. We visited the ossuary at Douaumont and Vimy where the Canadians are buried. I learned to distinguish between the thousands of white crosses for French soldiers, the rows of black crosses for German tombs and the sober aspect of British graves decorated with flowers in cemeteries dominated by tall stone monuments in the shape of a cross. That was not our first visit. Every year when we went up north to see my mother's family, we used to visit other places made famous by the bloody combats which took place there: the Somme, Hill 108, le Chemin des Dames, le Fort de Vaux and the bayonet trench at Verdun. We understood what those tragic places still meant for our parents; they had fought there and lost close relatives, friends, colleagues. Throughout our childhood, Maman had always made us pray for France and for an end to war. Alas, it was to start all over again, with forces ten times bigger and casualties seven times greater.

After that holiday, I went back to La Grive for the last time. As yet nothing had changed; on the face of it, our lives carried on just as they always had and our games lost none of their fascination. Our parents made a deliberate effort to appear calm and carry on as usual. Although the commercial situation was ominous, my father's factory was still in production, and my parents were hoping to obtain some state or regional support to help them through the lean times. But I could not help sensing an element of sadness in the atmosphere, catching a word here and there which troubled me deeply.

I had come back from Birmingham understanding English quite well and able to speak a little, so my parents decided to send me back on my own for another school year. When I returned to England for the autumn term in September 1931, the break with my childhood had effectively been made; I never lived at La Grive again. I remember my last night in our family home vividly; Maman came into my room, heavy-hearted, to kiss me good night and reassure me. Outside a storm was raging and the north wind was whistling down from the Alps, sweeping through our valley to become the mistral in Provence; it was the herald of winter. Even with the curtains tightly shut, we could see flashes of lightning streak across the night sky. Maman read me "The Traveling Companion," one of my favorite Andersen fairy tales, before we both recited aloud Marceline Desbordes-Valmore's delightful little poem, which was particularly appropriate that evening:

> Cher petit oreiller, doux et chaud sous ma tête,
> Plein de plumes choisies, et blanc, et fait pour moi,
> Quand on a peur du vent, des loups, de la tempête,
> Cher petit oreiller, que je dors bien sur toi.
>
> Dear little pillow, soft and warm 'neath my head,
> Filled with white, downy feathers, made just for me,
> When wind, wolves, or storms howl around my bed,
> Dear little pillow, I sleep well in your lee.[1]

---

1. My translation.

Had I been able to read the stars that night, perhaps I might have chosen to read another favorite story, not one of Andersen's tales but worthy of his anthology. With the help of Perrault's *Puss in Boots,* I might have been transported two thousand kilometers east, vaulting over some of Europe's great natural frontiers, the Rhône, the Rhine and the Danube, the snow-covered barrier of the Alps, the broad plains of Hungary and the countless rivers flowing in all directions from the Alpine glaciers and the Tatra Mountains. Together we would have discovered yet another mountain range, the Carpathians, a sweeping gigantic arc of immense forests and snow-capped summits; little known and isolated from Western civilization, forming a natural boundary between Central Europe and the vast territory of Russia, shielding other civilizations from a bygone age. Perhaps we might have caught a glimpse, Puss in Boots and I, of Bob's small village in the Carpathian foothills of Ruthenia, overlooking a fast-flowing and turbulent river, the village of Szlatina in the "White Lands" province of Maramarosh.[2]

But the sights I might have seen that evening were only familiar to me from the pages of my picture books, for that village was neither of our time nor of our age. It had remained fossilized in the eighteenth century, and its customs, traditions, language and way of life were completely foreign to the world I knew. Since the seventeenth century, the region had become the home of successions of Jewish emigrants, fleeing from massacres, famine and pogroms in their native Russia, Poland and Germany. They had settled in Maramarosh, establishing lively but inward-looking communities, living in harmony with the indigenous populations of Hungarians, Romanians and Ukrainians. They had preserved their common tongue, Yiddish, the language of the mundane and the sublime, and conducted business in it; the most sacred of texts, the Bible, the Talmud and the Psalms were also read and studied in Yiddish.[3] The adults also spoke Hungarian, the language of those who had ruled the

---

2. Slatzina is the village's Hungarian name; it is also known as Szlatinske Doly in Czech and Solotvina in Ukrainian. It means "the village of the salt" on account of the huge salt deposits that run underneath it. Maramarosh is the name given to the region including parts of Hungary, Romania and Karpatska Ukraïna, derived from "marmor" meaning white marble. Various alternative spellings.

3. Yiddish is a Middle Rhine dialect used by Jews in and from Central Europe which contains words from Hebrew and several modern languages. The Talmud is the body of Jewish civil and ceremonial law and legend comprised of the Mishnah and the Gemara.

region for hundreds of years, or Romanian, spoken by the inhabitants of their closest neighboring country.[4] As for the children, at the instigation of the new government of Czechoslovakia established in 1918, within whose borders Maramarosh lay, they were also required to learn Czech. So it was that Bob grew up amongst a people who needed to speak several languages in their daily lives. The linguistic skills he acquired as a young boy in Maramarosh, combined with his exceptionally good ear, were to prove invaluable in his future international business.

The Jews of Maramarosh had little interaction with society and deliberately cut themselves off from outside influences. Considering secular education a definite step on the path to assimilation, and determined to preserve their religious and ethnic inheritance, they tried wherever possible to maintain their own schools. All their children attended the *heder* (religious elementary school) from infancy and later went on to higher education, if their parents could afford it. The Jewish community's isolation in the Carpathian mountains, their minimal contact with modern society and their rejection of secular education doubtless all contributed to a general lack of economic progress. While the rest of Czechoslovakia was experiencing a period of economic growth, Maramarosh, probably the poorest area in the Austro-Hungarian empire before the First World War, was effectively at a standstill.

In the rural areas, Jews and native Ruthenians alike lived in extreme poverty. Their main source of income was derived from farming—breeding livestock, bee keeping, growing fruit, potatoes and corn. Others scraped a living as artisans or worked as lumberjacks—felling trees, sawing logs and floating them down the river. If the economic situation in Europe deteriorated, even very slightly, these rural workers were the first hit. Unemployment was always rife, and the Jew who had no land to farm was in most cases the worst off of all.

The Jewish community of Maramarosh was probably the most rural in Europe, and political changes had little repercussion there. The rebbes, or Hasidic religious rulers, held total sway over the population, meting out justice according to their own traditions and upholding rigorously the sanctity of the Sabbath. Only that day of

---

4. I am indebted to Professor Eliezer Slomovic for allowing me to read the manuscript of his as-yet-unpublished book, *Maramarosh: Sui Generis Among Hungarian Jewish Communities.*

rest and the other Jewish holidays allowed some sense of joie de vivre in an otherwise grindingly difficult existence.

For the village of Szlatina, however, all this was to change dramatically with the creation of Czechoslovakia at the end of the First World War. At a stroke, the community was cut off from Hungary, from its traditional markets and from its closest urban center. Szlatina, with its dubious privilege of being at the very heart of central Europe, was a village of extremes, brought about by the hand of both man and nature. Faced in Versailles with the political demands of the victors, those in authority had simply taken a map and divided the province of Maramarosh into three separate areas. Did they give any thought at all to the faraway peoples who were the subject of that decision or to its economic consequences? Had they the slightest inkling of the plight of the inhabitants in their daily struggle to survive? The winters were so severe there that old men's beards would freeze on their chins as they slept. Children would be sent to gather wood in the forest for home fires, and villagers would sometimes have to resort to burning their own garden fences to keep warm. The icy, snowbound roads were impassable for long periods and even sledges had trouble ploughing their way through. The frozen wasteland on either side of the river Tisa, which formed the frontier with Romania, would frequently resound with gunshots from nervous border guards trying to protect their territory from smugglers during the harsh winter months. The spring thaw brought with it a sea of melting snow and mud and the summers were sweltering hot. Autumn was punctuated by extraordinarily violent storms. The raging winds rattled the cob walls of the cottages, tore down gutters and uprooted the wooden lavatory sheds at the bottom of gardens. People went to bed early to save candle wax and kept warm by huddling together under the goose-feather quilt. Families of seven, ten or even twelve children were common and several generations might be housed under one roof.

So it was that grandfather Yankel Shlomowitz generously offered shelter to Bob's parents, his daughter Chanca and her husband, Mehel Hoch and their growing brood of children—Brana, Leiby (Bob), Chaim Hersh, Shenia, Sylvia, Zissel and Cipra—two would die in infancy. Yankel's house was larger than the average peasant's abode in the village and consisted of three rooms—a large living room with one smaller room on either side, one of which had a separate entrance. That was the room which Yankel allowed the Hochs to use, as it gave them more privacy. This was the center of their daily life where they cooked, ate, washed and slept, where the children did their homework and the family welcomed friends as best they could. It was sparsely furnished: a cast-iron stove against the wall, a wooden table and chairs, a clothes cupboard, two shelves for pots and pans, kitchen utensils, plates, glasses and basic cutlery. Pillows, homemade quilts and a few pairs of sheets completed the family inventory. Yankel's sitting room opened onto a wooden, covered verandah, and his bedroom at the back, overlooking a long, narrow garden, was comfortably equipped with a good bed and furniture which his grandchildren remembered as handsome.

Chanca's brothers and sisters had all left home before she was married and Yankel's offer of a home in his house was considered a temporary solution. But as times got harder and harder and the chances of setting up home on their own receded, they stayed on there, first with one baby, then two, three, four and finally with a family of seven children. Life in that living room was a constant battle: two beds, one for the parents and the other for the four girls who slept side by side, were separated by the table at which they ate. A wooden cradle was placed near the girls' bed so they could rock it at night to keep the latest baby quiet. After his wife died in 1929, Yankel allowed a mattress to be put on his bedroom floor, so that Bob, the only boy of the family, could sleep there. With so many people in such a confined space, there must have been a constant hubbub, which only quietened down at meal times, when food landed on their plates, albeit only the meager pittance that Chanca's ingenuity had somehow contrived to produce. Their usual fare was cabbage soup, cornmeal, beans and potatoes, bread and pieces of onion, with occasional eggs, cheese, herrings, fruit in season and cornbread when the ordinary bread ran out. For the Sabbath, the meals were slightly better—*challah*, fish from the Tisa or a chicken to be shared between nine mouths. A few times a year, Mehel would be paid for his labor in kind and would bring home a duck, a goose or a piece of kosher meat.[5]

Mehel's family was certainly amongst the poorest in the village. Yankel's other daughters had all married men with some property or at least a regular job, while Mehel's brothers were all relatively well-off, working as butchers. We cannot know for certain what circumstances had driven Mehel to such poverty, but it was probably a com-

---

5. *Challah* is a white bread specially baked for the Sabbath and holidays. *Kosher* means fulfilling the requirements of Jewish law.

bination of factors beyond his control. He came from a well-to-do family of butchers. Before the Great War, Grandfather Abram Leib Hoch had earned quite good money selling wholesale meat to the Hungarian army, and with the proceeds had bought some land and a fine, spacious house at Schwartzimmer (Bilacerkev). He had five sons and one daughter, who all had decent jobs, or married wives with good dowries. Mehel worked for some time as an apprentice butcher to his father, then when he died, continued working for his elder brother Lipman, thirteen years his senior, who carried on the meat business with his eldest son, Rachmil.

When the worldwide economic crisis of the 1930s made itself felt in the depths of Central Europe, Rachmil could no longer afford to pay a butcher's assistant; he had four sons of his own to provide for. Mehel's job then was to find cheap cattle for them to buy, and so began a life of endless exhaustion. He would set off at daybreak, walking the length and breadth of the region to track down a calf or cow, bargain for it and lead it back to Schwartzimmer. His pay was the animal hide, which he then had to resell to leather dealers. On his journeys he would sometimes be lucky enough to buy pelts of foxes, rabbits or other rodents, which he traded for money or goods. If he could find any, he would buy animals for the local Christian butcher, whom Mehel also helped. Because this meat was not kosher, Mehel could not accept payment in kind, even though he would then have been able to feed his family decently; once again, he was paid in animal skins.

To supplement his precarious way of earning a living, Mehel would also do some casual work, felling trees or chopping wood, in the sawmill belonging to his Shlomowitz cousins. In summer he helped with the haymaking on his sister Myriam's land in Sighet, over on the other side of the river. He never refused any offer of work, however menial, but it was a tough life, and there were many others like him, all trying to eke out a living and keep starvation at bay. All that hard labor brought in only the most inadequate of wages.

It's hardly surprising that Mehel himself was as thin as a rake. He was an exceptionally tall man, six foot four in height, and good-looking, with sparkling green eyes in a face framed with red hair. He was very devout and went to the synagogue as often as he could to study the Talmud with the other village men. He was even-tempered, but a man of few words, leaving Chanca to bemoan the injustices of a political system that prevented a good man from earning a decent living. He was interested in his children's education, especially that of his son, whose reckless side had already got him into trouble. Mehel had had occasion to inflict severe punishments on his young son, hoping to teach him a lesson he would never forget. But unfortunately Mehel's long journeys into the distant mountains, scouring the countryside for animals, meant that he was away from home for most of the week, so the children were more influenced by their mother. (Curiously, this pattern of home life was to be repeated in our own marriage with Bob's frequent absences when he was working in London or abroad.)

Chanca was intelligent and well informed; she followed national political developments with great interest, as she did the events in her own community. She was different from the other local women: in a community centered on the synagogue, dedicated to learning and adherence to the Torah[6] and deeply influenced by Hasidism (the pietist movement founded in the eighteenth century, which emphasized the need "to serve God in joy" and moved the faithful to mystical exaltation), Chanca's inclination was definitely towards socialism and the improvement of the masses through greater social justice. She was an active member of the Czech Social Democratic Party, no mean feat in those days for the Jewish mother of a large family. She was always reading—anything she could lay her hands on—and frequently attended political meetings. Very soon, she became a convinced believer in Zionism, the movement founded by Theodor Herzl in 1897 which sought (and achieved) the re-establishment of a Jewish nation in Palestine, thereby defying the Hasidic tradition of her generation. But despite her profound interest in the politics of the newly created Czech nation, she was also a very religious woman and never failed to attend the synagogue on the Sabbath and for religious festivals.

Herzl's Zionism came to that region through youth movements such as the Hechalutz and the Betar whose ideas were spread in the Zionist press.[7] The 1935 Zionist convention of the Hechalutz took place in a neighboring town, Mukacevo, and all the local youth movements sent representatives. Szlatina's delegation came back from that meeting filled with enthusiasm for the ideals of Halutziut,

6. The Torah is the will of God as revealed to Moses and is contained in the Pentateuch, or first five books of the Bible.

7. The Hechalutz was a Zionist youth organization for recruiting pioneers for Israel; the Betar was a revisionist Zionist youth organization founded by Vladimir Jabotinsky.

the pioneer spirit which inspired them with the hope of rebuilding Eretz Israel.[8] For the young people of the village, there was little prospect of a decent life or a normal existence in their native land. Full of the energy and optimism of youth, they longed desperately for activity and work. Yet they met with opposition from an older generation who failed to encourage them, preoccupied as they were with internal feuds between the Hasidim and the Misnagdim (Jewish religious leaders and laymen who opposed Hasidism and advocated an approach to God through study and learning and strict observance of the Talmud). In their commendable devotion to prayer, the Torah and religious tradition, the community's leaders were unable to see the need to adapt their way of life to that of the twentieth century. Perhaps it was this refusal to mix with society around them, this insistence on living in an ideal spiritual world, that blinded them to the storms gathering around their borders which would claim their beloved children as sacrificial lambs.

Somehow, Chanca had forebodings of the future. She knew that her son was unusually intelligent, quick to learn and keen on reading like her, and she was determined to ensure he would be a leader of men. He would become a great rabbi—that was Chanca's dream for him, a natural enough ambition in a community where rabbis were powerful men. She would mold his future, so that later on he would be ready to help the community return to Israel, where they would live and work in the dignity which had been denied her. She would make it her life's work, devoting all her energies to that end.

Named in Hebrew after his father's father, Bob's full name was Abraham Leib Hoch. He was known by his diminutive Yiddish name, Leiby, at home but was obliged to record his name as Ludvik Hoch in the Czech governmental registers. Whenever Bob talked about the early years of his childhood—and it was only rarely—what emerged most clearly was his great sense of shame and humiliation at his family's grinding poverty. His pride was deeply hurt by the need to depend on charity and the deprivation he saw all around him. He loathed the fact that his clothes were all hand-me-downs and his father and mother had to struggle so hard just to survive at the most minimal level. For the proud and intelligent boy that he was, it must certainly have spurred him on to succeed in life, come

---

8. Halutzuit refers to pioneering in Israel; Eretz Israel is the land of Israel.

what may, making him determined to achieve the material comfort and well-being he so lacked in those early years—and the social status that wealth could bring.

When I first met him in Paris, I was so fascinated by his compelling personality that I scarcely noticed his reluctance to talk about his past. Bob was very much a man of the present, alive to the endless possibilities of the future. We were on the brink of a new life together and the past had little importance for either of us. I accepted him for what he was and took his hesitancy to talk in detail about his family background as a natural reaction to the comparative wealth of my own family. I don't think he was really trying to conceal it from me; it was more that by the time I met him, there were so many more pressing events and emotions occupying his attention—his immediate anxieties about his future with a new regiment, his love for me and, although he never burdened me with it, his concern for the fate of his family. We had so little time together then and as far as he was concerned, the poverty of his childhood was already way back in the past. By nature, I am inclined to take people as I find them at the time, tending to let them tell me their innermost thoughts and secrets when they are ready to do so. I accepted as part of a past life what Bob had told me and which was now behind him and I focused much more intensely on the magic of a future by his side. The murder of his family by the Nazis was to prevent my ever knowing his parents or talking about a subject which by then Bob found too painful to discuss. For all these reasons, I had only the barest understanding of his early life until I gradually pieced it together over the next forty years. It was only when I started to work on the Holocaust myself and met some of Bob's cousins in America and Israel that I really became fully aware of the distance he had traveled in his lifetime.

Besides this material hardship, Bob would always talk about one other aspect of his early years—his mother's single-minded love and dedication. He would recall that he was given the best morsels from the table and remembered his mother teaching him to read and write at the age of four. She clearly pinned all her hopes for the future on him and would do anything for him. One day, he was watching the older boys having fun jumping into the fast-flowing river Tisa from the iron bridge that spanned its waters. Although he was only five years old and couldn't swim, he decided to have a go. Nobody remembers how on earth he survived, but somehow he did. Chanca, I am sure, was so relieved at the outcome of this near fatal adventure that she forgave him immediately, but Mehel gave him a belting he never forgot; the mere thought of it made him smart, even at the age of sixty! That was not the only severe beating Bob got from his father. There was another famous occasion when he inadvertently got himself blind drunk at the age of seven. He was in his grandfather's house one day, when he came across half a mug of alcohol, the kind that was smuggled in from Romania. Curiosity tempted him to gulp it down at one go and it was not long before he passed out in a nearby gutter. The gendarmes picked him up at three in the morning and took him back home, as sick as a dog. Once Bob had recovered, his father took off his belt and gave him a good thrashing. It was enough to put Bob off drinking spirits until the day he came face-to-face with a Tiger tank in Normandy in 1944 and took a deep swig of gin to steady his nerves.

Although he was very young—and very ill—at the time, Bob remembered clearly some aspects of another episode which bore witness to his mother's absolute devotion to him, when he was rushed to Berehovo hospital in the middle of the night on a sleigh hired from a Ruthenian peasant. How it was that he came to be kicked in the head by a rearing horse, we shall never know for certain. But we do know that the blow was so severe that it broke his lower jaw and Bob passed out, so that he had little recollection of the accident itself. Older members of his family filled in the details of the story later, but he did remember that Chanca had been obliged to sell her one and only goose feather pillow to pay for this expensive mode of transport. He left home, muffled in his mother's quilt and sandwiched between his mother and a neighbor, kept warm by the hay piled up on the sleigh. An oil torch mounted near the horse's head on the sleigh framework threw a fitful light on the desolate road ahead, blanketed in deep, fresh snow that had been falling all day. An emergency operation was performed as soon as they arrived, and for the rest of his life Bob's jaw was secured with a metal pin, leaving deep scars on both sides of his face, although his good looks amazingly were very little marred.

The Jewish primary school where Bob learned to read and write the Hebrew of the Torah was opposite grandfather Yankel's, in the house of the Schacter family, who rented out their main room for that purpose. At five o'clock in the morning, when it was still dark outside, Chanca would send her little lad across the road to absorb the word of God and the Holy Scriptures. At the age of six, he joined the village children at the local school where all the lessons were taught in Czech, although the pupils were a mixed bunch of Hungarian, Romanian, Polish or Ukrainian origin. The new government had determined to offset the Magyarization of the region by imposing compulsory free education in the Czech language for all children aged six to eleven. Szlatina's state school was opened in 1920, and so it was that Bob's primary schooling was all in Czech, although his maternal language was Yiddish.

Mehel and Chanca, as we saw, had been Hungarian nationals until 1918 and so it was quite natural for Bob to have picked up that language at an early age. Besides, Szlatina was also home to numerous Hungarians who worked in the local salt mine and the language was frequently heard in the village. In addition, the Hoch family had many relatives in the then Romanian town of Sighet, just across the river. Bob in fact spent a whole school year in Sighet, living at his aunt's house, and this meant that he also acquired a good understanding of Romanian, which he later also mastered.

School began at eight o'clock in the morning and although Bob would go home briefly at lunchtime, he didn't finish until four in the afternoon. He would then go straight back to the *heder* until half past seven in the evening, at last completing an extremely long day for a boy of his age. But there were, of course, holiday periods—the *heder* was closed for two weeks at Passover and for all Jewish festivals, while the Czech school broke up for the long summer holidays. So there was still ample time for play.

Toys such as I amused myself with in La Grive were unknown to poor children of Bob's region, but those young mountain lads invented all manner of games for themselves. In winter, they would build sledges and hurtle down the snow-covered hills or they would improvise primitive kinds of skis and race headlong down the slopes. The fast-flowing Tisa was naturally a constant source of fun—and danger. The bigger boys would fool around on the log rafts being floated down from the mountains, twenty to fifty logs wide, which three or more men would steer with difficulty to the various sawmills downriver. Another risky summer pastime, almost fatal to Bob as we have already seen, was to dive from the bridge at a particular spot where the water was always deep enough for this game.

Less adventurously, the children would go off into the woods and pick mushrooms or berries to supplement their restricted diet. But the favorite game of all, for the boys at least, was definitely football. All the survivors from Szlatina recall with great fondness their endless games of football beside the Tisa, playing bare-foot to preserve their shoes, with a ball made of *shmate* (rags). Bob was apparently a very aggressive center forward, and the other children liked to be on his team because they invariably won the match.

Mehel and Chanca's major preoccupation was feeding their large family. There was never enough food to go around for seven hungry children, and Bob, like all his village friends, had painful memories of his perpetual gnawing hunger. As children, they would pray for the day when they could eat their fill till their hunger was satisfied, and for the morning when they were not obliged to get out of bed! The whole family's unattainable and unfulfilled dream was to own a cow, for this represented supreme prosperity for a working man. If you had a cow, you never needed to worry about food; you had a source of milk and cream, you could make butter and cheese or sell it all if need be. Twice a year, an incredible bonanza would come to Szlatina from the JOINT, a relief organization set up in America by former emigrants, many of whom were originally from Sub-Carpathia. Money and gifts would reach the head of the community for subsequent distribution amongst the poorest families. Sylvia, the only member of Bob's family still living, can still remember flour being distributed to the community when food was scarce.

The men of Szlatina, unlike those of many small towns further north where Hasidism reigned supreme, did not dress in the traditional eighteenth-century Polish caftan and fur-trimmed hat, or *streimel*. They wore normal dark suits and felt hats, and only the rebbes and very religious men wore the caftan and wide-brimmed hats on the Sabbath and holidays. The men and boys would wear the skullcap, the *kippah* or yarmulke, all the time, much as most Israeli men do today. The modern dress of Szlatina was probably the result of centuries-long Hungarian occupation of the region, with traditions well established before the great influx of Polish and Galician Jews in the late nineteenth century.

Women wore ordinary dresses, skirts and pullovers, although the more elderly favored ample skirts right down to their ankles and long-sleeved blouses fitting tightly around the neck. Married women all shaved off their hair and wore kerchiefs on their heads during the week. For the Sabbath and the holidays, they would wear a wig and dress as well as their purse allowed.

The year was punctuated by the high holidays: Pesach (Passover), Shavuot (Harvest festival), Rosh Hashanah (the Jewish New Year), Yom Kippur (the Day of Atonement), Succoth (Festival of the Tabernacles) and Hanukkah (Festival of Lights). There would also be family festivities on the occasion of a *bris* (circumcision) or wedding, and, circumstances permitting, a tent or *chuppah* (wedding canopy) might be put up in the garden to welcome family and friends. On these special days, the women would endeavor to serve traditional fare: chicken noodle soup, gefilte fish, chicken liver pâté, a fowl or a joint of meat. Chanca's perennial problem was how to put food like this on the table. But she must have managed it somehow or other, because her surviving children all remembered her cooking as absolutely delicious. Much later, when I tried to cook some of my husband's favorite dishes from his childhood, I was for ever trying to emulate Chanca's consummate skill in the kitchen!

To celebrate Bob's circumcision, Mehel, who was certainly not known for flaunting the law, is reported to have hurled a kind of Molotov cocktail into the river and to have come back laden with fish—more than enough to feed all the relatives and friends who had come to celebrate this important event in the life of his first son. Distant relatives still remember Mehel's rare feat to this very day.

Other far more mundane events are also firmly imprinted in the memories of those who were children then. One was the regular arrival of the gypsies to empty the garden latrines, when the pungent odor would pervade the entire house and surrounding streets for a whole day. Mattress restuffing was equally unforgettable. Once harvest was over and the dry stubble available, the old straw stuffing would all be burned, along with the many lice and bugs that infested it. The covers would be washed and dried in the sun, and thick new mattresses of sweet-smelling straw would await you in your bed that night. Also in the short summer season, neighbors would gather to help Chanca spread a new layer of clay on the ground of the single room they occupied. In personal hygiene, too, the women of the family recollect the fun they had going together to the *mikvah,* the ritual bath, situated on the slopes going down to the Tisa, a short walk from Yankel's house. Apart from being traditional for all observant Jews, men and women alike, the *mikvah* was the only place that women from poor homes had access to a real bath. It must also have been a great luxury to be shaved to get rid of the accursed lice, so difficult to eradicate in overcrowded homes where there were no washing facilities to speak of.

Grandfather Yankel is remembered with affection by his surviving grandchildren and great-nephews. His ancestors had emigrated to Szlatina in the late seventeenth century; he was a respected figure and was related to nearly all the families in the village through his parents and brothers and sisters. His elder son, Chaim Leib, was later to become the religious leader of the community. Yankel himself was a very religious man who regularly rose at four in the morning to go to the synagogue. Indeed, his neighbors would chide him for getting up before sunrise, in that half light when you couldn't tell a dog from a wolf. He was renowned for his generosity, both to his family and the less well-off: he would often take a beggar back home for the Sabbath meal or give him lodging for the night. He had made his money as a cattle dealer, at a time when contraband was a way of life for most Szlatina men of his generation. He would buy his cattle in Romania and ferry them across the river at night. Even when he was an old man and no longer involved in such activities, he still allowed his back room to be used as a depot for alcohol smuggled over the border, especially when it was a friend who asked him for help, for he was known to be totally trustworthy. Within the village, any betrayal of smuggling deals—which for some were the only means of subsistence—was tantamount to high treason. The punishment meted out by the local rabbis could be severe, and on one occasion in the past a death sentence was known to have been passed: a Jew did not betray his neighbor.

Tales of contraband have animated every conversation I have heard amongst survivors from Szlatina, just as today they are the stock in trade of the French guides and ski instructors of the Tarentaise mountain resorts of Val d'Isère and Tignes, whose very livelihood before skiing took over, depended on smuggling cattle, tobacco and foodstuffs across the Italian border. After the creation of Czechoslovakia in 1918 and the establishment of the artificial border between Szlatina and its market town of Sighet, food prices went up by as much as 60 percent for a population that was already on the breadline. It is undoubtedly true that many villagers traded in manufactured goods from Czechoslovakia such as silk, socks and shoes or food products from Romania—bread, meat, eggs and of course liquor. Even the family of the upright teacher of Szlatina's Czech school, Shimon Sassoon, would smuggle kosher meat and everyday foodstuffs from Romania. Had the villagers not indulged in this kind of dealing, the majority of the Jewish population, who could barely scrape a living, would have died of hunger.

Stories of cattle passed across the frozen waters of the Tisa, their hoofs muffled in old rags, of eggs concealed under hats, of casks of alcohol floating freely down the river, shot open by Romanian guards and releasing a delicious odor downstream, of customs officers bribed to close their eyes to what was happening—I have heard them all, but never from my husband. On the contrary, he always maintained he had never witnessed anything of the sort, nor was he ever party to a deal of that kind. This, of course, is totally compatible with the known facts about Mehel's upright character. He would certainly never have taken part in such activities himself, nor tolerated his children's involvement in anything illegal, even if it meant that his family had to go without the bare essentials. Remembering the thrashing he gave Bob for a relatively trivial misdemeanor, I can just imagine how he would have reacted if he had the slightest suspicion of his son's participation in such escapades, let alone if he had inexplicably arrived home in the early hours of the morning.

There has been a tendency amongst Bob's biographers to attribute his negotiating and deal-making skills to early experience alongside his grandfather. But by the time Bob was old enough to remember his grandfather, Yankel was more than seventy years old, walked with a stick and had a terrible smoker's cough. He stayed at home most of the time or just walked down the street to *shul* (the synagogue). By the time Bob left home to study in Bratislava, Yankel spent most of his time protecting his patch of land from people trying to take a short cut to the synagogue, chasing away errant geese or hens intent on eating his beans or peas or safeguarding the well in his front garden, a major asset in a village where most people had to draw water from the street pump.

Village life took its rhythm from the seasons and religious festivals, but the Sabbath was the highlight of each passing week. The Hoch family was too poor to employ a Gentile to work for them on the day of rest, so Chanca would get up at four in the morning to start preparing the Sabbath meal. She would knead the *challah,* and after an early breakfast, the children would take it to the communal bakery since she had no oven to bake it in herself. Once everyone was out of the house, she would clean her modest abode thoroughly and lay out clean clothes for them all to change into. While it was still daylight, she would set the table and wait for Mehel to come home before lighting the two candles. Everything would be organized so that after sunset, she would have nothing more to do until Sabbath was over.

The traditional Friday evening meal was a blessed respite in a most arduous and difficult existence. The family would take their places at the table, with mother and father at either end. Mehel would say the opening grace, then with freshly washed hands, he would cut the *challah,* eat a piece, then pass it around before taking a sip of wine from the silver cup he had received on his wedding day. He would then hand the cup to his wife, and from her it went around the table to all the children in turn. Next, Chanca would ladle the chicken noodle soup into their bowls and they would sit down to eat the meal they had all been waiting for; for a brief moment, their hunger would be satisfied. Further prayers would be said after the meal, but this time Chanca and all the children old enough to know some Hebrew would join in singing the traditional melodies of the blessing, the halleluias and the amens. Sometimes a guest would share their frugal meal, for even though Chanca had so little to give away, she would never turn anyone away who was even poorer than herself—and there was no shortage of them in Szlatina. In the glow of the lamp, which burned much later on the Sabbath than any other night of the week, daily burdens would be forgotten just for a while in the warmth and love of the family. They would listen with pleasure as Mehel recounted Talmudic tales of old for the children, or discuss the week's events with their store of happiness and disappointment. On Saturday morning, everyone went to the synagogue and they would go back home with the rabbi's exhortations ringing in their ears and hearts, happy to have chatted with their extended family outside the *shul,* catching up with all the latest gossip.

When my husband talked about his childhood in Szlatina, he would sometimes recount anecdotes about his exploits with his best friend and cousin Volvi, his uncle Lipman's son who was the same age as him. The two boys were inseparable and always up to some mischief or other. They would go off into the forest to eat berries or climb trees. En route, as they walked through the Hungarian and Czech parts of the village, the other children would taunt them with the derisive nickname of "Moshe" (Hebrew for Moses), which would immediately get them into fights. Then they would stop for a moment, leaning on the railings of the salt mine. It was forbidden territory for Jews: they were hardly allowed even to look through the railings without incurring the wrath of the watchmen at the gate. Jews could not be employed in the mine, although it clearly brought trade to the village in supplying the needs of the thousand or so mineworkers. No wonder those mines were transformed into fabulous caverns in the minds of the highly imaginative youngsters. But the reality was even more incredible than they could possibly have imagined.

Fifteen years ago, Bob and I were able to return to Szlatina and we were taken down into those mines as VIP visitors. Clad in white overalls and safety helmets, escorted by the manager and a whole posse of officials, we were led into the depths. There Bob was privileged to see all that had previously been denied him, for successive Christian rulers had for centuries prevented Jews from working there. We were stunned by the astonishing spectacle which greeted us as we plunged down a steep shaft in an open lift. Glistening white crystals surrounded us on all sides, like frozen organ pipes in a vast Gothic cathedral, its vaulted roof shrouded in complete darkness. Four hundred feet below us, we caught sight of the scintillating marble floor with little black specks moving about, antlike workers carving out blocks of salt with pneumatic drills. The walls of that great cathedral towered around us, hard and sparkling, reflecting myriad twinkling lights like the facets of a diamond. Crystal columns jutted out everywhere, supporting yet more vaults, nave, transepts, chapels and cloisters, enhancing the breathless grandeur of that subterranean cathedral.

At the time, I remember wondering what was going through Bob's mind as he stood there, an honored visitor in a place that had been totally closed to him as a child. Did he spare a thought for the fate of his playmate Volvi? Forcibly enlisted in a Hungarian labor battalion, he had defected and escaped to join the Russian Czech legion. When the Russians eventually released him in 1945, he had headed for his home village, only to find that all his loved ones were dead and gone, and his grief killed him.

When Bob was not expending his energy on outdoor pursuits, he was studying either at home or at school. Following in his mother's footsteps, he read voraciously and early on joined the older boys in the Zionist youth groups that flourished in Szlatina. Thus for some time he was a member of the Betar, a paramilitary organization that emphasized physical fitness, taught Hebrew and extolled the merits of Eretz Israel and the pioneer's life. Many of his village friends joined the Hechalutz, another Zionist movement whose center of gravity was in Sub-Carpathian Ruthenia. These movements depended on new spiritual ideas and interaction was expected from the local base where lectures and discussions were held on the organization and its history, Israel and the Kibbutz movement.[9] Pamphlets were duplicated, passed around and read with great interest.

Chanca and Mehel could see that their son needed a more challenging intellectual outlet for his extremely active brain and they resolved to send him to the well-established yeshiva (Jewish religious secondary school) in Sighet. It was recognized as a center of Torah

9. By itself, the term *kibbutz* refers to the farming communities who settled in the land of Israel. It is derived from *Kibbutz Galuyot*, meaning "the gathering of the exiles."

learning and had trained generations of rebbes in all areas of religious scholarship. But before he could go there, he first had to improve his Hebrew, so was sent to stay with a family in Churst to join their sons' Hebrew classes. By the age of twelve, he had acquired sufficient knowledge of Hebrew to enter the yeshiva and moved to Sighet to live with his Aunt Myriam, his father's sister. His aunt's large home was situated beside the Tisa, and Bob had clear recollections of hearing the water splashing against the piers of the bridge during the night. Its comparative comfort made a deep impression on him; for the first time ever, he experienced the extraordinary luxury of having a bedroom of his own. It must have made him even more painfully aware of his parents' desperate situation, even more determined to make something of his own life and escape for ever from the constant humiliation of living in poverty.

Whilst he was in Sighet, Bob was taught by a highly influential Hasidic rebbe, Rabbi Teitelbaum, who detected his analytical ability and uncanny aptitude for learning and retaining what he was taught. Seeing great potential in the boy, he advised Mehel and Chanca that he should be sent to the Pressburger yeshiva in Bratislava, an institution of great renown in the whole of Europe and one of the few yeshivas authorized to train and ordain rabbis. That of course was Chanca's ultimate desire for her son, and so with the support of Rabbi Teitelbaum, they took the momentous decision to send him to Bratislava. It was a major turning point in his life.

After his bar mitzvah,[10] Chanca busily gathered together the clothes and necessities her son would need to take with him. He had only just turned thirteen when the matter was settled: he was to leave home for the capital of Slovakia, 500 kilometers away, an enormous distance in those days. He would have to fend for himself outside the protective cocoon of his family and in competition with other bright and advanced boys like him, many of whom came from other European countries. As events were later to show, this decision was also to save his life; but he was to pay a heavy price for his survival, and it was to mark him for ever.

Four years earlier, I, too, had been forced to cope with a complete upheaval in my world. Its consequences may have been less far-reaching for me than for Bob, but it was nevertheless to affect me

---

10. Religious ceremony at which a boy of thirteen undertakes to fulfill the commandments.

deeply. I had to learn to survive far from my family, completely on my own and without my sister for moral support, in the Birmingham convent where I had already spent five months. When I went back there in September 1931, no more allowance was made for the fact that I was French, and I was simply placed in the usual class for girls of my age. With a child's infinite adaptability, I did manage somehow to cope, although this time the pain of separation from my family was harder to bear.

My mother wrote to me regularly, so I would not feel too cut off from home, and I kept every one of her letters. She was clearly deeply saddened by our separation, but took courage from the fact that I seemed reasonably happy and well cared for. Those letters were full of interesting detail about their difficulties, hopes and plans, but also commented on significant national or political events. So, for instance, she wrote to me about the Spanish Revolution, the establishment of the Republic and the abdication of the King of Spain, advising me to commit the date to memory and hoping that the royal family would not suffer the same tragic end as Louis XVI or the Romanovs! She was always urging me to concentrate on my schoolwork and practice my music, and she used every one of my letters to her to give me spelling lessons! Till the day she died, my mother remained a teacher at heart; it had been her first job and she never lost interest in education. Even in her last letter to me shortly before her death, she could not resist correcting a spelling mistake I had made. She loved the French language, wrote it well herself and was a purist in matters of grammar and spelling. All those qualities she passed on to my sister, who continues to point out my spelling mistakes and the anglicisms of my modern spoken French. But whereas today I am grateful for my sister's help and interest, as a little girl, I hated Maman's perennial reproaches.

It was not long before my work was more or less of the same standard as my English friends, and the quality of my spoken and written English improved dramatically. All went relatively well during the term, when we were kept busy with activities after school. I had piano and violin lessons and prepared for the annual Associated Board examinations. We all had parts in the school play or represented the school in sports; we had to rehearse for dance displays or concerts, or embroider cushion covers and doilies as gifts for our parents.

But in the holidays when I was the only child left in the convent, I was homesick, in spite of a few invitations here and there. The nuns were sorry for me and infinitely kind and patient, but all their affection just could not compensate for the absence of my mother and my home environment. The result was that I became extremely naughty, perhaps to seek attention. I was rebellious and disobedient, an absolute pest really for those good nuns who were in no way responsible for the predicament I found myself in. We had to attend chapel every day and Mass once a week. I refused to genuflect or make the sign of the cross because as a very little girl I had been told that only Catholics did that: those outward signs of faith were not for Protestants. The nuns did their best to keep me amused and occupied. I have a strong recollection of one occasion when they kept me busy picking the petals off thousands of flowers for the procession of the Blessed Sacrament. The children of Mary (which I didn't belong to because I was a Protestant) would walk backwards, casting down those petals before the monstrance, held at arms' length by a priest bedecked in gold. The heady and slightly nauseating odor of those mounds of petals—of roses, carnations and other fragrant flowers—still makes me feel slightly sick as I write these lines.

Mealtimes, I remember, were another sore point, mostly because I didn't like the convent's English food and refused to eat it. I set such a bad example at table that I was often punished and had to stand in the corner of the dining hall, my plate full of food in my hands. Eventually, the nuns, who were not at all malicious, realized that it was simpler not to force me to eat. Instead, they made me read aloud during lunch, which was normally eaten in silence, giving me *The Lives of the Saints* as my text. At the time, it was a very widely used book in all Catholic institutions and convents and I remember discovering through it a whole new and unfamiliar side to Catholicism, because French Protestants do not pray to the saints canonized by the Roman Catholic church. Nor do they take seriously the Devil's incredible schemes to torment that poor priest of Ars by shaking his bed at night, or the many tricks he was supposed to have played on many other saints besides. As young as I was, the instruction I had received from Pastor Vinard and my father's family had certainly made its mark on me, because I felt no respect for Catholic pomp and ceremonial, and all that religious frippery which I was not used to left me completely indifferent.

I returned to France at the end of July 1932 and went back to Lyon and my mother's boarding house, which was our new home. Times were hard for my parents and the atmosphere at home far from cheerful, except on Sundays when all the boarders, who were foreigners and mostly advanced students, would join us for family games. We would play cards or mahjong and excitement reached fever-pitch—especially for my father who seemed to forget all his troubles for a while and recapture something of the old thrill of Monte Carlo! My happiest times were definitely spent either at school, the Lycée Edgar Quinet, or with my Girl Guide company, which met once a week and went camping in the summer holidays or when I was invited to stay with my Arnal cousins, in Saint Gervais les Bains in the summer or in Mérindol at Easter.

Once a week after school, I had First Communion classes with Pastor Durand Gasselin at the big Protestant church of La Guillotière. He was a learned and enlightened man who taught us the Bible in an attractive way. His approach was very different from the repetitive catechism commonly taught then to young Catholic girls, who took their First Communion at the age of ten or eleven. It was more like a course in ancient history given by an eminent professor to youngsters aged fourteen to seventeen, mature enough to benefit from his teaching. So I took my First Communion in Lyon, at the age of fifteen, a little younger than my other Protestant friends.

At school, I was good at history and geography, mediocre at Latin and hopeless at mathematics. In all other subjects, I was fairly average, except for English and French at which I excelled: I always won first prizes in these two subjects throughout my school career. In Lyon, I was lucky enough to have a first-rate French teacher for three years, Mademoiselle Delarouzé, who really inspired my love of my native language.

Since we lived in the suburbs of Lyon, I stayed at school for lunch. I can still visualize the headmistress, Mademoiselle Fontaine, a tall, slim lady, her white hair drawn back into a bun, framing a fine and regular-featured face. She was a lady of outstanding culture and savoir faire and enjoyed great prestige with the parents. She left Lyon to take up an appointment as principal of the newly opened Lycée de Vincennes in Paris but was arrested during the war for refusing to denounce Jewish students. She survived concentration camp and returned to resume her post until she retired. Although other headmistresses might have considered it demeaning to take on routine duties in school, she was always prepared to do them, in the interests of good discipline and behavior. She would patrol the corridors during breaks, preventing girls from running or shouting in an unseemly way. And at lunchtime, she never missed a single meal in the dining hall; she would stand there for the duration of the meal, keeping a watchful eye on our table manners.

We then went out into the playground and played volleyball

until we were completely out of breath. Sometimes, when the ball burst or it was too hot for running around, or for some other reason that stopped us getting rid of our surplus energy, I would lead my friends into forbidden pursuits and we would steal off to explore the prohibited territory of the school's basement areas. The school was an extensive, three-story building constructed around a square playground. One complete side was taken up with the headmistress's apartments and the gymnasium; otherwise you would have been able to run right around the corridors on all three floors and get back to your starting point. But the only place you could do so was in the basement, which was of course completely out of bounds. On the ground floor, there was a door leading downstairs at each corner of the building. The dare was first to go down at one door and come out at the next, then run around to the second door, then the third, without being caught going down or coming up, or encountering the caretaker who might give the game away. But the ultimate dare was to run right around the square and come out through the fourth door, next to the headmistress's office. I only did that once. Strangely enough, we were never caught. In our eyes, that basement was a fabulous place: it reeked of burning coal because of the huge boilers needed to heat those barracklike buildings. Then there were all kinds of theatrical backdrops, heaps of old desks, cupboards, maintenance workshops and so on. We did sometimes come across a few old maintenance men, but they were so surprised to bump into us down there that they never spilled the beans!

Apart from French and English, my schoolwork was not especially outstanding until I left for Saint Omer at the age of fifteen. I was quite lazy and after school preferred to stroll up and down the Rue de la République, Lyon's main street, rather than go home and get on with my homework. I can picture myself standing there looking at film posters (I wasn't allowed to go to the cinema) or walking up and down the street, my nose glued to the windows of all the smart shops, admiring all the things I couldn't possibly buy. I would often walk five or six stops of the streetcar journey to save some of the fare, and with the proceeds treat myself to dates or hot chestnuts in winter, or delicious caramels made by a street vendor before my very eyes. It was the bustle of life that attracted me. It was so much more fun than slaving at algebra or grappling with a Latin translation!

My mother, of course, soon discovered what I was up to, because I found it hard to explain why I was always home so late. After that, she made me stay at school for supervised prep and I then went home at half past seven in the evening, in the dark in winter. So my parents decided to send me to board with my godmother, Aunt Jeanne, in Saint Omer and attend the local high school, which was principally for boys.

Oddly enough, the only boys' state high school in the Pas de Calais was in Saint Omer, not in Arras, the county town of the department. Because there were numerous private Catholic schools for girls in the town, the numbers of girls needing state education did not warrant a separate girls' school, so arrangements were made for girls to be educated within the precincts of the boys' school. The younger girls were tutored by two or three private teachers, but the older ones preparing for public examinations were taught alongside the boys. I remember that there were five of us at the time, privileged to receive the excellent tuition of a school which prided itself on its academic reputation. Most of the pupils were weekly boarders who came from all over the area—Calais, Boulogne, Deauville, Le Touquet, Arras and a multitude of little Flanders villages.

I don't know whether it was the change that inspired me or whether it was the influence of Aunt Jeanne, who was so like my mother and very fond of me, or the presence of her daughter, Paulette, who though seven years my senior, was my favorite cousin. Or perhaps it was the fact that I was in competition with boys, which certainly spurred me on. For whatever reason, I suddenly began to work hard to make up for lost time and finished my fifth year very respectably. The following year I took my first public exam, which I passed with an A grade.

I was happy in Saint Omer. Every month, I would go to Arras to have my teeth straightened by one of my first cousins who was an excellent dentist. He was ten years older than me and as the months passed, we became close friends. He was really the first man I had met who did not treat me like a child. The only snag was that I had to stay the night at his mother's house—and she was terribly bigoted and unworldly. We used to have the most extraordinary conversations. She could not bear the thought that I was a Protestant and refused to go to Mass, and looked upon me as some kind of emanation of the devil! One day she taunted me by saying that unless I converted to Catholicism, I had no hope of salvation. I retorted that on the contrary, I was the one who would be saved, and all the Protestants along with me. That day, I really thought she would explode. In her most acid tone, her lips pinched in fury, she replied, "Never! That would be just too easy!" Dear old Aunt Clothilde, whom my sister and I irreverently called Clo-Clo, was married to my mother's eldest brother, a brilliant man, and was a good mother to her outstanding children. Her eldest son, my cousin Achille, became the head of the big seminary of Arras; he was as broad-minded and intelligent as his mother was not. Her youngest son first completed architecture studies, then, after being held a prisoner of war for five years, discovered a late vocation for the priesthood. He was absolutely charming, very refined, artistic; he was a saint and much too good a man for this earth. He died young in a drowning accident off the coast of Bilbao.

It is to him I owe my change of opinion about the existence of the Devil. He would sometimes come to London and visit me after the war. We would go to the National Gallery to view the early Flemish paintings, which he particularly liked, having been a student at the Ecole des Beaux Arts in Brussels. He would stand for hours in front of every painting, explaining the finer points to me; I really learned a lot from those private lessons. One day, he had been examining a particular Virgin and Child for ages and I was getting tired, so I sat down on one of the narrow benchlike settees which were then situated in the middle of the long galleries. As soon as I sat down, an extremely unpleasant man, dressed all in black, rather weird-looking and disquieting, came to sit beside me. I remember feeling so uncomfortable and so cold all of a sudden that I got up and walked the few paces which separated me from my cousin, who was still lost in contemplation of the picture. "I'm joining you because I'm frightened of the man sitting next to me," I said. But when we both turned to look at him, there was no one there; no sign of him. I just could not believe my eyes! We had a good view of the entire length of the gallery in both directions and there was nobody who fitted my description. I felt so ill at ease and embarrassed as I tried to explain that there really had been someone there. I was sure that Fernand would think I was mistaken and make fun of me. On the contrary, with immense composure he said, "Don't worry. It's the Devil, he's always pestering me, take no notice. Come and look at this exquisite painting." He then went on to explain that the forces of evil are all around us, that we have to try to combat them in every possible way; and if all else fails, we have to pray!

I have never been able to eradicate the memory of that uncanny apparition from my mind. It was totally inexplicable, illogical and very unnerving. Since then, I have experienced a number of similar encounters and have by now got used to those strange feelings, so I salute the memory of my saintly cousin and herewith make a public apology to the Holy Priest of Ars!

In the summer of 1937, my parents allowed me to attend a Girl Guide camp in England. I had remained in touch with my old Guide company in Lyon and heard that some of the girls were going to a big international Guide rally at Foxlease in Hampshire, where the World Chief Guide, Lady Baden-Powell, would be guest of honor. I arranged to meet them there and share their tent and arrived to find row upon row of army tents lined up with military precision, ready for the several hundred girls who were coming. We had a wonderful time: we were all good friends and there was the additional excitement of camping in a much more military style than we had ever done in France. While I was at Foxlease, I made friends with Lady Baden-Powell's daughter, Heather, and visited their home at Pax Hill. Feeling very happy to be back in England, I very much wanted to prolong my stay, and Heather found me an au pair's job in Devon, looking after the two small children of a friend of hers. Those two months in England did my English a power of good and helped me a great deal in my public exams in the following years.

Back at school in Saint Omer, all went well as we had really excellent teachers. The discipline was severe, but the school had high standards and we worked hard. It was in Saint Omer that I met Mr. Delandre, my Latin teacher, who later became a school inspector in Paris. He was a good-looking, man, tall and impressive with a sardonic sense of humor, but we all loved him and he and I remained friends until his death in the sixties. My French teacher, a young man barely older than we were, loved hearing me recite poetry. Whenever he needed to comment on a poem, or wanted the class to approve his choice of verse, he would always say, "Mademoiselle Meynard, please read." It almost became a classroom joke and whenever he uttered the words, "Mademoiselle Meynard," the entire class would say in chorus, "Please read." He told me I had a good speaking voice and should go on the stage. I certainly loved reciting poetry and talking, but was much too shy to act. I would never have been able to give way to my feelings in public. I strongly dislike public displays of emotion; I always have, and tried to train my own children to contain their own emotions unless they were at home—where everything was allowed, understood and forgiven. I have never believed in letting the outside world see my private emotions, whether of joy, or grief or indifference. My emotions have always been my private territory. Yet I am sensitive to good acting and displays of emotion on stage. I much admire fine actors and envy them their ability to evoke emotions in others, every night, over and over again.

With the passing years, my parents' affairs had improved considerably. My mother had been reinstated in the Telephone Service at a senior level, after a personal plea to Marshal Pétain who had decorated her in the war and still enjoyed immense prestige as the victor of Verdun. Papa, too, had managed to find a good position for himself, and they had disposed of the boarding house and school and now lived in a flat in the center of Lyon. Thankfully, they had managed to keep La Savane and were able to store there all the furniture from La Grive and their previous large house which would not fit into their small town apartment. A promising job offer in Paris for my father led my mother to seek a position there, which she obtained. They moved in the spring of 1938 and before very long were settled in a pleasant flat in the heart of the capital, on the top floor of a modern building in the Marais, very close to the Place des Vosges and a stone's throw from the Hôtel de Ville. My sister, who had already passed her medical exam to become a junior doctor in Lyon, decided to take the exam again for Paris, and was successful.

My mother decided it was time for me to be fully reintegrated in the family unit, so I, too, went to live in Paris and attended the Lycée Sévigné for my last year of school. We could study either philosophy or mathematics; I chose philosophy and passed my final exam commendably in the summer term of 1939. It was an excellent school whose building was shared with the Musée Carnavalet, right in the middle of the Marais, the heart of Paris's Jewish quarter. Most of my schoolfriends were Jewish and we got on well. I owe a great deal to the philosophy teacher I had there; she was also Jewish and introduced me to the works of Bergson. The family atmosphere was relaxed and I was welcomed home with as much pleasure as I myself felt to be back again. But I had acquired a taste for freedom and distance from the rather austere milieu of my aging parents. My childhood was already well in the past.

My year at the lycée in Paris was a great eye-opener for me. I discovered the thrill of intellectual argument, the joy of unlimited reading, the pleasure of writing French to my heart's content, unhindered by the need to grind away at physics or dreaded mathematics. The nearest I came to science in that last year was a course on cosmography and an advanced class in biology and I was able to take these in my stride without too much difficulty. I also discovered Paris, its numerous historical monuments, which had haunted my imagination since my first lesson in French history, its rich museums, theaters, musical and artistic dynamism. At long last I was living my life to the full. It was so exciting to be eighteen years old, on the threshold of life, with so much to live for. As soon as I had my exam results, I enrolled at the Sorbonne for the coming academic year and left with a light heart for the south, the sun and all the fun that lay in store for me. But the war was soon to cast its long shadow over my euphoria.

What was happening meanwhile to that young *yeshiva bokher*[11] as he prepared to leave his home for an exciting future, mapped out by his devoted parents? It had been difficult for Chanca to gather together everything Bob needed: the long black coat, or *kapote,* the matching long trousers, new shirts, underwear, socks and shoes, even a black soft felt hat. She had had to borrow funds for his train ticket and a small amount of pocket money for essentials. He had never owned such a wardrobe before, but it was the minimum required by the yeshiva where he was going to become a boarder. I remember seeing a photograph of him as he must have looked when he left home. He was quite chubby at the time, but already looked much older than his years with his side-locks and black hat and his V-neck *kapote* open to reveal a white shirt. The whole family went with him to the station as he set off on his two-day journey for Bratislava. It had been arranged that he would sleep and have breakfast at school, but since his parents could not afford full board, the rest of his meals would be shared between seven or eight families. It was a system known as *tägeessen,* whereby local families would take in the yeshiva students as guests, feeding them out of charity. Eventually a student refectory was established in the yeshiva by the last rector, but too late for Bob to benefit from it.

In later years, Bob often told me how much he had resented having to rely on other people's goodwill for his nourishment and it was to remain a never-forgotten humiliation for him. Some families were kind and welcoming, but others would remind him as he ate his meal that they were doing him a great favor. Editha Glazer, who as a child lived on the Hochstrasse in Bratislava (*hoch* meaning both high and tall) well remembers him coming to her house as a guest on the Sabbath. Bob described with evident pride his origins in the Carpathian

---

11. Student at a Talmudic school of higher learning.

mountains of "Podkarpatska Rus"[12] and talked of his parents and brothers and sisters. When she asked him what his name was, he replied with a pun, "Look at me Editha, my name is the same as the street you live in. I am called Hoch and I want to be hoch." Two years later, when he was selling cheap jewelry to earn a living, he went back to the Hochstrasse and gave a necklace to the lady who had so generously invited the young yeshiva student to her table. For her part, she barely recognized the clean-shaven, short-haired young man she saw before her.

School hours at the yeshiva were long and tiring. The day would start at 6 A.M. and the boys would still be working at 11 P.M. Even more stamina was required by those who also had to make their way twice a day to eat with various Bratislava families, sometimes at a fair distance from the yeshiva, but the students' travels to and fro did give them a glimpse of town life. After one year of this arduous routine, Bob went home to his parents and family, whose hearts burst with pride when they saw their son behaving like a true Jewish scholar. During those summer months, he was pleased to meet up with his friends from the Zionist movement and attended their meetings again, helping to distribute leaflets urging young men to join the Underground movement with a view to leaving for Israel. The devout and learned rabbi of Szlatina, Rabbi Haim Yitzak Eisik Halbersam, who along with Rabbi Teitelbaum, former rabbi of Sighet, had encouraged his family to send him to Bratislava, called the boy to see him to test his knowledge.[13] As the gossip of the little town reported, "He knew it all by heart, Torah, Talmud and all." While this is an exaggeration, the rabbi must nevertheless have been very impressed with his protégé's progress. Bob's retentive memory was phenomenal, and it is difficult for those who never knew him personally to appreciate the extent of his knowledge. Although patchy and selective, it was amazingly detailed and specialized in a great number of disparate fields.

---

12. Region situated between Poland, Romania, Hungary and Slovakia; also known as Sub-Carpathian Ruthenia or Karpatska Ukraïna. It was known as Podkarpatska Rus until 1944 and is now a part of Ukraine.

13. Rabbi Halbersam, the son-in-law of Rabbi Teitelbaum, was the last rabbi of Szlatina. He was a devout and saintly man who was tortured by Hungarian soldiers just before he was deported to Auschwitz, where he was murdered, together with his wife and nine of his eleven children.

Bob returned to the yeshiva in Bratislava in autumn 1937, where he resumed the normal routine of learning until the spring of 1938. At that point and for various reasons, he seems to have become disenchanted with the education he was receiving. He was concerned that he was receiving practically no general education, since yeshiva tutorials were confined strictly to the Torah and Talmud and, in his eyes, had little relevance to life going on around him. He must certainly have sensed the restlessness of the town and understood that the news from abroad was ominous after the Nazi's annexation of Austria in March 1938, and with the German army of occupation stationed in Vienna, not far from Bratislava. He started playing truant from school and decided to visit Prague, not an easy undertaking for someone who had no money. By begging and subsequently selling trinkets, he managed to make his way to the capital, but couldn't get into the city because he had no papers. As he made this journey, he discovered that the image of a *yeshiva bokher* was clearly something of a liability in a country where antisemitism was rearing its ugly head. At a stroke, he had his hair cut, got rid of his side-locks and the Jewish garb so lovingly prepared by his mother. In a state of total rebellion, he went back to Bratislava via Brno, but decided not to return to the yeshiva. In Brno, he had met other youngsters like him, also from Podkarpatska Rus. They would meet and discuss the political events of 1938, which deeply affected them all. Some of them were considering trying to escape to France, England, Palestine or the United States. A few volunteered to approach the Moravian military headquarters to ask if they could join the army—in order to fight the Nazis. One of the officers told them in Czech, "Go home, boys, we'll call you if we need you." They were intensely disappointed at this rejection, and Bob, one of the youngest amongst them, must have stood there grinding his teeth in anger. Some of them did manage to join the Allied armies; others, including the man who told me this story, found themselves marched off to concentration camps.

Through contacts he had made in Bratislava, Bob acquired a small amount of cheap jewelry that he started selling to raise the money for his train fare home at the end of the summer term. His sisters, who met him at the station in Szlatina, barely recognized their own brother as he stepped off the train. He had grown a great deal, acquired a completely new hairstyle—and, it seemed to them, a totally different personality. Anticipating their mother's reaction to such a transformation, they were petrified.

Chanca was devastated. All her dreams vanished the instant Bob arrived home. She just could not understand how the son on whom she had lavished all her love, all her care and hopes and for whom she had made untold sacrifices, could have changed so radically in such a short time. How Mehel reacted, nobody seems to remember, but his wife's response was immediate, loud and unequivocal. On the spur of the moment, the hurt and shame was so great that Bob had to leave home again immediately. This time, his younger cousin, Michael Tabak, went with him.

They left for Bratislava on foot, without any money at all and set out to find work. It took them two months to get there, sleeping rough, begging and doing odd jobs as they made their way through the countryside. Once they reached Bratislava, they managed to scrape a living by taking whatever work they could find, with Bob becoming a seasoned pedlar of cheap trinkets. They stayed there for a few months, but the political situation was rapidly deteriorating under pressure from Germany for the dismantlement of Czechoslovakia. In November 1938, the Czechs were forced to cede the territory of Sub-Carpathian Ruthenia to Hungary. The entire population of Szlatina instantly lost their Czech citizenship and became Hungarians once again. Slovakia was similarly obliged to hand over territories to Hungary, and in March 1939 declared its independence, placing itself under the protection of the Third Reich. Bob and his cousin Michael then realized it was imperative to leave Bratislava immediately, for fear of being arrested, and they decided to head for Budapest via home. Michael's clearest recollection of their hurried departure is that Bob left Bratislava laden with books which he would read all day long, regardless of their urgent need to earn a few coins working on a farm to buy food, and to find a place to spend the night in a barn or haystack. They finally arrived home after a month on the road.

By that time, home for the Hoch family was a new house provided by the generosity of one of Chanca's brothers who had emigrated to America and made good in the laundry business. On a visit to his father just before the war, he was so moved by his sister's poverty that he gave her $500—enough in the Szlatina of 1937 to buy a two-room house in the part of the village shared by the Hungarians and Romanians. For the first time in her life, Chanca had a home of her own, with a large garden full of fruit trees. They were able to acquire a goat, the poor man's cow. She had an oven and an outhouse which could be used for storage. What more could she possibly desire? Alas, Bob was there so fleetingly that he had no recollection of that new house at all. Home for him had always been his grandfather's cramped quarters and he was not to know the more comfortable life they now had.

He was by then a strapping lad of nearly sixteen. He was tall for his age, but very slim, perpetually hungry and used up all his energy trekking around the countryside. Although still a child by our standards, he mixed freely with men much older than himself. His aunt Dvora Davidovic kept a bar in the village and there he would listen to the latest news brought by older boys who had already been to Budapest, or others like him, who were thinking of going there to join the stream of Czechs hoping to escape the occupation of their country and flee to the West. He heard from his older cousin, Alec Davidovic, that he and his brother Joseph were considering leaving to join the Czech army abroad, but he himself was asked by his youth movement to go to Budapest and join the Underground. He already had a shrewd idea of what to expect from the Germans, for by the time he reached home for the last time, attacks on Jews were being orchestrated in all Nazi-occupied lands and puppet states. He had seen German Jews from the Sudetenland seeking refuge in Bratislava and, more recently, Czechs passing through the town on their way to Hungary, trying to escape the stranglehold that was beginning to trap them on all sides as the Germans encircled them in Austria, Poland and Slovakia. Every day, they would meet Poles who had fled over the Yasinya mountain pass and reached Szlatina by following the railway track through Rakhov. They, too, were making their way across Hungary, aiming to meet up with partisan movements that were helping Czechs and Poles to cross the border into Yugoslavia.

Bob shared all his apprehension and wild plans of escape with his mother, who by then had totally forgiven him. Chanca recognized that times had changed, that the fight for Eretz Israel and more equitable conditions for all peoples of Europe had to be led by other than pious and saintly rabbis. She was well versed in politics, and while she could not possibly have foreseen the fate that lay in store for her family, she certainly believed that Budapest was the safest town for him to go and find work, a possible way of reaching Israel—and ultimately an escape route to join the armies of the West. The Hungarians had at first been joyously received by a large part of the local Jewish population. Alas, subsequent events were to prove just how misplaced their confidence was. Hungary adopted anti-Jewish legislation before Nazi Germany and perpetrated the first mass execution of Jews at Kamenets Podolsk in the autumn of 1941, with a cruelty and brutality which surpassed even that of the

Germans.[14] A survivor reported the waters of the river Dnieper remained red for days with the blood of the martyred population.

So Chanca gave her blessing to her son's departure, sensing that it was the right course of action for him, believing fervently in his bright future but heavy-hearted and filled with foreboding. She was by now more accustomed to his absences from home, but found it hard to respond wholeheartedly to his enthusiasm and eagerness to leave. Bob and Michael Tabak left together in the autumn of 1939 to make their way to Budapest. That brief visit to Szlatina was the last time he ever saw his parents and siblings, except for Brana and Sylvia, whom he next saw again in 1945.

---

14. Over 14,000 Jews from Ruthenia, some from Sighet, Szlatina and surrounding villages, were deported by the Hungarians to German-occupied Ukraine and murdered by SS mobile killing squads, called *Einsatzgruppen,* in 1941.

2

I wonder by my troth, what thou, and I
Did, till we lov'd? were we not wean'd till then?
But suck'd on country pleasures, childishly?

JOHN DONNE, THE GOOD-MORROW

I was eighteen years old when war broke out in September 1939. At first, however, I was largely unconcerned by events on what seemed to me our distant northern borders. I had a place at the Sorbonne to study classics and philosophy and felt that my immediate future was secure. I can still see myself in that summer of 1939, on holiday in southwestern France, flirting demurely with my cousin Olivier who was an officer cadet at Saint Cyr, France's leading military academy.

He was more than a little in love with me, but his feelings were not reciprocated; I treated him more like a brother, much to his dismay. I had adopted him as my official escort, thereby acquiring much greater freedom of movement for myself than my strict and rather Victorian upbringing would have allowed. We played tennis, attended every house party and dance in sight and were invited to every country house in the neighborhood. I learned to drive in an old jalopy that one night I somehow managed to ram into a cow. I still have fond memories of that old car: we went everywhere in it, but it had a character of its own and was always letting us down in the middle of nowhere. That was how I came to have my first lessons in car maintenance and mechanics, when Olivier and I decided we would just have to learn how to strip it down and repair it. Then we would be prepared for all eventualities. I can picture myself now, hot, bothered and oily, grappling with bits of engine that were rather like a Chinese puzzle to me. The whole of that summer remains imprinted on my memory as an uninterrupted, sun-drenched, radiant idyll. I seemed to be in a permanent state of euphoria, living free as air, gorging on melons, hot semibaked prunes and purple sun-kissed figs, returning late at night from all our outings, feeling generally wonderful, on top of a world that was out there, just waiting for me!

By late September, it was time for those halcyon days to come to an end and I returned to Paris, ready to start my degree course at the Sorbonne. I was also taking a Cordon Bleu cookery course, a one-year Red Cross first aid course and singing lessons. I don't quite remember how I managed to cram all that in, but I did it somehow; I was so eager to live my life to the full. I have vivid recollections of those early student days: walking up and down the Boulevard St. Michel in the Latin Quarter of Paris, with a cosmopolitan band of fun-loving Bulgarian, Rumanian and French students, attending lectures in vast amphitheaters packed to the rafters with spellbound audiences, hearing Henri Bergson give a special lecture, burning the midnight oil cramming for tests on Latin classical authors and so on. But the real highlight for me was the interminable discussions that would go on late into the night on all kinds of abstract topics. I remember, for instance, a fierce and repeated debate on whether it was better to have great intelligence and no heart, or vice versa. The questioning, the thrust and parry of argument, the freedom to develop an idea, this was the stuff of student life and is my overriding memory of those days.

My Cordon Bleu course was an equally extraordinary experience, mostly because of the fascinating personality who energized the class. Dr. Pomiane de Pozersky, a descendant of an aristocratic Polish family, was well known as a physician at the time, but had taken to gourmet cuisine as his hobby. His class used to meet somewhere in the Latin Quarter; incongruous as it may sound, the class was held in a teaching convent where there was a kitchen specially fitted with the most modern equipment of the time. The course was exceedingly expensive and was really intended as a refresher course for Paris hostesses and society women who wanted to enhance the excellence of their table.

The daily pattern was always the same. Dr. Pomiane opened the morning session promptly at eight o'clock with an hour's lecture on nutrition in general and the food we were about to cook in particular. Then we would set to work in groups of two, each of us preparing a different course, but constantly peering at our partner's efforts to take note of what she was doing. We were a relatively select band of only ten students and the meal we cooked always consisted of an hors d'oeuvre, entrée, fish course, meat dish garnished with fresh vegetables and dessert. Once all the basic cooking was under way, we would lay the table, always under Dr. Pomiane's supervision. Then, at one o'clock, the great moment arrived and we would sit down to sample the most exquisite lunch, enhanced by the Doctor's sparkling conversation with his "guests." He was the most wonderful raconteur, with a fascinating repertoire of personal anecdotes about the many superlative meals he had eaten as a guest of the great and good of his time. One such story was his description of a dinner party at which the hostess had draped the table in a cloth of pink crêpe de chine, with matching napkins. Our gallant Dr. Pomiane saucily remembered that every time he wiped his mouth on that pink napkin, he would fantasize about kissing the little pink panties of his hostess. I was not yet nineteen, and these naughty tales really made me think I was catching a glimpse of Gay Paree.

My partner was a young Englishwoman, Emma Nikis, a charming, beautiful girl who had recently married a Greek. She tackled the course very dutifully and seriously, perhaps at the time not fully appreciating its slight eccentricity. When I came across her again later in life, I discovered that hers had been a tragic war: her husband had joined the Resistance, been captured by the Germans and died in a concentration camp. She had tried desperately to save him; she, too, had joined the Resistance, been caught and deported to Ravensbruck. It was a tragedy that had left her disconsolate for many a year, not so much because of her own suffering, but for the loss of the husband she adored. Awarded the Légion d'Honneur and the Médaille Militaire, she chose to remain in France after the war. Many years later, she was to marry Sir Charles Henderson, a prominent businessman and philanthropist, and settled with him on the Riviera.

For me personally, there was a far more memorable event in that spring of 1940. I fell in love with a Czech airman called Mihàlek. He was very handsome: tall, athletic, blond. He was shy, cultured, quietly spoken and gentle. Music was one of his great loves, and for him I made considerable efforts to improve my skills on the piano. Along with ten other airmen from the aeronautics school at Arvor, he had been sent on compassionate leave to the Cité Universitaire, the hall of residence for female students in the Latin Quarter of Paris, where I was living as a half-boarder. When the Czech airmen arrived, we were asked to befriend them, talk to them, go out with them when they were on leave in Paris and correspond with them when they went back to the war. It was all very innocent, certainly on my part.

One evening, when we were all having coffee at the Cité, the young men started to tell us the most ghastly stories. They described in graphic detail all kinds of tortures being perpetrated by the Nazis in their country: men imprisoned in cages, beaten relentlessly until they talked, burned with electrodes or savaged by dogs specially trained to go for their genitals. These young men were already pretty macho, and we girls all thought it was quite unnecessary for them to try to impress us even more with these horrifying tales. We had a great deal of admiration for them anyway and this assertive display of virility was completely superfluous. In short, none of us believed a word they said. I remember to this day their dejected faces. They never mentioned it again. It was only years later that I realized with hindsight that they had not been trying to impress us at all, far from it; they had actually been telling the truth, trying to warn us, to shock us out of our selfishness and childish insouciance.

Mihàlek and I corresponded regularly; he used to call me "ma grande de l'âme." His French was not good, his English not much better, and so our exchanges were necessarily limited. But one day he wrote to tell me that he was leaving and I should forget him. At first I did not really understand what he meant; I just thought he had found another girlfriend. It was only months later that I found out that all those young Czech airmen had left for England. Mihàlek was killed in the early days of the Battle of Britain, as were all his friends whom I had got to know in Paris. His plane was shot down as he pursued the German invader, but at the time I knew nothing of that. Much later when I came to England, I learned of his fate from a former Czech airman in their squadron who had survived.

My parents did not altogether approve of my very casual approach to my studies and were trying to curb my social life. They put a strict limit on my allowance, so I decided it was time to stop being completely dependent on them. I needed to find a way to earn some money. As it happened, I heard of a school in Vitry, a suburb about six miles from the Sorbonne, which was offering a reasonable salary to students in return for looking after the boarders in the evenings and at weekends. This sounded quite attractive to me, especially since it would leave me free to pursue my studies on weekdays, so in the spring of 1940, I applied for and got the job at the Ecole Départementale de Vitry. I had hardly taken up my post and got to know the fifteen- to eighteen-year-old girls who were in my charge (I was all of nineteen myself), when the Germans invaded the Low Countries on May 10, 1940.

These events precipitated an immediate order for all children in Paris state schools to be evacuated to the country, and we soon found ourselves under instructions to decamp to the safety of Normandy. Our journey by train was hastily organized and it was not long before we were temporarily settled in a summer camp near Cabourg, a seaside resort made famous by Proust's *A La Recherche du Temps Perdu*. Conditions were somewhat primitive; I lodged nearby in a lowly little farmhouse along with a new girl companion, Raymonde Debru, who was assigned to look after the younger girls. Raymonde was strikingly pretty, blond, tall, slim and willowy. She was terribly shortsighted, but refused at the time to wear glasses, and had a way of looking at men through her myopic haze that invariably bowled them over. She was extremely intelligent, well read, attractive and good company. We immediately took to each other and became inseparable. One of my cousins had also joined us in Cabourg; he was a chemical engineer and was completing a research project on a chemical compound. Believing he was on the verge of a momentous discovery, he had decided to find a place of refuge, both for himself and his precious collection of books.

For close to a month, we enjoyed the peace and tranquillity of the country, outside time and out of sight. The war seemed a long way off, and we were safe. But suddenly, the news broke that German Panzer divisions were thundering their way down the French roads from Belgium. Full-scale panic and hysteria gripped the population. You have to bear in mind that two generations of French children had been taught in school about the atrocities committed by the Huns in occupied Belgium and Alsace Lorraine in the First World War. They were reported to have raped women, slashed off their breasts and impaled babies on their swords. For the great majority of the French population, the Germans were barbarians. This explains to a certain extent the unspeakable fear which seized the whole of northern France at the approach of the German army. But another significant reason, of course, was the defeatist attitude of the retreating French army. Later, when forced to tramp the roads of Normandy, we came across thousands of unarmed French soldiers, all looking harassed, disheveled, totally weary and dispirited. Their story was always the same: they either had weapons and no ammunition or weapons with the wrong ammunition; and there was no point in carrying weapons if you could not fire them. The disorder of the retreat had to be seen to be believed. Of course, there were pockets of heroic resistance and other instances where the retreat was a strategic withdrawal, but this was certainly not the case for the regiments we encountered. As for the civilian population, there was no one left behind to take control and give orders; in every town or village we went through, the administrative heads had invariably been amongst the first to leave.

Looking back on this period, it seems scandalous that a government could leave an entire population to its own devices and instincts, conditioned as they were in this case by over forty years of the most appalling tales of barbarism. In children's picture books which I still have, German soldiers with their unmistakable peaked helmets are depicted like traditional ogres, with red faces, protruding teeth and fiendish expressions. To this day, I have a vivid recollection of one horrific picture: in one hand a German soldier is brandishing a dagger dripping blood, while in the other he holds the corpse of the baby he has just speared; on the road the baby's mother lies in agony with bleeding breasts which another soldier has just hacked through. Alas, harrowing scenes such as these were soon to become reality all over again, when the Nazi brutes in the death camps behaved true to form.

But this deeply ingrained terror of the Germans can offer no real excuse for much of the French establishment's shameful dereliction of duty. Numerous explanations have since been given, especially the infiltration of the administration, the army and the legislative bodies by fifth columns, a great boon to the Germans whose goal was to bring France down from the inside in order to make its occupation quicker and easier. Since then I have read a great many well-researched books on the subject, their accounts based on verifiable facts, but I can only talk about events as I saw or experienced them at the time.

So there we were at Cabourg with six hundred children aged between eight and sixteen, divided into four groups, in two primary and two vocational schools. In many ways, our stay there seemed like the last holiday of the prewar period. Food supply was just about the only thing which functioned more or less normally, and this was partly because the summer camp director was well used to the problems of feeding hundreds of children and somehow managed to provide substantial amounts of fresh, wholesome, well-cooked food. Marvelous, enormous slices of bread and butter formed the basis of all the meals, complementing ample helpings of tasty stew, pâtés, generous amounts of cheese, jams in abundance, slabs of chocolate and cider for the adults to drink. All the riches of Normandy seemed to contribute to the delicious sense of well-being which pervaded this camp of Parisian children, who were not too sure what was expected of them in this novel situation. In the meantime, we went to the beach every day, ate well and kept lessons to a minimum because we were short of books and paper. We were all in holiday mood.

But this relaxed and carefree atmosphere was abruptly interrupted one sunny June morning. Suddenly we heard a series of booming explosions and German planes with their unmistakable black-cross markings roared overhead. Before there was any time for explanation, the sky all around us turned as black as soot and we were engulfed in darkness. We just could not understand this phenomenon. It may sound amusing now, but I distinctly remember thinking it must be the end of the world! I was really so ignorant of anything outside my very limited experience of everyday life and academic studies. It was a traumatic ordeal for us all, children and adults alike. We could barely see one another at more than a meter away; the children began to cry and we had no idea how to begin to reassure them; we had been plunged into the depths of despair ourselves. Soon we were all covered in a film of black grease reeking of oil. Then at last we understood, or perhaps we were told, that the Germans had bombarded the oil refineries at Le Havre: all the wells and tanks were ablaze.

This pall of stinking murkiness lasted a whole day, and in the confusion we were ordered to pack our bags and be ready for evacuation the very next morning. At daybreak, a whole convoy of military trucks appeared on the playing field to evacuate us "towards the south." The children climbed into the trucks, with one supervisor allotted to each vehicle. Each child was carrying his or her little bundle of meager possessions: a change of underclothes, little personal treasures, bread and chocolate; and the supervisors were allowed to take their bicycles. When the signal was given, engines roared into action and off we went, destination unknown, just keeping ahead of the Germans who were hard on our heels.

All went well at first in the early hours of the morning, but by the time the sun was high, we soon became a target for enemy fire; from the air, of course, they had no way of knowing that this was a completely innocent cargo. Machine-gun fire rained down on us from above while we huddled in fear and confusion, not understanding what was happening. Suddenly the trucks lurched to a halt. The children were ordered to jump down quickly and make a run for the ditch on the other side of the road. There we crouched, panic-stricken and petrified, until the alert had passed. Then back we got into the trucks and the convoy moved off again. A few miles further on, exactly the same thing happened again and the whole performance had to be repeated. Several times over, along that road, the enemy opened fire on us, until in the end the captain in command decided the route was far too dangerous and gave the order to turn off the main road and head into the country. Just a few miles after this change of plan, the trucks suddenly came to a standstill and the captain explained he could not take us any further. He was under orders; he was already very behind schedule. He was sure things would sort themselves out.

So there we were, unceremoniously abandoned on the roadside, left to our own devices with a band of young children. Over and over again, we tried to hail passing vehicles, but it was no good. We were just beginning to feel desperate when thankfully a military convoy drew to a halt beside us. An officer got out of the first vehicle and began a confab with Raymonde who was at the front of our group. Somehow or other, we soon found ourselves loaded into the trucks of a Moroccan infantry regiment which was hurrying south to escape the Germans. Raymonde, sitting up front in the cab with the captain of this company, was doing her best to tell him our troubles—where we had come from and our present plight. He did not need much convincing. From high up in his truck, this young captain had already been captivated by her beauty; he had only stopped because of her. He had to drop us quite soon to continue his own journey, but in his heart he was absolutely certain he would see Raymonde again; in the twinkling of an eye he had made up his mind that she would be his wife—which later she did indeed become. They exchanged addresses, then the trucks left us near a little town where the captain hoped we would find help. And so we did. We had ended up near Condé sur Noireau hours after our journey began.

At this point, our headmaster was shaken out of his inertia. He got in touch with the mayor of Condé sur Noireau, who agreed to give us shelter in a former flour mill, now converted into a children's summer camp. As lodgings went, it was fairly basic, but nevertheless adequate. It was only at this point that we realized with growing horror that half of our group was missing. Somehow or other, long before the Moroccan infantry regiment had picked us up, our convoy must have got split into two, perhaps in the confusion, perhaps through lack of coordination between the drivers. To this day I can't fathom how it happened, but I do have vivid memories of our deep apprehension and concern for our colleagues and all the other children. Relieved to have reached a safe haven ourselves, we could not help worrying about them as we tried to settle the children down after the bewildering events of the day.

The building which was to be our home for the next two months was typical of many nineteenth-century factories—rectangular, elongated, with row upon row of small windows and a mill wheel, which now stood idle over a tributary of the Noireau. These rather dilapidated premises were huddled in a gorge at the foot of a high cliff. It was dismal; even the children's shouts and games did little to penetrate the gloom or make us forget the misery of our situation. The Greman army had now overtaken us and were occupying the entire region.

Raymonde and I were allocated a house that stood a little apart from the main buildings; and we shared it with Jacqueline Bergerol, the headmistress's daughter, whose mother had become separated from us with the other half of the school. The house was rather isolated, and nobody had been keen to live in it, so the headmaster finally decided to use it as the sick bay. Since I was the only adult with any inkling of first aid, however minimal, I was dispatched to sleep there to look after any sick children. Raymonde and I were delighted because this rather remotely situated house stood right beside the road leading out of the gorge and occupied a high position in relation to the other buildings. So when we were not on dormitory duty, we were able to get away from the group and chat in private about anything and everything, and especially what the future might hold in store for us. It gave us an opportunity to unwind, to forget our present anxieties and be young and carefree again. Sometimes our youthful high spirits would get the better of us, leaving us collapsed in fits of giggles.

After a few days, we were beginning to suffer from claustrophobia in this rather sinister place when an unexpected event changed everything—and was not without consequences for the future. It all started with a child being brought into the sick bay. My entire medical knowledge consisted of a first Red Cross certificate and a Girl Guide captain's first aid diploma, which in the event proved much more useful. But I recognized appendicitis when I saw it. What on earth could we do? Our only means of transport was bicycles and everybody was absolutely terrified: the men because they were in hiding and were afraid of being picked up by the enemy, the women because they were scared stiff of being raped by the Boches. Nobody wanted to volunteer to go and fetch help from Condé sur Noireau, a task they all considered hazardous to say the least.

I went back to the sick bay and found the child sweating profusely, with serious abdominal pains and nothing by way of treatment, not even ice. I decided I would have to ask the headmaster's permission to go on my bicycle to seek help. The Vitry school's headmaster held the rank of Academy Inspector and had accepted a post generally thought of as a sinecure: his only thoughts were of literature and a cozy fireside. He was a benevolent, meek man, not essentially a bad fellow, but like a fish out of water in a very difficult school. Vitry had originally been founded to cater to orphans after the 1914–18 war but had naturally seen its first intake progressively dry up as the years went by. After this, its pupils were drawn from "problem" families. Some children had been removed from negligent parents, others found delinquent by the courts. So the classes contained a high proportion of rebellious children from the most deprived Paris suburbs who needed constant vigilance and a very assertive teacher. Our poor headmaster was literally afraid of his own shadow, but he was even more frightened of taking any decisions which might not meet the approval of his peers. More often than not, he would pass the buck to the school's chief monitor, a rather embittered creature, underhand and surly, a real martinet of a man. We used to call him "L'affreux Jojo" (Jojo the terrible). To the headmaster's dismay, Jojo had been separated with the other half of the school, and we had absolutely no idea where they were or what had happened to them. I had no difficulty persuading him that he had no choice; he had to let me go.

I remember improvising a cape and a red cross; I borrowed a navy blue skirt and a white blouse and rigged myself out as a nurse as best I could. By now Raymonde had decided that she could not let me go alone. So, we got on our bikes and pedaled off towards Condé sur Noireau.

Our first realization of French defeat was the sight of the marketplace, all fenced off, with hundreds of French prisoners of war penned in the enclosure. After skirting around this distressing sight, I asked the way to the hospital. That was where I met "my first Germans." They were not dressed in their field green as I had expected, but were dressed in a grayish blue and were on sentry duty at the hospital gate. One of them directed me to the porter, and I described my problem to him. He in turn explained that the hospital had been requisitioned by the Germans, but that there was a French doctor I could speak to. So the doctor was called and he told me that the only vehicles available were German military ambulances and he would need permission from the German medical officer now in charge of the hospital. He signaled me to follow him and, with my heart beating furiously, I went into the German commander's office. Dr. Tauber was extremely courteous and understanding; he immediately gave orders for an ambulance to fetch the child, on the sole condition that I came back in the ambulance with him. I could hardly believe my ears. He walked back with me as far as the French doctor's consulting room, where he seemed very taken with Raymonde's beauty; she must certainly have appealed to his Aryan eye.

My mission had been successful beyond my wildest dreams. Leaving Raymonde and our bicycles at the hospital, I went to fetch the little boy in a military ambulance. Once we were back at the hospital, he was entrusted to the French doctor for an emergency operation to be performed by a German surgeon. As we were getting on our bicycles, Dr. Tauber himself suddenly appeared at the gate and said, "Don't worry, I'll be doing the operation myself, I have a little boy the same age as him." He then proceeded to give us some tickets for a concert due to take place that afternoon on the main square. Trying to refuse them, we explained that we would be on duty at school and that we could not possibly be released from work. He asked us nevertheless to do our best. Anyway, he said, he would be expecting us to come the next day for news of the boy. And this I agreed to do.

Once we were safely back at school, I recounted the entire adventure to the headmaster and all the other student monitors gathered to hear the tale. They simply could not believe we had actually spoken to the ogres and managed to come back in one piece! The next afternoon, we turned up at the hospital as promised to find the little boy in good shape. While we were chatting with the French doctor, trying to find out from him what was happening in the rest of France, Dr. Tauber suddenly appeared and invited us into his office. He had, apparently, something important to tell us.

Mystified, we followed him. As it turned out, that urgent message he had for us was nothing more than an invitation; he wanted to take us out to dinner along with an officer friend of his who was going to join us later. We hastened to explain that our work made it completely impossible. Anyway, there was a curfew on the roads and we would be arrested; it was quite out of the question. He then offered to come and speak to our headmaster, which we declined. He asked us what we did, how on earth we came to be in that dreary place in the middle of nowhere, then proceeded to tell us who he was and how he came to be there. He was an officer of a Luftwaffe regiment, supporting one of the Panzer divisions which were thundering down the coast road. The doctor commandant was a surgeon in Dresden; he didn't like the war, but he did like the French. It would all be over soon and everything would be for the best in the best of all possible worlds. Raymonde and I were both very innocent, but not quite as gullible as all that. The serpent and the apple flashed through my mind.

He then said, "When will you be going back to Paris?"

"In a few weeks, I expect."

"Where will you go then?"

"Back to school and the Sorbonne."

"Well, I hope all goes well. Give me your address, I'd like to have news of you and the boy; we'll certainly be in Paris soon."

They'll be a long way off in a month or two, I thought. So I gave him my address.

We stayed another two whole months at Condé sur Noireau. By that time, parents were beginning to agitate for their children's return, student monitors were anxious to get back to university and their families and the Seine Departmental School Inspectorate was becoming worried about the disappearance of one of its schools, without knowing exactly where it was. And so, at long last, our hesitant headmaster decided it was time for us to go home to Vitry.

At the beginning of September, we were transported by truck as far as Flers de l'Orne, where we boarded the train for Paris and Vitry sur Seine. When we finally arrived by coach outside the school gates, we were flabbergasted to see columns of German soldiers singing and marching in quick time, then, after a moment's pause, disappearing into the girls' primary school.

I have no precise recollection of who eventually sorted out this muddle, but I do remember clearly that in the end we had to share the premises with German soldiers until the Liberation. Every day we had to watch them march past singing in chorus—in tune and in three parts—all those German songs of the occupation: "Heidi i, Heidi ô," "Lili Marlène," not to mention the Nazi's preferred the Horst Wessel song, for good measure. They took over the two girls' schools, leaving us the two oldest buildings, the boys' primary and technical schools. We had to cram all the girls into the boys' technical school and all the boys into their own primary school. We were back home again, but the occupied Paris we had returned to was a very different city from the one we had left.

During the winter and spring of 1939–40, the city of Budapest, too, had quite a different feel about it and was then home to large numbers of foreigners and refugees, some making a living there, others trying to find a way of reaching the West. To get there, Bob and his cousin Michael Tabak had traveled the 350 kilometers from their native Szlatina. It was a long way to walk on very little money, but by then they were experienced hikers-cum-casual laborers, and they arrived without serious mishap. They had been given a few useful addresses back in Szlatina and had met up with Joseph Davidovic, Bob's first cousin, ten years his senior, who had already been in Budapest for some time with his younger brother Alec and a second cousin, Alec Pearl. There were quite a few young people from Szlatina and the surrounding area living in Budapest and they would meet in the evenings on the "Dob Ucca," the Great Synagogue street, where they exchanged information and helped one another to survive. It was through them that Bob and Michael found lodgings—if you can use such a grand name for the two or three rooms where up to forty young men would bed down for the night. Bob managed to get a job as a delivery boy for a hatter, but when he wasn't working, he would spend his time reading and keeping warm in one of the town libraries, or he would get hold of newspapers and read them from cover to cover as he walked along the pavement, at the risk of colliding with passersby. He soon succeeded in making contact with one of the many underground organizations which existed at the time, mostly unconnected with each other. Before long, he was working full time for the Czech mission and received subsistence money in return for helping to settle refugees in safehouses. Since most of the Czech refugees spoke no Hungarian, they had to rely on local resistance movements, some of which were supported by the French Embassy, which was looking after Czech interests following the Germans' annexation of Czechoslavakia. Their orders were to send Czech army volunteers to the West.

It was in the French Embassy at Fe Ucca that Bob, who had by now adopted the name of Jan Hoch, met Jan Toncar, born on the same day as him but four years his senior. As Jan Toncar wrote to me many years later, everyone seemed to be changing their names, even their identities, at the time—it was normal and quite unimportant. He and three of his best friends were also trying to make their way to the West, but while stranded in Budapest and speaking no Hungarian whatsoever, they were helping the Czech mission at the French Embassy, which would eventually ensure their escape. Without the local language, Jan Toncar could be of limited assistance, and so Bob, who spoke good Hungarian, was allocated to help him. Their task was to take refugees to their lodgings and pay the landladies with monies supplied weekly by the French Embassy from contributions given by Czech émigrés in the United States.

Bob soon graduated to accompanying refugees on their escape route. In all he would assist some twenty groups of men to the Yugoslav border and across. Such trips, which took place every day, were perilous for many reasons. Whereas Bob had proper Hungarian identity papers, that was not the case for the Czechs, who had become German subjects. They had no right to be in Hungary unless they had proper visas. Very few of the refugees had their papers in order, many had discarded them altogether and hardly any of them could speak Hungarian. The escort's role was to buy train tickets, food and drink, and generally act as lookout until they reached the Yugoslav border, which they would then cross on foot. Once in Belgrade, they would join the French Foreign Legion and transportation was then organized through Greece and Turkey to Lebanon, and from there by ship to the Foreign Legion barracks in Sidi Bel Abbes in Algeria. If they were caught en route, they ended up in prison and were deported back to Czechoslovakia. That is what happened to Toncar and his friends, but all of them managed to escape to Budapest again and finally reach France, where they eventually met up with Bob once again, by then a Czech soldier in uniform, known by his real name of Ludvik Hoch. They were all to sail to England on the same boat.

But Bob's route to France proved a great deal more hazardous. One day he failed to return from an escape mission. He and a few others had been betrayed, caught at the border by the Hungarian police, and were taken back to Budapest, accused of spying. Other Czech soldiers told me later that when leaders of escape groups were caught, they received quite different treatment from the men in their charge. They were generally beaten up over a period of weeks in the hope that they would reveal who they were working for, who was paying them and for what. In this case, Bob was the ringleader and was subsequently condemned to death. The French Embassy came to hear of his capture and sentence and, since they were still protecting Czech interests, remonstrated with the Hungarian authorities that he was a minor and therefore could not be given the death penalty. He was allowed to appeal and his trial was set for the end of January 1940.

As he was taken to court on the day of his trial, he managed to escape from his one-armed guard by hitting him over the head with his manacles. He then headed for the French Embassy where a young gypsy boy called Sandor, who spoke fluent Hungarian and who worked for the Czech Mission, enlisted the help of his mother to pick the lock on his handcuffs, which she did with ease. Sandor is still alive today to tell the tale and—small world indeed—he had been a schoolmate of Bob's back in Szlatina!

Bob had learned the ropes the hard way and now made good his escape via the underground movement he had previously worked for, leading a group across the border at Szeged to Belgrade and the French Embassy there. To greet and "vet" him on arrival was a young attaché, François Seydoux de Clausonne, a cousin of mine by marriage, who was later to become France's Ambassador to Austria and subsequently to the German Federal Republic. Bob and he would meet later on many occasions in Paris and in the various countries to which François was posted.

In this way, several thousand young men were saved from the jaws of death to become soldiers in the British army. Yet, although escape routes to the West from Eastern and Central Europe were broadly similar, each of these young men had his own story to tell and no two were ever identical.

By mid-1940, Czech forces in France totaled about 10,000 officers and men who formed the First Czechoslovak Division. They were stationed in a military camp at Agde sur Mer, near the harbor of Sète on the Mediterranean. Amongst them was Bob, known as Ludvik Hoch, transferred to the Czech forces from the Foreign Legion, in which he had been enrolled after his escape from Budapest via Turkey, Syria and Palestine. By then he had received basic training as a motorcycle sidecar machine-gunner.

Two Czech infantry regiments from Agde were dispatched to the front line. After helping to hold off the German advance, the first regiment was ordered back by the French High Command to the Loire, near Orléans. Its mission was to protect the French army's retreat, assisted by motorized reinforcements from its own division. But these forces were soon overcome by the speed of the German army advancing across the river and were forced to retreat. At this, many of their officers simply deserted, leaving the troops to their own devices at the height of the battle.

The Wehrmacht High Command, meanwhile, had issued orders that any Czechs captured while fighting for the Allies were to be put to death, and those identified as Jews were to be handed over to the Gestapo for summary execution. Knowing full well the price they would pay if the Germans caught them, the soldiers all headed for the Mediterranean Sea as their only means of escape.

En route, they slept wherever they could, and on one of the last nights of that forced march through France, Bob took shelter in the cheese caves of Roquefort. For the rest of his life, the pungent smell of Roquefort cheese so reminded him of those dank caverns and terrible times that he couldn't bear to have it on his table.

The British government had promised President Benes, head of the Czech government in exile, that all possible assistance would be given to evacuate the Czech units. By the time those weary, hungry Czech soldiers reached Sète, four British and three Egyptian ships were waiting to rescue them. Because of the utter chaos in France, only 1,600 of the original 5,200 infantrymen sent to the front line made it to Sète in time to be evacuated. Bob was amongst those who boarded a British destroyer and was then transferred, once they were a few hours out from the French coast, to an Egyptian boat, the *Mohamed el Kebir,* which sailed to Gibraltar. From there, they were shipped to Liverpool after a journey that had taken four weeks. So it was that Bob arrived in England in July 1940, speaking no English at all.

Life for me back at the school in Vitry resumed its normal pattern, but in abnormal cramped conditions caused by German occupation of our premises. This was not our only problem: all the male student monitors who normally supervised the boys had gone into hiding, for fear of being taken prisoner by the Germans. Monitors' jobs, both male and female, were always allotted according to seniority, with the result that Raymonde and I, both amongst the more junior employees, found ourselves assigned to the least popular jobs with the boys. Fortunately for us, we already had some useful experience with teenage boys from the days at Condé sur Noireau.

A boarding monitor's duties in this school were far from a rest cure. At first it was quite amusing to watch those big sixteen- and seventeen-year-olds adapt to a new regime. They had been well used to harsh treatment, even physical thrashings from their Corsican monitors, the "Mafia" who for years had dominated the reform schools of Montesson and Vitry. With Raymonde and me in charge, things certainly changed. The boys made eyes at us, carried our books and bags, repaired our bikes, waited for us in the corridors, blushing to the roots of their hair. At night in the dormitories, they took responsibility for discipline amongst their twenty or so peers, so that we could study in peace in the little glass cubicle positioned in the corner of the room.

The bed-wetters were by far the worst of all, those poor kids afflicted with incontinence who stank out the dormitories and endured the sarcastic comments of their friends. Every day started with the acrid stench of urine. But one day, the headmaster (I must give him his due) decided to consult a leading medical expert to improve the situation. This great doctor, who was immediately nick-named "Dr. Pipi" (Dr. Wee Wee), gathered all the monitors together for a complete course on the causes of the problem and the possible cures. The most effective was to wake the bed-wetters up three times a night and make them get up and urinate. If they had already wet their beds when we woke them up, then we had to give them clean sheets.

From that moment on, we never had another quiet night's sleep. I have nightmare memories of those late night and early morning sessions when the children positively refused to leave their fetal sacs, hated us for getting them up and hated us even more for putting clean sheets on their beds. But eventually, everything "went back to normal" and the bed-wetters carried on enjoying their nocturnal inundations until they reached puberty.

One fine day, the Corsican monitors came back. First one, then two, until Raymonde and I were finally repatriated to the girls' school. The first to come back was Pinelli, who before the war had a terror of a reputation. When he saw Raymonde and me managing to line the boys up, just by clapping our hands instead of using the prison warder's whistle, he mellowed. He really did not frighten us at all after that, although I must admit that he only had to look at the kids to make them toe the line. He fell in love with Raymonde immediately, just like all the other men who came anywhere near her. He would have done absolutely anything for her, and in fact did commit some offenses that very nearly cost him dearly. Raymonde, who was nearly six feet tall and painfully thin, was certainly not getting enough to eat, and Pinelli managed to get hold of some false ration cards, hoping to give her some extra food. But he was caught one day and sentenced to three months in jail. Prisons for men at that time were dreadful, dangerous places, especially since they were often the recruiting ground for the hostages the Germans demanded. I never found out how strings were pulled to get him out of jail; perhaps it was through the intervention of one of his well-placed uncles. The fact is that we never saw him at school again. Pretty soon all the Corsicans disappeared and were replaced by Frenchmen from metropolitan France, often university pals looking for jobs to avoid getting carted off for compulsory labor in Germany.

That was how I came to propose the nomination to our school of my university friend Jean-Claude Gourin, which was accepted, and he in turn brought in a Breton, Goavec. I managed to do this through my good friend, Professor Delandre, my classics teacher from my days at St. Omer, who was by now a General Inspector of Primary and Secondary Education with particular responsibility for the Vitry schools. These changes at boarding monitor level considerably improved the general atmosphere of the school. On the whole the new recruits came from family backgrounds where a child's wellbeing was considered important, and they looked after their charges with more warmth and sympathy.

The girls were now back under the aegis of Madame Bergerol, chief supervisor of the girls' primary school, who had returned safely from her own adventures with her young charges following the evacuation from Cabourg. She was in charge of boarders' discipline outside of normal school hours. She was friend, counselor, heroine and mentor to us all. We considered her quite exceptional, we loved her dearly and would have gone through fire for her. She had an extraordinary instinct for communicating with adolescents and winning their loyalty; she understood us, encouraged us in our intellectual pursuits and at the same time made us face up to our responsibilities at school, which were sometimes a very heavy burden for young shoulders. She taught us about life by talking to us in a way our parents never had. She listened to us, advised us, praised or criticized us; she was interested in all the minutiae of our lives. She had a warm heart and took care to share her love and influence in equal measure. She was particularly good at detecting unsuspected qualities in each of us, which she did her utmost to foster; she boosted our morale in times of depression—there were plenty of those—and managed somehow to inspire each and every one of us with her own special brand of enthusiasm. "My girls," that's what she used to call her favored inner circle, and I was proud to be amongst them. She was strict but fair, highly intelligent and well-read; it was through her I discovered whole sections of modern French literature. She was very broad-minded, without the slightest trace of pettiness, straightforward and outspoken. Unlike many in those troubled times, she never hesitated to show her deep sense of patriotism. Most of all, she really knew her pupils well; she had a wealth of experience as a mother and was a born teacher.

From time to time, she would let herself go and confide in us on more intimate matters. That was how we discovered a quite different side to her character: the hot-blooded, fiery-tempered Corsican, the woman who had dared to take great risks. No other woman had more influence on me in my youth. I was, I admit, quite envious of

Raymonde, who had pride of place in Madame Bergerol's heart since her only son, Pierre, was deeply in love with her. A graduate of the Ecole Polytechnique and an exceptional character, he was to die tragically in France's Indochina war, leading one of the unique native commando groups he had created, which bear his name to this day.

Without realizing it at the time, I was able to pass on to Jacqueline, Madame Bergerol's daughter, something of the enrichment her own mother had brought into my life. We first got to know each other when she was entrusted to me in the dark days of the exodus to Condé sur Noireau. Then we met again in their home and subsequently became firm friends during a Girl Guide camping trip. But I remained totally unaware of my influence on her until she told me so relatively recently. Yet I did feel a particular affinity for adolescents and later on deliberately tried to help them. Teenagers were attracted to me, felt able to talk to me, and I understood their anxieties and problems better than most, as they struggled to fathom what life was all about. It was quite fascinating to see the first faltering steps of a new confidence emerge from the timidity that paralyzes so many young people. Trying to advise them is such a responsibility; giving them an example to follow even more so.

So there we were back in Vitry after our evacuation, a good six miles away from the Sorbonne. Public transport was slow and completely inadequate. There were a few gas-fueled buses serving the town, but they were always crammed full. Vitry was in fact the least interesting part of the triangle formed by Villejuif Psychiatric Hospital nearest to Paris and the new cemetery at Thiais on the other side. We used to say jokingly that we were lodging in a Jerry barracks halfway between the mad and the dead. We would quip that you had to be one heck of an optimist to believe anything good could come of the budding delinquents we were in charge of. It's hardly surprising that we got on our bikes every day in search of the spiritual sustenance offered by our alma mater. But we needed an iron constitution: first there was all the physical effort expended on biking down towards Paris, then pedaling up Sainte Geneviève hill to get to the Sorbonne; then on the return journey, back down to the Place d'Italie and laboriously up the hill to Villejuif. But on top of that, we had to cope with all the exhaustion of working as well as being students, not forgetting that we were existing on a totally insufficient diet. So we were all as thin as Giacometti sculptures, but we were equally as tough.

Every second week, we were on "lighter duties," which meant that we could stay in Paris with parents or friends; it was a boon for our studies and social life. There was always a lot to catch up on. It was also possible to arrange a substitute, provided we organized it in advance. Everything seemed to happen on the spur of the moment in those days and the juggling necessary to make everything fit in was really quite phenomenal. We became experts at pulling the wool over Jojo's eyes, and we sometimes even managed to fool Madame Bergerol when we really had our hearts set on a date. It was amazing how many times we each had to go to the funeral of our grandmother, dear uncle, close friend. I'm not sure whether our superiors were taken in by these tales, but they certainly gave the impression they were. Especially in summer, nothing would induce us to stay in Vitry once our minds were made up; there were so many inviting outings to tempt us. Deserted riverbanks beside sparkling, crystal-clear waters provided perfect campsites we did not have to share with the Germans. A little cycling tour of Normandy gave us a chance to indulge again in the delights of real butter, fresh eggs or even a chicken. Luckily for us, the less well-off monitors were only too happy to be paid to stand in for us, not to mention those who were too scared to risk leaving the school premises. The risk, of course, was always the Germans. We were simply not free, especially the boys, who at any moment could fall victim to a roundup or a check on identity papers with a view to compulsory service. All men between the ages of twenty and forty were suspect. There was less risk for girls, but it was best not to stray too far from one's workplace or residence. The Boches were ever suspicious; they were always on the prowl for God knows who or what. It became more and more dangerous as the Resistance escalated its activities. Every time there was an attack, a train derailment, an assassination, the Germans would retaliate with a roundup, using French police to help them do their dirty work.

For the French, the way in which certain policemen connived with the Germans will remain an everlasting shame. I myself was more afraid of a Paris gendarme than I was of most of the Jerries strolling about in the streets. But the lairs of the Gestapo and the Kommandantur were a completely different matter; none of us went voluntarily anywhere near them.

One afternoon towards the end of October, I had just come on duty when I was called to the headmaster's office in the boys' school. That was quite a rare occurrence and as I crossed the no-man's-land between the two schools, I wondered what on earth I had done to deserve such a summons. I went into his office and came face-to-face with a German soldier in Luftwaffe blue. My heart skipped a beat.

The headmaster turned to me and said, "Dr. Tauber has sent this sol-dier for news of the little boy he operated on in Condé sur Noireau. He wants you and your friend Mademoiselle Debru to meet him in Paris at half past seven this evening. This soldier will take you."

I burst out, "But sir, we're on duty, we can't go."

"I'll see to that, let me phone Madame Bergerol."

Instead of protecting us, our coward of a headmaster was liter-ally throwing us into the lion's den. I couldn't think what to say or do and hoped with all my heart that Madame Bergerol would come to my rescue. She replied that she couldn't possibly let two monitors go out that evening. At which I remember commenting that I couldn't decently go by myself. Putting on his most paternal air, the headmaster looked at me and said, "You'll be perfectly safe. Don't worry, you'll be fine." I was aghast, but managed to blurt out, "You ought at least to make sure I'll be brought back. There are no buses in the evening and there's a curfew, after all!" After some humming and hawing, the headmaster insisted that I had to be back in the dor-mitory before midnight. Whereupon I left his office, hurtled down the stairs with the Jerry running after me, offering to take me in his car. I arranged to meet him at the girls' school at seven o'clock that evening.

I rushed to find Raymonde and burst into tears, begging her at least to come with me. It wasn't impossible; she of all people could have persuaded Madame Bergerol, she could have insisted on com-ing; she didn't. It was the first time she had ever let me down. We went back together to my room and discussed what I was going to say to Dr. Tauber, how I was going to repel his advances, how, in the headmaster's words, it was going to turn out fine. And what on earth should I wear? I tried on all my clothes and hers (we used to share them just like sisters) and we eventually decided on a chic navy blue suit I had bought before the war, with a red crêpe blouse. Teetering on a pair of navy blue high-heeled shoes, I looked, according to Ray-monde, like a girl of good family, and there was also a faint hint of the "nurse" I was supposed to be; my whole demeanor exuded respectability. At seven o'clock sharp, the German car drew up in front of the girls' school. Summoning up all my courage, I got into the back seat, wondering where all this was going to lead me and cursing my own stupidity. Why on earth had I put on such a brave act back in Condé sur Noireau?

The German soldier dropped me in the foyer of a big Paris hotel; I can't remember which one, I was so apprehensive and anxious. I sat down in an armchair. All around me Luftwaffe officers of all ranks kept coming in and going out, staring at me as they walked past. A handsome officer was sitting not far off, leafing through a German magazine and looking sideways at me from time to time. Surreptitiously, I was watching him as well. He was really extremely good-looking: typically Nordic, with a tanned complexion that made the deep blue of his eyes stand out even more. A wave of ash-blond hair showed beneath his cap. His full lips gave him a slightly disdainful air, almost sarcastic. Eight o'clock; time was passing and still no sign of Tauber. I was just beginning to think the whole thing was a hoax when the soldier who had driven me there came back into the foyer and bent down to whisper something in the handsome officer's ear. At this, he immediately got up and disappeared. Something was going on, but what? The officer then came back, eyed me scornfully up and down from his great height—well over six feet—and said in excellent English, "Are you Mademoiselle Meynard?"

"Yes, I am."

"My name is Werner Hoffmann, I'm a friend of Dr. Tauber's. Where is your friend?"

"I'm so sorry, she couldn't come; she couldn't get off duty."

"What a shame. I'm afraid I have some bad news for you. Dr. Tauber has been called out to perform an emergency operation and can't be with you this evening."

Hooray, I was thinking, I'm free. But he continued.

"We had planned to make a foursome and go out for dinner somewhere. Dr. Tauber sends you his deepest apologies and he's asked me to take you out instead. He's terribly sorry and hopes to see you another time. Shall we make the most of it?"

I was really furious. I felt trapped. I had no idea who this man was. I had had to drop some urgent university work to go on this blind date and I'd done it contrary to my every instinct and better judgment.

I retorted, "But we don't know each other, we've never met before. All I came for was to tell Dr. Tauber how his patient was getting on. We've probably got nothing in common and you'll have a rotten evening."

His response was cutting. "That's true of course. I'd much rather have taken your friend out. I hear that she's tall, blond and very beautiful. Anyway, Tauber fancies you and I wouldn't want to pinch another officer's girl."

I thought I would explode.

"Look here, I'm not Dr. Tauber's girl. Please have me taken back to the school; then your conscience will be clear and I can get on with my life."

"No, Hans is a major, I'm only a lieutenant. I have my orders and I have to carry them out."

And that was how we drove off to the restaurant: in the worst possible mood, apparently to obey Major Tauber's instructions.

Collaboration was of course deeply frowned upon during the occupation. The last thing you wanted was to be seen with Germans or dubbed a friend of the Germans. In fact there were hundreds of ways of showing your loathing of the occupation; most of my friends and I scored these little victories all the time, showing our noncooperation with as much exaggeration as we dared. When a soldier was coming along the pavement towards us, for instance, we would immediately step to one side and walk in the gutter. Those who were stupid took this as a mark of subservience; all those who had a bit more gray matter knew girls just didn't want to be seen walking anywhere near them. Any soldier who ventured to ask the way could be absolutely sure of being sent in the opposite direction. You could take the mickey out of a Fritz, every single time, without endangering yourself too much—and we did it all the time. Some good stories of that ilk did the rounds in Paris then. A famous cabaret singer-cum-satirist (not an easy job in those days) walks on stage one evening; he stands right in the middle of the stage, facing the front rows full of German officers and soldiers and gives the Hitler salute. He stands there with his arm right out in front of him for fifteen to thirty seconds until all of a sudden the German military decide to get up and return the salute. Then he says "Mesdames, Messieurs, we're in the shit right up to here," whereupon he lets his arm drop down beside his leg and all the soldiers sit down, totally nonplussed. At this the rest of the audience bursts out laughing—not only at the humor of the situation, but at his sheer audacity.

I felt extremely uncomfortable walking beside such a conspicuous German officer. Lieutenant Hoffmann took me to a restaurant packed with German officers, both male and female. As we sat down, he consulted me about ordering the meal. I told him I wasn't hungry, he could order what he liked. We hardly exchanged a single word. Then, suddenly, he got up and said, "This is just too stupid for words. Let's go for a walk, maybe we can reach some kind of compromise."

So he literally marched me out of the restaurant and we started walking down the Champs Elysées. Our conversation was desultory at first. He volunteered the information that he was an English teacher. That explained his fluent English, the language we communicated in, since I could neither understand nor speak German at the time. He taught in a high school in Dresden and that was where he had met Hans Tauber. He hadn't chosen to go to war, he said, he was just doing his duty. The war would soon be over. All the Führer wanted was peace and happiness for all the people of Europe. I told him I had already heard exactly the same line from Tauber, but the fact was that there was a war on; maybe we could be friends later, but it was just not possible then.

"I'll be dead later on. We're always sent to the front line, this is just a pleasant respite."

I remember remarking that he wasn't allowed to go out with French girls anyway. "Not if they're Jews," came the swift reply.

"Are you Jewish?"

"No, I'm Protestant."

"So am I, at least we've got that in common."

"What's wrong with Jews?"

"They're a different race."

"What do you mean, a different race?"

"Would you marry a black man?"

"I don't think I would personally, but what's that got to do with it? There were lots of Jewish girls in my class at school, they are just as French as I am."

"I can't speak for France, but they've done a lot of harm in my country."

"I don't know anything about that."

I have to admit that at the time I was completely ignorant about Jews, about politics, about Nazism. I had learned English and Latin at school, not German. I knew precious little about German history and even less about contemporary Germany. I was not equipped to challenge his statements. We were a Protestant, pro-Dreyfus family; we weren't at all anti-Semitic. As far as we were concerned, there wasn't a Jewish problem, so we didn't discuss it. Although we lived in the Jewish quarter of the rue Vieille du Temple and had many Jewish friends, we were not really aware of the Nazis' profound anti-semitism until the infamous yellow star made its appearance in Paris in June 1942, followed by the Vélodrome d'Hiver roundup in July of the same year.

I asked Lieutenant Hoffmann what he was doing at the moment. He told me he was in charge of ground transport and telephone communications. His regiment was stationed in Dreux at the time, but until they moved on, the men were allowed to visit Paris quite often. He and his friends had come to the capital on leave hoping to meet some decent girls. I tried to explain that this was out of the question as far as Raymonde and I were concerned; we both had jobs as well as being students, we had no time at all to spare and no transport. Vitry was south of Paris whereas Dreux was to the north; anyway, Raymonde was practically engaged to another student; last but not least, my parents would never let me go out with a German officer while the war was still on. All he replied to my protestations was that the war would soon be over; then we would be free. In the meantime, it was getting cold, I had no coat, would I agree just this once to go to another restaurant?

I was getting extremely tired of walking up and down the Champs Elysées in my high-heeled shoes. I needed to sit down, so I capitulated. It was getting late by now and the only restaurant to be found was a sort of nightclub where Edith Piaf was singing. I had never been in a nightclub before. I felt totally out of place, extremely embarrassed, ill at ease; I was drinking champagne, which I had also never done before.

Hoffmann asked me, "What's your name?"

"Betty."

"Betty, why won't you look at me, are you scared?"

"Yes, yes, I am scared, very scared. I shouldn't be here, I shouldn't be talking to you."

"Are you scared of me because I'm German?"

"Yes."

"You don't need to be scared. I think you're pretty, charming and innocent. I like your honesty and intelligence. I'd never want to hurt you."

After a little while, we left the club and I asked Hoffmann to have me taken back to Vitry, but he decided to drive me himself. When we were quite close to school, he stopped the car and said, "Let's talk." I felt reasonably reassured, knowing that home was just a stone's throw away, so we talked. He told me about his family and asked me about mine. I learned that he was single and twenty-nine years old. I remember commenting how strange it was that he wasn't married, because with his good looks he could have been quite a Romeo. Before the war, he said, he'd been too busy studying and earning his living to look for the right girl, and now he really regretted it. He told me he had enjoyed the evening in spite of the awkwardness, and that I need not worry, he would square it with Tauber. "In any case," he added, "Tauber has a wife and two lovely children, he's lucky and ought to be satisfied." It was nearly midnight. I told him that the school was full of German soldiers and guarded by German sentries; if I got in after the curfew, I would be arrested. His reaction was chivalrous; he would rescue me from any jail, he said, especially if the Wehrmacht had locked me in there. I retorted that I'd rather not get in there in the first place. So he deposited me on the doorstep, saying he had no regrets at all about the evening, even if it hadn't gone quite according to plan. He was determined to see me again, if only because he was very lonely and it had been interesting talking about France with someone forthright and educated.

I scurried back into school, up to the dorm where Raymonde was on duty and poured out the whole story. She was much more worldly-wise than me. She listened patiently to my rather breathless account and then concluded, "A fine mess you've got yourself into." "Yes, and it's all your fault," came my stinging reply. I remember flouncing out of the room, banging the door behind me. In the seclusion of my own room, I pondered the evening's events before falling asleep, miserable, puzzled and worried. The next day passed without incident and as the days went by, I tried to put the episode out of my mind.

But the two German officers just would not let the matter rest. They took to visiting or telephoning me every other week. The phone calls were really quite a performance: there was only one outside line that boarding supervisors could use for urgent calls, and that was over in the lodge near the school gate, a good five minutes' walk from the girls' school. The caretaker would ring through on the internal system, you had to be located and then run all the way to the lodge. This went on for several months and I was terrified that if I didn't take their calls, they would come in person even more often. Nobody could protect me; I was on my own because all those around me were afraid. Even when I asked her to, the caretaker did not dare say that I wasn't in. Everybody preferred to dodge the issue rather than have to say anything unpleasant to a German.

I really can't remember when or how this awkward acquaintance developed into friendship. Werner was intelligent and cultured and we found a common interest in discussing philosophy and the history of ideas. In fact, he would often help me plan and write my university essays. It was a constrained relationship, made all the more artificial by the fact that we conversed in English; it masked to a certain extent the fact that he was German. Yet there was an unspoken attraction between us. It took an incident I shall never forget to make me realize what was happening.

One day, Werner asked me to interpret for him in a shop in the center of Paris, where he wanted to buy a present for his mother. For the first time ever, he was not in uniform. I was completely unaware that a German officer had been killed in Paris that day and there was an early curfew. Twenty hostages were going to be shot at dawn in reprisal. As Werner and I were walking along, a military patrol screeched to a halt beside us and one of the soldiers tried to force me into the car, despite Werner's protests, which were hindered by his civilian clothes. Physically intervening between me and the car door, he spoke urgently to the officer in charge and finally, after the longest minutes of my life, managed to release me from their clutches. I was scared out of my wits but jolted back to reality: we were at the mercy of an army of occupation.

I knew that I had to extricate myself from this relationship, but I didn't know how. My relief was enormous when Werner telephoned one day to say that his regiment would soon be leaving for the "east." He called me again several times, the last time in December 1941 from the outskirts of Moscow. I could hardly believe where he was phoning from, but I was glad that he was so far away.

The occupation was more and more difficult to endure every day. All the foodstuffs the French had relied on at first, because they were not to the Germans' liking, all became scarcer and scarcer. In most large cities, especially Paris, food supply was now very difficult and haphazard. Our staple diet was a root vegetable which we called rutabaga. Before the war, this vegetable had been grown mainly for animal fodder, since its nutritional value for humans was minimal. The Resistance, meanwhile, was intensifying its campaign of attacks and derailments and the Germans were retaliating ferociously. You only had to go down in the Métro to see posters containing lists of the latest ten or twenty Frenchmen to be shot in retaliation for the death of one German. Roundups were becoming more frequent and people were subjected to all kinds of restrictions and humiliations.

In the midst of an appallingly cold winter, I would cycle furiously to and from the Sorbonne, work late at night huddled up in blankets, slaving over my Latin translations of Seneca, Horace, Ovid and Lucretius, but enjoying much more my reading of Bergson, whose books were on my philosophy syllabus. Through Raymonde and Madame Bergerol's son, Pierre, I was introduced to a group of law students who were also friends of my cousin Olivier, all of them living under the constant threat of compulsory labor service and police raids checking on identity papers. We would often meet at one or the other's digs for long discussions, sometimes till the early hours of the morning, not only about France's lamentable subjugation to an army of occupation, but more often on subjects that allowed our spirits and minds to roam freely in wider spheres. Despite the dreadful and uncertain future that confronted us, we would share in one another's studies and interests, and I particularly remember helping Jacques Gandouin, one of my closest friends, to put on a production of Molière's *Le Médecin Malgré Lui*. In those rather surreal times, exceptional ties of friendship were forged.

With unerring instinct, my parents sensed that I had just lived through some kind of crisis. They never asked any questions and I, for my part, could not bring myself to tell them the truth about my German admirer, knowing full well they would be very worried. My father and mother, for their part, were both deeply affected by France's humiliating defeat, but home was a haven of peace, wisdom and common sense. They were loving, kind and dignified and their quiet courage and refinement acted as a counterbalance to the harsh life of Vitry and our growing anxiety as the noose of enemy occupation tightened.

As those winter months of 1941 passed, a dreadful series of events brought home to me the terrible plight of the Jews. Their normal lives were being increasingly restricted; they were finding it harder and harder to earn a living. They were subject to a special curfew, so that if you invited Jewish guests for dinner, they had to stay the night or risk being arrested on their way home. My sister had several Jewish friends, medical students like her, who told us what was happening. More and more of them were trying to cross over into unoccupied France; many were caught at the border or denounced by their guides. Our Jewish acquaintances and contacts were progressively disappearing—my old schoolmates, a doctor we knew, my Polish dressmaker.

Then in May 1942, as I picked up my mail one day, I recognized Werner's handwriting on an envelope. He was at home in Dresden on leave and was writing to tell me that he was getting married. I never heard from him again, for the next twenty-six years. Then one day in 1968, his second wife managed to trace me through my sister in Paris (his first wife had deserted him whilst he was a prisoner of war in Russia). She and Werner wanted to know what had become of me. On my side, I was curious to know the end of the story, so I went to visit them one day when I happened to be in Frankfurt am Main for the annual Book Fair. They were both teaching English and spoke it perfectly. Our conversation naturally turned to events of the war years and particularly the crimes of the Nazis. I was interested to know how an intelligent and well-educated German had reacted to the "Final Solution." Had he been aware of the fate the Nazis had reserved for the Jews? How did he square the Holocaust with his conscience? When we had met in Paris, what had he known about the deportations? What were his thoughts now? I learned that he had become a lay preacher, that he was doing his best to atone for all that had been done in the name of Germany, for all that he had tolerated or allowed to happen without putting up any opposition. I then told him about my husband, the fact that he was Jewish, my move to England and about our children. Werner and his wife envied us our large family, since they themselves had no children. We parted on good terms and I kept in touch with them every Christmas after that until a few years ago, when they both died within a few months of each other.

I ended my second year at university with undistinguished results. It was at this point that I reached an important decision. Encouraged by my father and spurred on by my friends, I finally decided to change courses and study law. My father felt that studying philosophy was not going to get me anywhere in terms of a practical career. He himself was reading for a law doctorate, having embarked upon his legal studies at the age of fifty-four, and he clearly thought it would be a splendid idea for me to take up law as well; he would be able to steer me through the pitfalls, lend me his notes and books. So I took the necessary steps to enroll for a law degree.

In July, I joined my friends for a cycling-cum-camping holiday which took us to as many remote country hideouts as could be found north of the river Loire. This was exactly the break I needed from the chores of Vitry. Of the little group that set off that summer, Jacques Gandouin and Jean-Claude Gourin made their careers in the French civil service and have remained staunch friends of mine all my life; Pierre Bergerol was killed in the Indochina war and Raymonde married her infantry captain, who later became a director of Rhône Poulenc, a major French industrial corporation.

I remember that interlude as a joyful, carefree adventure—pitching and striking tents, foraging for food, skillfully cooking it on the campfire in the purest scouting tradition, swimming in the flowing, unpolluted river waters, basking in endless sunshine beneath skies of the purest blue. Alas, the holiday came to an end, and I returned to Paris in September, ready to start back at Vitry and the university at the end of month.

The year 1942 also saw changes in my personal life. I was

twenty-one on March eleventh. There wasn't much to celebrate, but I nevertheless did feel optimistic about the future. I don't know how they managed it, but my parents organized a party for me at a small Paris restaurant, and family and friends gathered for an exceptionally good dinner in those difficult times. As they had hired a private room, we were even allowed to dance, which had been forbidden in public places, at least for French people, since the occupation. In any case, in the Paris of 1942, our hearts were not set on dancing.

Having started my legal studies, I was enormously busy; the syllabus was very heavy in those days with five courses in Roman, constitutional and civil law, legal history and political economy. My duties in Vitry remained the same and just as arduous as before. Six months previously, I had helped Jean-Claude Gourin secure a housemaster's post at Vitry. At the time, he was looking for some kind of paid employment that would also allow him to continue his studies, and Vitry fitted the bill. He was already in his second year of law, so was able to guide me in my first year. He was the most attentive of my escorts, and we used to cycle into Paris together. I owe him a great deal for helping me pass my first-year law exams, written and oral, in June 1942. Delighted at my success, I could look forward to a summer of freedom and holidays.

The infamous demarcation line separating Free France from occupied France represented a tremendous hardship for all the French, dividing us not only physically but in many other less visible ways. This division was in fact actively encouraged by the authorities, on the one side the Germans and on the other the Vichy government, puppets of the Nazis in the so-called free zone. Had it continued, we might well have ended up separated like the two Germanies after the war. Meanwhile, many people lost their lives trying to cross illegally from occupied to southern France.

It has always been traditional for the French to go on holiday in the long summer break, especially since the introduction of paid leave. People would travel the length and breadth of the country: to the south, east or west if they were looking for sea and sun; and to the east if they were attracted by the mountains. So for the French, one of the greatest penalties of the occupation was the very fact that they could no longer move about freely. To these travel restrictions were added further humiliations of the meanest variety. Letters from one zone to the other were forbidden, except on partly preprinted postcards to which one was permitted only to add the briefest of handwritten personal messages—little more than yes, no, well, ill or other commonplace words of that sort. It was an absolute stupidity invented by some official in the Vichy government, eager to comply with the demands of occupying forces. But as an attempt at censoring letters, the scheme totally backfired. People thought of ingenious ways of getting around the problem, with the result that this official printed card soon became one of the Resistance's most reliable ways of passing coded messages.

I can't remember now exactly how my father managed to get hold of the pass that allowed me to enter the free zone for the summer holidays of 1942. I seem to recall that it wasn't too difficult for women, especially if they had really French sounding names and were born in France. It was quite the opposite for men, especially the younger generation; they hardly dared ask the authorities for the smallest thing they were so afraid of being picked up.

I boarded the train for St. Gervais les Bains, beside myself with joy. For a few months, I was escaping from the grip of the army of occupation; better still, I was going to see people and places I had been fond of since I was a child. That was how I came to be in the unoccupied zone when the Nazis perpetrated the most heinous crime against the Jews of Paris. I was only to learn about it from my parents when I returned, for of course newspapers in the free zone took great care to conceal the horror of those events. On the sixteenth of July that year, the Germans, with the collaboration of the French police, rounded up as many Jews as they could locate in the city and sent them to the Vélodrome d'Hiver, known as the Vel d'Hiv. More than twenty thousand Jews—men, women and children—were herded in the most inhuman conditions into the stadium, before being deported to Drancy and Auschwitz. There was no sanitation, children were separated from their parents, food was scarce and inedible. It was a scandal that can never be whitewashed and there is no possible excuse for French participation in it.

I shall never forget my parents' graphic description of the terrible events of that night, when thirty Jewish families were forcibly evicted from our block of flats. How they had screamed for help but were mercilessly ejected and marched off by German soldiers to an uncertain destination. How my father had tried to intervene, but had been roughly pushed back into his flat and told to mind his own business unless he wanted to be dispatched to Poland or Hungary or wherever all those foreigners came from. I remember vividly how appalled my parents were to think that people who had sought refuge in France were being sent back against their will. Had my mother and father then been told the truth, that the Jews were really being deported to death camps and gas chambers, they simply would not have believed it.

My own happy arrival in St. Gervais les Bains was unmarred by somber events of this nature. Holidays with Aunt Belle had always spelled freedom to me, even though when I was young that had meant nothing more than escaping from the constraints of parental authority. I can still remember exactly what I was wearing as I boarded the train that day. I felt quite well turned out in my smart suit of smooth brown velvet, which my favorite Jewish Polish dressmaker, moonlighting to bring in some extra cash, had made for me with material bought with upholstery fabric coupons. The jacket was very long, the skirt short and straight, showing off my legs, which I recall were much admired at the time! A silk blouse added the final touch of luxury to my outfit; again it had been run up by my home dressmaker, but this time from a bolt of fabric left over from the days of my father's silk factory. I was very slim and looked taller with my long, thick, brown hair piled on top of my head in the style that was then the height of fashion, perched up high on my cork platform shoes: those famous coupon-free shoes, which wore out very quickly but were not without elegance and originality.

So off I went to my aunt's Alpine chalet, Plein Champs, where I was looking forward to meeting up with my cousins from Marseilles; they always spent half their holidays in the mountains and the other half in the old family home in the village of Mérindol in Provence. Those were real holidays, the kind I have dreamed of ever since and tried hard to recreate, but their special magic quality has constantly eluded me. As I look back now and try to analyze why these memories remain so intense, I realize that for two whole months I was completely free of all responsibility. I had just passed my exams and my future seemed mapped out. I had enough money to treat myself to a trip which started in St. Gervais, continued at my godfather's on the Côte d'Azur, and ended at Aunt Yvonne's in the Lot et Garonne. In all these family circles, I was welcomed with the deep affection and absolute confidence which has always united our Protestant families. The weather played its part, too, with brilliant sunshine enhancing nature's radiance. Although the war was on our doorstep and the threat of occupation undiminished, we seemed to be experiencing one of those magnificent, deceptively calm periods, so often the harbinger of history's great tragedies.

Although I had just turned twenty-one, in some ways I was still quite naive. I was very childish, very selfish, untouched by tragedy and certain that I had an absolute right to happiness despite the dark clouds all around me. I had managed to escape all the relatively minor pitfalls on my path, so I felt strong, capable, sure that I was destined for an outstanding future to match my hopes and ambitions. With hindsight, I recognize that I was brimming over with incredible *chutzpah*—there was nothing in my life at the time to suggest what fate lay in store for me: it was all the product of my feverish imagination.

I arrived at Plein Champs in this euphoric state and found to my great delight that everything was exactly as I remembered it. Oh, the joys of breakfast toast with melting butter, savored with tea or coffee on the sunny terrace, against the unforgettable backdrop of the pinnacle of Bionassay, the dome of Miage and its glacier, bathing in the torrent nearby in spite of its glacial waters; the steep climbs up the Prarion and Voraçay in search of chanterelles, bilberries, wild raspberries and strawberries; coming back down again, singing as we went, heading for the dairy to buy real cow's milk and little hearts of mouth-watering soft white cheese topped with cream; going back up again to pay a visit to Alphonsine, the wife of the local carpenter who used to be our cook when I was a little girl; and that delicious, full feeling when we left her house, stuffed with fried puff pastries and thick pancakes.

This delectable routine was interrupted one day by my cousin Françoise Arnal, whose fiancé Pierre Walter, an air force cadet officer at the Istres base, had come to join us. She wanted to go climbing in the mountains and had made up her mind to do the circuit of the three passes (the Col du Tour, Fenêtre de Saleinas and the Col du Chardonnet). Pierre and Françoise had arranged to meet up with some Swiss cousins at the Aiguille du Tour, and they had promised to come with their bags stuffed with praline chocolate and Virginia cigarettes, both of which were unobtainable in the unoccupied zone; most important of all, they were going to bring a German camera for Pierre that could only be bought in Switzerland.

The slight risks we were taking only added excitement to our expedition; we were young, we were good friends and life felt marvelous. So, early one morning, we took a local train to Chamonix and began our ascent from the valley, following the mule track that would take us to the King Albert mountain refuge, where we would spend the night. All went well and, as we climbed, we got to know the people who would be on the rope with us as we crossed the glaciers. There was Pierre Walter, whom I had not met before (now a retired air force general), Robert Giscard, the brother of a Lyon schoolfriend of mine who took his first communion with me (a founding brother of the community of the Abbey of Taizé), Albert Laget, then an air force lieutenant and friend of Pierre's and Juliette Contandriopoulos, a friend of the Arnal family. Our equipment bore no comparison with what is available today. We were all sporting baggy plus fours. We had no crampons at all (they would have made climbing the walls of ice absolute child's play); all we had were studded boots on which we strapped a kind of spiked outer sole, which, if I remember correctly, had an irritating tendency to poke right through the fabric of our trouser legs. Pierre, Françoise and Robert made up the strongest rope; Laget, who was a terrific climber, led our group, going first on the ascent. As for me, I played it safe and stayed in the middle, definitely having the least training and being the most chicken on the ice. Juliette brought up the rear. We reversed this order on the descent, because then you needed the strongest person at the rear to stop the rope sliding.

Before our expedition, we had done a bit of training with Uncle Roger and my youngest cousin, Maryse. We had climbed once up Mont d'Arbois, reaching the high mountain pastures where my uncle used to go for fresh supplies of butter and cheese, which he bartered for Marseilles soap; another time we had been up the Voza pass (in those days you couldn't get up there by Jeep), but it was woefully inadequate preparation for the Parisian I had become. At twenty-one, though, you're game for anything. Some episodes of this trip are still remarkably fresh in my mind, especially the exhilaration of reaching the Col du Tour and literally racing towards the peak where our Swiss cousins were to meet us. It was such an invigorating feeling. Nobody knew we were there. We could easily have gone over the border then if we had wanted to. With hindsight, I realize that this would have been the right time for Pierre to make his escape; a few months later, he was to be caught by a German patrol as he tried to reach England via Spain. Deported first to Newengam, then to Buchenwald, he ended up in Dora, a less well-known labor camp not far from Buchenwald, where they worked on the V1 and V2 rockets in a huge underground factory. Having survived one and a half years in those camps, he returned to a career in the air force and fought in both Indochina and Algeria.

One other episode I shall never forget as long as I live: the ascent of the Chardonnet pass. It is situated at the top of a cliff formed by a crevasse between the Saleinas glacier and its rock face, and you have to climb it if you want to reach the valley that joins up with the Argentière glacier. Looking back on it, I'm convinced my cousins were quite foolhardy to take us on a such a hazardous escapade.

Laget climbed like a mountain goat, using his ice axe to cut giant spaced steps in the rock face, which was a wall of ice, pulling on the rope and shouting elegantly at me, "What the bloody hell are you doing down there?" Meanwhile the parties behind were hurling insults at us because as the ice melted, we were sending stones crashing down on their heads. Caught in the middle of these fiery exchanges flying up and down the glacier, I was scared stiff. With my nose pressed hard up against the ice, I was desperately forcing myself to put one foot in front of the other, trying to reach the footholds which were much too far apart for me. I reached halfway up, but then made the fatal mistake of looking down. For a split second, I was overcome by terrible vertigo at the thought of my precarious position; I was clinging like a limpet to the icy face, hanging from a lifeline which relied on the goodwill of a very impatient stranger and being pulled back towards the bottom by Juliette, who would never have been able to support me had I slipped. I can still remember the supreme physical and mental effort I had to muster. I kept telling myself that my life depended on getting to the top of the pass safe and sound, even if it did seem as daunting as scaling the Eiffel Tower.

When I finally reached the summit, I was elated. I felt as if I had won a gold medal in the Olympic Games; I really thought I had cracked it. We had a break for chocolate and cigarettes and then began the descent, in reverse order on the rope, with Juliette now leading. To my dismay, this was even more difficult than I had imagined. I tried to psych myself up, nose to the ice again. We now had to jump over crevasses, the worst of which were at the downward *bergschrund*. The crevasses looked gigantic to me, deep blue chasms, and I had terrible visions of falling in, dragging all my party with me and being found fifty or a hundred years later, totally intact, with all my companions. This had actually happened to a mountaineer in the previous century and I had to make a real effort to put the story out of my mind.

As soon as we got to the flat stretch of the glacier, we unroped and the boys unceremoniously dumped us, there and then, because we were too slow. Walking off without us, they shouted gleefully, "You'll have to get a move on, the last train leaves at eight o'clock." Juliette and I were getting more and more exhausted and it was only Françoise's endless patience that finally got us to the station in time. She coaxed us along, somehow managing to help us overcome our fatigue and paralyzing fear of jumping over even the smallest crevasses. We made it, and with no damage that a good night's sleep would not put right.

From St. Gervais, I went on to Mérindol where I planned to spend a few days, mostly to buy some fruit and vegetables to take with me to my godfather's on the Ile du Levant where food supplies were a real problem. I then made my way to Toulon, where I boarded a small ferry for the Iles d'Hyères, the most distant of which is the Ile du Levant. Although most of that extraordinary island was navy property, the western point had been let to a naturist colony. My godfather, Adrien Diederichs, a cousin of my father, was a retired manufacturer; he was a very keen amateur painter and deaf as a post. During the Belle Epoque, he had set up home with a dancer from the Folies Bergères, but his father refused to let him marry her. As soon as his intransigent father died, Uncle Adrien immediately got married. His wife Minou was charming; I liked her very much. She was cheerful and well-read, and my godfather had helped improve her culture on their travels together. At his side, she had developed a keen sense of observation, especially of people. She was a woman of few words and yet she spoke her mind and you knew exactly where you stood with her. They had decided to spend most of the year on the island, where they lived in a charming house overlooking a rocky escarpment. From their terrace crumbling under the weight of lush bougainvilleas, they had a splendid view over the creeks where little boats came to moor and beyond that, stretched the deep blue of the Mediterranean, as far as the eye could see.

The island's nudism was not at all aggressive. The men wore G-strings and most of the women wore skimpy bikinis, considered very daring at the time. Children, on the other hand, ran about completely naked and everyone swam in the nude. I could never bring myself to join in this nudism. I was by nature very modest and virtually lived in a two-piece swimsuit that covered me up as much as possible. Women like Aunt Minou who lived on the island all year-round were as brown as berries, so much so that they looked as if they were dressed. Paradoxically, white skin and bright red sunburn looked immodest.

All my memories of that holiday revolve around endless bathing in warm, clear water and my discovery of underwater fishing. That summer, a couple had also been invited who were friends of Minou's. The wife had been a dancer as well, and most of the conversation naturally centered on their reminiscences. My godfather, who was a perceptive man, soon realized that it must be rather boring for me to spend all my time with elderly people. So he introduced me to a young man who was "much older" than me: he was all of twenty-eight and was known to everyone as "le beau Combe." He was sun-tanned, with long blond hair like Tarzan, bleached by the sun and saltwater. He was a bit of a recluse and was only very occasionally to be seen at lunch or dinner gatherings. His remoteness naturally aroused my curiosity. Since we are generally attracted in life by anything that is slightly out of reach, I would often go for walks near his house, trying to cajole him into acknowledging my existence. My patience finally paid off and we struck up a peculiar sort of friendship. We used to talk about anything and everything, but I did most of the talking while he listened and observed. He didn't say much, but instinct told me that he was in hiding. Sometimes he would suddenly bring our conversations to an abrupt end on the pretext of an urgent appointment. On an island that was like paradise on earth, where nothing seemed to happen and life just took its natural course, I found these pressing engagements rather hard to believe. Then one day, my godfather and Aunt Minou took us for a swim at the other end of the island, where you could swim amongst the rocks that lay just offshore. There, I suddenly caught a glimpse of Combe in the distance, looking as if he were wearing some sort of short skirt that glinted in the sun. As I got closer, I realized that his "skirt" was in fact fish hanging from a piece of string tied round his waist like a belt. He was surrounded by other girls and boys. Greatly intrigued, I asked him if I could join their gang. "We'll see," he said, "Come to my house tomorrow."

Of course I needed no persuading and the next day when I arrived at his house, he told me to meet him in an hour's time at Garoupe lighthouse. "We're going fishing," he said, "so don't forget a hat and your sunglasses—and some Nivea cream." I flattered myself that these little personal touches were a good sign. Overjoyed at the turn of events, I hurried back to my godfather's to let them know where I was going and make sure they didn't mind. Then, bounding along the fragrant, stony paths lined with pines, I ran rather than walked the distance to the lighthouse creek. There I found Combe (I never knew his first name) with another young man and three girls. Two canoes were moored nearby and we set off, loaded with fishing paraphernalia, which was completely unfamiliar to me.

There were long steel harpoons with triggers and springs, lethal objects long since banned, underwater goggles, large nails, barbecue grills, wicker baskets and another larger basket containing bread, bottles of wine, salt and other picnic items. The men rowed and the girls relaxed, letting the waves sway them gently to and fro. We skirted the cliffs worn jagged by the elements, then after a little while landed in a secluded creek that was quite unseen from the footpath on the island. There the men got into the water, armed with their harpoons, telling us not to stay in the creek but to row out to the open sea and have a swim somewhere else; they would come back to the creek and join us later.

It was all very mysterious and exciting. As I chatted with the other girls, I found out that the boys were both very keen on underwater fishing, that they sold the fish they caught and that was how they made their living. They didn't want us to stay on shore because we might attract idle spectators to their favorite fishing grounds. All that seemed perfectly plausible to me. The other girls were clearly used to this routine, and once we were out at sea, they introduced me to the delights of underwater diving. They taught me how to empty the air out of my lungs and hold my breath so I could dive more deeply. Then, armed with goggles, we plunged into the sea, and I was entranced by the splendid, unexpected world that opened up before me. Sadly, the Mediterranean is no longer what it was, but in those days swimming around the islands, you came across whole shoals of extraordinary fish, whose big eyes stared inquisitively back at you, and strange, beautiful mollusks. Above all there was the most amazing flora: giant seaweed swaying in the currents, floating above fathomless chasms that fell away below, making you feel giddy. When you were closer to the rocky coastline, you were suddenly startled by the viscous branches of huge algae sweeping across your face and body. Nothing could have been a more perfect illustration of Snow White's headlong flight into Walt Disney's forest than the underwater depths of the Mediterranean.

At the appointed hour, we rowed back to the creek and suddenly the two men emerged from the sea, their bodies glistening with fish. They quickly lit a fire with some driftwood, placed the iron grids over the flames and began to grill the most exquisite fish I can ever remember eating. It was bass, the most prized fish around those coasts. They even played the classic joke on me which I fell for hook, line and sinker.

I was just about to sample the delights of the meal, when Combe said, "Don't eat that fish, throw it away."

"Why not?"

"It's not fresh."

"But how can you tell it's not fresh?"

"Can't you smell it?"

All I could smell was the exquisite fragrance of the thyme and savory that we had just picked to go with our grilled fish. I looked at them, wide-eyed, whereupon to my great embarrassment, they all burst out laughing. As we feasted on the beach, we got to know each other a bit better and I ventured to ask a few questions: where did they fish? how long did it take to net this catch? and so on.

After about an hour's siesta, the boys told us to go home in one of the canoes, after hiding the other in the cleft of a rock. It wasn't worth waiting for them: they were going in search of grouper and it would take a long time. I was delighted to be invited again.

The next day was a repeat performance. I was more and more intrigued by what the boys were up to, but I was having such fun that my natural curiosity was blunted. The day after that, Combe told me not to come because he was not going fishing. So I went again two days later. This time, we set off together and he told me one girl could not come any more because she was going back to the mainland. "Do you want to take her place?" he asked me. I was thrilled to think I was going to be useful to him. From that day on, I went with him every day. Sometimes, he was gone for hours on end and came back quite exhausted but with hardly any fish to show for his efforts. He was always telling me stories about grouper, which by now I took with a pinch of salt. The day came when I had to leave the island. I was convinced I was leaving behind me someone and something very mysterious, but I didn't know what.

Several years later, I met Captain Jacques Cousteau. I can't remember now how the conversation got around to the Ile du Levant, but I told him I had spent my summer holiday there in 1942.

"Really? We could easily have met. What were you doing there? Were you with the nudists?"

"No, I spent my time going underwater fishing with some boys; they were always after big grouper."

"Oh I see! You were one of Combe's gang?"

"Well, yes, if you can call it that. But how on earth did you know him?"

"Did he ever tell you who the big grouper was?"

"No, he never told me what he was up to."

"Well, I can tell you now. I was the big grouper. I was doing frogman testing for the French navy off the Ile du Levant; we were trying out the first oxygen tanks and I was training some men who were hiding on the island. We'd advised them to take some girls out with them so their jaunts wouldn't arouse suspicion. You were part of their cover. That's very good, you helped us a lot, he was one of the best divers we had. He got caught later on after he joined the Resistance and was shot."

I left the Ile du Levant at the beginning of September and went to stay at my Aunt Yvonne's château, Pechgris, in the Lot et Garonne. By that time her son Olivier had responded to Marshal Pétain's appeal by enrolling in youth work. He was champing at the bit and I sensed his anxiety and unhappiness. Although we were pleased to see each other again, our hearts were no longer in it and I stayed mostly with my aunt, doing the rounds with her visiting our numerous relatives in the area.

Olivier's father had walked out on Aunt Yvonne, leaving him without the benefit of paternal support. Partly because of this, he had became very close to a former St. Cyr tutor, Lieutenant de la Rochefoucauld, who became his mentor. I don't think we will ever really understand how respectable young people like Olivier, brought up to love their country and know their duty towards it, came to be completely misled by ultra-rightists, who urged them to join the enemy forces. It seems almost impossible that a member of a distinguished French family like de la Rochefoucauld could have advised the young men in his care to join the Militia. And yet that is what he did, and he was to pay dearly for it. Narrowly escaping a firing squad after the war, he was condemned to twenty years' imprisonment. I think he was eventually granted an amnesty after ten years, but I am not completely certain. As for Olivier, he was killed in 1944 in the bombardment of the Militia's Poitiers barracks by the Royal Air Force. For years after that, Aunt Yvonne regularly went to the prison at Fresnes, to visit the former officer who had been the last man to see her son alive.

Oh, *Le Chagrin et la Pitié*! Go and see that remarkable film, which was not released on French T.V. until some years after it was made. It describes so perfectly the political divisions that tore France apart before, during and after the war and that still rankle the country today. Alas, these animosities and ambiguities will continue for as long as there are people left who remember the unforgivable betrayals committed during the German occupation and the division of France, and the tragic settling of scores that occurred after the liberation.

Soon after this, I went home to Paris, back to my monitor's job and ready to start my second year of law at the Sorbonne.

This second year of study was very similar to the first, except that legal history was replaced by criminal law. If we had had enough time, I am sure that the comparison between the civil code (Code Napoléon) and the Roman law code would have been fascinating, but at that stage it was largely a question of memorization, as it was all the other subjects, apart from political economy, which needed a little more thought. It was simply an accumulation of dates, numbers of articles and their subsections, of changes in the law, additions and abolitions. We were lucky enough to be taught by eminent professors: one of the Marouzeau brothers for civil law (he joined the Resistance and was subsequently deported), Donnedieu de Vabres for legal history and André Siegfried for political economy. A delightful old man, Professor Giffard, taught us Roman law. He was well aware that 90 percent of his audience was bored to death by this subject but he was adept at using his fine sense of humor to capture our attention and succeeded in interesting the other 10 percent, who followed his lectures assiduously.

I began the autumn term of 1942 enthusiastically, and the wonderful memories I had of my holidays made me put my heart into my work. But this deceptive calm was shattered by an explosion—the German invasion of France's unoccupied zone on November 11, armistice day of the First World War. It followed closely on Montgomery's victory over Rommel at El Alamein and the Allied landings in North Africa. Despite the fact that the press and radio carefully concealed all news of Allied victories, or even told deliberate lies about them, we knew that the armistice and fragile agreements reached at Montoire between Pétain and Hitler had been broken. From that point on the whole country was totally under the German heel.

Thanks to my father who listened to the BBC every day, we were able to follow events from afar. At times the broadcast was completely inaudible because the Germans succeeded in "jamming" it; at others the clarion call of "Ici Londres" would reverberate through our apartment, making my mother live in dread of denunciation, even though my father muffled the sound under blankets so the neighbors could not hear. Although listening to the BBC was forbidden, it was a lifeline, keeping us informed about the Allies' progress in North Africa and of the turning points of the war as the initiative passed from the Axis to the Allied forces.

Nineteen forty-three was a terrible year. As Henri Amouroux writes: "It was the most difficult year of all—the year of great departures, of great actions, of great roundups and great sacrifices."

On February 2, General Von Paulus finally surrendered at Stalingrad after a bloody battle which had claimed some 150,000 lives, with more than 90,000 German troops captured by the Russians. These events were to trigger a whole series of measures on the part of the occupying authorities in France, which would, in turn, provoke an upsurge in Resistance activites and fierce countermeasures on the part of the Germans.

The month of March saw the formation of the Militia, a regular army recruited with Prime Minister Laval's approval and trained by career officers who were either First World War veterans or graduates of French military academies. Recruits came largely from right-wing elements of the population, from Catholics who loathed Bolshevism or from anyone prepared to listen to Marshal Pétain's advocacy of support for the occupation authorities in their "courageous fight against communism." The Militia's initial task was to enforce law and order, but very soon its members began fighting the Resistance alongside the Germans and inflicting terrible penalties on their own compatriots, inciting further retaliation from the Resistance.

In the same month, the Germans established compulsory labor service, the STO (Service du Travail Obligatoire). With the cooperation and assistance of the Vichy government, they ordered the deportation to Germany within the year of 250,000 men. Even these measures did not satisfy the German authorities' need for manpower. Daily roundups started to occur, with the authorities deporting at random anyone they could lay their hands on, keeping a percentage of the men as hostages against Resistance killings of Germans. It was to be called "the most successful recruitment drive ever for the Resistance": 36,000 young people would try to cross into Spain to join the Allies; 18,000 of them would be caught and deported.

The deportations also marked the beginning of a major influx into the Maquis movements, particularly in Haute Savoie, Vercors, Auvergne and in the southwest of France, with a consequent increase in acts of sabotage and harassment of the enemy by the Resistance. This in turn led to the Germans' responding with horrific reprisals against the civilian population. It was also in 1943 that the pursuit and deportation of Jews to death camps intensified.

At the same time, Allied bombing of industrial centers and railway depots near large cities escalated, and this, coupled with Resistance sabotage of railway tracks, exacerbated the increasingly acute problems of food transport and supply. Food stocks had already been seriously depleted by large requisitions for the German army and German population, and the simple act of feeding oneself had now become an endless daily struggle. Although my own "double life" was tough I did have some distinct advantages over most of my fellow citizens—we had better heating because we were sharing our premises with German soldiers and we were slightly better fed because the municipal authority was responsible for the children in our care.

All we could do to brighten up the dismal picture around us was to use our imaginations. Having been a Girl Guide since I was thirteen, I asked permission to form a company in Vitry and this, to my delight, was acceptable to both the school director and the Guide authorities in Paris. We were, of course, rather restricted in our activities, but we could at least leave school during my interminable duty weekends and go for long walks far away from our "prison." Dressed in our khaki uniforms, we would take a gas-powered bus as far as possible out of Paris and from there walk for miles in search of a distant farm. The farmers generally gave us a warm welcome, fresh milk to drink and sometimes even the rare delicacy of a real slice of bread and butter. Our regular bread was a terrible ersatz affair made up of 50 percent acorn leaf and bran. As for butter, we never saw any.

On these hikes beside the hedgerows we often used to find leaflets dropped by Allied planes, whole bundles of them, all damp and stuck together, describing what was happening outside France and telling us about the activities of the Resistance. They urged us to support the Resistance, telling young men to refuse STO and join the Maquis. They denounced the Vichy government as a pack of traitors and let us know that General de Gaulle had established the real French government in Algiers. They would give details of roundups, of shooting of hostages, of life for French workers in Germany, of anything and everything that the Germans were doing their best to keep hidden. I needed all my authority to prevent the younger girls from picking the leaflets up—if you did so and were found carrying them or divulging their contents, you could be sent to jail forthwith. But I would always manage to secrete one in my pocket or under my blouse, so that I could read it quietly in my room, learn it by heart, destroy it and pass on its contents by word of mouth to all those I knew I could trust.

As soon as term ended that year for the summer holidays, I took our thirty-strong Guide company camping for two weeks in the Loire region. Two other Guide captains came to help me, as did

Madame Bergerol's daughter, who was also a Girl Guide. From the main camp, I chose ten of the strongest girls to go on a two-day camping trip involving a sixty-kilometer hike. Our aim was to join up with a pilgrimage to the Abbey of St. Benoît sur Loire, a famous Romanesque and Gothic church, and also to visit the Carolingian church at Germigny des Prés, well known for its alabaster windows. I had arranged to meet Robert Giscard, my friend from the moun-taineering adventure, in St. Benoît. He was going to help steer our little group through the festivities, which included a pageant orga-nized in honor of the visit of Cardinal Suhard, Archbishop of Paris, who was going to celebrate high Mass and invoke the abbey's holy patronage for the salvation of France.

We were left with indelible memories: the Gregorian chant soar-ing upwards beneath the medieval vaults, the organ booming out its reply and the fervor of the many young people gathered there in response to the Cardinal's appeal to pray for France. Then there was the honest simplicity of the priest of Germigny, so proud to show us personally the architectural treasures of his unique church, the for-gotten peace of his typical presbytery garden, straight out of a pic-ture book with its flowers of all hues and species—hanging, climbing in profusion—old stone walls covered in greenery, trees laden with succulent fruit, little pathways leading nowhere.

Then there were the kindhearted farmers who twice let us pitch our tents on their land and in the torrential rain offered us the shel-ter of their barns, feeding us with delicacies unheard-of in those days. And there was our sheer joy and sense of achievement in walk-ing those sixty kilometers in two days, despite the fact that all the girls lacked the necessary training and had not been properly nour-ished for years. This store of treasured memories would help sustain us through the months ahead.

There were more foolish ways of livening up our dreary lives: the wildest ideas could germinate in the minds of young people whose only foreseeable future was extremely somber. Our counterparts in the formerly unoccupied zone had access to more reliable informa-tion and could more easily join the Maquis and ultimately risk a mountain escape from France. But in the occupied zone, the iron rule of the occupation imposed a regime of terror that you did not defy with impunity. We were bursting with pent-up energy, courage even, but there was no way it could usefully be channeled.

One day, for instance, one of our colleagues who was studying dentistry told us she had received an invitation to a medics' dance at

Corbeil Hospital. It was quite simple: we could catch a train from Juvisy station, which we could reach by bus from Vitry, and from there it was only a few minutes' walk. The mere idea of going somewhere different and dancing all night was just too tempting, so three of us, all monitors, made up our minds to go, come what may. It meant leaving the dormitories as soon as the children were asleep and coming back at dawn before Madame Bergerol arrived. With two girls left behind to keep an eye open for trouble it was a small risk to take and it seemed well worth it.

As luck would have it, the children were particularly unruly that evening and we could not escape until about nine o'clock. It didn't matter, we ran all the way to the bus stop—Mimi Deschamps from Saint Malo, with her big sea-blue eyes and constant talk of resistance (she became a stewardess and was tragically killed in an air crash); Colette, another colleague who married a top civil servant in the Ministry of the Interior, and me. We got to Juvisy but were very anxious when we discovered that we had just missed the last train. It was twelve kilometers from there to Corbeil. We couldn't possibly walk that far before curfew; never mind, we would manage somehow. We took the main road, which was the most direct route. Fortunately for us, it was pitch-black that night. Suddenly, headlights in the distance warned of an approaching car. At that time of night, it could only be Germans. We were frozen with terror and crouched down in the ditch alongside the road.

Our hearts pounding, we waited for the car to go past. Once the danger was over, we set off again, but suddenly more headlights appeared on the horizon. This time, it was a military convoy and we were glad to be able to take cover in the ditch again. This pattern repeated itself over and over again along the road to Corbeil. We did eventually reach the town, which in those days was much less built-up and populated than it is today. We had no trouble finding the railway line, which ran more or less parallel to the road and we then followed it to the station. We didn't know whether or not the station was guarded by German sentries and, after a great deal of conferring and hesitation, we agreed that I would go on my own to find help; if the coast was clear, I would signal to them. As I was crossing the tracks, I caught sight of a railwayman. By reputation, railway workers were patriotic, so I quickly explained the situation, telling him that we were looking for the hospital but not admitting that we were only going dancing. He offered to take us to within sight of the building and my friends came to join me. Somewhat reassured by this male companion, we finally arrived at the hospital gate and were let in without any difficulty.

Taken to the rooms of some junior doctors, we found a whole gang of young people, already fairly tipsy, who burst into noisy laughter on our arrival and dragged us off to dance a boisterous fandango. I soon found some of my university friends and explained our adventure to them, but they were quite unimpressed. I thought we had just done something quite splendid, but soon realized within minutes that we had risked being picked up, or worse, for the hell of it. The pointlessness of our escapade, which I had thought so heroic, took away my appetite for dancing; I was dead-tired and felt totally frustrated.

Yet that was not the only daring and stupidly dangerous expedition I got myself into in those days. Another such scrape involved going down into the catacombs of Paris with five other students. The term "catacomb" originally applied to underground quarries that housed bones removed from the Cimetière des Innocents in the heart of Paris just before the Revolution, and from other cemeteries later on, when the land was cleared for new building. By now, however, it was more loosely used to describe the intricate network of subterranean caverns and corridors that made up the various levels of underground Paris together with the sewers and the Métro. Someone in the Resistance had asked a medical student friend to check the feasibility of an underground route, from a private cellar near the river to a sewer outlet in a cul de sac near the rue Tombe Issoire. To cover up his mission, the medic decided to pass it off as a student prank, concealing his real purpose from us. But we were perfectly aware that we had no right to be there and instinctively followed his instructions to speak in whispers and tread softly.

The Germans were justifiably wary of the catacombs. Although they occupied a few of the vast, well-known intersections, they were loath to venture any further into the maze. They had no up-to-date plans of the area and suspected that bodies of soldiers who had mysteriously disappeared without trace might have been lost for ever in that unknown Hades. Fear still rises within me as I think of that group of six students, led by someone we barely knew through numerous tunnels and vaulted passageways corresponding vaguely to the streets above ground. Armed only with a rough map and a flashlight, we were nearing the end of our journey, walking past endless neat stacks of bones held in place by wire netting and topped with skulls and tibias for decoration. Suddenly we stumbled across a room blazing with bright lights. We could hear German voices and caught sight of soldiers in green uniforms. We held our breath, quickly retraced our footsteps and turned off into a different tunnel, hoping to find another way to the sewer outlet. The tunnels were getting smaller and smaller; we were hopelessly lost. Panic was fast taking hold when suddenly we heard more voices, this time speaking French. To our enormous relief, a gang of passing sewer workers came into view. They could not believe the risks we had taken but helped us to find the sewer outlet, warning us which intersections to avoid to escape German patrols. All told, we were down in those catacombs for about three hours, plenty of time for the foolishness and danger of our enterprise to sink in. When we finally emerged into the street as planned, it was dark; another student was keeping guard and we decided never to mention our escapade to a soul. Looking back on it now, I realize that of all the things I did in wartime, this was undoubtedly the most absurd. Had we been caught, what started for me that day as a student lark would very likely have ended in tragedy. I only hope that our foolhardiness did help others to find a much needed escape route.

I was perhaps tempted into such wild escapades because my emotional life was in a rut. First of all there were very few young French men in occupied France at the time. There were two million prisoners in Germany and deportations for compulsory labor service were becoming more and more frequent. All the other men had fled to the free zone. Some had joined the Maquis, some the FFI (French Internal Forces), others had been caught and deported when they tried to escape, and a great many were in hiding. I had a really good friend who was in love with me, with whom I flirted mildly but he did not correspond to my masculine ideal or my romantic ideas about marriage. He was full of all the qualities that go to make up lasting friendships, but he fell short of the dreams of adventure and the unexpected that had haunted me since the earliest days of my youth. When my mother questioned me about him, I would endlessly reply that I liked him a lot, he was a good friend, he was considerate, attentive, faithful but I just couldn't see myself attached to him for ever; I was afraid I would be bored. That charming young man followed his own destiny into the French civil service.

Life carried on; for my own part, I had to face the disappointment of failing my law exam in June. That meant I had to study hard for the whole summer. I passed the written paper but failed the oral in Roman law again in October. I then had no choice: I would have to do my second year all over again.

That failure was a factor in my decision to change the course of my life. One of the perks reserved for those who had spent three years in Vitry was special dispensation from taking the arduous competitive exam called the Auxiliariat de la Seine; it allowed you to teach in Paris and its immediate suburbs, a location of course very much in demand. So I made up my mind to apply for an official transfer to the teaching staff of the Paris and Seine area. From that moment, I was allowed to teach primary classes in Vitry to get myself ready for an "Inspection" and subsequent posting. Thanks to my friend Inspector Delandre, my application was processed quickly; I was inspected in November 1943 and posted to a primary school in St. Maurice, a Paris suburb which could be reached by Métro via Charenton.

I had very few regrets about leaving Vitry and going home to live with my parents. By that time, my mother and father had rented another small flat adjoining theirs and had linked the two together so I could live at home with some independence. So there I was, at home and a qualified primary school teacher. It was not exactly "glory," but I had certainly earned it the hard way.

I was given an intermediate class with two sets of pupils, not the easiest task for a beginner, so I used to prepare my lessons very conscientiously. My friend the Inspector, who had my interests at heart, invited me to go and see him to discuss my future and, whenever we were together we would invariably talk of happier times in St. Omer. He would ask me my opinion of Vitry and what improvements could be made there. On one such visit, he eventually asked me openly if I wanted to make a career in primary school teaching and I answered honestly that I did not. We then talked about my legal studies. Did I want to give up law? I told him that I intended to finish my degree while I was teaching. But finally we both came to the conclusion that this was not practical. He told me that he could help me to get a leave of absence from teaching, for as many years as I needed to finish my law course, without losing the advantages I had just gained. It was possible to do that in those days. My parents had already suggested I would do better to concentrate on my law studies, and so it was that I decided to abandon teaching at Easter 1944.

By then the Allies had intensified their merciless bombing campaign over France in preparation for the D-Day landings later that summer. Although it was creating havoc, I have to confess that we rejoiced at every single bombing raid. The Paris region was often the target of spectacular raids, mostly at night. If you were out in the street when the bombs started to drop, you would be forced to go down to the air-raid shelters, most of them in the Métro, and you would see the German soldiers head in the same direction; but if we were at home, my parents and I, or anyone who happened to be with us, would all immediately go to the terrace and watch the incredible fireworks display. We could hear quite distinctly the roar of the planes, see the tracer fire of the German "ack-ack" guns, followed by the massive explosion of the bombs and the gigantic fires on the horizon. Not once did we fail to congratulate the Allies in our hearts on their splendid efforts. We were not at all afraid; we simply did not believe German propaganda that the Allies were choosing to target the civilian population. We knew their objective was to hit industrial targets and the area where we lived, near the cathedral of Notre Dame, certainly did not fall into that category. The only time we did go down to our cellar was after the liberation of Paris when the Germans dropped a few bombs on the capital. On that occasion we were really afraid: we knew it was pure retaliation. Alas, one of those bombs did actually fall on our previous abode, killing some thirty people.

I went to the University every day and tried to concentrate on taking my law exam for the second time. It was not to be. The least one can say is that it was not easy to settle down and study in May and June of 1944. All the signs pointed to a dramatic end to the long conflict. The nightly bombings, however spectacular to watch, were enervating. It was impossible to get food; gas was severely rationed. We would meet the most extraordinary soldiers on the streets and in the Métro—Tartars, Georgians, Ukrainians, Mongols—all members of the Waffen SS who had been recruited to fight the Soviets and now found themselves in France. We learned from the BBC that the Allies were advancing in Italy and that furious battles were taking place there, that Mussolini had been arrested and then rescued by the Germans, that the Vichy heads of government were now in Sigmarinen. We heard on the bush telegraph about the latest exploits of the Maquis, in Grenoble, on the plateau of Glières, in the Vercors and the horrific massacre of the population at Oradour sur Glane. A growing fear of the Germans was gripping the population, yet at the same time there was elation at the distinct feeling that it would soon all be over.

At long last, on the evening of the sixth of June, we heard by word of mouth that a landing had taken place in Normandy. We spent our time on the telephone, trying to contact friends who lived closer to the field of action to find out if they knew any more than we did. Our efforts were always rewarded. The minute we heard any news, we would pass it on to friends and neighbors. Alas, progress was slow; the Germans fought like tigers and were able somehow to concentrate more troops on the Western Front as well as containing the Soviet armies in the east.

Although Paris had been in a state of ferment since the D-Day landings, we had to wait until the first days of August before the Paris uprising got under way, and that was despite CNR (National Resistance Committee) orders that nothing was to happen until proper instructions were given. By August 4, Paris had run out of coal as a result of the railway workers' strike; there was consequently no electricity, no gas, no train transport, no food and, stranger still, no police and no radio. Some roads and bridges were cut off. Too preoccupied in saving their own armies and skins, the Germans had clearly lost interest in the French population and, together with the Gestapo and their various HQ troops, had started to pull out. On August 10, Paris had a new German governor, General Dietrich von Choltitz, and some Resistance movements launched a call to arms with their slogan: "Block, destroy, attack, disrupt."

On August 12, General de Gaulle ordered Parisians back to work. Almost at the same time, Hitler instructed von Choltitz to blow up the gas, electricity and telephone centers of Paris, as well as the thirty-two bridges in the city and some thirty others on its outskirts. In the event, Paris seems to have been saved by general disobedience of orders! Contrary to de Gaulle's appeal, the Confédération Générale du Travail (CGT) called a general strike in solidarity with the railwaymen, and they were soon joined by staff and workers in many other key services—the post office, Métro, telecommunications, engineering, shops, banks, insurance, factories and the construction industry. As for von Choltitz, although he did have all the bridges mined, he did not order them to be blown, nor did he destroy any of the essential services. By August 19, the FFI and police force had recaptured the Paris police headquarters, and those of the gendarmerie and republican guard were soon likewise retaken. Barricades went up all over Paris and Molotov cocktails were manufactured in kitchens and distributed to all and sundry. By August 23, the FFI had taken control of most strategic points in the city, although the Germans still held nine important locations, including the Military Academy, Senate and Admiralty.

Finally, on August 24, blaring out on a radio system which the Resistance had somehow managed to coax back into life, we heard the news that we had waited for so long:

Leclerc's Division is in Paris! At this very moment, the first tanks have reached Notre Dame, and the soldiers of the Second Armored Division are right there with them! They are heading for the Hôtel de Ville, which has been in FFI hands since this morning. Citizens of Paris, this is a time for rejoicing. You, we, are all free at last! Go out on the streets to greet them, let the tricolor fly again with pride.

The broadcast erupted into every Paris living room, giving fresh heart to a population racked by hunger, since the routed German army had abandoned all pretense of feeding three million civilian enemy mouths. Of course, food supplies for Paris were not a high priority on the Allies' military agenda, either. Stepping up their relentless pursuit of the enemy, they were intent on encircling Paris in a broad, sweeping arc so as to cut off all possibility of German retreat; they could not afford to let civilian needs obstruct the momentum of their lightning advance. General Omar Bradley himself had sent word to the French General Leclerc that Paris was nothing more than an inkspot on the strategic map: if Parisians starved to death, then that was a risk of war, a risk they had to take. The army's mission was not to feed the French but to kill the Hun.

We could scarcely believe our ears when all of a sudden Paris echoed to the sound of pealing bells; from the belfries of 150 churches all over the capital, they rang out, led in their joyful carillon by the sonorous great bell of Notre Dame. The telephone never stopped ringing; everyone wanted to make sure that their relatives and loved ones had heard the good news. It had been so long in coming. Yet at the same time we could hear artillery fire in the distance and knew that the Germans still held some strategic positions in the city. We did not even dare to hope they might surrender the capital without any real resistance; only the Parisians' proverbial (and totally irrational) optimism sustained their dream that Paris might escape destruction.

My parents and I went to bed that night in a state of terrible agitation. Something my mother said at the time has always stuck in my memory; she was certainly no coward herself and in her old age still had a sound grasp on reality. We could, she told us, be absolutely certain of only one thing: that as long as the war was not over, the Germans were not to be trusted.

Early the next morning, we eagerly tuned in again to the "free" radio, which was still under Resistance control, and we heard that Allied troops coming from the west were already at the gates of Paris. Amongst these troops were the bulk of Leclerc's division, which the general himself had split into three sections, one of which had raced ahead into the capital the day before, quite contrary to the orders the General had been given. But the contingent also included the Fourth American Infantry Division, propelled towards Paris under the leadership of General Omar Bradley, reputedly furious at the slow pace of Leclerc's advance and unwilling to stand by and wait for the liberators to dance their way into Paris.

Leclerc's troops had in fact met fierce opposition, both from retreating German units near Arpajon and a more organized rear-guard action in the region of Versailles and Palaizeau. But they were also considerably slowed down by the delirious welcome they received from the inhabitants of every town they liberated. As General Bradley described in his memoirs, they "stumbled reluctantly through a Gallic wall as townsfolk along the line of march slowed the French advance with wine and celebration." As they finally motored into Paris, fighting their way through pockets of German resistance, unaware of or ignoring the cease-fire, the liberators went into battle, their faces smeared with lipstick!

The Allied tanks and armored cars swept on relentlessly, some heading for the Arc de Triomphe, some for the Eiffel Tower, and a third group for Notre Dame and the Hôtel de Ville. Like everyone else in Paris that day, I desperately wanted to rush out and greet the French soldiers. But where should I go to be sure of not missing them altogether? I gave it some careful thought, especially since I knew I would have to walk. No public transport was running that day: the Métro had been out of action for two weeks because of electricity shortages and the buses were on strike. I decided to head for Boulevard St. Michel in the Latin quarter, since I knew that district well. At this point a radio broadcast informed us that serious street fighting had broken out all over the city, especially in the vicinity of the Préfecture, the Place St. Michel, the Ecole Militaire, the Place de la Concorde and the Place de la République. This hastily armed Resistance was attacking German tanks with grenades and Molotov cocktails. The FFI's appeal had clearly been heeded; the uprising that had started in Paris the Sunday before was now at its height.

My father had been glued to Paris radio from the moment it started to operate freely. At this most recent news, he absolutely refused to let me go out, saying that it was sheer madness. I would not manage to see anything, I would only get myself killed. So I stayed at home, confined to our house in a quiet corner of the sixteenth arrondissement, seething with impatience, longing to be out in the streets with other like-minded Parisians.

I had to bide my time and be satisfied with a brief outing in my own very peaceful district. At least I could go out and buy the newspapers, which had recently started publication in the city, *Combat, Franc Tireur* and *Libération*, replacing *Paris Soir* and other collaborationist newspapers. No longer illegal, they were now being published quite openly, right under the noses of the sixteen thousand Germans still in Paris. The evening papers told us more about what had been happening: we found out that the FFI, helped by the Allies, had engaged in violent combat to liberate Paris and that General von Choltitz had finally given in after savage fighting around the Place de la Concorde. The act of surrender had been signed in Leclerc's headquarters at the Gare Montparnasse. De Gaulle was already in Paris and had made his way to the Hôtel de Ville. The next morning he would go to the Arc de Triomphe for a moment of quiet contemplation beside the tomb of the Unknown Soldier.

I telephoned a friend to ask him to go out with me that evening; I wanted to fill my lungs with the air of liberty. I pleaded with my father, who eventually yielded to my entreaties, reassured by the news in the press and on the radio. And that was how I came to be out on the streets about eight o'clock that evening, with my student friend Jean-Claude Gourin. Several million Parisians had the same idea and they were all, like us, heading for the Arc de Triomphe, symbol of our victories and freedom, defiled by the German army of occupation on its victorious sweep into Paris in 1940.

There had been no need for any kind of rallying cry; Paris had simply followed the dictates of its heart. As we walked from the Trocadéro not far from my home along the Avenue Kléber, we came across whole families quietly talking amongst themselves. There was no noisy euphoria or singing; it would have been completely out of place. The price of liberation had been too high in blood, death, treachery, cowardice and humiliation. The war was not yet over; millions of French prisoners of war were still in Germany; millions of Allied soldiers all over the world were still fighting on our behalf. No, it was not the moment for misplaced rejoicing but for a solemn kind of joy, for gratitude, for hope and for rebirth. Cars, proudly flying the French tricolor and with the letters FFI painted in bright red on their sides, sounded their horns over and over again as they tried to plow their way along that great avenue teeming with people. When we reached the Place de l'Etoile, it became more and more difficult to walk because of the throng, but our hearts were bursting with joy and pride at the sight of the Arc de Triomphe. It was bathed in the most extraordinary light, which seemed to radiate from it, a halo of incandescence in a shroud of deepening darkness. It was five long years since we had seen Paris lit up. We had had no electricity for fifteen days, no gas, no public transport, no food, but all our hardships were rewarded that evening. We scarcely knew why we had come; we just waited; we really didn't know for what. Never before had Paris witnessed such a spontaneous gathering of human warmth, understanding and harmony.

Our route brought us out on the Place de l'Etoile and from there we naturally made our way to the Arc de Triomphe. We wanted to see the eternal flame with our very own eyes, having been denied all access to it during the occupation. In an instinctive gesture of patriotism, we felt the need to offer thanks and prayers for all those who had sacrificed their lives for France. At this point we were just getting ready to go back down the Champs Elysées towards the Place de la Concorde; we longed to see it in all its glory, with the hated German hordes routed at long last and the French flag flying on the Hôtel Meurice and the Palais Bourbon instead of the loathsome swastika. But we were immediately pushed back towards the Arc de Triomphe by the thrust of an irresistible human tide originating from the Place de la Concorde. It seemed as if the entire population of Paris was determined to reach the tomb of the Unknown Soldier. There was absolutely no way of resisting this wave of physical pressure.

Suddenly I found myself separated from my friend. I was totally wedged in and could do nothing but sway backwards and forwards with the crowd. But I was teetering on the edge of disaster—the ebb and flow of closely packed bodies had forced me to the very brink of a chasm. Just beneath me lay a huge cement gully in which were three giant searchlights which, at that very moment, were illuminating the Arc de Triomphe. It was so deep that you faced certain injury if you fell into it; so wide it was impossible to leap across it like a mountain crevasse. And the searchlights were clearly much too hot to hang on to. I could see no way to avoid catastrophe. I remember the thought flashing through my mind that I was going to die like this, crushed in a grave of cement beneath hundreds of other people trapped like me; what an incredibly stupid way to die. I could see no way out of my predicament and was desperately trying to resign myself to my fate, when all of a sudden, from somewhere in the crowd, I was reprieved. "Don't push," went up the cry and the pressure was almost instantly lessened with the formation of a human chain, which succeeded in repelling the onslaught. It had been completely accidental, but so very nearly a tragedy. I have never been so physically frightened in all my life.

It took me some time to recover my composure. Luckily, I managed to find my friend again and felt very glad of his protection. The atmosphere of the crowd, my own fear and the very notion of freedom had left me feeling quite exhilarated, almost exhausted with emotion, and we decided it was time to go home. Jean-Claude faced a good hour's walk right across the center of Paris from the Etoile to the Place de la République, but he was undaunted. We had become so used to walking over the last five years; it had become an act of resistance, part of every Parisian's daily protest against the oppression of the occupation.

The next day was de Gaulle's moment of triumph. More than two million Parisians flocked to pay tribute to him. At eleven o'clock that morning, he was due to go to the Arc de Triomphe and from there to Notre Dame for the celebration of a Te Deum giving thanks for the liberation of Paris. Although we only lived twenty minutes' walk away from the Etoile, I was eager to get there early, determined to have a good view of the proceedings. So I set off soon after nine o'clock, taking with me our caretakers' two children, who were then aged about twelve. As we made our way towards the Champs Elysées, we realized that people were streaming into the capital from all directions and, when we finally got there, there was a good deal of pushing and shoving to secure our place. But the crowd was good-natured and cheerful, and we soon managed to elbow our way to a roadside vantage point. Behind us the façades of the buildings were literally swarming with people: some dangled precipitously from balconies, some had shinned up street lamps, others had a panoramic view from the lofty branches of the trees lining that broad avenue. We stood waiting, expectant, at the roadside. A tremendous roar went up: "Vive de Gaulle!" All the people around us, those above, those in the twenty-odd rows behind, those standing on stools or ladders, were all shouting at the tops of their voices: "Viiiive de Gaaaulle!"

We were all expecting to see him come down the Champs Elysées in a tank or armored car, but we were quite wrong. He walked down, flanked across the breadth of the avenue by the men he had selected as heads of the provisional Republican government, and by Resistance and FFI leaders. His cavalcade was led by some uniformed officers, mostly motorized army, and a similar contingent brought up the rear. But to all intents and purposes, he was completely without military protection. Towering above everyone else with his great height, he was quite unmistakable. As he walked, he raised his long arms towards the sky in the gesture that was almost to become his hallmark but was a complete novelty to Parisians that day. Turning to the left and right, he seemed to be offering his thanks and celebrating his faith in the people who had come to acclaim him. For all those gathered there, he was the living symbol of resistance to the enemy invader.

Numerous personalities followed behind, walking just in front of the tanks at the rear. Most were unknown to us since for the last five years, we had been denied news from abroad, especially about the leaders of the French Resistance. But from time to time, we would hear people say: "There's Bidault," "That's Fabien," "You see that one over there, that's Pisani." We watched the parade pass by, our hearts singing with joy and pride; soon, even when we craned our necks, all we could make out was the mass of people rushing to follow in its wake. Caught up in the excitement and atmosphere, I decided to do the same; I made my way to Notre Dame in the hope of catching one more glimpse of the hero we had all been waiting for. But when we got as far as the Champs Elysées roundabout, shots began to ring out. The terrified crowd dispersed in an instant, taking refuge under the trees lining the side roads. It was difficult to see where the firing was coming from, but clearly some Germans were shooting from the rooftops opposite the Grand Palais. My instinct was to run towards the river and try to reach the banks of the Seine. I thought I could find a safe shelter there.

Taking to my heels, telling the children to follow me closely, I started to run towards the embankment. Most of the crowd seemed to have the same idea. When we reached the Pont des Invalides, the gunfire intensified; I automatically threw myself on the ground, but the children kept on running and I quickly lost sight of them. A few minutes later, with bullets whistling all around, I decided to risk running a bit further. I was still aiming for the river and had not given up all hope of reaching Notre Dame. Unfortunately, some German snipers had positioned themselves on the rooftops and were picking us off like sitting ducks. That was how several people were killed or severely injured that morning. But luck was on my side and I escaped without a scratch. I carried on running, diving for cover every now and then under the arch of the nearest bridge. Before long, rumors began to circulate amongst the people on the streets: shots had been fired in Notre Dame; de Gaulle had been injured! There was, fortunately, no truth in this and the general had remained upright and impassive, heedless of the potential danger. At this point, I decided I had better get back up on the embankment and make my way home; I was especially worried at having been separated from the children.

As for them, they had run as fast as their legs could carry them and had arrived home safe and sound—but their arrival had precipitated a wave of anxiety about me. When I did eventually get home, in a state of high emotion, I told my parents the whole adventure, and they seemed to lap up every last detail. I was so happy I could have cried; so happy to have taken all those risks to catch sight of the one man who had never lost hope in the hours of darkness, the man who embodied for us all the spirit of Free France.

Yet the indescribable happiness of those days of liberation did nothing to dispel the danger which still threatened us all: the war was not over, far from it. On the following Sunday, I went to my own parish church, the Protestant Church of the Annunciation, where Pastor Boegner was leading a service of thanksgiving both to God and man for the liberation of the city. During the occupation, the pastor had taken a courageous stand against the Nazis, and in his sermon that day he recalled the terrible price in suffering that had been paid to secure our freedom and which was still being borne by all those remaining in detention: the prisoners of war, political deportees, Jewish deportees. It was a service of thanksgiving and gratitude, but also an appeal for tolerance, a warning against any premature euphoria.

Listening to the pastor's message, I resolved that the very next day I would find a way to contribute and do something positive. Although I was still completing my law degree, my heart was no longer in my studies. I spoke English fluently and felt sure that I could find a job where my second language would come in useful. It was at this point that I found out about the Welcome Committee for Allied Officers, which required bilingual staff. I decided to go straight away to their offices and was taken on immediately. Little did I realize how much this decision, taken in the enthusiasm of the liberation, was to determine the course of my life.

In the England of 1940, Bob had landed in Liverpool and from there had been taken to Cholmondeley, near Chester, where the remnants of the Czech army were assembled under the control of Benes's Czech government in exile. Soon after their arrival in Cholmondeley, a rebellion broke out, led by the Communist Vlado Clementis who had played a leading role in the Spanish Civil War, becoming foreign minister of Czechoslovakia under the Communists and later executed by them for his virulent nationalism and opposition to the Soviet Union. The rebellion was supported by some 150 Jewish soldiers who had experienced antisemitism at the hands of their Czech officers. Five hundred rebels, one-seventh of the Czech forces, broke from the rest of the Czech army, refusing to obey the orders of officers they felt had abandoned them in battle in France, escaping before them to Britain. Bob joined the rebellion, although he was later to say that he was too young to understand the politics of the situation. The rebels were insisting that the Czech government in exile court-martial the officers or they would refuse to serve under them. Instead of the officers being court-martialed, however, the rebels were segregated, surrounded by British military police and taken first to Oswestry, then to another camp in York and finally to a hastily built military prison camp in Sutton Coldfield, near Birmingham. They were subsequently discharged from the Czech legion.

It was while he was in Sutton Coldfield that Bob met Hazel, a young lady who taught him English. As he was later to relate, he met her in a tobacconist's shop where he regularly went to buy cigarettes, and they struck up a friendship. She was surprised at how quickly the young Czech picked up the language, but it was only many years later, in the publicity surrounding my husband's death, that she realized Bob Maxwell was none other than the young Czech Ludvik she had gone out with in 1940.

As soon as he arrived in Sutton Coldfield, Bob made it clear that he was interested in fighting Germans and volunteered to join the British army. Along with his compatriots, he was offered a choice: he could either remain confined as an undesirable alien or apply to join the Pioneer Corps. He chose the latter, mistakenly thinking that "pioneer" meant "engineer." He enlisted on October 9, 1940, having given the year of his birth as 1921 and not 1923, so as to be old enough to join. Stationed first in Ilfracombe in Devon for a brief, basic training period, he was then moved to other towns around the British Isles and soon discovered it was not a fighting regiment he had signed up for but the "pick and shovel" brigade. He stuck it out, however, unlike a number of other rebels from Cholmondeley who rejoined the Czech Legion, under strong protest from the Czech military command, taking advantage of the amnesty declared by President Benes, "for Czechoslovak citizens who had refused to serve in the army or had been dismissed." For almost three years, he toiled alongside Germans, Austrians and Hungarians, men much older than himself, quarrying stone and building roads, huts, military barracks, ammunition and petrol dumps all over the country, including a stint of several months in some Welsh slate quarries.

Bob was always complaining to the army doctors about his tummy troubles and, after a few months, he was given a brief respite when he was taken off work and sent to hospital. There it was decided that he needed to have his appendix removed, and after the operation was performed in December 1940, he was sent to a convalescent home for British soldiers in Ely, near Cambridge. He was the only foreigner there and was to make quite an impact on one of the nurses who looked after him. She was later to describe the impression he made on her:

He enchanted, fascinated, infuriated and, above all, baffled the lot of us. His character was mercurial, mostly exuberant but sometimes deeply melancholy. At times he appeared almost illiterate, but at others he displayed such a breadth and depth of knowledge that he might have lived a hundred years. No one who knew him could ever forget him.

They fell in love and remained close to each other for almost two years. It was Bob's first love affair in England and had a deep and lasting effect on him, for through this young nurse, he came into contact for the first time with an English upper-middle-class home and family. He was welcomed and liked by her parents and it was here that his transformation into the personable young man I met in Paris really began. Bob was quick to notice the standards of manners, language and behavior of her family and copied them immediately, thereby acquiring a polish that had been lacking in the rather wild young man from Szlatina. One trait of his character which she remembered well from those days was his willingness to have a go at absolutely anything—even if he had no previous knowledge or experience of it:

One day the resident corporal could not be found to meet a new nurse arriving at the station. Ludvik volunteered for the job and I went with him as a welcoming committee. He was seventeen and I don't believe he had ever driven a car in his life. After a bit of jiggling around with the gears, we suddenly shot out of the garage backwards, across the main road. We then proceeded to the station in a series of swoops and jolts and life was preserved due to the fact that the little traffic there was, after alarmed glances, gave us a very wide berth indeed.

After his stay in the convalescent home, Bob was posted back to his unit and his life in the Pioneers resumed its normal course. But it was not long before he broke his thumb in a fight with another soldier and found himself back in hospital in Cambridge, followed by a second spell of convalescence in Bedford. This was another episode of great significance for his future.

It was whilst he was in Bedford that he met Mrs. Tillard, a

charming lady who had lost her only son, an air force officer, in a bombing raid on Essen. She took a great interest in Bob and acted as a mother to him for many years. Through her, he was to come into contact with the headmaster of Bedford public school who in turn introduced him to a widow called Sylvia who was to play a leading part in his life for the next two years. As Bob later described it:

We met in the bar of the Bridge Hotel. We talked half the night, we fell in love at first sight. She was a very beautiful and intelligent woman. Although much older than I, I was very much in love with her. She represented for me the dream of my youth. She was the turning point of my first life. With her, I turned from an adolescent into a man, and with her I left behind all that was unsettled in me, all my youth.

Through Mrs. Tillard and Sylvia, Bob again came into contact with refined and educated families, a world he had glimpsed with his first girlfriend's family, but of which he was still largely ignorant. His determination to find out more about the culture of those who opened their homes to him, and the history of their country, became a driving obsession. He read extensively, borrowing books from anyone and everyone, questioning, inquiring, learning and his excellent command of English struck all who met him as unusual. Bob's intelligence, his curiosity about life and insatiable thirst for knowledge fascinated people and they vied for his friendship. I have thought a good deal over the years about how it was that a penniless, uncouth young man, uncultured by British standards and "bullish," as he was described when he first landed in England, should have encountered such enormous goodwill and assistance, often without specifically seeking it. I have come to the conclusion that men admired him and women fell for him, not because he could offer them wealth or social advantage (he clearly had neither), but simply for his natural gifts and a strength of personality that was immensely appealing to all who met him. People were attracted by his innate grasp of any situation, by his concern for others, by this ungainly, bearlike, infinitely lovable youth whom women found irresistible and men envied. They recognized his daring, his courage, his originality, his vitality, the magic that emanated from him and the magnetism he exercised over others.

Bob's emotional life was clearly flourishing, but this did little to relieve the frustrations and monotony of service with the Pioneer Corps. He desperately wanted to join a fighting unit and it was Sylvia who helped him achieve his ambition by introducing him to

Brigadier Carthew-Yorstoun DSO MC, the former battalion commander of the Scots Guards, then commanding a Brigade of infantry,
the 59th Division. Impressed by Bob's linguistic knowledge and
eagerness to kill Germans, Carthew promised to help him as he was
to do throughout Bob's military career. By June 1943, the Brigadier
was able to write to Bob:

I have been held up waiting for a letter from your CO which only reached me
two days ago. Now that the business has started, I do not think it will be long
before we can get things through. I hope to see someone in the War Office on
Sunday with the object of getting a move on [with] normal procedure. Don't
worry; we'll get you out quite quickly now.

By October, Carthew had arranged Bob's transfer, first to the
Somerset Light Infantry in Colchester and then to the North
Staffordshire regiment, stationed at Cliftonville near Margate. Along
with other foreigners from German-occupied countries, Bob had to
be given a new name in case he was captured. So it was that Ludvik
Hoch became Leslie Ivan du Maurier—named after his favorite
brand of cigarettes.

Then began a period of intense training in preparation for what
turned out to be D-Day. Because he was a good shot and, being
rather young, foolishly fearless (in his own words), Bob was made
Battalion Sniper Sergeant, whose job was to go into no-man's-land
and pick off targets of opportunity.

Of his four years in the British army that saw the transformation
of Private Ludvik Hoch to Sniper Sergeant Leslie Ivan du Maurier,
and the few months of bitter fighting in Normandy from which he
emerged as Lieutenant Robert Maxwell, he told me very little when
we first met. He never bragged to me about his exploits, which were
many. Although he was certainly mortally afraid at times, his
courage was instinctive, his powers of leadership inborn, his
charisma undeniable. Most men who fought alongside him have told
me repeatedly that they preferred him to any other officer around—
with him they felt sure of pulling through. In their eyes, as the
French Moroccans would say, "Il avait la baraka!" (Fortune smiled
on him). I learned more about "his" war over the following years as
I came to meet his wartime comrades and friends, and after Joe
Haines's biography of Bob was published in 1988, many other former soldiers came forward, adding their personal stores of memories
and anecdotes. What these had in common was recognition of his

bravery and innate capacity for leadership. Some of them were quite blunt, "Mr. Maxwell did not invite affection, but he was what England needed at that time," said a man who fought with him in Normandy. Another wrote to me, "The chances that man took in the war were unbelievable. Luck was definitely on his side to get away with it."

Soon after he arrived in Cliftonville, Bob was made a lance corporal and recommended for a commission. He attended a three-day War Office selection board but failed to pass the exam. Nevertheless, his military career progressed and he was made a corporal in April and a sergeant in May, in charge of the sniper section of the battalion. North Staffordshire comrades, whom I met in Derby in September 1987, remember the newcomer as a tall, skinny but handsome lad, who was physically very fit. Even then, he seemed to "get away" with things without incurring the usual reprimands. He could, for instance, speak with great familiarity and impunity to a brigadier but he was disliked by some of the junior officers, though not by Captain Edward Abbotts, OBE. Known as "Crash" Abbotts, he was the intelligence officer of the 59th Division, in charge of training snipers before the invasion of Normandy and he well remembers his first meeting with the young Czech soldier:

I expected to encounter a hard-bitten regular soldier who had probably served part of his time as an instructor at the Small Arms School or some similar establishment. In the event, I found myself confronted by a slim, athletic-looking twenty-year-old who, at first glance, looked as if he could have come straight from school rather than be charged with the destinies of a Division's marksmen. At second glance, however, and after he had begun to speak, his strength of character and dedication came through. . . . If he had not made me aware of his Central European origin, I would have classified him as a native-born Englishman who spoke standard English with no trace of a regional accent. He outlined his training program and I realized at once that there was nothing I could add to it. He already had a good team and his whole emphasis was on motivation. His war aims were the same as mine but a thousand times more intensely personal.

By July 1944, Bob found himself in Normandy, moving up for his first engagement with the enemy since the retreat through France in 1940. The village of La Bijude near Bayeux was to be his first trial in battle as a member of the British army and he was scared throughout, as he later recorded. His commanding officer, however, thought he did "rather well" and recommended him for a commission in the field, but it was turned down on the grounds he was not a British-born soldier. After that, Bob recalled that the most memorable battle he was involved in was the crossing of the Orne River near the forest of Grimbosq, where for forty-eight hours he definitely thought his end had come. By that time, Captain Abbotts had received disturbing intelligence reports that the Germans were dispatching prisoners from the occupied countries to concentration camps as political prisoners or traitors, rather than treating them as bona fide prisoners of war. Calling for Bob along with other refugees serving in the division, Crash warned them of the danger they faced and advised them they were being withdrawn from the line. As he recalled:

I sent an urgent message to the 6th Battalion of the North Staffordshire Regiment, in which du Maurier was serving, asking him to be sent immediately to see me. An hour later, he stood before me and I gave him the news that he had to be withdrawn from the forthcoming action.... He looked at me in utter amazement, as if I had been guilty of naiveté in the extreme, and pointed out that his own firsthand experiences of Nazism had left him with no illusions about sportsmanship, rules of war or any such refinements. He knew only too well the sort of enemies we were fighting and he had joined the army with the precise object of fighting against such an evil. He finished by asking permission to ignore the instruction to go to the rear echelon and to be allowed to take what he considered to be an acceptable risk and return to his post at the front. In the circumstances I released him from the constraints of a direct order but repeated that I was advising him most earnestly ... to take advantage of the directive from Corps. He thanked me and left without saying whether he would take the advice or not....

It was to be nearly forty years before Captain Abbotts saw Bob again, on the occasion of Bob's sixtieth birthday party, but he did hear from another intelligence officer that the young soldier had taken no notice of Crash's warning—he was in the thick of the fighting on the bridge.

At that murderous battle for the Orne bridgehead in July 1944, an eighteen-year-old Royal Engineer who was helping to raft light ammunition across the river witnessed an example of his courage firsthand. Field Marshal Montgomery had decided to launch an attack across the Orne by way of a feint in order to draw off the 11th SS Panzer Division, to enable him to mount a massive army attack to close the Falaise gap. The plan succeeded: the Panzer division was drawn off by the 59th Division and the Falaise gap was closed. But the British brigade was decimated. At one stage, the bridgehead had shrunk to virtually nothing and there was panic because German tanks supported by infantry were overrunning the

British positions. Practically all the officers had been killed or wounded. In the face of a fierce German counterattack, British troops were fleeing across the bridge to escape enemy fire and Bob stood there, gesticulating and shouting, "Go back and pump bullets into those Jerries or I'll turn my machine gun on you." At that instant, an almighty mortar explosion wounded the landing Raft Commander, leaving the young lad on the opposite bank transfixed and totally shell shocked. Bob caught sight of the youth, paralyzed with fear. He rushed down the bank under constant shelling, picked him up and ran with him on his shoulder as far as the cellar of a house where he left him to receive medical attention. That, wrote the grateful soldier forty years later, was true compassion.

Although Bob told me little about his actual exploits when we first met, he would talk more generally about the emotions he experienced in battle and all those more refined and human feelings that fighting men harbor in their hearts, enabling them to survive the cruelty and bloody demands of war. One can hardly begin to imagine the thoughts that must have passed through a twenty-year-old soldier's mind when he saw two men, ostensibly British since they were in khaki, signal a Cromwell tank forwards, only to witness a hidden sniper knock it out immediately, killing all the crew with his Panzer-faust. Or how he felt as he turned his captured Schmeisser machine gun on them, dispatching all three German SS soldiers at a stroke. Or how he reacted to the murder of his own lieutenant quartermaster, shot in the head by a sniper, dropping dead at his feet just as they stood together. Eight young men of his age, all killed within the space of five minutes and three by his own hand.

In the few traumatic weeks that followed the Allied landings in Normandy, the North Staffordshire regiment had taken part in the major operation that resulted in the defeat of the 7th German army. It had fought against all manner of German military units, including SS and elite Panzer regiments, and had faced every known form of German weaponry. It had also, alas, been blasted by rockets from our own Thunderbolts, machine-gunned from the air and pounded by 500-pound bombs dropped on the unit while it was in a rest area. The battalion suffered horrific casualties: 555 officers and men either killed, wounded or missing. After the Normandy campaign, there was no alternative but to disband the regiment, disperse the remaining men and assign them to other regiments.

Shortly after the crossing of the Orne, Bob was recommended for an immediate commission. Such promotion was hardly surprising considering the decimation of young officers in his regiment and his evident leadership qualities. But his name, exploits and nationality were mentioned on the radio by a Canadian commentator and he was consequently withdrawn from the line on the order of the division commander, Major General L. O. Lyne. So it was that for reasons of security, Bob was given the temporary new identity of Leslie Jones.

It was at this point, as he waited for his commission to come through and upon the recommendation of Captain Abbotts, that he was sent by the divisional high command to Arras. He was to join a section of the intelligence service responsible for interrogating prisoners of war. His knowledge of several European languages would clearly be an asset, especially his fluent German, which he had perfected in his daily contact with German-speaking soldiers in the Pioneer Corps. By then, the Allies had liberated the north of France and Belgium from the German army in retreat and hundreds upon thousands of German soldiers had given themselves up and become prisoners of war. Intelligence service personnel were in charge of debriefing them. It was a foretaste of the work he would be asked to do after the German surrender, when the task of Intelligence was to weed out Nazis from public life in postwar Germany.

Whilst still in Normandy Bob had captured a large German motorcycle and sidecar and had been allowed to keep it because mobility would be an advantage in his new job. From Arras he was sent to Brussels to be briefed on future missions. He stayed there just long enough to dislike the atmosphere of the town, which at the time was like a huge transit camp, although he did meet a charming and cultured girl who expressed her love for him in beautiful, literary prose.

It was not long before he managed to obtain seven days' leave and make his way to Paris. There he was to have another stroke of luck, for by then Brigadier Carthew-Yorstoun was head of British troops in Paris. After those terribly hard weeks of battle, the French capital was a very sweet haven indeed. As Bob wrote some years later:

It was no more the glittering city of world fame, we were still too near the occupation, but it held for me all the fascination of a jewel. . . . On Brigadier Carthew's recommendation, I went to the French Welcome Committee, hoping to be introduced to French people who could describe to me what life had been like on the continent during the German occupation. When I arrived, there was a large crowd of officers, a still larger crowd of civilians, all talking at the same time across this overpopulated room. Standing behind a large desk, I saw a girl whom I immediately noticed. I stayed in the doorway gazing at her. She was pretty, very vivacious, she was slim, well-built; above all I could not take my eyes off her face. There shone, sparkled, the most lovely pair of blue eyes I had seen. She had a lovely look of slight childish desperation as she was talked to by so many people at the same time. I loved her dearly there and then. From the minute I saw her, I wanted her for my wife.

3

I remember thee for the affection of thy youth,
The love of thine espousals,
When thou wentest after me in the wilderness,
In a land that was not sown.

JEREMIAH 2:2

She lov'd me for the dangers I had pass'd,
And I lov'd her that she did pity them.
This only is the witchcraft I have us'd.

SHAKESPEARE, OTHELLO

I suddenly realized how long we had been sitting there chatting in the corner of the hotel lobby and told Bob that I really had to leave. He asked me if I would go out with him again that evening and suggested we might go to the cinema. After his kindness to me, I did not want to hurt or rebuff him, so I agreed.

We had English-style tea and then I went home. I felt the need to think more calmly about what had just happened, to distinguish between the reality and strangeness of the situation. I was aware that the man with whom I had spent the afternoon was more than fleetingly interested in me and I knew instinctively that I was dealing with a very determined character who would not be easy to get rid of if I got tired of him. Did I really want to embark on an adventure in which I might lose the upper hand? So far I had been lucky: I had been able to stay in control of all my amorous affairs, and I rather wanted to keep it that way. Was I rushing headlong into an adventure which admittedly had its attractions? Could there be any future in such a relationship? We were two people from such different backgrounds and upbringings, from such totally different worlds and traditions. Would we ever manage to bridge the yawning chasm between us?

The film we saw that evening left no impression on me. What really struck me most forcibly was Bob's behavior. Unlike most of the soldiers I had gone out with before, he did not make a pass at me, nor even try to kiss me. At the time I was greatly relieved, but he also left me puzzled. He was certainly different! After the cinema, he took me out to dinner. We talked a little of this and that; he asked me how I came to be working with the Welcome Committee, what I had done before and so on. We spoke English, and I remember how charmed he was by my French accent and intonation. He smiled as I stumbled over the pronunciation of his name, Ivan, a difficult and rather awkward combination of sounds in French, and was immediately agreeable when I asked if I could call him Ian, the Celtic form of his name. He was quite thrilled at the suggestion because Jan was the name he had chosen himself when he was working for the Resistance in Budapest. So from then on, I called him Ian until some years later, when the name Bob took over. A few moments later in our conversation, he returned to the subject of names with a twinkle in his eye. To his ear, Betty was very odd-sounding—Betuska was the way he thought of me, and that became his name for me in the early years of our marriage, before I became just "Mummy."

As we laughed and chatted that evening, it was not long before I realized he was smitten and definitely wanted to see me again. At the time, I was reluctant to get involved in a steady relationship; I was determined to enjoy my freedom and play the field in search of the adventure that would satisfy all my longings. I was quite open about this to Bob, but he just retorted that I need look no further: he was the beginning and the end of my search!

I didn't want to be rushed into things by a complete stranger, so I told him about my dreadful habit of playing a little game I had invented called What Makes You Tick? I would make friends with people, men and women alike, spend some time finding out what they were like then drop them once my curiosity was satisfied. I wasn't especially proud of that, but at least it was the truth. I was determined not to hurt him, and said it would perhaps be wiser to end our acquaintance there and then since it seemed to have so little future: so many things separated us, the end of the war still seemed a long way off, and whoever he was, his world was very different from mine.

He was interested in this game of mine and asked how it had all started. I told him that since the days of my philosophy studies, five years before, I visualized the soul as a dry cuttlefish bone that you picked up on the beach: lovely, white and smooth on the inside and hard on the outside with rough edges. Thinking at the time that everyone imagined it like that, I had been quite startled when my teacher had made a great fuss in class about the originality of this image. Ever since then, every time I lost interest in an acquaintance, I had a mental picture of stringing another fishbone onto the thread of my experience. Bob was quite amused by my explanation. I remember his immediate rejoinder, "Well, you won't string me on that thread of yours as easily as all that, just you try!"

As soon as we ordered dinner, he startled me by declaring, without any preamble, that he was in love with me, that he had fallen in love the minute he saw me and wanted me for his wife and that was that. He asked me if I had known many men. I replied that I had known a few but until recently I had little chance to meet many. I had been in love before, but if he meant "know" in the biblical sense, then the answer was no. He carried on relentlessly: "I love you as you are. Whatever might have happened to you before, whatever you did or didn't do, whoever you met, whatever you thought, whatever your ambitions were, your successes and your failures, I want you as you are now. Life starts all over again with you."

It was certainly the strangest declaration of love. A bolt of lightning had just struck, and out of the smoke, just like in the film *Les Visiteurs du Soir* had stepped a strange and mysterious being who had just landed on our planet. There he was next to me, powerful, extremely seductive, persuasive, piercing me with those blazing eyes of his, which in turn coaxed and cut me to the heart. He did not even let me get my breath back, my heart was pounding, my throat was dry; I felt as if a hand were gripping my stomach, and my legs were like jelly even though I was sitting down. He had not even touched me, not even kissed me, and I was gasping, suffocated by this tempestuous love, completely at his mercy. I had totally lost my appetite and the filet mignon he had ordered was choking me. I couldn't swallow anything. I saw myself being bowled over, along with the virtue I had taken such great pains to preserve.

It was late and he took me home by taxi. As he left, he asked me to think over what he had said, and anyway, he would see me again for lunch the next day. He did not even try to kiss me good night on the pavement outside my front door. That would certainly have pleased my old aunts, who considered the modern habit of smooching on the doorstep completely lacking in class.

I couldn't get to sleep that night: I tossed and turned in bed, conjuring up in my mind his splendid physique and appealing personality. I knew that I was sliding off the straight and narrow, but it was delightful and I really wanted to let myself go. "Love, that terrible game in which one of the players loses self-control"—nobody had expressed as well as Baudelaire exactly what was happening to me.

Bob had one of those mysterious and attractive faces, a face of extraordinary mobility which captured your attention magnetically but could suddenly be transformed into a strange, steely mask, sending a chill right through you. It was impossible to discern the color of his slightly slanting eyes: they shone with moonlike, imperious radiance, sometimes dark and fiery, sometimes extraordinarily soft and childlike.

The shadow of his destiny lay heavy on his strong shoulders, encircled his slender, energetic physique, traced a dark and slightly bronzed ring under those bewitching eyes framed by jet-black, heavily arched brows. His prominent cheekbones accentuated his penetrating gaze, the determined outline of his chin, the broad and voluptuous curve of his nose, sensitive to the slightest odor wafting on the air and his expressive, sensuous mouth. A sudden devastating smile could crease his whole face into an expression of abandoned mirth and the ensuing deep, chesty explosion of laughter would seem to rock the whole room. Although he seemed much older, he radiated the energy and virile strength of a twenty-year-old and moved with all the suppleness and agility of a feline. There was an overwhelming impression of dominance and masculinity, reinforced by the resonant speaking voice from deep down in the diaphragm, confident and self-assured. When he spoke, his swift-moving lips, thick and red like two ripe fruits, evoked luxury and youthfulness; yet sometimes, thin as filaments of blood, they depicted death and carnage.

War, combat, and bloodshed had forged that restless mind and muscular body, a body of such perfect and harmonious proportions, capable of enduring the most excruciating suffering without yielding. He had breathed the fetid air of a prison cell and had felt the deep-seated fear of the escapee and the exhaustion of retreat. He had known those muted, haunting eves of battle, the ponderous clanking of tanks breaking the stillness of the early morning, houses crumbling beneath mortar shells, the sudden, encircling tongues of flame around the dugouts. He had known hand-to-hand combat and the bitter, lucid struggle which is the arbiter of a man's personal fate; he had stared into the enemy's gleaming eyes. He had known the roughness of the rifle butt on his palm, the monotonous bursts of machine-gun fire, the smell of powder and of blood. He was used to death; he knew her well.

The next morning an English soldier brought me a brief note which read: "Terribly sorry, darling. I have been called away on a job which I cannot delay, I will come and see you at the Cercle this evening." It was the first of many such notes I was to receive in the course of the next two months.

By the evening I had regained my composure to a certain extent and we went out again. I tried hard to tell him that I was not used to being taken by storm, that I needed more time to think it over. But this did nothing to deter him; he was quite confident that I would come round to his way of thinking. We continued to talk and exchange information about each other, our past and present lives. Then, before he left me that evening, he told me that he had to leave Paris for a few days, but that he would come back to see me and hear my reply.

Although I was obviously attracted to him and intrigued by his forceful personality, I had not altogether given up going out with other young men. I had met an American officer from Los Angeles who was a professional dancer. I loved dancing—any time, any place! With this young American, I really improved my ballroom skills. He taught me all the fashionable dances, paso doble, tango, rumba, java and of course the waltz, which he danced with immense panache. In those days we made a striking pair and occasionally the whole dance floor would clear to watch us. Bob could not dance at all then. Sometimes, he would find out where I had gone to, appear from nowhere, tap my partner on the shoulder, attempt a few steps with me then whisk me away in the sidecar of his huge German motorbike.

Since we were spending more and more time together, I decided to invite him home and introduce him to my parents. I must say truthfully that they were not impressed. As far as they were concerned, he spelled adventure and everything they most feared for their daughter. They were even less impressed when he brought me back home one day after an accident which could have had serious consequences.

We had gone out for a ride with Bob astride his motorbike and me in the sidecar. Winter had come early that year and it was freezing cold. The streets of Paris were icy. We were roaring along, when suddenly we skidded. Bob jammed the brakes on hard and we finally came to a halt after we ran into the back of a truck with iron pipes protruding dangerously from the rear. I was so badly crushed that I was having trouble breathing. Bob made a U-turn and rushed me to the Hôpital de la Pitié, where I was X-rayed immediately. Although my chest was imprinted with marks and bruises from six-centimeter piping, thankfully nothing was broken. He then drove me home to my parents who were none too pleased with this eccentric young man who had nearly killed their daughter. But Bob now had the perfect excuse to visit me to make sure I was making a good recovery.

He would come to see me and take me out whenever he was in Paris. As I got to know him better, it became obvious that he was quite unusual—extremely bright and totally different from anyone I had met. At least with him I would never get bored, quite apart from the fact that he was immensely good-looking and attractive. Whenever we went anywhere, girls literally fell over themselves to catch his attention. As the weeks passed, it was also clear that he was head over heels in love with me. I found myself falling in love, too. He started to talk about marriage.

Life in Paris was progressively returning to some sort of normality: food supplies improved, even if they were still painfully inadequate, and although there was strict rationing, coupons could at least be exchanged for decent food; bread at last became edible again. People who had fled to the free zone started to come back, including members of some Jewish families who had mercifully survived. Theaters were coming back to life and becoming more daring. Performances had never actually stopped in Paris during the occupation. The Germans had encouraged intellectual, artistic and social activities, wanting the French to believe that the Nazis were educated and civilized, and all highbrow cultural events throughout the war were always packed with German soldiers and high-ranking Nazis. But now they started to produce plays which the Nazis had forbidden. Cinemas showed *Gone With the Wind* and all the great American and English films which were completely unknown to the French, amongst them Charlie Chaplin's *The Dictator*. Cabarets were springing up everywhere and Edith Piaf and Yves Montand topped the bill. As for me, I carried on working at the Welcome Committee, but with less enthusiasm as my thoughts turned more towards the mysterious man with whom I spent most of my free time.

He would appear at the office surreptitiously and take me out there and then, and my employer, Madame Maloubier, allowed him to whisk me off like that, such was the prestige he enjoyed as a result of his friendship with Brigadier Carthew-Yorstoun. We would go out for tea or have dinner in one of the officers' clubs that he now had access to, where they served a variety of food that would still be out of reach to most Parisians for many long months to come. Sometimes, we would drive out into the country near Paris and go for long walks in the woods. We had discarded the sidecar after the accident and I now rode pillion behind my fearless soldier on his motorbike, which we had affectionately christened "The Horse." In the evenings, we would go to performances given by popular singers. Our favorite by far was the legendary Piaf, particularly when she sang "Mon Légionnaire," or "Celui que mon coeur a choisi," and we greatly enjoyed Yves Montand and his big hits "Elle a des yeux, c'est merveilleux" and "Mais qu'est-ce que j'ai, à l'aimer tant," songs that echoed all the sentiments of our nascent love.

The war was no longer on our doorstep, but we nevertheless followed anxiously the progress of the tough battles taking place in Belgium and Alsace as the Allies fought their way to the Rhine and beyond. Sometimes I would take Bob home. During the winter of 1943, my family had moved from the Rue des Francs Bourgeois to a large private house in the sixteenth arrondissement. It was a delightful nineteenth-century residence, typical of the district, with a garden in front and a caretaker's house at the back. My sister Vonnic had just qualified as a gynecologist and shared the house with us; my parents and I occupied the first floor, and she lived on the top floor and had her consulting room on the ground floor. I can still picture my spacious elegant bedroom with its predominantly blue décor.

Bob and I were becoming more and more intimate. I felt myself being swept along in a whirlwind of intense physical attraction. I made no effort to resist it; I had no real reason to, nor did I want to. On December 3, he wrote me a letter which was to have profound consequences for us:

... the only thing I know is that inside me there is something stirring, something warm, something young and glowing like a flame in the dark. It's asking and knocking on my heart as well as on my brain, they are both saying the same thing, something that I have been afraid of, something I tried to fight but knew it was a losing battle against that one little magical word, love. I must now admit that I have lost that battle irrevocably. I am in love with you; as from now my fate is in your hands and I know not of better hands in which to put it than yours. Guard it well, my sweet, it's all that I possess.

That evening, Cupid favored us with his protection: my parents had gone away for a whole week. I rustled up a snack and opened a bottle of wine for him. We had a cigarette, a du Maurier of course, and its delicious scent of Virginia tobacco not only spelled liberation to me but filled me with a sense of euphoria. I showed him to my room. I felt at ease there, surrounded by familiar furniture, comfortable armchairs, my desk and books. It was cozy and warm; we started talking. The contrast of that war hero in my feminine surroundings was exhilarating. I was living a dream, I was the heroine of a story and Mathilde de la Mole, Julien Sorel's lover in Stendhal's novel *Le Rouge et le Noir* had nothing on me that evening. Bob talked of his love for me, of his dreams for us both. Soon we started kissing, then he moved me to the bed and he started undressing me, gently and with extreme modesty. Although he was ablaze with desire, he did not rush me. I was ready for love, eager to be at one with him and we made love. But despite my readiness, it was a painful first experience. He was in tears at the thought of having hurt me. Nothing was ever to move me more than my husband's tears, and by the time I next felt them mingle with mine, a full ten years of togetherness would have gone by.

The silly bourgeois conventions of our generation would not permit him to stay the night with me. My sister was looking after the house for my parents and would simply not have allowed it. So we pulled ourselves together; I went into the bathroom next door to tidy my appearance and comb my hair, and he did the same. We then went into the dining room, where I made some instant coffee, a gift of Bob's and a great delicacy in wartime Paris. We lit another cigarette and sat there, gazing into each other's eyes. Soon after, my sister came home to find a pair of cooing lovebirds, but she would never have guessed what had just happened.

All that week we saw as much of each other as our respective duties would allow. We usually ended up in some hotel or other, which, like Cinderella, I would leave on the stroke of midnight so that my poor sister, detailed by my parents to keep an eye on me, would not go berserk. One night, I did not go home and Vonnic was justifiably furious, accusing Bob and me of abusing her trust. I tried to calm her down by telling her that I was going to marry the guy anyway, but that only made her more worried. When my parents came back, Bob went to see them and formally asked for my hand in marriage. They insisted that he should at least produce some kind of birth certificate, together with a recommendation from his commanding officer.

He left for London that day. He was to meet high-ranking officers at the War Office to discuss his military career following his recent promotion. He would have to be transferred to a new regiment, since his own had been disbanded, and this would take a little while. In any case, it was customary for a soldier commissioned in the field to be posted to another regiment.

Much later on, I discovered that he had also gone to discuss his latest Intelligence assignment, which involved being dropped behind enemy lines to pass on information about German preparations before the final Allied assault. He felt, rightly as it turned out, that it was a suicidal mission, but eventually the German counterattack in the Ardennes prevented those orders from ever being carried out and he continued with his Intelligence Service assignment in Paris, reporting on Communist activities in the capital.

He had also gone to London intending to "tidy up" his life and bring to an end his affair with Sylvia, the widow who had befriended him in 1942. He had been wanting to do this for a little while, and now that he had met me, the time had come. He wanted to be honest about it and break off the relationship in a manly way—which he did.

Before he left Paris, Bob had arranged for Brigadier Carthew-Yorstoun to come home to meet my parents in person. He gave Bob a most glowing character reference and told my father that if he had a daughter, he would be proud to entrust her to his hands. That did it, and the very same day my parents agreed that we could celebrate our engagement officially on New Year's Eve 1944.

Bob returned to Paris on December 24 and slipped an engagement ring on my finger. We spent Christmas together: it was to be the first of forty-six such celebrations, which come hell or high water we would manage to spend together, with or without our children. Our engagement party took place at home on New Year's Eve, and we saw the New Year in with the family in traditional French style, with Bob's ingenuity greatly enhancing the celebratory fare—he turned up with a goose! I beamed with happiness the whole time, as did Bob. As for my parents, they were slightly more reserved: they had lived through a bloody war themselves and were only too aware of all the dangers which still lay ahead of us. Besides, at the time they were still rather dubious of a future son-in-law about whom they knew so little, except that he was wildly in love with their precious daughter.

During the last few days of his leave, before he returned to the front and his new regiment in Holland, we met almost daily, reluctant to miss any of the treasured hours we could spend together. He could not always meet me at the appointed hour and sometimes arranged our rendezvous in the most far-off suburbs, but we were both so much in love that no place was too outlandish, no time too absurd, to mar our joy at being together.

It was a period of adjustment on my part, both physical and

moral. I felt slightly guilty about sleeping with Bob before our wedding, knowing for certain that my parents would strongly disapprove. This inhibited me to a certain extent; although I was twenty-three, I was rather prudish and completely inexperienced sexually. Bob was quite the opposite and, as in other domains, very mature for his age. Whereas in intellectual matters I was to be the dominant partner for many years, guiding him in the general education and social upbringing he had missed, in matters of the flesh I had everything to learn. He was the one who aroused my desires, satisfied them and taught me love play. He was, I think, quite amazed and strangely moved to have met someone who had known no other man, and he was immensely considerate and gentle. For me those few days after our engagement were a time of constant excitement and childish wonder at what love was all about. We were both walking on air, almost oblivious to the tragedies of war and all the hardship that was yet to come. It was youth at its best, bursting with health and vigor, filled with enthusiasm, passion, optimism and daring, thumbing its nose at ill fate and displaying inordinate belief in its lucky star. Such confidence was hardly justified by the horrors Bob was soon to endure. Those few fabulous days were to sustain him through two months of grueling battles when he was repeatedly in danger of losing his life.

January 6, the day Bob was to leave Paris for Brussels en route to his new regiment, was upon us in a flash. It was a bitter winter that year: snow was falling heavily and a blizzard had iced over all the roads, giving an Arctic feel to the whole of Northern Europe. He had spent the night at his hotel and came home early in the morning to say a last good-bye.

Over his battledress, he was wearing a voluminous waterproof overcoat, mid-calf in length, which seemed to envelop him completely except for a brief glimpse of his lace-up boots. Black leather gauntlets went halfway up his arms. Close to his body were two pistols in their holsters, hanging from a belt around his waist. On top of his headgear and driving goggles, he had pulled on a khaki-colored woolen balaclava left over from the last war, given to him by my mother. The effect of all this gear was to double his normal girth and height and make him look rather like the ghost of a legendary Spanish knight, fully armed for battle.

Beside his kitbag in the sidecar, under several layers of blankets, sat a thickset black Labrador—to whom I had not yet been introduced! Although Bob was very attached to him, the dog had definitely taken second place during our whirlwind courtship and had been left "on leave" with a kind acquaintance in the suburbs. Bob claimed that this stray, which he had picked up in Normandy, could actually sniff out Shu mines, the small German antipersonnel weapons that could easily blow your foot off. His war comrades, who remember the dog well, had actually seen him do it. Alas, one day, that brave canine was killed when he failed to detect a land mine, but his sacrifice saved Bob's life, giving him the vital split second to throw himself clear of the impact. Ever since that time, I have been very fond of Labradors and kept them as pets for many years.

Shivering in the blizzard, all my family gathered on the pavement outside our garden to watch that gigantic war machine captured from the enemy disappear, backfiring deafeningly, into the thick white curtain of snow. Off they went, those spectral emulators of Don Quixote and Sancho Panza, hurtling towards Holland on their Rocinante. But they were not going to tilt at windmills. It was the start of a great adventure for me—my family and I felt it intuitively.

After the tornado that had swept through my life over the last few weeks, the days of his absence stretched ahead of me, dull and interminable. The next day was a Sunday. I stayed long in bed, then pulled myself together to go to morning service with my father. I liked our church, which was led by two of the great Protestant ministers of Paris, Marc Boegner and Pierre Maury. I had taught at Sunday school there, and after the service met members of my family and friends. I also wanted to make an appointment with Pastor Maury to ask him to bless my marriage.

Once we were home again, my parents and I began to make plans for the wedding, which we hoped could be arranged to coincide with my birthday on March 11. It was only two months away, and it would take all our efforts and ingenuity to organize it in time—especially in a city that had just been liberated, where everything, from the most basic foodstuffs to luxury goods, was still in short supply.

Although I have always been good at organizing and am certainly a woman of action, my head was no longer as well screwed on my shoulders as it was before Bob's eruption into my life. A future beckoned that I sensed would be different from anything I had known in the past. I was living an adventure, but wasn't that where all my reading and feverish imagination had led me? Part of me was fiercely determined to break free from the constraints of my upbringing and emerge from my shell, and that was precisely what made me accept an uncertain future with a man I barely knew. He had offered me glimpses of a forbidden paradise and visions of the world that made me giddy. The promises he had made when he proposed to me appealed to the imaginative side of my character: "I shall win a Military Cross, I shall create a family, I shall make my fortune, I shall be prime minister of England and I shall make you happy to the end of your days." All my life, I had reveled in an atmosphere of make-believe, and there I was, all of a sudden, ready to share my life with a man who was going to make my dreams come true.

Before he left for the front, Bob and I had sworn that we would stop whatever we were doing at half past eleven every night, come what may, and think of one another with such intensity that we would feel close, in spite of the distance and all else that lay between us. We kept this nightly rendezvous faithfully until peace was declared.

We wrote to each other almost daily, but writing from France to an English soldier was by no means simple! Whilst the motherland gave priority to letters for troops in the most distant corners of the world, the same did not apply to countries recently liberated from German occupation, where censorship amounted simply to the non-dispatch of mail. Within the Intelligence Service, there was total paranoia about the civilian population. Everyone was suspected of being a Fifth Columnist left behind by the enemy or a Communist; if not, you were in the Resistance. It was black and white—there was no "in-between"; it is a perception of the French during the war that has barely altered for the British public to this day. The first ten letters I sent him via the French postal service never reached him. It was a disastrous start to our fledgling relationship, when, as is commonly known, letters from home are almost as vital to fighting men as ammunition. Bob assumed that I simply hadn't written to him, and although the matter was eventually resolved, he held it against me until his dying day.

It did not occur to me at first that my letters might not reach their destination, and so that very evening, I sat down at my desk in the room that had witnessed our first lovemaking and wrote the first of "A Thousand and One Letters" which I would write to him over almost fifty years. At the time, I did not have the command of English which I have now, and I found it painfully difficult to express the subtleties of my feelings in a language he understood. Sometimes I would lapse into French. He had told me he understood it very well, and I suppose his knowledge of Romanian did help him somewhat, but there was a definite communication problem between us at the beginning, exacerbated by the loss of my earliest letters and some of his.

Our war years' correspondence depicts our growing love, our hopes, our fears for each other and above all the unmitigated ferocity of the combats on the Roer and the Ruhr. It was the enemy's last stand, and he was determined to fight to the death. Almost every day, I would sit at my desk and write to Bob, hoping and praying that he would be spared injury and certain that I would soon receive some news from him. A whole month elapsed before either of us received our "first" letter. I was elated, I kissed it, I carried it on me everywhere and I know that he did the same. Those flimsy sheets of paper were all we had to sustain our love, to express our longing for each other, our despair at being separated and voice our anxieties at the carnage taking place in the Low Countries. Through those pages, we expressed our dreams, our ambitions, and we created an image of each other which gradually lost touch with reality.

Reality, for soldiers on the front in Holland, was a terrible winter with a coldness that paralyzed body and soul, alternating with thaws that made the dykes overflow, bogging down tanks and men in a sticky clay mud that concealed treacherous land mines. In those appalling weather conditions, Bob and his company moved up towards the Roer to reinforce other units engaged in repelling German counterattacks. It was part of Operation Blackcock, a Seventh Armored Division attack planned by Montgomery to wipe out a deep enemy salient west of the Roer, where the German army was still entrenched. Bob was no stranger to combat and his hatred of the Boches was undiminished. He was, however, joining a new unit with comrades-in-arms he did not know.

The military world that had been his up to then was a closed book to me. I knew nothing of the army vocabulary for the formation of units, for weapons and ranks, which would have been familiar to any English girl, whether a WAAF, a WRNS, a WRAC or a nurse.[1] I did not even possess the basic knowledge of military terminology which every English civilian must have acquired after four years at war, reading newspapers and listening daily to radio broadcasts.

With hindsight, I realize that my feverish preparations for our

---

1. Women's Auxiliary Air Force, Women's Royal Navy Service, Women's Royal Army Corps.

wedding obscured my mind to the carnage in Holland. As Bob prepared his men for the Blackcock assault, news reached them that their own battalion's B company had been all but decimated in the grim battle for Susteren. In all, sixty-eight men were killed, wounded or missing; amongst them were all the officers of the company and its commander, who had sustained serious injuries.

By that time, Paris was completely protected from enemy attack and used as a forty-eight-hour leave center for Allied personnel. Censorship still affected our knowledge of events and bad news was deliberately camouflaged to keep up the morale of the troops on leave. How was it possible in such a situation to be on the same wavelength as those fighting men who were enduring hell? It was only through soldiers' private letters that we had any inkling of what was really happening.

28 Jan 1945 British Liberation Army 1/5 Queen's

My darling Betuska,
It is now 8 o'clock and of whom should I be thinking but you, my love. I hope this letter is not going to be read by the censor.
I have got to tell someone my thoughts and to whom but you, my one and only, could I tell them? As you will have guessed, I am in the front line again, this time in Holland. I am commanding about 30 men and for the first time tomorrow I shall take them into attack. When talking to them or giving orders, I am my usual strong and confident self, but inside I am anxious. Will I do well? I pray to God that he may give me wisdom and strength, so that I may come out victorious in the ordeal ahead. The chaps I am commanding seem to be a hard and difficult lot, but I believe that I have already gained their confidence, which is the most important thing. All that I have got to show them tomorrow is that I am also a good fighting fellow, and the rest is easy.

31 January 1945

My own Betuska,
I have stood the test. I am now sitting in a house and trying to write a letter to you. I have to make a great effort not to drop the pen, as I am still suffering the effects of the previous battle. We took a village on the morning of the 29th after some opposition. We made our hole, and now we have to hold it. Apart from the usual artillery and mortar fire, nothing happened during the day, but at night around 10 o'clock after a stiff barrage, the Boches put in an attack with orders to retake the village. This I learned from prisoners I interrogated after the battle which lasted till 2.30 A.M. Most of the men were very brave.

When I received this letter, I had no idea that Bob was describing an action in which he personally had done something extraordinary. His brief and matter-of-fact description of the battle did not seem any different from similar accounts in many other letters. One month later, I was to discover that in this very first action with his new regiment, he had been awarded the MC. Within a matter of weeks of leaving Paris, he had already fulfilled one of his promises. I was stunned, and my faith in his extraordinary capacities doubled. It was only much later that I learned from his comrades and the MC citation itself the extent of his bravery that day.

It had all happened during the attack on Paarlo on January 29. Certain that the Allies were planning a major offensive across the Roer River, the Germans had launched a battalion-strength offensive directed at the front line held by Bob's new battalion. His platoon was one of those in the front line. When the platoon on his right was overrun, the company commander, Major Watson, ordered Bob to retreat, saying that the position was untenable with heavy German fire against them. Bob's reaction was quite the opposite. He immediately told the commander that he could not obey because he believed that Lieutenant Baker and some of his men from the other platoon might still be alive. He was determined to lead a counterattack to see if they could repulse the Germans and free their comrades. The major left him, saying that it was a stupid enterprise, and that he may have to face a court martial if he came out alive. Bob organized his remaining forces and counterattacked. The Germans were so surprised by this unexpected effort that they began to fall back, and Bob and his men did indeed find Lieutenant Baker and a few of his men who had survived in a farmhouse. Bob's action—foolhardy as it may have seemed—had saved their lives. As the official citation reads:

During the attack on Paarlo on 29th January 1945, Lieutenant Maxwell was leading his platoon when a heavy artillery concentration fell on and near the platoon, killing and wounding several men.

The attack was in danger of losing momentum, but this officer, showing powers of leadership of the highest order, controlled his men with great skill and kept up the advance. During the night, another platoon of this company was counterattacked and partially overrun. An attempt to restore the position with another platoon failed, but Lieutenant Maxwell repeatedly asked to be allowed to lead another attempt, which request was eventually granted.

This officer then led two of his sections across bullet-swept ground with great dash and determination and succeeded in contacting the platoon who had been holding out in some buildings.

Showing no regard for his own safety, he led his sections in the difficult job of clearing the enemy out of the buildings, inflicting many casualties on them and causing the remainder to withdraw.

By his magnificent example and offensive spirit, this officer was responsible for the relief of the platoon and the restoration of the situation.

My childhood home,
La Grive, Isère

parents, Paul and Colombe Meynard, 1917

Aged twenty months

Vonnic and I in our English school
uniforms, Acock's Green, 1931

Aged sixteen

With Françoise Arnal, Pierre
Walter, Robert Giscard and friends
on a mountaineering expedition in
the French Alps, 1942

Bob being decorated with
the Military Cross by Field
Marshal Montgomery, 1945

Bob outside Hamburg, 194[5]

Bob and I on our wedding day in
Paris, March 14, 1945

Bob's sisters, Brana and
Sylvia, Iserlohn, March
1946

Broomfield, Esher, 1950

Bob and I in Berlin
with Michael,
Christmas 1946

With Elisabet and
Ferdinand Springer on his
seventieth birthday, in
Heidelberg, 1951

Bob and I at Broomfield, with Michael, Philip, Anne,
Christine, Isabel and Karine, Christmas 1954

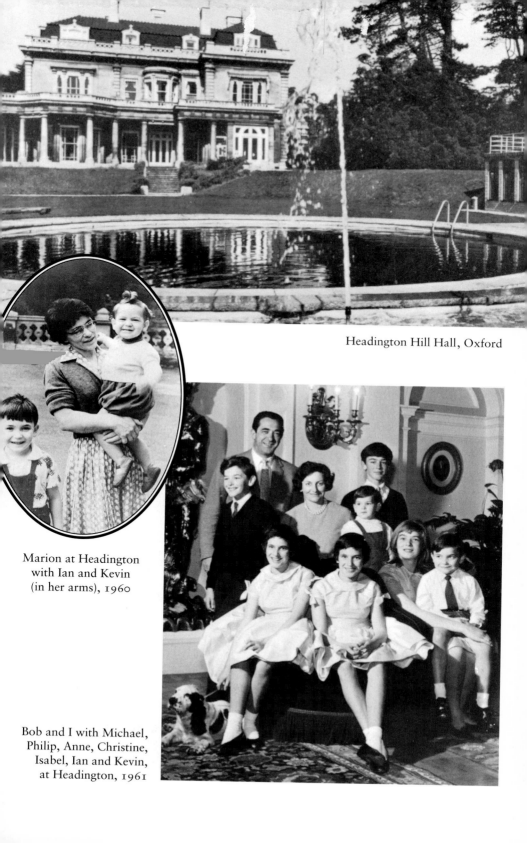

Headington Hill Hall, Oxford

Marion at Headington
with Ian and Kevin
(in her arms), 1960

Bob and I with Michael,
Philip, Anne, Christine,
Isabel, Ian and Kevin,
at Headington, 1961

Victory parade in Buckingham after winning the 1964 General Election
(courtesy North Bucks *Times*, Bletchley *District Gazette*)

Campaigning in Buckingham, 1966 (courtesy *Oxford Mail & Times*)

YOU KNOW
LABOUR GOVERNMENT
WORKS

It was Field Marshal Montgomery himself who presented Bob with his MC. Bob wrote to me on March 26:

> I was decorated yesterday by Montgomery. He asked me all sorts of questions and was apparently pleased with my answers. His photographer took a picture of us when he was pinning the medal ribbon on my jacket and Monty said that he will send me this picture with his autograph on it.

Soon after I started going out with Bob, I left the Welcome Committee to work at the American Officers' 48-Hours' Leave Club. The salary was much better and included lunch—a real bonus at a time when food was still scarce, but the atmosphere was uncongenial. We worked in a huge hall rather like a modern railway station, and the job was extremely repetitive and boring. It consisted of handing out K rations (packaged meals) to departing officers, acting very much like conference hostesses and interpreters, and answering the hundreds of questions put to us by bewildered, exhausted men we would never see again. As soon as the date of our marriage was fixed for mid-March, I decided to leave this job and devote all my energy to the final preparations for the big day.

Nothing was easy in those days: shops were empty and food supplies haphazard. Textiles were virtually unobtainable, and even if you were lucky enough to find some, they were invariably unattractive and of an inferior ersatz quality. Lace and tulle were the only pretty materials which were freely available, so I bought as much as I could afford, not stopping to consider that even if I used layer upon layer of them, my dress would still be transparent and need a lining. When Bob and I first talked about marriage, long before I had given any thought to my wedding dress, he had suggested that he could probably get hold of a used silk parachute. So it was that some time before he left in January, one of those very fine, beautiful silk parachutes arrived on my doorstep, which I was able to convert into a multilayered petticoat under the wedding dress which a girlfriend of mine had designed and made up for me.

My parents had dealt with the wedding invitations, which they had ordered before the news of Bob's Military Cross had reached us and before we had been able to decide on the exact date of the wedding, since we did not know when he would be able to come to Paris. I can still see my mother working slowly through the pile of printed invitations, painstakingly adding by hand the letters MC after Bob's name and the date of the wedding.

He arrived late on March 11, my birthday, which just the two of us celebrated, by candlelight, in a little restaurant. The next day, we visited Pastor Maury, who had insisted on seeing us both before the religious ceremony. He already knew me well but wanted to feel sure that my fiancé fully understood the consequences of marrying a Christian. Bob reiterated what he had already told me: that he was not ashamed of being a Jew, that he had lost his faith way back in 1939 when he gave up his religious education, that he would put no pressure on me to change my religion and had no objection to his children being baptized and brought up as Christians.

Had I been superstitious, I would perhaps have paused a while to consider what was written in the stars and contemplate our signs of the zodiac: Bob was a Gemini and I was born under Pisces. Any astrologer will confirm that this is the worst possible combination for a marriage, since people born under those signs tend to have dual personalities. In the case of Gemini, it is a split personality of the Jekyll-and-Hyde type and for Pisces a series of conflicting desires and talents. It is difficult enough for two people to get on, but in our case I had the distinct feeling that there were four of us! I never knew which of my Geminis was likely to come home in the evening—the fiercely dogmatic, imperious, autocratic master or the adoring, love-starved, fun-loving boyfriend. Equally, he would never know whether to expect his incurably romantic and daydreaming Betuska or the forceful, super-active organizer of the Maxwell tribe-to-be. How could such a union ever work? But considerations such as these were the last things on my mind, two days away from my wedding with Prince Charming at my side.

We were frantically busy over the next two days with all the last-minute preparations. Bob had to sort out all the necessary military permits for his leave to be spent in Paris, make arrangements for his eventual return to the front and contact his military friends in Paris who had been invited to the wedding. He also managed to turn our wedding breakfast into a feast, with wonderful presents of food from his own British HQ mess, where they were pleased to help give a suitable send-off to a young, recently decorated officer about to return to the inferno of the front. For my part, I had to attend to all those decisions that are the prerogative of the bride—prepare my going away outfit and luggage and many such mundane details.

We were married in our local town hall on March 14, in the presence of only my close family and Bob's witness, Gary Carthew-Yorstoun. Since the Revolution, only civil marriages are recognized by law in France, but although this is the only binding legal contract, those who are religious look upon this event as a formality to be complied with and reserve for the church ceremony the sacredness of the vows, the emotion, pomp and pageantry. During that civil ceremony, a strange incident took place which would have lasting consequences in my life. Seeing a British officer before him, the mayor simply took it for granted that I would adopt my husband's nationality. He was right in the middle of the standard declaration "and the said Elisabeth Meynard states that she chooses to adopt her husband's nationality," when all of a sudden I intervened with a loud "Non." Bob was startled, as was my family who all thought I was having second thoughts about the marriage at the last minute! It was nothing of the sort, but in a split second, I realized that because Czechoslovakia was then part of the Grosses Reich, Bob had become de facto a German citizen. Although I had no objection to becoming British, I certainly did not want to become German. From my legal studies, I was aware that I had the right to retain my own nationality, and on the spur of the moment knew I had to exercise that right. So it is that my marriage certificate makes specific reference to my refusal to take my husband's nationality; it was, I believe, quite rare at the time since very few people knew about the law or the choice they had. That quick reaction in March 1945 later allowed me and my children to have dual nationality, an advantage which anyone who lived through the last war will appreciate.

I left for the church accompanied by my father who, for a man of seventy, cut a fine figure in his black frock coat. When I went into the church, filled to capacity with all my Paris family and friends and Bob's military comrades, I could not take my eyes off the dashing officer standing near the altar. Resplendent in his new service dress completed by my father's Sam Browne belt, he really looked like the hero of my dreams. In the pews just behind him, standing in for his parents, were Gary Carthew-Yorstoun and Lady Moore, a prominent executive member of the Overseas League Club whom Bob had met in London. Pastor Maury took as his text a verse from Malachi: "The Lord hath been witness between thee and the wife of thy youth." Throughout my marriage, those solemn words were to be my rudder in times of doubt.

In spite of the time of year, the sun shone gloriously for the photo sessions and for the rest of the afternoon. My mother had prepared a sumptuous wedding lunch, remembered by everyone present as an almost impossible feat at the time. Although our greatest wish was to be on our own, Bob and I stayed till five o'clock and then set off by car for Versailles and our first dinner and night as a married couple. We spent four brief days together, making one surprise visit to Paris for dinner and a good film. Most of the time we made love, talking endlessly in between and walking in the woods in the afternoons. I was no longer inhibited by conventions and just abandoned myself to the sheer pleasure of lovemaking. Bob was exultant. We were discovering each other and dreaming of our happiness after the war. For a fleeting moment, the war and all its attendant horrors were forgotten. We were both blissfully happy.

When the time came for us to part and I accompanied him to the station, I cannot recall anything that we regretted. The dominant emotion for both of us was dread at the thought of separation. I went home that day feeling intensely lonely and bewildered. I sat at my desk and poured out my heartache at his departure and my happiness at being his wife. We had agreed that I would leave for England as soon as possible. In the following days, every minute of my time would be taken up with acquiring all the necessary travel papers, which in wartime was no easy matter. It was not long before I received a letter from him. It gave me the courage I needed to brave the trauma of leaving home and the protective environment of my family for a country at war, still being shelled by rockets, where I didn't know a soul.

21 March 1945

My beloved petite darling wife,
How are you? The sight of your body disappearing from my view as the train moved out from the station is still too vivid and hurts like an open wound in my heart. That last au revoir still echoes in my ears, I shall never forget it for as long as I live. During those brief few seconds where I could still see that adorable little hand waving good-bye, tears came to my eyes, such sincere tears as I have never shed in my life. At that moment for the first time I realized as I have never realized before how deeply and truly I love you and it gave me strength and courage to face anything that may come. I wish to remind you once more about those few words I spoke to you before I left. Let the hope of my return and the certainty of our future happiness be the guide for all our actions. It is nearly 11.30 P.M., I will close now. Good night my own and remember that I am always with you wherever you may be and that my only thought is to come back to you as soon as it is humanly possible.

England was where he wanted me to be; that was where I would go. From that moment on, there could only be one captain on our ship. After a great deal of red tape from both the French and British authorities, I secured a crossing on April 17. The war was not yet over. My own sacrifice paled into insignificance compared with the hell he was still enduring every day.

27 March 1945

My darling Betuska,

I am quite well and very much in love with someone you know perhaps and miss her as much as I miss 30 tons of armor around me because for the last half an hour all hell has broken loose over here. It's misty and it's cold, but that and more will not stop me from finishing my letter to my wife. Over here the going is pretty hard, but it can't last very much longer now because the foe is getting a hell of a time too. Shells are falling all around me, but I have got a very nice and deep hole which some German must have spent at least two days to dig and so I am not worried. Dearest I must finish now, a shell has just dropped in a hole where I have three men. I must go and see what I can do . . . I am OK, back in my hole and the shelling has stopped.

6 April 1945

My own Betuska,

I will just steal a few minutes to let you know that I am fit and well, and very deep inside Germany advancing on a main road. The town I wrote to you about has been taken at last. It was defended by about 600 officer cadets from the school of officers, Hanover, all of them fanatics, so most of them died. We are off again and I am dead tired; I haven't had my clothes off for weeks now and no sleep for 72 hours, but still it will not last very long now.

9 April 1945

My beloved wife,

Just a few lines to let you know that I am well and in good health and still fighting. Today there is a very difficult job for me to do, we have got to rush a bridge across a biggish river. We hope to go that fast that the Boches will have no time to press the lever and blow the bridge while we are getting across or just after we are on the other side. But I know that God is looking after us so do not fear my beloved.

Later the same day:

I am once more safe and sound, in good health and in most excellent spirits after a very successful day of fighting a few miles from Bremen. The Germans have brought up SS formations to defend the town and this was our first encounter with them. I was leading my platoon into a village. I had to fight for nearly every house, and the hardest fight I had was in the cemetery. The outcome was that I took the village after four hours' fighting. I lost one man killed and one man wounded. We killed over 20 and took 19 prisoners. I have ordered the Germans out of a very nice house and installed my HQ in it. Firing has just started, most probably a German patrol trying to sneak in. I must go outside and see what I can do.

12 April 1945

My beloved darling wife and little Betuska,
I have just received two of your letters where you tell me that you will be arriving in London on the night of the 17th. My dearest, you have no idea how much I admire your courage and how proud I am to know of the confidence you have in me. If I needed any proof of your love, you most certainly have given it by the biggest sacrifice you could possibly make, short of giving up your life, namely by leaving the security your family gave you for so many years and going to a foreign country, where you don't know anyone and where you have to take on the struggle of life alone and unaided. That to me, my beloved darling, is the biggest demonstration of courage and confidence I have yet witnessed and no doubt is one of the reasons why I love you so reverently. My love for you is like a flame, but not an ordinary flame which consumes and then fades out, no! my flame is eternal.

17 April 1945

My darling wife,
How are you? What sort of journey did you have? How did the immigration officer treat you? And how did Mrs. Straton-Ferrier receive you? Did somebody meet you at the station? Please answer all these questions in detail as I am very anxious to know how you are, and how you got on. Your photograph is smiling at me so sweetly from the table, and I don't know what I would do if I lost it. If you saw at times how I talk to your image, tell it my fears, hopes and all sorts of things, you would think I have gone nuts, but I am sure you would forgive me since you know how madly I love you.
Your adoring husband

By now I could answer all his questions! When I arrived in Dover, I was grilled for a whole day by immigration officers before I was finally allowed to land as a "British subject." The trouble was that my marriage certificate was made out in the name of du Maurier but by then Bob had changed both his name and regiment. Why had he changed his name? Why had he moved to a new regiment? The questions rained down on me from all sides and I had to tell the story right from the beginning. I felt as if I were fighting the whole Normandy campaign! I had to explain that he was a Czech and therefore under threat of execution if he were taken prisoner by the Germans; hence the need for the first name change from Hoch to du Maurier. Then, after he won an immediate commission in the field, his name and nationality had been divulged on the radio by the Canadian war correspondent Chester Wilmot, so his name had to be changed again. For a brief period, he then became Jones, before he was officially given the name of Robert Maxwell when he joined the Queen's Royal Regiment. I also had to clarify that we were married as du Maurier and not Maxwell, simply because his new identity papers had not reached him in time to meet the deadline for applying for a wedding license. All of this was crystal-clear to me, but it certainly was not to the immigration officials; nor would it ever be to those who later implied that my husband reveled in concealing his true identity. If that were not complicated enough, I don't think the immigration authorities had ever come across a case involving a non-naturalized British officer, so my story must have seemed highly suspicious.

Having eventually managed to convince them of the truth of my tale, I made my way to London where Mrs. Straton-Ferrier was waiting for me. She had been at the station all day, wondering what on earth was happening to me and had even phoned the authorities in Dover to try to release me from their clutches. She recalled having met at last "a solitary figure, a girl with her luggage, looking patiently out into the dreary London gray dusk. She was thin, almost transparent and for some days, she could hardly eat at all." She took me home and settled me in an adorable minuscule room at the top of her house, which I immediately christened the "pigeonnier."

Mrs. Straton-Ferrier was a warmhearted, charming Australian. Her husband was an officer in the air force, stationed in London, her eldest son a subaltern in the Welsh Guards fighting in Holland, and her youngest son, Brian, a naval officer on a destroyer in the Mediterranean. She worked as a hostess at the Overseas League, where she welcomed lonely Allied soldiers. That was how in 1943 she first met Bob, "the devastating Czech with a lovely speaking voice" and came to be dubbed his "Mother Two." At night, she would don her tin hat and walk down the road to take up her post as an air raid warden, a voluntary job she did throughout the Blitz until the end of the war. She was kindness itself to me, as she was to an incredible number of "strays"—nicknamed the "menagerie" by her sons. She opened her wonderful heart and her ramshackle, bomb-damaged Victorian house to an assortment of people whom she saved from utter desolation and despair.

In the room next door to me there was an English girl who was accommodating to more than one lonely fellow in the house and who later married a Lord, and in a room across the corridor lived a shell-shocked English officer who kept me awake half the night telling me his troubles. He had been advised to consign them to paper and insisted on reading aloud to me from his well-thumbed little notebook. On the floors below, besides the family, lived a Belgian who had a certificate to say he was not mad, another very prim and proper French-speaking girl who later went to work at Buckingham Palace, senile old Mrs. Cameron who would not go down to the basement during air raids because she could not find her pretty pink bed-jacket, an old girl called Vera, christened "the silly Coco" by the patient, hardworking, kind Chinese housekeeper who managed to keep that extraordinary household clean, tidy and fed throughout the war. In the basement lived Hilda and Leslie Rogers whose only son was in the Inniskillings' regiment and who lived in perpetual anxiety that he might be killed, and Mad Maggie Vessey who lived on garlic pills and charcoal biscuits. Many others came and went.

I soon found myself a job at the French Embassy as a secretary in the Transport section. My "boss" was Chinita Abrahams, a strikingly handsome, chic, attractive and distinguished lady who spoke perfect French and worked there as a volunteer. She was endlessly patient with me and became my role model for many years to come. It was at her home that I had my first Passover dinner with Bob, all those years ago, and we have remained friends ever since. Those last days of the war were amongst the most punishing for Bob, and now that I could follow the news directly, my anxiety for him increased daily, lest he be killed when the end was in sight.

20 April 1945

My dearest darling,
At last I may have a few minutes to spare before once more the army claims me to do something. This last week we have been fighting or advancing continuously and we are now very close to Hamburg and the going is harder the closer we get to the darned place. I am waiting for a letter from you very impatiently. I haven't had any news from you since the 10th.

23 April 1945

My darling Betuska,
I had a very lucky escape last night on patrol; a big shell landed half a yard in front of me and failed to go off! Believe me I felt very weak at the knees for a few minutes after that, but I got my few Jerries for the day and returned to my position at 05.30 this morning. I am sorry my love that all I ever seem to write about is this beastly war. But as long as I am doing what I am, war is all I can write about.

27 April 1945

Hello Betuska,
Just a few lines, my beloved darling, to tell you that I am well and that I have received your air mail letter this afternoon, which was a great relief for me. You simply must write to me every day because I must have this little bit of

daily happiness to save me from getting drowned in my surroundings, which consist only of hate, fear and destruction. I have now been moved to a more dangerous part of the front, still near Hamburg, but the Boches are only 150 yards away which means you have to be awake all night and sleep in daytime if you can. My feet are burning like hell and it is exactly a month today since I had my boots off or clothes off and I am really beginning to feel the strains of it all. I must have a bath tomorrow even if I have to get the water under sniper fire, but don't worry I won't take any unnecessary risks.

29 April 1945

My darling wife,
I am writing this in a hurry so that it will go off today. I am well but in the same place and especially at night it's rather nerve-wracking. They put in a counterattack with 200 men, one tank and several self-propelled guns. Fighting went on all night and by the morning they had had enough. They lost 47 killed, 56 captured and no doubt quite a few were wounded, but the Germans managed to evacuate them. We lost 7 killed, 20 wounded and 18 got captured.

Later the same day:

I am writing this letter in my "foxhole" by the light of a Boche paraffin lamp. It's 11.30 now and your picture, for which I have dug a little hole of its own so that I can look at it every time I lay down here, is looking so beautiful and majestic in the shadow strewn by the lamp. I can't help wondering what good I have done in this world yet to deserve such a beautiful and good wife. That question I cannot answer myself, but I am most certainly grateful to the Lord for his kind guidance.
I must go and see to my sentries, whether they are awake and doing their duties. I have got 12 men on guard during the whole night and it is a very good thing from the point of view of my men's morale to show them that even though it's gone midnight I am not afraid to go and inspect the most forward sentries of my platoon which is about 60 yards from the Huns' positions.

4 May 1945

My darling Betuska,
The war is over!!! It's just been announced, 8.20 P.M., it's true, it's over! and I am still in one piece, thank God. Oh my darling, our dream is not so far off now, we shall soon be together once more and for ever. I must close as I have just been told that we are pushing on to Kiel right away.

As ill luck would have it, we were both victims of the vagaries of the mail again. Many days were to pass after my arrival in England, and even after the cease-fire, before I heard from him that he was alive and would soon be coming home. Cease-fires had already been declared on several fronts, but it was not until May 4 that the German armies in northwest Germany, Holland and Denmark surrendered to Montgomery. On May 8, Prime Minister Winston Churchill broadcast a businesslike statement of victory at three o'clock in the afternoon. Upstairs in my *pigeonnier*, I was crying and feeling sorry for myself when Brian Straton-Ferrier, who had arrived on leave a few days earlier, knocked on my door and invited me to go and celebrate with him in the streets of London. I refused at first, saying I was truly not in the mood, but he persuaded me that it was unpatriotic not to, that he was sure Bob was safe and that I should not let the postal service get me down.

So it was that Brian and I set off in great expectation for Hyde Park Corner, plunging in amongst the sweltering millions gathered in front of the palace. The sun beat down on that colorful throng, and over and over again, the cry went up, "We want the King" or "Come on George." The royal family took their time to come out while the balcony was being decked out and organized, but the roar that welcomed them when they appeared was deafening and moving. The King was in admiral's uniform and smiled as he waved his hand in a gesture that became familiar as the years went by. The Queen and Margaret Rose were in turquoise; Elizabeth charmingly unostentatious in khaki. The crowd just would not let them go, but eventually they did retire, at which point we wandered through the human rivers that were the West End, beneath the myriad colorful sun-lit flags, to Whitehall, and saw Winston appear with his cabinet to address us briefly. "May God bless your all!" (loud and prolonged cheers). There followed a lot of excellent rhetoric about "Never in all our long island history was ever a day so great as this" (more loud and prolonged cheers). He cut it short in the end with another happy, half-embarrassed "God bless you all," drowned by a wild acclamation, a roaring, triumphant, tumultuous tribute to this extraordinary man who had saved the free world in its darkest hour.

We then followed the crowd via Trafalgar Square to Piccadilly Circus where we met with French naval ratings beside Eros, and rolled down arm-in-arm, ten abreast, to Hyde Park Corner singing the *Marseillaise,* "Les gars de la marine" and other French songs. The singing was general; it was spontaneous and seemed to relieve in everyone the tension that had accumulated over five years. We then returned to the palace along Constitution Hill to join the throng, which by then had doubled in size, in requesting further appearances of the royal family. They came again and again as we kept shouting, "We want the King, we want the King!" while the searchlights did victory circles overhead and bonfires lit up a very happy, though strangely sober, London. After an exhausting walk back to Gloucester Road, we arrived home tired but elated to find Brian's brother Johnny there which completed the happiness of a memorable day. We were really worn-out, but still found the energy to talk until four in the morning, getting tight on gin and orange kindly left for us in the garden room by Mother Two.

London was still a strange wartime city when I first arrived. There were bomb sites everywhere, most of them filled with water to be used for firefighting. Buildings gaped open, torn apart, their twisted girders still supporting rotting mattresses and bathtubs hanging crazily by their pipes. Wooden fences had been erected everywhere to hide the devastation caused by the last V2 rockets or doodlebugs. People were still wearing tin hats and carrying gas masks and at night you groped your way in the pitch dark of the blackout. Yet what struck me most was that hotels were offering dinner dances every night of the week and everything seemed geared to keep morale high and entertainment going. For me, it was exhilarating to find shops full of goods, total luxury after the lean years in occupied France. Food coupons were always honored and allowed me to buy more than I could eat. There were admittedly long lines of customers, but as I usually went shopping early in the morning, they did not worry me unduly. On Saturdays and Sundays, I would walk to the Overseas League in Piccadilly where Mrs. Straton-Ferrier always needed help, or to the Allied Circle or the Lansdowne Club, where I was sometimes invited for lunch by people I had met at the embassy. Many of them were Jewish businessmen, returning to France for the first time since war broke out, who were naturally apprehensive about what they were going to find and which of their relatives might still be alive. They were only too happy to have some company and comfort while they were in London and were anxious to hear what France had been like during the occupation. It was an anxiety I could readily understand.

Looking back now over our war correspondence, I can detect a noticeable change in Bob's letters at this time. Whilst all his letters up to then had been written "under fire, in the forward line or whilst on the move," he now had more time to think and to describe his love and immense longing for me.

11 May 1945

My adorable little darling,
Thanks a thousand times for the most beautiful letter ever to reach me. How much hard work it must have been for your gentle little hand, 2,269 words and each one then set like a sparkling jewel in its right place. Its love and

its vitality, its love and sincerity shine from it like the sun out of a burning sky on a hot summer day. This letter has jerked me on a point where I thought I could no longer go any deeper, namely in my utter determination to make you, to make us, the happiest couple that ever got married on this God's earth; but somehow as soon as I had understood everything that you had written in this letter, I felt something stirring inside me and all of a sudden it became an avalanche, the same as if you add petrol to a fire. Darling, I swear to you that I would give my right arm now to be near you, to tell you what I feel at this moment, how much I love you, how much I desire you, how much I adore you and how certain I am that we will succeed in building the strongest and happiest castle of love of any man and woman since creation. Of that I am certain, as it is certain that the sun will rise tomorrow morning. If only I could be there with you now to pour my heart's thoughts out to you, the only one to whom I really could, if only I could be with you, if only I could. God speed this transfer of mine please; do not keep me separated from my beloved any longer; have mercy upon us. Darling, I must stop for a little while, my emotions are too highly strung, my hand shakes. I am too much in love with you.

13 May 1945

My own beloved darling,
It is 10.30 P.M. and I just came inside the house where I have my HQ. It's very quiet in here just now because all my men are outside sitting around a big bonfire singing and drinking tea, but I myself could not enter into the spirit, and that awful hollowness inside me would not and could not be filled by just sitting around a fire and singing. All of a sudden I felt miserable and wretched, lonely and terribly unhappy. Darling, my heart bleeds for you, my body craves for you, my brain demands you, my whole being loves and desires you more than anything else in this world. Dearest, forgive me for such a gloomy letter and please understand that now that my life is no longer in danger, you my only one are on my mind without pause during the whole of my waking day and for most parts in dreaming at night, and sometimes that pain of loneliness hits me so hard that its weight becomes almost unbearable. When there were Germans to fight, I could turn that loneliness to hate, but now, who else can I come to for consolation but you?
Your ever and always adoring husband

24 May 1945

My darling wife,
I am terribly unhappy and disappointed because it looks as though it will be a few months now before I will be able to hold you in my arms and whisper to you how much I love you. The one thing which we must constantly bear in mind in order to help us overcome these lonely nights and at times the almost unbearable physical desire, is our mutual love. It is our strongest asset and our future happiness is certain with these two fundamental pillars, the one which springs from the heart and the other from the mind. No sacrifice or hardship will ever be too much for me and those two points at the same time help me to brush aside all physical temptations which the women around

here can offer. You see, I look at it like this, for me it's a test of my willpower and character and if I slipped away or let myself be carried away by my impulse, I could never face you again; and this is what I say to myself, if you haven't got the will and strength to resist that physical impulse, how can you have the will and strength to fulfil all the promises which you have made to your wife whom you love so much and who is in fact yours? To me this is the answer to this problem.

I remember receiving this letter and being immensely moved by the expression of his love, yet at the same time I felt desolate and struggled to adjust myself mentally to the long wait ahead. I had just tidied my little *pigeonnier* when I heard someone running up the stairs three at a time, and as I opened the door, there he was. He took me in his arms and suddenly we were spinning around and around on the tiny landing outside my door. He carried me over the threshold of the *pigeonnier,* our first home, and set me down in front of him for a brief moment as we stood and looked at each other. He was very sunburned and seemed taller and slimmer (in spite of his broad shoulders) than I remembered him. The last two and a half months of grueling combat and stressful responsibilities, coupled with more abundant fresh food and some well-deserved rest since VE day, had somehow changed him. The youth I had married had become a fully grown man.

We then locked in a tight embrace. So intense was our emotion at being in each other's arms that we stood there, not wanting to let go, the warmth of our reunion dispelling all the horrors of war which Bob had just experienced. His mouth was crushed hard against mine and we were literally suffocating with happiness. At last he stopped to catch his breath and hurtled down the seven flights of stairs to fetch two enormous suitcases crammed full of presents he had bought in Germany: a little typewriter, a camera, a vanity case and other small and much coveted items. At the same time, dear Mrs. Straton-Ferrier came upstairs to tell us that we could use a double room on the floor below for the duration of Bob's leave. It was a great relief—I had been wondering how on earth we were going to manage in my little room that barely measured twelve-by-thirteen, and especially in my single bed!

Bob's leave, originally for ten days, was extended by another fortnight, an undreamed-of length of time in those early days after the war! Through the personal intervention of my boss, the French Embassy was exceedingly generous in granting me exceptional leave as long as his. It gave us a chance to get to know each other better.

As I wrote to my mother after he left, "He is undoubtedly very intelligent, extremely mature for his age and has a real talent for business. He has boundless energy, bags of self-confidence, is very hardworking and adores me!"

We went on a shopping spree and he bought me a smart black suit and a new pair of shoes. He took me out once or twice to dinner dances at the Berkeley and Grosvenor hotels, which then had the finest dance bands in London. I would wear my wedding dress, which I had turned into a strapless gown trimmed with navy blue velvet, and Bob looked distinguished in his service dress. At dances during the war, you would find a few people wearing black tie or long dresses alongside other men and women wearing service and battle dress; no one was ever refused entry if they were not in formal evening dress. We spent a few days in Margate and went for long walks along the seashore. Bob had been stationed there before D-Day and we managed to recover some belongings he had left behind.

But most of our time was spent in bed! We just could not stop making love. Our need to feel close to each other was insatiable, and as I think of those days now, I remember so well Bob's incredible energy, well matched by my own. It was as if he needed to assuage all his pent-up desires and realize all his dreams, as if our carnal pleasure were the living proof that life had prevailed over death. Some days, we did not even leave our room, and had it not been for Mother Two, who dispatched a guardian angel in the shape of Nanny with coffee, tea, sandwiches and fruit, we would not even had eaten. The letters I wrote after this leave and subsequent ones reveal that I was discovering the power of sexual attraction and that I responded well to his expectations and the fire he had kindled in me.

24 June 1945

My darling husband mine,
I am madly, passionately in love with you and my physical desires, so long suppressed, are now intensely aroused, obsessive, imperious. Yes, I love you, my precious darling. You are now the life source from which I derive all strength, all courage and all hope. I want to be happy, I will be happy, I will make you happy! I will do everything in my power to ensure that this constantly renewed happiness of ours lives and thrives long after we have exhausted the entire spectrum of sensual delights. Talking of those physical pleasures, I know you will fulfill my every longing, for you are certainly the most perfect lover, the lover all women dream of yet never find. Through you I have discovered the passionate side of my nature, and I realize now that I would have been terribly unhappy if marriage had fallen short of all my expectations.

24 July 1945

My dearest darling,

If I dared, I would like this evening to write you the most erotic and passionate love letter ever. If it were not for my innate modesty about sexual feelings, I would tell you of my growing, insatiable, uncontrollable desire for you.

Darling, perhaps you can help me understand why I simply dare not commit to paper all my ideas and dreams, all the desires that fill my heart. I am by upbringing ashamed to admit them, and that is quite ridiculous. I cannot see why I should have scruples about loving my own husband and craving his physical love. And yet I fear you may be shocked by such a letter; perhaps you might think that I am only concerned with carnal love.

I want you to know how my love has developed and intensified until I feel totally at one with you. In those first days when I knew you, I did not think about your physical body. Even in the early days of our marriage, I longed for the sensations I experienced through you, rather than for your body itself. All that has changed. Now it would give me infinite pleasure just to feel you there next to me, look at you, caress you, cuddle up beside you. I would so love to cover you in kisses until every nook and cranny of your body were as familiar to me as my own. I want to lay claim to your body, make it sing in harmony, send a thrill through every fiber of your being, adoring you in silence until you can bear it no longer and cry out in desire and love. I want my lips to tell you in silent kisses all that words are powerless to express.

Physical passion is the way given to us to convey our feelings when words are transcended. I would like to place my lips on yours, kiss your eyes, whisper words of love in your ear and drink from your cup of life in loving ecstasy, worship even, were I not afraid to mingle divine love with our earthly passion.

Bob's love was equally eloquent, and he left me in no doubt that it was strong, all-embracing and exclusive. He assured me that I was the first and last woman he could be happy with, that he loved me reverently and passionately for ever and always, that I had given a worthy purpose to his life.

17 February 1946

Dearest,

You are the only woman I love and by whom I wish to be loved and cared for. Oh Betuska, how I wish to hold you in my arms right now so that I could tell you of the tower of strength from whom I am drawing inspiration.

Anything without you is just blurred, unreal and unbearable. Oh my beautiful Betuska, I love you with all my strength, with all my heart, with all my soul, and this will never be otherwise until my death. Please my own adorable wife, look after that love because that is all I treasure above everything else that this or the future world can offer me.

Berlin, 27 October 1946

My ever most adorable and for ever beloved Betuska,
Your last most beautiful and sincere letter has stirred me no end and made
my heart and soul go out towards you like they have never done before. I was
so moved and touched by its truth and beauty of self-expression that for a
moment it gave me an inner glimpse of myself and helped me to realize how
deeply and sincerely I love you. It shook me out of my perpetual overwork and
tiredness and made me long for you physically till I nearly went crazy. Never
before have I felt like that and never before did I realize that I love you so
deeply and reverently, or even that I was capable of bearing such a love for you
in my body, soul and heart. Thank you, Betuska, for this most wonderful reve-
lation, and believe me I have never loved you as passionately as I do now.

The pattern of our married life, however, was extremely difficult
and not conducive to the development of a normal married life. In
our first year of marriage, we barely lived eight weeks together;
apart from Bob's twenty-three-day leave after VE day, all his other
visits were for ten days at the most. Exploration of our feelings, discovery of our respective characters, likes and dislikes, discussions
on politics, religion, talk of our priorities in life, our hopes and
dreams, all the essential process of adjustment between two people
from such diverse worlds—all of this had to take place through the
letters we exchanged. To complicate matters still further, delivery of
mail was still highly irregular. Crucial letters filled with the out-
pourings of our hearts would go astray or turn up a month late. At
the time of our worst anguish whilst the war was still raging, we
were sometimes up to twenty days with no news from each other.
We would begin to dread the worst, accuse each other of laziness or
callousness, let our imagination play havoc with reality and indulge
in hurtful thoughts, when all the time we should both have been
more aware of the enormous difficulty of communications in
wartime.

One of the major handicaps, I discovered much later, was that my
earliest letters were mostly written in French, which Bob had assured
me he understood perfectly. It took me over a year to realize that this
was something of an exaggeration. Whilst he certainly had a reasonable command of everyday spoken French, he did not at the time have
the depth of understanding and knowledge which he later acquired. It
was impossible for him to comprehend the subtleties of my letters, and
this largely accounts for his recurrent reproach that I did not trouble
to find out about "his war" or encourage him sufficiently in all his
enterprises or, worse still, that I did not really love him.

February 1948

I have been wondering for some time now whether you truly understand my letters in French. Perhaps it is too nuanced a language for the tough boy you are. It is a language for dreamers and romantics, a language as gentle as the climate, as steeped in musicality as Debussy's arabesques. It is a part of me that you cannot understand, because fundamentally we are not of the same race: you are a realist who wants success and goes straight for your goal. I am a dreamer who likes music and poetry. Besides, the vocabulary of the two languages is completely different and similar words do not have the same meaning or implication.

In addition to this fundamental language difficulty, our letters make it clear that when we were apart, we created an image of each other that corresponded more to our dream of an ideal partner than to reality itself. We were blinded by our love, and the next time we met we invariably had to face the fact that reality fell short of our elevated aspirations. The little time we were able to spend together was simply not long enough for us to adjust to a more realistic idea of each other.

Berlin, 24 April 1946

Darling Betuska,
I would not survive if once more my hopes and dreams for our happiness are but a mockery; never again do I want to experience the torture of having my hopes and visions, which I so carefully nurse whilst away from the only being I love, shattered upon coming face-to-face with the reality that I have been nursing an illusion.

I am haunted with past disillusionments of the happiness for which I prayed, schemed, imagined, desired and worked whilst away from you. Each time when I returned from a leave I soon forgot the unhappy hours which we went through. The only thing that I constantly remembered were the words that you love me or your seductive little curls tickling my face, or an image of you putting our few belongings together; in short I only remembered the nice things: that you are intelligent and will surely begin to love me in that selfless way in which our happiness and salvation lie.

I was quick to respond to his reproaches, angered by his thoughtlessness so soon after I had given birth to our first son:

Little Brickhill, 29 April 1946

You are convinced that I have failed in my duties as a wife, partner and lover, you think that I do not love you in a selfless way. It's very hurtful for me to read that I have shattered your illusions, spoiled your anticipated joy in coming home on leave, in short ruined everything. But by far the most painful thing for me is that none of this was my intention, I really thought I had done quite the opposite. You were so hard, so terribly harsh, and the pain you have inflicted goes deep. You have left me distraught and disappointed; you have wrecked everything; and you thought fit to make such a scene when our son was only two weeks old.

A great many things would never have happened if we had been living together normally. Ever since I have known you, you have been more than just a husband or lover to me, you have been a god. For me, you represented the very best I could dream of, but my dreams, like yours, are shattered. I don't think I have been as thoughtless as you said. I'm afraid I'm not a Romanian peasant; in my country the usual way of thinking is that a young mother needs a lot of tender loving care and understanding!

We would hurt each other dreadfully, yet we loved one another to distraction. It is certainly true that Bob was madly in love with me right from the beginning, whereas my love for him took longer to mature. I tried hard to convey the profound changes which were affecting me, but I was unable to convince him, simply because I failed him in some of the more mundane details of his material needs. They seemed to me so trivial, but he attached great importance to them, and all my subsequent efforts in other domains, however grandiose, would constantly come up against the perennial stumbling block of my inattention to detail.

27 June 1945

Betuska my love,
You most certainly have made big strides towards becoming the perfect partner through the things you have done like washing my clothes, or darning my socks or all the other hundred little kindnesses which you have shown me time and time again. Although by themselves they may seem trivial and matter-of-fact, do not be deceived by that because they constituted the demonstration of the love which we have for each other, and to me they are of the highest value, for without them our love could not live.

Little Brickhill, 18 August 1945

My dearest beloved husband,
Natures like mine are unwilling to lay themselves bare impulsively and without reserve. My feelings have to be sifted through the process of my judgment, but once I have made up my mind, then action is my watchword. The love you have aroused in me is growing, slowly, surely, faithfully. It is increasing and will reach fabulous proportions unknown to those who love first and reflect later. I swear that you will not be disappointed. I know that I am far from perfect, that I am very selfish, but I have in me a tenacity which refuses failure and a depth of fidelity of which you have no inkling. By fidelity, I do not simply mean remaining faithful to you, for that is surely its most inferior form; what I mean is

fidelity in the constant development of my love for you, in my total confidence, devotion and gratitude, and my certainty that together we will attain the happiness you aspire to. I am changing a little every day without having total control of all that inner turmoil. Keep your faith in me, it is in good hands.

Little Brickhill, 11 September 1945

My own dearest love,

The revolution that your love has roused within me has touched the very deepest recesses of my subconscious. Through you, for you, I am becoming a different woman. My entire being longs to correspond to your ideal of a wife. I want to give you convincing proof of the effect you have on me.

From the earliest days of my childhood, I wove fantasies almost continuously; reluctant to reveal my innermost thoughts, I wanted only to disclose to others what I was prepared to give away. I built my life on fiction and invention to the point where I could no longer recognize myself. All that stopped when I met you! Do you remember your very first declaration of love? Well, I took you seriously. I swear to you with a clear conscience that I have never told you a single word that was not the honest truth, ever since our souls and bodies are united as one. I live my life so there is never anything I want to hide from you. Between me and you, there is not a single bridge you need fear to cross lest it prove unsteady. You gave me the opportunity to become myself again, because neither my faults, nor my eccentricities nor my true character made you recoil. From the moment I decided to marry you, the only condition I imposed upon myself was to build anew, something pure, something solid, for all eternity.

I want you to know that up to now my unique aim has been to attain that perfect union of my dreams, that absolute mutual confidence without which all relationships founder on the rocks. My confidence in you is truly limitless. I have staked my life on it, all my hope of a pure, unblemished, marvelous life in your hands. I can tell you my weaknesses; you are the only person in the world who really knows them, and will always do so; I am not afraid to reveal them to you. I have confidence in your love, perfect confidence. Before I gave myself to you, I had to feel absolutely certain that I could live in your thoughts, in your body, in your heart, and know that I was as essential to you as you would become to me. We had to be able to construct our lives on the crucial basis of our gift of mutual love. Without that, I was incapable of surrendering myself to you completely in the way you desire above all else.

I sometimes wonder whether I assume too much, whether I will ever succeed in making you understand how much I love you, especially if trivial details can make you doubt my love so much. I have often asked myself if you really love me, if you understand me, if you can look beyond my failures to provide for your material comfort.

24 September 1945

My own adorable Betuska,

First and foremost, I knew from the first time I met you that between us we have got the raw material necessary for the happiness we both crave so much (by raw material I mean ambition). As I got to know you better, that belief strengthened itself into an obsession and I realized that you are the woman for whom I could do, and give, everything to make you happy. Although I was aware when you accepted my proposal to marry me, you did not do so because you were deeply in love with me, that did not make me change my mind, because I was certain that, sooner or later, you would realize that I am as indispensable to you as you are to me, and I now believe that you have arrived at that stage. God knows that I love you beyond anything in the world.

Bob's desperate need to be loved was so great that he tortured himself and in turn almost convinced me that I was incapable of loving anyone but myself. At first he almost persecuted me to arouse my love, and when I finally reached the point of being deeply in love with him, he simply would not believe it and carried on with his perpetual doubts. It was a story rather like Crommelynck's "The Magnificent Cuckold," although Bob's doubts were never in the realm of the flesh. Whenever he came home on leave, there was always pain and hurt somewhere. He was incredibly sensitive: an ill-chosen word, a chance remark or an unimportant oversight of his needs on my part was enough to send him into a sullen humor, which he would only snap out of in bed.

7 September 1945

My dearest Betuska,
Ever since I came back I seem to be unable to do anything constructive, I feel incapable to concentrate. I am worried and I don't know about what because I am worried about so many things. I am worried about you, can it be true that you really love me? Can it be true that I have at last got someone to whom I belong?

He was so madly in love with me that he was frightened himself when he realized it; he became afraid of the hold I had over him (although on my part it was not at all deliberate) and worried that I would "destroy his dream."

15 November 1945

I cannot understand how and why I have so completely fallen for you; of course when I say I don't understand, I don't mean *understand* in a physical way, because I could name a thousand and one reasons why I love you, but that in my selfish moments is not enough and I don't like it, and yet I am happy as I have never been before.

At times he was aware that his insatiable quest was hurtful, and he would comment on it, but with little indication that he wanted to abandon it or try to change himself.

26 June 1945

Darling,

I love you more than anything in this world and I miss you terribly and although I do realize that it's too late now to do anything about it, I do want you to know that I feel terribly guilty for making you unhappy at times, and I beg you to forgive me.

20 September 1945

Haven't I been more than selfish, in fact cruel, with you, when I seem always to be pointing out the things that displease, and taking the good things from you as a matter of course and giving very little praise for them? Please, darling, do forgive me if at times I have acted in such a manner, whenever my selfishness tries to take charge of my reason.

What he wanted was total surrender. There was something almost messianic in his quest: "Come to me and I will give you eternal life" was replaced by "Come to me and I will give you eternal happiness." If I was prepared to commit myself to this unconditional act of faith, then I would be born again.

February 1948

My darling Betuska,

Please believe me that I love you and that my only object is to make you realize that I want you to learn how to feel and love, to love me. I am sure that once I have succeeded in bringing a permanent feeling of love into your little heart and soul, then I will have caused you to be born once again. Once my Betuska is reborn, then I am sure that because of our genuine and true love for each other, we shall help each other to strive to become better and more worthy human beings than we are today; and when the day will come for our departure from this earth, then we shall both know and feel that we have fought a hard battle with ourselves for our own life, and won.

I just could not understand how this total communion was compatible with retaining my own personality and originality, which he certainly loved. I tried many times to surrender myself completely into his hands, but I never succeeded. For a few days, it would be sheer bliss, as if someone had lifted all responsibilities off my shoulders, but then everyday decisions needed to be taken and I was brought sharply back to reality. I would become confused, uncertain of my role, losing confidence, and I realized that living like that was just not feasible.

February 1948

My darling husband,

It has become terribly difficult for me to write to you: for quite some time now, you've never once failed to ask me if I meant what I wrote, to the point where I wonder if I ever mean what I say, what I write, what I think. With your endless doubts about me, you are making me go completely crazy. I really do have to be alone to collect my thoughts, to pull myself together, to persuade myself at least to my own satisfaction that someone I think I love dearly does exist. When we are together, far from being at ease, our souls butt against each other like two wild bulls.

I am sure we should feel more carefree about our relationship and more relaxed in each other's company. Let us have more joy and less "inner thinking," because in this incessant desire to dissect everything as on the coroner's table, we are killing our love as surely as you suffocate a duck by wringing its neck. For my part, I know that after each of these horrible arguments, I am so distraught, so unhappy and depressed, that far from giving me the strength to go on, they leave me totally disorientated. I can only draw strength from a strong and stable basis of love, confidence and hope, not from this chaos that destroys every part of me, even my confidence in my own intelligence.

Total surrender was quite contrary to my own contentious nature. My own feeling was the opposite: that each of us lives according to his own inner compass and intuitions, and to abandon that in favor of someone else's spells danger and insecurity. I was still determined to live my life according to my personal instincts. Looking back, I will never know what would have happened to our relationship had I allowed my will to be totally dissolved in his. Yet to avoid confrontation, I did submit to him entirely in all major decisions, and in the solution of many other problems, I would often concur with a blanket judgment that "Daddy knew best." This was to change later on when I felt I had to protect the children from his excesses, but otherwise I never felt belittled by deferring to his authority.

For most of our married life, he treated me with love and respect and acknowledged my supremacy in domestic matters without question. But in our emotional relationship, we battled right to the end. He was for ever searching for that indefinable "something" which he sensed I was holding back. For my own part, I was convinced it was precisely that very *chasse au bonheur*—the chase for love so clearly depicted in Stendhal—that would keep him interested in me. In love as in friendship, I firmly believe we should all retain an element of mystery, a small, impenetrable corner of ourselves, a last reserve of original thoughts we can draw on in times of need.

Throughout our married life, nothing I could say or do would ever convince him for very long that, given my multiple roles as wife, lover, mother of a large family and helpmate, I was doing my best to love and cherish him and attend to all his needs. I have pondered many times on what I could and ought to have done to try and relieve the pressure and deep unhappiness about our relationship which would obsess him from time to time. I think it was an impossible task. Our life together fell very early into such an abnormal pattern with his incessant traveling and my many pregnancies. He had taken on his young shoulders the immense burden of a large family, together with responsibility for his two sisters rescued after the Holocaust, and he was ambitious for success in the business he had created from scratch. When he took time to reflect on what we had really achieved together, his love came shining through, warm and uplifting, and for these glimpses of paradise, I adored him and would have gone through fire for him.

30 March 1949

As you know, sweetie, this month was our 4th anniversary and when I look back on the four and a half years that we have known each other, I swear to you that I don't ever regret the moment in Paris at the Welcome Committee when my fate brought me face-to-face with you, my future wife and partner for the rest of my natural life. I wanted you from the first moment I saw you and as we kept on meeting each other for the next few weeks, I conceived a great love for you. Although I realized that you on your side were not ready to love me (or for that matter anyone else but yourself), I said to myself that with time and a lot of patience, you too will discover that you have a heart that is capable of love, if only it can be assured that it is being loved and will never be hurt.

Well, darling, since we have joined our life together, I have changed from a young, impulsive and irresponsible boy into a full-grown man with a lot of responsibilities. I have changed outwardly both as far as you and the world is concerned, but inwardly I swear to you that I both know and feel that I love you more and deeper than I have ever done before. I implore you to believe me that I love you more than anything in this world, and if at times I made you feel that you have become second fiddle and I have placed my business before my love, then please put it down as your particular sacrifice and help in the tremendous struggle that I have taken on my inexperienced shoulders for the material well-being of our family.

Dearest Betuska, it is exactly two years this month that your young and inexperienced tiger came out hunting in the open jungle (business world) without money, friends or knowledge. In this jungle the law since eternity has been "catch as catch can," no holds are barred and only the fittest can survive. This struggle has therefore demanded of me the continuous concentration of all the faculties and powers at my disposal; it has given me very little time for anything else, but don't think that there has not been many a time when my heart, soul and body did not demand of me and admonish me to return to you and stop working and fighting. I had, however, to be stronger and resist with all my strength the temptation to cease working and fighting, because there are a lot of sharks who have been waiting for me to do just that.

Please, darling, don't think I am crazy when I think all this. I swear to you that it has been impossible for me to show you my deep love and devotion whilst I was under the tremendous pressure and stress of building up what I have done in the last year. However, I can now say that I have reached the stage where I feel secure and sure that I cannot be knocked down easily. I feel terribly tired both mentally and physically, and I am terribly lonely and desperately need you to tell me that you love me and that you are proud of what I have achieved in such a short while, although you had to suffer at times. Please consider it as part of your contribution to the hard fight. Now that we are on top of the hill, as soon as I bring you back from Paris I would like us to start living as befits two people who are in love.

This search for happiness and love was always paramount in our minds and formed the backdrop to our lives. The difficulties we experienced in our relationship were inherent in our characters and upbringing and were, after all, commonplace problems for newly-weds. But they were compounded tenfold in our case by the great disparity of our cultures, traditions, social milieux, maternal languages and religions, by the economic hardship of the period, the instability of communications, the atrocities and anxieties of war and above all the perpetual separation. Isolated from each other, we both endeavored to find our feet in the chaotic climate of the post-war years, hoping to lay the foundations of a stable future together.

In my post at the French Embassy I was receiving basic secretarial training. It was fairly menial at first, typing, filing and so on (although efficient filing, I discovered then, is a crucial element of a well-run secretariat). But Chinita, soon introduced me to the more sophisticated art of public relations. All our "clients" were important and influential people who were either returning to France after some personal trauma or traveling from France to resume cultural or business contacts with America. They were nervous, apprehensive and impatient. My role was to soothe their ruffled feathers and make the waiting time more bearable whilst Chinita attempted to expedite the necessary visas and permits from the various foreign administrations. I gradually became more proficient at keeping all the balls in the air, quietly and discreetly, leaving the ultimate honor of handing over the precious travel documents to my boss.

I remember coming into contact with many interesting people, amongst them the writer Georges Bernanos, who was returning from Rio de Janeiro. I was familiar with his works on saints and heroes and had been influenced by his oscillations between love and anger and his intense dislike of mediocrity and indifference. I also met Eve Curie, daughter and biographer of the scientist Marie Curie, who was making her way back from America after working there for the

French Resistance. Many such personalities passed through our office in those days—the conductor Charles Munch, whom I had already met in Paris, a bevy of continental princesses, diplomats (including several of my own cousins), scientists, professors, actors and well-known musicians.

Once peace had been declared and transport to and from France had returned to normal, Chinita Abrahams decided that the time had come to end her voluntary work. I remember being quite shocked at the way the embassy parted company with her. Instead of marking her "retirement" with a small party and a token of their appreciation, the French authorities simply sent this very wealthy woman £150, her "wages for one month's work" after the end of the war. She was deeply hurt, and rightly so, and I felt ashamed of my compatriots. If that wasn't bad enough, they then proceeded to offer me her job at the attractive salary of £35 a week, but I declined out of loyalty to my friend and contempt at the way she had been treated— although in those days an increase of £7 a week would have made all the difference.

By that time I was expecting my first son, Michael, and the need to find decent lodgings became more urgent. The maximum we could afford was five guineas a week, and although I literally spent days on end running from one side of London to the other, I just could not find anything suitable. It was always the same story: all the good, cheap flats for rent in London were snapped up long before they were advertised, and I eventually realized I would have to go much further afield. I had seen an advertisement for unfurnished accommodation at two guineas a week in the village of Little Brickhill in Buckinghamshire. It was almost the opposite of what I was looking for—miles from London and unfurnished—but I was getting desperate and so decided to have a look at it. It turned out to be a converted land army hostel for girls called The Clock House, and I was soon won over by the thought of having a home of my own and bringing up my baby in the fresh country air. Luckily, I managed to persuade the owner to rent the property furnished at five guineas a week. The only snag was that the furniture, originally from the adjoining manor house, was all piled up in a nearby garage since the manor itself was being used to house German prisoners of war. Left to extricate whatever furniture I needed from this store, I was grateful for the help of the village constable and his wife, who took pity on my plight and later became good friends. The rooms in The Clock House were vast, and I had four bathrooms in a row, but somehow or other I succeeded in transforming that barn of a house into decent living accommodation. I bought a little wood-fire cooker to keep the kitchen-cum-living room warm and spent all my time sewing curtains and bedspreads, building my nest for my husband's next homecoming and the birth of our first baby.

Bob, meanwhile, had been sent to Berlin as part of an advance party to arrange billets for his battalion and was on loan to the Military Government. As soon as the soldiers arrived, they were drilled for the many parades that took place in the devastated German capital, displaying the might of the victorious armies of Russia, America, Great Britain and France. This was all to culminate in the great Four Power Victory parade held on the Charlottenburg Chaussée on September 7 to celebrate the victory of the Allies over Germany and Japan. The Russian Marshal Zukov, whose armies had captured Berlin, took the salute, flanked by Winston Churchill, General Patton and other great military figures of the day. First to march past were the Russians, then came the French contingent, followed by the British troops led by a detachment of the 1/5th Queen's with my Maxwell at their head; leaving the American Eighty-Second Airborne Division to bring up the rear. For Bob there can have been no greater sense of achievement than this, leading the British victory parade along the once proud main thoroughfare of Berlin, where the Nazi troops had themselves paraded before launching forth to invade the whole of Europe, spreading war, devastation and desolation.

For the soldiers in Berlin who had spent the previous six months in a state of great tension, demanding total physical alertness, sudden bursts of exertion and immense physical courage, life was suddenly very boring. Reconstruction of Germany's civilian life had not yet started and it was up to individual officers to invent tasks to occupy their men's time. They would involve them in sports competitions and mock exercises, but the troops no longer had their hearts in it and most preferred going to ENSA[2] shows or fraternizing. Bob, who was keen on neither, took to improving his Russian and French, using the opportunity he had to practice with his opposite numbers in the other occupation armies. It was the best way for him to kill time while he waited for a transfer to the Intelligence officer post he had applied for.

He now had time to think about his family and, overjoyed to hear that one of his sisters had been seen in Prague, hurriedly obtained permission to go to Czechoslovakia. But when he finally

---

2. Entertainments National Service Association.

reached Prague in late October, survivors from his village told him that two of his sisters, Brana and Sylvia, were indeed alive but had left for Germany two months before in search of him. Crestfallen, he made his way back to Berlin and was delighted to learn upon arrival that he had been appointed Intelligence officer at a civilian interrogation camp in Iserlohn where high-ranking Nazis were being debriefed. Bob found this new job fascinating and seems to have achieved considerable successes. Amongst the Germans he interrogated were Hitler's adjutant, von Below; one of Ribbentrop's interpreters who was a Hauptmann in the SS; Major Willi Johannmeier, who had been present in Hitler's bunker just before his suicide and been handed a copy of his will; Friedrich Flick, the steel magnate and one of the principal financial supporters of the Nazi party; and Lieutenant Colonel Hermann Giskes, chief of German counterespionage in the Low Countries and northern France until the end of 1943.

In mid-November, Bob was reunited with his sisters in Iserlohn, but their search for him had taken its toll: Sylvia, then only fifteen years old, had nearly died of blood poisoning in a displaced persons' camp near Munich. His older sister Brana, who had survived the ordeal of two concentration camps, had exhausted all her remaining energy in caring for her younger sister and looking for her brother. In discussions about their future, they came to the conclusion that Brana would probably be happier living in America, but that Sylvia, still a child in need of education and motherly love, needed to be part of our own family in England. Bob began the lengthy process of applying for immigration permits. Seven months later, in June 1946, both sisters arrived in England; Brana had been given permission to stay with us until her U.S. permit came through and Sylvia was to begin a new life with us.

I was a young mother with a baby only three months old and suddenly I also had to cope with the problems of a rebellious teenager and the serious psychological trauma of a young woman of much my own age who had survived Mauthausen and Buchenwald. From the moment of their reunion, Bob acted as a father to them, doing all he could to keep their morale high, housing, clothing, feeding them and above all grieving with them on the tragedy that had robbed them of their parents, siblings, entire family and home. This additional responsibility on our young shoulders brought further complications to our relationship, but we both accepted it as a completely natural course of action. Seeing Bob and his sisters together for the first time, sensing their pain and all their unspoken sorrow, I loved him all the more.

4

The people who get on in this world are the people who get up and look for the circumstances they want, and if they can't find them, make them.

BERNARD SHAW

Bob arrived on leave in December 1945, and for the first time in our married life, we were just the two of us in a real home. I vividly remember my feverish preparations for Christmas, putting into practice all the skills and knowledge I had learned in Dr. Pomiane's Cordon Bleu course. We had a wonderful festive lunch: goose stuffed with chestnuts, baked *à l'ancienne* in the cast-iron stove, Christmas pudding and cake—all that just for the two of us! We ate heartily, went for a brisk walk then had tea and retired to bed. At three o'clock in the morning, we both woke up hungry and went to the kitchen, polished off the goose then went back to bed and more lovemaking. That Christmas day was one of our favorite memories of those early years of marriage.

At the end of his leave, Bob went back to his interrogation job in Iserlohn, but in March 1946, after his promotion to captain had come through, he rejoined his regiment in Berlin as adjutant to the commanding officer, a responsible and demanding job, with a personal staff of six soldiers and German secretaries. Our first baby was also due in March, but Bob was not able to come home until three weeks after the birth. Luckily, we had foreseen this eventuality and my parents had come from Paris to be with me. Michael was born in Queen Charlotte's hospital in London on my birthday, March 11, and we named him after Bob's father. He was a little mite of just over five pounds with delicate features and a lusty cry. We were both overjoyed, and I was proud to have given my husband tangible proof of our love and an assurance that despite all the Nazis' efforts, his lineage would be perpetuated.

When Bob came home in April on "passionate leave," as we fondly called it, we had both decided that he was not really cut out for an army career and that instead he would join the Allied Control Commission in Berlin. This would give him more training, time to think and a better opportunity to find a civilian job in which his languages and leadership qualities would be a real asset. By now his sisters had joined me in Little Brickhill and we were trying to settle down to a normal family life. The question of nationality was also soon resolved, when on June 19, Bob's naturalization certificate came through, topping the list of those processed after the end of the war, and I acquired British nationality a few days later. By mid-July, Bob came back to London, his demobilization papers in his hand, with authorization for eighty days' leave. His former commanding officer, Major General L.O. Lyne, provided him with a reference to be proud of:

Captain Maxwell is a born leader of men and some of his exploits were quite remarkable. He certainly earned his Military Cross several times over. He inspired the men under him to great feats of endurance and bravery, and was quite one of the most successful young officers whom I met during the whole course of the war. I can confidently recommend him for any position demanding self-reliance, leadership and initiative.

He had also received a tempting job offer in Berlin as a Temporary Officer Grade III in PRISC (Public Relation and Information Services Control), which he decided to accept.

During that summer leave, he was particularly active. As usual, he visited his Czech friends in their London haunts, especially the Czech restaurant on Edgware Road. It was here that he first met the businessman Arnold Lobl, who was looking for a partner in Low Bell Ltd., a small import-export business he had created in December 1945. Bob agreed to join the venture and used part of his army gratuity in September to buy 90 shares in Lobl's firm, whilst Arnold himself had 192. Once Bob had invested in Low Bell, we realized that we needed to move back to London, one of the reasons being that I could work for the firm as Lobl's part-time secretary for £2 a week. Living in London, we thought, would also make it easier for me to find a suitable school for Sylvia and see to all her needs as a new boarder. Brana was still waiting for her U.S. immigration visa and was happy to look after Michael whilst I went to work. So it was that we all moved from Little Brickhill to a two-room flat in Notting Hill.

After investigating a number of educational establishments, I located a lovely school in Somerset which offered a general education with special emphasis on acting and dancing, since Sylvia had told us of her ambition to become an actress. We all agreed that the school was exactly what Sylvia needed at the time and decided to send her there as a boarder. She could speak, read and write in Czech, Hungarian and German, but otherwise she had everything to learn. When she first walked into my life, I was twenty-five and she was sixteen and she lacked discipline. At the age of twelve, she had had her first taste of freedom working for two years in Budapest as an apprentice in a knitting factory. In March 1944, she had narrowly escaped being transported to Auschwitz as she boarded a train to return home to her parents after the Germans occupied Budapest and started to arrest Jews if they ventured outside the ghetto wearing the yellow star. Sylvia owed her escape from deportation—as did many other children like her—to the action and protests of Raoul Wallenberg and others. He would go to the station in person and physically reclaim all children under the age of fifteen, or arrive with a pile of Swedish identity papers preventing "his own nationals" from being taken. Then, as happened to Sylvia, he would shelter them in Red Cross homes. In the same home as Sylvia were three children from Romania, and when their mother came to collect them in January 1945, she took Sylvia with her to help on the journey back home. Sylvia then stayed with them for six months until the end of the war. On their farm, she spent most of her time horse-riding and reading Shakespeare and other classics in Hungarian. She then made her way to Szlatina, in search of surviving members of her family. No wonder she had difficulties in adjusting to a normal life when she arrived in England. It would take a great deal of time and patience to remedy the situation, but Sylvia was extremely fortunate because her school in England prepared her to gain entrance to the Royal Academy of Dramatic Art, and she was thus able to fulfill her ambition to become an actress.

I only wish I had known then what I have since learned about the horrors her family had to endure and the consequences of this trauma for young survivors. I was far too young and inexperienced to handle such immense problems, and I found it hard to deal with this beautiful, untamed teenager, at the height of her adolescent rebellion, whom I so wanted to love. Despite all my misgivings,

Sylvia has kind memories of all I tried to do for her throughout my life, and we became close friends.

On September 1, 1946, I went to Low Bell's tiny offices in Grand Buildings on Trafalgar Square to start my part-time job. There was no daylight at all inside because the window was completely obscured by a large advertisement for Ivor Novelo's show *Perchance to Dream*. After a week's experience there, I was writing to Bob with news of my new job, telling him that import-export seemed to be mainly about travel, letters and telegrams, with letters counting for 65 percent of the work! At first Lobl dealt mostly in Czech goods such as beads, small objects in glass, crystal and wood, pencils, safety pins and the like. It was all on a very small scale. As soon as Bob had a hand in it, the business exploded in a hundred different directions.

Another Czech, Ladislau Skaloud, acquired 420 shares in the business within a month of my starting work there. At the time Bob had been offered the opportunity to increase his shareholding, but he was reluctant to do so because he felt he was bringing in all the business while his partners quietly raked in the profits. He had offered to buy the business outright, but Lobl was not quite ready to sell. There seemed little point in my continuing to work for little pay, with little benefit to myself or to Bob, so we decided that I would join him in Berlin until he had a business of his own.

I was delighted at the thought of family life with my husband and baby son. Bob set about finding us an apartment, eventually settling on a delightful flat in a block in Kastanien Allee, right underneath that of his commanding officer, Major George Bell. It was our great good fortune that Anne and George were a charming, quiet and cultured couple. We liked them enormously, got on well together and remained staunch friends throughout our lives, even though George's career took his family to Pakistan, Nigeria, India and other far-flung Commonwealth countries.

Life was cheap in Germany for occupying troops and their families. Whilst the basic salary was the same as that of a comparable grade in the UK, there was a generous supplementary allowance for service abroad and fully furnished accommodation was provided rent-free; all food could be obtained at no charge from special shops for Allied personnel; staff were easy to find and their wages were low. It was quite possible to enjoy a high standard of living yet save most of one's salary. It was certainly an attractive prospect, but above all I was thrilled at the thought of being reunited with my husband. In great excitement, I set off with Michael for Berlin on November 17, sailing to Cuxhaven and traveling for a full two days to get there. Bob and I were overjoyed to set up home for what we thought would be a full year together.

By now he was extremely busy in his post as censor to the newly revived Berlin press, whose main paper, *Der Telegraf,* was edited and managed by Arno Scholz. Bob would work at the office late at night to "put the paper to bed," but would then stay at home until after lunch, enjoying family life and the antics of his baby son. For the army of occupation, life in Berlin in those days was a constant whirl of social activities. We would go from one party to another, giving parties ourselves and attending them in all sectors of the town, enjoying French, American, British and Russian hospitality while our young German nanny looked after Michael. There was little else to do: the city was rather like a ghost town, desolate and utterly devastated, its people ashen and starving, living mostly in derelict cellars. The weather was bitterly cold, public transport was minimal and there was no question of fraternization with the Germans at the time.

On one occasion, George and Bob went off together in blizzard conditions to visit the first postwar Leipzig Book Fair, then in the Russian zone. Anne and I spent the time together in her flat talking until the early hours of the morning, waiting for our husbands to return from what was then a hazardous trip. Through those hours of anxious waiting, we got to know each other better and became close friends. When the men finally came home, I think we all felt that there was a bond between us that would never be broken. It was the first time Bob ever went to the Russian zone; he was not to go behind the Iron Curtain again until 1951.

One night, as we came back late from dinner with the Bells, our key refused to turn in the lock. With his prudence born of wartime, Bob let the dog in first after he managed to unlock the door. There behind it stood a burglar with all my jewelry in his pocket! Bob tackled him on the spot and proceeded to interrogate him while I rushed upstairs to ask for George's help in calling the military police. After that episode, whenever Bob stayed late at work, I could never go to sleep unless I had Barry, our superb Alsatian, curled up beside me on the bed. He had been the last stud dog left in the kennels used by Hitler and Bob had acquired him through the Führer's dentist, Dr. Eibisch. When Bob eventually arrived home, Barry would relinquish his place on the bed with the greatest reluctance.

By January 1947, Bob was beginning to show signs of boredom

with his job and to question the wisdom of continuing to work in the Control Commission. Whether the trip to the Book Fair with George Bell had sparked a greater interest in books and heightened his discontent, I do not know for sure, but he certainly started to talk more and more of handing in his month's notice so that he would be free to develop his own business. It was in this state of mind that he traveled to London in February to see what was happening to his "investment." He decided the time had come to accept the financial help offered by my father and his friend Mr. Rague to increase his Low Bell shareholding to equal that of Lobl. He also created a new company called EPPAC—European Periodicals, Publicity and Advertising Company—whose primary objectives were to help prominent German publishers restart exports of scientific, technical and medical publications, import German newspapers, and sell them to German prisoners of war and explore the market for scientific publications. By that time he had made a great many contacts in Berlin and in the Control Commission and could sense the countless opportunities available to those who could grasp and exploit them.

As soon as Bob came back to Berlin, we discussed the latest developments in his business career. Agreeing that it would be best to go back to London, Bob resigned his post. Michael's christening had been arranged for February 17 and his godfathers, Gary Carthew-Yorstoun and Major Nick Huysmans, were coming, along with my relatives, the Seydoux de Clausonnes, as my cousin Beatrice was standing in for his godmother, Jacqueline Arnal. Amongst our other guests that day was another good friend, Colonel Christopher Rhodes, who was a fluent French speaker. I was always delighted to talk to him in my native language, and when I inquired how he had mastered French so perfectly, I discovered he had been dropped as an agent near Bordeaux in occupied France and had lived there under cover as a teacher while working for the Resistance. For his quiet bravery, he had been decorated with the Distinguished Service Order and Croix de Guerre. I remember being fascinated by his story, especially since he had no French ancestry at all, but Christopher was always very modest about his achievements. We had also invited George and Anne Bell, and a number of PRISC colleagues, together with a whole band of Germans, amongst them Arno Scholz, Kurt Schumacher and Erich Ollenhauer.

Once the christening party was over, we made plans to leave Berlin just after my birthday, on our wedding anniversary, March 14. We left for Paris in a Dodge, a car Bob had managed to buy very cheaply from the manager of Mercedes Benz, Lothar Hennies.

Besides the three of us, we also had our dog and all our worldly goods squeezed into every available nook and cranny of the car! My parents were so pleased to see us that I decided to stay for a few days and leave Michael with them until we had sorted out our immediate future, especially somewhere to live. Bob left for London, intending to find a flat and register his new company EPPAC, which he had set up in partnership with Mr. Rague, the same friend of my father's who had lent him money to invest in Low Bell Ltd. Once I returned to London, I resumed my work for Low Bell, but all my spare time was devoted to house hunting. I'll never forget that desperate search for an apartment and the series of Kensington garrets we lived in before we finally found a basement flat in Stanhope Gardens, which we shared with the rats of London.

By that time, my father had opened his own import-export business in Paris, which was totally separate from a fruit and vegetable business he ran with a partner. Daddy had many friends in the Paris business community, who were all beginning to get their firms off the ground again after the war. Most of them had capital but very little know-how. Amongst them was a Turk called Mr. Denker, whose best friend was a Turkish general, the cousin of the Turkish Minister of War. Denker had been asked to cooperate in a project to reequip Turkey's industry at a time when both the UK and the United States, keen to get back into the export market, had agreed to supply a large amount of goods on credit, on condition that the items were really destined for Turkey. My father was also friendly with another Turk, Nissim Zacouto, a Jewish businessman of distinguished ancestry. His family had once lived in Spain, where a distant ancestor had helped finance Christopher Columbus's expedition to the New World, but they had returned to Turkey as the Spanish Inquisition got into its stride. Zacouto had been the largest Oriental carpet dealer in Germany before the war, with headquarters in Berlin, but all his stock had been stolen by the Nazis. He was determined to recover some of it, or at least obtain compensation. During the war, he had been in hiding in the French unoccupied zone and, despite his misfortunes, was still a very rich man. We remained friendly with the Zacoutos and their son, a distinguished scientist and inventor of a heart pacemaker.

It was originally through Zacouto's contacts that my father launched into the famous Turkish boots deal that kept us all in suspense for a year. The Turkish army needed one million pairs of leather boots and the leather was to come from England. All seemed to be proceeding quite smoothly; we had the order, we had the letter of credit, we had the leather, what could possibly go wrong? Then came the snag. As I described in a letter to Bob, who at the time was in America:

The boots' deal is kaput! And why? Bignals [the agent] wants confirmation from the Board of Trade that he is allowed to sell the boots, the Board of Trade wants confirmation from the leather people that they are going to provide the skins. The skin people want confirmation from the Turks that the Turks have ordered the boots and the Turks, before they send their confirmation, want confirmation from us that Bignals is going to deliver them.

There were so many fly-by-nights trying to make a quick buck that people were over cautious, and you could not truly blame them. This kind of problem happened all the time.

Another famous imbroglio concerned a shipment of caustic soda from France to China. French regulations at the time did not permit the export of sodium hydroxide, or caustic soda, but the French themselves had found a way of circumventing the problem by labeling the goods "sodium chlorate." Once again the deal had been struck and everything was poised for a shipment of fifty thousand tons of caustic soda. We had confirmed that the manufacturers were French, that the goods were actually available in the warehouse, that it really was caustic soda and that the letter of credit was correctly worded. We had explained the problem to the Chinese, who understood perfectly and had agreed to the solution. We were ready to go ahead when suddenly they started to get cold feet. First they argued about the labeling of the goods, then they started to worry about the concentration, then the quality. At this, the French intermediary washed his hands of the whole affair like Pontius Pilate, leaving us with nothing to show for a great deal of effort.

Whilst we were offered impossible caustic soda deals like the one quoted FOB Bombay and payable in Swiss francs, which never actually materialized, we did make good money on smaller regular consignments of caustic soda from ICI (Imperial Chemical Industries), which Bob had contacted directly, and on other chemicals and dyes such as acid fast green, acid leather brown, indigo, diazodis blue and benzol, and on various items like eucalyptus oil, kapok, cider taps and many other disparate goods. There was a huge demand for all kinds of things and incredible orders found their way onto Bob's desk: 20 to 30 stonecrushers, 20 to 30 crushers for small stones, 20 to 30 bulldozers, 30 to 40 tractors, 80 to 100 trailers. Some of these gigantic orders were pie in the sky, but others did come to fruition, bringing in a great deal of money.

I have clear memories of the two best deals of those days, since I was working in the office at the time and was closely involved in their success. One was a contract for the purchase of many thousands of tons of coffee beans and the other a $1 million contract for paint. Both were needed for the German market, which was greatly shored up by Marshall Plan aid. I can still see Bob thumbing through the telephone directory, lighting on the names of "RIDGE, Coffee Merchants" and "LEWIS BERGER, Paint Manufacturer." Before long, he had made appointments to see the managing directors of both firms, from which he emerged with both contracts in the bag. Nowadays, unless you are a well-known exporter, you would simply be shown the door, but those were different times. Even then, however, talk of an order for several thousand tons of coffee must have seemed quite preposterous when it was difficult to sell one ton, especially in England where rationing had virtually cut off all demand. Talking in terms of thousands of tons must have been beyond anyone's wildest dreams, an absoulte impossibility. But for Ernst Breminer, the Czech owner of Ridge who had emigrated to England before the war, the impossible was to happen when Bob walked into his office. They took an instant liking to each other, and Ernst was later to name his own son after Bob. For my part, I became friendly with his attractive Czech wife, who had the most striking sapphire blue eyes I have ever seen. She was artistic, amusing, talented in many ways, but was constantly bullied by her domineering husband; I really felt for her. In those early years, Bob and Ernst were to conclude several such contracts; indeed, Ernst dined out on this story of thousands of tons of coffee beans for the rest of his life! After his death in 1952, I kept in touch with his partner, who had worked on those early deals, and with his children, who came to stay with us many times, especially after their mother had also died.

In much the same way, we remained friends with Bill Berger after the completion of the paint contract. He remarried late in life after parting from his first wife, Flo, who had been unable to cope with the success of her wiry, astute, fun-loving husband. His second wife was a much younger, charming French woman with whom he went to live in St. Tropez. I remember wondering then what happens to all the loyal Flos of the world, swearing that I would never let my marriage deteriorate to such a point.

Those were heroic days in Grand Buildings: we were all so full of enthusiasm and dreamt of making our fortunes! One deal often led to another. The paint contract, for instance, not only brought in a great deal of money itself, but it then precipitated a need for paint-brushes, swiftly followed by a need for bristle for the brushes. They were all excellent contracts that contributed healthily to our early fortunes. The word passed round quickly in refugee circles and amongst demobilized soldiers that our minuscule offices in Trafalgar Square were a hive of activity. People came and went as they pleased, some with offers of goods, others looking for a job. Those who were taken on stayed to form the nucleus of our early staff. Amongst them was Eileen Straton-Ferrier's husband, John, a retired bank manager who wore a monocle and used to sit behind an enormous desk occupying half the available space, looking totally inscrutable like the oracle of Cumae. He was to become our self-appointed "bouncer," liberating us from all the hangers-on who frequented our office and wasted our time, like the curious gentleman who insisted on wearing a kilt for business and only came to use our telephone. John's unflappable composure was the perfect foil for our youthful enthusiasm, and although his commercial experience was limited, his presence lent a great air of respectability to our venture. I was fond of him and we got on well. Then there was the Czech, John Kisch, a former PRISC press officer who had been in charge of supplies and licensing in Bad Oynhausen. On a trip to Berlin in search of desperately needed newspaper supplies he met Bob and later became his first employee in EPPAC, responsible for selling German newspapers to prisoners of war. Using the old Dodge, he would set off to make the deliveries himself, then disappear for the best part of the day, taking his girlfriend for long joy rides. He was also involved in the affairs of Low Bell Ltd., and I have hilarious memories of him talking long distance to Brazil in his inimitable Czech accent, trying to find out the latest exchange rate of the cruzeiro against the U.S. dollar. From that moment on, we affectionately nicknamed him "Cruzerio." In the midst of all this hubbub, another refugee, Eric Eiser, laboriously tried to work out the figures, half-deafened by the clatter of the typewriter as Sadie Dancer's fingers flew over the keys at a furious pace. Then there was another Czech, Victor Sassi, who later became the owner of the Gay Hussar restaurant in Greek Street; his job was to collect the German newspapers from the airport in a hired van. John Kisch had also introduced his friend Vic Sherwood, whose wife kindly baby-sat for me. Many years later, he was to find himself working for Bob for a second time in one of the subsidiaries of the British Printing Corporation. As for me, I was fully occupied answering the telephone, pacifying impatient or angry customers, supplying endless cups of tea and coffee to that perpetually thirsty bunch and typing letters at a much more sedate speed than our secretary, whose generous bosom had earned her the sobriquet of "The Sex Machine."

To escape this madhouse briefly, at the height of summer Bob and I would often catch the bus to Hyde Park, go for a swim in the Serpentine then sit on the bank, eating sandwiches we had bought on the way. If we felt rich that day, we would hire a rowing boat and have our lunch "far from the madding crowd." Simple pleasures meant a lot to us; we worked hard and our life was full of love, excitement and promise. Bob's fertile imagination and immense energy ensured there was never a dull moment, and no two days were alike. But it was a far cry from the flashy life of luxury described in later years by people who did not even know us then.

In that summer of 1947, Bob made his first trip to America, where he stayed for the whole month of June. In New York, he visited his mother's brother, Nathan, and also followed up a great many introductions he had been given by friends in England. Chinita Abrahams had put him in contact with Larry Lesavoy, a wealthy businessman with whom Bob subsequently did important deals. It was Larry who gave Bob a Chrysler, which previously he had had shipped to the UK. It was costing him a small fortune to garage it in London and the understanding was that Larry would use it on his trips to England, but it was ours for the rest of the time. Two years later, he shipped over a Cadillac and the same arrangement continued. That Cadillac was a superb car, but it was so wide that we had trouble maneuvering it around the narrow streets of Piccadilly and the City. Like the Chrysler, it absolutely guzzled fuel, but it was still cheaper for us than buying a car of our own. It wasn't at all to our taste, and we certainly regretted the amount of money that disappeared in gasoline, but, as the saying goes, you don't look a gift horse in the mouth. By 1949, Bob finally balked at the expenditure on fuel and decided to buy a secondhand Jaguar, but it was not long before another Cadillac arrived from Lesavoy, continuing an arrangement which was proving more and more costly. It was not until 1954 that we bought our first new car, a Humber Super Snipe, which we used almost exclusively for travel to and from the airport.

Whilst Bob was traveling abroad, I would hold the fort as best I could, writing daily letters to him to seek his guidance and advice. I was totally inexperienced in business and would sometimes panic at the thought of all those commodities flying around in all directions, especially when I saw the resulting pile of paperwork which landed on my desk.

In late December 1947, I went back to France, taking Michael with me, to give birth early in the New Year to our daughter Anne. By that time, my sister had just opened her own maternity clinic in Maisons Laffitte and Anne was the first baby to be born there. On Anne's fortieth birthday, she was also to be present at the clinic to celebrate my sister's retirement, the fortieth anniversary of the clinic and the birth of the 15,000th baby delivered there, my grandson Xavier, born forty years to the day after Anne.

On the day before I left for France, we had a ghastly accident in our basement flat. It was infested with small black rats that were particularly attracted to the kitchen, especially at night. We were just about to settle down to dinner when I went into the pantry to fetch a small item I had forgotten. To my horror, I was immediately set upon by a band of rats—they had absolutely no fear of me. Bob was so furious that he was determined to kill some of them, and seized upon the nearest bottle as a weapon. I took refuge behind the door, but suddenly heard a loud explosion. The next minute, the door swung open and all I could see was Bob covered in blood and several dead rats on the floor, also oozing blood. The bottle Bob had snatched up in the heat of the moment contained chlorine bleach. When it smashed, it exploded like a small bomb, showering shards of glass everywhere, killing four rats and lacerating Bob's hand severely. After I had dressed his wound and cleared up the mess in the pantry, Bob swore that he would find us somewhere decent to live. He had made up his mind that we would never live in such miserable conditions again.

Whilst I was away in France, he set about flat-hunting in earnest and eventually found a lovely home for us in Addison Crescent. We returned to a spacious, sunny, modern three-bedroom apartment where we spent two happy years. We became friendly with the other family who lived in the house, Jim and Vivian Gear, an architect and painter, respectively. Their daughter, Chloe, was the same age as Michael, and we have remained in touch by letter to this day.

With two babies on my hands, Bob constantly away and my own work in the office, which I wanted to continue, I had to consider looking for some help at home. My first thought was to find a cook, but when I discussed the problem with my mother, she pointed out that whenever I was tired of cooking, we could always have sandwiches or go to a restaurant. Children, on the other hand, demanded constant, active attention, so in her opinion it was better to look for a nanny. It was one of the best pieces of advice she ever gave me. So it was that Marion Sloane became part of our family. By the time she came for her interview, I had already seen two oldish, rather uppity Norland nannies whose first request was to see "the pram." I remember looking at Marion's references and asking her why she had left her last position after four years there. Without any hesitation, she replied that she had been rude to the lady of the house. I was so surprised at her complete honesty that I decided to engage her on the spot, and we came to a mutual agreement on a three-month trial period. In the event, she stayed with us for sixteen years, until she died of cancer in 1964. Marion loved my children as if they were her own. She was discreet, loyal, hardworking and totally devoted to our family. Over the years, we became close friends; throughout our long association, I cannot recall a single angry word passing between us.

Two months before I left for France, at the end of 1947, Bob managed to conclude a very advantageous contract with Springer Verlag for the exclusive worldwide sales and distribution rights of their books and journals, including back issues. To implement this enormous task, he had moved his business premises to Studio Place, off Kinnerton Street, and several more refugees were added to the payroll. One of the first to join was Peter Orton. During the war, he had been a subaltern in the Pioneer Corps, serving in the same unit as Vernon Baxter, who was also later to join Bob's staff. He managed to return to his native Berlin at the end of the war, working on a military government assignment, and it was there that Bob met him for the first time. Although he may have been useful to Bob right at the beginning of their association, especially since he was older, he was later to become a burden. The problem was that he never seemed to complete satisfactorily any task he was given, nor conclude any business successfully. As Bob would say, "He had no balls," and this was not helped by the fact that he was an avowed homosexual at a time when such things were not flaunted. He often went to Paris where he would blatantly entertain young boys overnight in our own flat. Some years later, just before Christmas, Bob was on the point of giving him his notice and severing business connections, when I persuaded him at least to wait until the New Year. But Peter was killed in a road accident near Oxford that December 1955. He had just returned from a business trip to the Far East where Bob had agreed to his return via Hong Kong so he could meet his brother, whom he had not seen for sixteen years.

Nearly all the people who joined Bob's staff at that time were Czech or German refugees, since it was essential to be German-speaking. Most of them were extremely well qualified, holding doctorates in law, literature or mathematics from their own countries, but their diplomas were of little use in postwar Britain. They were delighted to find some employment and several of those early employees of fine intellect who started off as packers and dispatchers eventually graduated to more appropriate jobs and continued to work for Bob for twenty, thirty or even forty years. Amongst these, I remember Vernon Baxter and Detlev Raymond best of all. Vernon, with whom I still correspond, had a great sense of humor and excellent English. He wrote a moving yet very amusing book about his years in the Pioneer Corps, which, to my great regret, was never published.

Detlev had met Bob in Berlin in 1945 when he was a trainee editor at *Der Berliner.* Their first encounter took place when Detlev, then only eighteen years old, went one Saturday to take an "illegal" hot bath in some deserted military quarters. Bob had just arrived to take over the premises for his battalion and came upon the young, good-looking German having a long soak. "You ought to be shot for this," bellowed Captain Robert Maxwell, but by then the war was over. Instead, Raymond was promoted on the spot to the post of liaison editor between the British Military Government and *Der Berliner.* As he used to put it, from that day on he became "part of the spoils of war and for better or worse, the Captain's favorite German vassal!" For years afterwards, Bob would alternately call him "Stulpnagel" (a derogatory nickname, after a well-known German general in World War II) or "Mein Goldener" ("my golden boy"), depending or whether he had performed badly or to his satisfaction. With Detlev, Bob got up to the last pranks of his youth, since they were both roughly the same age. Detlev himself had an inexhaustible stock of stories about their antics, which he would recount with the greatest pleasure, leaving us all in hysterics. Throughout his career, he was efficient, hardworking and completely loyal, and the business relationship-cum-friendship between the two men never diminished over more than forty years until Detlev's death in 1988, soon after he came over to England with his wife to attends Bob's sixty-fifth birthday celebration.

By June 1948, Bob had signed distribution contracts with some of the most prestigious German scientific, medical and technical publishing houses, headed by Springer Verlag, whose publications had been famous for decades all over the world. EPPAC had already begun deliveries to customers and libraries via Her Majesty's Stationery Office at a time when EPCOM, the official Enemy Publications Committee set up by Churchill in 1945 expressly to import the huge cache of German classified scientific information, had still not even managed to fix an appropriate exchange rate.

Bob first met Dr. Ferdinand Springer, the owner of Springer Verlag, known to all in the business as "the Kaiser," in the Berlin of 1946. Before the war, Germany had led the world in science, especially in mathematics, physics, chemistry and engineering, and Ferdinand had become the world's leading publisher of scientific books and journals. His authors included a remarkable array of distinguished scientists, including many Nobel prizewinners who contributed to his celebrated Beilstein series. Being half-Jewish, he was not allowed to own or direct his business after the infamous Nuremberg race laws were passed, with the result that his company was managed during the war by a Prussian "Aryan," Tonjes Lange, whom Bob had also met at the time he met Springer. Ferdinand had been hiding in the country but was taken prisoner by the Russians as they advanced on Berlin. His miraculous "escape" story deserves to be retold. Some weeks after his capture, by a stroke of extraordinary luck, he was taken for interrogation before a Russian officer who was himself a scientist and remembered Springer's publications well from the days of his own studies. After they had talked a little about scientific matters, the officer wanted to be certain that this was indeed Ferdinand Springer, so he asked him how many scientific journals he actually published. The total at the time was around one hundred. The Russian officer then sat him down at a table, gave him pen and paper and asked him to list all the titles. By the time Springer had reached the eighty-second journal, the officer was convinced of his identity and revealed that he was in great danger of deportation and would certainly end up in a gulag. But that Russian officer took it upon himself to put Ferdinand on a tank and have him sent back to the Western zone in Berlin.

After her husband had been marched under military escort from his hiding place and nothing was heard of him for several weeks, Elisabet Springer felt certain he had been shot and tried to commit suicide by slashing her wrists. Fortunately, she was saved in extremis by a faithful maid. She was Ferdinand's second wife and a Hungarian of striking personality. She positively worshiped Ferdinand and devoted her whole life to him; everything else took second place. They had two very intelligent sons, neither of whom showed the slightest interest in the publishing business, and they each had a child from their previous marriages. She had a daughter called Rösi and he a son, also called Ferdinand, who was completely ostracized by the family.

Bob was to develop a deep and close relationship with both Ferdinand and his wife, and he frequently stayed at their home in Heidelberg, where the Springer business was relocated after the war. Elisabet would speak Hungarian with Bob and was always telling him how much she longed for a son like him. He was welcomed in their home like the prodigal son, and Elisabet would go to enormous trouble whenever he visited, cooking special Hungarian dishes which she knew he liked. In fact, he came to look upon her as a surrogate mother and constantly held her up to me as an example of the perfect wife. She used to send me recipes of the dishes she suggested I cook for him, and every time I saw her, she would try to give me advice on how to handle my relationship with Bob. She definitely had a great influence on him and I felt as if I had acquired a mother-in-law. In the evenings, Bob would talk business endlessly with Ferdinand, their Jewish backgrounds forging a link between them which could never have existed with the Prussian Tonjes Lange, who was the epitome of Hansi's caricature of the Germans. Yet I hasten to say that he in no way behaved like the proverbial Hun.

It was Ferdinand Springer, not Tonjes Lange, who had a significant influence on my husband. Indeed, Bob came to look upon him as a father figure. He was always dressed in black, with impeccable white shirts and pale gray ties. There was something very Germanic about his bearing, yet he had lovely soft eyes and a kind smile. We invited him to become godfather to our second son, Philip, born in 1949, and he was pleased to accept, but he suggested that we also ask Tonjes, which we did. Later on, it was Lange who undertook most of the traveling for Springer Verlag and Bob went twice to the States with him. He would occasionally come to London and we would all go out for the evening together. Sometimes we also met in Paris, where he liked to go to the Lido or the Folies Bergères. But Bob's relationship over the years with Lange was more of a business relationship that developed into a distant friendship. It never had the intimacy, the respect nor the refinement of his friendship with the Springers in those formative years of the business. There was, it is true, an appearance of joviality, with Bob calling Tonjes "Onkel," and later on Charlie, but it was really more of an amusing, long-standing joke than an indication of real closeness, although Bob never failed to admire Lange's loyalty and deference to "the Kaiser" until the former's death in 1961. Our friendship eventually waned, not only because business ties were ultimately severed, but because Lange was finally able to marry his ladyfriend of many years after her husband died. Traute was pretty, elegant and charming; she was good company as well as an accomplished housewife. Tonjes then discovered the joys of married life with a wife who could entertain his friends and be entertained by them. He was no longer the solitary bachelor we had known for a decade. In the late fifties, Traute Lange was officially invited to the Springers for the first time. Although she had known Tonjes for years before that, moral attitudes and hypocrisy dictated that your best friend's mistress was not someone you brought home to socialize with your wife!

As the years passed, Springer came to rely more and more on Lange and other loyal employees to run the business. His elder son, a scientist, emigrated to Canada; his youngest boy, an endearing dreamer, was playing the eternal student and the family business did not interest him, although he officially became a partner in the firm in 1963 and did take an interest in the field of life sciences in the seventies. Meanwhile, Ferdinand's first-born son from his previous marriage, now a well-known painter in his own country, was largely ignored by both his father and stepmother. Ferdinand really cared only for those sons he hoped would succeed him in the publishing house. As for his wife, she did not want young Ferdinand near them for fear he would exercise his right of primogeniture in the publishing house and "oust" his two brothers, as the Kaiser himself had done, driving out his brother Fritz from the family firm in connivance with his cousin Julius. This state of affairs had been compounded by the Nuremberg inheritance laws, which cut the younger Ferdinand out of his father's will because, although only a quarter Jew himself, he refused to divorce his Jewish wife in 1937. A financial settlement with his father was agreed upon at the time, but not honored. During the war, Ferdinand Junior had lived in unoccupied France with his Jewish wife until 1942, when he escaped to Switzerland. Both he and his wife were charming and immensely talented, but were eking out a Spartan existence in Paris. Towards the end of his life, the older Ferdinand did show some regret about the situation and Bob offered to mediate. I was sent to visit them in Paris, where I found them living with their young son in a poky, unheated hotel room, struggling to make ends meet, as is often the lot of artists striving for recognition. When I described all this to Bob, I begged him to use his influence with Ferdinand to remedy the situation. I had promised his son I would do this, and I am glad to say that Ferdinand did offer him an ungenerous part of the original settlement money, although by then the Nuremberg laws were no longer in force and Ferdinand Junior should have reverted to his legitimate position as heir. This never happened, not even after the Kaiser's death. The amount he received was nevertheless enough for this unfortunate trio to buy a decent apartment on the lovely Place des Vosges, which in those days was not as fashionable as it is today.

I used to entertain the Springers when they came to London in the late forties, and I would go to immense lengths to serve them dinners worthy of the culinary reputation of Elisabet. She reminded me at the time of the well-known statues of Queen Victoria with her regal bearing, generous bust and deep cleavage. I shall never forget one evening at home when Elisabet explained how diamonds sewn into the hem of her skirt had saved their lives on various occasions during the war. Not only that, they had also rescued the business, as we well knew. Ever since then, Elisabet told us, she would never allow herself to travel anywhere without the rock-solid reassurance of valuable precious stones on her person. As she uttered these words, she proceeded to extract a small leather pouch from between her breasts and empty its contents onto the white linen of the dining table. To our utter amazement, out rolled the most enormous diamond rings and single gems, as Ferdinand looked on fondly.

Our partnership with Springer Verlag was to be successful for many years. Bob had helped Ferdinand to reconstruct his business in 1947 by offering him commercial facilities for export to England at a time when other publishers seemed unable to cope with the restrictions and red tape which dogged all transactions in the postwar era. In the years when Germans were not permitted to travel freely, Bob traveled one million miles on their behalf, selling their books and journals all over the world. I remember one instance when he went to the United States in June 1950 and managed to prevent American libraries from carrying out a threat to boycott Springer publications. He addressed four large gatherings in Atlantic City, Boston, Washington and New York, explaining the benefits for the world of sharing the results of scientific research, even if it was German in origin. There were, admittedly, some difficulties along the way. At first, EPPAC's inexperience in dealing with a huge mailing list caused some minor problems, but they were easily remedied after Springer dispatched some of his most trusted lieutenants to teach them how to manage it properly, and especially after the creation of Lange Maxwell & Springer (LMS), which was well run, with Springer directors and executives regularly attending board meetings and Annual General Meetings (AGMs). Later on, Springer felt with some justification that Bob was much more interested in building up his own publishing venture than in looking after their interests. But despite these disagreements, Springer was the first to recognize wholeheartedly the immense assistance Bob had given him when they were struggling to restart their business in conditions of great hardship. For his part, Bob readily acknowledged that this close relationship with Springer Verlag not only brought him great financial advantages but enabled him to lay the foundation for his own publishing house, Pergamon Press. It had been indeed, as Bob wrote to Lange, a "momentous decade during which we have shared and suffered many things together."

As trade restrictions were gradually lifted and commercial relations returned to normal, Springer Verlag no longer needed an intermediary to sell its publications. After negotiations that lasted over a year, a settlement was reached in February between Springer and Bob. Although the closeness of our relations with the Springers waned as Ferdinand progressively passed on the reins of his business to his executives, we corresponded with them until the death of Elisabet in 1963. We entertained the Langes at home in Oxford and Bob saw them in Berlin shortly before Tonjes's death in 1961. At the same time, they were justifiably concerned that the growth of Pergamon would bring with it intense competition for their own business, since Bob had realized that it was more financially advantageous to publish books and journals than to act as an agent for another company. Knowing Bob well, Ferdinand could foresee that competition was inevitable; he had trained a rival and the pupil might very well overtake the master. When Bob went to Heidelberg in 1959 for a reception in honor of Tonjes Lange, Elisabet's last words to him said it all: "What a pity you were not our son!" She died in 1963 and her husband followed her three years later.

Bob had learned the rudiments of successful scientific publishing from Ferdinand Springer: the importance of publishing series that scientists needed, the value of back issues, the significance of journals. From Tonjes Lange, he had acquired experience of the mechanics of publishing and the editorial quality required. By the time Bob parted company from Springer Verlag, the basis of Pergamon Press was firmly established, and Bob was to develop and expand on all he had learned. His methods were dynamic, responding to the immediate requirements of scientists and the need for rapid dissemination of their research, fostering close relationships with authors and editors, and personally supporting work in new scientific fields which hitherto had not been recognized. His crucial role in creating a new scientific publishing industry for Britain, much praised by the academic and scientific communities, cannot be denied.

During those early years in London, I was working as a secretary in the office, but at home I was also chief cook, which naturally involved doing all the shopping myself. Because of world shortages, all essential foodstuffs—milk, butter, cooking fats, cheese, bacon, meat and so on—were still severely rationed. Fresh eggs were a luxury, and nobody at the time would have dreamt of using them for baking cakes when dried egg powder was quite adequate. Tea and coffee continued to be precious commodities, as was rice; spaghetti and noodles did not exist in England at the time. Fruit and sweets were both restricted, and I can still remember when bananas first appeared in the shops in 1946. Even potatoes had to be rationed at one point. There were always long lines of customers for everything and a lot of time was wasted, even to buy common fruit and vegetables such as cabbage, carrots, Brussels sprouts, tomatoes and apples when they were in season. You had to use your imagination to vary the menus. When coupon-free whale meat was introduced to the market I courageously gave it a try, as I also did horse meat, but they were both so tough that even if you minced the meat, it was still impossible to chew. Bob joked that since both were non-kosher anyway, they had to come off our menu for good—although in reality he was never troubled by such considerations. Other essential commodities were also in short supply, including coal, fuel, soap, clothes, fabrics and shoes. It was difficult and a nuisance, but there was no real hardship for our household. Nevertheless, we would always scour the daily paper for the latest ups and downs of rationing, and our weekly domestic joys and doldrums would consist of one extra ounce of cooking fat or two gallons less of fuel!

I would come back home carrying back-breaking loads of food and essentials. Although I was thin as a rail in those days when I wasn't pregnant, I certainly had muscles! One of the advantages of being pregnant was that you had priority in the long lines. The trouble was that because I was so slim, people could not believe that I was expecting a baby and would give me furious looks, hating me for pushing to the front. On more than one occasion, I had to show my ration book to make them stop grumbling, but I would stand my ground and go to the front of the line. I don't really know whether there was a black market in England at the time. Compared with the shortages I had experienced in the German occupation of Paris, I found the rations allotted sufficient and the system fair. If you were careful, you never lacked for anything. In fact, as the years passed, rations did increase and there came a time when it was no longer necessary to buy all that we were entitled to. Rationing remained officially in force until July 1954, but by the time of the Coronation in June 1953, it had been greatly relaxed.

Some of our personal and family problems had been solved by the late 1940s. Brana had finally received her immigration permit and left for the United States, and Sylvia was happily settled in Taunton and seemed to be making up for lost time in her education. Bob and I were now living under one comfortable roof. In theory, we should have been enjoying that unfulfilled dream of being closer together, but our hopes were thwarted yet again by Bob's constant traveling and my constant pregnancies. Even when Bob was in England, he would stay late at the office, dealing with his myriad problems, not least of which was the second move of his offices, this time to much bigger premises above a banana warehouse in Neal Street, Covent Garden, where they were to remain for the next four years. When he was abroad, which was at least 50 percent of the time, we wrote to each other regularly, and Bob would phone or cable whenever possible, but in many ways we were back to wartime separation, with my old anxieties about bombing and shelling now replaced by all the risks associated with travel. Sometimes when Bob came back home, I was just about to set off for France and my latest confinement. I insisted on having my babies in my sister's clinic near Paris and always left a few weeks before the event, taking Marion and the other children with me; they were then entrusted to the care of my mother, who now lived nearby. All told, we would be away from home about two months each time.

When he was abroad without me, Bob would never do any sight-seeing, all his time was spent on business matters. He took pride in the fact that he never once traveled for the firm without bringing back some business and making enough money to cover his travel expenses ten times over. By the time he died, he had gone through twenty British passports, which he used to give me as souvenirs once they were no longer valid. His six earliest passports, between 1948 and 1956, contain 150 or more entry and exit stamps, to Frankfurt, Berlin and Vienna, Paris, Basel and Geneva, New York, Boston and Washington, Toronto and Montreal, Moscow, Tokyo, Singapore and Sydney. I remember that Philip's first words were "Good-bye, Daddy" and he would say them regardless of whether Bob was just setting off or coming back. As far as he was concerned, a daddy was someone you saw from your mother's arms, standing on the doorstep!

Despite all these necessary absences, Bob would try very hard to spend some time with me and the family. He was conscious of the fact that I was often alone and unhappy about it, so one day he came back home with one of those early enormous television sets with the minute screens, so that I would have some distraction whilst he was away. He had also made up his mind that he wanted to learn to dance with Victor Silvester's televised dancing lessons! We would clear the furniture in the drawing room to one side and have such a lot of fun, trying to follow the instructions to the tunes of Silvester's orchestra. We would inevitably collapse in laughter, and after most sessions would end up making love on the carpet. In those days, Marion did not live in, but sometimes she would baby-sit for us whilst we went to a dinner dance to put all we had learned into practice!

When I found myself pregnant again only seven months after Philip's birth, I became very depressed and sought refuge with my Aunt Belle at La Bourdille. I was certain she would understand how I was feeling, since she herself had had four children in quick succession. She welcomed and cosseted me and gradually my batteries were recharged and I felt able to face the demands of my life once again. After two months' rest, I came back to England, but I had only been home a matter of weeks when I discovered that Bob was planning a long trip to the Far East. Not wanting to be alone, I took Marion and all the children to Saint Gervais in the Alps to be near my favorite aunt again, since she always spent the summer months there. Bob then came to fetch me two months before the baby was due. Marion and the children stayed with Aunt Belle. After spending a few days with the family, we set off for Paris with Bob at the wheel. For the first time ever, he took it very steadily rather than driving like a maniac as he usually did. We even paused on the way to buy fishing tackle, stopped near a river and Bob went fishing while I sat beside him watching and knitting.

Bob then left me in Paris in my sister's care and went off to America, planning to return in early August in good time for the expected birth. By that time I was absolutely enormous, and after examining me, my sister was certain that I was expecting twins. She decided not to tell me until she had seen the X-ray, a common procedure in pregnancy in those days, and sent me off to see a radiologist friend of hers. I can still hear that doctor telling me that he wanted to take a second X-ray, since the first was not as good as he had hoped. I remember inquiring innocently, "Can you see the position of the baby?" whereupon he answered brusquely, "Of course I can. You've got two in there!" At this, I asked him to let me go with the one picture he had already taken and went back to Maisons Laffitte in a state of shock. Vonnic herself had given birth to twins, and I felt sure it would not happen twice in the family. I just kept going over the radiologist's words in my head. I couldn't think straight at all. Where would they sleep? How on earth were we going to manage? What would Bob say? He was already on his way home on the *Queen Elizabeth* and although telephoning a ship at sea was quite difficult, I did manage to have two minutes' conversation with him to give him the news. In a letter posted in Cherbourg, he told me that he had been stunned for a couple of hours, that he did not sleep a wink that night but assured me of his love:

> I love you and feel that you are my one and only possible partner in life. You have changed so much in the past three years that it's hardly believable. You have already given me so much of you, so much happiness and purpose in life. I promise you, darling, that we shall buy our house as soon as you are back.

In the event, things were not quite as easy as that. I went into labor early, then had a long and difficult confinement and finally went into postnatal syncope, which left me very weak, but the three of us pulled through the ordeal. The girl twins, Christine and Isabel, were six weeks premature and weighed around four pounds each. Hearing the news, Bob hired a small plane and traveled from Croydon to Le Bourget the next day, but since the twins had been safely delivered and I was in good hands, he decided to go back to London. Three weeks later, he visited us again as he drove to Frankfurt and Berlin. It was after this visit that disaster struck when the twins were taken ill with toxicosis. They were unable to keep any food down and were rapidly becoming more and more dehydrated. In two days they lost a whole pound each in weight. Bob was in constant touch with me by phone, and when he heard how serious matters were, cut short his business trip and raced back to Paris. My sister had told him that there was only one doctor who could save them, Professor Lamy at the Children's Hospital in Paris. Bob immediately tried to get in touch with him, only to discover that he was away on holiday. With some difficulty, he eventually managed to locate this famous pediatrician, explained the urgency and agreed to fetch him from his country home and bring him to the clinic. From there, Bob rushed us all to the Children's Hospital at 100 miles an hour over the cobbled streets of Paris with the police in hot pursuit. They did stop us, but when they realized that we were racing to the hospital against the clock, they led us through the traffic, with sirens blaring. As soon as we arrived, Professor Lamy dispensed with all the red tape of registration and the twins were immediately given injections of Aureomycin, a common enough antibiotic today, but at the time only just available to hospitals. They were then put into oxygen tents and all we could do was wait. I cried my eyes out while they remained on the danger list. Thankfully, they did survive, although they had to stay in special care for two months. Bob's intervention definitely saved their lives.

Once the twins were well and truly on the mend, I left the children behind with Marion and set off for England to furnish and supervise the redecoration of the house that Bob had just bought in Surrey. He had found Broomfield, where we would live for the next ten years. It was a superb Georgian-style modern house, set in four acres of landscaped gardens in the smart suburb of Esher, part of the stockbroker belt. It seemed ideal for us; there were good schools nearby, nice neighbors, frequent trains to London with a travel time of only twenty minutes and Northolt Airport, in the light traffic of the day, was a bare forty minutes away. It was such a relief to have a real home of our own at last. We paid a deposit from our savings and took out a combined mortgage and life insurance policy, which ran for the next twenty years.

The deposit on the house had taken nearly all our savings, so we had to be careful in furnishing it. In addition, England was still in the grip of postwar austerity; only limited supplies of newly manufactured goods were available for the home market, so you had to keep your eyes open for secondhand furniture or export rejects. That was when I met Raymond Shard of Davies and Sons, owner of an antique furniture business in Tottenham Court Road. He had just lost his father and, still very young, had inherited a business which was just picking up after the war. I went into his shop one day looking for a small armchair. This first encounter was to be the beginning of a long and fruitful association.

I had seen a few reasonably priced pieces of furniture I liked and took Bob with me to the shop to have a look at them. He liked my choice and went on to tell the proprietor, "Mr. Shard, my wife likes you, so I want to do business with you. She has good taste, you have good furniture. I can pay you a sum on account, but you'll have to wait till next year for the balance. Is it a deal?" It was. Much later, when I asked Raymond why he hadn't shown us the door forthwith, he told me that my husband's magnetism and self-assurance had given him an instinctive feeling of confidence that here "was a man of the future." Bob then left me to make my final selection with the words, "Good-bye and get on with it," and we did.

Raymond was a superb draftsman and designer and had a remarkable knowledge of antique furniture for such a young man. Later on, I added a new dimension to his business when I introduced him to some artist friends in Paris and launched him in interior design. Over the forty years that we "got on with it," he helped me to furnish and decorate more than thirty houses, flatshouses, flats and offices where Bob and I lived and worked during that period. Raymond and I have often thought back to that first meeting and still laugh about it today. It was Raymond again who supervised my move into the two-bedroom house where I am temporarily living in London, lending me some of his own furniture to add a touch of the elegance to which he knew I was accustomed.

By December 1950, the house was ready for occupation and the family all returned to England. It was a delightful home, sparsely furnished, but that was going to be remedied in the New Year when my parents gave us some pieces of furniture that had been in my family for decades. The house was welcoming and warm, with large bay windows letting the sunlight stream in, and it was surrounded by a large, safe garden, where the children could play to their heart's content. By then I had five children under the age of five and only Marion by way of staff. We had our hands really full, especially with twin babies, but work never frightened me and we just coped with everything. We were happily married, our business was growing nicely and Bob could at last try to put the loss of his family behind him as he lavished care and love on me and the children. I knew that we would be happy at Broomfield.

5

We were impatient to gather our brood around us in our new home, so we decided to bring them back to England in time for Christmas. I set off for France intending to get everything packed and organized, and then Bob joined me on December 10 to drive us all back to England. The huge Cadillac was a blessing. Marion and I sat in the back seat, each holding one of the twins, and Philip was sandwiched in between us. Michael and Anne sat in the front seat (which was allowed in those days), and all the bags and cases were piled up in the huge luggage compartment and pushed into every available corner of space. The children could hardly contain their excitement. They had been away for several months, were overjoyed to see Bob and myself—and were longing to see Broomfield.

We left early in the morning, crossed the Channel at Dunkirk and reached Esher around teatime. I had worked extremely hard on the organization of this large new home. When we arrived there, it was just as I had hoped and anticipated. The children stepped over the threshold and instantly loved the house and the rooms I had chosen for them. Overnight, the pitter-patter of children, their laughs, shouts and high spirits brought the house alive. It was to be a happy home, and I know that the older children remember it with love.

That first Christmas at Broomfield was of great significance for us and set the pattern for all our future family Christmases. Since the days of my own childhood in La Grive, I had indelible memories of the magic of Hans Christian Andersen's fairy tales. My godfather had given me an illustrated edition of his stories one Christmas; it was a huge tome and I could barely lift it, but it had made a tremendous impression on me. I knew almost all the stories by heart and the picture of a happy family gathered around an illuminated Christmas tree, just like the one at La Grive is still imprinted on my mind. It was that special magic that I wanted to re-create for my children. Bob took an almost childish delight in helping me in all my plans. Even though its religious significance was not part of his tradition, Christmas was the Christian festival he was most ready to accept. For the two of us as a couple, it was also a significant time of year: we had celebrated our first Christmas together during the war just before our engagement, then there was the famous Christmas of the goose in The Clock House, then our Christmas in Berlin with our first-born son, Michael. That was when we had acquired our first Christmas decorations—silver bells on strings of tinsel and a little wax angel with wisps of blond curly hair, robed in gold-pleated paper and holding a lantern. Our third Christmas after our marriage had been spent in France, awaiting the arrival of our first daughter, Anne, and the next year we had celebrated in London, with a little Christmas tree set up in the drawing room for our toddlers. But because we had moved so many times, we had not yet established a family Christmas tradition of our own, which I was longing to do.

There were only two weeks to go before Christmas and—even though I say it myself—I worked miracles in that short time. I set up a lovely Christmas tree just inside the drawing room door and dressed it with new baubles and decorations I had bought specially for the occasion. But I also made sure to use the Berlin silver bells and the little angel on the very top of the tree, which were to figure on every one of our Christmas trees until the last one we decorated, in Oxford in 1989. The children looked eagerly for them every year; the tree would not have been the same without them.

Then I began the tradition of taking the children to see Father Christmas at Harrods. I would also bake a Christmas cake and make the Christmas pudding, which—in true English fashion—I later learned to make two months in advance. I bought nuts, oranges, tangerines and dates. Some dishes I prepared in traditional French style—goose liver and turkey with chestnut stuffing, just as it had been done in my family for generations. I bought chocolate, sweets and crystallized fruits. I chose toys for the children: a first tricycle for Michael, a baby doll for Anne so that she could play mother as we looked after the twins, a cuddly teddy bear for Philip, whose fur he took to plucking off until it was quite bald. Even when Philip's godfather, Uncle Lange, gave him a brand-new one, that mangy teddy bear was affectionately retained. On Christmas Eve, Bob arrived home laden with drinks. Everything was ready for our first real family Christmas in our own home.

For Bob, I had found a beautiful pullover and a pair of furry gloves. He gave me a dangling gold charm bracelet, full of symbolic and sentimental associations—a donkey carrying a pair of heavy baskets, which evoked for Bob the burden he was shouldering for us all; a fish swimming endlessly inside a little circle, which reminded him of his favorite Pisces constantly encircling her brood; a Huguenot cross and a star of David. Later, on his many travels, he would buy me gold charms to add to my bracelet—or to commemorate an event of personal significance. Most of the charms he bought me then were much more elaborate—they had a chime or a light, or they opened and closed. I am sure that Bob had as much fun buying them as I had receiving them, but eventually the bracelet became so heavy that I had to ask him to switch to buying costume jewelry brooches, which I have always loved.

That first Christmas at Broomfield, I was so busy with cooking preparations that I decided to leave the presents until late on Christmas Eve. I can still see myself with Marion, waiting till the children were all safely asleep before starting to wrap the gifts. It was to become the pattern for many years to come. As the years passed and the family, staff and acquaintances grew in number, I cannot recall a single Christmas without whole nights spent completing all the festive preparations. On Christmas Eve, the children would ask Daddy for his socks and hang them up in great excitement.

On Christmas morning, very early, we would hear shouts of delight as the children discovered their stockings filled with tiny presents and tangerines, followed by little footsteps going down to the drawing room to see whether Father Christmas had left any presents. Then we would all have breakfast, put on our best clothes and sit around the Christmas tree. I would read St. Luke's story of the birth of Jesus in Bethlehem (later on, Michael, then Anne, would read from the Bible), we would sing Christmas carols and then the children rushed to the tree, ready to distribute the presents. It was all very joyous, very warm, the best memories we have as a family. The children played with their new toys until lunchtime when we all gathered in the dining room, suitably decorated with holly and mistletoe. We would start with smoked salmon and foie gras garnished with truffles. Then I would bring in the turkey on a platter and carve it at the table. Bob would always be given a whole leg, enough to fill his plate completely, and he would pick it up and grip it in his hand, tackling it like the Henry VIII we saw on film. At this, the children would roar with delight. Bob would soon revert to using a knife and fork, but we all had a good laugh, and it became a ritual family joke. He would serve us with German wine to accompany the foie and French red wine with the turkey. When we all had done justice to this sumptuous fare, we would draw the curtains and the Christmas pudding would be set alight. We would savor its rich fruitiness with traditional rum and butter sauce and wash it down with a glass of champagne in the lovely flute glasses that my parents had given us.

There would just be time to rush to the study to hear the King's speech on the radio (or, in later years, the Queen on television). We would sit around the hearth with the children on the carpet in front of the log fire. When the royal speech was over, we would all go out for a walk, coming back in time for tea, and then Bob would play riotous games of his own invention with the children. The two best-loved were called Rouscous and Wolfie, but Wolfie was the absolute favorite. By that time the house would be dark and Daddy would play the part of the big bad wolf. All the children would scuttle off to hide somewhere in the house and Bob would prowl around, searching until he found their hiding places—then the children would squeal with pleasure as he scooped them up in his arms and literally "ate them up" with kisses.

Rouscous was a more complex game, and I never quite understood the ins and outs of its rules, which I am sure they made up as they went along. But the children understood it—or pretended to—and adored it. I would generally excuse myself from Wolfie and Rouscous so that I could have a little rest away from all the excitement, leaving father and children having a whale of a time. Later on, when we moved to Oxford, those games developed on a grand scale, and if we had guests for Christmas, they would be roped in, too. The whole house would reverberate with the laughter of the adults and slightly mystified guests and the shrieks of the younger children. Not quite understanding exactly what was happening, those little ones would run up and down, bemused and a little anxious at the thought of being devoured by Wolfie. Those Christmas games certainly brought father and children closer in those earlier years when they were not as frightened of him as they would be later on.

So the pattern was set in Broomfield—largely by me—for all the

Christmases of the rest of our married life. Bob simply loved it all. I think it was one of the rare occasions when he became a child again. Over the years, the ritual for the festivities became absolutely sacrosanct and the family was reluctant to introduce even the smallest changes to the tradition. I did add a few new features: the Christmas tree became bigger and bigger, the decorations and presents more lavish, but I was never allowed to forget anything. Even when they were grown-ups with families of their own, the children would still look for the Berlin silver bells on their bits of tinsel, by now tarnished and pathetic-looking, and the little old angel with her lantern that my eldest sons had managed to equip with a tiny electric bulb.

On Boxing Day, Bob would always go to a football match. In those days, offices worked normally in the week before New Year, which was not then a bank holiday, so Bob would go back to London, although we generally spent New Year's Eve together, dancing or going to a show. He would be at home for New Year's Day and then invariably set off on his travels.

The festivities were hardly over after that first Christmas at Broomfield before Bob left for Germany and Berlin. Bob's travels played such a major role in our lives that I feel the need to look more closely at them—at their pattern, purpose and results. Were they prompted by sheer wanderlust, or—as some writers would have us believe—by other more sinister motives? Many are the fictions about Bob's life which aim for the sensational so loved by readers of the popular press, playing to the lowest common denominator and reaching for the easiest explanation of his many trips abroad—he had to be a spy. But those authors lacked the ability or knowledge to plunge back into the atmosphere of the early postwar years and remember the scale of opportunities available to those intelligent enough to see them. Nor do they give any credit to a man who undoubtedly had an unusual breadth of vision in those days. It made a better story for their readers to have the hero turned villain before the appointed time—even if it were all lies.

Before 1949, Bob's traveling was largely confined to Europe. On the one hand, he was doing business as a bookseller, importing German scientific books to Britain for export to the rest of the world; on the other he was trading and bartering in commodities needed by the entire world after the war. By the time we moved to Broomfield in 1950, he had made more than fifty trips, mainly on behalf of Springer Verlag, to Germany, Austria, France and Switzerland. If you add to those journeys two trips to New York and a trip to Japan, he had been away from home for half of all those years.

The early 1950s witnessed a real upsurge in Bob's business activities. By then he had signed further distribution contracts and was acting as official export agent for the books and journals of Wilhelm Ernst and Sohn, J. F. Bergman of Munich, Walter de Gruyter & Co., Urban and Schwarzenberg and Verlag Chemie GmbH, as well as Springer Verlag, of course. Before Lange Maxwell & Springer (LMS) came into being on September 1, 1949, founded in partnership with Springer Verlag, all these early contracts were signed with EPPAC, but they were soon transferred under the umbrella of LMS. To these initial agreements were added others with clients such as Standard Chemie AG, now operating from Basel, as well as the Johnson Reprint Corporation of America, Butterworth Scientific of the UK and other European and American companies who were now ready to import or export but were hampered by the complicated legislation in force at the time. LMS, however, already understood its mysterious complexities and had the advantage of leading the field. From that point onwards, EPPAC was gradually phased out, although it did retain some activity because it was the holder of the precious original import-export license, difficult to obtain in those days before trade with Germany and Europe was freed of all restrictions. Those stalwart early employees of EPPAC were in no doubt as to the impending death of the company. "De mortuis nil nisi bene"— do not speak ill of the dead—commented my old friend Baxter, the day after the new company was launched, but they soon transferred their loyalty and enthusiasm to the new company, LMS.

Bob's indefatigable work to build up his LMS catalog of books and journals, his skill as a salesman and nonstop traveling, all combined to increase his sales turnover from £250,000 in 1949 to £600,000 in 1950. His catalogs were carefully compiled by a learned old Czech professor and bookworm called Niderlechner, who always reminded me of a wizened Merlin! Those catalogs offered precisely the books and periodicals that scientists outside Germany, researching in the fields of chemistry, mathematics, medicine, physics, and other sciences, were desperate to lay their hands on and research libraries would pay handsomely for.

As early as 1946, the British government had shown great interest in German science and had set up a top-level scientific advisory committee to encourage aggressive and effective British scientific publishing to rival Germany's Springer Verlag, and at the same time learn and borrow from their editorial expertise and sales techniques. So it was that Butterworth, an established British publishing firm, was encouraged to foster these aims and started two publishing companies. The first was Butterworth Scientific Publications and the second, more relevant to our story, was called Butterworth Springer, founded in April 1949 as a joint venture with Ferdinand Springer, with the help of his former editor Dr. Paul Rosbaud. It soon became clear, however, that both Butterworth and Springer were ambivalent about their joint venture. Butterworth was required to invest considerable capital without guarantee of profitability, and also felt that Springer had the most advantageous part of the deal. On the Springer side, there were reservations about sharing control of English-language publishing. In addition, both sides were now dealing with Bob because LMS was the distributor of Butterworth Springer publications, so that he had influence and leverage both with the new company and with Springer. In any event, Butterworth wanted out and began to consider disposing of their interest in the company.

Protracted negotiations between all the parties were then held. One of the intermediaries was Count Frederick (Fanny) vanden Heuvel, who was chief of the Secret Intelligence Service (SIS) station in Geneva and a Count of the Holy Roman Empire, a character who reappears later in our story. In this context, however, he poped up in the negotiations because he had been responsible for the acquisition of a remarkable scientific journal called *Spectrochimica Acta* from the Vatican and also knew Charles Hambro of Hambro Bank, who had originally lent money to set up the Butterworth Springer venture.

Sir Charles Hambro, a member of a distinguished line of bankers who had emigrated from Denmark to Norway, was the first head of the Scandinavian Section of the Special Operations Executive (SOE) until 1942. He was a tall imposing man, athletic and broad-shouldered; he had great charm and was immensely likable. He would put you at ease immediately, taking time to hear what you had to say, never displaying impatience. He was not known to have any enemies, a rare attribute in the City, where his memorial service had to be held in St. Paul's, so great was the number of people who wanted to pay their respects. Hambro had already met Paul Rosbaud in Berlin just after the war; but it was vanden Heuvel who introduced Bob to Charles. There was an immediate rapport between the two men, and Charles demonstrated his confidence in Bob's ability not only by entrusting him with money without any guarantee when he started up in business but by rescuing him later with a much greater sum of money, at a time when no one in the City was prepared to help. Legends in the City about Charles's first encounter with Bob are legion, but some eyewitnesses are still alive to tell the real story. Charles apparently listened to Bob for a quarter of an hour without interrupting him, then called for a subordinate and ordered a checkbook to be given to him, with a facility to draw up to £25,000. A former legal liaison officer of the bank who was present at that momentous meeting, told me, "Bob always appeared to know where he was going. He seemed to foresee the questions and answered them precisely, explaining how he proposed to get there. He'd thought out the whole journey from start to finish." Charles's death in 1963, at the age of sixty-six, was a personal blow to Bob. He had immense respect for him and at a stroke had lost a good friend, a financial mentor and wise and respected advisor who was able to influence his thoughts and actions.

Butterworth finally agreed to sell their interest in Butterworth Springer to Bob. In 1951, with the help of Hambro's bank and family money lent by my father and Uncle Nathan in America, Bob paid £13,000 for Butterworth's shares in Butterworth Springer. He became managing director and the name of the company was first changed to Parthenon Press, but when it was discovered that this name was already in use, the name Pergamon Press was finally adopted, along with a colophon depicting the face of Athena, goddess of wisdom, found on a coin at Herakleia. The name seemed particularly appropriate: the famous library of Pergamon had literally saved the knowledge of the Mediterranean world after a disastrous fire had destroyed the library of Alexandria in C.E. 200. As far as Butterworth was concerned, they were glad to conclude the sale. Perhaps, however, they may have begun to regret their decision when Paul Rosbaud joined forces with Bob as Pergamon's scientific director, followed by who, then Eric Buckley, another of their employees, became Pergamon's production manager. As part of his negotiations with Springer, Bob had acquired the Springer Verlag share in the joint company. The net result was to give Bob a controlling holding of 75 percent in Pergamon Press, the other 25 percent being held by Rosbaud.

Dr. Paul Rosbaud was an Austrian scientist who had been working as an editor for Springer Verlag when war broke out. His position in the publishing firm had brought him into contact with many top-level scientists, not only in Germany but throughout Europe. He was a highly intelligent man and an inspired editor with an extensive knowledge of the scientific research in progress at the time. He counted amongst his friends or acquaintances Otto Hahn, Lise Meitner and Max Born in Germany, Niels Bohr in Denmark, Victor Goldschmidt and Odd Hassel in Norway, Sir John Cockcroft in England and the Russian Peter Kapitza whom he had known in Cambridge along with the entire Rutherford laboratory team, including recent immigrants from Germany—Rudolf Peïerls, Otto Frisch and many other present and future Nobel Laureates.

He was a most intriguing and remarkable man, who, "like Raoul Wallenberg, saw the evil of their time, struck against it and were almost forgotten."[1] I do regret that at the time I knew him, I had no inkling of his enormously courageous activities as a self-appointed spy during the war for Britain and the Allies. Had I known then of his involvement in a far-reaching spy network that passed on scientific and armament information, I would have found it easier to understand and accept some of the less attractive facets of his personality. But it was only very much later that I read about how he had perfected his alibi in Berlin as a high-ranking Nazi officer, often seen in uniform, womanizing and enjoying Berlin's famous night life and decadent "high society." At the same time, as scientific advisor at Springer Verlag, he was also visiting his scientist friends in their laboratories, finding out what they were working on.

In 1938, Rosbaud had been instrumental in publishing Otto Hahn and Fritz Strassmann's paper describing nuclear fission in Springer's journal *Naturwissenschaften,* so that the non-Nazi scientific world would have access to this latest research in full. The new age of nuclear energy had begun and Rosbaud had certainly played a part in bringing it forward. He had had the foresight and courage to publish the paper before the German military had realized its significance, probably before any other scientist had grasped the vast destructive potential of Hahn and Strassmann's discoveries.

In his book on the subject, Arnold Kramish claims that intelligence supplied by Paul also contributed to the Allied decisions to carry out the successful 1943 bombing raid on the V2 rocket manufacturing site at Pennemunde. His exploits were in fact so audacious and his double life so credible that he was also able to save many Jews from deportation and smuggle Jewish scientists to safe havens. At the time of the July 1944 plot against Hitler, he escaped discovery thanks to the help of a well-known Nazi officer. Paul had a sixth

---

1. Arnold Kramish, *The Griffin: The Greatest Untold Espionage Story of World War II* (Boston: Houghton Mifflin, 1985), p. 17. I am greatly indebted to this well-researched book for information on World War II British and Norwegian intelligence services, and to the author for our subsequent talks.

sense that helped him to be in the right place at the right time—or to leave it before danger struck. At the end of the war, he was nearly taken prisoner by the Russians, but was spirited out of Berlin under the cloak of a British army uniform and secretly flown to England.

All spies who worked on behalf of Britain were, of course, sworn to perpetual secrecy, and most of the information now available on Rosbaud has been gathered from other countries or by piecing together information from his family or friends. Paul himself never breathed a word about it, or if he did, it was in such veiled terms that it shed no light on the mystery. Even when the SIS files are finally opened, it is doubtful whether there will be much to substantiate his enigmatic life. Equally, Britain could never recognize or acknowledge his heroism, and he died in January 1963 an embittered and impoverished man, leaving his wife in great need—for although he was a brilliant scientist, he was a hopeless businessman, uninterested in money. The many people he had helped during the war remember him well, but he was completely forgotten and unrewarded by the country which owed him so much.

Until the mid-1950s, Bob and Paul were very close. I can still see Paul, curled up in one of our armchairs in Addison Crescent, plotting the future with Bob. They would talk until the early hours of the morning and I would fall asleep in the same room, only to be woken later by the sounds of their laughter and the pair of them babbling away in German. I would then give them some sustenance in the form of appetizing sandwiches or savories, accompanied by coffee or spirits. Bob was never a heavy drinker, but Paul could gulp down a whole bottle of gin in one evening. I found it hard to believe how much he could get through and still remain compos mentis; alas, it would greatly damage his health in later years. Like all those I knew who were actively engaged in intelligence work during the war, he was very secretive and tight-lipped. When he was really drunk, he would be slightly more forthcoming, but he never revealed any secrets from his past.

He certainly enjoyed Bob's company and there is no doubt, whatsoever, that Bob owed a great deal of his scientific understanding of the postwar and nuclear era, as well as some of his early insights into scientific editing and publishing standards, to Rosbaud. Like Paul, Bob was a strategist, and their combined insights as to where scientific discoveries would take the world in the third millennium were quite extraordinary. Many a time, I felt as if I was hearing a lost work of H. G. Wells, when Paul would sit, his narrow eyes half-closed, pondering Bob's latest extravagant vision of the new atomic miniaturized world. Paul introduced Bob to many of the great scientists of the day, some of whom we would become closely acquainted with. Paul also cleared Bob in the worlds of the SIS, SOE and XU (Resistance Intelligence Organization), allowing him to cooperate at the height of the cold war with scientists involved in top-secret work on both sides of the Atlantic and behind the Iron Curtain. As two of Pergamon's early authors observed in the forti-eth-anniversary history of the press, Bob and Rosbaud together formed an "excellent complementary pair, Bob with his entrepreneurial ability and a degree of single-mindedness that preceded the days of his wider interests and Rosbaud a renowned scientist who com-manded the respect of academics."[2] Paul's daughter, Angela, came to work for Bob and stayed for many years as an assistant in his office. She was good at her job at Pergamon, and I know that Bob's support helped her to settle down to proper and regular work, overcoming the serious psychological problems which had resulted from her par-ents' estrangement, her original move to England as a little girl, her separation from her father during the war years and subsequent tense relationship with him. Immensely kind and loyal, Angela became a personal friend of my family, and it made me sad to learn that she died prematurely a few years ago.

Although Pergamon was later to play a dominant role in both our lives and Bob recognized that it held the key to his future. In the early 1950s, however, he was so involved in creating capital in the other side of his business, in part to provide adequate financing for the publishing house, that he was unable to give it his undivided attention. As things turned out, Bob was to find himself extensively occupied with bookselling matters from 1951 to 1955 and was con-tent to keep his finger on the pulse through his frequent evening dis-cussions with Rosbaud. In the early fifties, however, Pergamon Press was a small-scale operation with a small share capital; yet starting with the original Butterworth Springer list of only five book titles and three journals, it went on to build up a high-quality list with futher textbooks and an important new journal, *Chemical Engineer-ing Science.*

Bob's bookselling activities with LMS were growing rapidly worldwide, especially in the Far East—in Singapore, Hong Kong,

---

2. Contribution of Professor J. Richardson and Professor J. Coulson, *Robert Maxwell and Pergamon Press* (London: Pergamon Press, 1988), p. 199.

Tokyo and China, which was then one of our largest customers. In fact, this trade consisted mainly of successful reselling of what is known in the business as antiquaria. In the early fifties, useful science reference books and valuable back issues of research journals were mostly no more than fifty years old, and Bob started to create his own antiquaria department, either by purchasing private collections or by printing excess copies of Pergamon titles. He was, of course, also selling Springer's collections, the proceeds of which were to give Ferdinand the necessary capital to rebuild his own empire. Rosbaud had helped Springer to save the precious antiquaria he had stored in a castle in Bavaria and handled the transfer of those valuable collections to the West, where they were kept in our warehouses. I recall row upon row of neatly stacked German books, impeccably cataloged by the learned Czech staff who were well aware of the value of what looked like piles of worthless paperbacks. Immediately after the war, the world had been deprived of the results of German scientific research and was keen to make up for lost opportunities. I remember orders for large sums of money from Guozi Shudian in China, and I have in my scrapbook a photocopy of a check for £25,000—the equivalent of £250,000 today. Our excellent relationship with the Chinese survived even the Gang of Four's coup, and when in 1979 I entertained for a second time Mr. Cao Jianfei, director of Guozi Shudian, whom Bob had first met in 1955, he brought with him records of our longstanding commercial relations, showing transactions between us to the last penny.

Apart from an early foray into Germany's Russian zone in February 1947 to attend the Leipzig Book Fair, contrary to all the rubbish printed about my husband's alleged links with the KGB, Bob did not travel behind the Iron Curtain until 1951. In that year, he went to Belgrade with Peter Orton to buy 1,190 copies of a scientific book recommended by Springer, *The Atlas of Operative Thoracoscopy*, for which we became sole agents worldwide. He did not make his first visit to Moscow until 1953, but after that would go roughly once a year for the rest of the decade. It was a time when Russian scientists were starting to travel again to meet their counterparts in the West, and UK researchers were urging the renewal of the scientific cooperation that had existed with the Russians before the war. There is no doubt that Bob showed great foresight in these early contacts with Russia. He was convinced that the West was making a serious error of judgment in underestimating the value of Soviet research in many fields and had already resolved to start a major program of translation of their books and journals, which was much appreciated on both sides of the Iron Curtain. When, on October 1, 1957, the Russians launched their Sputnik into space, the world was astonished, and the Americans, who for years had disparaged Russian scientific knowledge and research, were stunned. Russian successes in the space race continued. In that same year, they sent up the first animal, a dog called Laika; then in 1959 the Lunik satellite which sent back to Earth the first photos of the far side of the moon; but their greatest triumph over the Americans came in 1961 when they launched the first man into space, Yuri Gagarin. By that time, Bob had long secured the cooperation of academician Topchiev, secretary of the Russian Academy of Science, and a leading petroleum chemist. He had obtained permission for some of their best scientists' work to be translated into English and for some of Russia's eminent scholars and academicians to travel to the UK and join the editorial boards of our international series and journals. For more than a decade, the Russians had been undervalued by the scientific community of the West, so they were never to forget the man who helped to correct this misconception. Instead of looking for sinister motives for Bob's cordial relations with Russia, any serious biographer can easily trace the origin of his business relations, just as the Western scientific community did some thirty-five to forty years ago.

Bob returned to Moscow as part of a trade delegation in 1954 at a time when traveling to Russia was still a complex operation. First you had to travel to Berlin and make your way to the Russian zone; then you took a plane from the airport in the then German Democratic Republic and flew either direct to Moscow or, as in Bob's case, via Leipzig if you wanted to visit the famous Book Fair. From 1957 onwards, I accompanied my husband several times to Moscow, Leningrad, Baku, Novosibirsk and Akademgorodok. I was present at most of his meetings, taking notes of the proceedings for him, and attended all the dinners and private interviews. Not once did I hear anything but business being transacted, but if sometimes more general questions were asked, it was invariably from the Russian side. They were always interested in Bob's career and were convinced that he was in the pay of the Secret Intelligence Service, being simply unwilling to believe—until Gorbachev brought perestroika and glasnost into their lives—that anyone who was not in the pay of a government could travel freely, take decisions of major importance and decide on capital expenditure without having to ask someone's permission—or at least report on it first. The Russians took to Bob immediately. Not only could he speak their language—extremely rare for any businessman or scientist forty years ago—but for them he was the epitome of the capitalist Westerner, for which they undoubtedly had a secret hankering. For years, though, it was obvious that they kept strict tabs on his activities whilst he was in Russia. We were constantly aware of it, although it was difficult to pinpoint. We used to whisper in our bedroom at night or talk under the blankets in bed, certain that our room was bugged. As for other Iron Curtain countries, Bob first visited Hungary in 1957, Yugoslavia in 1958, Poland in 1959, Czechoslovakia in 1963, but did not go to Romania until 1980. By 1955 he was already traveling three or four times a year to America, Canada and the Far East, and as the years passed these trips would become even more frequent.

When we first lived in Esher, Bob would come back home from London every night, however late it was. Often we would set off from Broomfield for the airport and have a wonderful forty minutes together in the car without interruption. But it soon became clear that commuting every day was tiring and impractical and we decided that Bob needed a pied-à-terre in London. He then rented a service flat in Park Lane where I would join him at least once during the week or whenever we were going out to a dinner or a show. Later on, he found a one-bedroom unfurnished apartment in Three Kings' Yard, just above the archway leading to the mews behind Claridges, which we turned into a little love nest. With Raymond Shard's help, I furnished it with great care and I would go there twice a week, leaving home by train after the children had had their baths. It was a peculiar time in our lives. I felt as if I was making clandestine visits to my lover! We would go out for dinner, then dance till the early hours at the Ambassadors' Club in London, rubbing shoulders with the heartthrobs of cinema and theater—Clark Gable, Marlene Dietrich, Humphrey Bogart, Rita Hayworth and Margaret Lockwood—who all seemed much less dazzling in the flesh. The trouble was that Bob traveled so much that even those rather glamorous visits were irregular and too few.

The future augured well, however, and except for the usual daily struggles, life was proceeding smoothly. Bob had all the excitement he needed in his efforts to build up his business and remain on top of his work, in spite of all the ups and downs which were the hallmark of the postwar world economy. Invariably, something unforeseen would result from his travels or he would meet new and fascinating people. On one of his journeys to America, for instance, he was traveling on the liner S.S. *United States* and met Senator Benton, president of Encyclopaedia Britannica, in a bar. He took a liking to Bob and it was to be the start of a long and fruitful relationship. The senator invited Bob to a cocktail party on board the liner to meet the then president of the United States, Harry S Truman, and his wife. This encounter was to lead to other meetings with the president and his daughter, Margaret, a coloratura singer whose help Bob later sought in some charitable work. All his life, Bob seemed to have an uncanny knack of meeting interesting people purely by chance, who in turn introduced him to their friends. Outside the scientific community that he mostly met through his work for Pergamon Press, Bob built up an amazing circle of acquaintances, purely on this kind of chain reaction.

As his schoolteachers had discovered, he had a prodigious memory, which served him well until the latter years of his life. He would remember names, faces, the most minute details of a conversation, and he possessed amazing store of data gleaned from his constant reading or talks with people from all walks of life. Bob always insisted on seeing copies of all Pergamon publications and later on kept the major reference works in his office. His reading of Pergamon journals and books supplemented the knowledge of scientific fields and trends that he acquired from his contacts with editors and his own awareness of competitors' activities. Even if he did not understand the intricacies of the scientific research described in the articles, he would try to grasp its key aspects; where it was leading, why it was being carried out and who would benefit from it. He was quick to pick up concepts and jargon from the scientists themselves and alert to new opportunities for publishing projects involving international scientific collaboration. If it was a subject which fascinated him—and many did—the next time he met the author or editor of the journal, he would ask for further explanation.

Whenever Bob attended congresses or symposia and met new authors, they were often surprised by the extent of his knowledge in their field and would sometimes ask him which university he had attended. I heard him asked that question a number of times. Exactly the same happened in the trading business: if he was selling cement, wood houses or dyes, he would learn all he could about his products so he was able to talk knowledgeably on most of the subjects he was dealing with. Of course, he had no classical culture, so there were gaping holes in his knowledge, and he would readily accept that literature and the arts both fell into this category. He did not generally like novels, but loved biographies and history, particularly analyses of the two world wars, Greek philosophy, and political thought. On holiday, however, he would devour whodunits at a fantastic rate. His knowledge of classical music was entirely self-taught; he would listen to records, later on to tapes and CDs, whenever he had a minute to himself, and his memory permitted him to do what some of us find difficult—identify the composer and title of a piece immediately, whether we were listening to Beethoven's Sonata No. 17 in D minor or the Violin Concerto No. 5 in A by Mozart, Bob's favorite composer. He had acquired this great liking for Mozart after hearing *Don Giovanni* over and over again when one of his companies, Harmony Films, was filming it in association with Paul Czinner. He also loved the Czech composers Dvorak and Smetana, the Russians Stravinsky, Shostakovich and Prokofiev, the Finn Sibelius, and the Hungarian Bela Bartok, but apart from Gershwin and Bernstein, Bob was not a fan of musicals or jazz. I introduced him to baroque music with Vivaldi and Albinoni, and French music with Debussy and Ravel, but when, on a Sunday morning, he would ask one of us to put on some music, we all knew better than to indulge our own taste.

Although in the later years of his life, no one could get a word in edgeways and he would dominate all conversation, it was not always so in the two decades immediately following the war. Bob still had everything to learn—and he knew it. But he never had much time for chitchat or small talk. If he met someone working in a field he was unfamiliar with, he would not make ordinary conversation, but would literally interrogate that person, who was generally flattered by Bob's interest. In that way, he would learn in detail, straight from the horse's mouth so to speak, all about a trade or a business or a complex financial deal. It is important to remember that when Bob began his business career he was twenty-four and the majority of the people he was doing business with were a great deal older than him. Most of them were father, if not grandfather figures: this was true of Dr. Ferdinand Springer, who was born in 1880. For this reason, Bob represented neither threat nor competition, at least not in the scientific community, for by the time you are in your sixties or seventies, you are ready to pass on your experience and knowledge to up-and-coming young people; by then you have attained "mentor status." So for thirty years Bob was able to benefit from the know-how of countless older people—especially scientists—until his turn came to pass on what he knew to the younger generation when they came to seek his advice. In the last decade of his life, he gave generously of his time and knowledge, and numerous people sent him letters expressing their gratitude for his help and counsel.

Not a day of his life would pass without Bob reading from cover to cover various newspapers and weekly magazines from several countries. He would then tear out any articles of interest and pass them on to his staff for filing under an appropriate keyword of his own choice. As far back as I can remember, the only time either of us stayed in bed much after seven in the morning was on Sundays—and even then I could not really sleep because of the constant paper-tearing going on beside me. It was as if a rodent was at work! I used to find it exasperating, but tolerated it as best I could because I considered it part of Bob's education. Through this daily reading, he acquired a formidable general knowledge and became extremely well informed on politics and foreign affairs, both of which fascinated him, as well as technology and business opportunities. Until the last years of his life, he was able to draw at will on this vast personal data bank and, combined with his analytical turn of mind and unusual capacity for synthesis, would often use it to devastating effect in conversations.

In this respect, the 1950s were formative years for Bob: his thirst for knowledge and his ability to use and apply it were exciting to watch. In those days, he could be enormous fun to be with; his enthusiasm for life seemed to know no bounds. You never knew what to expect next from his inventive mind—but invariably he would come up with something to sort out, redress or change a situation.

He also received some terrific knocks, mostly because he acted rashly and tended to plunge headlong into things without fully considering their consequences. Whilst his instincts may have been correct, he would always put too much trust in people's ability to see matters his way and carry the plan through. It would take him some years to understand how difficult it is to lead people in the right direction and keep them there, for people are inclined to take the line of least resistance and many are fickle. They prefer the words of the soothsayer to those of the prophet, especially when it is a question of swallowing a painful truth and knuckling under a more demanding solution for a while. It was also the first time Bob realized how full of sharks the business world was and how the close-knit "establishment" worked in cahoots for its own benefit, with a ruthlessness difficult to match anywhere in the world—determined to keep outsiders out at all costs.

When Bob made the decision in May 1951 to invest his money in Pergamon Press, he may well have realized that the kind of import-export deals and bartering he was doing would come to an inevitable end one day, as would the favorable bookselling terms he had with the Germans. As part of the deal to acquire Springer's share in Butterworth Springer, LMS had had to give up its worldwide monopoly in distributing Springer's publications. Pergamon Press, though promising, was still small at the time. At this point a completely unsuspected offer came Bob's way when John Whitlock, co-managing director of Butterworth and a business colleague whom he had originally met through vanden Heuvel and Hambro, approached him with a proposition which sounded tempting, a challenge Bob was unable to refuse. Whitlock introduced Bob to Jim and Chris Pitman, owners of Sir Isaac Pitman & Sons Ltd., the well-known publishers and printers who were also running Simpkin Marshall.

Between the wars, Simpkin Marshall was the British book wholesaler par excellence. It then held sufficient stocks of all important publishers' lists to be able, so the company claimed, to meet all single-copy and small-value orders from booksellers. Its slogan was a proud one: "Anything that's in print, we've got in stock." But it received a fatal blow in December 1940 when its premises were hit by a German bomb, destroying four million books. The Pitman brothers, one of the largest publishers at the time, were talked into rehousing the firm in one of their warehouses and took on this albatross as a service to the trade, because such a clearinghouse seemed essential for efficient book distribution. By 1950, after losing a great deal of money in the operation, they had had enough and decided to avoid liquidation by offering the company for sale as a going concern. They needed a white knight. The dashing twenty-eight-year-old Maxwell seemed to fit the bill to perfection. Most British publishers were keen that Simpkin should continue, because it offered a service which they themselves could not possibly afford to give. The publisher Stanley Unwin strongly encouraged Bob to take on the business, promising his full support and the cooperation of the major publishing houses, and agreeing that a larger discount on their books was necessary if Simpkin was to run profitably.

Before making any final decision, Bob asked his accountants to investigate the company. They concluded Simpkin could become profitable, notwithstanding the large sums owing to the Pitman brothers and other creditors, provided it had the full cooperation of publishers. This was promised and that was how Bob was led to believe that he could make it work: he signed on the dotted line. A financial agreement was reached with the Pitmans: Bob would immediately come up with £50,000 of his own money, Hambro would lend £90,000 and the rest of the debt would be reduced to a lesser sum, payable in installments over several years.

Despite the fact that they needed Simpkin services and wished the company well, the majority of publishers not only refused to increase the traditionally slender wholesale margin on the price of books but also stabbed the new enterprise in the back by offering better terms to retailers, thereby reducing their incentive to buy from Simpkin. As Arthur Coleridge, MD of Simpkin in the pre- and post-Maxwell eras, wrote to *The Bookseller,* everyone said they wanted to see the old firm prosper—as long as it wasn't at their own expense. But by then booksellers were going directly to publishers for the bulk of their worthwhile business and relying on Simpkin only for books which were difficult to obtain.

Rashly, as it turned out, Bob moved Simpkin's stock in 1954 from its cramped quarters in Rossmore Court to a larger building in Marylebone Road, a renovated brewery. It was an expensive move, and the trade union involved was not cooperative. They had at first seemed to welcome it, but the minute the books were transferred to the miles of bookshelves installed in the new premises, they asked for wage-rises from a company they knew to be in difficulties. Reluctantly, Bob had to agree.

For four long years, Bob worked like a Trojan to try and rescue Simpkin. He never drew a salary but kept on pouring money he was making on barter deals and through his other companies into this doomed enterprise. He made efforts to expand the market outside Great Britain by buying a substantial share in the British Book Center, New York, through the Conservative MP Peter Baker. He thought it would be a useful outlet for the vast book surplus accumulated by Simpkin (most publishers did not allow sale or return in those days) enabling the British Book Center to repay longstanding debts to British publishers. Unfortunately, none of those plans was ever realized. Peter Baker fell on hard times and Bob never recovered a personal loan he had made him, unaware of his financial troubles. In lieu of this debt, Bob acquired Baker's shares in the British Book Center, but far from helping, its financial difficulties were to bedevil us for years. Had there been less greed on the part of the publishers, a little more patience from booksellers whilst teething-troubles were sorted out and a modicum of cooperation from the unions, Britain could have had a prosperous single-copy house, run on the very successful German model.

Within three years, Simpkin was bankrupt and the creditors voted for liquidation of the company. The receivers' report catalogs the reasons for the failure and apportions the blame fairly: there was inadequate capital throughout, the trade margins were grossly insufficient for the business to be viable; neither the costly move to larger premises nor the acquisition of a shareholding in the British Book Center should have been contemplated. Finally, the report concluded, it was doubtful whether the company had been solvent at any time: it should certainly have been liquidated much earlier. The truth was that instead of selling Simpkin to Bob, the Pitman brothers should have closed it down there and then. It is no credit to the ten directors party to the sale of Simpkin, some of them famous publishers with vast experience of the market and its postwar ramifications, that they sold Bob an enterprise they knew was not viable without fundamental changes in the book trade. Everyone lost: nearly all the publishers to a greater or lesser degree, the booksellers who lost out on the single copy trade they would now have to take on themselves, the union whose stubbornness and lack of cooperation helped to lose hundreds of jobs, a host of unsecured creditors and Bob most of all. Not only did he pay a heavy price financially, but—worse still—his reputation was sullied for ever by the very people who had contributed to his failure, and who declined publicly to acknowledge their share of the guilt. Subsequent events were to show just how seriously his health had been damaged by all the worry and stress to which he was subjected.

Jim and Chris Pitman always exonerated Bob and, through the media, castigated the book trade in forceful terms for its lack of honesty and foresight. Their own rescue effort had been described as the "most unsordid act" in the history of the book trade, so they, better than anyone else, were aware of the price that they and Bob paid. They remained friends and, as a printer, Chris went out of his way in the late fifties and sixties to help Bob with Pergamon Press. It was a way of making amends for what they knew themselves had been a rotten and damaging piece of business.

Bob was to pay dearly for the poor advice he was given and the shabby deal he received at the hands of the publishers, but of course, one is always so much wiser with hindsight. He once acknowledged publicly that Simpkin Marshall was his first big business mistake. In my view, it was more than a business mistake: the saga in itself was bad enough, but it was compounded by a series of tragicomic events which brought into our lives the ubiquitous Dr. Wallersteiner, also known as Kurt Waller. This introduction, courtesy of John Whitlock, was in many ways unfortunate in that it distracted Bob from the matter at hand. With the help of Hambro and his advisors, he could possibly have found a way to force the publishers and booksellers to fulfill their promises to him, or else make the decision to close Simpkin much earlier, saving himself all the ensuing misery. The connection with Waller, however, brought with it a whole new scale of activities. Although Waller had a serious side to his character (he had studied organic chemistry in Vienna), he was responsible for some of the biggest laughs we ever had through his preposterous large-scale bartering—of which he was a past master—in the postwar period. He was a past master at it.

An Austrian by birth, Wallersteiner controlled an international group of companies, including a London merchant bank, the Anglo-Continental Exchange Ltd., and the Watford Chemical Company. As we soon discovered, he had serious cash-flow problems because all his money was tied up in goods and materials all over the world, waiting to be bartered for other commodities. His assets, although tied up in this way, were estimated at some £50 million of today's money, but he was having trouble bringing any deal to a successful conclusion and converting his goods into cash. He was looking for a bright entrepreneur with experience of the barter trade who would have the know-how to move the goods, compelling all the fly-by-nights he was trading with to come up with the money. With his problems increasing, he had confided in Whitlock. John's immediate thought was that Bob was probably the ideal person to help sort out Waller's tangled affairs. His reputation as a tough negotiator and successful postwar wheeler-dealer had preceded him. Bob and Waller met for the first time in the spring of 1953 and decided it was in both their interests to join forces. As Bob would have to devote a great deal of time to Waller's affairs while also facing the difficulty of Hambro's pressing for repayment of their loan to Simpkin, Waller agreed to take over the Hambro's debenture at a fixed interest rate for five years. For his work, Maxwell would receive 20 percent of the net profits from Waller's companies and a £50,000 advance of his fees would be paid straight away. They signed an agreement spelling out these conditions in July 1953, after which two nominees of Anglo-Continental sat on the Simpkin board. Bob himself was still dealing in various commodities which were mostly connected with barter deals. By then he had enlisted the help of Bill Hickey and Paul Lassen, two fellow officers he had met in the Control Commission, and there was a steady flow of cash resulting from a number of transactions, not all as spectacular as the earlier deals I described, but worthwhile nevertheless. But this bartering never formed any part of Bob's scientific book business, which was well taken care of by his deputy Tom Clark, Paul Rosbaud and Eric Buckley.

So it was that Bob got involved in trying to sort out Dr. Wallersteiner's messy businesses. To describe all his deals in their complexity would fill an entire, hilarious volume. They encompassed every conceivable commodity the world needed after the war—foodstuffs, chemicals, houses, building materials, household goods, clothing and office equipment. The original barter might start with Argentinian pork bellies intended for England but refused an entry permit by the Ministry of Food; they would then be shipped to Holland for canning and half the quantity sold to Austria in return for prefabricated wooden houses, which in turn would be sold to Canada. The remaining half of the canned pork would be sold to East Germany in return for cement, which was also sold to Canada for the foundations of the Austrian houses. Waller had been particularly successful in trade with China, which at the time was opening up again to foreign trade following the bitter Civil War. Bob loved telling the story of the order for 100 tons of indigo-blue dye, which through the clerical error of an inept Chinese official became 1,000 tons (roughly equaling world output at the time). The deal netted millions of pounds for Waller, not to mention condemning the Chinese to their famous blue uniforms for the next twenty years. Then there was the Chinese silk—somehow Waller managed to obtain huge shipments of Chinese silk, flooding the market in England. He even presented me with a sample bale, which because of my proverbial thrift forced me and my family to wear Chinese dresses and dressing-gowns for many years to come.

Stories of this kind, which I heard from Bob or John Whitlock, were just endless and illustrated the milieu Waller worked in: he surrounded himself with people who were all fishing in troubled waters and trading with totally unreliable characters. Bob got to the bottom of many of these affairs with his usual tremendous energy, having devised a proper plan to clean up the mess and bring the money in. First he ordered an investigation into all outstanding debts in England, then he pursued all the deals relentlessly. I still keep in my scrapbook a letter from Waller's legal advisor, which Bob passed on to me so that we could laugh about it in our old age. On Bob's initiative, one of Waller's companies, Dermine (which Bob soon nicknamed Vermin), was justifiably trying to recover some bad debts. Upon investigation, the lawyer had discovered that orders had been placed by an eighty-eight-year-old man whom he described as "an associate of thieves." He went on to say: "Through his agency, the orders were placed by fifteen individuals, none of whom carried on a proper business at all; two are now in prison and seven have police records. In my mind, there is evidence to suggest that this was a concerted attempt at relieving Dermine of several thousand pounds' worth of goods." At which the lawyer could only point out the need for proper credit control and suggested that the sums be written off as bad debts!

There was also a hilarious letter which Bob found when he was clearing out the mail of one of Waller's companies. In the later years of his life, he would always ask me to find the "schidt and rice" letter on special occasions when he tried to evoke those epic times for the younger generation. I hope my readers get as much fun out of it as we have had over the years!

(LETTER FROM GENERAL FOOD CORPORATION, GREEN RICE PURCHASING DEPARTMENT)

To: Messrs Lykes Bros Steamship Co.
Houston, Texas.

Sir,
   We quote verbatim letter received from our client, Hans Gruber Wilhelmstrasse, Hamburg, Germany:
   "Der last two schipments uf rice ve get from you on der Lykes Schip vas mit mice schidt mixt. Der rice vas gut enuff, but der mice durde schpoils der trade. Ve did not see der mice schidt in der sample vich you sent us.
   "It takes too much time to pick der mice durds from der rice. Ve order Kleen rice, und you schipt schidt mitt der rice.
   "Ve like you to schip us der rice in vun sak, und der mice schidt in anoder sak, und den ve mix to soot der customer.
   "Please rite if ve should schip back der schidt und keep der rice, or keep der schidt und schip back der rice, or schip back der whole schitten verks.
   "Ve vant to do ride in diss matter, budt ve do not diss mice schidt business like.

Mitt much respects,
HANS GRUBER.

As Bob tried to put Waller's affairs in order in his various companies, including the Watford Chemical Company (alias the Comical Company), he disturbed a great many people who thought they were safely ensconced like rats in their larders. They hated being found out and tried their hardest—at times successfully—to sow poisonous untruths about Bob in Kurt's mind. Bob had an incredible sixth sense and would follow his intuition to the very source of the mess, unfailingly putting his finger on the dubious elements in a shaky enterprise. Very soon, all those deceptive little tricks which abound in badly managed firms were brought to light. It was a pattern which was to be repeated many times throughout his business life, culminating in 1981 with the rescue of the British Printing Corporation.

Waller was a tall man, with myopic, bleary eyes. He was aloof, and I found him a difficult man to talk to, but he was a well-mannered gentle giant. Although he seemed to live perpetually in the clouds, he was undoubtedly creative and the originator of several serious money-making deals. The trouble was that he was a poor judge of character and surrounded himself either with spineless, inefficient assistants or with wily crooks he entrusted with a great deal of money. He undertook so many deals simultaneously that he could not follow them closely enough to ensure that each and every transaction was properly accounted for. On the other hand, I suppose that in the world he operated in, there were no rules. If you were bright, as he was, you made your own rules. Bob and Waller never became close friends, and Waller never came to Broomfield, even though they were business partners for two years. When Bob joined Waller and started bringing in chartered accountants, lawyers and bankers, he soon realized that in 1954 Waller was operating as if it were still 1948. By then the climate had changed completely and the whole edifice would soon crumble, with Waller himself ending up in trouble. Our connections with him stopped completely with the demise of Simpkin. Waller recovered all the money he had lent, both to Simpkin as a preferential creditor and to Bob, whom he could thank for the recovery of a large part of his frozen fortune. They parted on reasonable terms. Bob remained grateful to Waller for helping him in his efforts to save Simpkin Marshall, and if Waller felt aggrieved, he certainly forgot it with time, if I am to judge by the letter he sent me after Bob's death.

After Bob bought Simpkin in 1951 he was projected into the limelight overnight. Social invitations literally poured in from everywhere. I remember two of those early parties particularly well: one was the Booksellers' Association annual dinner and dance held in Brighton in the summer of 1952, where I first met all the book trade moguls I was to come across regularly over the next few years. That night, I felt like the belle of the ball and I was flattered when the next president of the Association, Peter Cadness Page, who was later to join our staff, personally sought me out to lead me on to the dance floor. The other very memorable party was a ball given at Dropmore by Lady Helen Berry, Viscountess Kemsley, where I met all the press barons of the time, along with members of the aristocracy and royal family, who were studiously left alone. Once you had been received in line by the hostess, you were free to roam through the palatial state rooms of that spectacular great house, meeting whoever you pleased. It was in July; the park and formal gardens were lit; there were several orchestras inside and out, drinks and food everywhere. I remember encountering Princess Marina of Kent, the Queen's aunt, sitting completely alone on a couch, with people passing by without giving her a second glance. We fell into conversation. It was the first time I had met her and at the time I had no notion of royal protocol. She had a deep velvety voice with a hint of an accent, difficult to pinpoint on first hearing. She soon discovered that I was French and we continued our conversation in my native language. It was to be the start of a special relationship with her, and later on with her daughter, Princess Alexandra, which always remained formal in nature but nevertheless gave us pleasure on our subsequent meetings. These two lovely, attractive royal ladies would later attend many charitable or cultural functions which Bob and I helped organize, and we would invariably slip into French whenever we met either of them.

The ball at Dropmore was to set my entertainment standards for life. It had a quality of extraordinary elegance, very akin to Alain Fournier's magical descriptions in *Le Grand Meaulnes,* along with a relaxed and carefree atmosphere which can only be achieved by a perfectly planned party and a great hostess. I have attended dozens of great parties in my life, but none of the others left me with that inordinate sense of pleasure and timeless perfection.

It was not long before I started to give parties at home—many informal lunches and dinners, cocktail parties, formal dinners, for which I prepared all the food myself, with the help of my cook and an au pair. Dr. Pomiane's teaching certainly came into its own then, and I would go to endless lengths to please my guests, preparing chaudfroid de poulet in aspic, salmon en gelée, lobster thermidor, turban de soles, ice cream, babas au rhum. Nothing was too much trouble and the reputation of my table really dates back to those days when the type of food I was offering, requiring two days' preparation, was virtually unknown in English private houses after the austerity of wartime. I was not actively seeking to create a good name for myself and my cuisine; I just loved doing it and believe that I kept that reputation right up until Bob's death, after which there was no call for entertaining on my part.

At first we would generally invite five or six people—an absolute maximum of twelve—which I manged on my own, but when numbers began to rise, I used to hire two waiters from Searcy's, in those days the best-known and most reliable West End caterers. Even then, we rarely entertained for the sheer pleasure of it: business was always the underlying reason. My first guests included the Springers, Tonjes Lange, the Coleridges, the directors of Butterworth and Hugh Quennell who enjoyed some prestige at Butterworth though he was, in my view, an insufferably arrogant and xenophobic Englishman of a type I have met many times since—the very people, in my opinion, responsible for the loss of the British Empire! I frequently entertained the vanden Heuvels; Harry Siepmann, the then chairman of Pergamon Press; the film director Paul Czinner and his film star wife Elizabeth Bergner; the Pitmans, executives of Hambro Bank and our lawyers, as well as partners in the early deals; Bill Berger; and the Breminers. But from 1955 onwards, we started to entertain Pergamon authors and editors, especially overseas guests who expected to be entertained—from America, Belgium, France, Norway, Holland, Sweden, Russia, Canada and Italy.

They would often come to England accompanied by their wives, and Bob would dispatch me to show the ladies some of the beauty of the English countryside. By the end of the fifties, there was barely a single monument, museum or place of interest in London I had not visited several times; barely a National Trust house, castle or park for a hundred miles around I had not explored. That was really how I came to know the south of England and Midlands so well.

Looking back on those years of frenetic activity, I wonder sometimes how I coped with so many children, a demanding husband, a career acting as a travel guide and keeping an open table! Yet as the children grew and started to attend local private schools, I would also take my turn in ferrying them to and fro. When first Michael, then Philip, became boarders at Summer Fields, a preparatory school in Oxford, there were also the two-and-a-half hour trips to and from Oxford at the beginning and end of term, at half term and visits in between. Somehow I also managed to take the girls to dancing classes and to riding lessons, where I learned to ride, too. During the holidays, I would take them all ice-skating at Richmond and would skate with them. Once a week I would go shopping at Kingston market, packing my car full of bags of potatoes, vegetables and fruit, buying as keenly as I could so as to be able to spend the savings on extra activities for the children.

Twice a year I would take them all to Harrods in London to equip them with school uniforms and other necessary items of clothing. We would spend almost the entire day there and return home exhausted, the children pleased with their new shoes and clothes and excited from running about in that enormous department store. I remember one such trip with terrifying clarity. We had finished our shopping and piled into the car, cramming it to the roof with all of us and our packages, when suddenly I realized I was one child short! I ran all the way back to Harrods in complete panic—my stomach still churns at the thought of it. But I was soon able to retrieve Philip, who had wandered off when we were not looking. Luckily, a kind and watchful assistant had spotted him, looked after him and contacted the "Lost Property" department to report his whereabouts. Philip was always a wanderer: one day, aged three, he left home on his tricycle to be found by a police patrol car as he pedaled along the Portsmouth road!

Bob and I were both living our lives to the full; we were young, healthy, in love, bursting with vitality, ambition and hopes. National events were very much part of our personal lives. Bob was deeply affected by the death of King George VI, whom he greatly respected and to whom he had sworn allegiance. I remember he stood in line for several hours to file past the King's coffin where it lay in state in Westminster Hall. Bob did not attend funerals, except those of his own family, preferring to follow Jesus' saying, "Let the dead bury the dead." But he waived this self-made rule to attend the lying-in-state of both King George and Winston Churchill, the latter embodying for Bob the spirit of resistance during the war and indomitable leadership in the struggle for freedom against the forces of evil.

We also attended the Queen's coronation procession, viewing it comfortably from a first-floor apartment in Piccadilly which also had a television set. That way, we had the best of both worlds: we missed no detail of the ceremonial transmitted on television yet were able to share in the enthusiasm, excitement and roar of the crowd just below. In that well-orchestrated pageantry, one of my clearest recollections is that of Queen Salote of Tonga, regal in an open carriage, laughing and waving to the cheering crowds beneath the pelting rain, refusing all protection from the weather until the return journey to Buckingham Palace.

The unrelenting pattern of Bob's working life was astounding. When the rescue of Simpkin was compounded by daily involvement with Waller's affairs, his travel schedule increased twofold and he worked in his office well into the night. In the normal course of events, we barely saw each other at all, so we decided in the spring of 1952 to take ten days' holiday, just the two of us, in the south of France. On Charles Hambro's recommendation, we booked into the then small and select hotel of La Réserve in Beaulieu, which also boasted a famous restaurant. In those days, the hotel had only thirteen bedrooms or suites and its privileged clients were only accepted if they were known to the owner, Mr. Pot de Fer, or personally recommended to him; once there, guests were cosseted as if they were staying in a private and highly luxurious home. Bob and I spent some truly memorable days at La Réserve. We would make our way to the swimming pool shortly before lunch, then eat outside on the terrace; I would water-ski in the afternoon and then we would change for an invariably exquisite dinner in the hotel's restaurant overlooking the Mediterranean. Later in the evening, we would go to Monte Carlo where Bob liked to play roulette. He was unashamedly lucky or skillful—I'm not sure which. Although he did lose sometimes, on the whole he won enormous sums, and we would go back to the hotel around three in the morning, padded with wads of money. We would then order a light dinner accompanied by champagne and make love till we finally fell asleep until lunchtime, the next day!

For a few days, all worries were forgotten and we made up for all the frustrations of living and working apart for most of the time. We talked endlessly. We were in love and very happy. We had made a conscious decision, for a while, not to take the children on holiday away from home. We had had a swimming pool and tennis court built at Broomfield, preferring to have fun with them and their friends in our own comfortable home and garden. Besides, in those days a great many hotels advertised "No Children Allowed," just as today you might see "No Dogs Permitted"! But we did take them to stay with my relatives to learn French, and Marion would take one or two of them to her parents' farm in Ireland when she went home on holiday. Everyone seemed pleased with these holiday arrangements, and it was not until 1965, the summer after Bob entered Parliament as MP for North Bucks, that we chartered a yacht for the first time. Up till then, Bob and I would steal a few brief days' together at La Réserve every spring. One year we met Liz Taylor and Mike Todd at the gaming table in Beaulieu. Although she was pregnant at the time, she was quite ravishing. I was struck by her eyes: they were like two enormous pansies of a deep, rich velvety purple. I had never seen eyes like those before—nor since. A few years ago, I met Liz Taylor again several times; although I still found her very attractive, her eyes had lost that arresting purple glow and are now a deep brown.

At La Réserve we always seemed to meet people in the news and often struck up friendships with them. In April 1953, I caught a first glimpse of the most beautiful, enormous yacht on the horizon; it was called the *Shemara* and was heading towards La Réserve. It soon anchored at a distance and a motorboat brought Sir Bernard and Lady Docker ashore. Their arrival created quite a stir, with both of them looking the part in impeccable white and navy blue. Bob looked at the yacht and told me, "One day, I shall bring you ashore just like that to this very restaurant." I forgot all about that incident in the following years, until the summer of 1968 when we ourselves chartered the *Shemara*. True to his word, Bob took me ashore just like Lady Docker in front of La Réserve—and I played the part, putting on my best navy blue and white for the occasion. But despite these happy memories, ominous storm clouds were gathering in our own sky.

Bob was working fifteen hours a day. All his life, he was an early riser and he would start his working day at 6 A.M. and finish at 11 P.M. Until 1964, he would at least take Sundays off to spend with the family, but after he became a member of Parliament, his only relaxation consisted of changing activities. He continued to travel, and when he did touch base, his days were crammed full of business meetings as he took stock of events with his colleagues and senior staff. He was also a prolific letter writer. On average, he would dictate sixteen letters a day, which means that some days he actually dictated thirty or forty letters—his record for one day was sixty-five! Between 1955 and 1968, the thirteen crucial years in which he built up his publishing empire, Bob dictated over 50,000 letters, 90 percent of which were directly concerned with the creation or continuing expansion of scientific journals and book series. Reading this business correspondence provides a fascinating insight into his flair for scientific matters, as well as his keen interest and extensive knowledge of them. It was precisely these qualities that would help him establish Pergamon as one of the world's leading large-scale scientific publishing houses.

By 1953, I was pregnant again and our sixth child was due in November. Bob was spending more and more time in London and I felt extremely cut off from his activities, although with all the children growing up, I had little time to spare. Soon after we returned in May from our annual holiday at La Réserve, Bob accepted an invitation to spend a week on Conrad and Chinita Abrahams' yacht. So it was that I came to be alone at Broomfield with the children when fire broke out in the early hours one morning. The previous day had been hot and sunny and the sun had streamed into the house, as it always did. But the convex bow windows of the drawing room had apparently acted like a magnifying glass and the sun's intensity had been enough to set the curtains on fire. By eight o'clock next morning, I was woken up by a resounding clatter from downstairs and rushed to see what had happened. The sitting room was ablaze and the noise I had heard was the curtain rods crashing to the ground. I lost no time in waking up Marion and the children, then calling the fire brigade, who arrived promptly and dealt with the blaze. Although most of the furniture was destroyed, by some miracle or other my Blüthner grand piano was saved. This was the first of five serious fires I had to cope with on my own in the forty-six years we were married: by coincidence Bob was abroad every single time.

With Bob away so frequently and my pregnancy advancing, my parents came to stay with me for two months, and their company was a great help and comfort. I left for France and my sister's clinic at the beginning of October and Bob returned just in time from Madrid in early November to welcome his new baby daughter, Karine, into the world. She was the image of her father, and we were both overjoyed. By the first week of December, I was well enough to travel back to England and Bob came to take us home, although he then set off immediately for the United States and Rio de Janeiro. But he was back for Christmas, which we spent in our traditional family way.

Early in January 1954, he was off on his travels again, this time to Moscow, accompanied by his private assistant. He was aiming to build up the two-way traffic of scientific and technical publications between East and West, and in fact did return from that trip with the UK publication rights to some fifty Russian scientific, technical and medical titles. Not only that, but the Russians had promised to buy more British books and Khrushchev himself had promised to look into the Russian copyright position, a vexed question at the time. But the business success of the trip was not uppermost in my mind. Bob's private assistant had been working for him since July 1950. By 1953, relations between them had certainly gone beyond those of employer and personal assistant, much to my dismay. She was undoubtedly devoted to Bob and worked long hours to organize and manage a well-run office. She was distinguished-looking and well-spoken and had worked for the Foreign Office during the war. She introduced Bob to some of her friends, but whilst they were pleasant and charming, they had no real weight or consequence in the worlds of business or politics, except for Francis Noel Baker, who in turn introduced Bob to his father Philip, the Labor MP for Derby South. It was through Philip, later knighted and a Nobel Peace Prize winner, that Bob first met Hugh Gaitskell, later leader of the Labor party, who was to die at a tragically early age on the verge of power.

She was rather inclined to blow her own trumpet to Bob and exaggerate out of all proportion the significance of her role in assisting him, which after all is the normal duty of any good PA. She was clearly very fond of him and certainly helped other people to recognize the best in him. For his part, Bob acknowledged that in her early years with him, she had worked extremely hard and for long hours, including through the demise of Simpkin Marshall. In the six and a half years she actually worked for him, she only came to Broomfield on a few occasions: she did not like me; there was no affinity of any kind between us, only the necessary, routine contact between the secretary of a busy man and his wife.

Thinking back on that episode, I realize that there was nothing very new about the situation: a boss falling for his secretary and vice versa. It was classic: an attractive young man, working till the early hours of the morning with an intelligent, able girl who was fast becoming indispensable in running his expanding office. They traveled together and the business they were creating was a compulsive and binding interest. They both had a sense of humor and appreciation of the fun generated by all the surrounding circus of new postwar businesses. As for me at that time, I was burdened with children; I always seemed to be either pregnant or nursing a new baby. There was no way I could measure up to his secretary in taking an interest in the day-to-day affairs of the business, and Bob would often accuse me of not showing sufficient concern for all his struggles.

I was so stupidly naive and trusting that I could not believe Bob would let himself get into the kind of situation he despised in others, without thinking of the terrible pain it would cause me when I found out. Nor could I understand how a girl would allow herself to fall in love with the father of six children under the age of eight, whatever the circumstances. It was not the kind of moral code I had been brought up on, and I can say in all honesty that I have never allowed myself to fall in love with a married man. As I met them at the airport early that Sunday, I sensed, with the unerring instinct of a wife in love, that I had to fight back to oust an intruder from my patch. But I kept my cool and said nothing, deciding this was the best course of action for the moment. When we arrived home, Bob told me a little about Moscow, then asked me to pack a bag and go with him on a business trip to Canada, leaving in two days' time. I was torn at the thought of leaving my baby behind and retorted that I would have to think about it, which seemed to make him angry. By the time he left for the office the next day, I had made up my mind to go, hoping that during the trip we would have the opportunity to talk. Perhaps I had imagined things.

Although Bob never admitted to me that his relations with her had been anything for me to worry about, he realized that I would have no peace of mind until she was out of the office and our lives for good, and took immediate measures to remedy the situation by offering her a post in his New York office. Soon after our return from Canada, she left for an extended stay in Tibet for health reasons. Later on, she worked for Bob in the United States but found the job unsatisfactory and handed in her resignation early in 1957. When she requested adequate financial compensation for her years of service with him, I encouraged Bob to make a generous and suitable arrangement for her future, and she left with two years' tax-free severance pay which ran until 1958. She finally settled in South Africa.

One day, I received a strange telephone call from an unknown lady who seemed to know all about their "affair" and asked me how I had managed to disentangle my husband from his former PA. I pretended I had no idea what she was talking about. By that time, as far as Bob was concerned, it was a thing of the past, but it was still hurtful to me. After that phone call, I was so distressed that I wrote to him, pouring out all my pent-up sorrow at the way he had shattered my blind faith in him. He answered me as follows:

I have been suffering terribly and have tortured myself into a stupor because of the terrible pain and unhappiness that I have caused you. I do not say this because I wish you to lavish any sympathy on me but so as to show you how deeply sensitive and affected I am whenever anything seriously happens to cause you misery or harm. Like you, I have made myself sick over this matter but try as I may to find absolutely foolproof evidence that I have not ever betrayed you, I find this physical evidence impossible of procurement and must fall back on my love for you, of which I am completely certain.

I swear I love you and only you, I have not betrayed you. I love you, believe me, please.

Well, I did believe him. I persuaded myself that I had grossly exaggerated what I had surmised and decided never to mention the subject again. She came to England two or three times after that and would meet Bob in his office, for old times' sake. The last time she tried to see him, a couple of years before his death, her phone calls were never put through (because of the utter incompetence of the girls then running his office), and Bob heard from a stranger that she was in town. He concluded that she had come with harmful intentions, which was absurd and untrue. By that time, so much water had gone under the bridge that I no longer harbored any ill feelings and I felt sorry for them both.

After she left Bob's office, he only had two private assistants, along with some six deputies, right up to 1986, all of them extremely able, and my personal relations with them have remained close and friendly to this day. That regrettable episode taught Bob just how easy it is to become ensnared if one is not vigilant. For as long as he could still exercise some self-discipline, he endeavored after that not to "dirty his own nest," as he put it, and never gave me cause for concern. It is possible that he had the odd fling now and then in the late seventies, but I never knew nor were they of any consequence to our relationship. The assaults on our mutual love came from inner and not outer forces.

Our trip to Canada lasted a whole month, its main purpose being to sell a ship full of cement, which for one reason or another had been dispatched to Vancouver before it was sold and no one wanted to buy. On a personal level, it was a great success: I acted as Bob's secretary-cum-hostess-cum-wife and we managed to get our relationship back on a sound footing after it had been badly shaken. Businesswise, Bob made contact through Waller's associate, General Critchley, with a great many Canadian businessmen and managed to disentangle several of Waller's complex deals. We also met Waller in Montreal and Ottawa, where I gradually got to know him better. He was a curious mixture: painfully shy and sentimental, yet at the same time a teller of dirty limericks and a cold and calculating businessman. From Ottawa we left for Toronto with the Waller circus, twenty pieces of luggage and a large retinue. We then flew over the Rockies back to Vancouver, in one of the most hair-raising flights I have ever experienced in my life. Weather conditions were poor and the plane wings iced over badly in the bitter cold, with the result that the underside of the plane was sometimes perilously close to the mountain peaks as the pilot tried to find warmer air to melt the ice. At one time we really thought we were going to crash into the Rockies, but we finally landed in a much milder climate, ablaze with blossoms of all hues.

During 1954 Bob had his first encounter with the film world. Through Harry Siepmann, chairman of Pergamon Press at the time, he was introduced to the film director Paul Czinner, husband of the celebrated prewar film star Elisabeth Bergner, famous for her starring roles in *Catherine the Great* and *Escape Me Never*. At the time,

Czinner was contemplating a new and original project; he wanted to film Furtwängler's last performances conducting *Don Giovanni* in Salzburg that summer, using three cameras simultaneously. Bob was excited by the idea, promptly formed a company called Harmony Films Ltd. and we were both present for the filming sessions in Salzburg. The cast was superb; there was Cesare Siepi in the title role and Lisa della Casa and Elisabeth Grümmer as the leading ladies. At its premieres both in England and America in 1955, it received excellent reviews and is still seen on television. This first film venture was then followed by an unforgettable film of "Giselle," danced by the famous Russian ballerina Ulanova, leading the Bolshoi Ballet. After the Queen left the Royal Opera House one evening, film crews moved in to work through the night, despite the fact that Ulanova and the rest of the cast had already danced one performance.

I attended several premieres of these films on Bob's behalf. It was a pleasant interlude, and I can still see my twin daughters on one occasion shyly presenting two halves of a bouquet to Princess Marina, and my daughter Anne, on another occasion, offering flowers with a little more poise to Princess Alexandra.

But Bob's prodigious activity, sadly, could not make up for the basic flaws of the Simpkin Marshall business; in spite of all his best endeavors, the final blow came in March 1955 when the company went into liquidation. It happened just as he had arranged to join a trade delegation to China, but he decided to continue with his travel plans, acting there on behalf of the book trade, his own bookselling activities and Waller.

In late 1954, it seems that Bob was focusing more of his mind on Pergamon Press. At a board meeting in January 1955, he asked the directors to aim at publishing 100 books a year by 1957, and in March the board agreed to a systematic expansion with the aim of doubling output within a few years. It was probably at this point that Rosbaud's objections began, which were to lead twenty months later to the rift in their relationship. Bob was clearly not content to keep Pergamon on its slow expansion path. He was eager and ambitious for it to become a large-scale international and dynamic science publishing house, and once he was back from China in May 1955, channeled more of his energies toward Pergamon's development. He had earlier moved Pergamon's small offices out of the huge Simpkin premises in Marylebone Road into its own headquarters in Fitzroy Square. It was a significant move, both psychologically as well as logistically. The new offices were situated on the elegant side of the square in a Regency building that had previously served as two residences. They soon became a hive of activity and were to remain the center of operations until Pergamon moved its headquarters to Oxford in 1960. Even after this move, Bob kept some offices and a town apartment in Fitzroy Square until the building was sold in 1970, when he moved for a few years to Montpelier Square in Knightbridge.

August 1955 brought Bob an outstanding opportunity to develop his new ambitions and vision as a science publisher at the First United Nations Conference on the Peaceful Uses of Atomic Energy held in Geneva, which we both attended, along with Paul Rosbaud. Bob had rented a villa overlooking the Rhône with a steeply sloping garden which led down to the river. He had somehow managed to install his own office in the United Nations building where only government officials, scientists, administrators and those closely connected with the conference were normally allowed. Bob was at his promotional best there, full of his usual *chutzpah,* using his tremendous energy to great effect as he signed up authors for books or persuaded them to become editors of Pergamon's journals. He was so successful at this that the UN Secretariat apparently included a paragraph in one of their daily bulletins to the effect that "the conference proceedings were to be published by the UN and not by Pergamon."[3]

In retrospect, the Geneva conference laid a foundation stone for Pergamon's growth under Bob's leadership, setting a pattern for years to come. It was really the moment when he came into his own as a science publisher. He attended many receptions and meetings, recruiting new authors and editors to work. We also gave a series of cocktail parties and dinners for Pergamon in our villa, to which we invited the luminaries of the conference, including some very famous scientists, most of whom are no longer alive, as well as the younger generation, amongst whom we made firm friends. Bob met leading UK and U.S. Atomic Energy specialists, as well as distinguished scientists from America and Europe who had flocked to the conference, knowing or sensing that the fusion and fission of the atom would affect all science from then on. He also made the important contact with academician Topchiev, who was to invite him to Russia the following year.

This great UN conference at Geneva must certainly have broad-

---

3. Contribution of Professor Michael Williams, *Robert Maxwell and Pergamon Press*, p. 242.

ened and confirmed Bob's instinctive understanding of the need for scientific communication to be truly international—reaching out to European, American Russian, and all other scientists. Results were evidently flowing from the world's laboratories, and the concept of international scientific communication for peace must have seemed an especially worthwhile ideal in those early years of the cold war, both to Bob and Paul and all the scientists present there.

Yet if Geneva 1955 marked Bob's coming of age as a science publisher, it also seems to have accelerated the breakup of his partnership with Rosbaud. Bob had discovered in Geneva that he could deal directly with leading scientists and did so—very successfully in some cases. This was difficult for the scientifically educated Rosbaud to accept. Until then he had been largely the scientific architect of the company. But the pace of expansion on which Bob was now insisting implied pressure and encroachments on his functions as scientific director. There was a marked generation gap between the two men: Bob was only thirty-two years old, whilst Paul was fifty-eight and there was also a clash of education and respective styles. The older man was naturally more reserved and secretive whereas even in those days, Bob was not publicity shy. His supreme confidence in approaching even very senior scientists, seemingly unabashed by his lack of formal education, irked Rosbaud considerably. Sadly, Paul had neither the patience nor the forbearance to train a raw, immensely impatient, but very bright, willing and able new colleague, and at the time I did not have the wisdom or knowledge to use my influence to nurture their relationship.

The actual issue over which they later ostensibly split up—a complex dispute about Paul's insistence on maintaining a contract for a textbook on optics—seems to me probably to have been only the superficial reason. The crux of the matter was, I think, that Bob wanted to be able to expand Pergamon dramatically and increasingly take publishing decisions himself. According to Bob, Paul had resisted the idea of expanding Pergamon so fast and predicted that Pergamon would go bankrupt. By October 1955, two months after Geneva, Paul had sold Bob his 25 percent share in the company, but remained with the company under his service contract.

The final split took place in October 1956. In later years Bob failed, I think, to give adequate recognition to how much of Pergamon's and his own success was built on the excellent scientific and editorial foundations laid down by Rosbaud. On the other hand, Bob understood better than his partner, and indeed better than any other Western publisher, the extent to which postwar science was expanding exponentially—and how much the world needed the launch of new specialist books and journals in many different fields of science.

Around the time of the Geneva conference, Bob also managed to make another very valuable scientific contact who was later to become a key advisor to Pergamon. Dr. J. Herbert Hollomon (Herb), who during the war had been a brilliant young professor at the Massachusetts Institute of Technology, and was in a leading research management position with the General Electric Company in Schenectady, New York. Bob and Herb got on extremely well, and this friendship led Herb to steer the very great publishing prize of *Acta Metallurgica* towards Pergamon.

In October 1955, Herb became one of Bob's principal consultants on new journals and the selection of editors, and he naturally introduced Bob to other leading American scientists. He was instrumental in bringing Bob and the physicist Harvey Brooks of Harvard University together (although they had already met in Geneva), and Harvey agreed to become editor of a new and important Pergamon journal, *The Physics and Chemistry of Solids*. Not only that, but the Hollomons and Brooks were soon firm family friends and have remained so ever since.

Bob's experiences in Geneva and the contacts he made there confirmed what he already knew, that the international network of scientists in industry and academia needed outlets for publication of their research results worldwide. This was the thriving, innovative and rapidly growing circle of scientists, often supported by government and industry, which Pergamon Press served as publisher, and on whose work its success was based. From this burgeoning network came not only authors and editors but readers and purchasers who needed access to the published research results of universities and laboratories. Bob was quick to understand that it was a two-way traffic: scientists and researchers needed science publishing, and science publishers set out to fulfill this demand and profit thereby. Alas, at the moment when he was poised to launch himself wholeheartedly into further developing this market through Pergamon Press, disaster struck.

6

Higher still and higher
  From the earth thou springest
Like a cloud on fire;
  The blue deep thou wingest,
And singing still dost soar, and soaring ever singest.
PERCY BYSSHE SHELLEY, ODE TO A SKYLARK

I shall never forget the day in September 1955 when I found him sitting at his desk, pale, drawn, anxious and racked with pains in his chest. I immediately called our doctor, who prescribed hot poultices to relieve the discomfort, but there was no improvement and Bob was dispatched to have X-rays taken in London. An eminent radiologist detected tumors in both lungs, which, in his opinion, were almost certainly due to secondary malignant deposits in each lung. Sir Stanford Cade, called in for consultation, diagnosed secondary cancer of the lungs. In an icy-cold and detached manner, he told Bob that in view of his six children and the important business he was running, he felt it was his duty to tell him that he had no more than six weeks to live. He should waste no time in putting his affairs in order.

Bob and I were stunned. We both sat there, tears running down our faces at this unexpected and devastating blow. The nursing staff were crying as well, distressed that such a handsome young father should be condemned to such a short life. They allowed me to sleep in his room at night, and I lay on a mattress beside his bed. We talked endlessly and made plans. I kept holding his hand all night; I wanted him to go to sleep knowing that I was watching for Death, that I would not let her steal him away without his knowledge. On the wall opposite his bed, I had hung a Chinese picture of a prancing wild horse, a black-ink drawing on a traditional rolled parchment. A present from Guozi Shudian, it had arrived shortly before Bob's illness and we had all felt it was in some way symbolic of Bob. That picture now came to signify life itself and Bob would look at it with tears in his eyes.

We immediately made arrangements for Michael, who was by now at boarding school in Oxford, to be brought to the clinic to see his father, and the five younger children came with Marion. Bob so desperately wanted to see them all. Anne remembers her father looking at a single rose on his bedside table and pointing to its intense beauty and color. It was as if he was seeing it for the first time: he had never had time before.

It never occurred to us at first to question the verdict of such eminent physicians, but I did telephone my sister in Paris and we decided to ask for a second opinion. Vonnic recommended a French physiologist, Dr. Roger Kervran, whom we managed to persuade to come over to England to examine the patient and look at the X-rays. Dr. Kervran himself expressed some doubts about the diagnosis and recommended that under the circumstances a completely new team should be brought in. Now we decided to consult Sir Clement Price Thomas, the surgeon who had operated successfully for lung cancer on George VI a few years before. Price Thomas came to see Bob and he in turn recommended the King's radiologist, Peter Kerley, who performed a tomography, a series of X-rays of the body, enabling it to be viewed from different angles.

The results of that tomography were to reintroduce a slender ray of hope into our shattered lives. What had been diagnosed as a tumor in the right lung was, according to Kerley, the shadow of an excrescence on a rib. There was, it was true, a tumor on the left lobe of the left lung, but until it had been removed and examined, we would not know whether it was malignant. The next step would be an exploratory operation to remove the upper left lobe, to be performed by Sir Clement himself at University College Hospital, London. The diagnosis had been slightly altered, but nevertheless we were still terrifyingly close to disaster.

Bob was not a religious man, and although he did see a rabbi and consulted a friend of mine who was a Christian Scientist, religion was of no comfort to him. In fact, I am proud to remember that I was his greatest help and faith then. Not only did I refuse to believe the verdict which condemned him, but somehow I willed him to live and have faith that his time had not come. Yet we took all possible measures in case the outcome of the operation should prove fatal. Bob was allowed a "last weekend" at home. He was particularly concerned to make plans for the children's future education and he had asked Summer Fields school to send Michael home for the day, accompanied by a master young enough to see all our sons through their prep school careers. So it was that Pat Savage, who later became headmaster of the school, came to Broomfield and agreed to help me with the boys' education, in the event of Bob's death.

After Bob had discussed the situation with Pat, we went into the dining room and were joined by some eminent scientists and doctors to whom Bob was giving instructions about the future of Pergamon and the business: if the worst happened, I would have to run the business with their help. As Pat and I had coffee in the drawing room, we could see the children playing in the garden, riding around and around on their bicycles like goldfish swimming in a bowl and running about with the wind streaming through their hair. Pat remembers thinking at the time of those lines by Thomas Gray:

> *Alas, regardless of their doom,*
> *The little victims play!*
> *No sense have they of ills to come*
> *Nor cares beyond today.*[1]

We talked meanwhile of the great responsibilities we would share in the children's education, in the event of Bob's death. Michael was then taken back to school, oblivious to the impending catastrophe, since we had decided to tell the children only that Daddy needed an operation and had to go back to hospital. But I saw the agony in Bob's eyes as he said good-bye to all the little ones for what he really thought might be the last time.

The day of the operation arrived. I had driven to town the night before to be near Bob until the last minute. I finally left him, late at night, although we had decided that I would go to hospital in the morning and wait until he was wheeled into the operating room. The operation lasted several hours: lung operations were then—and still are—bloody and lengthy. Early in the afternoon, I rang Peter Kerley, who gave me some details: the operation had been successful; they

---

1. "Ode on a Distant Prospect of Eton College," II, ll. 51-54, *The New Oxford Book of English Verse* (Oxford: Clarendon Press, 1972), p. 439.

had removed the upper left lobe as planned and sent a sample for biopsy. Bob had come around from the anesthetic, but Peter did not advise me to visit him until the evening, or better still, the following morning. I decided to wait until the next day.

When I first saw Bob, he was still groggy but managed to make me laugh by telling me that our own GP, a kindly, war-trained but not especially brilliant doctor, who had insisted on being present at the operation, had fainted at the first sight of blood and had to be wheeled out of the operating room and sent home! The image he conjured up of this six-foot-four giant stretched out cold was very amusing in the circumstances, but laughing was terribly painful for Bob and he ended up laughing and crying with pain at the same time. But he was alive! Some anxious days of waiting followed during which Bob, now mentally alert and in dreadful pain, became despondent and just did not seem to recover the will to live. That was when I realized the damage the great pundits had done him, from which he would never fully recover. After nine interminable days of anxiety, we were told to our indescribable relief that the tumor had turned out to be non-malignant. From that day on, Bob's attitude totally changed and he improved very fast, subjecting himself to painful physiotherapy in his determination to build up his strength.

There was a strange coda to the drama we had just lived through. On one of his trips to Japan, Bob had bought me a magnificent opal which I had received with some qualms because of the superstition of bad luck attached to the stone. When I told Bob about it, he said, "Nothing I ever give you will bring you bad luck." With those few words, he dispelled all my anxieties and I wore the ring with pleasure for several years. But when I heard the news of Bob's likely death, I told him I wanted to get rid of that opal, and he agreed. A friend of mine offered to sell it, but because of the superstition she only managed to get the ridiculous price of £92, which was paid to her in cash and handed on to me. Before Bob left hospital, Sir Stanford Cade presented his bill for his consultation at the London Clinic: it came to exactly £92. My first reaction was to send it back to him, telling him what he could do with it, but on reflection I had a better idea. I took the cash I had received for the opal, put it in an envelope and had it delivered to his home, secretly hoping it would bring him bad luck. I agree it was not very charitable, but his erroneous pontificating had cost us too dear for me not to harbor some bitterness, and I eased it in that way.

Bob was advised to convalesce in a warm climate, since catching a cold after a lung operation could have serious consequences. So we left for Jamaica directly after he came out of hospital on December 6 and stayed there for a month. The sun and warm sea, coupled with the excellent food of the Round Hill Hotel, contributed greatly to a swift recovery, but above all we were lucky enough to meet in the same hotel a well-known American chest surgeon, Irving Sarot, who was a personal friend of Sir Clement Price Thomas. They had both trained under Dr. Robertson, father of chest surgery at the Brompton Hospital. Bob and Dr. Sarot took to each other immediately and his encouragement and friendly concern greatly helped to keep his morale up throughout his convalescence.

We had survived an agonizing crisis. Its consequences, some beneficial, but most detrimental, were to affect our lives for ever. In his young life, Bob had faced death with immense courage many times, but there is a world of difference between confronting death with a sporting chance of using your skill and judgment to escape its clutches, and being informed that you will be dead in six weeks' time.

Those weeks spent in Jamaica gave a fresh impetus to our mutual love. We had been so close to each other during Bob's illness and felt immensely grateful to rediscover the joy of being together, reaffirming our hope in a future which was all the more precious because it remained so precarious. During Bob's convalescence, we heard of the deaths of Hugh Quennell and Peter Orton. The death of the latter gave Bob quite a shock; although Peter had little real commercial sense and Bob had already made up his mind to part company with him, they had worked together for some ten years. Since Bob himself had just had a close brush with death, it brought home to him all the more forcibly the fragility of human life.

I had never been to the tropics before and fell in love with what seemed to me to be paradise on earth: constant blue skies, cerulean sea, soft sand, warm water, luxuriant vegetation with a profusion of bougainvilleas of every hue, orchids, poinsettia and hibiscus, banana and palm trees, glorious shells and brightly colored fish, beautiful young black bodies glistening in the foam of the waves.

At first Bob behaved almost like an adolescent, rediscovering all the little joys of everyday life. When we arrived, we found that the hotel we had booked into was full of noisy Americans and we asked to be transferred to a quieter beach compound of rather primitive-looking huts. Our first night was disturbed by giant mosquitoes, enormous rodents running along the wooden beams, fat, red cockroaches nestling in our slippers and lizards creeping out from under the beds! I was horrified, but Bob thought it was hilarious and laughed as much as his unhealed wound allowed without too much pain. We soon moved again, this time to the luxurious Round Hill Hotel in Montego Bay, where the staff of friendly, jovial Jamaicans gave the hotel a lingering, old-colonial flavor. We stayed in a secluded bungalow with a glorious view over the coastline and the Caribbean sea.

Every day that passed brought an improvement in Bob's health. He was getting stronger, his scar healed completely within two weeks in the sun and he acquired a good suntan. He started to bathe in the warm gentle waves which lapped the hotel's silver sand beach and went fishing every day in a small boat, coming back with the strangest of fish, such as yellow-tail and silk-fish. We would go out in a glass-bottomed boat and explore the coral reef swarming with fish of fluorescent yellow, red and blue. The climate was perfect, the surroundings heavenly, the whole setting unreal. We just lazed in the sun, holding hands. We even danced at night to the tunes of the latest American and English musicals and then walked along a small stone pathway through heavily scented gardens to our private bungalow.

Most of the guests staying at the hotel were well-known English and American actors or business people. I remember meeting Laurence Olivier, Noel Coward and Ed Sullivan, all seeking to escape the hurly-burly of London or New York for the Christmas break. Bob and I were happy with our own company and never tired of talking to each other. By that time, I was expecting my third son, Ian, but because all my thoughts and actions were concentrated on Bob, and not on myself, I was hardly even aware that I was pregnant, and unlike all my preceding pregnancies, did not suffer the usual nausea and morning sickness. It was then that I realized the power of the mind over the body and the extent to which physical discomfort of the kind I had previously experienced originates in the brain. After that, I never felt any nausea or sickness in my last three pregnancies, and from that realization, derived enormous strength which was to help me all my life.

We came back home early in January 1956 and Bob had hardly landed in England before he was back at work, accepting an invitation to visit Moscow in March. He was to meet leading Russian scientists there, and it was following these discussions that he and Sir Robert Robinson created the not-for-profit Pergamon Institute and initiated a large-scale program of translation for Russian books and journals. He also organized a trip to Washington and New York in

April. He was unstoppable; far from slowing down his activity, he was convinced that he would not live long and embarked upon an incredible race against time to expand Pergamon Press and establish it as the premier scientific publishing house of its kind. All book-selling activities were left largely in the hands of Tom Clark, who had joined LMS as chief accountant in 1951 and retired as vice chairman of Pergamon Press in 1988. Although Bob retained a creative interest in Harmony Films with the world premieres of *Don Giovanni* and *Giselle* with the Bolshoi Ballet, which thankfully provided him with some diversion, he concentrated with incredible single-mindedness on the development of Pergamon.

As a consequence of his illness, Bob decided that I needed to be more involved in business matters. But our new working relationship could not begin until after the birth of our seventh baby, Ian, the child Bob had seriously thought he would never know. He was enormously moved by Ian's birth and was looking forward with great excitement to the success of our new partnership, both professional and personal. I was going to travel with him and help him and Pergamon in the sphere of editorial liaison.

We had decided, on doctor's advice, that Bob should again spend most of the winter in a warm climate, which would also force him to take a break from work. So we left for Barbados on January 20, 1957, traveling via New York as Bob had received a personal invitation from President Eisenhower to his inauguration ball. General Eisenhower had remembered asking Bob in a handwritten letter in 1949 to transport some streptomycin from America to England to save the life of his wartime friend Colonel Gault. He had assured Bob of his lasting gratitude at the time and it was generous of him to remember him again in his hour of triumph. So we attended one of those typical American extravaganzas in Washington and on the next day left for Puerto Rico where Bob was to attend a symposium on Atomic Energy at the University in San Juan.

I spent a few hours getting a glimpse of the Puerto Rican capital and visiting the old Spanish fortress, but soon we were off again for St. James in Barbados. It was raining, which did not augur well, and soon after our arrival, we were still deciding what we would like to do when we were handed a telegram from Marion. At home in Broomfield Karine had fallen ill with a high temperature and had been taken to hospital. Bob immediately tried to telephone home but was unable to get through. We were beside ourselves with anxiety and decided to go home straight away, full of foreboding as we traveled back on that interminable flight, which in those days took almost twenty-four hours. When we arrived, our doctor told us the diagnosis: Karine had leukemia and had been taken to Guy's hospital.

I remember feeling how unfair it was that so soon after we had overcome one major trauma, fate should strike again so soon. But this time it proved a real tragedy, which ended in the death of our little daughter, two weeks later, from acute leukemia. She was only three and a half years old. Bob, Marion and I mounted vigil at her bedside night and day. Bob was determined to move heaven and earth to save her life. He wrote to every conceivable specialist all over the world to seek a cure. Sidney Farber, who had founded the first leukemia clinic in Boston, had agreed to take her as a patient, but she died in Bob's arms on February 8 before any arrangements to move her could be made. We were both prostrate with grief and cried in each other's arms, but after that Bob did not express his sadness openly; he seemed to contain it within himself just as he had for his own family. He was, however, deeply affected. As he wrote to a friend: "I don't think in all my life I have ever suffered a worse blow than to have this beautiful and intelligent girl snatched away at this early innocent age." I could not believe that the little daughter I had left in apparent perfect health had wasted to nothing in a matter of weeks and died in such appalling pain. My heart was torn apart. Karine was the first cherished member of my own family whose death really hit me. Later, of course, I was confronted by the death of my loved ones over and over again, but, as Dylan Thomas wrote, "After the first death, there is no other."[2] For years after her death, I shed many tears, and I would never cease to long for that impish little girl full of vibrancy and laughter. My father's death a few months later was an added blow. He had never been ill in his life, but felt unwell one day in his eightieth year, took to his bed and died soon after. He had remained alert and on the ball until the last two years of his life, but then his brilliant, sparkling brain had gradually deserted him. We were very close and for me it was another immense loss.

Action was to be our salvation. Bob and I both took refuge from our sorrow in punishing work schedules. Bob continued his unswerving concentration on science publishing and refused to let himself be

2. "A Refusal to Mourn the Death, by Fire, of a Child in London," *The Poems* (London: Everyman, J. M. Dent & Sons, 1971), p. 192.

diverted from this aim. He truly built an idea into a publishing empire. From 1955 onwards, he became a focused industrial pioneer in science publishing, in contrast to his later years as the tycoon of a multimedia communications conglomerate. There is an enormous difference between the two, not merely in scale, but above all in style, concentration, milieu and, in the end, enduring achievement. Scientific and technical publishing is a totally different kind of business from newspaper publishing, partly because of the structure of science and education and the institutions that support it. Growth in scientific knowledge is long-term, steady and systematic. Daily news is the other extreme, short-term, speculative, fashionable and ephemeral.

The nature of Pergamon Press was fundamentally serious, as are the disciplines involved in science publishing. In those days, Bob had only one headquarters and the overwhelming focus of his life was on this one core business. Equally, there was only occasional press publicity, nothing like the enormous excesses associated with press tycoons. No helicopters, no planes, no boats, no PR men. There was no diversion from the central purpose, only a consistent attending to day-to-day office business, when he was not traveling abroad on specific company business. But his approach consisted of much more than devoting his acknowledged energy to the task at hand; he had a thoroughly international outlook and good business sense. He combined these qualities with an ability to communicate, to persuade eminent scholars to publish their research with Pergamon, to gain and retain their esteem, loyalty and friendship. It was to be long-term and inter-disciplinary work, with high standards in both production and presentation. Bob and the staff were justifiably proud of their achievements and the growing international reputation of Pergamon.

It is a fact that most of Bob's biographers and obituarists, almost certainly because of unfamiliarity with these years of achievement and with the industry itself, have seriously underplayed and undervalued Bob's pioneering success as the founder, managing director and publisher of Pergamon Press for over forty years, as compared with his much shorter but more controversial careers as a wholesale bookseller, printing tycoon, newspaper publisher and global media mogul, each of which lasted less than a decade. It would also be interesting to compare the space biographers have devoted to his role in UK politics or in football to that they allotted to his more than forty years of cumulative work at Pergamon Press.

Because I was at his side during the two early and most vital decades of his business, I witnessed firsthand the explosive growth of Pergamon under Bob's energetic leadership. A measure of its extremely rapid expansion is that by 1988, some thirty-seven years after Bob acquired it, Pergamon Press had grown to the point of having over 3,500 books in print (and some 7,000 out-of-print titles as well) and was publishing the rather startling total of some 400 journals a year. Whatever else may be said about him, Bob did succeed in developing Pergamon Press into one of the world's leading science publishers, a British equivalent of Germany's Springer Verlag.

One of the keys to his success as a science publisher was his creativity in the company of scientists and editors, and his ability to establish and sustain fruitful partnerships with many of them. Brian Blunden, managing director of PIRA—the Paper Industries Research Association—considered Bob to be especially sensitive to changes in science and technology and wrote: "One has only to spend a short time in his company to observe the empathy he has with creative thinkers. He possesses that rare gift which engenders a bond of creativity and at the same time guides original thought into practical business."[3]

In founding and sustaining science publications, all manner of problems would arise requiring communication and agreement between publisher, advisors, authors and editors. Bob was extremely attentive to all such communications and in meetings he was proverbially quick to propose solutions, adopt recommendations, correct errors and take advantage of opportunities which arose. One distinguished scientist records his amazement at Bob's reaching a decision before he had even completed the presentation of his argument!

To help plan new developments, Bob relied not only on his own hunches but actively sought the ideas and advice of existing editors and authors and the guidance of a smaller number of scientific advisors, many of whom became long-term consultants and friends: Walter Owen, Harry Wasserman, Derek Barton, Alan Sartorelli, Corneille Radouco-Thomas, John Coales, Saul Penner, Guy Ourisson and Ian Sneddon, to name but a few. Amongst these many advisors and friends, probably the most significant for Bob was Sir Robert Robinson OM. An outstanding organic chemist and Nobel prizewinner, he had met Bob early in 1956, but a trip by liner to the United States in the following spring sealed their friendship. The two men got on extremely well, played endless games of chess and discussed the progress of organic chemistry, enjoying each other's company and

---

3. Contribution of Brian Blunden, *Robert Maxwell and Pergamon Press*, p. 43.

sharp intellect. That meeting was to trigger the birth of Pergamon's specialist organic chemistry journal *Tetrahedron,* after Bob persuaded Sir Robert to work with the rising star in the field and equally distinguished American chemist, Robert Burns Woodward. The launch of *Tetrahedron* was to mark an important milestone for Pergamon because, unusually at the time, the publication was totally independent of any national learned chemical societies. More than any other postwar Western publisher, Bob grasped the need for rapid communication journals, where the process of reviewing manuscripts and their publication would be far quicker than for research work submitted to the organs of long-established learned societies. This, coupled with Pergamon's outstanding marketing and worldwide distibution networks, greatly attracted scientists, and Bob's created literally hundreds of new journals on the cutting edge of science.

Another innovation which Bob introduced on a large scale was his emphasis and insistence on the thoroughly international membership of his journals' editorial boards. From the mid-fifties onwards, he strove to bring together Russians, Europeans and Americans at a time when science was still very nationalistic and few other publishers realized how valuable this could be, both for science and world peace. He liked to participate in editorial board meetings held throughout the world where, as one scientist observed, "An extraordinary gift for languages frequently allowed him to break sudden barriers by communicating with editors in the language of their choice."[4] It was clearly not all plain sailing bringing together groups of individual scientists and getting them to work together. The Pergamon editor, Dr. James Lodge, amusingly highlighted one very extreme case:

There were about a dozen members of the board, Wes Eckenfeider as editor, and a few representatives of Pergamon. As I walked into the room I looked about in horror, recognizing that however well Wes may have chosen his board members for their expertise, each of the 12 board members was the mortal enemy of the other 11. We sat down and tried to get started, but the board members virtually refused even to agree on that. For about 15 minutes or so there was absolute chaos; the sensation of being there is best described "like being bitten to death by a flock of ducks." At this point, Bob walked in, excusing himself for being late on the grounds of being tied up on the transatlantic telephone. By sheer force of his presence, he got them quiet and then spoke to

---

4. Contribution of Professor Corneille Radouco Thomas, *Robert Maxwell and Pergamon Press,* p. 354.

them without notes for about 20 minutes. . . . There was absolutely nothing that the board members could do but rubber-stamp his statement of purpose, snarl at each other over lunch and then go home, completely cowed.[5]

The years from 1955 to 1960 were also the time Bob contributed to making Russian research available to the West through translated journals and books. The experience was not without its lighter moments, which often arose from amusing translation howlers. Professor George Herrmann, for instance, remembers receiving a manuscript with the enthralling title of "Necking in a Bar," which for reasons of propriety, not to mention accuracy, was amended to "The Necking of a Bar." Then there was the translator from Russian to English who managed to transform a "hydraulic ram" into a "water goat"! Both these blunders remind me of a story attributed to the great Theodor von Karman, who mentioned laughingly that someone had translated a title of a paper, probably from German, as "The Flapping of Turbine Shovels" when it should have read "The Flutter of Turbine Blades."

But it was not only works in translation that Bob was keen to make available. He also published a great number of new monographs and textbooks aimed at the needs of research and graduate students, and played an important entrepreneurial and organizational role in commissioning major scientific reference works. Pergamon was to publish eleven such encyclopedic works in the 1960s, three in the 1970s (when for several years Bob was no longer Pergamon's publisher) and ten in the 1980s.[6] These twenty-four multivolume publications were models of their kind requiring substantial investment, planning and coordination. They are testimony to Bob's publishing flair and his willingness to risk large sums of money on his publishing intuition and the skills and hard work of his editors, a point which many Pergamon authors and editors emphasize. They knew that he did not shrink from taking risks, once he was convinced of the need for a publication and the quality of the enterprise. He was also ready to innovate in completely new areas of technical publish-

---

5. Contribution of Dr. James Lodge, Robert Maxwell and Pergamon Press, p. 504.

6. Such works included the nine volumes of *The Encyclopaedic Dictionary of Physics* 1961–1964, the five volumes of *Comprehensive Inorganic Chemistry* 1973, the six volumes of *Comprehensive Organic Chemistry* 1979, the ten volumes of *The International Encyclopaedia of Education* 1985 and the eight volumes of *The Encyclopaedia of Materials Science and Engineering* 1986.

ing. Captain Fred Weeks, editor of *Seaspeak*, the prize-winning maritime communication language, remembers vividly Bob's almost instantaneous decision to give financial backing to his publishing project at a time when funds were very difficult to obtain:

All present were delighted when Bob arrived, listened to the proposals and then entered into the proceedings with gusto. Within minutes, he said, "This is something that must be done. How much do you want? I have my checkbook in my pocket." The Seaspeak Project was under way.[7]

There were, of course, the inevitable detractors, complaints and criticisms. Pergamon journals and books were often said to be too highly priced, libraries criticized the price differential between personal and library subscriptions (yet other publishers were later to follow Bob's example) and in the early days particularly, payments and royalties for book authors were insufficient and staff overworked. There was perhaps an overproliferation of monographs and conference proceedings, leading in some cases to second-rate books or journals, although the latter sometimes died a natural death if they were not up to standard. Other serious criticisms can be leveled in the later years, concerning the lack of sustained marketing of book and journal titles and the unacceptable delays of publishing decisions, when Bob had become involved in too many other pursuits. At that stage, he was no longer in close communication with editors and authors, failed to delegate adequately and neglected Pergamon to some extent. It could also be said of those later years that there was insufficient plowing back of profits into Pergamon itself. But in the 1950s and 1960s, criticisms often resulted from Bob's innovative approach. Paul Streeten, director of the World Development Institute at Boston University, explained some features of Bob's approach in a generous 1988 tribute:

An elemental force meets with obstacles, and the obstacles do not like being pushed out of the way. One hears many people virulently criticizing Robert Maxwell. I sometimes think that this is the way the feudal lords must have felt in the rush of capitalist progress. Innovation implies the removal of deadwood, and the deadwood is sometimes alive enough to squeak. But they are puny squeaks against the powerful and imaginative innovations that Bob initiates.[8]

---

7. Contribution of captain Fred Weeks, Robert Maxwell and Pergamon Press, p. 238.

8. Contribution of Paul Streeten, *Robert Maxwell and Pergamon Press*, p. 745.

Over the intervening years, with all the adverse publicity concerning Bob's newspaper activities, it is easy for his forty years' contribution to science publishing to be belittled or forgotten. But, as many hundreds of eminent scientists have testified, Pergamon was a solid and lasting achievement, and Bob's talents crucial to its success. Professors Derek Barton and Harry Wasserman, the two immensely distinguished chemists, summarized the feelings of many of their colleagues in their letter to *The Times* in December 1991: "Robert Maxwell was a man for the times. Through his style and bravura, he captured the imagination of scientists and led them into bold and successful innovations in publishing. He was a catalyst, sparking exploration and experimentation and enabling scientists to take huge leaps over the barriers to communication."

Life at Bob's side during the early years of his rise to success was both exhilarating and rewarding, but it imposed choices on my part and enormous sacrifices in our family life, in my isolation from ordinary friendships and pleasures and produced an increasing strains on our emotional life. Everything was sacrificed on the altar of Bob's genius, and in the end the children and I were to pay a heavy price. At the time of his illness, however, when I feared that I would lose him, I promised myself that if he pulled through, I would devote the rest of my life to loving, cherishing, helping and working both for him and his happiness, convinced that in turn it would bring happiness to me and the children.

That was exactly what I set out to do, to the best of my ability and for as long as Bob himself wanted me to carry on. The path was far from smooth, however, and I found it hard to repress my own will and desires and submit to his needs and ambitions without losing my own personality and originality completely. Knowing that it was one of the qualities in me that Bob found attractive, I had to hang on to my individuality at all costs, yet I also had to avoid constant confrontations.

Traveling with Bob became part and parcel of my life. Although I found it hard to be separated from the children, I had complete confidence in Marion's ability to cope in my absence and we would write to each other regularly and at great length. She would tell me every minute detail of my children's lives, what they had been doing at school, the funny little things they had said, all the ups and downs of their young lives, and I in turn would describe all the places of interest we had visited, the people we had met and the general aim of our trips. During those years, I visited nearly every European country with Bob, along with Canada, the United States, Russia, India, the Middle East, the Far East, Japan, Australia and Africa. And whenever we were back home, I held open house for all our authors and editors, most of them from abroad. It would be an unenviable task to recount the many incidents which occurred in that period of discovery of new countries and encounters with their leaders and scientific communities. Some anecdotes, however, stand out in my mind and have remained conversation pieces in the web of our family lore. On those travels, I would sometimes make terrible faux pas which would infuriate Bob, but afterwards he would roar with laughter every time he told the story publicly at the dinner table. At other times, he would ask me to undertake missions of diplomacy which I would manage to accomplish to his great surprise and delight. This earned his rare praise for my audacity, courage or cleverness, or whatever other quality the mission had required which I had been able to muster. We were definitely a good team in those days, in spite of the tumult of our love life, which resulted largely from his changeable moods and my absent-minded inattention to the detail of his personal and everyday needs, which he invariably interpreted as proof that I did not love him enough.

The year 1958 was a momentous one in our lives when Bob took me to five major scientific meetings, following which Pergamon founded some twenty-eight journals in new areas of scientific research. In March we visited Palermo on the island of Sicily for the third NATO/AGARD meeting (Advisory Group for Research and Development), chaired by the father of modern aeronautical sciences, Professor von Karman, who had organized the meeting there in part because he also wanted to spend a few days visiting the Greek temples on that beautiful island. We flew to Naples, visiting Pompeii en route, then joined the 200-strong contingent of American scientists, many of whom had traveled all the way from California simply to spend a few days with the celebrated professor. Von Karman's colleagues, most of whom had also been his own students, respected him enormously and indeed almost revered him. By that time, the professor had difficulty walking, and if he wanted to speak to you, would virtually summon you to his presence, and such was his prestige that his orders were immediately obeyed! I found myself summoned like this several times. Von Karman liked Bob and was intrigued by him, and I sensed he was trying to figure him out, with my help. In fact, it was von Karman who first dubbed me Madame Pergamon, a friendly nickname which some authors adopted over the years. In Palermo, Bob struck up a friendship with the well-known American professor of engineering physics, Saul Penner, and we also met Professor A. K. Oppenheim, the celebrated authority on combustion and founder of the journal *Acta Astronautica,* which later came within the Pergamon stable. One day, we visited Luigi Napolitano, a wonderfully warm and talented Italian, in his superb laboratory on the Island of Ischia. He used to refer to Bob as "Roberto Il Magnifico" in recognition of his efforts in this particular branch of science—supporting the International Astronautical Federation, helping to create the International Academy of Astronautics and promoting the dissemination of space technology and knowledge through *Acta Astronautica.* At every subsequent AGARD meeting, in Greece and in Turkey, we would meet these marvelous friends who had by then become Pergamon authors and editors.

By the summer of 1958, Sputniks and the promise of space exploration had engendered a worldwide level of excitement about new technology that has hardly ever been equalled since. It culminated in August of that year with two consecutive scientific symposia held in Moscow in the space of three weeks, both of which Bob and I attended: the final meeting of the International Geophysical Year and the International Astronomical Union. To everyone's surprise, the weather in Moscow that summer was idyllically sunny and warm. We were staying at the Hotel Ukraina, a tall, massive structure in Stalin-Gothic style, along with Professor Fred Whipple, discoverer of the Whipple comet, and his wife, Babbie. I remember that we all went swimming in the Moscow River (which reminded me of the ill-fated Napoleonic invasion), having overcome the problem of lack of swimsuits by improvisation, whilst the Russians all swam stark naked. It was enough to earn us a reputation for complete eccentricity at the time, although I couldn't help feeling that many others would secretly have liked to join us!

Everything about Russia in those days was new to the Western contingent, but recent Russian success in the space race made us accept day-to-day deficiencies as quaint rather than annoying. Although foreigners' movements were quite restricted then, I joined in all possible sight-seeing trips and Intourist tours, discovering the Kremlin, the art galleries, monasteries and smart dachas of the apparatchik hierarchy, and of course we made the compulsory visit to view the corpses of Lenin and Stalin, lying side by side in the Red Square Mausoleum. While Lenin looked very much like a greenish-colored waxwork, Stalin was smiling and rosy-cheeked, almost as if he were going to wake up any minute.

It was on that trip to Moscow that we met many of the scientists who would become associated with Pergamon's drive into the fields of astronautics, geophysics, planetary and space science. Here began a lifelong friendly relationship with Sir Granville Beynon, cofounder of one of the greatest ever worldwide scientific collaborations, the 1957–58 International Geophysical Year, for which Pergamon was official publisher, along with the forty-eight volumes of the International Geophysical Year Annals. We also met most of the famous Russian scientists who would form the nucleus of our first five-year translation program and future international scientific book series. Foremost amongst them were Professor Kapitza, director of the Institute of Theoretical Physics, and Professor Landau, one of the giants of theoretical physics, who had been imprisoned in a gulag by Stalin and Beria and saved by Kapitza's courage.

Bob and I were invited to lunch by Topchiev who was to become a staunch ally in promoting scientific publishing links with the West, and I was the only lady present alongside ten men. We sat down to eat at noon and were still at the table at five P.M., having eaten and drunk almost nonstop. I had never before—and have never since—eaten so many courses, washed down by so many wines. First there was a variety of hors d'oeuvre of black and red caviar, salmon and assorted fish, cold meats and shrimps and an endless choice of salads, green salads, tomato salad, cucumber and cheese. Then came the famous Russian borscht, followed by eggs and mushrooms, then shellfish thermidor and roast beef en croûte. The meal was constantly interrupted by toasts, which are a standard feature of Russian entertainment. "First," said our host raising his full tot of vodka, "We must drink a toast to our friend, Captain Maxwell, who came all the way from England with his lovely wife to visit Great Mother Russia—bottoms up." We had scarcely touched the dishes on the table groaning with food before another toast was under way. Raising his glass of Georgian chardonnay, the man on Bob's left got up and said, "Let us drink to good and friendly business between us and Pergamon Press—bottoms up." And so it went on, with the toasts getting friendlier but still remaining rather formal. By the time the sorbet appeared, I had done great justice to the sumptuous lunch and thought the meal was at an end. But I discovered to my dismay that we had only reached the pause in the middle and my host explained that the really scrumptious food was to follow! Whereupon, everyone got up from the table and proceeded to the toilets! The situation called for drastic measures and I then did probably the most disgusting thing I have ever done. Following a tip I had been given, which at the time I thought was a joke, I pressed my fingers on my tongue and made myself vomit all that I had eaten in the first four courses, then went back to my seat, not feeling too much the worse for wear, and willingly accepted a small vodka which took away the remains of the unpleasant taste in my mouth.

By that time, the men were merry, having drunk liberally of the vodka and several different wines during the break in the proceedings. As soon as we were all sitting down again, the most exquisite salami of pheasant appeared on the table, served in individual silver saucepans and accompanied by a good Georgian red wine; then came fried sturgeon accompanied by exquisite potato dumplings and a kind of curled potato fritter, the like of which I have longed for ever since. This was followed by the celebrated chicken à la Kiev, which Bob especially enjoyed. By then the whole table knew that Bob was born in a village that was now part of the Ukraine, so he had instantly become "one of us." The whole atmosphere was suddenly much more matey, the toasts became more personal and at one point, quite ribald. We drank to longevity and world peace, we drank to good business and making money, we drank to the beauty of Ukrainian and French girls and their reputation for making love and having babies. Bob was sitting on Topchiev's right and I was on his left. Topchiev seemed to be amazed at my eating capacity and plied me generously with wine and vodka, which he encouraged me to swallow in one gulp, miraculously settling my stomach! At the same time, he was beginning to ask me insidious questions about the source of Bob's money, insinuating that he must be paid by the British secret service. We had reached the cheese course, which was followed by dessert with its endless variety of ice cream, cakes and fruit, accompanied by coffee and cognac to wash it all down. By this time, all the men were under the table! Bob's companion on his right had almost passed out, Bob himself was unusually loud and merry, although still compos mentis, and the only people in complete control of their faculties were Topchiev and myself.

By then I understood the whole game. I was completely on my guard, alert, witty and jovial, very much on the ball. Topchiev was oozing charm and generous with his compliments. Eventually, in reply to his persistent questioning, I heard myself say, "Academician Topchiev, I will let you into a secret: Bob gets up at six every day of his life, he works nonstop till nine at night, he travels for Pergamon, he eats Pergamon, he drinks Pergamon, he makes love to Pergamon and the money just pours in! That is the truth." Whereupon, he turned to Bob, who was by then rather befuddled and said, "Mr. Maxwell, I know your secret, your wife has just told me." Jolted out of his torpor, Bob instantaneously recovered his sangfroid. "You're a lucky man, Mr. Maxwell, you have an exceptionally strong and capable wife. I congratulate you."

It would be fascinating to know whether the results of my grilling by Topchiev reached the archives of the KGB, but I don't think the Russians ever asked questions after that as to the source of Bob's money. I felt quite certain that Bob no longer worked for Intelligence, so I must have sounded honest and straightforward. But a curious incident just after that rather puzzled me.

One sunny morning, Babbie Whipple and I were talking in my hotel room planning our day, when Bob suddenly burst in carrying a huge parcel wrapped in brown paper. In a completely detached manner, he told us, "I've managed to obtain sixty-three pages of important book titles available for translation. I haven't got a photocopier, but I need to take a copy and I have to return the package before lunch without fail. Do you think you could photograph it?" I couldn't imagine how on earth we could do this, but at that moment Fred Whipple came in and suggested we try their 16-mm movie camera on its tripod, using the best film available and tripling the normal exposure time. Even then, we would have to carry out the entire operation on the tiny hotel balcony, photographing the sixty-three pages in broad sunlight. Babbie and I then proceeded to do the work as requested, not without some trepidation in case we were discovered doing something that looked slightly suspicious, or that the rooms were bugged and Bob's request had been overheard. Babbie was operating the movie camera one shot at a time, whilst I handed her the sheets and placed the finished ones on a nearby table. As I was putting the sheets back in order, I noticed that they were written in German and that what we had been asked to photograph were lists of "Die deutschen Firma, deren Einrichtung demontiert und zur Ausfuhr nach der Sowjetunion bestimmt sind" (German firms whose equipment is to be dismantled and transported to the Soviet Union).

I remember feeling cold all over when I realized they were not lists of books. By then we had just reached page thirty-two. I finished the job in a cold sweat, but never said a word to Babbie, who was concentrating on working the camera. We had hardly completed the job when Bob walked in, repacked the lists in the brown paper and disappeared. I never talked to him about this episode, having instinctively remembered my training way back in 1944 when I first met him.

Years later, Bob told the *Sunday Times* that he had been opposed to the dismantling of German plants by the Soviets, which was contrary to Ally policies. Although he knew that it was happening, he had not at the time been able to secure proof of systematic disman-tling. His superiors at PRISC had not believed him and he had been told to drop the matter. How he had stumbled upon the proof some ten years later, or who had put him on to it, I do not know and never asked, but the truth is that he had, and back in London, I assume that he was able to prove the truth of what he had told them after the war. Bob kept a set of the photographs and years later some of them found their way into my archives. Looking at one of those pho-tos as I write this, I tell the story with sincere apologies to Fred and Babbie Whipple who, as I had at first, innocently believed what Bob had told us at the top of his voice, most probably for the benefit of the "buggers." At any rate, it was totally in keeping with his Intelli-gence training to never divulge any more than was necessary, always operating on the "need to know principle."

We left Moscow soon after and visited the great city of Leningrad with its magnificent seventeenth- and eighteenth-century buildings and unique setting on the Neva. We also spent several hours in the rich Hermitage Museum with its Scythian gold trea-sures, the Fabergé collection of eggs, jewelry and precious objects, and high up under the roofs of the Czar's Winter Palace, a fabulous collection of French Impressionists. There, hanging so close together that you could scarcely see them, were paintings by Manet, Monet, Bonnard, Gauguin, Matisse and many others, including fairly mod-ern Cubists. I believe that admirable collection has now taken pride of place in various galleries, as have all those paintings which used to be considered decadent Western art and remained stacked in the cel-lars of Moscow's Tretiakov gallery, which I was privileged to see in 1988 on the authority of Raisa Gorbachev.

In the late summer of 1958, we rented a small château overlook-ing Lake Geneva on the French side of the water and attended the Second International Conference on the Peaceful Uses of Atomic Energy. Bob consolidated the impact he had made three years earlier, at the first such conference. Since we were also celebrating the tenth anniversary of Pergamon, we decided to give a party and invite the top scientists from all over the world who had come to Geneva for the conference. I had taken our London butler, John Jenner, to Geneva to help me with all the entertaining, which is a vital compo-nent of any good publishing house. We called him Jen-Jen, and he was the nearest replica of a live Jeeves I have ever come across in my life. We were all very fond of him and appreciated his incredible resourcefulness—he was a bit like a magician and literally seemed able to pull a meal out of his hat. But at the same time, he was clearly a roaring queen, which had its drawbacks. Bob had asked me to drive his car to Geneva. At the time, we had a rather antiquated Rolls-Royce which had previously belonged to Aristotle Onassis. I had taken our three eldest children with me and planned to arrive around seven in Saulieu, a town on the way to Lyon well known for its gastronomy, intending to stay the night there. We were only about forty miles away when we suddenly had a puncture on a totally deserted stretch of road. I can still picture myself in my light-gray Dior suit, standing by the roadside, emptying the contents of the car with Jenner's help. We were going to be away for a month and it was absolutely crammed full of all the clothes needed by the family, not to mention a hundred and one other things that might come in useful at the château. The spare wheel, of course, was stored underneath all that, along with the jack and other tools! Once the entire contents had been heaped on the verge, I then had to remove the wheel and maneuver the jack into position, with my eldest son Michael, then all of twelve years old, trying to help. At that precise moment, the heavens opened and the worst downpour imaginable forced us all to retreat to the car. Once it had abated, I decided to carry on changing the wheel on my own, but was thankfully rescued by a passing truck driver who stopped to give me a hand. By that time, I was soaked to the skin, my suit was covered in oil, my hair was dripping all over my face, and Jenner stood beside me, elegant in his gray gloves and spats, trying to shelter me under a huge umbrella, shaking his head and saying over and over again, "Oh that Madam should have to do a thing like this." It never seemed to occur to him that he could have helped me change the wheel.

By the time we arrived at the inn in Saulieu, it was 10:30 at night. I have very clear memories of preparing mentally what I was going to say to obtain food and lodging at that late hour. So as I walked in, I said, "I'm sorry I'm so late, but we had a puncture. I've got a car, a butler and three children. We're all starving and I need a bath. Can you help me?" Those wonderfully kind people did just that. But they told me they only had three rooms and asked whether that would do. I told them that the only caveat was that I couldn't sleep with the butler, but any other arrangement would be fine! They then apologized for not being able to give us their usual three-course dinner, but proceeded to serve us with exquisite poularde demi-deuil (chicken prepared with black mushrooms, truffles or morels), followed by profiteroles in chocolate sauce. It was a welcome treat.

The next day, we arrived at the château, a comfortable and elegantly furnished eighteenth-century house, and I met the Swiss owner who, upon seeing the children, was naturally concerned for the safety of her pink Sèvres ornaments and other objets d'art. I told her not to worry at all, because I would put all valuables and break-ables away immediately, which I did with the butler's help. I had hired a Spanish couple to help me since the house was also going to accommodate two authors and their wives, together with the Perga-mon staff working on the conference proceedings.

One of my overriding memories of that summer is my feeling of total exhaustion as I tried to accomplish all Bob wanted and Perga-mon needed at a time when I was once again in the early months of pregnancy, this time with my eighth child, Kevin. I managed some-how or other, even though in the daytime I had to look after my own children, do all the food shopping, entertain the wives of our editors and authors and take them sightseeing, and in the evening accom-pany Bob to numerous parties and receptions given by all the inter-national organizations, embassies, universities, industries and science institutes of that great city. But in spite of my fatigue, our time in Geneva was exciting and culminated in a resounding success for Pergamon.

As the day of the anniversary party approached, the Spaniards, Jenner and I worked nonstop for two whole days preparing a three-course dinner for 150 people. It was very hard work, but if we had employed outside caterers, the dinner would have cost ten times as much, the food would have lacked the home-cooked taste I liked and the occasion would not have had that family atmosphere which would become the hallmark of all our parties. Our children were a great asset that evening, helping to serve our guests and on their very best behavior. Michael's comments in a letter to Nanny back at home were well observed: "The party is drawing near, all we hear are hur-ried discussions about whether the champagne table ought to be inside or outside and whether the lights ought to illuminate the lawns or not. You can see the state we're in. But anyway, by the sounds of it, it's going to be pretty good. . . ."

I had found a local four-piece band and after coffee on the ter-race overlooking the city, we danced in the flickering light of Chinese lanterns. There was a wonderful atmosphere that evening, and the scholars relaxed and loved it. All went well, except for one extremely crass remark made to me by an eminent scientist who shall remain nameless. He had not been an easy guest and at one stage I asked him if he was enjoying the food, to which he replied, "Oh, it's OK for me as long as it's clean." Recalling how much love and skill I had lavished on the preparation of the dinner, I was hurt for a moment, feeling that I was really throwing pearls before swine. This rude remark was to go down amongst the family's stock of standard maxims!

The time soon came to leave Geneva. About an hour before we were due to depart, I unpacked the owner's precious china and returned the two large pink Sèvres vases and jardinières to their rightful positions on the drawing room mantelpiece. The children were running around as we made all the final preparations for departure, when suddenly I heard an ominous crash in the drawing room. I rushed in to see what on earth had happened, only to find one of those precious pink vases lying smashed to smithereens on the floor. Michael and Philip were white with shock. Following a rowdy chasing game, one of the buttons on Michael's cuff had apparently got caught in the lace runner under the vase and brought the whole thing crashing down. Luckily for him, Bob had already left by plane that morning. I can still see myself frantically rushing to the owner's lawyers in Geneva and negotiating a replacement fee.

In September 1958, we launched *Tetrahedron Letters,* which, along with its sister publication, *Tetrahedron,* remains to this day the Koh-i-noor diamond of the Pergamon crown. Robert Robinson was once again its founding editor. He had just remarried at the age of seventy-one and his new wife, Stearn, was a slightly eccentric American widow, twenty-five years his junior whom he had met on his travels to the States. After their wedding, they spent part of their honeymoon with us in the Alps, where we all went climbing. After a choppy start to their partnership, she turned out to be a devoted wife and companion for close to twenty years, helping him to continue traveling the world almost right up to his death, even after he had gone blind. Later, after we moved to Oxford, the Robinsons became regular weekend visitors and sometimes Bob and I would go for dinner during the week to their home in nearby Great Missenden. Robert was our son Ian's godfather, and whenever he came to visit, he would draw rebuses for the children and show great patience in listening to them. Stearn had great zest for life and her creative talents came to the fore in her invention of the TV cartoon, "Dodo, the Kid from Outer Space," coproduced by Bob, which was so much ahead of its time that it was not a great success then, but may now be revived.

For the launch of *Tetrahedron Letters,* Stearn had decided to use me to model one of her creations: a dress designed in a sort of three-dimensional diamond shape, like a tetrahedron. Bob's quizzical smile as he inspected my outfit confirmed my worst suspicions that I looked like a clown, and I exclaimed, "Boy oh boy! The things I have to do for our publishing house." I have to admit, though, in spite of its unmatched eccentricity in the rather staid scholarly milieu of the launch party scholars, the outfit looked stunning on me and was certainly a conversation piece.

Early in the new year, 1959, it was time for me to go to France again since my pregnancy was nearing term. Soon afterwards, Bob came to Maisons Laffitte to see me before attending to some business in the center of Paris. Whilst he was there, however, he felt unwell and phoned me from our flat in Paris, feeling rather sorry for himself. Although I was heavy and cumbersome myself, I made the effort to go to the flat and look after him. He soon felt better for my ministrations, and after a good night's sleep, was able to carry on the next morning with his scheduled business meetings. Later that day, I went to the Paris office, intending to see Bob off to the airport for his return flight when he went back to England, but he phoned in the afternoon to say that he had already missed the three o'clock plane and could I please change his booking to the five o'clock one. I waited and waited. That plane came and went, and eventually I received another phone call, this time asking me to secure a place on the seven o'clock flight. So again I waited, until at seven he phoned me, asking me to jump into a taxi and rush to Le Bourget Airport north of Paris as fast as possible, taking his suitcase with me. In the meantime, he would make his own way there. But he never arrived. The next I heard was another phone call at eight from Orly, south of Paris, twenty-five miles away! I felt utterly dejected, wondering how he could possibly treat me like that, only two weeks away from the birth of my eighth child. But after an incident like this, I would receive a letter that melted away my anger:

Betty, my dearest, I shall always remember that you came to see me at the flat last Sunday in spite of your condition and the physical effort that meant. Your arrival dispelled my pain completely and you and I passed a happy evening. This is love, I love you, you love me. You and I must plan to live more closely and intensely together, enrich each other, help and make life more fascinating and fuller for us and our family.

The pace of life was unrelenting, baby or no baby. Soon after Kevin's birth, I was off on my travels again. This time we would enact one of Bob's favorite dreams: we would take the car to the Continent and visit Vienna, Budapest, Warsaw and Berlin. We were going to drive there in leisurely fashion like two young lovers, combining arduous business with sightseeing and the pleasure of being together. We had decided to travel to Poland via Slovakia, visiting Auschwitz on the way to Warsaw, since it was of great significance to us both. But on the day we were due to start our journey, Bob was suddenly detained by business and asked me to drive the car to Vienna, where he would join me. Well, it wasn't the first time that had happened, so I agreed, but it was a long journey to face alone. I stopped off in Paris and in Geneva and finally reached Vienna, where, according to my instructions, I made my way to the Sacher Hotel in the center of the city. By late afternoon, I arrived to find Bob waiting, happy to see me, with an unmistakably mischievous look on his face.

Having left both car and luggage with the concierge, we went up to our room. The Sacher dated from Imperial times, with high ceilings, rococo décor and rich period furniture. Passing through a huge double door, we found ourselves in a large anteroom where Bob made me sit down and wait till the bellboy had brought up all the luggage. I was intrigued. While we were waiting, he asked me about my trip and rang down to ask for a bottle of Dom Pérignon to be brought to the room at seven. It augured well. He then opened the doors, which led to a second anteroom, then with an almost theatrical gesture, flung open yet another set of doors to reveal the most gigantic bedroom I have ever seen. Far away, across the other side of the room, was an enormous bed, and Bob said to me, "Let's run for it!" Like two crazy youngsters, we hurtled across the room, leapt onto the bed, fell into each other's arms and made love as if we were newlyweds. As night gradually filled the room, there was a discreet knock at the door to tell us that our champagne had arrived. We bathed, changed, then shared that delightful refreshment before joining in the nightlife of that bewitching city.

Bob had work to do in Vienna, but he did take some time off to go with me to the famous Spanish Riding School with its stunning Lipizzaner horses. On that first visit, I went on a quick sightseeing tour of the city, but I was to return there many times in the future, since it became a favorite venue for congresses amongst the international scientific community.

The following day, we continued our journey to Budapest, where Bob was to meet scholars at the Biological Research Institute. We were entertained there by Akademiai Kiado, Hungary's leading scientific publishing and printing concern, which had collaborated in the production of some sixty Pergamon titles. Our host was George

Bernat, a native of Maramarosh, with whom we remained friends for the next thirty years.

Budapest owes much of its beauty to the majestic Danube, which flows right through the city, its banks lined with baroque buildings. Bob took the trouble to show me certain parts of the old city, not without great personal emotion, for Budapest had represented all the hopes of his youth, yet it was also there that his adolescence had been so tragically cut short.

But my most memorable recollection of that first trip to Hungary was our visit to Lake Balaton. Bob very much wanted to see "the Hungarian sea" and Bernat immediately suggested a scenic tour, to include lunch at a well-known inn, renowned for its local fogash fish and Tokay wine, and a drive around the lake. After an excellent meal, Bob was keen to hire a boat and sail across the lake. Intent on pleasing such an important customer, Bernat immediately hired a local sailing boat and we took to the water, with me quite unsuitably dressed for the occasion in my high-heeled shoes. All went well at first and we greatly appreciated the magnificent landscape all around us, but suddenly the wind got up and the water started to become choppy. Before long, we were in the midst of a raging storm and our little boat was being tossed up and down like a cork. Bernat showed some anxiety and Bob asked him to look after me, while he went to help the sailors steer the craft towards dry land. Bernat, meanwhile, made me stand next to the mast and threw his arms around me so that I would not be swept overboard. I am not easily frightened, but I did think for a moment that we were going to die a stupid death, drowned in Lake Balaton. I've never been so grateful for the physical strength of a Magyar! The waves lashed my face and the boat keeled over to one side, with its mast almost parallel to the water. Although for most of the time, Lake Balaton calmly reflects the beauty of the surrounding wooded hills, it is known for its sudden, tempestuous storms which can rapidly transform its placid waters into surging waves. By the time we did eventually manage to get back to the jetty, I felt more dead than alive!

After that hair-raising experience, we finished off the evening in one of the city's famous restaurants where we were serenaded by the haunting tunes of gypsy violins. Bob was happy and kept asking them to play songs which evoked his youth, "Ochi Chornaya" and the Volga boat song. The next day, we left Budapest for Poland and Cracow, making a detour to visit Bratislava, where once again Bob walked the streets of his youth. It was all rather melancholy. At the time, I knew much less than I do now of those terrible years which saw the annihilation of the Jews of Mitteleuropa. It was difficult for me to imagine what life had been like for Bob. I tried, as sensitively as possible, to get inside the black hole of his mind, but he simply refused to let me in, resenting my every initiative in that direction. Everything to do with his past was still an open wound and the slightest intrusion caused him untold pain.

As we made our way to Cracow, we stopped just before the natural border formed by the Tatra Mountains and walked in silence into the woods. We sat at the edge of a wood, looking down on the little villages on the plain below. Nearby, a mountain stream rushed downwards, splashing over small boulders. Bob turned to me and said, "The mountains and forests near home were just like this." That was all he said, but I knew he was desperately sad to be so near home and not be allowed to go there, since it was out of bounds to all foreigners. It was late by the time we arrived in the medieval city of Cracow. Although its historic monuments remained intact and its university was flourishing anew, the city still had a rather battered appearance after years of German and Russian occupation, neglect and poverty. We were met there by Adam Bromberg, director of the Publishing House of the Polish Academy of Sciences, who was handling huge printing contracts for Pergamon Press.

The next day, Bob and I went on a pilgrimage to Auschwitz, sixty kilometers away. We did not exchange a single word as we walked around, both lost in our thoughts, overwhelmed by a depth of sorrow which weighed us down like a coat of lead. Few people visited the death camp in those days. We had been obliged to accept the presence of a non-Jewish Polish guide who showed us in great detail around the original camp, uttering an endless stream of platitudes. But it was not the camp we had really come to visit; we wanted to retrace the path trodden by Bob's family in their last few hours on earth, remember their suffering and quietly pray to God for the peace of their souls. It was in nearby Birkenau, known as Auschwitz II, that they had tragically lost their lives, along with most of their relatives and friends from Szlatina and the surrounding area. On Bob's insistence, the guide then took us to the vast compound of Auschwitz II. Numbness overcame me as I walked the road to death taken by those millions of victims. Not only did I feel bereft of any normal human warmth, but it was almost as if Nature herself had abandoned me. One might be tempted to ascribe those feelings to auto-suggestion, from what I have heard and read, but that was really not so. In those days Holocaust literature barely existed and my knowledge was limited apart from newspaper war reports and accounts of the Nuremberg trial. Endless gray clouds seemed to hang over the rows of remaining wooden huts where prisoners were once herded, or over the vestiges of their foundations. It was as if the smoke from all those millions of calcinated corpses still hovered between heaven and earth, refusing to disappear lest the world forget. We walked from one crematorium to another, then followed overgrown tracks leading to a marshy woodland pond. A dilapidated metal structure still stood there, above the level of the water. A rusty wheelbarrow had long since tipped its last cargo of ash into the murky depths. We knelt beside the dull gray waters and Bob plunged his hands into the mire, pulling out a handful of grayish mud full of calcified, pulverized bones. He took a white handkerchief from his pocket, carefully placed those macabre relics in it, then burst into tears. I could not say a word. Only silence was appropriate in the face of such anguish.

Since then, I have been back to Auschwitz several times, and the feelings I experienced then have been transformed into anger and a fierce determination never to allow mankind to forget the horrors it is capable of committing. But I never again felt the heartrending emotion of that first visit, the completely inconsolable despair which seemed to pierce its poisoned dagger into the heart of the man of my life, to whom I had become both wife and surrogate mother. That day, in a place that has come to symbolize the world's shame, I understood as never before how much I loved him. But at that very moment, by the cruelest of ironies, I experienced a feeling of guilt that nothing would ever assuage and sensed for a moment that I was perceived as an outsider: the execrated *goyim,* the poisoned source of all those evils. In Bob's eyes, by marrying outside his religion, by not fathering Jewish children who would take up the torch, he had failed in this most profound duty towards his martyred family.

Our hearts were exceedingly heavy as we left that scene of utter desolation and disgrace. When we returned to Cracow, Bob asked Bromberg all manner of questions about the deportations to the camp and what exactly had happened to people from the moment they tumbled down half-dazed from the overcrowded cattle cars onto the infamous Auschwitz ramp. Bromberg suggested that Bob should see *Nuit et Brouillard,* the first film on Auschwitz made in France by Alain Resnais, but it was so harrowing that Bob could not take it and we had to leave. At dinner that evening, a glass of wine was accidentally spilled on my dress. For a fleeting moment, I thought it was blood and screamed in fright. Bob was furious. I could not explain what had come over me, except that I was still reeling from the shock of that visit to the death camp, combined with the horrifying realism of the French film. But this was not the time to ask for sympathy.

We ended that part of our journey in Warsaw, where Bob took an hour off business to go with me to visit the site of the famous Warsaw Ghetto, which in those days was still a vast wasteland set around Nathan Rapaport's commemorative monument. Bob then decided to fly back to London, leaving me to drive the car back home. It was certainly a tall order, a drive of 2,000 kilometers all by myself, through territories Poland had newly acquired from Germany, from which all the original German population had been moved and replaced by Poles in the postwar shifting of peoples and borders. I had counted on my smattering of German to help me out, but the people I met on that journey were all Poles who had not seen a Western civilian car for years. The drive through Poland was difficult and rather scary, but that was nothing compared with the terrifying fog-bound motorway between Cologne and Aachen. Conditions were so bad that day that all you could do was follow the car in front, bumper to bumper. But there was worse to come when we came to a standstill and the German driver behind me decided to try and pick me up! His opening gambit was not very original: "Sie sind alle allein Fräulein, sie sind schön, komm mit mir in meinem Wagen" ("You're all alone, you're pretty, come and join me in my car"), but it was enough to make me very nervous. I tried hard to keep my cool, fobbed him off as best I could with a mumbled answer about staying in Aachen, then at enormous risk to myself, accelerated to overtake the whole line of cars, hoping to get rid of my ill-intentioned German. I arrived at a hotel at three o'clock in the morning, still feeling so frightened that the ghastly man might catch up with me that I pushed the wardrobe in front of the bedroom door and barricaded myself in!

I eventually arrived home and recounted the whole journey to Bob. His only reaction was to tell me there had been ten unresolved murders on that stretch of motorway that year. Many times in my life, when I was convinced I had accomplished a heroic feat and merited a pat on the back, I would be cut down to size by Bob's lack of appreciation. It certainly taught me humility, and although I craved his admiration, I had to be content with my own assessment of my worth. On the few occasions when he did acknowledge my achievements, I really valued his compliments, although the rarity of his praise also contributed greatly to my perpetual inferiority complex.

Other people would sometimes express admiration of my actions, but I just took it for flattery and did not believe them. It was Bob's praise I longed for; to quote Henry de Montherlant, what did it matter that I counted in the universe of others? Bob would sing my praises to other people, but rarely to my face, yet that meant so much to me. I never quite understood why he took me so much for granted. As the years passed, however, I learned to find my reward in the very fact that he asked me to undertake projects or tricky missions, or simply asked my advice or my impression of people and events.

In the course of 1959, Bob made two major decisions which were to change the course of our lives completely. He decided to enter the political arena and to move his business, and consequently our home, to Oxford. That year was also to bring me the great personal sorrow of my mother's death in the summer. She had become very frail; she had never really recovered after father's death two years earlier. From the moment I had exchanged the secure haven of our family home for married life in England in those tempestuous postwar years, she had been a constant source of encouragement and support, and her letters are a remarkable diary of her love for me. But in that summer of 1959, I had little time to brood over my loss, for with Broomfield sold and a general election looming, I needed to make urgent arrangements for the family. The older children were already away at boarding school and we decided to send the younger ones to stay with Marion in my parents' house in France until our new home was ready. Of course, schools then had to be found, bags packed for an absence of several months and I had to go and help get them get settled. Bob and I then proceeded to fight a general election and prepare for our move to Oxford.

I must say truthfully that I regarded Bob's entry into politics with some apprehension. From my own childhood, I had unhappy memories of all the unpleasantness associated with my father's campaign to be elected to the County Council. My father was a Radical Socialist, roughly equivalent to the moderate wing of the present English Labor party. The opposition at the time was the right and extreme-right, who ran a strong campaign, targeting my father with inflammatory language and obscene posters, stuck on the walls opposite our house. I felt unable to raise objections to Bob's political ambitions, having accepted them so long ago when he proposed to me. And, as always, once we had decided on a particular course of action, I really gave it my all. I knew little at the time about English politics but had been brought up with the humanist ideals of my

father, who had inherited his views from his Protestant and bourgeois industrialist backgrounds. His paternalist concern for the dignity of man and belief in social responsibilities beyond the exploita-
tion of the working classes had been passed on to me at an early age.
From my mother, I had inherited respect for people from different
social milieus and a rather uncritical compassion for the less privileged. But I was really ill-equipped to be thrown into the den of local
politics and parochial in-fighting.

Bob was selected as prospective Labor candidate for North Buckingham (North Bucks) in August 1959, after their much-respected
candidate, Dr. Gordon Evans, was badly injured in an accident.
There was some opposition amongst the local Labor party about the
fact that Bob had only been a paid-up member of the party for one
year. There were even rumors that he was not a Labor party member
but a Tory, who in the past had applied for nomination to a Conservative seat, but the Tories would not have him! The truth is that
Charles Hambro had suggested that Bob was just the sort of energetic young man the Conservatives were looking for to rebuild their
image after the Labor landslide victory of 1945. But Bob felt unable
to entertain such a prospect and declined. He was raised on socialist
ideas and well remembered the arguments of his politically active
mother, who ascribed the indignity of unemployment to the government of the right. Perhaps even more important, Bob considered at
the time that any right of center party was potentially fascist.

By September, his candidature had been endorsed by Labor's
National Executive Committee (NEC), and he began campaigning
with all his usual energy and originality, in preparation for the election on October 8. His mobile headquarters was a borrowed trailer,
painted red and white, from which he bombarded the electorate of
North Bucks with "Maxwellgrams," duplicated bulletins and messages relevant to the villages we passed through every day on our
campaign trail. During the course of three intensive weeks of campaigning, Bob and I certainly got to know the winding roads, quaint
little villages and three major industrial towns of North Bucks!

The Conservative candidate, Sir Frank Markham, had been MP
for North Bucks since 1955 and the Tories were determined to
return him to Parliament. They put up a vigorous fight which degenerated into a nasty smear campaign centered on Bob's foreign origins
and the Simpkin Marshall affair. A prominent Labor party member
even went so far as to endorse the Tory candidate's nomination! On
polling day, there was a nationwide last-minute swing towards the
Conservative party and Bob lost to Sir Frank by 1,746 votes, the

Liberal candidate having contributed to his defeat by polling over 4,000 votes. Bob was disappointed, but his performance was judged to be commendable, especially considering that Labor only managed to win one seat from the Conservatives in that election, and a Scottish seat at that. In a very short time, Bob and I had learned a great deal about the problems of "our" constituency and we had got to know its people and local Labor supporters. In the postmortem which inevitably followed, it became clear that the lack of postal votes from absentee Labor voters was a significant factor in defeats. Conservative activists conveniently forgot to nudge the elderly people they knew were Labor supporters, and Labor had lost almost every vote that could have been cast by locals who had moved away or by newcomers to the area who had forgotten to register for their vote. Those were hard-learned lessons which would not be forgotten next time around.

We returned to Esher, where my most immediate task was to organize our move from Broomfield to Oxford. I was not without misgivings about leaving a home where we had spent so many happy days as a family, but there were some compensations. Our new home would be close to the boys' school in Oxford, and because Bob's business premises would be literally a stone's throw away, we would see much more of him than we had in past years. I was also aware that Oxford was a center of learning which academics and scholars would automatically visit when they came to England, whereas Esher was too far from London and altogether inconvenient from the point of view of entertaining. But the major reason for the move was decisive: our warehouse in the Elephant and Castle district was going to being pulled down and we had to find new premises to house our antiquaria. It had proved impossible to find the kind of space we needed at a reasonable price in London; the only possible solution was to move away from the capital.

Bob resumed his active life in Pergamon, although he remained closely involved in Buckinghamshire local politics, hoping that he would have another chance to stand in the next general election. He even managed to get me involved by persuading me to stand as Labor candidate for the Newport Pagnell ward in the local County Council Elections of April 1961. The Labor Party General Management Committee (GMC) had decided to contest every seat in the constituency in order that Tory activists would be spread thinly in each town, thereby relieving the pressure on Bob and his political agent, Bryan Barnard, who were standing as candidates in adjoining wards. I hadn't the slightest hope of winning against a well-known and respected local lady, especially when the decision to run was made so late that I had only three weeks to campaign, receiving no help from the local Labor party who were opposed to the GMC's decision. I was thrashed but my defeat left no ill-feelings either way and I was nevertheless pleased to get back to a more normal routine in Oxford.

Our new home was a magnificent Victorian mansion built in 1858 for a local brewer, James Morrell. Standing on the site of previous Georgian, Tudor and possibly Roman houses, Headington Hill Hall was situated in fifteen acres of wooded parkland, with a magnificent view over the dreaming spires of Oxford. It was owned by Oxford City Council, who were looking for a tenant to take over this white elephant. When I first visited it, I could see immediately how other buildings on the site could be converted into new headquarters for Pergamon, but as for the Hall itself, I really wondered whether it could ever be turned into a home. During the war years, the house had been transformed into a Red Cross rehabilitation center for brain-injured servicemen and all the lawns had been dug up to grow vegetables. By 1959, it had been unoccupied for fifteen years and was completely dilapidated. The ceilings had collapsed in some rooms, the floors in others, the walls were painted in wartime cream and green and were peeling badly. Every single door was damaged, there were giant, ancient radiators everywhere and bathrooms with the most antiquated water systems imaginable: it was a real mess. Bob called in the builders, I called in Raymond Shard, now affectionately known as "Treaj" (Treasure) because of his resourcefulness, and we all set to work to rebuild that house. In the course of my thirty-two years of living there, the roof was completely retiled with small handmade tiles, the lead gutters replaced and the water and drainage systems extended so that bathrooms could be fitted both at the back and front of the house. The whole plumbing system was brought up to modern standards, as was the electric wiring. Walls were replastered, marble and carvings repaired, columns and balconies reinforced, several hundred cracked window panes replaced. The original plan of the house was reinstated, a modern elevator installed, two internal staircases built for access and as a fire precaution and the gardens were redesigned and replanted. None of all that happened of its own accord! All renovations are painful and protracted, but with Bob in a hurry, I had no alternative but to move into the house to urge along architects, foremen and workers. So it was that in February 1960, I moved into the only habitable bedroom on the top floor. It was rather spooky all by myself in that fifty-room mansion, but I went to bed cheerfully the first night, poring over the plans of the twenty-three rooms we had decided to use for the family and Bob's office, determined to be up early the next morning to energize the army of rather unmotivated workers who seemed to amble aimlessly around that huge barracks of a building.

As I was dozing off to sleep about eleven o'clock, I was suddenly awakened by the wind howling around the house and the noise of a window rattling, so I got up and wedged it with a piece of paper, mentally noting that all the window latches would need to be checked. I had hardly gone back to sleep when I was awakened yet again, this time by a terrible creaking sound. It was rather like a door slowly swinging open on rusty hinges, except that the noise didn't stop, it continued, as if the door was closing again, but with even more difficulty. By then, I was wide awake and determined to investigate this noise which seemed to come from somewhere outside my bedroom. I put on my dressing gown, went along one corridor, then another. Sometimes the noise seemed to get closer, at others it was further away. I went down the backstairs, opened one door, then another. I was getting closer. The noise was becoming unbearably loud. I traced it finally to a cupboard, which I opened gingerly to find an antiquated mechanism grating around and around on its rusty cogs. It turned out to be linked to an ancient weather cock on the roof, which transmitted wind direction readings to a huge circular dial in the entrance hall! Feeling immensely proud of myself, I made my way back to my bedroom, elated at having located my first "ghost."

As I walked back upstairs, something attracted my attention to a door on the landing which led to another part of the house, and I distinctly saw the door handle move up and down. I froze. I could not believe my eyes and stayed glued to the top of the stairs, scared out of my wits. After a little while, I recovered sufficient sangfroid to run back to my bedroom and barricade myself in just as I had done in Aachen, with the wardrobe against the door and my bed against the wardrobe! I was absolutely positive that I was alone in the Hall, and this time I knew for certain that I had a ghost for a companion. I was in a cold sweat and only relaxed enough to fall asleep as the first light of dawn pierced the darkness of the night. Afraid of being laughed at, I decided not to tell anyone about my ghost and gradually got used to the idea of sharing my nights with a spirit.

Soon afterwards, however, there was a much grimmer ghost story to recount. By that time, the house was almost ready for the family to move in, all the wallpaper was up, new carpets were laid and the hall freshly painted. One stormy afternoon, I was going up the main staircase when I realized that water was cascading in from a point in the ceiling at the top of the stairs. I immediately called in the architect, Mr. Underhill, whose brusque manner had prompted Shard and me to give him the rather disrespectful nickname of "Unterberg." He duly arrived the next day, inspected the problem and with a great deal of complicated explanation, told me that the leak resulted from a fault in the original construction of the house. There was little he could do, but he would investigate thoroughly, and hopefully find a way of putting it right.

The following week, however, after the ceiling had been given another coat of paint, exactly the same thing happened. I was furious, picked up the phone and complained at Unterberg's failure to solve the problem. He arrived at the Hall almost immediately and launched into a passionate diatribe, explaining that he had located the fault in an elbow pipe in the stonework and that you would either have to pull the house down or be a ghost to be able to put it right! He left in a state of great agitation. The next Monday, Raymond Shard telephoned me and asked me if I was sitting down. After I had replied in the affirmative, he blurted out, "Unterberg has hanged himself!" I was exceedingly shocked and proceeded to recount the story of my last unpleasant encounter with him the previous Friday. The curious thing was that from that day on, rain never poured in again on the stairs, and for the next thirty years I lived there, I fervently believed that Unterberg's ghost blocked the leak in the drainpipe. I even used to say good night to him as I passed by and looked up at the ceiling, thanking him for his dramatic but successful intervention.

Whilst I was fully occupied turning that ramshackle Victorian pile into a family home, Bob was busy organizing the relocation of Pergamon staff to Oxford. Although it was one of the most traumatic periods in the history of our ten-year-old company, it proved in the long run to be a wise decision. Key executives were quite happy to move their homes and families to Oxford, but the move was much more difficult for many of the other employees, especially for women whose husbands had jobs in London. I can still see the full-page advertisement Bob placed in all the local papers, with its big banner headline, COME AND WORK IN OXFORD FOR LONDON RATES OF PAY. That ad did the trick, and soon workers were leaving Oxford University Press and other local firms to work for us. There was the added attraction of free parking facilities and working only fifteen minutes away from the center of town with good public transport facilities. The staff operated at first from four large Nissen huts built in the grounds during the war for the Red Cross, and from the former stable block of the mansion, a handsome three-winged building constructed around a vast paved courtyard. But it was not long before we obtained planning permission to build new modern headquarters on the site, which were completed in record time. Pergamon was able to attract first-class personnel, most of whom stayed with the company for twenty or thirty years or more. Their loyalty to Bob and Pergamon was immense, and they soon got to know me and the children personally. We would hold regular Christmas parties at home for all the employees until the number grew so large that we had to move the function to a hotel in town. This close relationship between staff and family emphasized the family aspect of the firm, a feature our authors and editors particularly liked and frequently mentioned.

I soon found myself acting almost as a social worker, for whenever there was a family or staff problem, in some ways it affected us all. Employees would find their way to my office in the privacy of our home, and I rapidly became the agony aunt, hearing an endless saga of marriages on the rocks, adultery, babies born out of wedlock, serious medical problems, financial troubles and all kinds of shenanigans amongst in-house staff. I would do my best to help them with advice and a sympathetic ear, calling upon the wisdom of my experience, common sense and compassion for all that causes human suffering. I can boast a few repaired marital relationships and numerous successful approaches to Bob for financial or medical help or transfer of staff from one department to another to ease working tensions. I had a friendly relationship with most members of staff at all levels, which has endured to this day.

By the end of March 1960, the house was at long last ready for occupation and I fetched the children back from France in time for the Easter holidays. They spent hours and hours exploring the infinite resources of that wonderful house. There was nothing they didn't do: not a place they didn't investigate, not a tree they didn't climb. It was a real paradise for them. I had to keep calm when I caught sight of the boys clambering on the roof or when they reconnoitered the dangerous subterranean passages which, in their opinion, once linked the house to Magdalen College a mile or so away, although it was more likely that they led to underground water tanks. It was impossible to stop them from going into the offices and making friends with the staff, who loved the informality of it all. And then there were the pets—the dogs, cats, ponies and donkeys—

beloved by the children and spoiled by the staff. Once upon a time we had peacocks in the grounds and we would go to bed to their strident chorus of good night screams. They were joined by deer and squirrels, by foxes who chased the rabbits who in turn played with the magpies, by blue and green woodpeckers and ducks who nested in the bulrushes and took their ducklings into the swimming pool. There were goldfish in the pond and herons who came to gobble them up. It was a real menagerie and we all loved it.

The years ahead were to be outstanding ones for Pergamon. My own role as a hostess for the company increased dramatically. We started entertaining editors and authors for dinner after the annual general meetings of their journals, until the journals themselves became so numerous that we had to delegate some such functions to our very able journals director, Gilbert Richards, and his colleagues, although we always dealt personally with new or specially significant publications. It was about this time, too, that Bob started sending me to represent him at international conferences. So it was that I attended the 1960 AGARD meeting in Turkey where I met our now good friends in that field.

I love Istanbul and find it a magical city. Its setting is unique, with the Bosphorus, Golden Horn and Sea of Marmara encasing it like a jewel in lapis lazuli, and century upon century of civilization greets you everywhere. There are unusual monuments from Greek and Roman times, foremost amongst them the Basilica soft-water cistern built by the Emperor Justinian, which has a special place in my memory. It takes the form of an endless crypt filled with the purest green waters of an underground lake, which you reach by walking down a flight of steps, then embarking two at a time on a little craft rowed by a Charon-like boatman at the helm. You glide along, in the light of resin torches, casting enormous shadows on the distant walls, through a forest of Roman columns of green granite and pink porphyry, their antique colors reflecting in the transparent water. Alas, tourism has taken its toll and you are no longer allowed to visit the cistern like this. Then there are those moving earliest Christian churches of St. Eirene and St. Saviour in Kariye, whose Byzantine mosaics, unequaled in the world, are mercifully preserved by the layers of plaster with which the Moslems covered them. There is the glorious Byzantine cathedral of St. Sophia and the seventeenth-century mosques with marble carved like lace and tall, light minarets standing out against the constant blue sky and the unique marble sarcophagus, said to be of the young Greek conqueror Alexander. And all around, the unforgettable sight of endless cemeteries with their Moslem gravestones warmed by the sun and carpeting the hillsides which slope down to the sea. Over the years, I was to return to Istanbul many times, and I never tired of its beauty. Every time, I would visit other favorite sites, the Blue Mosque of Sultan Ahmed, the Topkapi palace and the Süleymaniye mosque.

Bob was to join me towards the end of the conference, but for a week I was on my own, holding the fort for Pergamon, who were as usual going to publish the AGARD proceedings. There was political unrest at the time in Turkey and I was looked after by a young military attaché. On one occasion, our Turkish hosts took me out for lunch to a restaurant on the Bosphorus, along with five other ladies. Before the main course arrived, we had already been generously plied with rather sugary and sickly Turkish delight. As I am not keen on sweet food, I was beginning to feel rather nauseated, and when asked what I would like to drink, decided to ask for vodka, knowing its powerful digestive qualities. At this, I was told that the Turks had an excellent equivalent of vodka called raki, which I simply had to taste. The drink soon appeared on the table, served in a small glass and looking precisely like vodka, and I immediately reached out to pick up the glass. But the naval officer caught hold of my arm and prevented me from taking it, leaving me to puzzle over why I wasn't allowed to drink. By the time the first course appeared, I was feeling decidedly sick and tried again and again to pick up my glass, but every single time, my escort gently prevented me. As the meal neared its end, I seized hold of my glass in a determined way and gulped it down in one go. In less than five minutes, I was overwhelmed by a most curious sensation; I really felt as if I were floating on air. The Bosphorus, which was on my right, suddenly appeared on my left and the restaurant's palm trees seemed to be rushing headlong into the water. I realized I was drunk. All I could think of was the shame I would bring upon Pergamon Press, my husband and myself and I resolved that somehow or other I just had to survive. It took all the willpower I could muster to stand up and walk back to the car unaided. I remember half-dozing in the car, hoping and praying that I could cope until I got back to my hotel. I still vividly recall climbing the flight of stone steps leading into the Istanbul Hilton, walking with great concentration to the reception desk and asking them to call me at six, in time to change for the evening banquet. I took my room key, managed to open the door, then fell on the bed and passed out!

At six, I was woken from my torpor, took a bath, put on my makeup and evening dress and made my way to the banqueting hall, where I was sitting on the right of the evening's Turkish host, Pasha Ulug, who was later to be hanged in the military putsch. When the meal was about to start, the dreaded raki appeared on the table again and I discovered the proper way to drink it. I watched as people picked up the small glass in front of them, poured a little of the alcohol into a larger glass, which they then filled with water, just as one does with Pernod. I decided to try it like that and was just about to empty some water into the glass when the Pasha caught hold of my hand, just as the naval attaché had done earlier, and said in excellent French, "Oh non! Je sais que Madame boit son raki pur" ("Oh no! I know that Madame likes her raki neat"). News of my adventure had already done the rounds and from then on, the hotel manager, bellboys, porters and any other Turk I met, would all, according to their station in life, bow or kiss my hand as a sign of respect for the woman who could hold her raki!

Bob joined me for the last two days of the conference and took me on a pilgrimage to Heider Pasha where he had embarked for Lebanon and Haifa in 1940 to set sail for Europe. From Istanbul, we flew to Israel and visited Jerusalem and Tel Aviv. It was the first time either of us had set foot on Israeli soil and we spent a week there, at a time when Jerusalem was still a divided city and dangerous for visitors. It wasn't possible to do much sight-seeing in those days, so we took a few days' holiday, sunning ourselves on the beach at Tel Aviv.

As I think back now over that period of our life, I realize what an incredibly busy and productive time it was for both of us, cramming in arduous careers, a busy social life, increasing traveling for Bob and the growing responsibilities of a large family for me. I would regularly drive the fifty miles to Marlborough College to fetch Michael, Philip and their friends and take them back home for a Sunday or weekend. The other children were day pupils at schools in Oxford and I was constantly busy with after-school activities for them. By 1961, I was pregnant again, for the eighth time, and the baby was due towards the end of December. Bob and I were overjoyed at the thought of a new baby. Neither of us had quite come to terms with the loss of Karine and we longed for another baby girl. We had also been saddened in 1960 when I suffered two miscarriages, probably brought on by overtiredness and the fact that I was approaching forty. I left for my sister's clinic in France as usual, having organized the family Christmas festivities, children's holidays and entertainment in advance. My disappointment at not being with my husband and children for Christmas was more than offset by the arrival of a new baby, our youngest daughter, Ghislaine, born on Christmas Day.

Two days later, our eldest son Michael was invited to a Christmas dance at a friend's house. On the journey home, the car in which he was a passenger was involved in an accident on the Bicester Road, near Oxford, and Michael was all but killed. For the next seven years, after undergoing brain surgery, he was to be kept alive in a coma in an Oxford hospital.

The bottom dropped out of our lives. The consequences of such a tragedy were incalculable for us all. Michael was a very good-looking young man in his sixteenth year and, being the eldest, was maturing quickly. He was responsible, gifted, an endearing child and the apple of my eye. I just don't know how one finds the strength to survive such a catastrophe. There are times when all you want is to die yourself; there is no possible consolation for the loss of a child. Perhaps the condolence letter which touched me most came from a Moslem friend of mine who assured me that time, being one of the attributes of God, would heal my wounds and one day my searing pain would give way to the sweetness of memory. I remember being appalled at the thought that my suffering might one day be forgotten. I was wrong. The bitterness of the pain has passed and I will never forget that wonderful child who excelled in all he did and showed such sensitivity and promise. All those years ago, our whole family was torn apart by grief. I cried so much then that I seemed to have exhausted the source of tears within me and have not been really able to cry since.

For a whole year I spent every morning at the hospital, and sometimes I would visit twice a day in the hope that if I kept talking to him, Michael might wake up from his deep unconsciousness, but he remained my sleeping prince for his last seven years on earth. For the whole of that first year, he was kept in an emergency ward at the Radcliffe Hospital in Oxford until the doctors decided to move him to a neurological unit at the nearby Churchill Hospital. I would do anything to stay beside him. I did the work of a ward orderly, talked to other patients and their parents. I saw people with horrific injuries, parents driven mad by their heartrending sorrow. Somehow I seemed to find words which healed, words I myself would have liked to hear. I learned from experience that encouraging people to express their grief was therapeutic, for them and for me. I remained close friends with the admirable sisters and nurses who devoted their lives to helping both patients and families and showed such love for my darling Michael. He was never once able to smile again nor express his gratitude. He never recognized me, nor Bob nor any of his brothers and sisters.

Bob was shaken to the very core of his being. He could not believe that fate had dealt him such a cruel blow after all he had already endured. Michael's closest brother, Philip, who worshiped his elder brother, suffered deeply and began a prolonged struggle to accept his loss. Anne lost her natural companion and an older brother she adored. Her security was shattered and it would take her years to come to terms with her grief. The twins clung to each other and allowed no one to penetrate their world. Ian was found playing endlessly with cars, ambulances, little figures in white coats and making blood-spattered drawings. The two little ones were seemingly unaware of the tragedy, but Ghislaine, who should have been the center of our love and attention, was hardly given a glance and became anorexic whilst still a toddler. One day, aged three, she planted herself in front of me and said simply, "Mummy, I exist." I was devastated, and from that day on, we all made a great effort with her, fussing over her so much that she became spoiled, the only one of my children I can truly say that about.

Each of us survived the trauma in our own way, some better than others. With hindsight, I realize that I should have had some counseling, since I did not really appreciate the burden it was for some of the children, especially the two older ones. Perhaps we should have brought Philip home from Marlborough—a boarding school—to be near us. At the time I really thought it would be best to leave the children in as normal surroundings as possible, but looking back now, perhaps I was mistaken. At first Michael's brothers and sisters would go and visit him in the hospital in the hope that their presence might bring back a spark of memory, but I realized that it was a harrowing and pointless ordeal for them. From then on, I took it upon myself to be Michael's only regular visitor, so that everyone else could return to a normal life, knowing that I was watching over him. But I know that when Philip was a student at Balliol College, he used to go to the hospital from time to time and I also discovered from Bob's drivers and Bryan Barnard, that Bob would sometimes turn up at the hospital, late at night on his way back home from London or the constituency, although he himself never told me this. For me, it was as if 1962 never existed. I have practically no recollection of events in that year. Later on, people would come and talk to me about things I said and did then, but I could not remember them. My diary of our India trip, begun on the day of our departure from England, December 27, 1962, is very revealing in this respect: I had dated it neatly December 27, 1961. For me, time had stopped then, on the day of Michael's accident, and it would take that journey to India to bring me back to the world of the living.

It was Michael's neurologist, Dr. Ritchie Russell, who realized the extent of my own needs. After I had carried on my daily routine of hospital visiting for a whole year, he came to see my husband. In his opinion, he told him, Michael was so strong that he might survive for years; I, on the contrary, would inevitably collapse if I carried on virtually "living" at the hospital in the totally vain hope that Michael would recover. He advised Bob to take me away for at least a month to help me recover some mental equilibrium. Bob followed his advice, and took me with him to India and Australia, where he was going to launch Pergamon's new Commonwealth Library of Science and Technology.

At first I was reluctant to go, feeling guilty at leaving Michael unconscious in a hospital bed. But Thelma Howell, the Staff Sister on the Radcliffe Emergency Ward who had supported me through an abyss of despair, persuaded me that I had to go to recover the strength I needed to carry on looking after Michael. She promised me that she would watch over him with the utmost love and vigilance, just as she had done for the past year. So we left exactly a year after Michael's accident for a long tour of India—Calcutta, New Delhi, Agra, Benares and Bombay, continuing via Columbo, Singapore and Jakarta to Darwin, where we started an Australian journey.

India left me with an overwhelming impression of earthen colors: of sandy, dusty, roads, fawn cotton suits and cashmere shawls worn by men sitting on donkeys, low dwellings made of yellowish clay, browny-beige humped cows ambling haphazardly in search of food and endless caravans of tawny camels. Even the splendid terra cotta-colored forts and palaces and the occasional striking stone buildings with their intricate lacy-patterned marble windows, enhanced the feeling of sunbaked Mother Earth. Flashes of women in brightly colored saris on their way to the village well, balancing shiny golden water vessels on their heads, stood out like colored gems against this attractive background of browns, yellows and ochres. Traveling along the roads, we would come across other women patiently walking behind two or three wandering cows, collecting their precious dung, then flattening it out immediately in their hands and leaving it to dry in the sun for fuel. As we drew near villages or towns, there would invariably be throngs of dusky-colored people milling about on both sides of the road, all busy selling and bartering in a seemingly endless bazaar of little stalls, supplying the daily needs of a community whose simple life seemed to take place mostly in the open air, for all to see and hear. Snake charmers would attract an enthusiastic audience and children would gather to watch mongooses in cages.

We were entertained in Calcutta by Professor Mahalanobis, director of the Institute of Statistics, whose wife, Rani, had been a favorite niece and secretary of the Indian Nobel-prizewinning writer Rabindranath Tagor and had translated his works into English. They were splendid hosts and their vast home with servants galore gave us a taste of highborn Indian society under the Raj. There was a huge lake in the grounds of their house, surrounded by luscious tropical plantations. I can still feel the cool of its deep green waters and remember all the fun I had floating and splashing about after Rani had a banana tree chopped down and thrown into the water to use as a raft. I loved listening to her tales of travels and conversations with Tagor; I was fascinated by her hundred-year-old collection of saris and all she taught me about India. Their palatial home was in stark contrast to the abysmal overcrowding and poverty of the city of Calcutta, struggling beneath the burden of a flood of newly arrived refugees from Pakistan, where people were skeleton-thin and many would just die of hunger, every day, on the streets.

Soon after, we left for Benares, where our visit early one sunlit morning to the Ghats, those flat stone steps leading down to the Ganges, moved me greatly. As we walked, we were met by a crowd of beggars, holding out their leprous stumps in ancient gestures of supplication. There were countless old people waiting for death beside the funeral pyres, whose acrid wreathing smoke carried away the souls of the departed. Men clad only in loincloths walked up and down from the river bearing sacred copper vessels which they had just filled with holy water. Men and women washed in the waters of the great river, that giver of life which cleanses you of your sins and transports the ashes of the dead inexorably downstream, towards the sea.

Our journey also took us to beautiful Agra and the unforgettable Taj Mahal. I had already heard so much about this palace, one of the Seven Wonders of the World, that I thought I might be disappointed, but it was quite the opposite; I was entranced. Nothing could have prepared me for the impact that monument had on me. Our hosts had arranged for us to see it three times, first at dawn when the main dome was iridescent in the pink rays of the sun, then at midday in golden sunshine and beneath the most glorious blue sky and finally at midnight, on a night in January when the full moon was at its brightest and picked out the marble of the dome and four minarets in a translucent pearly white. A great sense of calm and peace radiated from the Taj Mahal: the Emperor Shah Jahan's sorrowing love poem to the memory of his adored young wife, who died aged thirty-seven, having given him fourteen children. His plan had originally been to build a black marble tomb for himself next to hers, but his own son had held him prisoner and prevented him from building a second folly, and he is said to have died on the balcony of his palace, on the other side of the river, looking out towards the white Taj.

From Agra, we went to visit Fatehpur Sikri, the legendary sixteenth-century city built as a ceremonial capital by Akbar the Great, one of the best known emperors of the Mogul dynasty, on the site where his Hindu wife had given birth to his son Jehangir. Some five thousand people had moved there to help build and populate the new city, but after sixteen years it had ceased to exist, doomed for ever when the nearby lake dried up completely. Tropical vegetation quickly took over and before long all recollection of the Imperial Palace vanished from human memory until its rediscovery some three hundred years later by an English officer. But that long, undisturbed sleep had preserved the fabric of an architectural masterpiece, an exquisite blend of Moslem and Hindu styles, seen particularly in the great entrance door, the Sultana's palace, the audience chamber and the great mosque. I could not help associating this melancholy tale with Charles Perrault's story of Sleeping Beauty, written some hundred years after Fatehpur Sikri had "fallen asleep."

New Delhi was our next destination, where Bob already had an appointment with Prime Minister Nehru and hoped to have an opportunity to meet the president. He was also going to meet the Minister of Science and Culture and give two lectures, as he had in Calcutta, on the Administration of Science and Education, which he dictated to me for typing and retyping. By the time we reached the capital, news of Bob's trip had been well publicized in the newspapers and the phone never stopped ringing. As I was acting as secretary, I had barely any time for sightseeing and just managed to snatch a half day here and there to visit the splendid fort and palaces of that great city. But as we came and went from the splendid Ashoka Hotel, we would be ushered in and out by magnificent porters dressed in the uniform of Bengal lancers, which gave me quite a thrill as if we were bit players in the famous film of that name. Every day, I would welcome Bob back after his day full of appointments by handing him the letters I had typed and passing on all the telephone messages I had taken. There were always so many that in the end he found them wearisome, especially since most of them were of no importance whatsoever. But I had no way of assessing their significance. All the people I spoke to announced themselves with grandiose sounding titles, the Managing Director of the New Delhi Emporium, President of the National Engineering Company, Chairman of this or that Institute. After a while, Bob told me to stop taking the names of all these people. "Any more calls like that, just say I can't see anybody as I'm leaving for Bombay." Relieved at the thought of not having to worry any more, I followed his instructions in earnest the next day, which was as usual incessantly interrupted by numerous callers.

When Bob returned that evening, he asked me, "Any interesting phone calls?"

"Oh no, only the usual rubbish. You wouldn't believe it, but one of them actually called himself the president of India, no less!"

"But he *is* the president of India! When does he want to see me?"

"I said you couldn't see him as you were leaving for Bombay."

Well, I leave you to imagine the rest of the conversation! Bob immediately got on the phone to the president's office and tried to repair the damage, blaming the misunderstanding on me and my imperfect knowledge of the English language! I had obviously not understood what was said to me.

The next day, a phone call came through from the president's aide-de-camp, who gave Bob an appointment and added, "The president particularly requests that Mrs. Maxwell should come with you." At this, Bob remarked sarcastically that the president was clearly curious to meet a wife who could be as foolish as that. Anyway, my stupidity had earned me a meeting with President Radhakrishnan. When we arrived, we were first of all shown into the aide-de-camp's office by smartly uniformed lancers, then at five o'clock precisely we were introduced to the president, who offered us tea. He was a tall, lean, imposing man with a sensitive, worn and intelligent face. A philosopher, he had taught for several years at Oxford and was dressed as a Punjabi, all in striking white, like the Pope. Our appointment was scheduled to last twenty minutes but actually lasted forty-five, during which Bob swiftly and succinctly explained his mission in connection with Pergamon's Commonwealth Library, which he was in the process of launching. But when he mentioned Kashmir, a sensitive issue for any Indian politician, we were given an unforgettable lecture on the Kashmiri situation with a few generalities of high politics thrown in for good measure.

Whilst we were in New Delhi, Bob met several Indian ministers and we were received by the High Commissioner for India, Sir Paul Gore-Booth, at his official residence, and by the American Ambassador, John Galbraith, whom we were to meet again in 1971 when Bob was a Fellow at Harvard University. Bob also made contact with the largest local publishers and booksellers and visited various educational establishments, amongst them Dr. Deshmukh's Institute, a center of learning for scholars the world over. There we met Mrs. Deshmukh, a member of the bar of the Supreme Court who had been party to the drafting of India's Constitution. As a follower of Gandhi, she had fought alongside him in the cause of independence for women, which landed her in jail for three years. Through friends of mine, we also met the Maharaja of Baroda, whose enlightened father had introduced into his state as far back as 1896 compulsory education and medical care and abolished child marriage and the Hindu practice of suttee (when a widow immolates herself on her husband's funeral pyre).

It was soon time to leave for Bombay, where Bob was to give a lecture. We were also invited to the Tata Institute of Fundamental Research by its director, Dr. Bhabha, who was hosting the Executive Committee of the International Union of Pure and Applied Physics, many of whose members Bob already knew. The most memorable event for me of that stay in Bombay was the invitation to dinner we received from the Governor of Maharashtra, Mrs. Vijaya Lakshmi Pandit (Nehru's sister), who was installed in splendor at Government House on Malabar Hill. Tall Indian palm trees were softly lit against the night blue sky and from her house we had the most stunning view over the bay of Bombay and the so-called "Queen's necklace"—the twinkling string of lights illuminating the bay. Mrs. Pandit was a delightfully elegant and feminine woman, yet she was known to have great strength of character, which helped her to achieve high office as the first woman Minister in India, first woman president of the United Nations General Assembly and Indian High Commissioner in London. She was a highly approachable person, and forthcoming in conversation. In the following year, I had occasion to entertain her myself in Oxford and these subsequent meetings confirmed my initial impressions.

Whilst we were staying in Bombay, I also managed to fit in some sightseeing to the Elephanta Caves and other places of interest, but my recollections of individual Indian monuments are a little fuzzy. They all seem to have merged in an endless blur of sun-baked, beautifully carved pillars, of statues of gods and goddesses: Lord Shiva, his wife Parvati and their son Ganesh, the elephant-headed god of wisdom; together with a whole pantheon of minor gods, depicted in the most complicated physical positions with multiple arms and legs, symbols of religious or heraldic significance or associated with the most contorted lovemaking imaginable. I loved India, felt at peace there, and believed that in a previous life I could easily have been a blue scarab, sitting on the warm stones of a temple. But the time had come to leave India for an altogether different world, the continent of Australia.

I was soon to discover, however, that Australia was not for me, but I had to agree that it was the most marvelous country for young and adventurous people keen to seize opportunities for themselves and their families. Although we were welcomed with open arms in Sydney, Melbourne and Canberra, I must confess that my most vivid recollections are not of people and places, but of strange animals! The platypuses, which my lisping hostess called "platyputheth," pandas, emus, koala bears and of course kangaroos—it was only when I had seen hundreds of them in the country around Canberra that I realized what a pest they were for farmers and what devastation they caused. We had been invited there by Mr. and Mrs. Osborne, wealthy owners of 18,000 acres of grazing land and 20,000 sheep, who drove us for miles through the bush, then took us up in a little plane to give us an idea of its extent and the sparse distribution of sheep stations. It was whilst we were there, on the other side of the world, that news of Hugh Gaitskell's death reached us. Bob was shocked and it took him some time to shake off the shadow cast by the untimely demise of a friend who would certainly have made an excellent prime minister. Despite being lavishly and warmly entertained in Australia, I found the land and its people altogether too vast, too rough, too brash, too uncouth, too wild—just too much! I am certain that my sweeping generalizations do gross injustice to that great and generous country. I would have welcomed an opportunity to go back there at my leisure and discover it in another light, but I never had the chance.

We visited the universities of Sydney and Canberra, and in the capital, the distinguished neuroscientist Sir John Eccles and his wife gave a splendid and useful cocktail party in our honor, allowing Bob to make contact in a single day with most of the Australian scientists he wanted to meet. I liked Lady Eccles immensely and we found we had similar tastes. She was kind enough to invite me to her home, where we talked about her large family and my recent tragedy. By now Bob had accomplished most of his aims for the trip, and for me time was beginning to drag. I was homesick and couldn't take my mind off Michael. We decided it was time to head for home, stopping off en route for three days in New Delhi, then flying back to England.

As soon as I was home, I rushed to the Radcliffe Hospital to see Michael. Nothing had changed, and I knew that I just had to start living again for Bob and the other children. During our extensive travels, we had been drawn closer together in our long talks about Michael's accident and the family, and were able for the first time to contemplate a future without our eldest son. We had also realized that our plan to move to the constituency was now out of the question, even though Bob was spending a great deal of time there. It was essential for me to be near the hospital where Michael now lived. But I also wanted to help Bob and be near him, so we decided that I would take on some activities in the constituency.

Although we had originally envisaged a part-time involvement, for the next fourteen years politics were to occupy a great deal of my time and bring a new dimension into my life. As the months passed, the country was expecting a general election to take place in the spring of 1964, but in the event it was postponed until the last possible moment, October of that year. Bob decided to use those extra months to turn Pergamon into a public company.

July 16, 1964 saw the public offer of 1,100,000 Pergamon shares, 29 percent of the share capital, designed to finance further expansion and acquisitions. The offer was an immediate success, opening and closing within one minute and oversubscribed twenty times: the least one can say is that buyers didn't have to be dragged in! The media had ample time to analyze the proposed offer and did not hesitate to do so. Some commentators found the shares cheap and attractive, others considered them too risky, there was a whole gamut of opinion. The tabloids tended to focus on Bob's personality and his rags to riches story, describing him as "roguishly handsome" and pointing out that he collected more abuse and envy than any publisher since the Copyright Acts were passed. The more serious financial columns agreed that there was an expanding market which Bob had known how to capture, and wished him well in his venture.

I talked recently to Sir Michael Richardson, a much respected financial figure in the City who was with Panmure Gordon, the brokers who handled the issue at the time. Because Bob was a virtual newcomer in City terms and the sour memory of Simpkin Marshall's demise still lingered, they had been extra careful in examining Pergamon's previous annual report and accounts, making a point of talking with Bob's bankers. They found no grounds to justify any of the innuendoes or downright lies about this period of his business life, which have appeared in print since Bob's death. The issue was completely above board and the shares were in fact conservatively priced. The fact that they went up by 20 percent on the first day of trading confirms the general feeling of the market that they were a good investment.

The success of Pergamon's share issue added to Bob's desirability as the new darling of London hostesses. He brought good looks and liveliness to their parties, along with an aura of mystery, which always fascinates women. Although he never had the refined social manners to which I was accustomed, he had acquired an acceptable standard from my teaching and his own observation and any lapses were quickly forgiven because of his brilliance in conversation. Sadly, in the last few years of his life, when I was no longer at his side to remind him constantly that "manners maketh man," he tended to overlook this aspect of social intercourse. I remember one amusing instance when we were invited for dinner by Sir Isaac and Lady Wolfson. By then, Isaac was in his late sixties; he was a highly respected businessman and philanthropist and could speak with justifiable authority on economics and business. That evening, he was pontificating on economic measures he considered detrimental to the country, punctuating every one of his statements with a rhetorical question, "Can someone tell me why?," then carrying on with his lecture to a captive audience. When this performance had gone on for some time, Bob interrupted forcefully, using all the strength of his voice, and said, "Sir, if you will only switch off your sender and turn on your receiver, I'll tell you why!" Sir Isaac stopped midstream, his mouth wide open in astonishment and all the guests were stunned at such audacity from a young upstart. Bob then proceeded to answer the question. I was extremely embarrassed, but sneakily proud of Bob's courage. Sir Isaac must have forgiven him, because we were invited there again and later became friends with his children.

Our life in Oxford during the 1960s was overshadowed by Michael's fate, but it was extraordinarily active and, for the business, highly successful and productive. Pergamon was becoming a name to reckon with in the international world of learning, Bob's image as a successful entrepreneur and a man who got things done was to win him a seat in Parliament, Pergamon's successful public issue earned him the respect of the City and continued confidence of the banks; the stability of his family life was an added security. His understanding, compassion for people's sufferings and generosity towards many charities brought acceptance in social circles, and his attractive physique coupled with his enigmatic past, charisma and money opened the doors of famous London hostesses of the period.

England was at long last emerging from the dreariness of the post-war years. "You'd never had it so good" claimed the Tories. Gaiety was in the air and British rock ruled the pop world, with new music and songs being created all over the kingdom, led by the Beatles and Rolling Stones. Shop windows glinted and glittered. Clothes were extravagantly beautiful and ladies' fashions went from the midi, the calf-length day dresses of wartime, to the era of the miniskirt, dry-cleaned by the inch and sometimes so short that nothing was left to the imagination! London was the swinging capital par excellence: young people rushed to Carnaby Street and the King's Road to buy the latest hippie gear and gathered together at huge pop festivals, where "flower children" set themselves free with pot and the pill. America elected John F. Kennedy, who captured the world's imagination and raised morale with his famous "Ask not what your country can do for you but what you can do for your country." The Kennedy frontier extended to Europe, epitomized by his much-quoted "Ich bin ein Berliner!" His assassination in November 1963 stunned the world, as did those of his brother Bobby and Martin Luther King, Jr. barely five years later. The world itself seemed to shrink with ever bigger jets flying more miles nonstop, yet it extended immeasurably when the Russian Yuri Gagarin was the first man to orbit the earth and America's Neil Armstrong the first to set foot on the moon.

Those were great years with great expectations. Britain was trying to modernize its economy and we at Pergamon were part of it. We were a growth company based on scientific research and were exporting most of our output at a time when earning foreign exchange was a key aim of UK economic policy. It would not be long before Bob was also in the thick of it at Westminster.

7

Would Eleanor really have been able to explain the deep motivation behind a great deal of her behavior? How far was she in control of the varied roles she played in the course of her long life, and how far did she slip into them unawares?

D. D. R. OWEN, *ELEANOR OF AQUITAINE*

It all began at 11 A.M. on Tuesday, November 3, 1964, the day of the State Opening of Parliament with all its historical pomp and splendor, the day when Bob first took his seat in the House of Commons as a Labor MP in Harold Wilson's new government. I had been lucky enough to be offered an invitation to watch from the Royal Gallery leading to the House of Lords, where the monarch traditionally performs the ceremony after the summer recess or a general election. It was a splendid vantage point—from there you saw the glittering procession make its stately way from the Queen's Robing Room to the Prince's Chamber and into the House of Lords. Preceding the monarch were the Royal Heralds robed in all their finery, their titles dating back to medieval times: Rouge Dragon Pursuivant, Bluemantle Pursuivant, Gold Stick in Waiting and a host of lesser heralds, gentlemen ushers, kings of arms and equerries. Just ahead of Her Majesty walked the principal peers of the realm, then came the Queen herself, followed by members of her Household, her pages of honor, the Mistress of the Robes, Ladies of the Bedchamber, Lords in Waiting and assorted aides-de-camp.

The Queen was attired in a long dress of heavy brocade, encrusted with jewels, set off by a fabulous necklace of enormous diamonds and matching pendant earrings. She was wearing the gold imperial state crown, a replica of Queen Victoria's state crown adorned with three thousand diamonds, sapphires, emeralds and pearls. She walked slowly, her whole being sparkling and glistening as she moved, her coat of red velvet embroidered with gold and trimmed with ermine, trailing behind. Thick, gold bracelets studded with gems glinted against the whiteness of her long gloves. Standing in the splendor of the Royal Gallery, I followed Her Majesty's movements as she made her way through the Prince's Chamber and into the House of Lords. When she disappeared from view, I could picture her slowly ascending the steps to take her place on the throne whilst her ladies in waiting skilfully arranged her train in a curve in front of her. As I waited there, I felt immensely privileged to witness such impressive pageantry firsthand, long before television and photographs had made the ceremony familiar to all Britons. That day, I had to be content with Bob's description of the scene in the House of Lords, although two years later I was to see all of the ceremonial in the chamber itself from a seat in the Strangers' Gallery.

Along with other Members of the House of Commons, Bob followed behind the Speaker, the Prime Minister and Black Rod,[1] and took his place in the tight squeeze behind the Bar of the House of Lords. From where he stood, the Queen looked a diminutive and lonely figure, almost dwarfed by her heavy crown. The judges, resplendent in their wigs and impressive robes, were packed together on the Woolsack.[2] To the right were the bemedaled foreign ambassadors and high commissioners clad in uniform or evening dress. Hundreds of peers bedecked in red and ermine occupied the center of the house in front of the Queen, while peeresses in ceremonial dress and tiaras crowded the side benches. Up in the Strangers' Gallery sat specially invited guests, amongst them the Prime Minister's wife, Mary Wilson, and other wives of members of Parliament, in their smart day dresses with matching hats and gloves. It was a truly magnificent sight, a tradition scarcely changed since the days of the first Queen Elizabeth. That State Opening in November 1964 was not only highly

---

1. Ceremonial official of the House of Lords who acts as messenger from the Lords to the House of Commons.

2. Large red cushion filled with wool that the Lord Chancellor sits on in the House of Lords.

significant for the Labor Party—back in power for the first time since 1951—but for Parliament too, since the coming session marked the seventh centenary of Simon de Montfort's Parliament.[3]

The time came for the Queen to read her speech. All eyes were riveted on her, and the chamber echoed to the recurrent, "My Government will ... My Ministers will ..." It lasted a full fifteen minutes, whereupon the entire ceremony was reversed, so to speak, with the Queen escorted out of the chamber. All told, it had lasted well over three hours, and I had thoroughly enjoyed every minute. Two years later, when I was fortunate enough to be present again, I witnessed an unchanged pageant, except that Prince Philip, the Duke of Edinburgh, accompanied the Queen that time, and Admiral of the Fleet Earl Mountbatten of Burma was Gold Stick in Waiting.[4]

That imposing spectacle was an unforgettable reenactment of history and tradition at a time when royalty had not yet been debased by the younger generation behaving as if they had forgotten their motto, "Noblesse oblige." In recent years, they have mistakenly believed that conducting themselves like commoners would win them greater popularity, when in fact their unguarded behavior has contributed to the demystification of the royal office and the disaffection of the public, especially the young in search of heroes. Bob and I both respected the Queen immensely, and he would not tolerate a single word of criticism of the royal ladies in his presence, nor of Prince Charles or the Duke of Edinburgh. His loyalty was total, and in later years he landed in hot water over the Commonwealth Games, trying to protect the Queen's good name. He was, however, much less tolerant of the antics of the younger members of the Royal Family.

Nearly three weeks had elapsed since Harold Wilson had been elected prime minister and Bob had won his seat for Labor at Buckingham. Soon after the opening of Parliament, Bob's political agent, Bryan Barnard, introduced him to the Deputy Speaker, Dr. Horace King, whom he knew well. Bryan later told me how Bob came to be

---

3. Simon de Montfort, Earl of Leicester (c. 1208—1264), was leader of the English Barons in England's Civil War of 1264. His great Council—or Parleyment—was England's first truly representative Parliament.

4. The Gold Stick in Waiting is the carrier of the gold stick, or gilt rod, used on state occasions.

the first Labor MP to deliver his maiden speech on the very day he took his seat. Bob apparently asked Dr. King his advice about how and when he should make his first speech, to which the Deputy Speaker replied, "You should seek a good attendance record, listen carefully to experienced debaters and then when a subject you know something about is up for debate, you make your maiden speech." Bob retorted, "I've certainly not come to the House to be a rubber stamp," and he proceeded to ask if he could speak that afternoon. Somewhat taken aback, Dr. King agreed to call him about 4:30. That gave him two hours to write his speech, which was not to exceed eight minutes.

Immediately after the Speaker had selected two Labor back-benchers to "move the Loyal Address" to Her Majesty, thanking her for her gracious speech, Dr. King nodded in Bob's direction and he rose to his feet. Following tradition, he began by praising the work of his predecessor, focusing the first half of his speech on the problems of his constituency. In the second part, however, he argued strongly for government assistance in applying science to industry and criticized the waste of scientific and engineering manpower—not to mention taxpayers' money—on defense research programs. It was a forceful maiden speech which, while antagonizing some, earned Bob the respect of distinguished politicians. The periodical *Nature* quoted his words almost verbatim, urging the government to take advantage of scientific research and concluding, "The opinions and ideas of Mr. Maxwell are what we have been awaiting for a considerable time." Bob had chosen to ignore many aspects of Dr. King's advice, but he did at least speak on a subject he knew well, an area—science and technology—which had featured prominently in Wilson's election campaign.

From the moment Bob stood up to make that maiden speech in Parliament, he was irrepressible. In his first sixteen months in the House of Commons, he made two hundred interventions. Harold Wilson, who became a friend over the years, was later to write to me:

It was quite clear from the outset that Bob would make his mark in the House of Commons because he was a vigorous speaker with something to say, and he usually attracted quite a lot of attention. I for one always went in to listen to his speeches. Nevertheless, the House of Commons does not take kindly to those, who, notwithstanding their undoubted ability, attempt very early to impress such ability upon the House. . . . But even if he had taken a more subdued role, while still showing that he had real talent, I think that his independence of spirit would probably have prevented him from attaining high office.

Bob and I had agreed that once the formal opening of Parliament was over we would meet briefly before I made my way back home, leaving him to go on to the House of Commons. I was still reflecting on the dazzling splendor of the occasion as I walked back to my car and set off for Oxford. But as I started driving, my mind went back to the grueling three years which had paved the way for Bob's victory. I remembered the election defeat of 1959. We had realized then that if Labor was to stand a chance of winning the seat, every single Labor voter would have to be identified and wooed, and in particular, Labor postal votes had to be dramatically increased. Bob and his agent concluded that a complete recanvassing of the constituency was necessary if they were to do justice to the postal votes. But it needed someone in charge prepared to devote time and energy to this undertaking. Somehow, my name was suggested, and before long I found myself even more deeply involved in Bob's campaigning as official Postal Votes Officer.

I embarked upon my new job with enthusiasm, but also with trepidation. The agent gave me his unqualified support, but he already had his hands full with general administration and running the local weekly tote, and was pleased to hand over this time-consuming job to me. Our house in Bletchley, the largest town in our constituency, was to become my second home. We bought the house in 1963 and often stayed there, especially at election times when it became our full-time home. First I set about organizing a survey of the whole constituency, working late into the night to analyze the results and prepare the next day's work. It was a laborious job. My own efforts, of course, would have been in vain without a network of dedicated helpers, who were to form the nucleus of the Socialist Women Circles I founded in the constituency, which remained active for the next twelve years. My French taste in food encouraged Labor women to meet over cheese and wine, in candlelight, as opposed to the traditional sausage and mash.

Every evening, we would enlist the help of some twenty to thirty members and go canvassing. I even persuaded my son Philip to help, along with many friends and Labor supporters from Pergamon Press. I gave teach-ins in many of our North Bucks towns and villages and taught new members how to canvass, having learned all this myself from wonderful stalwarts in the 1959 election. I also made real friends in the constituency—hardworking and generous people. I drank endless cups of tea and heard countless stories and streams of gossip. I shall never forget the storm that ensued when one local wife discovered that her husband had registered for his own postal vote, but had done nothing about hers! As he wrote to me a few days later, "My wife threatened to axe me for failing to register her. You have now brought peace and quiet to our little abode." Nor shall I forget the afternoon I sat for hours having tea with a local resident, who, as I got up to leave, said to me, "So nice of you to call, Mrs. Kellett" (the prospective Conservative candidate). There was a great spirit of brotherhood at the time and my life was enriched by the comradeship that prevailed in the North Bucks of the sixties. By the time the day of the 1964 election came, there was hardly a door in the whole constituency of 58,000 voters on which I hadn't knocked personally. And we were finally rewarded by a total of 1,750 Labor postal votes in an 86.5 percent poll, one of the highest in the country, helping to ensure Bob's majority of 1,481.

Whilst I and my constituency friends were pursuing this unglamorous assault on the postal votes, Bob was working tirelessly in the limelight. He would drive to the constituency every evening to attend even a minor Labor meeting in the back of beyond, as well as address major crowds in the factories and bigger towns. Greatly helped by the results of our canvass, he would make a point of calling personally on the waverers or "don't knows."

By the time of the final meeting before the election, the scent of victory was in the air. That was the famous occasion when a Conservative activist, totally misjudging the general mood of the meeting, tried to reintroduce the old Tory hobby horse of Bob's Czech origin.

"Isn't it true, Mr. Maxwell that you're only an Englishman by nationalization?"

Gales of laughter greeted his unwitting malapropism. The five hundred Labor supporters packed in Wilton Hall that night could hardly contain their glee. Bob intervened in his deep and resonant voice, obviously enjoying a chance to have some fun at the Tories' expense.

"Now, now, now, we're all here to have a good time, give the gentleman a chance, I'm ready to answer his question."

Silence fell and Bob addressed the man he knew well. "Tell me Mr. Wheeler, did you have to make an effort to be born?"

"No, none at all!"

"Did you choose to be born in this country?"

"No! of course not! How could I?"

Then Bob thundered,

"Well, sir, I did both, I chose this country and made an effort to become British."

Bob had the audience in the palm of his hand. As he left the meeting that night, a member of the audience handed him a letter which read, "You deserve to win," signed "A Tory." And win he did, defeating the Tory candidate, Mrs. Elaine Kellett, by a comfortable majority for a marginal seat.

It was a great victory and a crucial one for Harold Wilson's government with its slender winning margin, although two years later another general election was to reelect Labor, giving the prime minister a safe majority and Bob an increased vote under a slogan suggested by the television star David Frost—"Let Harold and Bob finish the job!" Bob had fought hard against determined opposition; he had won and was radiant with success. What a long way he had come from Szlatina! I remembered his promises when he proposed to me. He had already won an MC, re-created his family and made a fair-sized fortune. Was it really possible that he was also going to become a political figure of note?

After the election, our schedules became quite insane. Besides my work at Pergamon, and the fact that after Michael's accident I only allowed Marion and myself to drive the children anywhere, I was also heavily involved in charity work. Starting with the Royal College of Nursing, I had become interested in leukemia charities after Karine's death, and with Michael's accident, added Mencap (the Society for Mentally Handicapped Children and Adults) and other charities dealing with brain research to my activities. On top of all that, I now had to give interviews, attend women's meetings, political meetings and civic functions and found myself constantly "on show" on constituency platforms. I had to open schools, bazaars, fêtes, garden parties and barbecues, start races, present silver cups, guess the weight of cakes or the number of sweets in a jar, draw tickets at raffles, visit hospital wards and keep an eye on all the elderly people I had visited regularly when I wanted their votes, not wishing to abandon them after they had helped me. I became interested in the welfare of the old and founded a senior citizens' club in Wolverton where I cooked a hot meal once a week for sixty people. At the other end of the age range, I recognized the need for a large preschool playgroup in Bletchley when I discovered that most of the local children had nowhere to play but the streets and many of their mothers not a single hour to call their own. With the help of fifty volunteers and eight paid and qualified staff, the playgroup took in eighty children under the age of five, in four groups of twenty, and was to continue for the next twenty-five years under my chairmanship. I also went regularly in the evenings to the Strangers' Gallery of the House of Commons, listening to the debates when my husband was speaking and trying to understand what it was all about. I shall never forget my first experience of the House of Commons at work—it was an absolute bear garden. I didn't have a driver in those days, so would make my own way everywhere. I would drive Bob back from the House of Commons to Fitzroy Square, sometimes steal a few hours of lovemaking, then return to Oxford in the early hours of the morning. I had a constitution of iron, but I more than needed it.

During the first two years of Bob's parliamentary career, the government majority dwindled to one and it was crucial for all Labor MPs to be present for every vote. Bob would frequently have appointments to speak in the constituency and I would suddenly find myself representing him at a minute's notice, expected to speak publicly and knowledgeably about the latest local conflict or problems. Perhaps the most nerve-racking episode of this kind occurred in the autumn of 1965 when Bob was guest of honor at the centenary anniversary meeting of the Union of Vehicle Builders in Wolverton, who had the distinction of making the carriages for the royal train. Bob had already phoned to let me know that he would only just make it in time and had asked me to hold the fort until he arrived. I arrived as late as was decent, hoping against hope that Bob would soon be there. As I walked into Wolverton Hall, I realized immediately that it was packed full of high-ranking union officials.

The proceedings began and still no sign of Bob. First one chap got up and started haranguing the crowd, then a second, then a third. I was getting more and more uncomfortable, dreading the moment when my turn would come. The chairman then turned to me and whispered, "What do you think? Is he going to come?" I nodded, trying to look confident, and asked him to let everyone else speak first. When there was no other speaker left the chairman got up and made a brief speech to introduce me. The assembled members already knew me well, but what they didn't know was that I was petrified of them that evening! Ever since I had taken my place on the platform, I had been racking my brain to find one useful piece of information I could pass on to them in my speech, since I knew next to nothing about unions in general or theirs in particular.

I walked slowly towards the lectern, praying for a miracle, or failing that, for the earth to open up and swallow me. I knew that I was going to ruin my own credibility in their eyes and, worse still, my husband would lose all their votes next time around. I began by reminding them of the political circumstances which had forced Bob to delay his arrival, then blurted out a most unfortunate sentence, "Had my husband been able to make it tonight, he would have wanted to talk to you about . . . " I had no idea what Bob would have wanted to say and I ought to have said just that; at least it would have been honest. Realizing my blunder, I was just about to faint (this seemed the only way out) when the double doors at the back of the hall opened and Bob walked in. It was the miracle I had prayed for. I had willed him to come and there he was. He ran down the hall, vaulted onto the platform and kissed me unashamedly to thunderous applause. He had saved me—by a hair's breadth. But I learned an important lesson that night. From then on, I never attended any public event without first having done my homework.

An MP's wife leads a strange life. She has no official status, so at every social function in the House of Commons, I would introduce myself as the "Member for Buckingham's wife." It could hardly be more clear that one was a mere appendage. Then there was the problem of actually meeting your husband when he was in the House. There was nowhere to wait apart from the draughty Members' lobby where, like any other constituent, you had to sit on the hard benches lined up along the walls. If you wanted to see your husband, you had to send a green card via the duty policeman, and with any luck, he might appear an hour later. When finally I managed to get hold of him, Bob might then take me to the Harcourt Room for a cup of tea, unless he was summoned by one of the constant division bells; or if he was due to speak, he would obtain a ticket for the Strangers' Gallery for me.

It was a completely different matter in the constituency where people had seen me at work and respected me for my efforts on Bob's behalf. Yet even there I was always expected to be well turned out and available for a long list of local functions. People were apt to forget that I also had a husband and large family to look after. The endless litany of balls, dances, dinners and opening ceremonies of all sorts in North Bucks and in London brought me the eternal female problem of what to wear. I discussed it with Bob and we agreed that I would have to invest in a reasonable wardrobe, so that at least I would be spared that problem on top of all the others. I was lucky enough to be introduced to a French dressmaker, Madame Fausta, who had previously worked for Lanvin and Nina Ricci in France, and had a small clientele whom she looked after personally. She used to go to Paris twice a year to see the latest collections, where she bought exclusive designs with her special clients in mind, an approach which today would be unthinkable because of the staggering prices the great couturiers command. That dressmaker made really lovely clothes for me, elegant, becoming, fashionable but never "over the top." Over the years, we became close friends, and until she died in the late 1970s, she would come to Oxford twice a year to sort out my wardrobe. Together we would decide which outfits could be remodeled, which ones would have to be discarded and what new dresses and coats I would need in the forthcoming season. In those days, hats were "de rigueur" and by wearing them with matching accessories, I could wear the same outfit but look completely different.

Those wardrobe-sorting sessions were great fun. My dressmaker knew the type of life I was leading and gave me superb advice. Without her resourcefulness, I doubt whether I could have solved all the problems posed by my multifarious activities. How could you be suitably dressed for a busy day which started in the constituency at eleven in the morning with the opening of a new leisure center, continued at midday with the opening of the first house on a new estate, followed by the selection of a local beauty queen, before a lunch at Woburn Abbey with the Duchess of Bedford and a visit to the playgroup at three in the afternoon? As if that was not problem enough, I might then have to get into the car and drive to London to attend the Speaker's tea party at five o'clock in the House of Commons, go on from there to a cocktail party at the Russian Embassy in honor of a trade delegation then end the day in full-length evening dress at a formal dinner and dance. The sheer logistics involved in such a day would sometimes make it impossible for me to go to our London apartment to change. Fortunately for me, I had struck up an acquaintance with the keeper of the fourth floor lavatories in Harrods. She would help me to change, zip me up and lend me cosmetics or a hairbrush if I had forgotten my own. One day she picked up my handbag containing all my jewelry, which in my haste I had left on the toilet seat. When she returned it to me the next day, I naturally gave her a reward for her honesty, but her reaction was one of surprise. She was apparently constantly giving back diamond rings and earrings to their rightful owners, and one day had even returned a huge emerald pendant as big as a pigeon's egg to a well-known Indian maharani, but as a rule barely got so much as a thank-you for her pains. That Harrods lavatory attendant used to help countless women like myself, and I believe she eventually wrote a book. She was a real godsend to me in those hectic days.

Tearing around like that, it was hardly surprising that occasionally I came unstuck. One night I was due to meet Bob at the Russian

Embassy. I got into a taxi and gave the driver the address, 13 Kensington Palace Gardens. Once we arrived, I walked straight up the flight of steps at the entrance to one of those magnificent mansions on that exclusive road. I went inside the embassy, joined the throng of people in the main reception rooms, helped myself to a drink and started looking for Bob. I noticed that there seemed to be an awful lot of dragons, snakes and Chinese lanterns and I remember thinking that the Soviets had gone very Eastern in their taste. I looked and looked, but couldn't find Bob anywhere, although it did strike me that there were a great many guests with Oriental features. I began to feel uneasy. I stopped a passing waiter and asked him if I was in the Russian Embassy, to which he replied with some amusement, "Oh no, Madame, this is the Nepalese Embassy, the Russian Embassy is just across the road." I hurried out, already very late to meet Bob, and made my way to the right embassy, where once again I was able to walk in without anyone checking my invitation. As I went in, I caught sight of Bob, who by this time was wondering where on earth I was. When I explained why I was so late, Bob laughed, scolded me for being such a scatterbrain, then to my great embarrassment, proceeded to regale our amazed Russian hosts with an account of my adventure.

One of my French dressmaker's creations I remember with particular affection. I had been invited to a charity premiere of the film *Dr. Zhivago* and we had concocted a wonderful idea for my outfit that evening—an exact copy of the costume worn by Dr. Zhivago's future wife as she stepped down from the Paris train in Moscow. The film was already showing in London and my dressmaker sat through nine consecutive performances to make a perfect copy of that glorious pink suit complete with muff and collar of gray marabou. It was a great success and I wore it for many years with pride.

Madame Fausta also introduced me to a corsetière used by the Queen and later on, in the eighties, I came to share one of her couturiers, Ian Thomas. They were both very discreet, but as they got to know me better, secrets of the royal bust or royal manner would filter out, although I kept these stories to myself. Ian and I had both known Balenciaga and we would often share our memories of that great Prince of Couture, sometimes inspired by his pencil-portrait which hung in Ian's salon. I had been introduced to Balenciaga in Paris in 1960 by a mutual friend whose sculptures we both admired and purchased, and I remember our first encounter particularly well. Balenciaga took us from the salon up to his flat above the fashion house. I remember it was elegant, but in a unique way: its walls were entirely covered in rough natural silk material and there was not a single painting. The only decorations were the sumptuous flower arrangements, which he did himself, and the most exquisite furniture of the Directoire era, unadorned and pure in line. That day, I was wearing a simple pale blue cotton shirt-dress bought for £5 from Marks and Spencers. I must admit that I felt slightly naked before that giant with piercing eyes. I apologized for being so inadequately dressed in such illustrious company, to which he replied, "No, not at all. Your dress is simple, it's unpretentious, it's perfect." He then went on to explain how all his life he had to deal with rich materials vibrant with color and that was why at home he wanted quiet, peaceful surroundings and particularly no color. Later on, I was to meet him several times more and was invited to his country home near Fontainebleau. Bob knew how much I admired Balenciaga's designs, Bob gave me a present of a suit and one of his famous "little black dresses." That was the only time in our married life that Bob came with me to choose clothes. For the next ten years, I wore both items of clothing with pleasure and have always kept the "little black dress" as a memento. But in those days, I couldn't afford Balenciaga's prices, and in any case considered it almost obscene to spend thousands of pounds on one dress. Even in the late eighties, I never spent that kind of money with Ian Thomas. The Queen would not agree to extravagant expenditure on her clothes and neither did I. Even when prices went through the roof, Ian managed to keep his at a reasonable level in England and opened another house in Japan in order to survive.

Beyond my work in the constituency, my involvement with Pergamon, through entertaining on behalf of the company, stands out most in my recollections of the sixties. I can truthfully say that in the thirty years I lived at Headington Hill Hall, until Pergamon was sold in March 1991, hardly a week went by without one, two or even three days being dedicated to extending hospitality to our authors. I was really running a small but busy hotel, with the important difference that I also had to act as hostess at most of the lunches and dinners. The organization required was intense and exacting and I could never have done it without the hardworking and devoted staff who helped me achieve this perpetual tour de force. But I worked just as hard as they did and, by shouldering the burden alongside them, won their respect and loyalty. We had two live-in staff and a daily help, but for dinners or lunches with more than twelve guests, I would enlist the aid of my own secretary, Pergamon switchboard operators and maintenance staff who would turn themselves into waiters and waitresses after hours. Having trained the staff myself, I felt confident they knew exactly how I wanted things done, and they supported me to perfection, most of them for fifteen years or more. Until twenty minutes before the guests were due to arrive, I would still be in the kitchen putting the finishing touches to a sauce. Then I would rush upstairs to my bedroom where my clothes would be laid out ready on the bed. I would have a bath, get dressed and put on my makeup in eighteen minutes flat and then go downstairs again, passing through the dining room on the way for a last check on place settings. If guests arrived early, Pergamon's good-looking West Indian carpenter, transformed for the occasion into an impeccable butler, would offer them drinks and make them feel at home. One of the Filipino maids would welcome guests at the door, take them through to leave their coats in my study, then show them the way to the reception rooms, where I was waiting to receive them.

My children and staff always marveled at the way I could come down the cantilevered staircase, leaving all my cares behind, looking elegant and outwardly unruffled. It was, I suppose, rather like being an actress, but I was not born with that gift, I had to learn it the hard way. It was Bob who instilled in me the first principles of being a successful hostess. In the early days, I would get terribly worried in case something went wrong in the kitchen or some serious hitch occurred which I could have avoided. Feeling responsible for all the preparations, I would be nervous and could not relax until the evening was over. Bob soon sensed my anxiety and taught me that once it was time for the show to begin, the most useful thing I could do was to switch my attention entirely to my guests, make them feel welcome and enjoy their company. Bob himself would arrive—always at the last minute—and say, "Let me look at you, you look beautiful, the house looks superb, everything is fine, let's enjoy it." All my confidence would be restored and I felt ready to play my part. If, as sometimes happened, the guests were known to be difficult to entertain, then we would just look at each other and tacitly agree to make the best of it.

But ultimately my reputation as a good hostess resulted from hard work, attention to detail and meticulous planning; I know no shortcuts to success. I would pick up tips from other parties or dinners we attended and adapt them to our lifestyle. I remember observing how Evangeline Bruce, the wife of the American ambassador, made sure that her guests were introduced to one another or were engaged in conversation by well-trained embassy staff. She was the best hostess in London in the 1960s and was also a great success in

Paris and Bonn, captivating everyone with her beauty, elegance, wit, culture, knowledge of current affairs and excellent table.

Those years were truly memorable: most of our guests were challenging, intelligent, well read, often with sparkling and original conversation. Good food and excellent wine would put most people in good humor, and I have vivid memories of lunches and evenings where some of the best brains of the world would spark off novel ideas and create striking new projects, helping to ensure that Pergamon remained at the forefront of science publishing. The assembled company would quite often be mixed, and became even more so through Pergamon's textbook publishing program, the Commonwealth Library of Science and Technology, which rapidly expanded to cover virtually the whole scope of human endeavor. Besides our usual quota of scientists and academics, we also entertained classical and jazz musicians, artists, painters, philosophers, novelists and not a few politicians.

All my life I mostly entertained for business, but people tell me that my dining room was rather like one of those celebrated Parisian salons where eminent people gathered for the sheer pleasure of exchanging ideas. Our guests felt free to talk openly, without worrying that their uninhibited comments would be made public, and Bob was at his best on these occasions. In those early years, he would not monopolize the conversation as he took to doing later, but would throw out an idea to those sitting beside or opposite him, and that would set the tone. That was what was so marvelous about that period of my life. We were able to enjoy and share brilliant conversation, the launch of new concepts, challenging ideas being thrown into the arena, and all this in a wholly private environment which hardly ever made the papers. Journalists were far too attracted by the other side of Bob to understand that the best part of him was not on public display. It was only much later that our parties became more widely talked about.

Everything seemed to happen at the Hall: one professor went down with appendicitis and had to be rushed to hospital, others would arrive with dreadful colds, toothaches or migraines and I would dose them with miracle-working French medicines, which they swallowed without asking any questions. Another famous scientist was visiting with his young girlfriend called Sally and had a minor heart attack during his stay. Bob's diagnosis, however, was that he had "Sallyitis" and should get a few nights' real sleep before returning home.

In the summer the pattern of entertaining would be altered, and I would give barbecue lunches or dinners; on very hot summer days, all the guests would go for a swim in the pool afterwards. I remember one August when we were due to entertain a whole host of distinguished scientists, amongst whom were the Nobel prizewinner Lord Florey and the physicist Harvey Brooks. It was also our twin daughters' seventeenth birthday, which they happened to share with Harvey's son. Since I had organized a barbecue, I took the risk of mixing adults and children. There were simply not enough days in the year to do justice to private and public life separately, so our children were well accustomed to celebrating their birthdays with the extended Pergamon family. By the time the barbecue was well under way, the youngsters started getting a bit boisterous and pushing each other into the pool. I was standing at the poolside, balancing a glass of champagne and a bowl of strawberries and cream and talking with Lord Florey. I could see that he was greatly amused by their antics, but what worried me was that he was gradually edging nearer and nearer to the exuberant teenagers. I was beginning to panic at the thought of my distinguished guest being unceremoniously thrown into the water and did my best to protect him by getting dangerously close to the water myself and gently steering him back onto the lawn. Some months later, Lord Florey died, and when his wife replied to my letter of condolence, she told me that our summer barbecue had been the highlight of her husband's last year, that he had enjoyed himself enormously talking to all the guests, young and old, and he had frequently referred to the good time he had had with everyone that evening. He had, however, one regret: he would dearly have liked to be thrown into the pool! When I remembered my superhuman efforts to avoid what I thought would be a minor catastrophe, I decided that you can't win them all.

Dinners and lunches always had an element of surprise which resulted not only from my own pleasure in meeting new people, but also from the originality and creativity of most of our guests. One memorable evening in the late spring of 1964, we were entertaining a group of famous scientists, amongst whom were six Nobel Prize winners. It was a truly brilliant gathering and my dinner partner, Professor Daniel Bovet, remarked on it. An Italian chemist, he had won the Nobel prize for his research on the derivatives of the substance curare (which were eventually used to relax Michael's paralyzed muscles), and he also spoke perfect French. At first we talked about our families and I confided my worries about my youngest daughter, Ghislaine, who was anorexic. It had probably started as a bid for attention in the days when Michael's plight had preoccupied us almost exclusively, but by now was a matter of serious concern.

Daniel told me, "You must treat her just like I treat my rats." Puzzled, I queried his comment and he told me about his scientific experiments with twenty-four genetically similar white laboratory rats: how he had fed twelve of them regularly each day, according to the accepted standard diet for rats—a certain amount of grain, cheese, nuts and so on—whilst the remaining twelve received their entire week's food supply in one go. In the first week of the experiment, the rats which had a free choice had rushed towards the nuts and eaten them all, then headed for another food and done the same thing, then another, then another. By the second week, however, he noticed that they were rationing themselves quite wisely, with so much of this and so much of that. At the end of the six-week experiment, these rats were all thriving, whilst the regularly fed group was not doing as well.

"But I don't follow what this has to do with Ghislaine's problems," I said, and Professor Bovet went on to outline a strategy that might help us. What was needed, he suggested, was a complete change of her environment, especially in connection with mealtimes and anyone normally involved in feeding her. I was not to lay her place at table and to let her eat whenever and whatever she wanted. As we were about to go on a cruise and Marion was setting off for her annual holiday in Ireland, it was a perfect time to try it. I followed his advice to the letter, but remember looking at Ghislaine in disbelief as one day she stuffed herself with chocolate, and on the next with so many peaches that I was certain she would get diarrhea. This went on for a whole week, just as with the rats. After that, she began to roam around the table at mealtimes, picking off our plates, a chip here, a salad leaf or piece of meat there. Then one day, she asked me why she wasn't eating at table with the family, to which I replied that it wasn't possible because she didn't eat like the rest of us. "But I want to eat like you!" she howled. By the very next day, she was seated at the end of the table, asking to be served with exactly the same food as us. From then on, we never looked back. I remain eternally grateful for my good friend's advice, and Ghislaine loves to tell the story of how she was coaxed back to health after being treated like the experimental rats of a famous professor.

Not a day passed without leaving its mark: with all our guests, the staff and the children, there was plenty of scope for drama. As I relive the full life that we led, some high spots come immediately to mind, but there were so many more I am forced to leave untold. I could write another book about my life and illustrate it with a completely different set of anecdotes, but let me rescue one more story, just for the fun of it. This was a lunchtime I remember particularly well because—as quite often happened in those days—I had two lunches going on simultaneously, one in the dining room for the VIPs and another in the breakfast room for accompanying younger officials or researchers, presided over by Pergamon's vice chairman, Tom Clark. I had taken special care that day in seating all our guests in the big dining room: they were a motley collection of important authors from eight different European countries, most of whom spoke more than one language, although not always English. After careful thought, I managed to solve the puzzle satisfactorily so that everyone would at least be able to communicate with the guests sitting beside them. At the last minute, however, all this painstaking planning was thrown into utter confusion when a constituency Labor Party member turned up unexpectedly, having been given an open invitation by Bob to drop in for lunch if he ever found himself in Oxford. My latest guest was a Bucks train driver who could only speak English. So I placed him between Bob and an English professor who could also speak German to his Russian neighbor. The Russian in turn spoke German to an Italian, who spoke English to a Norwegian, who then spoke English to me. I then spoke French with my Belgian neighbor, who spoke German to a Pole, who spoke Russian to a Hungarian, who spoke Hungarian to Bob. You can imagine the chain of conversation that had to go from the guest on Bob's right all the way around the table and back again if any story was to be successfully communicated to everyone present. It was just like playing Chinese whispers.

It wasn't always quite as difficult as that, but there were many occasions when linguistic snags cropped up in the cosmopolitan life we led. As the children grew up, they also took part in our business entertaining, and this was a great help as they added first Italian and Spanish, then Japanese to the eight languages Bob already spoke. I could always rely on them to lend a hand if Bob was away. I remember bargaining with them—if they came and helped me at a lunch or dinner, I would help them in return with the French translation or essay they currently had to do. But that was later on. In the 1960s, they were still at an age when it was difficult to stop them from making fun of our guests at the slightest opportunity. Entertaining two celebrated Russian and Austrian authors of a bestselling book on the theory of space, time and gravitation, Professor Focke and Dr. Penish (whose names were actually pronounced "Fuck" and "Penis") was enough to send them into hysterics. They would pass the nuts around, going out of their way to say, "Have some more nuts, Professor Fuck," or "Another drink, Dr. Penis?" I myself would find it hard to keep a straight face confronted by the mischief written all over their faces, seeing that they were ready to burst into laughter.

In those days, it was always the Americans who were difficult to mix at table with their European counterparts because they rarely spoke any language other than English. Not many Russians spoke English either, but a number knew German and a few could speak French. The Chinese who visited us either spoke English or French, which they spoke fluently after being sent expressly to Paris to learn it. As the younger generation took over, however, most scientists spoke English, the lingua franca of the scientific community, as it is in the worlds of banking, business and communications.

From time to time, I had to organize large-scale parties, the first of which was held on a warm sunny day in May 1962 to celebrate Pergamon's launch of the Commonwealth and International Library of Science, Technology, Engineering and Liberal Studies. Its ambitious aim was to publish a thousand textbooks to meet the needs of every level of student, ranging from twelve-year-old schoolchildren to university postgraduates. A distinguished editorial advisory board was recruited under the chairmanship of the Nobel prizewinner Sir Robert Robinson in order to ensure the high quality of the books. Sir Robert's counterpart in America was President Kennedy's commissioner on education, Dr. Athelstan Spilhaus, dean of the Institute of Technology at the University of Minnesota. Some of the books were to be translated into French, Russian and German and special arrangements were made for a number of them to be published in India, specifically to meet the growing demand for reasonably priced textbooks in that country. The first book of the Commonwealth Library was published in 1963, the 100th in 1964, the 200th in 1965 and the 1,000th in 1970. In all, the series totaled 1,100 volumes.

The launch party was hosted by Sir Robert Robinson, Athelstan Spilhaus, the Lord Mayor of Oxford, Bob and myself. Our guest of honor was Mrs. Pandit Nehru and the 250 guests included interesting and interested educationalists, headmasters, teachers, professors and booksellers from around the Commonwealth. My staff and I had worked extremely hard the previous day to prepare an appetizing cold buffet. I cooked my first large salmon and hams for the occasion, decorating all the various dishes early on the morning of the party. In later years, I would hire chefs and specialist personnel for that kind of grand celebration, but in those days we would do all the preparation and cooking ourselves. With the arrival in 1970 of two Filipinos, Oping, a first-class cook and Mary, a devoted and hardworking housekeeper, we became quite a professional team. I would concoct new dishes or revive favorite recipes inventing special names for them based on significant events in our lives. Some dinner menus came to be known by the name of the principal guest, and I would just say to Oping, "Let's have le dîner de la duchesse," referring to a dinner I had given for the Duke and Duchess of Bedford, prepared with extra special care since Nicole herself was a fine hostess and cook. Or I might say, "Let's have the *Daily Mail* lunch," a meal prepared when Lynda Lee Potter of the *Daily Mail* came to write an article about my skills as a hostess. I would often give dishes names with special significance for the guest of honor and that always went down very well. Oping and I both enjoyed the great displays we managed to produce, and we received many compliments for our home-baked and prepared cuisine. We gradually built on the experience we acquired as large-scale entertaining became more frequent: launch parties for international book series, buffet lunches for scientific conferences, staff Christmas parties, dinners and dances given for our journal editors, authors and business contacts.

Bob's birthday on June 10 was always an occasion for one or two parties. Our first really large-scale birthday event was held one weekend in June 1968, with a great many friends present from the worlds of science, publishing, printing, politics, the national press and the City. We had decided to celebrate Bob's birthday with a ball on the Friday evening, then hold a dance for our eldest children on the Saturday; these parties were to set the pattern for the next twenty years. I remember that Bob and I paid particular attention to the seating plans, trying to mix our friends so that they had an opportunity to meet people from other walks of life. We would place bankers next to scientists, architects next to politicians, publishers next to artists, and the ensuing conversation was always fascinating. My French dressmaker had outdone herself with a striking creation for that party. It was a red chiffon pleated sheath dress which left one shoulder bare and I set it off with a magnificent costume jewelry necklace of emeralds and diamonds. My four daughters were all dressed alike in long Victorian-style dresses made by Gina Fratini in the days before she was well known, trimmed with white lace and narrow velvet ribbon. It was an enchanting party with a special atmosphere our friends greatly appreciated. One friend wrote "It was something to shake everyone out of a feeling of gloom and remind us that Britain is prospering when managed brilliantly."

Another remarked, "Your lovely house and garden made a perfect setting for a fairy-tale evening." My favorite thank-you letter came from the *Times'* journalist Nicholas Tomalin:

Thank you for what was undoubtedly the most enjoyable ball I have ever attended. I always felt I did not enjoy such occasions, but you organized the party so superbly I was confounded. I also thought, being awkwardly middle-aged, that I would feel out of place amongst the young. But your husband was so exuberantly youthful, and your children so mature and kindly competent, that I didn't feel the generation gap at all.

Over the years, as the number of guests gradually increased, we started renting marquees which were set up around the swimming pool and linked to the Hall. This raised the logistical problems of entertaining by a power of ten. In later years, the pool would be covered over and formed part of a splendid decor with an island of flowers and plants as a centerpiece. The marquee company would arrive a week before the party to erect the tents: two huge marquees and a series of smaller ones to house the kitchen and preparation rooms, staff rooms, sculleries and cloakrooms. The whole area was connected through covered walkways to the reception rooms of the Hall. I remember that the boys used to call it "the Saracen encampment," and it certainly did look rather like that, viewed from the terraces of the Hall. This expression enriched the Maxwell family vocabulary, and over the years, the rules of lexicography applying, it engendered new terms and expressions. "Have the Saracens invaded yet?" came to mean, "Have the guests arrived?" Over the years, these annual parties acquired a Gatsby-like flavor, but behind that dreamlike atmosphere lay a military-style campaign.

We were always lucky with the weather: for me entertaining in the summer will always conjure up warm evenings under the starry sky, welcoming old and new friends from many countries of the world, enjoying good French cuisine and wines in a Victorian English setting, laughter of carefree guests drinking one another's health in champagne poured from gigantic Jeroboams or Methuselahs, very English-looking men in dinner jackets leading their partners onto the dance floor, women looking beautiful in their fabulous or exotic ball gowns, the sparkle of real or costume jewelry beneath the crystal chandeliers, couples wandering off into the depths of the garden for a romantic embrace, beguiling soft music enveloping everything, a magical, enchanting ambiance set against the magnificent backdrop of the floodlit spires of Oxford.

But it was not only at home that I was called upon as a hostess by Pergamon; I would also be sent abroad whenever really important guests had to be entertained. It might be a cocktail party in Tokyo, dinners in Washington, buffet lunches in New York, dinners and receptions in Paris, Geneva and Stockholm. There was even a famous reception for 150 Pergamon authors in Moscow, which happened to coincide with a gigantic military parade in Red Square in honor of Titov, the second Russian astronaut launched into space, which we were able to watch in comfort from the first-floor vantage point of the Hotel Metropole.

Another job that landed in my lap was supervising the literary luncheons inaugurated for publicity purposes by our bookshops. These would take place in the grand assembly rooms of Oxford Town Hall. They were quite fun at first but eventually petered out after Bob made the decision to close our Oxford bookshop. Situated on the wrong side of Magdalen Bridge, it had been plagued with constant pilfering and never properly got off the ground despite some innovative ideas such as the inclusion of a coffee bar and record shop. I would preside at those luncheons, with the author whose book we were promoting seated on my right. Our guests of honor were many and varied and the conversation fascinating—there was Robert Carrier with his new cookbook, the Duke of Bedford launching his *Book of Snobs,* Iris Murdoch and Nicholas Montserrat with their latest novels, the American theatrical producer Margaret Webster, Dame Rebecca West and Winston Churchill's doctor, Dr. Moran, whose indiscretions about his famous patient shocked me.

Another type of entertaining—again largely at Bob's instigation—involved a constant stream of extended family members coming to stay at Headington: friends' or authors' children who were going through difficult phases at home, damsels in distress whom Bob met on his travels or youngsters from abroad who came to learn English or be educated here, to whom we sometimes became guardians. Most adolescents benefit from a stay outside their own family circle, where they are able to show facets of their personality which have perhaps remained hidden or unappreciated at home. Over a hundred such youngsters passed through my hands, most of whom are now married with teenaged children of their own. Many of them are still in touch with me and tell me they have fond memories of their stays and of our long discussions on all manner of subjects—relationship problems with their parents, emotional entanglements and their longing to assert their independence. Some of those youngsters have remained very close to my heart, others have become the subjects of family sagas or much loved anecdotes. Such, for instance, was the case of the Mexican girls attending an English school, who came to spend the holidays with us on strict instructions that they were never to be allowed out without a chaperon. They asked me one day if they could go and see the sights of London. As there were three of them and they were all sixteen years old, I decided there was safety in numbers and allowed them to go, but told them firmly that they had to be back by 8 P.M. at the latest. By ten o'clock that evening, no Mexicans; by midnight, still no Mexicans. I was worried stiff and eventually telephoned the police, but they had no more idea than I had where to start looking. The girls turned up at ten o'clock the next morning and I asked, "Where have you been?"

"In Piccadilly."

I had immediate visions of them being picked up.

"What were you doing in Piccadilly?"

"Sitting on the steps of the statue talking to other young people."

"Where did you sleep?"

"At the Grosvenor Hotel."

"Why didn't you phone, didn't you realize I'd be sick with worry?"

"We couldn't remember the phone number."

What could I say? I was so angry that I sent them to their rooms to think about the stupidity of their actions and their complete lack of consideration. I wasn't used to that kind of behavior with my own children, who would always let me know if they were going to be late, even if it was only by half an hour.

Other young visitors would just come to my study in the evenings and pour their hearts out, mostly complaining that their parents did not understand them. I always did my best to defuse the situation by trying to make them aware of better ways to approach their parents with their worries. Many of those youngsters, especially the sons of eminent scientists, were so afraid of disappointing their parents if they could not follow in their footsteps, even though they might be talented in another field. It was often a question of having the courage to change course. I remember one young man in particular who was studying natural sciences, not very successfully, to please his parents when all he really wanted to do was electronics and computer science. Once he had overcome the obstacle of telling them how he felt, he never looked back and is now at the forefront of his chosen field. Another one kept failing his law exams to the great disappointment of his internationally reputed lawyer father, but is now a thriving publisher. Another young girl also hated law and is now a successful actress. But of all those youngsters who came into my life, the one who remained closest to my heart was the little Japanese boy who came to be educated in England at the age of nine. My heart melted when I first met him; he spoke not one word of English and was so tiny that his feet didn't even touch the ground when he was sitting in a chair. I looked after him as if he were my own son and saw him through Summer Fields prep school, Eton and Balliol College, Oxford, after which he left to become "a man of the city." As a little boy, he would come to me and say, "Mrs. Maxwell, will you play with me?" and I would join in his games, teaching him mahjong, playing in the snow with him or simply exploring the treasures of the house. He has recently married a charming American girl, and his parents, who looked after our son Ian when we sent him to Japan, have remained good and supportive friends.

Most of those youngsters were the same age as my own children and lasting friendships were forged. They brought a breath of fresh air into our lives and a strong flavor of cosmopolitanism, even if at times they increased my already heavy burden of work. In my memory, they are like a kaleidoscope of vibrant joyous youth and they certainly added to my discovery of the great potential of the younger generations of the sixties and seventies.

But if nonstop entertaining was my scene, incessant traveling around the globe was Bob's. As my duties in the constituency and in Oxford increased, Bob traveled much more frequently on his own, although I would still find myself doing my fair share, mostly to represent him and Pergamon. Occasionally, Bob would spring a nice surprise and whisk me off for a few days when we could relax, just the two of us, far from the madding crowd.

I recall a few lovely weekends like that in the the sixties. On one occasion, Bob suddenly announced that we were flying to Paris for a gala evening to celebrate the international première of *The Longest Day*, a film reenactment of D-Day produced by Darryl Zanuck. It was one of those grand galas that Paris stages so magnificently, held in the floodlit Trocadéro, opposite the Eiffel Tower. An impressive military parade and a detachment of mounted Republican Guards preceded the arrival of the French Minister of Defense, accompanied by a large contingent of Allied generals, ambassadors wearing white-tie and decorations, and the great and good of Paris decked out in their finery. After the *Marseillaise* had been played, the film started. It was a poignant reminder of those terrible days preceding the liberation of France. Bob was very moved and found it very realistic, as near as one could get to actually being there and taking part in the savage fighting on the beaches and in the coastal villages of Normandy. As we emerged at the end of the show, we were greeted by a fabulous fireworks display illuminating the entire skyline of Paris, followed by Edith Piaf singing her heart out from one of the levels of the Eiffel Tower before the city she had come to personify. Never did she do more justice to Jean Cocteau's moving tribute to her:

She is inimitable: there has never been an Edith Piaf before, there will never be another. . . . She is a solitary self-devouring star in France's night sky. . . . She is greater than herself, greater than her songs, greater than their music and lyrics, greater than we can comprehend: the very soul of the street invades every room in the city; it is no longer Madame Edith Piaf that we hear, but the rain falling, the wind blowing, the moon spreading its halo of light.[5]

Bob and I had always been Piaf fans and we ended the evening listening to her in a night club, feeling nostalgic and remembering our wartime years.

Another time, Bob drove us down to Rye where in those days you could put your car on a little plane and hop over the Channel. We had been invited to the races in Deauville by our lawyer friend, Isidore Kerman, who had a horse racing there that weekend. I believe it was the one and only time that the mare ever won a race. Bob had backed it to the hilt and made a killing on a little-fancied runner—as he also did in the casino that night. In the afternoon, we went to the beach at Deauville where I met Harold Lever and his new wife, Diane. Harold Lever was Chancellor of the Duchy of Lancaster in Harold Wilson's government. He had lost his first wife and was left with a young daughter, who became a good friend of my daughter Isabel. He was very much in love with Diane, a woman of ravishing beauty, petite, charming, elegant and kind. Having grown up in the Lebanon, she spoke perfect French and we soon became friends. I also loved Diane's mother, Marcelle, a kindhearted and refined widow, devoted to her five daughters, who lived in four different countries. Marcelle would spend a month in Canada, a month in Switzerland, a month in Paris and the rest of the year in England, being closest to Diane and to Diane's youngest sister, who was still a student in London. Marcelle became another role model for me, especially in her compassion and close relationships with her children.

---

5. Edith Piaf, in *Texte de Jean Cocteau*, recorded on compact disk by Europe 1, 1993. My translation.

But for me the highlight of our stay in Deauville was meeting Gregory Peck and his wife, who is also French. At the time, there was a striking resemblance between Bob and the famous actor, although Peck was taller. I have a photo of them taken together— they could almost have been twins. Stranger still, Gregory's wife looked like me. That night, the two of them played roulette side by side and people crowded around the table, attracted by the cele- brated heartthrob. Because Bob was sitting next to him, many of the guests commented on the likeness and wondered if Gregory Peck had come with his brother!

On another occasion, we spent a pleasant few days in Bellagio on Lake Como where Bob was attending an international biochem- istry conference. It was in the casino there that we bumped into Simone Signoret and Romy Schneider. It always struck me how much easier it seems to break the ice with perfect strangers in hotels abroad. Whereas you wouldn't normally start up conversations with people you don't know, the mere fact that you are staying in the same hotel in a foreign country, meet regularly at the swimming pool or gaming table or perhaps speak the same foreign language, seems to facilitate things somehow.

I also enjoyed attending the Nobel Prize ceremonies in Stock- holm, magnificent affairs held in the month of December. They began in the morning with the formal presentation of prizes by the King of Sweden and acceptance speeches from the prizewinners, and in the evening a spectacular banquet took place in the capital's grand neo-Gothic ceremonial hall. Men wearing white tie and decorations, ladies in long evening dress and tiaras, if they had them, creating a shimmering scene. (I was always taught that you either inherit a tiara or "marry" one; you don't just buy one, however much you would love to sport it on such an occasion.) The prizewinners and their spouses would be seated at the King's table, sandwiched between all those lovely Nordic princesses, whilst their family and friends would sit at tables placed at right angles to the King's. Bob had been hon- ored by the Nobel Foundation for his work for science and was later decorated with the Royal Swedish Order of the Polar Star. Through this association, I was to meet Gustaf VI and his grandson Carl Gustaf on several occasions in Stockholm.

One of the more dramatic times I lived with Bob occurred on a visit to Spain in 1962 for the International Publishers Association Conference in Barcelona. It was a sunny day and we decided to go and see a *corrida*. It was the first time we had attended that tradi- tional, well-loved but bloody Spanish sport and I must admit that I found it most unpleasant and gory. In the second fight, after the ban-derillas had been stuck in, the picador was not particularly skillful in impaling the bull and his clumsiness prompted catcalls from the crowd; when it came to the kill, the toreador made a disgraceful job of it, plunging his sword again and again into the dying beast. All of a sudden, I heard a thud and turned to see Bob falling off the bench. I rushed to help him and found he had passed out; he was com-pletely green and drained of life. When he had recovered enough to walk, we left the arena and made our way back to the hotel, dis-cussing our impressions of the bullfight. The unnecessary murder and all that blood gushing out had totally disgusted him; it had evoked images of war and that, combined with the heat, had made him faint.

The conference started the next day. Franco was still at the height of his power and censorship was a dominant feature of his dictatorship in many spheres of Spanish life, especially the written word. At one point that afternoon, a Portuguese publisher stood up and harangued the whole assembly of foreign publishers. (Portugal at the time was suffering Salazar's even more repressive dictatorship.) How could we possibly come, he asked, to celebrate the freedom of the word in a country where people were thrown into jail at the slightest criticism of the regime? It was such a powerful regime that he himself faced certain imprisonment back in Portugal for his denunciation of its savage censorship. Did we condone that kind of repression? Bob's notorious courage showed up on that occasion. He rose to speak after him, urging the assembly to support this belea-guered colleague and show solidarity by refusing to accept the invita-tion to shake General Franco's hand in Madrid at the grand finale of the conference. The hall was full of Spaniards; there was a stunned silence at Bob's audacity. From that moment on, Bob and I were completely ostracized by the entire Spanish contingent, who were all quaking in their boots lest they should be seen talking to the man who had so openly defied the great dictator. The English delegation did not behave much better and thought it would be "rude" to reject an invitation from the head of state. Before long, Bob was receiving foot-long telegrams from London advising him not to rock the boat and not to encourage others to upset the Caudillo. It really was dis-graceful. No one dared to be seen next to us, our material life was made extremely uncomfortable and it began to look as if we might even be arrested. Soon after, we were told that we were personae non gratae and asked to leave Spain forthwith. Our great triumph was to learn that on the pretext of a sudden "malaise," the Caudillo canceled his invitation to the conference delegates. If nothing else, Bob had achieved that much. It was only when King Juan Carlos came to power in 1975 that we were able to return to Spain. From the day of his accession, we were invited regularly by the Spanish ambassador and met the King in London. Later on, he received Bob twice at his palace and telephoned him quite informally on several occasions.

During those years, I was befriended by one of Bob's old flames, Mimi Mengers. Born in the Austro-Hungarian empire, she spoke Hungarian, but had lived in Vienna in its heyday where she had been courted by famous men and married several times. She was by then in her sixties, but looked much younger with her pretty blond hair, vivacious eyes, beautiful complexion and bone structure and fastidious attention to grooming. She was elegance itself, full of charm and gaiety and always had a roving eye for a handsome man. She had met Bob soon after the war and they became friends, partly through the strong bond of the Hungarian language and their great nostalgia for Budapest and central Europe. For most of my married life, I found myself landed with Bob's female admirers and Mimi was no exception. She would come to Esher and Bob would occasionally drop in on her for coffee—the best you could get in London, he said. When we moved to Oxford, she would often phone me, and in her heavy Viennese accent invariably begin, "Betty? Mimi here. Betty, you no phone, you no come, you no love me no more. Daling komm mit mir to de opera." Accepting her invitation for myself and sometimes for Philip or Anne as well, I would meet her at her home, have a drink there, then go with her to Covent Garden where she had a regular box. She was a great connoisseur of music and listened with a critical ear to the singing. During the interval, she always had a special table of refreshments set up in the middle of the foyer and treated me to smoked salmon and champagne whilst commenting loudly on the people around her. She was a real character, but thanks to her I acquired a good knowledge of London's operatic repertoire. I grew fond of her, especially as she became lonelier and and less able to fight the ghosts of the past. For her, the past soon became the present and I listened to fascinating tales of Vienna, the balls she had attended in royal residences and Venetian palaces, the Emperor Franz-Joseph and "her" princes and princesses. I even met one of her lifelong admirers who had been one of the Emperor's Ambassadors. One day, as I was describing an event she had invited me to, I summed up, "It was thrilling," and she replied, "How can you be trilled with dat? De only ding dat trill me anymore is a castle on de Lido, full of diamonds." To this day, the Maxwells often start a family conversation with, "You no phone, you no come, you no love me no more!" and the expression "A castle on the Lido full of diamonds" has passed into our everyday language. We still remember Mimi with great fondness and have remained friendly with her family.

In trying to telescope fifteen years of one's life into a single book chapter, one invariably tends to remember the highlights, giving the impression that life consisted of one long stream of parties and travels, and relegating the constant humdrum routine to the background. The phenomenon is best illustrated by comparison with a few minutes' television report covering hours and hours of soccer. After watching the football highlights for many years in that truncated form, I shall never forget my amazement when I was first invited to Wembley to attend the Cup Final. It was my first live football match and I couldn't get over the players' apparent sluggishness: nothing seemed to happen for ages, when I was used to seeing three or four goals scored on TV in as many minutes. Our own life was anything but sluggish, but the other side of the coin was the unremitting hard work, difficulties in safeguarding my relationship with Bob, and above all trying to preserve a sensible and secure environment for the children to grow up in, at their own pace and with a minimum of upheaval.

Bob and I had taken great care to place the children in schools best suited to their needs and temperament. With Bob's constant and my not infrequent absences abroad, I insisted on the boys' going to boarding school. As they grew in physical size and wilfulness, it was difficult for me to cope on my own, and I felt it would be best for them to be in a disciplined environment offering maximum scope for their inquiring minds and plenty of sports to develop their physical strength. So it was that after prep school at Summer Fields in Oxford, they went on to Marlborough College and from there to Balliol College at Oxford University. My eldest daughter, Anne, first went as a boarder to a girls' private school in Oxford, then became a day girl when we moved to Oxford and finally gained a place at St. Hugh's College, Oxford. The twins attended an Oxford grammar school, and from there Isabel went to St. Hilda's College, Oxford, whilst Christine studied at an American university, then returned to do postgraduate teacher training at Lady Spencer Churchill College in Oxford. Ghislaine went to public schools in Oxford and Somerset, then went on to Marlborough College after it began admitting girls, and from there followed the boys to Balliol. Thus my children all shared a common alma mater, but I cannot claim that their successes were achieved without tension at home, far from it.

Even with the excellent discipline that the boys acquired in their prep and public schools, I did sometimes find it difficult to enforce good behavior when they were at home and would often find myself on my own confronted by these strapping, headstrong lads. The most memorable of these confrontations occurred with Ian when he was fifteen. Generally well-mannered, he had been extremely coarse and insolent at the lunch table one weekend when his father was away. I asked him to leave the table and he refused. I knew that it was a show of strength and willpower, and that I had to win, otherwise I would lose the other children's respect. I remember getting up, taking him by the shirt collar, toppling him off his chair and telling him to come to my study in five minutes' time. When he duly appeared, I asked him whether he realized just how ill-mannered he had been, and he agreed that he had been both rude and impertinent. I then gave him a choice—he either took three of the best from me, or the same punishment from his father when he came back from abroad. I remember Ian asking how he could be sure that I wouldn't tell his father even if he took his punishment there and then, and my replying that all I could give him was my word. After momentary reflection, he decided to take the beating from me. It was the first time I had ever beaten any of my children. I hated doing it and needed all the courage I could muster to perform such a hated punishment with the twins' riding crop. I remember breaking down afterwards, thinking how pitiful it was to have to resort to such extremes and wondering where I had gone wrong. From that day on, however, Ian always showed me the utmost respect, never once ventured a word of insolence and we have remained the best of friends.

When the children were very young, Bob enjoyed even the little time he was able to spend with them, but as they grew up, he took a much more active role in their education and upbringing. Conscious that he himself had missed out on a good education and parental guidance, he was determined to give the children all that fate had denied him. He also wanted to pass on to them all he had learned the hard way through being pitted against the dangers of war and uprooted from his native country. His basic principles were excellent; it was the way he applied them that left a good deal to be desired. His impatience and heavy-handedness were at times counterproductive, although he did achieve extraordinary results with some of the children. Some recognize that they acquired principles from their father which have stood them in good stead all their lives, yet they cannot erase the memories of humiliations and harsh treatment that went with them. Bob was totally inflexible with school reports and scholastic results and simply could not accept that any factor other than laziness contributed to a poor level of attainment. The mere word *careless* was enough to send him into a terrible rage, which invariably led to the culprit being caned. He was always ambitious academically for the children and nothing short of excellence would satisfy him. In a way, one can understand his reaction: there he was, working nonstop to ensure that the children got the best education money could buy, and in return he expected them to make full use of all the opportunities he was offering them.

There is absolutely no doubt that Bob loved his children dearly, but his relationship with them began to change soon after he became a Member of Parliament. The difficulties were really caused by the fact that he wasn't living at home regularly, so there was little normal daily contact between them to counterbalance the peaks of crisis and drama. Essentially he only saw them on Sundays when he made a point of being at home, insisting on the children's presence irrespective of any other commitments they might have, even when they were adults. Even on Sundays we were rarely on our own as a family: there was the inevitable contingent of Pergamon authors or business people, as well as the children's own school or college friends whom we encouraged them to invite. It was invariably in the presence of this mixed and generally learned assembly that the children were, so to speak, put on trial. The conversation would start normally and one of the children would be asked to answer Bob's query on such and such a topic. If they hummed and hawed, didn't speak to the point or gave the wrong answer, Bob would then ask them which of the principles he had drummed into their heads they had forgotten to apply and why. By this, he was referring to some of the rules for life that he had coined and encapsulated in easily remembered mnemonics like the 3 Cs—Concentration, Consideration and Conciseness—or WWWH, a simple way of answering questions, especially in exams: What? Why? When? and How?

Lunchtime was too short for all the children to jump through the hoop, so Bob would pick on one who became the scapegoat for the day. It was always painful in the extreme. Everyone around the table was made to feel uncomfortable, rooting inwardly for the child under attack and trying to put in an occasional word in his or her defense. If we had a distinguished stranger in our midst, the dressing down would be curtailed and the children, dismissed from the table, would rush off as fast as possible and stay out of range until it was time for them to go back to school or college. At other times, Bob would not let go, and lunch would be ruined for those present with one or two of the children ending up in tears, punishments being doled out, the whole family disconsolate and taking sides. I soon realized that somehow Bob needed to create a sense of drama around him. He would shout and threaten and rant at the children until they were reduced to pulp. Then came the reconciliation scene when he would eventually forgive them, tears would be dried and smiles returned to their faces. In the eighties, things got a good deal worse and we all came to dread Sundays, knowing in advance that every week we would witness what I came to call the "Maxwellian Drama."

There were good times, however, when family gatherings were not as fraught and conversation at table was enjoyable and enlightening. On New Year's Eve, for instance, Bob might invent a kind of panel game which we played around the table, setting us topics for debate about the major events or personalities of the past year, the last decade or century or what was to come in the future. It was stimulating to see all those young brains at work, and Bob would make a splendid quizmaster, adjudicating on the various opinions and adding another dimension with his own contribution. After dinner, he would join in great family games of Monopoly and Risk, thoroughly enjoying the strategies involved in buying and selling properties and moving vast armies across the world. He seemed happy and relaxed then, as he also was in the holidays when we took to chartering a yacht for the whole family.

Those cruises were always quite an odyssey, generally lasting for a month. We would leave by train from Victoria Station loaded down with some thirty pieces of luggage and travel to Cannes. There, we would be met by crew members who then drove us to Antibes where the boat was lying at anchor. The first yacht we hired was the *Sister Anne,* a French ship manned completely by Yugoslav sailors, which caught fire a few years later and sank off the French coast. On that first day, we would take on board all the nonperishables we needed for the cruise, as well as enough perishables—meat, groceries, fruit and so on—to last a few days. It was always my job to supervise supplies, decide on daily menus and arrange for fresh food to be bought at our various ports of call. Then cabins would be allocated and we would set sail for Italy that evening, calling at Elba, Corsica, Sardinia, Naples, Capri, the Aeolian islands. After that we would head for Greece via Malta, Paxos and Anti-Paxos, the Corinth Canal, Athens and a number of Greek islands with their picturesque little harbors. We followed that itinerary several times, varying the harbors, islands and coastal towns we visited. Later on, we would fly out from England, join the boat in Athens and visit Istanbul, the coast of Asia Minor and the island of Rhodes. In other years we went to the Caribbean and visited most of the islands there.

Once we were on board the holiday mood took over, Bob was immediately more relaxed and less domineering, allowing the children to water-ski, swim and visit the sights. From time to time, however, we would disagree on the time allotted for such and such excursion and I remember visiting Delphi and having literally to run all the way up to the Acropolis and famous stadium. Although on holiday Bob was generally much more tolerant than usual with the children, I remember a famous occasion when he forced Kevin, then age seven, to eat French beans (which he absolutely loathed), on pain of being shut up in his cabin until he did so. Kevin stubbornly resisted for two whole days and finally gave in under the threat of being lashed with a rope. I can still see him, in floods of tears, his words interrupted by convulsive sobs, saying to Bob, "I give in, but only because you are bigger and stronger than me, and for no other reason." My own heart was torn to shreds. I knew that the whole thing could easily have been solved with a different approach, but that was Bob's way of doing things and I felt it was important to maintain a united front before the children. Once Bob and I were alone, I would often try and make him see things from the children's point of view. Later on, when he became really unreasonable with them, I would always intervene to protect them, and this invariably led to the most painful confrontations, ending with Bob accusing me of dividing the family and alienating the children. As far as he was concerned, if you weren't for him, then you were against him: there was absolutely no middle way, and whatever happened, I couldn't win.

Whilst we were on the cruise, we each had to take our turn at writing the daily "log book," a kind of extensive holiday diary. Years later, these still make interesting reading. The children didn't object too much and I made it more attractive by suggesting that they stick in postcards, pictures, flowers, photos or their own drawings. Then at breakfast next morning, the author of the narrative would read it out loud and the odd forgotten detail would be added by the others. After that, Bob would take out the map, show us where we were, outline plans and ask us what we would like to do that day. The children and I would often read up in the guidebooks about the sites we were going to visit, making sure that we didn't miss some famous monument or antique sculpture. Well trained in this by my own father, I was an indefatigable sightseer and passed on my love of antiquity to the children. Bob approved of this interest in history and sometimes participated in my expeditions himself—or even planned his own. On one occasion when we were sailing past the Cape of Sunion he woke us all up at five in the morning because the guidebook had recommended seeing the sun rise over the celebrated monument. Despite the rude awakening, it was a glorious sight as the rays of the sun bathed the temple in the pink hues of early morning. Another time, he kept us all awake till midnight to see the moon shroud the sacred columns in its spectral light, and the unforgettable sight soon dispelled our tiredness.

In the early days, the communication systems of these yachts were quite poor, and whenever Bob wanted to make a telephone call to England, he would take the boat into the next biggish harbor along the coast and head for the nearest telephone booth. He would be stuck there for a while, unable to get a decent connection, but would eventually lose interest and forget about whatever business it was. English newspapers were equally unavailable in the far-flung islands we visited, and for once even politics took second place. So for a few days, we had Dad to ourselves, relaxed, playing with the children and enjoying being away from it all. The whole family remembers those early cruises with pleasure.

One of the great yachts we chartered was the *Shemara*, owned by the Docker family, in her heyday the greatest yacht afloat in European waters. She had a crew of thirty-two, and enormous engines, which by the time we hired her were already beginning to give trouble. We joined her in Malta, where she had been in dry dock for repairs, and then sailed on to Venice, Dubrovnik and along the Yugoslavian coastline to Greece, Turkey and Rhodes. The luxury of that yacht was beyond belief. The chief steward, whom the children nicknamed "Roly," had been trained in the old school and would lay the table every evening as if we were expecting the Queen. All the best china, crystal glasses and silver cutlery would be laid out in splendor. One night when the sea was rough, we heard an almighty crash and rushed to the dining room to find the entire display smashed to smithereens. Roly called in the under-steward to pick up the silver from amongst the debris, then seized hold of the linen tablecloth by the four corners and hurled the lot straight through one of the portholes into the sea. The children and I just stood there open-mouthed. It wasn't only that he made no attempt to rescue the dishes that were still intact or the tablecloth itself, but we were shocked by the way he used the sea like a dustbin. Roly would also entertain the children with tales of previous charterers, generally well-known but eccentric Hollywood film stars. It seemed the charterers before us had hardly ever asked the captain to sail the yacht which had stayed most of the time at anchor in the Bay of Villefranche near Monaco, sleeping all day, going ashore in the evenings, then returning totally drunk to play golf with ice cubes all over the decks!

We had a wonderful time on the *Shemara* and certainly made the most of her, sailing through the night and using her facilities to the full in the daytime. We had all kinds of exciting adventures, the most exotic of which was the day the children landed in Albania on water skis without realizing where they were. Albania was absolutely forbidden territory in those days and a few people had found themselves thrown into jail for trespassing on their border. At first, the children were welcomed by old women dressed in black who had never seen such a phenomenon before and made the sign of the cross, wondering whether they had witnessed new Jesuses walking on water. Militia men soon arrived, however, machine guns at the ready, whereupon the children hurried towards the powerboat and back to the yacht as fast as it would take them.

For Bob and me, those cruises were the only time in our crazy lives that we had some weeks on our own, with something approaching a normal husband and wife and parental relationship. We would take time to discuss the perennial problems of our relationship: Bob would reproach me for my carelessness, my inattention to his needs, siding with the children against his decisions, my lack of concentration on his business problems—in short, what he termed my levity. I would retort that he overlooked how hard I worked and the endless demands made on me and complained of his constant absences from home, which made him truly an absentee father. We would return home full of renewed desire and heartfelt promises to work towards overcoming our difficulties.

There was never any doubt in my mind about Bob's love for me. It was real, radiant, tempestuous, omnipresent, demanding, but he idealized me to such an extent that it was almost impossible for me to correspond to the paragon of virtue of his dreams. In many respects, his behavior towards me was like Pygmalion with his statue: he wanted to mold and shape me into the perfect woman of his imagination. I never doubted his intentions and responded to them as best I could. The sad thing was, however, that no efforts on my part ever seemed to satisfy him and he would return again and again to my shortcomings, unable to accept a compromise or admit that I had defects inherent to my personality. If I did alter and improve—which I am sure I did in many ways—he was never content for long, but would always come back to the same theme. Yet I took all that as an expression of his love. I was completely smitten and desperately wanted to please him. All I strove for was his approval, his appreciation, his acknowledgment that I was making a huge effort to become a better person. I never stopped trying to meet his expectations as long as he continued to show his love for me in one way or another. Until 1987, he used to telephone me every single day and never once refused to accept a call from me. Even the day he had Mrs. Thatcher in the office, he still spoke to me, told me why he couldn't talk at the time and promised to call me back later. This daily telephone contact was Bob's way of answering and commenting on the letters which I wrote regularly, but he had little time to answer. He did still send me letters every now and then, reaffirming his love. He would often write a letter for my birthday, to accompany a gift at Christmas or when he was traveling abroad and had time to reflect:

11 March 1962

Betty dearest,
I salute you on your forty-first birthday. You are wonderfully young in body and spirit and you are to me and everyone else a more attractive and lovable person as our years together grow. . . . I love you very much.

Christmas 1966

Betty my dearest,
It gives me as great a thrill to give you this present, as I hope it will be for you to receive and wear it. On this occasion, I feel that it is appropriate (because I hope that you will allow the children to read this letter) for me to enumerate some of your major achievements in our nearly 22 years of married life together.
Your continuous struggle to become a better character and person, in particular during the last 5 years, and especially your most recent efforts which look like bringing you and us lasting results.
To have borne with great courage and without fuss 9 children and have helped mightily in their upbringing, showing them great love. They are a living credit to you and to the family as a whole.
For the tremendous hard work and mutual effort you have made in all the years, on my behalf and for the family, keeping us all well-housed, fed, clothed, taught, entertained, loved and when necessary scolded.

You so seldom complain about the little time that I have been able to devote to you in recent times because of my business and political work.

For the indispensable help and hard work that you contributed in my three elections to Parliament.

For the great efforts you have made to help Anne win a place at Oxford and the twins to pass their O Levels.

For often looking after and helping Aunty Brana, and thus helping to save her life and sanity.

For helping us with your courage and example to overcome the terrible tragedy of our Michael's accident.

For looking so slim, young, beautiful and well dressed, in fact you look better than most women who are 10 years younger.

For the love you have given me and the children, for the millions of sacrifices, big and small, that you have made on our behalf and for the many, many years of happiness I and we all hope to have with you.

Your ever loving Daddy

1966

Betty, my dearest,

Thank you for your two letters from your heart. I am amazed and delighted with what strength of feeling, wonderful logic and great beauty of language you write. I love you and feel that we have many years of wonderful life ahead of us. I too feel very close to you and miss you very much. In spite of all the criticism, believe me, I love you.

But whilst he expressed his love for me in letters or over the telephone, when we were face-to-face his discontent and bad moods became insufferable. He would come home totally exhausted, and at some point I would invariably fail to satisfy his desires and ruin his hopes of a loving, peaceful and restful time. It only needed something quite trivial for him suddenly to become very bad-tempered, and after that it would take great efforts on my part and any amount of resourceful ingenuity to make him snap out of it. Sometimes, I would take my pen to remind him of the facts of our life, trying to convince him that if life at home was going to be pleasant for all concerned, then he too had to make an effort. Shortly after moving to Oxford, I wrote:

I find it a sorry state of affairs that on one of the finest Sundays of the year, you decided to show a most detestable facet of your character; You behaved in a completely callous and self-centered way and were totally oblivious of other people around you. I have also had a tough two years in which—just to remind you—I have given birth to a baby, lost my mother, and had a consequently difficult summer sorting out our family affairs in Paris. We fought an election, I moved from Broomfield and was separated from my children for six months, I had to organize the refurbishment of this house followed by the move, with all that it entailed. I had two miscarriages, no doubt brought on by rushing around and my complete exhaustion. I am at the end of my tether, and so are you, through too much work, going out every night of the week and driving for hours in this life of politicking which has become your hobby.

Bob would promise to try and curb his moody temperament, and I, like Sisyphus to whom I often compared myself, would push my heavy rock back up the mountainside only to see it roll down again, mostly because it was impossible to sustain these constant efforts towards saintliness.

Despite this sporadic tug-of-war love, my own affection for him grew steadily stronger, as did my yearning to match his expectations, even at the risk, to paraphrase Gide, that he would esteem me a little less as I loved him a little more. He was never out of my mind. As I wrote in December 1960:

Whilst in Paris, I never stopped thinking of you. I felt with uncompromising compulsion that you are my life. I now do everything—live, breathe, talk, buy, build, think only around you, and all that I do is aimed at securing for you, for us, respect, strength, friendship, comfort or pleasure. I crave for you. Life with you is full, exciting, worthwhile; at least one won't have any regrets that one could have done more. The minute you have gone from my life, it's got no taste and no kick unless the things I do are for you or because of you.

I had long believed that if you are not in your husband's life, then you are out of it. As I see it, if you are not prepared to share intimately in what your husband considers essential for his work or enjoyment of life, then you have no right to claim his exclusive attention. That was essentially why I decided I had to take part in Bob's political campaigns, even though I was not naturally attracted to politics.

Life on the home front also claimed my constant, if not undivided, attention. The health of Bob's elder sister was deteriorating rapidly and she would telephone me three or four times a day. As a result of an untreated infection contracted in the concentration camp, Brana suffered from a cardiac complaint which had become so acute that she needed to have an artificial valve inserted. Before she went into hospital for surgery, she became extremely anxious, both for herself and her children. She was full of contradictions, one day wanting me to find her a companion and another totally refusing any help when I had found one. Then there were my own children's needs: the girls were taking secondary school entrance exams, then O levels and A levels and needed help and supervision in their homework and revision. The twins had been given a pony and had to be taken to riding lessons, local pony club events and gymkhanas. The boys needed transport to and from school at half term and holidays, a job I insisted on doing myself. I was still visiting Michael in hospital every week, sometimes twice a week, and our dear nanny Marion was dying of cancer.

I should have been able to share all these burdens, but Bob had his own problems and I found it difficult to make him listen: all that was my responsibility, and I just had to get on with it. With Marion's death in autumn 1964 and Bob's election to Parliament, the little time we could spend together was even further reduced and the difficulties of communication between us were exacerbated. When he did come home, he was absolutely worn out; nothing and nobody pleased him, although his complaints were mostly about my behavior towards him. He never queried my running of the home, the decisions I took concerning the children or any of my basic actions. As I wrote in December 1965:

At your request, I have tried many times to look back at myself, locate all my many shortcomings and alter my manner of acting or speaking.

Since the election, our relationship has deteriorated to such an extent that our life has become an impossible dialogue. It seems to me that you have no joy in coming back home and, when you are with us I live in fear of saying the right thing the wrong way, or saying the wrong thing; of saying nothing when I should speak, or speaking when you want to be left alone. The children hope to catch you on the right leg but prefer to keep away because most of the time they find you on the wrong one. I am so intensely miserable that I have decided to confide my thoughts to paper in order to concentrate and force myself to think what I can do to remedy the situation, and also to draw your attention, if you will bear with me, to your attitude toward your family and me.

We are living a kind of suspense with Michael, which is proving too much for you and for me, at a time when you are overworking and facing many problems, old and new.

I am living through a crisis at home, where my presence has been sadly lacking for two years at the very time when Marion's capacity for work was fast diminishing, allowing the children to have too much freedom. Objects and clothes seem to have invaded all available space in the house like fungi.

We are both mentally and physically exhausted. We have not been able to unwind for years—the physical strain of the election, the daily car journeys, the mental wrench of the tragedies which have hit us, the strain over Brana's illness and that of Marion, culminating in her death in my arms in Ireland.

It affects us in different ways: you have become exceedingly short-tempered, snappy, nagging, despotic. Your weight has gone up, you sleep badly. Your use of uncouth language does you no credit, nor does your complete lack of respect for what I represent, notwithstanding all my failings. You must curb your intemperate, short-lived but wounding judgments of my every move and utterance, control your excessive swollen-headedness and show some appreciation for my great devotion to you alone, throughout our lives. I note that you are unstinting in your compliments when you need me and yet so stingy with your reward when the battle is won.

I am prepared to do without friends, entertainment, joy of any kind in my own pursuits. The only thing I am not prepared to give up in life is you. I love you. You wanted me for what I am, you have got me for keeps.

Despite all our ups and downs, I worshiped Bob and never stopped hoping that I would eventually be able to convince him that I was the partner of his dreams. But as the business expanded, I became more and more worried that all his new acquisitions and the additional work they entailed signified an automatic reduction of our time together:

What frightens me is that I had not realized you had another million pounds involved in Layton, so I suppose when you have managed to straighten out and organize Chambers, you'll have to start all over again with Layton. It is obvious that much more of your time is going to be spent in London and therefore our life needs rethinking if we are not to live in a state of perpetual readjustment, great strain and separation. We fare better when we are together.

I would also rebel at times at the ridiculous way he allowed our private affairs to be conducted. Immediately after his departure in January 1967 for his longest trip to the Far East, I wrote expressing my frustration at his whirlwind lifestyle and lack of adequate time for me:

I cannot reconcile myself to the fact that you have left me for six weeks for an adventurous journey, with all the risks attached to such an expedition, and I have not been gratified with two minutes alone with you. Surely that cannot be right and I must protest most strongly and beg of you to consider this in the light of our lives together. I am ready to make every concession to all your commitments in life, your ambitions, your desires, your love of challenge and the driving force that pushes you forwards to achieve some lasting results in life. I accept all of this because living with you is exhilarating and a unique experience which no other partner could have given me, but I refuse to be "squeezed out" of your life.

It was a ludicrous situation we found ourselves in—with you almost boarding the plane, yet still instructing me on vital issues, telling me the most significant things, dictating to me at a hundred and fifty words a minute in the final three minutes before your departure, as we walked between two doors. It is just not possible and we must not tolerate this kind of thing any more.

Sometimes, sadness at these constant separations at the airport would hit us both, and in those fleeting moments, we were fully aware of how much we meant to each other. As I wrote:

I was so moved to part from you in that melancholy mood. Never before did I feel with such pain what severance it would cause in my very flesh, were we never to see each other again. It was totally unbearable and so rare to see you sad on departure. Old memories come flooding back to me of all those many years when I used to take you to the airport from Esher and fetch you back at night, how my heart used to pound until I saw your dear face emerge from that narrow, angled corridor, towering above all the other anonymous, bewildered wide-eyed humans.

You have been the man of my youth and no one can ever take that away from me; I have loved you every day of my life. I have loved you day and night, even in the days when I was very cross or very sad, very lost or utterly despairing. I have always loved you and have never gone to bed without you in my thoughts, in my eyes, in my dreams. I have wanted you, called you and willed you out of the night, out of the sky when you were flying around the world, out of towns, plains and mountains. I willed you out of hospital and from near death, out of the inferno of the war, out of the reach of the sirens' songs, out of your enemies' clutches.

I myself had exceptionally good health and a strong constitution, but I did get very tired as a result of all those long hours of work, the endless demands made on my body and mind and most of all Bob's unceasing requirement for my self-perfection, which I came to think of as his own personal quest for the Holy Grail. I would try to bring more practical and attainable goals to his attention, whilst still retaining my conviction that it would be wrong to surrender myself completely.

However well you think you know another human being, there is always a dark corner that is not open to investigation, a last secret and impenetrable bastion of the mind, a kernel of imponderable individuality that is unique to us all, unintelligible, inexplicable, sometimes unacceptable to others, which explains why one is finally always alone. It is the gradual erosion of this unknown quantity that helps make a success of a relationship, but keeping a marriage on the right track also requires constant vigilance, sacrifice, a joint judgment of priorities, honest exchanges, confidence and a genuine, mutual desire to hoist oneself above the common lot of indifference.

I continued to write to Bob frequently up until 1969, partly because we had so little opportunity to meet and partly because I knew he loved receiving my letters and needed them, even if I chastised him at times. In his heart of hearts, he knew that my complaints were justified and that the little time he managed to devote to family life was quite insufficient.

Since you entered politics, time seems to have shrunk on the one hand and consequently your judgments have had to become sharper, snappier. You are now surveying much larger horizons and in the intellectual, financial, economic and political spheres you inhabit with your peers, you survey our world like a god. The down-to-earth realities of my daily life are always trivialities and you, perhaps more so than others, have forgotten that the mountain from which you survey us is but an ants' hill made up of the labors, sweat and daily strife of the likes of me. My luck is that you chose me to be the queen of the ants.

We seem to have a breakdown in communications. I ask you to forgive me for the lapses of my tongue since any more pressure on my head and heart would literally destroy me. The very slender equilibrium in which I live, the tautness of the cord is such that it would take very little from you to make it snap. Your displeasure is agony to me. I'll watch communication, you watch consideration.

My head is empty and I have a curious sensation of my skull being on my shoulders but of my brain—or rather my dull grey matter—being in front, floating, before my eyes. I am immensely tired. It is only when the children are in bed that I can start working. You do not know what it is to try and think straight with little children around you.

By the late sixties, Bob was at a pinnacle of his career: Pergamon's share price had gone up spectacularly, the newspapers praised Bob's achievements and he had fulfilled his ambition to become an MP. Poised as he was on the crest of the wave, he should have been happy, if by happiness one means personal success and victory in the face of great difficulties. Yet he was not. And he managed to convince me that I was the cause of his fundamental dissatisfaction. As I wrote to him:

I love you more than anyone ever will on this earth. It is not possible to have wished you more success, to have prayed more for protection against adversity, to have manifested more loyal admiration of your intelligence and generosity, to have given oneself for more love of your handsome and virile body, to have given birth to more lovely children, toiled longer hours at home, tackled a greater diversity of tasks, counted more hours of loneliness—and all for the advancement of your own destiny and that of your tribe, and solely for love of you. Yet I have failed ... and I know where. I can explain it better than you could ever understand it yourself because, as the poet Tagor wrote, "I have laid my whole life bare before you, that is why you do not know me ... My heart is as near to you as your life itself, but you will never know it completely."

In order to retain his love, I was prepared to abandon my own personality completely:

I want to live for you, I want to drown my soul in your desires. This requires all my attention and all my strength, there is no time to do anything else. You will only need to say what you want and it will be done, or to express a desire and I will satisfy it. Perhaps you will discover that the half-flayed creature you have stripped naked still deserves to be loved.

But it was still not sufficient to make him happy. He would constantly revert to the same old theme—that I did not look after his material needs to a standard he considered acceptable and was therefore incapable of ensuring his happiness. Sometimes there would be a button missing on a shirt or I would forget his evening shirt studs or black tie when I packed his bag. He would complain that his cupboards were not impeccably tidy or that I hadn't got his summer clothes out early enough. The right item would be in the wrong place or something would be missing from his case when he was traveling abroad. What he wanted me to do was to "assist, bolster and serve him and the children." But whilst it was a perfectly reasonable request, I felt that I was already doing my best to fulfill it:

> I am trying to analyze why I have not been able to satisfy your material needs in every way. If I were doing all these things for myself, then it would be true to say that I care only for myself, but I don't. The truth is that I don't like this aspect of household work, i.e., I don't like mending, ironing, sewing on buttons, tidying cupboards, but since it has assumed such importance for you, then I am wrong and shall force myself to focus on your material well-being.
>
> As to your question, "Do you not know that your happiness is critically bound up with the degree of affection you can get in return from me when you love and serve me?" Yes, I do know that, with absolute certainty. It is in knowing how to satisfy you that the difficulty lies.
>
> With the children, I feel that I could have acted better or more efficiently at times, but in my heart I do not reproach myself very much. I have tried to give them the best I could and have worked tirelessly for their moral and material welfare. If, as you say, the reward is the degree of appreciation and love I can get in return, then I am fully rewarded. I know that the children love me, respect me and appreciate my endless toil for them, very often well into the night. Their love is not merely a badly severed umbilical cord; it is a grown-up, deep-rooted extraordinarily close relationship for which most mothers envy me. Their vital need of me even after they have flown the nest is clearly demonstrated in their letters, for they feel that I should know their lives, hopes, joys and sorrows in the minutest detail.

I would apologize for my shortcomings and try to win his forgiveness by emphasizing just how much I was coping with, but sometimes I felt it was impossible to please him. If, at business lunches or dinners, I happened to engage in conversation with my neighbor rather than helping to focus attention on him, or if I ventured to introduce an extraneous topic which might distract from the purpose in hand, he would accuse me of disloyalty. He also thought I talked too much and monopolized the conversation. In time, I did manage to correct this fault, but I think that overall I helped more than I hindered. I would never accept his allegations of disloyalty and fought like a tigress to defend myself.

Despite these difficulties, our relationship was never really under threat until September 1967 when Bob suddenly decided to take me to Ireland for a few days' rest. He had some business to transact in Dublin and from there we made our way to Killarney. We chanced upon one of those appalling weeks when the rain came down endlessly the whole time. We were both poorly equipped for such weather and had to buy trench coats and boots to wade through the muddy country lanes. Bob was in a foul temper and vented his anger on me. We had an almighty quarrel one day which went on late into the night, resurrecting old ghosts which I thought had long since been laid to rest. But since we spent most of the rest of the time in bed, we soon made things up. On the day after we returned to Oxford, Bob was up early as usual, preparing to leave for London. Suddenly, like a bolt out of the blue, he walked into the bathroom and told me that he wanted us to separate because he needed his freedom. I can still remember the physical impact of the shock—like a vicious punch in the stomach. I went completely cold and it took me a while to recover my equilibrium. But by then Bob had set off for the office and my only option was to pick up my pen and write him a letter. When I next saw him, a few days later, it was as if the whole thing had never happened.

After that it became a recurrent phenomenon of our lives that every time Bob reached a peak of success in his business or political careers, he also felt an immense desire for freedom, and this would invariably be accompanied by threats of separation from me. It was not that he wanted to abandon material responsibility for me and the children, nor that another woman was involved. He always stated quite specifically that he did not want a divorce. I tried so many times to analyze why these crises occurred, especially since they did not necessarily follow a particularly difficult phase or new development in our relationship. Over the years, I came to the conclusion that it was rather like the lone wolf syndrome—he simply wanted to return to the wild. Whenever such a drama occurred, he would talk of shackles, of being continually tied to a cart that stopped him from going forwards. Although I fought tooth and nail to maintain a loving relationship, my love for him was so great that in a strange way I did understand this desire to be free. I could never forget how longingly we had both admired the freedom and joy of the prancing Chinese horse in one of our favorite pictures at the time when we thought he had only a few weeks to live.

There is little doubt that Bob's political life added intolerable pressure to our relationship. I was certainly not alone in that predicament; it is well known that the rate of affairs, separations and divorces amongst MPs is high. Lucille Iremonger, writer and MP's wife, described the lot of MPs' wives in her book, *And His Charming Lady,* published shortly before Bob entered the Commons. She also examined how the wives of well-known politicians of old had fared, discovering that nothing had changed in the hundred years since Catherine Gladstone learned that:

She did not have his company when he [William] was away, did not have it when he was at home, did not have it when she went out, did not have it when she took the children on holiday and did not even have it in those moments when he might seem available to her. For he worked, as she put it, "like a dragon, furiously." She could only, desperately, seek to fill her own life with other matters—with her family, with any friend or stranger within her orbit who fell ill, with sudden trips here and there, with all her charities and a constant bluebottle buzz of activity—and to force herself as near to him as she could get, as often as possible. So we find her his attentive shadow everywhere, in his study when he is absorbed in his work, on his platforms when he is on tour, in the Ladies' Gallery when he is in the House . . . and where she could not go, she followed him with letters, letters, letters. Instinctively she must have recognized that the surest way to his heart, good as it was, and the best way to claim his attention, was a passionate admiration of him, and she supplied it.

Neither of us had anticipated the pressures we would be subjected to, intensified by the slender majority of the first Wilson Government. On the first day Bob entered the House, October 27, 1964, he sat down and wrote me a letter full of love and hope for the future:

Darling Betty,
To you I write first from this place. Thank you for your great help to get me here. Thank you for being my wife, lover and helper for nearly 20 years and for putting up with me in spite of all the difficulties and vicissitudes, and for being so cheerful most of the time.
I love you very much and will try to make our next 20 years as eventful as those just passed, without causing you too many frights.
Your ever loving Bob

What he had not foreseen, I think, was how compulsively he would be attracted to the business of the House, which covered all spheres of human endeavor and responded to his insatiable curiosity and passionate desire to live life to the full. He became a vigorous and indefatigable speaker in the House and would intervene on all manner of topics ranging from Charolais cattle to the computer industry, from exports to the use of synthetic estrogens in agriculture, from education to the sale of council houses, from the state of the economy to the nuclear program, from the Sea Slug and Sea Dart to land reclamation.

Crossbencher of the *Sunday Express* soon dubbed him a "gasbag" and would repeatedly advise him to "belt up," but perhaps the best description of Bob's eagerness to be constantly in the thick of things came from the pen of the *Daily Mail*'s political writer, Eric Sewell:

Mr. Maxwell came into the Commons with flattering promptness on the first day of the present Parliament, made his maiden speech two and a half hours later and hasn't stopped talking since. He has speechified, questioned, interrupted, attacked and defended with passionate relentlessness, on topics from cancer to brick supply. Equipped with a self-confidence verging on brashness, and a deep powerful voice that can outcry all irritated protests, he has yet to find a parliamentary situation into which he fears to put his foot.

In his first year in the Commons, when everything was so new, Bob would recount his numerous interventions to me, giving me the weekly Hansard reports so that I could follow his life in the House. Those detailed reports of debates made good reading, without the press's subjective and partisan interpretation. Sometimes, however, newspaper cartoons or headlines brought the whole affair alive for me, as on the famous occasion in November 1964 when Bob, a convinced proponent of European unity, asked Harold Wilson to seek an early opportunity to discuss Anglo-French policy differences with de Gaulle. French newspapers carried headlines like LABOR MP ORDERS "GO AND MAKE PEACE WITH DE GAULLE" while Cummings's cartoon put it all so graphically—there was de Gaulle, tall, dominant, masculine alongside a short, dumpy, female version of Harold Wilson, each of them carrying their Entente Cordiale briefcases, shaking hands across the divide of the Anglo-French aircraft industry. The caption, from the mouth of de Gaulle reads, "Ah ma chérie, we must stop the divorce—we've got to think of the children!"

Some of Bob's early contributions provoked pandemonium in the House and developed into first-class rows, accompanied by the traditional jeers, heckling and laughter which Hansard mildly describes as "interruption." There was, for instance, the episode in December 1964 when he queried the fact that some £60 million of supplementary estimates of government expenditure was being passed without proper debate, "on the nod," as he put it, which degenerated into an argument about rubber-stamping and whether it was in order for an MP to read his speech rather than talk from notes. A general commotion ensued, with so much noise that Bob couldn't be heard and the Speaker, Dr. Horace King, had to try again and again to bring the House to order as other MPs stood up to intervene, raising dubious points of order.

Then there was another hilarious occasion in March 1965 when a matter of seemingly little importance—the misinterpretation of a shorthand outline in a Hansard report twelve months before—provoked a first-class row. It was out of all proportion to its significance, especially compared with the issues of Vietnam and immigration which had aroused only a ripple of calm concern, but it illustrates perfectly the classic House of Commons row which has now became familiar to Britons through television. It all started in a debate on army estimates when Bob wanted to know how the word *detached* made in a defense debate by Mr. James Ramsden, then Secretary of State for War, had become "attached" in the bound volume of Hansard. The difference was not insignificant—it amounted to something like fifty soldiers per battalion and gave a very different impression of peacetime defense forces. The speaker patiently explained how the mistake might have occurred, concluding firmly that the correction had been quite properly made by Mr. Ramsden. The matter might have rested there, but for the fact that two MPs insisted that Bob should make a public apology. This he promptly refused to do, maintaining that he had not impugned Mr. Ramsden's honor, merely suggested that the former government, a bunch of "incompetent twerps," had no objection to cooking the books where defense was concerned. Up jumped Ramsden amidst the uproar, who indignantly denied the allegations, claiming to detect the "hairy hand of George Wigg" in the matter (which was quite true as it was George, paymaster general and a former colonel, who had put Bob up to it). The Tories were infuriated and just wouldn't let the matter drop. Even the former prime minister, Alec Douglas-Home, felt incensed enough to protest, but was told that he would have to put up with it! Finally, on the third day, a group of Tory MPs tabled a motion of censure on Bob, countered by another one from Michael Foot, Labor MP for Ebbw Vale, and sixteen other Labor MPs. Through it all, according to the *Times* political correspondent, Bob sat relaxed and smiling, "shrinking from controversy like a flower turning its head to the sun" and enjoying all the fun produced by the play on words, "cooking the books" and "booking the cooks." He had set out to anger the opposition and succeeded beyond his wildest dreams.

Bob clearly enjoyed being deliberately provocative, breaking some of the rules and pinpointing some of the absurdities of Parliament, and this quickly earned him the reputation of an upstart. But as he told a reporter from the *Illustrated London News*, "I've come into the Commons as a modernizer—to halt the retreat of this country which has been going on for the past fifty years. . . . This government came in to modernize, and they should start right here in the Houses of Parliament. It's archaic—completely out of keeping with this country's needs." He was eager to get on with the job, wanting, in his own words, to shake people up, to release their energies and make them excited again about being British. Transport House, the Labor Party headquarters, came in for his criticism, as he recognized the urgent need for more full-time agents, better professional surveys and research facilities, more modern equipment and increased subscriptions. It was, Bob said, "A ramshackle affair," and Labor would never be able to persuade people that it was capable of modernizing Britain until it could successfully modernize itself. As he wrote in the *People* newspaper, "Harold Wilson's 'rusty penny-farthing' crack is an under-statement. In comparison with the Tories we haven't even invented the wheel." It was, alas, to take another twenty years or so for that modernization to get off the ground successfully.

If Bob's irrepressible speechifying irked some members, his courage and ability to home in on the crux of a complex issue and transform it into practical political thinking endeared him to others. There was a good deal of genuine comradeship in the House and some of the unspoken public school rules definitely applied amongst members of the Labor Party. You upheld your side, irrespective of right or wrong. Several times, Bob was asked to chip in for an MP who was in trouble. His natural open-handedness with money, generosity of spirit towards the failings of his fellow man and total discretion were all well known. He would never betray a secret and wasn't in the least inclined to gossip, which was certainly not true of many MPs. At a time when pairing[6] was almost impossible because

---

6. Pairing is a permanent arrangement made with an MP of the opposite party not to vote on chosen days, thus allowing both MPs to travel or attend to constituency or business matters. The arrangement must be approved by the Chief Whip.

of the slender majority, Bob did his best to play by the rules of the House and made some good friends, people we kept in touch with long after he left the Commons. Amongst these was the Chief Whip, Ted Short, whose authority Bob accepted like that of an officer and to whom he wrote in October 1964, "The life of the government is in your hands." Another very colorful figure was George Brown, whom he had met before he became an MP and who became successively Secretary of State for Economic Affairs and Secretary of State for Foreign Affairs in the Wilson government. They got on extremely well: Bob appreciated George's undisputed intelligence and talents and learned a great deal from him about the early days of the Labor party and unions. George was original, creative and courageous. He would often finish the evening at our home in Fitzroy Square or drop in at Headington on his way to Donnington, the foreign secretary's official country home. In February 1966 he came to Pergamon to open our newly built headquarters and, a few months later, present the company with the Queen's Award to Industry for export performance. Sometimes he would come for lunch in Oxford or for dinner in London, with or without his wife Sophie. If he was in a good mood, he could be great fun as a guest, but all his qualities were marred by an incredible lack of elementary manners and a tendency to exhibitionism. Over the years, I learned to humor him when he was on a high, laughing off his antics if all of a sudden he pulled my hair, pretending to see whether I was wearing a wig or not.

At other times, humor was quite out of place. I remember one highly embarrassing lunch in Oxford, when George announced he was coming at the very last minute. I was entertaining my cousin Patrick Vieljeux, Maurice Couve de Murville's son-in-law, who had brought his daughter Georgina to stay with us for a month to improve her English. Although Maurice later became France's prime minister, he was at the time foreign minister, that is, George Brown's counterpart. Patrick himself was not a politician but an influential member of a family shipbuilding firm, in one of the largest shipyards in France. We had hardly sat down for lunch before George, completely without provocation, lashed out about Couve de Murville, shouting at Patrick in the most menacing terms, "And you can tell that to your father-in-law, and that and that." Bob tried to explain to George that my poor cousin was really not in a position to answer his criticisms and it would be better for him to speak directly to his French colleague. I was shocked and looked at Patrick, wondering if he would leave the table at such an offensive attack, but he was a perfect gentleman and was certainly not going to embarrass me any further. Assessing the situation better than I did, he just remained silent. I had never witnessed such an undiplomatic and ill-mannered outburst by an English foreign minister, damaging in every way both to George and good relations between our two countries. I had not realized at the time that George might be drunk. Alas, over-indulgence in alcohol was to prove his downfall. Whenever he came to see Bob at Fitzroy Square and I happened to be there, I would go downstairs with him and the butler to see him off in his Jaguar. Although we tried not to ply him with drinks, he had usually already had a fair amount before he came and by the time he left was truly the worse for wear. But he would say, "Don't worry, I'll get there, just point me in the right direction!"

His misbehavior at important banquets was notorious, but I think the best story that did the rounds of London's French community at the time concerned an evening when George attended a grand dinner at the French Embassy. The ambassador then was Baron Geoffroy de Courcel, friend and Chef de Cabinet of De Gaulle from his war years in London who later served as his Secretary-General from 1959 to 1962. His wife, Martine, was pretty, cultured, elegant, and a superb hostess. At that dinner, she had the Minister for Foreign Affairs on her right as her guest of honor. Soon after the guests had sat down, George's hand started straying under the table towards Madame de Courcel's thigh. Very discreetly, she took hold of his hand and firmly put it back on his own thigh, but to no avail as the hand soon started straying again. At this point, Madame de Courcel ventured a timid "Oh! Minister," to which George responded, "My dear Madame, don't tell me this is the first time you've been courted like that!" "Oh no, Minister, but never before the soup!" came Martine's reply.

Having suffered a great deal himself from George's volatile temperament, Harold Wilson predicted, "He won't last long. He'll trip over himself sooner or later and destroy himself." And that is exactly what happened. As he gradually deteriorated, his wife Sophie suffered it all with immense dignity. I felt enormously sorry for her.

Although Richard Crossman was not a close friend, Bob and he got on well and at one time saw quite a lot of each other. He came home for lunch once or twice, and although I found him abrupt, Bob did not mind his manner. With Dick, he said, you always knew where you stood. I suppose it was because of this relationship that Dick called on Bob in March 1967 to help him with a problem. Crossman, then Leader of the House and Chairman of the Services

Committee, decided to bring Bob in to sort out the terrible financial mess of the Commons' catering department. As he records in his diaries:

I soon had to go out to the Services Committee where I had to get agreement on a draft report on how we should meet the £60,000 deficit on the kitchen account. We just dare not publish the report of the accountants or of the Treasury O and M until we have a concrete policy. What we finally decided was to bring Bob Maxwell to the Committee and put him in the chair. When I first heard the idea I was shocked but John Silkin swallowed it and persuaded Bob Maxwell to accept and to my amazement the Tories on the Committee accepted him too. . . . I think they realized that one has to get a businessman of experience and courage and that Bob is the only businessman in the House who will be prepared, out of sheer vanity and ambition, to spend a couple of years saving the House of Commons' kitchen from corruption and bankruptcy.[7]

Bob reluctantly agreed to take on the chore of chairman of the Catering Subcommittee and was soon to discover the lamentable state of its finances and general management. As Crossman readily agreed, it had been going downhill since 1956 and losing thousands through utter incompetence.[8] Four months into his new job, Bob was writing to Crossman to report on reality and progress:

I do not think that anybody realized the terrible mess and complete lack of financial or any other management control in the Catering Department of the House of Commons. Since I took over the Chairmanship of the Catering Sub-Committee, I have spent some 400 hours on dealing with its problems, which is more than the total number of hours I have been able to spend on behalf of Pergamon Press and the rest of my parliamentary work.

Bob had already taken steps to reduce wastage and improve security. He had dismissed four employees for misfeasance, brought in a catering financial controller and experienced staff manager, tightened up on overtime, stopped over-investment in wines and liquor and started to realize capital locked-up in the famous Commons' cellar. By then the department's losses, which had been run-

---

7. Richard Crossman, *The Diaries of a Cabinet Minister*, (London: Hamish Hamilton & Jonathan Cape, 1976), March 7, 1967, pp. 267–68.

8. *Ibid*, p. 278.

ning at £3,000 per month, had been halted and it was able to increase pay once the government standstill on wages was over. To emphasize the serious trouble the department was in, Bob went on to explain that there were twenty-five people with prison records on the staff—the only people they could get at the current low rates of pay. Encouraged by the Chancellor of the Exchequer's promise to clear the overdraft with an interest-free loan and pay an annual grant in respect of periods of recess, Bob had set about his task with his usual tireless energy. It was the start of the revolution of Chairman Ma (a nickname probably invented by George Brown), which is still remembered with amusement and outrage by those who were MPs at the time.

Reopening Annie's Bar, the place where political journalists and Members of Parliament could meet as equals, was a popular move amongst the press, but it was not long before other changes or new ideas brought howls of protest. Perhaps the most audacious of them all—which was never implemented—was the suggested installation of vending machines in Westminster Hall! Bob Mellish, Minister of Public Building and Works, and a good friend of Bob's, wrote to him in September 1967, registering his shock at the thought of such newfangled equipment in such a historic and revered location, ending his letter, "You must be stark raving mad to think of this one!"

It was also the start of a long and often amusing series of questions and comments in the House centering on the quality, cost and efficiency of the catering services provided. Bob had to field questions on the use of powdered milk in tea, the cost of banqueting charges, the poor quality of Commons catering, the availability of avocado pears or oeuf en gelée, why lamb cutlets were cold, the cost of the ingredients of a ham sandwich or a corned beef salad, the ban on tipping, the price of a pork pie, why wine was bought from shippers in France, the ban on foreign cheeses, complaints about Portuguese spoons in the MPs' tearoom and about paper napkins and protests at the varieties of biscuits available. It was an endless saga, and became a kind of game in which certain MPs loved to indulge. My new "Tsar of Catering" loved to regale me with all these stories and we would laugh so much at the funny side of these episodes. It also prompted Bob to take an interest in my recipes, what ingredients I used, how much they cost and whether or not I would contemplate using powdered eggs or powdered milk in my cooking, which I certainly would not.

By December 1967 the Catering Subcommittee was reporting a profit and, although the jocular sniping continued, things quietened down considerably. Bob continued as chairman until he tendered his resignation in March 1969. Although the *Sunday Times* was later to publish a one-sided and derogatory article, denigrating Bob's successes in Commons' catering, his Parliamentary colleagues at the time recorded their deep appreciation of his services, thanking him for reorganizing it on a profitable basis. Crossman himself wrote a personal letter to the *Sunday Times'* then editor-in-chief, Denis Hamilton, pointing out in forceful terms that the paper's investigative team "Insight" had not reported one iota of all that he had taken the trouble to tell them in great detail, nor how he had persuaded Bob to take the "suicidal" course of accepting the chairmanship of the Catering Subcommittee nor what a marvelous job Bob had done.

Amongst the range of his work in Parliament, Bob himself considered the Clean Air Act of 1968 as perhaps his greatest success. Well aware of the problems of air pollution from the local brick and cement factories of his constituency, he introduced a Private Members' Bill, the Clean Air Bill, early in 1968. It was designed to tighten controls on air pollution, giving government and local authorities greater power over smoke control and emissions from industrial premises. One of his sponsors for this bill was Gerald Nabarro MP, author of the Clean Air legislation of 1955, who was pleased to support the strengthening and extension of his original Act. After a comparatively easy passage in its early stages through the House, the bill ran into difficulty after its second reading with unlimited spurious objections from the opposition. It took a government decision to make time for a special debate before the bill eventually passed its committee stage in the Commons after a large number of amendments, many from Bob himself, were debated and agreed. It then sailed through the Lords with little problem and became an Act of Parliament later that summer. As Nabarro himself summed up, through this clean air legislation of 1955 and 1968, "Thousands of lives will have been saved, millions of lives prolonged and limitless rewards derived from greater fuel-burning efficiency applied gainfully for all our people."[9]

---

9. Gerald Nabarro, *NAB 1: Portrait of a Politician*, (Oxford: Robert Maxwell, 1969), p. 298.

It was also in 1968 that events in Europe interrupted our family holiday cruise when Parliament was recalled in August for an emergency debate on the Russian invasion of Czechoslovakia. Bob flew back to London. He really spoke from the heart that day, urging the government to condemn the "rape of Czechoslovakia," but not to be panicked into "fanning the embers of the cold war." It would, he argued, be utterly wrong and against Czech interests to give up the encouraging progress already made towards détente. Fearing that the Czechs were about to get rid of all their old Stalinists and create a completely refurbished Communist party, opposed to the Kremlin's central authority, the Russians had decided to take action before this new spirit of freedom became too firmly established. As Bob said, "They were afraid to let the shaft of light into their own party. After fifty years of communism, they felt unwilling and unable to speak any other language than that of the tommy-gun and the tank." He then went on to discuss what could be done to help the Czech people, calling on private citizens and businessmen to give Russia the cold shoulder, urging everyone to voice their protest and admiration of the Czechs' spirit of Resistance. His former countrymen were in effect telling the Russians, "You may well have managed to occupy our territory, but you do not own us. You cannot command us and will not control us. We will only take instructions from our legal government." The Russians clearly had to be shown that the strong-arm method was no longer acceptable amongst civilized nations.

Bob was also extremely proud of two major reports that he wrote for the Labor Party, in which his political life and business expertise overlapped. I remember them very well too for the simple reason that the whole family somehow got involved in helping with heaps of photocopying, meticulous proofreading and checking of references. Through his work for Pergamon Press, Bob was already conscious of the need to harness the results of scientific research for use in industry and was involved early on in the development of Labor's science and technology policies. In 1963, before he was elected to Parliament, he became chairman of Labor's working party on science, government and industry which was set up by Harold Wilson and reported to Richard Crossman. Wilson had promised to lead the nation into "the white heat of the technological revolution" and the phrase became the platform to launch the 1964 election campaign. Unfortunately for Britain and for science, it soon became apparent that nothing very tangible resulted, although this policy

My hostess days, in the dining room at Headington, 1966
(courtesy Bryan Heseltine)

Family group on the occasion of my doctorate, 1981

With Philip, 1984

Kevin, 1987

With Bob at Headington
on his sixty-fifth
birthday, 1988

Receiving the
Sir Sigmund Sternberg
award from Cardinal
Hume in 1988, for my
contribution to furthering
Christian-Jewish relations
(courtesy Mike Maloney)

Being presented to the Queen at the Council of Christians and Jews reception,
St. James's Palace, 1989

With Ian and Mrs. Thatcher at George Thomas's eightieth birthday celebration, 1989

With Bob at Malcolm
Forbes's seventieth birthday
party, Tangiers, 1989

In conversation with Prince Charles, 1989 (courtesy Desmond O'Neill)

Addressing Chancellor Kohl and the International Council of Christians and Jews Executive Committee, Heppenheim, 1990

Bob with the *Lady Ghislaine,* 1990 (courtesy Mike Maloney)

With most of my children and grandchildren at Headington on my
seventieth birthday, March 11, 1991

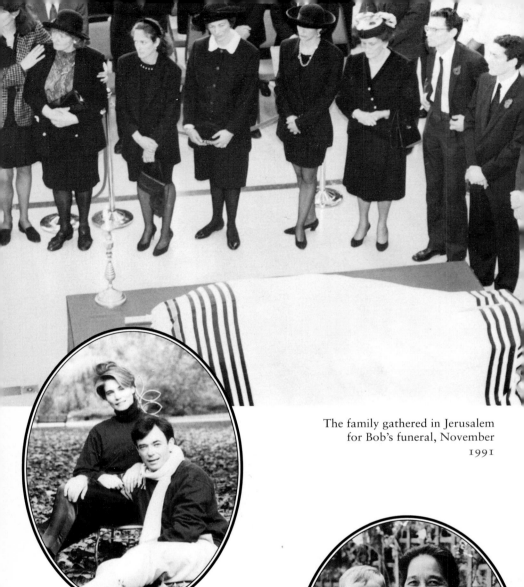

The family gathered in Jerusalem for Bob's funeral, November 1991

Ian and Laura in Saint James's Park, London, October 1993 (courtesy Canetty-Clarke)

Oping with my tenth grandchild, Fleur Holve, June 1994

could have put us at the forefront of Europe. As Joe Haines put it, "The white heat soon cooled."[10]

In the scientific sphere, Bob submitted an important paper for discussion after examining Britain's problems with many distinguished scientists, including President Kennedy's scientific advisory staff. Much later, Crossman was to write of Bob's report: "Throughout his work on science, where I regretfully let him set up a group of very powerful scientists, he has been unfaultable. I can't find him putting a foot wrong. The paper he and his group have produced is by far the best."[11]

Reading sections of that paper today, I am struck by how topical it seems at a time when science is still generally underfunded and undervalued. Whilst many of Bob's suggestions were recognized as valid and practical, many years would still go by before they were put into practice.

As the MP Tom Dalyall wrote in the *Independent*, "And had Bob Maxwell's ideas been implemented—for instance on the power of public spending to promote science, or on European Cooperation (he was vice-chairman of the Council of Europe Committee on Science and Technology)—then the whole industrial history of the Wilson government might have been more successful."[12]

Bob's second report, on the subject of public sector purchasing, was similarly long in receiving recognition. During 1963 and 1964, Harold Wilson had repeatedly stressed the enormous power which modern government has if it is prepared to use its great strength as a buyer. By November 1967, Bob had made a detailed study of this potential, putting forward sixty proposals on public sector purchasing. His report was distributed widely to ministers, MPs, civil servants, academics and industrialists. More than 160 people sent him letters of congratulation on his effort, recognizing the value of the research and commenting on his recommendations. Tony Benn called it "an impressive and wide-ranging study." Sir Sigmund Warburg wrote, "I am much impressed by the comprehensive and clear-cut

---

10. Joe Haines, *Maxwell*, (London: Macdonald, 1988), p. 217.

11. Richard Crossman, *The Backbench Diaries of a Cabinet Minister* (London: Hamish Hamilton & Jonathan Cape, 1981), p. 1017.

12. *Procurement Weekly*, November 15, 1984.

way in which these papers deal with the chief economic problems with which we are faced." But despite this praise, it would be many years before some of Bob's suggestions were put into practice, and even then it was subsequent Tory governments which adopted them. When in 1984, a government report advocated a senior body to coordinate government purchasing and oversee the training of civil service buyers, Bob was delighted to see how closely these recommendations followed those set out in his report of 1967. I remember that about a year before the government reported its findings, a member of the Tory research party wrote to Bob asking if he could purchase a copy of his report. I was asked to find one in the cellar and it was duly forwarded to him. As Bob told *Procurement Weekly* magazine: "It's taken seventeen years. . . . I'm flattered, but I don't mind as long as somebody at last will organize the government's buying power in order to do good for both the taxpayer and for the country at large."

Another of Bob's campaigns—I'm Backing Britain—was to win him much greater publicity. A simple, patriotic cause, it was to win the hearts and minds of countless ordinary workers around Britain, starting with five secretaries in Surbiton, Surrey, who decided in January 1968 to work an extra half-hour without pay to help Britain. Public response was amazing and people all over Britain were soon doing their bit to buy British and help Britain. I have vivid memories of that campaign spilling over into my own life and kitchens, with Bob banning all foreign cheeses and insisting that I change my French car for a British one. With his usual boundless enthusiasm, he did manage to tread on a few toes, but on the whole his input was appreciated. Richard Crossman was to comment:

I had to go back and see Bob Maxwell, who had come to see me about his Buy British campaign. What a miraculous man that fellow is. However much people hate him, laugh at him, boo him and call him a vulgarian, he gets things done. If it wasn't for Bob Maxwell we would have got nowhere with this campaign. He was rebuked and he got a terrible snub from the CBI—who said this was an anti-export campaign—but then he modified it to a Help Britain campaign and persuaded the CBI to support him. Today he was bringing me the drafts of his advertisements. And though these adverts will be big and vulgar, at least they'll show people wanting to help Britain, and wanting not to be anti-Wilson and supporting us in the post-devaluation climate.[13]

---

13. Crossman, *Diaries of a Cabinet Minister,* p. 681.

But it was probably as a constituency MP that Bob really came into his own. By the time he was elected to Parliament, he knew his constituents extremely well, along with all the problems they faced in the constituency. He was accessible and soon gained a reputation for getting things done for local people. He was never more relaxed than amongst his constituents, at his busy Saturday morning surgeries, at local rallies, in the marketplace and on the doorstep. Judy Ennals, Bob's political secretary, told me a lovely story which illustrates clearly this genuine concern for his voters. At one particular surgery in Bletchley, an old man came shuffling in carrying a bundle of letters wrapped up in an old newspaper and told Bob that he had been summoned to a tribunal on a social security issue. The old man was anxious and not a little overawed at the thought of answering questions before such a tribunal, so Bob read through the latest correspondence, grasped the gist of the problem and said, "Right, I know your problem. Now pretend I'm the chairman of the tribunal. Go to the door and knock." There was a knock at the door. "Come in. Now, go out again. Come in and say 'Good morning, sir,' and then sit down." So patiently, Bob went through a complete rehearsal of the man's lines, helping him prepare for the ordeal. Some months later, the old man wrote to thank Bob. He had won his case.

One of the major events in the constituency when Bob was its MP was the development of the new town of Milton Keynes. He was closely involved in its conception and planning, not only in obtaining adequate compensation for farmers dispossessed of land, but also in helping to convince Richard Crossman, Minister of Housing and Local Government, that the town of Wolverton should be included in the proposed new town. I still have vivid recollections of that day in December 1966 when Crossman visited the constituency and Bob took him up in a helicopter to convince him of the geographical reasons for including Wolverton.

Another red-letter day was the royal visit in April 1966, the first such visit to Buckingham for almost four hundred years. The town spared no effort to welcome its monarch. Flags and bunting fluttered from almost every building, shopwindows were decorated, schoolchildren were given time off and huge crowds gathered to welcome the Queen and Prince Philip on their whistle-stop tour of the town and constituency. The weather had been sunny and quite warm that week and Bob and I had spent the night in Bletchley so as to be sure to be there on time. A platform had been erected in the middle of Buckingham town square, and Bob and I, the mayor of Buckingham and all the council dignitaries were asked to be in place an hour before the

Queen was due to arrive. My outfit that day was a new oatmeal-colored suit and a wide-brimmed hat, which later became known to our constituents as "the Queen's outfit." It was the first time I had been introduced to Her Majesty, but I would be privileged to meet her on many subsequent occasions. That day, she was wearing a mink coat, which I envied, not for the coat itself, which was rather old-fashioned, but for the fact that she had had the foresight to dress for the weather, which by now had turned bitterly cold. She was snugly wrapped in her fur while I was shivering with cold on the drafty platform. She talked to Bob for a short while, congratulating him on his election result, then had a brief word with everyone on the platform. On many occasions since, I have marveled at the Queen's knowledge on an incredibly wide range of topics and her ability to put people at their ease with a few simple words that they cherish till the day they die.

As soon as Bob became an MP, we were also automatically invited to other royal occasions, the Trooping the Color on the Queen's birthday in June, and the royal garden parties at Buckingham Palace. Our social engagements, of course, increased tenfold in those years, headed by invitations to Number 10 Downing Street. When in 1965 Harold Wilson issued an invitation for drinks to new MPs and their wives, it was the first time I had ever been into that historic house, used as both office and residence by the prime minister. Since then, I have attended many social functions there, often for a special charity or cause supported by the prime minister of the day. On other occasions, Harold's wife, Mary, would invite MPs' wives for tea or entertain businessmen and their wives to interest them in a charitable cause. I got to know her well over the years and liked her very much. She is refined, cultured, completely honest and without any artificial social mannerisms. When she talks to you, she is really listening and does not let her eyes wander. Although I have never read any direct criticism of her, the press has generally dismissed her as something of a mouse, totally overtaken by events, but it is an opinion I consider hasty, untrue and without foundation. Unostentatiously, she has been a pillar of strength to her family and a steady calming influence on a man whose brain was constantly on the move, who spent his whole life in politics, invaded her home with his "kitchen cabinet" and carried on longer than any prime minister, other than Mrs. Thatcher, with the heavy responsibilities of the affairs of the nation. Unfortunately for me, I did not know Harold well until he was old and already a victim of Alzheimer's disease. By then he had lost most of his spark, but as I often sat next to him at functions, I heard his favorite stories many times. I would often try to make him tell me about famous Labor party characters like Aneurin Bevan, Ernest Bevin, Clement Attlee or Sir Stafford Cripps, but he always preferred to recount his meetings with Ian Smith or President Kennedy or Nikita Khrushchev.

Besides attending the usual civic balls and official dinners in the constituency, we were constantly invited to banquets in the various City Halls of London, not to mention evenings spent with old friends or the new ones Bob made in the House. We also attended many charity or social lunches and dinners, two or three of which still stand out in my mind. Two of them involved Jennie Lee, whose husband, Aneurin Bevan, had served as health minister in the Attlee government and been responsible for the reform of the health service of Great Britain, making it freely available to all. She had become friendly with Bob after he agreed to help Center 42, the arts foundation under Arnold Wesker that aimed to buy the Round House. Interested in this venture by Bob, the wealthy industrialist and diplomat Nubar Gulbenkian (who was one of our constituents) gave a lunch at the Ritz Hotel at which Jennie Lee, then arts minister, was guest of honor. At the end of the lunch, the traditional separation of ladies and gentlemen, still current in those days, took place over coffee and brandy. I remember taking the opportunity to go to the ladies where I came across Jennie Lee, absolutely furious at not being treated like the men. She was after all the minister, didn't they realize she could not be treated like a housewife? She told me in no uncertain terms that she would not be going back in; on the contrary she was heading straight back to the Commons. That would teach all those snobs a lesson. Could I please tell our hosts just that? By the time I joined the other ladies, Mrs. Gulbenkian had realized that something was wrong. When she asked me where Jennie Lee was, I am afraid I told her a white lie. I just couldn't bear to offend a nice woman who had obviously done her best, so I told her that Jennie, suddenly remembering an engagement at the House, had asked me to make her apologies and say good-bye for her as she didn't want to break up the party.

At other times Jennie could be quite magnanimous, as on the occasion we were invited one cold December evening to Yehudi and Diana Menuhin's home in Highgate. They had gathered together a number of rich and influential friends, again with Jennie as guest of honor, to help them raise funds to launch the Menuhin School of Music. Whilst we were all having dinner downstairs, a thief broke in on the upstairs floor and escaped with all our fur coats and wraps. Lew Grade's wife lost a beautiful honey-colored mink, another guest a full-length white mink coat, and Jennie Lee her own mink coat. But that day, she never complained. She simply laughed it off, not wanting to add to poor Diana's anguish. Our poor hostess already felt that all her efforts that evening had vanished along with her guests' fur coats!

For Pergamon Press, the two years since its public flotation had been highly satisfactory. In 1966 the company had expanded greatly with the acquisitions of the educational textbook publisher Wheatons; C & E Layton, the old-established blockmakers and typesetters; the Religious Education Press; the well-known booksellers Bumpus, Haldane; and the Book Society. In 1967 Bob continued this expansion, with the purchase of an increased holding in the History Book Club; Speedwriting Ltd.; shares in Thomson Press (India); Caxton Holdings, the encyclopedia sellers and a 50 percent stake in International Learning Systems Corporation (ILSC). By October 1967, the opportunity arose for Bob to make a £5.3m bid for Butterworth, the publishers from whom he had originally bought Pergamon Press. He was very keen to proceed, seeing Butterworth's legal publishing business as a cornerstone in his plans for an information storage and retrieval system for the legal profession. Butterworth, on the other hand, did not want to be taken over by Pergamon at any price. Fear of Bob was rife, and in order to achieve their ends, they were prepared to stoop to trumped-up allegations to damage his reputation. In the ensuing lawsuit, however, they were forced to admit the falsity of their claims and the gross impropriety of their actions and had to make a groveling apology. But Bob's takeover bid had failed and the International Publishing Corporation (IPC) eventually bought the company. It had been an intensely personal battle, the first in a long line that were to darken the coming years.

For the whole family 1968 began with deep sorrow when Michael died, aged twenty-three, at the Churchill Hospital, seven years after his tragic road accident. Unbeknown to me, Ritchie Russell, the neurologist looking after him, had come to see Bob in the late autumn of the previous year. They had come to the inevitable conclusion that Michael was brain dead and had agreed that although nothing should be done to shorten his life, nothing beyond good nursing should be undertaken to prolong it. So it was that when Michael developed meningitis, although the antibiotic Penbritin could have saved him (as it had many times before), it was not prescribed and he died of this infection.

For seven long years, I had sat at his bedside, hoping and praying at first that he would recover consciousness, then gradually accepting that his brain had been damaged beyond any possible recovery. I would sit there, beside my sleeping prince, remembering the bright, exceptionally gifted and considerate child who had now grown into manhood without knowing it. Shortly before his accident, when he was nearly sixteen, he had come home from school and, seeing me heavily pregnant and tired, had acted like a man and head of a large family. "Mummy" he said, "Don't bother to cook lunch, leave the tribe to me, I'll take them all to Headington for fish and chips; they'll love that and you can have a rest." He had a passion for go-carting and that Christmas before his accident, we had given him a secondhand cart, which he was only able to enjoy for three days. Immediately after he heard the news of Ghislaine's birth, he wrote to me, "I don't know why but I think that this is the first time I really thought and worried about what was happening and I was terribly relieved when I heard that everything was all right." The next day, he was all but dead.

I would sit beside him, pondering, shedding tears for what was never to be, searching in vain for an explanation that would help me understand his situation. Michael needed thirty-two people to keep him alive and care for him day after day: nurses, doctors, physiotherapists, pharmacists, nutritionists, masseurs, barbers, and yet to all intents and purposes he was dead. How could that be allowed? Why should such life-and-death decisions be left to the grieving parents of a brain-dead child? Why did the medical experts not have the courage to take the responsibility that their knowledge and expertise surely dictated? Did we need a new definition of death? I understood then that death really occurred with the death of the brain, not of the heart. But from there I would find myself in great spiritual conflict. Since Michael's brain was no longer with him or with us, where was it? In limbo? It was the greatest challenge yet to my faith and I had no one to help me. No one apart from Bob could really understand what I was going through, and his own faith was very shaky at the time, for very similar reasons. He was wondering what kind of God could permit the murder of most of his family, then punish him further by the deaths of two of his own children.

When Michael was finally allowed to die, it was surely a relief for him, but it came seven years too late. This totally abnormal situation had had untold consequences for us all, particularly for Michael's closest brother, Philip, whose grief was never to be assuaged. After his death, we gave permission for an autopsy of Michael's brain to be carried out and this, along with observations

378 / ELISABETH MAXWELL

made during his seven-year coma, allowed doctors to establish a better-defined picture of the human brain. I was also to derive some small consolation from the fact that experimental use of the wide-spectrum antibiotic Penbritin on Michael was to pave the way for its release for general use. It was then in a trial stage, but when Michael first developed meningitis, Bob had pleaded with the company producing it and they had finally agreed with Michael's neurologist that his case was so borderline that the hospital could use it. After its amazingly successful results on him, it was subsequently given to several patients in the emergency ward who had caught meningitis and whose lives were saved.

Later in the year, another spiteful episode was to plunge us further into gloom. For years, Bob had harbored ambitions to own a national newspaper. As far back as 1964, he had attempted to save the Labor *Daily Herald* before it was succeeded by the broadsheet *The Sun*. Then in May 1968, he made a brief attempt to revive the *Sunday Citizen,* former newspaper of the Cooperative movement,[14] but this was merely a forerunner of his major bid to acquire the *News of the World,* which was also to end in failure after an acrimonious battle and dispute with the Takeover Panel.

It all started in October 1968 when Jacob Rothschild made it known that he was seeking a buyer for 25 percent of the *News of the World*'s shares owned by Professor Derek Jackson, an eccentric cousin of the newspaper's chairman, Sir William Carr. Bob's £26 million takeover bid, made to Hambro, the Carr family's advisors, on October 16, 1968, took them completely by surprise and created enormous excitement on the stock exchange, pushing the shares to new and dizzy heights. Whilst the Carr family, owners of a 27 percent shareholding, contented themselves with a brief statement advising shareholders to take no action for the moment, Bob told reporters he felt confident of success, but he had reckoned without the dirty tactics which Carr and the *News of the World* would stoop to in the forthcoming tussle.

Four days after the bid was announced, the *News of the World*'s editor, Stafford Somerfield, launched a virulently xenophobic attack

---

14. The Cooperative movement was a British political party established in 1917 which grew out of the idea of voluntary mutual economic assistance developed in the nineteenth century by Robert Owen. It became closely integrated with the Labor party.

on Bob on the front page of the newspaper. It was a disgraceful outburst that shocked even Carr's supporters in its open display of anti-semitism: "Why do I think that it would not be a good thing for Mr. Maxwell, formerly Jan Ludwig Hoch, to gain control of this newspaper which I know has your respect, loyalty and affection—a newspaper as British as roast beef and Yorkshire pudding?"

Maxwell had, the editorial continued, no newspaper experience. He was a Socialist and there was no chance his promise of impartiality could be maintained if he became the paper's owner. "This a British paper, run by British people. Let's keep it that way," he thundered in conclusion.

Unfortunately for Bob, the same kind of dirty, defense tactics were to be adopted by Carr's professional advisors in the City. Bob's bid was also among the first to be regulated by a new Takeover Code of practice and supervisory panel under the chairmanship of Sir Humphrey Mynors, which was determined to show its teeth in policing takeover battles, yet in the end proved ineffectual.

In spite of Somerfield's editorial, all still seemed on course; there were no rival bids and other press comment was generally favorable to Bob's takeover. But everything changed dramatically on Monday, October 21, when Hambro adopted new tactics. By making £750,000 of their own money available to buy up *News of the World* shares on the stock market, the view was widespread that Hambro had breached the spirit of the new code. But the Takeover Panel exonerated the bank from breaching the letter of the code and they continued unimpeded, buying and obtaining pledges of support from shareholders, and could soon guarantee the Carrs control of 48 percent of the shares. Bob's advisor, Robert Clark, who had been one of the authors of the new code, was astounded at this behavior. To counteract this approach, Bob immediately raised his bid to £34 million and Clark sought help from Mynor's panel, but it was soon clear that the City establishment would offer Bob no protection.

Even more ominous was the arrival of Rupert Murdoch on the scene. Hearing that the Carrs opposed Bob's bid, the Australian press owner, keen to expand in Britain, had rushed to London to propose an alternative deal: he would buy enough shares to tip the balance in Carr's favor if Hambro persuaded Carr to accept a merger with him. Murdoch would become managing director, and Carr would remain chairman. They were to prove empty promises, and recognizing a way to foil Bob, Carr was tempted. By the following day, Murdoch had hit the headlines, having already bought more than 3 percent of the shares. Despite Bob's complaint to the panel and the suspension of share dealings, Carr had already achieved majority control. What he didn't realize until too late, however, was that Murdoch was not prepared to invest anything like the £34 million Bob had promised. Not only was Carr selling his paper for a great deal less to satisfy his own prejudice, but his own position would now be severely jeopardized.

At the end of October at the shareholders EGM the Panel made a belated attempt to save its reputation when Mynors persuaded the three merchant banks involved not to vote the 15 percent shares they had bought after Bob's bid. It was a move that gave Bob fresh hope, but dirty tactics were to come to the fore again. Murdoch's Australian newspapers began to carry lurid stories about the methods of the encyclopedia salesmen employed by ILSC, a Pergamon company. Yet again, the battle reached an intensely personal level, focusing on the "foreigner" issue. By this time, all that seemed to matter to Carr was defeating Bob at any price.

Bob of course fought back vigorously, but not with the same tactics. He publicized the advantages of his bid and sought injunctions and damages, but as the battle reached its height, unsubstantiated rumors in the City about ILSC's profits began to depress Pergamon's share price. Bob did his best to keep the price high with large share purchases by his private companies; he even made a brief takeover bid for Murdoch's group. But the writing was on the wall. Despite personal telephone calls to dozens of *News of the World* shareholders, telegrams to others and taxis to bring people to the January shareholders' meeting, Bob's bid failed.

The fateful meeting took place at the Connaught Rooms, London, on January 2, 1969. The hall was packed with hundreds of Carr employees brought in specially for the occasion in company buses. Murdoch walked in smiling and confident with his wife, Anna. Bob was dignified, although determined to fight to the bitter end. There were jeers, boos and catcalls as he attacked Carr. Shouts of "Go home" echoed around the room, hecklers voiced their clear dislike for the "foreigner." It was all to end in uproar and victory for Murdoch. Yet for Carr, it was a hollow victory, for both he and his editor Stafford Somerfield were soon unceremoniously deposed. Shortly before he died in 1977, Carr wrote to Bob, regretting what had happened and wishing that he had sold Bob the company. It had been a bruising, nasty battle where quite shameful tactics had been employed. Many other people wrote to Bob at the time to express their disgust at the way he had been treated, their disapproval of the carefully packed and rehearsed meeting and their appalled reaction to the "roast beef" editorial. Sir Harry Verney's words were typical: "You have come out of it with credit. They have behaved badly. You have not. You have gained the sympathy of many who do not know you." Bob Edwards, editor of the *People,* quipped: "At least Mr. Murdoch has taken Sir William to the cleaners!"

Bob was exhausted and frustrated but, as I told the *Guardian* financial journalist William Davis immediately after this failure, he soon recovered to fight another day: "He came limping home and I put him to bed. He was terribly disappointed, but the next day he decided to shrug the whole thing off. He still has Pergamon, and his seat in Parliament and he says his experience will come in handy during the next takeover battle. Nothing gets him down for long."

There was an immediate consequence of the *News of the World* affair that certainly set me thinking and thanking my lucky stars that Bob had failed to win the paper. Had he bought the *News of the World,* I might not have been as lucky as Anna Murdoch! In December 1969, Muriel McKay, wife of the senior director and deputy chairman of the *News of the World,* was kidnapped and a ransom of £1 million was demanded. Although the kidnappers were later arrested, Mrs. McKay was never to be seen again and her body never recovered in spite of a systematic search of several acres of farmland. At the kidnappers' trial in October 1970, it became clear that their intended victim had really been Rupert Murdoch's wife. It was a horrific crime: Mrs. McKay had been captured, assaulted, killed and her body disposed of on the pig farm belonging to the two accused. There was even an attempt to implicate Bob in the affair when the older brother invented a cunning lie that Bob had actually visited their farm, but he had simply made up the story because of Bob's involvement in the *News of the World* takeover bid. The Hosein brothers eventually received life sentences for the cold-blooded kidnapping and murder of Mrs. McKay, and the whole business left a sour taste in my mouth for many months to come. Bob might have lost the *News of the World,* but I felt as if I had escaped being murdered and my body thrown to the pigs.

What I did not know then, however, was that we would soon be involved in yet another bitter takeover battle, which this time would blight our lives for the next seven years and damage Bob's reputation for ever.

8

But little time will be left mĕ to ponder upon my destiny!
The circles rapidly grow small—we are plunging madly
within the thundering of ocean and of tempest, the ship
is quivering—Oh God! and—going down.

E. A. POE, *MANUSCRIPT FOUND IN A BOTTLE,*
TALES OF MYSTERY AND IMAGINATION

The loss of the *News of the World* was quickly followed in January 1969 by an approach which caught Bob's imagination. Telephoned by Saul Steinberg, owner of the American company Leasco, Bob listened to his plans for a rosy future that linked Pergamon's enormous information output with the computer storage facilities of Steinberg's company. Together, their combined resources would create a vast scientific data bank of easily accessible information, the happy and successful marriage of hardware and software. Bob was excited by an idea which appealed to his own vision of the great potential of data storage and retrieval. Although he had some misgivings about Leasco's proposed acquisition of Pergamon, Steinberg was promising to make him president of Leasco's European operations, and Bob decided to continue discussions and exchange information. After talks throughout the spring, Leasco representatives came to England in May, when Bob was also preoccupied with a brief bid to buy the *Sun* newspaper, another round which he eventually lost to Rupert Murdoch.

He finally traveled to New York for four days of nonstop negotiations beginning on June 13. By June 17 Steinberg and Bob had reached agreement on a £25 million bid by Leasco for Pergamon, valuing Pergamon's shares at 37 shillings each, approximately 11 shillings more than their quoted price on the London Stock Exchange. According to one of the terms of the agreement, Bob undertook to sell Leasco his own shareholding and to secure acceptance by family trusts for theirs. For their combined 34 percent holding in Pergamon, Bob and the trusts would accept payment largely in Leasco stock, which he was persuaded would soon rise from its current level of $37 to $50 a share. Steinberg's company, he was also told, had $60 million Eurodollars on deposit and was on the point of obtaining a further $100 million from its acquisition of Reliance Insurance. Bob was later to admit that he was not shown any current financial statements, because he was told they were "unavailable." At this point, his impulsiveness led him to commit a fatal mistake as he overruled his advisors' counsel not to sign the agreement before further information was provided by Leasco. He chose to disregard their advice and plunged on with the proposed merger. The deal appeared to be done, and I must confess that I felt some bewilderment at the thought of Bob no longer controlling Pergamon. But he easily convinced me of the multiple advantages of the merger.

Saul Steinberg and other Leasco representatives came to Oxford in May and early July 1969 to have a thorough look at Pergamon's books and Bob told me they were satisfied in every respect. I entertained them all and even took them to Woburn Abbey where Nicole de Bedford gave us all a sumptuous lunch. Saul, accompanied by his wife (the first of three), came for lunch: she had nothing to say and spent her time before and after lunch working furiously on a small tapestry, which in the circumstances was extremely impolite. Saul, on the other hand, kept on admiring the house, saying how nice it would be to live there, which made me feel uneasy to say the least. Apart from that encounter and another time I met the Steinbergs at his birthday party in New York, they left little impression on me at all, except that of a youngish, bright but self-opinionated and ill-mannered couple.

About this time, without telling Bob, Leasco had started buying large blocks of Pergamon shares on the open market, even though they had intimated to him they would not acquire more than 10 percent before they made a formal offer. Concerned at these purchases, Bob was told not to worry—it was simply a way of saving money since the shares could be bought at less than the agreed price of 37 shillings. Leasco continued to acquire Pergamon shares until it held a stake of 38 percent, over and above the shares pledged to them by Bob.

It was not long before problems arose over the sale of family shares in Pergamon held by trustees in the United States. Steinberg flew to England and the difficulty was ironed out, but it was only a temporary respite. By August 13, Bob was off to New York again to prevent the whole arrangement from breaking down and reluctantly agreed to a revision of the transaction. The problems rumbled on as Leasco began to question Pergamon's profitability.

Matters finally came to a head on August 22 when the American company announced it would not go ahead with its bid, citing amongst its reasons doubts about profitability and the composition of Pergamon's published forecast earnings for 1969. Bob was aghast. Aborting a bid at this late stage was virtually unprecedented and he immediately called on the Takeover Panel to make a statement. By August 24, he was accusing Leasco of having run out of cash. The *Sunday Times* further undermined confidence in Bob with a highly critical "Insight" article. The Takeover Panel under Lord Shawcross sat for three days to examine the affair, but by August 27, Leasco had put a new offer on the table, although there was no longer any guarantee that the price would be as much as the original one. Examining whether or not there had been full disclosure by the Pergamon board, the Panel concluded that there was "no suggestion of personal misconduct" but questioned whether Pergamon shareholders had been given all the necessary information about the affairs of their company. At the time, we could have had no idea of the future consequences of this Panel hearing, for it was this conclusion that led to the subsequent appointment of government Board of Trade inspectors to investigate Pergamon's affairs.

The negotiations continued, however, until September 13 when Leasco once again decided not to proceed with its bid. Although he later denied having said these words, Steinberg was quoted in the *Wall Street Journal* as saying that his company had "accomplished its purpose of taking over the British concern without having to pay the $60 million it had expected it would cost." Meanwhile, at the initiative of a number of institutional shareholders concerned by the turn of events and anxious to protect their investment, intensive behind-the-scenes negotiations took place between merchant bankers representing respectively the institutions and Leasco from the end of August right through September and into October. In their efforts to ensure that Pergamon did not collapse in a welter of strife and litigation and that Leasco rapidly make a full bid, the institutions concluded that Bob had to be removed from control at Pergamon and an investigation instigated to determine the real value of the company's business.

The final act of the Leasco fiasco was again to take place in the Connaught Rooms, scene of Bob's discomfiture over the *News of the World*. I shall never forget that Pergamon shareholders' meeting on

October 10, 1969, which was to see Bob ousted as a director and chairman from the company he had built up from scratch and loved. The majority of shareholders present were overwhelmingly on his side and made this perfectly clear as they slow-hand clapped for Steinberg's representatives. But they were powerless against the combined votes of Leasco and the City institutions in favor of a series of resolutions which called for the dismissal of all the existing directors and the appointment of Leasco nominees and two "neutral" directors. When the result of the voting was announced, I shouted "Shame!" But it is Bob's final words at the meeting that day that come back to me vividly across the years and I still remember the catch in his voice as he spoke of his deep sorrow and fear for Pergamon, his love of his company, its business, authors, customers and staff, all of whom he would never forget.

Words of sympathy poured in from friends everywhere, voicing outrage at the way in which twenty years of Bob's hard work could be demolished in a few hours. Professor Scorer's reaction was typical of that of many Pergamon authors and editors, "Events leave me flabbergasted. The authors, for whom Pergamon Press has been the means of much creative activity and realization of ideas and dreams, seem helpless when shareholders let themselves be manipulated."

Woodrow Wyatt wrote: "I am sure that your energy and brains will secure victory from defeat in the end. . . . Although the campaigning against you has often been very unpleasant . . . the British sense of fair play will ensure that it is eventually counterproductive."

The Pergamon editor of *Biorheology*, George Scott Blair, concluded, "I'm afraid that your fate shows the rottenness of the whole system." Well-wishers expressed their disgust, as one writer put it, at seeing the maggots crawl upon what they fondly imagined to be the corpse of a fallen giant. Eric Ogden, MP, suggested the image of the phoenix for Bob's future coat of arms, certain as he was that Bob would rise again. Although the hour seemed dark, many of those who wrote to Bob were convinced that with his energy, originality and dynamism, he would bounce back again with renewed vigor.

On the following Monday, Sir Henry d'Avigdor Goldsmid, the newly appointed independent chairman of Pergamon Press (by now nicknamed "Goldshit" by Bob and the children) drove into Headington and immediately asked to be shown Bob's office, his drinks bar and his Rolls-Royce, but since they were all privately owned, his requests were met with a negative response. Bob, meanwhile, was on his way to London to talk to various journalists and appear on television. Just over a week earlier, he had already appeared on Cliff

Michelmore's TV program and given a remarkable performance of dignified courage and fighting spirit in the face of unsympathetic questioning, which had won him a great deal of public sympathy. Those who wrote to him after the program admired his courage and stamina, generally expressing the view that the whole Establishment was arrayed against him. One man wrote, "My own guess and hope is that your image and tenacity when you battled alone after your advisors had run like rabbits will be remembered when everything else is forgotten." An author friend summed up the whole affair: "It must need one hell of a lot of guts to face the world on TV and say 'There goes my dream.' The country will be worse off if the dream really has gone pop!" Lord Aldington wrote to me, "As I told you on that extraordinary and unhappy day, there is so much in Bob which not only I but many others admire—unquenchable courage, equally unquenchable energy in mind and body, foreseeing ideas and great human compassion and unselfishness."

It was difficult for us to absorb the enormity of what had happened, but events so far were nothing compared to what lay ahead as a direct consequence of the Leasco debacle. The Board of Trade's inspectors, Owen Stable QC and Sir Ronald Leach, were appointed in September 1969 and the ramifications of their investigations were to dominate the next seven years of our lives. In the meantime, the immediate impact on me was Sir Henry's arrival at Pergamon Press and the implementation of certain restrictions on our freedom of movement at Headington. As soon as the new management was in place, an iron gate was erected in the basement of the Hall, preventing access to the cellars used by Pergamon Press for storage, where the central heating boiler was also situated. At the same time, new locks were placed on the doors between the Hall and the adjoining offices. It was all very childish and, as far as the boiler was concerned, dangerous. In my ten years at the Hall, I had had no reason to go through to the offices but often had to control the central heating system and cope with the odd flash flood. I immediately took my pen and wrote a terse note to David Hunter Johnston, one of the new directors appointed to represent shareholders' interests, asking him to telephone me. When he delayed until six o'clock in the evening before doing so, I was absolutely furious and told him that these ridiculous barriers were endangering me and my family. He offered to come and see me to discuss the matter and I received him with all the icy haughtiness I could muster. We went down to the basement and I showed him what had been done. I was so incensed that I did not even feel able to offer him a drink, and faced with my total silence, he made his exit from the Hall in great embarrassment. Having slept on the matter, I wrote him a short note the next morning, thanking him for "the courtesy he showed me in attending personally to an intolerable situation" and suggesting we find a modus vivendi "without loss of dignity or charity on either side." He replied immediately, thanking me in return for my friendly letter, adding, "We are all of us in a difficult position—you especially so, I feel— and we have to try and live at peace with one another. At any rate, please do not regard me as an enemy, but at worst as a neutral and at best a friend."

It was to be the start of an amicable correspondence between us and by November 13, David was summing up with some humor the complexities and absurdities of the situation we were facing: "It is a horrible business altogether and not getting any easier. I would really have liked to say all this to you; but I hesitate to call at the Hall lest we should read a report in the papers the following day that you and I were engaged in secret negotiations!"

He tried in vain to end the conflict, but eventually decided to resign. Before he left, he wrote that I could rely on him "to work consistently for an end to strife and litigation and for a just and constructive solution to the Pergamon problem." From further correspondence between him and Bob, I concluded that he was one of the protagonists who had best understood the whole situation and, having assessed Bob's qualities and his flaws fairly, had the courage to tell him exactly what he thought.

We had lost Pergamon and the future looked ominous. The events and consequences of the Leasco affair had been an enormous strain and Bob was in desperate need of a holiday. We needed time together, time to reflect, time to gather our strength and ponder on the future. So it was that in late October, we set off for Kenya and the Treetops Hotel, where Princess Elizabeth had spent part of her honeymoon and learned of her father's death and her own accession to the throne. We spent a quiet two days there, talking and watching the endless procession of large and small wild animals going to drink at the water hole just below the hotel terraces, built literally amongst the trees. I sensed, however, that Bob was anxious and restless and knew that he was preoccupied with the need to safeguard his American interests. After just two days' rest, he decided to fly to America immediately, which as it turned out, proved to be a crucial move in his attempt to retain control of Pergamon's American subsidiary, Pergamon Press Inc. Bob felt there was little point in my accompanying him since he would need to devote all his time to business affairs, and suggested I could either go back to England or remain in Africa by myself. Having traveled all that way to a continent I had not visited except for a brief trip to Egypt, I decided to stay and at least get a flavor of that great, bewitching land. That was how my African adventure began, a time of great discovery and new experiences, yet also a time of deep reflection and soul-searching for me.

I saw Bob off at the airport and a wave of panic washed over me as soon as he had left. For a moment, I couldn't find the driver who had taken us to the airport and was suddenly petrified at the thought of being all alone in the heart of Africa without my natural protector. I felt totally lost and kept thinking of Bob on the plane, of all our problems and upsets and the unpleasantness of other people towards us at the time. Overnight, we seemed to have become pariahs; the dozens of invitations we used to receive every week had dried up completely. Suddenly I realized my tremendous dependency on Bob's love and how he had protected me from the nastiness of the outside world. It struck me then how defenseless I was without him and what a heavy burden the family must be for him, especially when he needed to concentrate every ounce of his effort on his own—and our—survival. Alone in my hotel, I went over and over events of the last years in my mind, wondering how I could have supported Bob more and what I could do now to help him. Such thoughts were to preoccupy me for the whole of my stay in Africa.

By the next morning I felt less gloomy as I organized my sightseeing trip and set off on my safari in a hired Mercedes. My driver was a small man named Aaron, black as ebony, a Kikuyu who spoke better Swahili than English. Heading along the main north-south thoroughfare, our first destination was Tsaropark, a vast national park of some 80,000 square miles. As I looked out of the car window, I had the distinct impression that the whole of Africa was "on the march," for the road is the very bloodstream of that enormous continent, the pulse and beat of life. Men and women alike walk to and fro in seemingly endless lines on either side of the road, like a procession of ants, and in Kikuyu country, it is the women who do all the porterage, carrying mountains of goods on their heads, whilst the men walk empty-handed.

Aaron took me first to Mzima Springs, a favorite haunt of hippos, where crystal-clear, sparkling waters gush forth from lava soil and spread into a series of small lakes. From there, we drove at tremendous speed along a track road of red earth, which seemed to me to go on for ever. I was beginning to feel a little uneasy, alone in this immensity with a native, maniac driver at the wheel, but I was soon to discover the real qualities of that true boy of the jungle and of all his fellow Africans. They are totally in tune with their surroundings, unlike we Europeans who seem stupid and clumsy in their environment. Their body smell, which to us may seem pungent, is perfectly matched to the odoriferous scent of the flowers and shrubs of their own country. Indeed an African friend once told me that they describe us as long-nosed and smelling of corpse! They are physically fit and have an inborn capacity for survival in a difficult and hostile environment, where their fast reflexes and acute senses of sight and hearing come into their own. They make excellent drivers because they seem able to avoid or bypass obstacles we would scarcely have time to notice. Aaron could spot a wildebeest or herd of elephants a thousand yards away, and with his help, I saw elephants galore, lions, zebras, zebus, bush gazelles, antelopes, giraffes, ostriches and a huge variety of brightly colored birds.

I shall never forget my first impressions as we made our way gently down towards the sea, with coconut palms, magnolias and lush green grass welcoming us to Mombasa and the Trade Winds Hotel near the coast. The sight of that wonderful beach, stretching for miles, was quite extraordinary. I can still picture the Africans' beautiful dark bodies glistening in the sun, the clear blue waters, the coral reef, the shells, the coconut trees bending in the wind, the tide washing up its crop of curios, leaving behind a sand of silvery white powder, the sun, the heat and the birds. It was divine. For a few hours, I was able to banish my worries to the back of my mind and enjoy that paradise, but even then I couldn't help wishing that Bob was there to share it with me. I stood on the fine, smooth sand, watching the waves break on the reef and die gently at my feet. I found some beautiful shells and swam near the reef, catching sight of shoals of tropical fish, blue, red, purple, turquoise and yellow, some of them as big as carp. In Mombasa itself, I was fascinated by the way Arabs, Indians and Africans mixed freely dressed in their traditional garb: some women veiled, others bare-breasted, some completely clothed in black with only their eyes to be seen, others in a riot of brilliant colors.

That evening, I was alone in my ground-floor bedroom when the velvety curtain of night suddenly enveloped me, as it does at the Equator. The waves relentlessly pounded the shore just below the terrace and a handsome Ashanti outside watched over my safety, prowling around with the stealth of a cat in the darkness. I sat at the desk and wrote to Bob, trying to put on paper all my impressions of the sights, sounds and smells of Africa, and adding in conclusion:

I love you deeply. It was kind, thoughtful and generous of you to encourage me to stay in Africa. I have made the most of it and, as always after a trip to another continent, I will never be quite the same person again. One just becomes humbler, more broad-minded and more tolerant. Like the man in the desert, I am happy! But I am so unhappy that there is no one to say it to. I am, of course, also worried stiff, not knowing whether you won your fight in New York, and I feel guilty being here, enjoying God's creation whilst you are battling with your life. I really want to be near you to help if I can.

The next day, Aaron and I left Mombasa by car for Melindi and Voi Lodge, where we were due to spend the night. The road was clearly marked "open" and all went well for the first twenty-five miles or so, until the road started to get narrower. All of a sudden, the car began to zigzag before coming to a complete standstill. It was only then that I noticed the terrible state of the road, still deep in mud after recent heavy downpours. Every time Aaron pushed the starter, the engine roared but the wheels skidded, and the car refused to budge an inch. Just as I got out to see what could be done, Aaron tried the starter one more time and the car lurched forwards a few hundred yards, leaving me stranded in the jungle, running behind as fast as my heavy, mud-clogged sandals would carry me, eaten alive by terrible horseflies, which settled on me and drew blood the minute I stepped out of the car. With enormous relief, I finally caught up and we drove on for a few miles.

It was only a matter of minutes before the same thing happened all over again. This time, alas, there was nothing doing: the Mercedes would move neither forwards or backwards. Protecting myself from the horseflies as best I could, I got out and suggested it would be better to switch off the engine to save the battery. "How far are we from the nearest lodge?" I queried. "Seventeen miles" was Aaron's ominous reply. This time we were well and truly stuck. The only possible way out was to construct some solid track under the wheels. I could see that Aaron was sweating profusely and starting to panic. I knew that I would have to take charge, even though I was more frightened than he. "Come on, Aaron, if we help ourselves, then God will do the rest. Fetch me some branches and I'll find some stones and try to clear the mud off the wheels." Whereupon I set to work with my bare hands, on my knees in the mud. Aaron, meanwhile, was working painfully slowly and I realized he was afraid to venture any further than ten yards away from the car. The fact was that we were stuck in no-man's-land between villages, where wild animals were abundant. I could hear elephants trumpeting in the distance and peculiar barking noises made by wild dogs which filled me with primeval fear. Suddenly, Aaron had a bright idea and suggested using a big piece of wood as a kind of primitive jack. It worked! Very soon, the first front wheel was free of mud and we were able to follow the same procedure for the other three, placing a layer of stones and twigs on the road surface to give us some traction. At last, after unloading all the luggage and spare wheel to make the car as light as possible, we were ready to try to move. Aaron got into the driver's seat, I pushed from behind and both of us offered up a prayer.

To our great joy and relief, once again, the car shot forwards and I was left standing barefoot in the mud beside a pile of luggage. Seizing three of the bags, I ran towards the car as fast as my bare sticky feet would allow, then Aaron dashed back for the rest of the luggage and spare wheel. All told, we had been at our little game for two solid hours. I was coated from head to foot in thick, clinging mud, but I did notice that the horseflies were no longer interested in me! It had also crossed my mind several times that I might have to spend the night in the car with Aaron, at the mercy of wild beasts and with one coconut to share between us.

Once we reached a dry section of road, Aaron reverted to his usual breakneck speed even though it was pitch dark. Then we heard a terrific bang on my side of the car, almost as if someone had hurled a huge boulder at us. It turned out to be a massive horned beast, which Aaron had hit, and it left both doors on the passenger side dented. As we drove along, the headlights lit up a frightening array of wild night life—red snakes on the road which sent shivers down my spine, mongooses, a multitude of mice, rabbits and small, unidentified felines, as well as large owls and other beasts. Then we started encountering herds of elephants—suddenly there was a herd ahead of us, blocking the road, and another one just behind us. We switched off the lights, not wanting to frighten them in case they stampeded towards the car. It seemed like an age before they finally lumbered away into the darkness. It was a tense and terrifying journey, but we finally managed to bribe our way through the locked park gates and reach Voi Lodge, looking like a pair of tramps, with me caked in red mud like a Tanagra statue and Aaron's once white uniform now a dirty brick color. I shall never forget climbing into the bathtub with my dress still on—it was so stiff with mud I couldn't peel it off my body. From the dining room balcony later that night, I saw herds of elephants, wildebeests and hyenas drinking at the floodlit water hole. I felt so pleased to be back in civilization, content to watch the animals from a safe distance. My experiences had taught me that there is no romance about the jungle: it is a question of sheer survival.

I went straight to bed after dinner, mulling over all the recent events in my mind, especially my own madness at undertaking this expedition so ill-prepared, with no food or water, just believing in my lucky star and abandoning my fate to the hands of a perfect stranger. I felt ten years older, wiser, calmer, and had learned a valuable lesson. But I had never stopped thinking about Bob and all the problems we faced.

We left the park next morning and traveled for a few more days through the vast desert of Ashanti country, where I ended my safari in a tented hotel at the foot of Mount Kenya. On that last evening, I sat beside an enormous campfire beneath the starry African sky, talking to the other guests and the hotel manager, with Ashanti warriors all around us for protection. Our conversation that evening revolved around the jungle, freedom and solitude. They wanted to know where I came from, whether I had a family, where my "man" was and how on earth a white woman like me came to find herself alone in darkest Africa. Wasn't I afraid? I was most definitely afraid, but told them I was never alone. I could call on God who could see me, as he now saw them talking to me. My words seemed to impress them and gave me confidence to go back to my tent, reasonably sure I would not be raped, but I must confess that the Ashantis guarding that camp frightened me much more than those herds of elephants poised to charge the car a few days before.

Next morning, I got up early, went to the lounge with its magnificent prospect of Mount Kenya knowing exactly what I had to do. For days on end, I had been wondering how I could help Bob in his present crisis. My night's rest had brought me the solution I had been searching for since my arrival in Africa. I asked for writing paper and wrote to him.

29 October 1969, Mount Kenya Safari Club

My love, my Lev, you are a lion. I offer you your freedom. Civilized countries protect lions as an endangered species. Others kill them and display their heads on the wall as trophies. Whenever I see one of these proud beasts impaled, I am sad and dream for him of the sun-drenched bush where he can roam alone, the wind playing in his mane, before repairing in the evening to the water hole to quench his thirst and meet his lioness.

For twenty-five years, for better or for worse, we have stuck together to bring up a family. You have every reason to be proud of the children. Each one, enriched in his or her own way by your understanding and teaching, will now travel through life knowing what they can contribute to it and obtain from it.

For some years now, I have realized, at first with bellicose sadness, then with hurt pride and at last with victorious serenity, that my usefulness to you has come to an end. I am now certain that I am in your way. You are still a very young man, you are really incredibly healthy. Because of the unfair treatment you have received at the hands of the most hypocritical of societies, you have been denied the laurels you so richly deserved. You are now poised at the peak of your intelligence, made wiser by your experiences of men and matters, with the whole wild and mad world around you tearing at your soul.

I love you and will always love you till the day I die. If the world wounds you, my heart, my head, my lap and the cradle of my arms will always rock you, heal you and comfort you. At all times of the day or night, my door will always be open to you, for a talk, for food or simply for a rest.

I have searched night and day in my head and heart and now understand that the only present that can prove my love to you after twenty-five years is, paradoxically, that I should give you your freedom. I have not reached this decision lightly. More than half of me has fought it tooth and nail, but believe me when I say that I offer it with serenity, with no strings attached whatsoever.

Perhaps no one else but you will understand and believe that for me this is the supreme sacrifice, the most excellent expression of my love for you. I do not ask my freedom in return, for I do not wish for any man other than the one of my youth. My home, wherever that may be, will always be yours. I will always be waiting for you, even if you never return.

I will make things easy for you, and the children need never know until such time as you might wish to have your freedom "legally" and then this can be done quietly, if ever.

I think that the way in which you have just been treated by the world has precipitated things. I have always tried to protect you from yourself and the world, often in a clumsy fashion which you have not cared for. All of a sudden I realized that you really want and need no protection, you must literally be let free like the prancing Chinese horse in your bedroom in London. You cannot be caged in by regulations, the need to conform, family or even love. As a supreme act of my love for you, I will make no more demands on your physical and mental love and I relieve you as of now of any sense of guilt that might creep in. I know that if ever I am in difficulty or in need of advice, you will never deny me your help, because what we have cemented between us in twenty-five years, neither I nor you nor the Lord can undo. I have not thought at all of material details. What I want you to understand is that if you need me, I will be available anywhere in the world, anytime, to do anything, but *need* will be the operative word.

My heart was heavy as I returned to Nairobi and boarded my plane back to London, wondering what the future held for me, for Bob and our children. I knew that he would understand I wasn't trying to escape the bad times, but sincerely trying to help him. But I hardly dared predict what his response might be. I settled into the comfortable luxury of the great planes of those days (as opposed to the sardine-tin compression of modern air transport), drinks were served and the London papers passed around. I remember asking for the *Times* and *Financial Times* because I liked to look at Pergamon's share price. Perhaps you can imagine my shock at seeing our name splashed on the front page of the *Financial Times* in huge bold type: MAXWELL SUED BY LEASCO FOR $22M DAMAGES. My heart missed a beat. I could not believe what I was reading. Above all, I could not comprehend why I was named in the suit as a defendant with Bob. What could I possibly have done to Saul Steinberg to justify this personal attack? I was stunned and in a total panic. I had visions of toiling away for the rest of my life to repay a huge debt which read like a telephone number, and which I knew I did not owe. But what emerged clearly from the turmoil of my mind that day was a new determination to protect my future and that of my family. I knew that my French university qualifications were of no use to me in England and realized that if the worst came to the worst I would have great difficulty in finding anything other than a poorly paid administrative or secretarial job. That was when and why I decided that I had to acquire an English university degree, at whatever cost.

Soon after I returned from Africa, Bob came back from America where he had managed to counter Leasco's strategies and hold on to Pergamon Press Inc. Although he had considered and appreciated the extent of the sacrifice I was prepared to make, he assured me that he needed my support and the children's. He asked me to forgive the comments he had made under stress in the past about regretting marrying me, wanting to separate and the burden the children and I represented. He wouldn't hear of having his freedom; he had me and the children, and with love, hard work and good health, we would pull through, of that he was certain.

By the time we saw each other again, I understood much more clearly the extent of the damage caused by the Leasco fiasco and Bob's isolation—not only from his City "friends" who were abandoning him in droves, but also from the life that had been his for the past twenty years. For days Leasco had been trying to serve a writ on him and instead of behaving decently with the usual notification through solicitors, had literally mounted a siege around our London offices in Fitzroy Square, which up till then Bob had been able to outmaneuver using the various entrances on two different streets. After that, they tried to deliver the writ inside the House of Commons, pretending to be Buckinghamshire constituents.

It had never been my intention to abandon Bob. All I wanted was to relieve him of the pressure of marital life so that he could start afresh without impediment, perhaps in a new career or country. Whatever differences we may have had, one thing was absolutely certain—we were in this together! That was never clearer to me than the morning I was alone at Headington, preparing a meal in the kitchen, when the doorbell rang. I was dressed in work clothes, looking rather untidy, and was loath to answer the door until I saw who it was. I looked discreetly through the glass pane of the front door and saw a man I didn't know who kept taking a long envelope from inside his jacket and putting it back again. I smelled a rat immediately and went to open the door prepared for action. "Are you Mrs. Maxwell?" asked the man, to which I replied in my worst broken English and heavily accented French voice, "I am zee maid. Madame iz not 'ere, Madame in London, 'ave you got appointment?" The man looked terribly crestfallen, took out the long legal envelope and said, "But I have come a long way and I must give her these documents." "Sorry, Madame not 'ere, Madame see nobody wizout appointment, you 'ave to phone for appointment, Good-bye." I slammed the door and rushed to the phone to let Bob know what had happened. I was terribly upset that Leasco had tried to serve me with a writ as well, but felt no guilt at my play-acting. Steinberg's action against me was wholly vexatious so I felt fully justified in protecting myself as best I could. Bob was shocked at their underhanded tactics and tried to reassure me that since they were false allegations I had nothing to fear; his lawyers in New York would soon have the action dismissed. I was temporarily reassured, but the whole episode was extremely unpleasant.

Soon Christmas was upon us again and the children were home. They gave us great strength and in spite of the ominous clouds gathering over our heads, we remained strong through the storm. Bob's gift to me that year was accompanied by a sweet and loving card, with a form of endearment he had not used for decades:

My darling Betuska,
I thank you for all the hard work you have done,
Your Bob

But as the 1970 election drew nearer, all the publicity surrounding the Leasco affair was becoming a matter for serious concern. After the date of the election was announced, our campaigning machine went into action and I was once more made responsible for postal votes. Although publicly Bob expressed confidence, he was finding it more difficult to work with his new political agent, Jim Lyons, who, besides doing little to keep the party machine in good shape sided with the "lunatic left" of the party, which included a number of new members who came to live in our constituency with the establishment of the Open University in the town of Milton Keynes. Several of this hard-left "clique" who were Communist party card-holders had infiltrated the local party and were creating bitter divisions amongst us. Bob tackled his campaigning with his usual energy, touring villages and towns as he had always done, bombarding the electors with Maxwellgrams and supported by visits from George Brown, Jim Callaghan and Lord Shackleton. The rest is history—an unpredicted last-minute national swing towards the Tories confounded the latest opinion polls and Bob, along with several other Labor MPs, lost his seat. It was yet another blow and Bob was intensely disappointed, although I had already detected the trend through my canvass and was not that surprised by the result.

Kind and supportive words were written by Bob's political friends. Harold Wilson expressed his deep regret, his thanks for all Bob had done in the last Parliament and sincere hopes that he would be back soon. Jim Callaghan said the odds had been stacked against Bob, and Richard Crossman commented how sorry he was at the result "despite a terrific poll to which I give your dear wife a large share of credit." John Silkin was "terribly distressed"; Jack Ashley told him he would be missed in the House; and Tam Dalyell wrote "Bluntly, it's a fucking shame ... you're a loss to the House." Sir Geoffrey de Freitas hoped he would not give up politics; Sir Samuel Fisher said, "I feel that your absence will create a void and certainly reduce effectively the prestige of the Jewish community which had relied so much on your work and efforts." Many constituents wrote to express their sorrow and their gratitude for all he had done for North Bucks.

Those were difficult and demanding years for the whole family, and there were many times when I wondered how I would find the strength to carry on. Our whole world seemed to have fallen apart. We had been successful, admired, envied and courted; now we were cold-shouldered, abandoned by many of our friends and facing financial ruin. Our eldest son had died after seven long years in a coma-vigil. Bob had been frustrated over and over again in his takeover bids with ever-increasing slurs on his character. He had been ousted from Pergamon, the company he had built from nothing into a thriving and respected business. He was under suspicion, facing a Board of Trade investigation for his management conduct. He had lost his seat in Parliament and his future looked bleak and uncertain. My heart went out to him. My own sense of security was also badly shaken and I could take no more. My work at Pergamon was in jeopardy with Bob no longer in charge. I was struggling to sustain Bob's morale and protect the children from the worst of the pain. Bob was becoming ever more difficult as he fought to clear his name and survive financial ruin. Worst of all, there seemed to be little I could do to help him in a positive sense. I felt alone and bewildered. Somehow I had to find my own passport to sanity and survival.

The early seventies were overshadowed for me and to a lesser extent the children by the endless horror of lawsuits which became a dominant feature of Bob's life after the Leasco takeover, as he struggled both to regain control of Pergamon and to fight against the inflexible and unfair procedures adopted by the Department of Trade inspectors. All those ghastly battles merge in my memory into a miasma of gloom and desperation. The entire DTI episode altered the course of our lives irrevocably, leaving Bob with a deep well of bitterness that he had never been allowed to state his own case properly before judge and jury and shaking the family to its foundations. To recollect all that happened in those difficult years, I recently forced myself to read extensively on the subject, and I also discussed the whole affair with a number of the protagonists who are still alive today. As soon as I began this research, the magnitude of the events of those dark years—for Bob and the whole family—came back to me with resounding clarity.

When in September 1969, the Board of Trade appointed inspectors to investigate certain aspects of Pergamon's affairs, Bob promised them his full cooperation. One month later, however, Leasco, advised by its banker, Jacob Rothschild, and a group of City institutions brought about Bob's removal from the board of Pergamon, and this, together with Leasco's subsequent lawsuit in the United States, put a very different complexion on their investigation. To me, it had all the hallmarks of a conspiracy, and whatever good intentions the institutions may have had, the manner in which Bob's removal was accomplished and the viciousness of the attacks mounted against him ensured that whatever goodwill he may initially have had in assisting the inspectors and new directors, was irretrievably lost. The complete lack of understanding by the new Board and its advisors as to how to run a scientific publishing business and the lack of impartiality and common sense of Pergamon's new chairman resulted in the company's fortunes going from bad to worse.

At the same time, the arrival at the company's headquarters in Oxford of this new Chairman, Sir Henry d'Avigdor Goldsmid, engaged us in another fierce controversy over our way of life at Headington Hill Hall. We were living on the same site—the Pergamon offices were barely a few yards away—but Bob was locked out of the firm he had created; there were even ridiculous, short-lived attempts to fence off the company buildings from the house. I remember waking up one morning to the sound of hammering and looked out to see workmen busy driving in wooden posts linked by huge rolls of barbed wire. The geography of the premises made such moves ludicrous and I recollect taking my pen to write and ask the new directors why on earth they were transforming Pergamon into Colditz and how exactly they planned to divide the grounds. Had they considered all the problems involved? What about the cats and dogs, the rabbits, squirrels and deer? Had they found a foolproof way to stop them from straying into forbidden territory? And what about the ducks who could fly but also liked the swimming pool? The family and I had a hilarious time composing a seemingly serious letter asking them how they intended to distinguish Maxwell rabbits from Pergamon rabbits. But my letter was not without effect. The fences disappeared immediately and an agreement was soon reached to rationalize the location of office space. After that, all the offices in the house were occupied by Robert Maxwell and Company (one of Bob's private companies, which he was still running) and all the Pergamon staff decamped into the main Pergamon building at the top of the drive.

On a more serious level, one of the immediate problems was that Bob no longer had access to Pergamon documents, so it was difficult for him to look back and verify facts for himself and for the inspectors. Bob's lawyers then advised him not to appear before the inspectors unless they told him the procedures they intended to follow and gave him notice of allegations against him. The inspectors declined to provide this information. So began the first of a series of lawsuits aimed at clarifying the role and procedures of the inspectors.

The first round took place in the Companies Court in April 1970 and in the Court of Appeal three months later. Although agreeing that the inspectors had to be fair, the judges decided that they must be masters of their own procedures. The appeal judges were impressed by the inspectors' apparent commitment to give individuals the right to answer criticism and Lord Justice Sachs concluded that this showed "they were going to do exactly what was right—to give, at the appropriate later stage to anyone in danger of being criticized, notice of the potential criticisms in general terms sufficient to enable him to know what the allegation was." Nothing was to be further from the truth, but Bob was now obliged to answer their questions.

Before these interviews began in the autumn of 1970, however, there was another major blow in August when the accountants Price Waterhouse (PW) produced their independent review of Pergamon Press's accounts for 1968 and the first nine months of 1969. It made gloomy reading. Using different accounting techniques, a 1968 pre-tax profit originally stated as over £2 million was reduced by PW to a mere £140,000 and the first nine months of 1969 showed a pre-tax profit of only £29,000 when, at the height of negotiations with Leasco, Bob had been forecasting profits in the millions. Deeply disappointed, Bob voiced his disagreement with the treatment of the accounts, as did the auditors Chalmers Impey, commenting that accounting was not "the exact science which some of us thought it was." But as far as Leasco was concerned, the Price Waterhouse report confirmed that Leasco had been duped. By November, the Americans announced they would not proceed with a bid for the whole of Pergamon Press and press comment speculated widely on the future of the company. Was there a chance that Bob might be able to mount a cash bid to regain his business?

Bob, of course, was hoping to do this and had been negotiating with Sir Henry Goldsmid, with Lord Aldington acting as mediator, to find a way of settling his differences with Leasco and working together for the good of the company. He also traveled frequently to the United States to look after the affairs of the American subsidiary Pergamon Press Incorporated, of which he had managed to keep control. At the same time he was preoccupied with the DTI investigation. Between September 1970 and June 4, 1971, he gave evidence to the inspectors on a dozen occasions, expecting to be given a general idea of any matters of potential criticism. Indeed, without knowing it, he was still giving evidence to the inspectors after they had already signed their first report on June 2, 1971! When the inspectors published that first highly critical report on July 13, Bob was stunned. They considered him to blame for virtually every transaction which had been investigated. They had accepted as totally reliable the evidence of disgruntled former employees, people whom Bob had discovered to be dishonest and sacked, and he was given no opportunity to show that these witnesses had faulty memories or were blatant liars. An important element of that first report was the reliance placed by the inspectors on the testimony of a witness named Hedley Le Bas, former chairman of Caxton Holdings, despite the fact that a lawyer had given them proof that his memory was at fault. Hedley Le Bas had a drink problem and Bob had fired him after receiving a confidential report in October 1968, from a well-known firm of accountants, commissioned by Bob to look at the expense accounts of Le Bas along with those of another employee. The report concluded that Le Bas had been claiming lavish and unauthorized expenses and sales commissions and described his extravagant lifestyle—entertaining almost every day, substantial car hire bills even though the company had already purchased an expensive vehicle for his exclusive use, cigars and cigarettes on account and so on. Another employee allegedly had an apartment maintained for him in London at the company's expense, which his mistress occupied when he was not around. Worse still, he had persuaded her to compromise some of the salesmen using a tape-recording machine under the bed. And these were the men the inspectors chose to rely on without question.

The conclusions of that first report were damning: "We regret having to conclude that, notwithstanding Mr. Maxwell's acknowledged abilities and energy, he is not in our opinion a person who can be relied on to exercise proper stewardship of a publicly-quoted company."

Bob was furious at the publication of this report and its conclusion. The overall DTI enquiry, he was later to contend, had offered him no "real opportunity to meet accusation after accusation" and the entire report had become "a vicious partisan attack" on his reputation.[1] Worse still, few people realized that the inspectors' report had no legal validity and was merely an opinion. The publication of such an opinion with the worldwide publicity it received and with no right of appeal was extremely damaging. But its timing was devastat-

---

1. *They Must Be Fair: Robert Maxwell's Reply to the Department of Trade and Industry's Reports on the Affairs of Pergamon Press Ltd,* (privately published, 1973), p. 139, paragraphs 255 and 256.

ing. By April 1971, Sir Henry's negotiations with Bob had reached a positive conclusion. Realizing how important Bob was to the future success of the company, Goldsmid was ready to settle all differences, bring him back as a consultant on publishing matters and support his reelection to the Pergamon board as a non-executive director. To that end, Bob had also decided to end his outstanding litigation with the *Sunday Times* over the defamatory Insight articles published in 1969, accepting a compromise settlement. Leasco's American litigation against me had been summarily dismissed by the judge as frivolous and without substance. The future was looking hopeful as the *Sunday Times* published an article at the beginning of May under the headline THE WEEK ROBERT MAXWELL BOUNCED BACK, and the *Daily Telegraph* talked of "the most remarkable reconciliation since the Prodigal Son." Friends wrote to express their delight at the latest moves, commenting that it was the end of a bad chapter, that his influence had been sadly missed at Pergamon and that they had never doubted he would rise again. But the publication of the first DTI report was to extinguish all those hopes at a stroke, preventing Bob's reelection to the board, even though he did become a consultant to Pergamon.

Once again, friends supported him in a wave of positive letters— Sir Derek (now Lord) Pritchard wrote: "You know that you always have my full support and it never entered my head that all this hoohah was anything but grossly unfair." Lord Clancarty commented on how much the company had rallied since Bob had returned as a consultant and referred to the "extraordinary and somewhat venomous way" in which the inspectors had acted in their "long drawn-out vendetta."

Bob immediately appealed against the inspectors' procedures. Declining to assist them further, he began proceedings for an injunction on the grounds that they had not complied with the rules of natural justice, and the application came before Mr. Justice Forbes in September 1971. Although he refused the injunction, Mr. Justice Forbes was critical of the inspectors. They had, he said, moved from an inquisitorial role to an accusatory one and virtually committed the "business murder of Mr. Maxwell":

This conclusion stands against Mr. Maxwell's name and amounts to banning him permanently from business life, for no body of shareholders would be wise to appoint as a director a man against whom this criticism stood. It is a fundamental rule that before being convicted of any offense a man should know the substance of the charge made against him. For myself, I cannot see how this rule can be satisfied unless a man knows both the fact that he is being charged and the identity of the charge that is being made.

The trial judge, he continued, would probably find that the inspectors had acted contrary to the rules of natural justice.

Bob came back from court greatly encouraged by this opinion, and subsequent press comment critical of the inspectors' procedure reinforced his hopes. For instance, under the headline INQUISITION OR INQUIRY?, the *New Statesman* concluded on October 22, "by his vigorous counterattack against the Department of Trade and Industry, Mr. Maxwell may already have ensured that he will be the last person to be subjected to this kind of administrative 'fishing expedition' masquerading as a legal process."

Bob decided not to waste time appealing against the refusal of the injunction, but to press on with this action against the inspectors which came before Mr. Justice Wien in November 1972. In the meantime, there had been further developments on the Pergamon front: in February 1972 Sir Walter Coutts, the last Governor-General of Uganda, had replaced Sir Henry Goldsmid as chairman of Pergamon and the Inspectors' second report had been published on April 11, focusing on the affairs of Pergamon's book subscription division. Bob was abroad at the time it was published, but once again he was shocked that they had issued a report without giving him a chance to refute the accusations.

Sam Silkin QC represented Bob before Justice Wien in November 1972. Philip, Anne and I attended the hearing, having spent many desperate hours in the Savoy Hotel the night before, helping to sort out the masses of documents Bob or his lawyers needed. The first days of the hearing were stormy as Silkin continually tried to draw the judge's attention to matters of fact which showed the inspectors to have been wrong. Silkin showed all the deference due to the judge, but he had a rather laborious manner, and I wondered at times if the judge was even listening. I could see that Bob was constantly close to exploding as Justice Wien refused to consider Silkin's arguments. After three tough days, the inevitable eruption occurred. As a result, Bob and Silkin decided amicably that it would be better if Bob conducted his own case. That way the judge would have to allow him rather more latitude as a personal litigant. Those were difficult and stressful days for Bob, and he worked continuously way into the night to prepare for court the next day. It was all to no avail. At the end of the action, Justice Wien ruled that Bob had failed to substantiate his allegation of unfairness, although he did pinpoint his dilemma in the words of his judgment:

It can truly be said that the Plaintiff has no other course open to him if he wishes to clear his name of the stigma attached to it by the publication of the report. He has no right of appeal and if the inspectors acted in accordance with the principles of natural justice, he cannot take the matter any further. Parliament has made no provision for his doing so, and I express no view whether Parliament ought to do so.

Once again, Bob went to the Court of Appeal, but it took the same view as Justice Wien, with Lord Denning concluding: "To my mind the inspectors did their work with conspicuous fairness. They investigated all the matters with the greatest care. They went meticulously into the details of these complicated transactions. . . . If there were one or two points which they overlooked, these were as nothing in relation to the whole field which they covered."

It was a conclusion Bob found totally unacceptable. He had still not had an opportunity to demonstrate in a court of law that the inspectors had reached the wrong conclusions. He felt he had had no real chance to defend himself, that he was not allowed to hear the evidence given against him nor contest that evidence. Above all, he had not been sufficiently informed by the inspectors of specific allegations or potential criticisms against him. In terms of punishment and suffering, the consequences could not have been worse had he been charged with and convicted of a criminal offense.

By June 1973, Bob was again giving evidence to the inspectors, but in such a hostile atmosphere that he finally declined to give any more evidence in person. He was then given fourteen days to provide written submissions, which he did as far as possible in the short time available, with some of the family getting involved again in typing, photocopying and proofreading. Sir Walter Coutts, meanwhile, had become convinced that Bob's presence was vital to the success of Pergamon and called a special shareholders' meeting to reelect him to the board. As he wrote to shareholders on June 1: "Robert Maxwell has unique personal contacts with a large number of editors and authors on whose continued efforts the whole lifeblood of the company depends."

In the event, the meeting was inconclusive. Although the small shareholders supported Bob, Leasco remained firmly opposed to his reelection and the City institutions preferred to maintain the status quo until the DTI had issued its third report. Pergamon's editors, meanwhile, had been working steadily in the background to secure his return. Many of them had written to the directors in June supporting Walter Coutts's initiative. Dr. Dunworth wrote, "What I can say is that the success of the Pergamon Press journals is very largely due to the qualities which Mr. Maxwell has brought to bear." Professor Bates said, "Robert Maxwell has great gifts as a scientific publisher." Professor Miles's feeling was that "Although he was very ambitious and, as a businessman, motivated by a desire to build up a profitable business, he shared with us a desire to play a role in science and its communication. We thus had a feeling that we were partners in a common enterprise." These moves by editors and authors were to set the stage for the next act, the decisive editors' meeting at Imperial College, London, in October 1973.

After Bob was ousted from the board in 1969, many of his senior editors kept in close touch with him. Bob's personal assistant, Jean Baddeley, remembers their visits to the house he rented in Montpelier Square when they voiced their obvious dissatisfaction at the way their books and journals were being handled at Pergamon. They were becoming more and more disenchanted with the new management and watched with frustration all the abortive moves to bring Bob back on the board. The company's authors were equally dismayed. Charles Plumpton, for instance, a well-established mathematics author and editor, wrote in January 1971:

As far as I am concerned, the sooner you return to put some sense and order in the Company the better. As an author of long standing with Pergamon Press and, in fact, having put some seven or eight thousand hours effort towards the success both of the Press and of myself, I have no desire to see a spread of the death-wish which seems to be overwhelming the Company lately.

Two months later, the physicist Harvey Brooks expressed his grave disquiet at the new management's poor performance in handling journal subscriptions—Pergamon's lifeblood—and its failure to keep promises. He had been editor of the *Journal of the Physics and Chemistry of Solids* for fifteen years and was considering taking his publication elsewhere. As he concluded, "In the face of a threat to the continuity of the Press and of the *Journal*, I wonder whether I can in good conscience continue to have the *Journal* published by Pergamon, unless unity in management is restored and I have some assurance that Pergamon is not in danger of folding up or severely and arbitrarily contracting its operations."

Others would come to visit us at Headington and I would hear firsthand how unhappy they were with the new regime. I entertained the eminent Belgian biologist Zénon Bacq, editor of one of Pergamon's most successful journals, on one occasion when Bob was away in America. Around ten o'clock one morning, I received a phone call from Zénon: he was on his way to Pergamon for a meeting but was stranded at London airport since no one had been sent to meet him. I quickly apologized for Pergamon's mistake and told him, "Don't worry, take the train to Oxford and I'll let them know you'll be arriving at the station." I passed on the message to Pergamon immediately. About midday, the phone rang again: this time, Zénon was at the station in Oxford and there was still nobody to collect him. "Just stay where you are, I'll be with you in ten minutes," I told him. When we finally arrived back at Headington, I phoned one of the directors and asked for someone to collect Professor Bacq from the house. A few minutes later, I could hardly contain my anger when I saw that they had dispatched a very junior employee (who even needed reminding of basic courtesies) to collect this distinguished scientist. But Zénon left with a brave smile, telling me that he would probably have finished his business by about five and would come back to see me. About one o'clock, the doorbell rang again and a totally dispirited professor walked in.

"Is everything all right?"

"Far from it. They want me to go back this afternoon, but the atmosphere there is so awful, I'm not sure I want to. If there weren't so many problems to solve on the journal, I'd leave straight away."

"Zénon, have you been invited to lunch up there?"

"No."

"Won't you come and join me?"

"I'd love to, I'm very hungry."

Over lunch, we discussed not only the future of his journal and the whole sad saga of Pergamon Press, but Zénon told me he had brought with him the manuscript of his new book. He left for his afternoon appointment with Pergamon staff and returned at six even more crestfallen. No plans had been made for his stay: there was no hotel reservation, not even an invitation for dinner that evening. Without any hesitation, I offered him one of our guest rooms, and knowing him to be something of a gourmet, I ordered the finest dinner we could muster at short notice. I did my best to soothe his pride as we ate by candlelight, remembering with nostalgia all the wonderful dinners we had shared there. Zénon was not only a renowned scientist, but an immensely cultured man and fine pianist. After dinner, he sat down at the piano and gave a wonderful recital. Before he left next morning, he handed me his new manuscript, which he had intended to offer to Pergamon. "Tell Bob to publish it himself," he said. "And I've got a big reference work in progress. Do you think Bob might be interested in that as well?" I assured him that he certainly would be.

Incidents like this illustrate why the senior editors and authors felt so frustrated and why a group of influential editors decided to band together in October 1973 to support Bob's return. His consultancy appointment was due to expire that month and Leasco's aim was to terminate his involvement with the company, whereas many Pergamon editors were openly supporting plans for his reelection to the board. They had already written to Sir Walter Coutts to express their concern:

We consider the involvement of Robert Maxwell—whose life work Pergamon represents—essential to the restoration of confidence in the management of the company. His past record indicates that he will bring the required leadership to the publishing management. . . . Without him, we shall be forced to reassess our relations with the company and make alternative publishing arrangements.

A meeting was finally scheduled at Imperial College on October 31, 1973, under the chairmanship of Professor Brian Spalding, editor of the *International Journal of Heat and Mass Transfer*. Many of the American editors had arrived the day before and had already talked to Bob, along with their British colleagues, at Montpelier Square. On the day of the meeting Heathrow Airport was plunged in fog, delaying the arrival of Steinberg and the Leasco team, who remained inflexibly opposed to Bob's reelection. By the time Steinberg finally arrived, the meeting had begun. Sir Walter Coutts had already made plain that in the absence of a Leasco bid for the whole company, he regarded Bob's return to the board as essential. Sir Harold Thompson had made an impassioned plea in support of his reelection, although Norman Freeman, representing the institutional shareholders, had recommended waiting until after the publication of the final DTI report. But Saul Steinberg instantly rejected any possibility of Bob's returning to the board. When Professor Sam Eilon, one of the distinguished editors present, voiced the editors' view that Bob should definitely be reelected, Mr. Steinberg was plainly contemptuous in his reply: he did not need the current editors, he said; editors were two-a-penny and he could line up dozens of editors to take the places of those who chose to resign or who would be sacked.[2]

Professor Eilon's response was quiet and dignified: if that was Steinberg's attitude, he could have Pergamon, but it would be an empty shell because all the editors present—and many more besides—would take their journals elsewhere. Thus the meeting broke up, with Steinberg having completely lost credibility in the eyes of the authors and editors there that day. Bob, meanwhile, had been in Professor Spalding's office three floors below, dictating press releases to his secretary Colleen (now also the professor's wife) and irritating her immensely by putting his feet up on the professor's desk.

By November 8, Sir Walter Coutts was writing to shareholders to convene a meeting to resolve the problem, leaving them in no doubt that many powerful editors would only continue to be associated with the company if Bob was a member of the board. Sir Walter's view was plain:

I have read all the reports of the inspectors and taken full account of the comments made by them. I doubt if it is publicly understood in what role I wish Mr. Maxwell's ability to be used. I consider that the Company needs at this time his entrepreneurial flair for recognizing publishing opportunities in the international scientific world and I am unaware that the inspectors have criticized this part of his work.

The DTI's final report was published only a few hours before the Extraordinary General Meeting on November 20. But despite further criticisms of Bob's management, he was appointed an alternate director to John Silkin, thus allowing him to attend board meetings and cast a vote in Mr. Silkin's absence. The battle for Pergamon was virtually over, but Bob's fight against the injustice of the DTI inspection system was still continuing.

When the third DTI report became public, Bob's reaction once again was to challenge the accuracy of the inspectors' conclusions. As he wrote in an affidavit, "To my mind it was absolutely full of errors and omissions apart from many glaring instances showing how unfair the inspectors had been to me."

---

2. Contribution of Professor Sam Eilon, *Robert Maxwell and Pergamon Press* (London: Pergamon Press, 1988), pp. 639–40.

Part of this third report was devoted to showing that a number of private Maxwell companies which were not owned by Pergamon were, in October 1968, substantially indebted to it. This conclusion rested on accountancy evidence which, when inspected closely, showed that the inspectors had misread a debit entry as a credit entry which omitted entirely a substantial sum (£94,000) owed by Pergamon to one of the private companies.

As Bob told me many times, if a fraction of the inspectors' accusations had been true, he would have committed many criminal offenses. Yet the Department of Public Prosecutions had looked into the affair and the Solicitor-General, Peter Archer, stated in the House of Commons on May 13, 1977, that after lengthy and extensive police investigation, "Counsel came to the conclusion that proceedings against anyone concerned would not be justified. The DPP agreed with that conclusion. Having studied the opinion and relevant papers and discussed them with Counsel and the DPP, I am of the same opinion."

Yet the stigma remained and Bob was to fight for the rest of his life to recover his reputation and demonstrate the unfairness of a procedure which allowed many accusations to be leveled at him without any real opportunity to counter them. Bob immediately published his own 141-page detailed response, *They Must Be Fair,* and had it distributed to all the major newspapers even before they received their copies of the third DTI report. In it, he highlighted the major areas in which he claimed the time-honored safeguards for the rights and reputation of the individual were ignored. The inspectors at the time gave no prior notice to the person of the particular areas they would be questioned on. No papers, documents or letters were provided in advance to witnesses who were expected to deal with them on sight. The witness was questioned by the inspectors, but not allowed to question any other witnesses or read the transcript of their evidence. Testimony of reputable, independent witnesses buttressed by contemporaneous documents was brushed aside in favor of that of unsavory and unreliable characters. As Bob said, "I have been tried, convicted and sentenced in my absence without having a chance to defend myself or appeal against the inspectors' opinions and conclusions."

Richard Briston, professor of accounting and finance at the University of Strathclyde, was also to come to Bob's defense in an article published in the journal *Accountancy.* Talking of the first report, he was to conclude that "whatever else he may have been, Maxwell was unlucky." Of the second report he commented that "the accounts had received a clean certificate . . . the inspectors had the benefit of hindsight." He went on to say, "Maxwell adopted commercial practices which were far more common than the City or Institute cared to admit. . . . When the City, in order to postpone the threat of an SEC, had to make an example of somebody, it turned out through a series of unfortunate circumstances to be Pergamon and Robert Maxwell."

Bob was not, of course, the only person to suffer at the hands of DTI inspectors. Angus Ogilvy, Princess Alexandra's husband, was to be damaged in much the same way a few years later by a DTI report issued on Lonrho, of which he was a director, and Lord Boardman resigned as Chairman of the National Westminster Bank, following the DTI's report on its investigation of Blue Arrow. The whole issue of Department of Trade investigation procedures was reopened with the case of the Al Fayed brothers (owners of the House of Fraser and Harrods). In March 1990, the *Daily Mirror* editorial on the subject went out under Bob's name:

If the Al Fayed brothers are dishonest, liars and deceivers, the place for them to be arraigned is in the High Court, not in the findings of trade and industry inspectors who act as judge, jury and executioner. There is no natural justice in these inquiries, as I, Angus Ogilvy, Lord Boardman and many others have found to their cost. No opportunity to cross-examine hostile witnesses. No jury to reach a fair and just verdict. . . . Parliament should change this bad law and, until it does, inquiries of this kind should be treated with contempt.

Four years later, the Al Fayeds took their fight to the European Court of Human Rights and distinguished lawyers are still calling for reform of a system that denies citizens an effective remedy if they find themselves branded dishonest and criminal by government inspectors, without the right to a fair trial. As David Pannick QC wrote in the London *Times* in March 1994: "Whatever the conclusion reached by the European Court, there is a very strong case for Parliament to reform English law to confine the discretionary powers of inspectors and to impose higher standards of procedural fairness."

A few days later, the *Times* editorial was to comment on "The British Inquisition," arguing that as far as possible, reports that may lead to prosecution should be "investigative rather than determinative." They should establish facts, make modest recommendations; they should not be an opportunity for "vitriolic attacks or extravagant prose." Individuals under investigation ought to be informed if they are suspected of any criminal or civil wrongdoing and told the identity of relevant witnesses. Within reason, they should also be given the right to reply to a report that is critical of them before it is submitted to the government.

These are long-overdue reforms which would have made a big difference to Bob in the 1970s. The basis then on which the DTI reached its judgment was flawed; and the fundamental unfairness of its procedures of enquiry has hardly diminished over the years. The damning verdict that Bob could not be relied upon to exercise stewardship of a publicly quoted company was tantamount to his business murder. Whilst the inspectors' conclusions were to come back to haunt him time and again until his death, Bob's subsequent achievements, particularly in restoring the fortunes of Pergamon Press, BPC and then the Mirror Group, were all given substantial public recognition. Today, in the light of the collapse of the Maxwell Group in December 1991, many commentators and public figures have resurrected the DTI's conclusions. Time and the facts may well prove that Bob was not fit to run a public company *at the time of his death,* but the events of 1991 do not validate the inspectors' conclusions reached in 1971 nor provide post facto justification for the defects of the DTI's system of enquiry.

9

> *You promised me blue skies, and I cared for you like my*
> *own father. You tormented me, you tore me apart. I would*
> *have put the world at your feet. Look at me, Look at me!*
> *When will I ever be able to tell you: it's over! When that*
> *day comes . . . I dread it. How much longer? How much*
> *longer? How long?*
>
> KURT WEILL, *WIE LANGE NOCH?*

The impact of those long, dark years on the family was almost immeasurable. By then, the older children, Anne, Philip and the twins, were in their twenties, but the younger ones were still at impressionable ages—Ian was thirteen, Kevin eleven and Ghislaine only eight. Although we hardly expected the younger ones to understand events fully, they did realize that something was amiss when we brought them home for the weekend after Bob was voted off the Pergamon board. As gently as we could, we tried to explain recent events and their consequences, telling them that Bob was going to fight back and would hopefully one day regain control. The children remember that weekend vividly. Philip, by then a graduate working as a fund-raiser for Third World First,[1] had followed the news in the papers and also learned firsthand about some events from Bob. At one point in March 1970, he recalls, his father became so dejected that he desperately pleaded with Philip to drop his pres-

---

1. A student organization founded by a group of students including Philip and supported by Oxfam that encouraged students to give a percentage of their income to Third World aid projects. By its second year of operation, Third World First had 27,000 student members; it remained active for the next twenty years.

ent activity to help him. That was how he came to work as manager in the Robert Maxwell bookshop in Oxford, more a move of psychological support for his father than one of practical benefit to either of them. Philip was to leave this post within seven months to work again with Oxfam, this time as a fund-raising consultant in the United States.

For Anne, who was in her final year at university, and Isabel, in her first year, the pressure and challenge of university life insulated them to some extent from the gloomy atmosphere at home, and this was even more true for Christine, who had just started at Pitzer College in California. At Marlborough College, Ian's housemaster and his friends did their utmost to protect him from the fallout, but he was very unsettled by all that he read in the newspapers. He wrote a moving letter to his father which ended "I understand how bad things are for you at the moment, but I am doing all I can to get a first-class report, as I know it will give you pleasure." Of all the children it was probably Kevin who was most directly affected. He was at Summer Fields in Oxford at the time and had the school job of "paper delivery boy." This meant that he had the opportunity to read the newspapers before delivering them to all the boys around the school. Glaring headlines about Bob would tempt some boys to make callous and even anti-Semitic remarks, which in his case was quite absurd. I had a letter from the headmaster, Pat Savage, telling me how sorry he felt for Kevin and us all, and assuring us that he was doing his best to protect him from the cruelty of the other boys.

As for little Ghislaine, although she could not really understand what was happening, she did start seeking attention by behaving badly at school and letting her work deteriorate. Her headmistress, although a distinguished philosopher, had a poor understanding of the psychology of small children. Her conclusion was that Ghislaine was not very bright and, because she was also a disruptive influence, she recommended we remove her from the school and enlist the help of a psychotherapist. I promptly took Ghislaine to a specialist in Oxford who conducted a series of tests leading to a very different verdict. The child, he told us, was highly intelligent and was clearly giving poor results because she was in the wrong type of school. What she needed was a complete change of school environment, preferably a boarding school so that she would be away from home. Bob and I decided to follow the specialist's advice. I looked around for a school where I felt Ghislaine would thrive and eventually chose a mixed prep school in Somerset which had an excellent reputation and catered to individual talents. She was happy there and her behavior changed almost overnight, although it took her longer to improve her academic standards. In the end, however, she graduated successfully from university like all her brothers and sisters.

We were all very shaken but bonded together by an incredible tribe spirit, which is common in large families, and the family came through this terrible period intact. My own initial reaction was to love my beleaguered husband more than ever and shield my children as much as possible. I spent a great deal of time with the younger children in those years, drove them regularly to and from school, never missed a single school event and brought them home for weekends as frequently as was allowed. It was during those dark times in the early seventies, partly in an effort to extricate them from the gloom of home, that I started taking the children for camping holidays throughout the British Isles, inviting friends or cousins to join us. I remember the first of these expeditions to Ireland in 1970. Our first destination was to our former nanny's family farm in County Cavan where Ian and Kevin had spent some really happy times as youngsters. We traveled in two cars: I drove a Land Rover packed with five of us, with all the camping equipment piled up on the roof, while the rest of the party followed behind in my car, driven by a good friend of Philip's. My experience as a Girl Guide was invaluable on those holidays. Every night, we would find a place to camp on farmland, often with spectacular views over the Irish Sea. We would pitch five tents in a semicircle around a campfire, including one very large one with an awning, in which Ghislaine and I slept and in which we could all eat if it was raining. Farmers were welcoming and provided us with milk and eggs. The children loved those carefree holidays and particularly enjoyed having their French cousins with them—they seemed to add an extra dimension of mischief to the trips. I remember for instance one hilarious pillow fight when we literally couldn't see across the tent for a thick cloud of feathers.

The highlight of that stay in Ireland was a visit to the medieval castle owned by Colonel Sean O'Driscoll, a Pergamon author and friend. Having made a small fortune in the space industry, he had bought Castle Matrix and restored it with love, great skill and knowledge. It was one of those enormous square medieval keeps with walls so thick that the spiral staircases leading to the upper floors were actually built into the walls themselves. Sean had decorated the castle with period armor; the floors were laid out like chessboards with gigantic Welsh slate flagstones; the kitchen had a French electric-powered spit large enough to roast an ox. The most impressive room in the keep was a splendid library with a unique collection of antiquarian books on weaponry and the restoration of medieval buildings. All the rooms were furnished in Elizabethan style with beautiful oak four-posters in the bedrooms. Sean wanted me to stay in the castle, but I decided I would rather stay with my brood, so we camped at the foot of his ramparts like the armies of Cromwell had done three hundred years before, piped to sleep and woken in the same way in the morning from the battlements. When the time finally came to say good-bye, the plaintive tune of bagpipes accompanied our departure.

In subsequent years, we had the same kind of camping holiday in Wales, then in Scotland, where we again visited old friends, the Straton-Ferrier family who had looked after me on my arrival in England. Dear old Mother Two was getting on in years, but she welcomed us all with open arms to her border castle. One day, she took us to the top level of the tower where the names of her Scottish ancestors were carved on a seemingly endless genealogical tree curling round and round the tower walls and going right back as far as Adam and Eve! The children were fascinated and it prompted interest in our own family origins. Ian, who has always shared my enthusiasm for history, greatly appreciated this touch of medieval pageantry, as well as all the tales of border feuds which the Straton-Ferriers recounted as we sat around a huge log fire. These are amongst the few happy memories I have of family life during those painful years in the wilderness.

What dark years they were, though. I remember that first year without Pergamon in 1970 as one of the bitterest and most difficult times we lived through as a family. We seemed to be under attack on all sides and constantly losing battles one after the other. In order to survive, we would pool all our small successes, sharing anything that was positive to keep our spirits up. I took ten days off in February to go skiing in Courchevel, France, with my sister. As I went up on the lifts or down the slopes, my mind would invariably return to Bob. I wrote to him every day, telling him my thoughts and how much I loved him:

I have thought quite a lot, going up the sunny or snowy or blizzardy slopes about what I could say to you to give you back some courage, as you sounded so sad on the phone the other night. The essence of what I wish to tell you is that I love you, irrespective of your worth in terms of cash or otherwise, irrespective of the ill-winds that might have passed between us at a time when we were both tired and under the stress of very heavy pressures, irrespective of what our future might be. I love you for the exceptional life you have already given me and the privilege I have had to share your life for twenty-five years and be loved by you for all that length of time.

I am not afraid of work and even if I had to live in a semi-detached house and work from 9 to 5 and again from 5 to 1, I would not reproach you but go on loving you and working to educate our children. I would not like you to take decisions thinking that you must save me or protect me to your own detriment. Work really and truly does not frighten me, nor people's gossip, nothing save that I would like to complete the little ones' education to give them the better chance in life that we gave the older ones. If you feel that we must give up Headington Hill Hall and live elsewhere or emigrate to China or live underground or on a treetop, I am game. No waves are static and I would much rather swim and have swum with you than vegetated with small, unintelligent and uninteresting beings.

These were memorable times. I well remember Bob's sharing his joy with us when a specially bound copy of the 1,000th volume of the Commonwealth Library, the publishing venture he had initiated, was sent to him privately by a Pergamon manager. We were all greatly cheered in October when Bob was offered a Kennedy fellowship at Harvard University to lecture and research on science and government in the spring term of 1971. When the first letter on this subject arrived from the dean of Harvard, Bob wrote back saying that there must be some mistake and they must have the wrong Robert Maxwell as he had little more than a basic primary education. His letter provoked a swift response, "No, we have the right fellow." He was just the kind of man they wanted, with experience in both business and politics. The children and I joined Bob at Harvard for Easter. It was a welcome diversion, and the Brooks, Whipple and Hollomon families, together with other Pergamon authors who lived around Boston and Harvard, could not have been more hospitable.

That same year, 1970, we also celebrated our silver wedding anniversary, but in very subdued fashion. There was little call for a great fanfare or big dinner and dance. It remained a family affair, mainly orchestrated by the older children, with as many of our close family as possible gathered at home in Oxford. I had organized a surprise for Bob by ordering ten dozen bottles of a special cuvée of Dom Pérignon, his favorite champagne, specially labeled by the producers in honor of our silver wedding. Although a few tears were shed that night, we were quietly happy to have survived so many years together, mixed so much with joy and sorrow notwithstanding the storm clouds all around us.

* * *

During the spring of 1970, I had enrolled to take English A-level at the Oxford College of Further Education. It was a rather ambitious move since I had to cram two years' work into two months before the examination in June, but I managed to pass, albeit with a relatively low grade, and the whole family celebrated my first success in an English examination at the age of fifty. At the same time, I had already approached St. Hugh's College, Oxford (where Anne had been a student) to see whether there was any possibility they might accept me as a mature student to study modern languages. We were all delighted when I was eventually offered a place for the following autumn term, and Bob was supportive of my plans to read for a degree. I remember there was great hilarity when it came to filling in all the necessary forms, especially the question, "Do you wish to share a room with your husband in college?" The mere thought of Bob sleeping in a college single bed with me . . .

In that first year, I worked mostly at home where I turned one of the small rooms into my study, placing my desk in front of the large window with its magnificent view of the spires of Oxford, whose bells chimed the happy or sad hours of my life for thirty-six years. As long as I live, I shall remember the dawn rising behind the house, shrouding the spires first in pink, then gold, until they were finally ablaze with light against the green background of Boar's Hill and Botley Hill. At the end of the day, the glorious sunsets à la Turner were equally unforgettable, enveloping the entire horizon in a riot of gold, orange and purple, with the spires etched out against the creeping darkness of the night. In the foreground lay the lush, old-world garden of Headington Hill Hall with its centuries-old cedars and yews, rambling roses, heavily scented lilacs and syringas and sloping green lawns. The following autumn, I was to share digs just opposite St. Hugh's with my other student children. But that year, with its first university examination, was the hardest of all for me. There was the agony of starting the day at 5 A.M., then spending nights bent over my books and the difficulty of coaxing my brain into academic routines after so many years of lying fallow. Besides that, I had to resurrect my Latin, which I hadn't studied for more than thirty years and had never found easy. I tussled with Seneca's letters, Horace's poems, Tacitus and some obscure texts by a late Empire writer, Jerome. I passed my preliminary exam in French, but failed in Latin and had to retake it the following term, which was an immense bore. It later transpired, however, that I need never have taken it at all, since the passing of my French university exams all those years ago gave me exemption. For the next three years, I would get up at dawn, drive to my digs and spend the morning working at my studies or attending lectures and tutorials. I could occasionally study again in the afternoon, but more often than not, my time was taken up by family or continuing constituency affairs and I would only be able to return to my books in the evening, burning the midnight oil to keep abreast of my work. In those years, I would invariably miss a whole night's sleep every week to write the weekly essay, then carry on as best I could the next day.

It required much discipline to accommodate my two separate lives. My room in Oxford was sparsely furnished, like a monastic cell. I wanted no material clutter. The only painting I hung there was an oil by Jean-Claude Janet, depicting a hand touching a luscious pomegranate, a symbolic representation of forbidden fruit, be it knowledge or sex. For the next four years I never read a newspaper, never went to the cinema or theatre, never listened to music and never read a book which was unconnected with my studies. Working in my digs, I was like another person.

I can still see myself in subfusc (Oxford academic dress), walking along in the spring through Oxford's narrow streets, breathing in the heady odor of lilac and wisteria, which hung in heavy clusters from the ancient college walls. For a moment, my cares vanished and I was young and free, as if I were back in the Paris of my youth, feeling the fervor and enthusiasm of an eighteen-year-old student all over again. I was so eager to be punctual that I would run all the way to my tutorial if I was a few minutes late and one rainy morning, my eagerness landed me in trouble. I was on my way to Christ Church College for a tutorial with Professor Krailsheimer, a distinguished authority on Pascal, when I tripped on the old flagstones outside the college. I went sprawling on the ground, with my possessions scattered around me in the mud, my black stockings torn and my knees badly grazed. My eminent tutor soon noticed the holes in my stockings and my bleeding knees and I must admit that I felt a fool explaining what had happened. But the affair was soon forgotten as we set to work to discuss the complexities of Pascal's thought. He is, in my tutor's own words, "an exceptionally difficult author and the constant references to religion and philosophy are not matters to be lightly brushed over." Unlike some of my younger student friends, I was fully aware of my tremendous luck in being taught by such a notable scholar. Many years later, this brilliant man was to record his recollections of the time in a souvenir volume prepared for my seventieth birthday. To my surprise, I discovered that we were both the same age when I read his memories of "a coeval who was fleetingly 'in stat. pup.'[2] to a Christ Church tutor."

My greatest joy was that my Oxford years coincided with those of several of my children, and this brought me very close to them. When you have been brought up abroad, it is difficult to integrate fully in the life of your adopted country. Oxford gave me another chance, and my relationship with the children in those years also had the added dimension of our being college friends. I would help them with their French essays or translations and they would reciprocate by correcting my written English or lending me their essays from previous years. I remained "Mum," but they started to look at me with different eyes and became my best friends.

Christine, however, deciding she wanted to take Latin-American studies, which at the time was not available as an undergraduate course at a British university, succeeded in obtaining a place at Pitzer College in California. Bob and I both missed her enthusiasm, joy and tenderness. On a trip to America in the spring of 1972, Bob spent a few days with her, wanting to make sure that she was settled and happy. As he told me in a letter, she helped him to forget for a few days "the Board of Trade, Steinberg and the pack of vultures that have been after me for so many years now." Our greatest worry was the drug problem in America and the high "drop out" rates of students—we had actually been told by Christine's professors that only 50 percent of the students completed their degrees in California's universities. I was greatly relieved, therefore, to read Bob's assessment, "Christine is OK and in every way, her success and her survival are a miracle which she herself helped to create, making full use of what you and I have taught her and the advice we gave her when she left for Pitzer; she is slim, smart and lovely."

At home, Ian's enthusiasm and exuberant personality helped to make Christmas 1970 much happier than that of the preceding year. When I was feeling rather halfhearted about the festivities, he would jolly me along, help me buy and wrap presents and decorate the house in the traditional way. As I wrote to Bob in my Christmas letter that year:

I love you very much. All on my own last night in the kitchen, whilst I was struggling with my twenty-fifth Christmas turkey, I thought of all the years gone by, all our happiness, all our tragedies, all our struggles and all the things that

---

2. *In statu pupillari*: in a condition of pupillage.

bind us together for ever. I did it with more care than ever before, certain that there is some virtue in tradition and in the repetition of familiar acts, perhaps because in their very continuity, they spell security. . . . I think a special thank you must go to Ian. Without him, I doubt there would have been a Christmas this year; he bore the brunt of the shopping, wrapping and all the decorating, and his enthusiasm managed to permeate every one of us. He reminds me so much of Michael at times that it is impossible not to think of that lovely, cherished child who, like Ian, had started to take the lead in so many fields at home and school and had an infectious joy which echoed in his laughter. After it was silenced, the house was not able to laugh for years. Yet that is life and it is up to all of us to carry on living with a brave smile, in spite of all the mortal blows we have had to endure, because we know that there is an imperishable love and warmth that radiates between us, through to the children and back to us again. We are still amongst the very lucky ones, thanks to you.

In those early years of the seventies, Bob was constantly traveling to America for the affairs of Pergamon Press Inc., and I wrote to him regularly with all the news from home. At the beginning of the autumn term 1971, I reflected on my life and love for him:

There are no startling developments anywhere, all the pots are boiling. I wonder what you are doing in Jacksonville? Since you have no real business there, I wonder if the hunting Maxwell of the good old days has returned, when you used to go out just to sniff the air for new ideas, opportunities and possibilities.

I think of you a great deal, conscious that I can do little to help you in this ordeal except by smoothing your sidewalks, trying to keep life on a fairly even keel and myself in an urbane temper. My studies help me a great deal because they really are an escape of a kind, but a rewarding one. The ancients had great wisdom which we seem to have lost on the way. And reading through the centuries, it is humbling to see that human endeavors are eternally the same. It makes you feel more contented with your own limited ambitions and the fulfillment of a life three quarters over. I often look back on our life and ponder how swiftly it whizzed by. I remember the times we quarreled and regret it bitterly. I try to remember only the achievements, not the failures. I amend my judgments of human beings and events. Many people have been abandoned by the wayside, many desires put to one side, many ambitions cut down to size, but overall—and thanks to you—we have lived a totally extraordinary life, original, eccentric, extravagant, rich and incomparable. For me you have dwarfed all other men and taught me so much. You have made me a better person and for all these achievements and for my children, I thank you. Even with their failings and shortcomings, I would have no others. They have much that you should be proud of. Perhaps if you saw more of other people's children, you might be less hard on your own. So really, I am happy and love you. I think you are quite a man, although you are far too elusive and too busy surviving to think of other smaller matters which are at times necessary to enhance happiness.

I have 12 essays to write in 8 weeks (one and a half per week), 56 books to read and 8 translations to boot. If I survive, I hope to see you before Christmas.

During my years at Oxford, my fulfilment in my studies and closeness to the children often prompted me to reflect on the life I had led so far. I was absorbed in something that gave me a real sense of satisfaction, I had my own student friends and, for the first time ever, a life that was separate from Bob and the business. Because of this, I gradually acquired a degree of detachment that allowed me to analyze events more objectively. When my daughter Isabel, who had shared my first two years at Oxford, left for a long trip to South America, I wrote to her:

All of a sudden I realized you had gone, the room was awfully bare, its soul had vanished, along with your books, your posters, your laugh and your chatter, but the memory of those marvelous years lingered on. I had a big lump in my throat and had to sit down and consider how attached we can become to our cozy happiness, our environment, our bits and pieces, how really foolish we are to try and build eternity during our brief passage on earth. And yet, like the bees and the ants, we untiringly start to build our nests everywhere.

I thought of the extraordinary wisdom there is in monastic rules, where not a single possession or item of clothing is your own and you can be shifted from one convent to another at a moment's notice. It highlights just how foolish it is to love one's earthly possessions. If you think about it, the whole evil of the world stems from there. One should really treasure other values, those one can carry in the heart. Yet the thoughts which assail me this morning are not nostalgia of comfort and material goods but all the joy and love you gave me. I will always cherish those wonderful hours of shared anxieties and pleasures, of endless talks and discussions, successes and failures. If you in turn have also been enriched, then my joy will be complete.

I did not expect the additional good fortune of sharing this exhilarating time with my children. As you know, the reasons for my taking a degree are
a) to escape to a certain extent from the horrors of Daddy's business entanglements and remain sane
b) to secure a financial safety net for myself in case everything turned sour and I had to earn my living in order to finish educating the little ones
c) to realize a lifelong ambition to consolidate my superficial knowledge of literature and philosophy
d) to achieve a mastery of French and improve my English so as to be able to write excellent French, and at least passable English.

Last but not least, after twenty-seven years of constantly looking after others, giving freely of my ideas, my zest for living, my enthusiasm for projects, my capacity for organization and my love to tutti quanti, I felt literally pumped dry. I desperately needed to replenish my own vital sources and prove to myself that I had a mind of my own.

There is one fantastic compensation in getting older, you become very wise, you really do. You are more detached, much more objective and less concerned with trivialities. You see it all in better perspective and would so like to pass on your wisdom. "Si jeunesse savait, si vieillesse pouvait" [If youth but knew, if old age but could] as the French say. As you get older, you become more selective and that is why at the moment I am hibernating. At this time of great mental upheaval, I want to be on my own, I want to think for myself, I refuse to be bullied for any reason whatsoever, emotional or otherwise. If I can't make up my mind now, I never will. It's only when I'm in this kind of retreat that I begin to realize how much I've exerted myself on other people's behalf and how desperately I need to rediscover and revitalize myself if my natural strength and energy is to be restored.

There were times when I felt guilty at being able to evade the gloom of our daily life by retreating into the world of academia whilst Bob was fighting for his life and ours. I was very aware of my luck and grateful that Bob's continuing hard work enabled us to carry on living at Headington Hill Hall. As I wrote to him,

It is one of those very beautiful English pre-summer days, the sun shines at intervals through a few evanescent white clouds, the traffic has subsided, all the hues of green in the freshness of newly born leaves provide a fitting background for the vivid yellow of the broom, laburnum, forsythia and glorious magnolia.[3] Instead of being green, the lawn is white with daisies and here and there patches of uncut grass show up dark green against the rest.

None of the small crawlers who nibble at your shoes or at times wander up your socks have any idea of who you are: you are beyond their comprehension. In the City, the cowards were so excited to be in on the kill when they were all in a pack, but when they see you, limping but erect, lonely but proud, towering over their yapping, their own smallness shatters them.

You are a man, you are not afraid, you fight, you shoulder an antagonistic world on your own. You are brave, you are not shy about admitting you have made mistakes. Your eyes are a little sadder, less whimsical, but just as caressing, soft and piercing at the same time. You smile, your brave smile is still there and your words still spell an awful lot of sense. They have at the moment to be more precise for they carry such weight, and they must be cautious. Do not let them carry magic, but just affirmation, cold denial or irony. Do not try your charm on the inspectors, keep it for me. Your brain is unimpaired, it is as vivid and exciting as ever. Times will come again when, given back your wings, you will contribute to further happiness. I will think of you all day and send you every ounce of energy and love I can muster. You have a tendency to be over generous in your judgment of the people around you. Curb yourself of this generosity when you meet the inspectors, they are after your blood for no reason other than it is their job. May God and all the concourse of people who love you and wish you well help you to face this ordeal with a clear brain and flowing tongue. I know that you will pull through.

I feel lonely and terribly frustrated that the only way I can help you is by keeping things as normal as possible. I miss you.

---

3. Headington's grounds contain a rare pink magnolia thought to be well over two hundred years old.

By the spring of 1972, I was writing,

When one recalls where we all were in October 1969 and the seemingly bottomless abyss of despair we seemed to have fallen into, it is a remarkable achievement that we have been able to carry on as we have. We have lived in style in our beautiful house, the children have been educated for three more years in expensive schools and universities, the business has been pruned and is floating on a reasonably even keel and you have managed to do all that in the last year. Considering that all along you also had to face court cases, lawyers, unpleasant newspaper articles, the Board of Trade vendetta and Transport House witch hunt, it's bloody miraculous!

My allusion in this last letter to the "witch hunt" brings me back to events in the constituency, where the situation was rapidly deteriorating following problems with the Labor party agent, Jim Lyons. After the 1970 election defeat, the president and executive committee of the local party were dissatisfied with Lyons's performance and asked him to leave, but with his union's support, Lyons refused to go. This disagreement was to provoke almost four years of unrest during which the constituency machinery disintegrated. There was an extensive inquiry by Labor's national executive committee, which eventually found in favor of the agent. Whilst they acknowledged that Lyons had failed to prepare adequately for a general election, they censured both Bob and me severely for interference in party affairs. It was a strange and rather ridiculous situation: since I had been elected vice-president of the local party, chairman of my own ward and postal votes officer by the General Management Committee and, as such, it was my duty to be involved in all local party affairs. I had also kept the flag flying in the villages which Lyons, on his own admission to the regional agent, had "written off as not worth bothering with." But we were dealing with determined troublemakers who were active in several constituencies and became known as the "lunatic left," with members of Parliament, as well as prospective candidates like Bob, suffering at their hands. They were never willing to talk to you face-to-face but disrupted gatherings with ridiculous points of order and prolonged executive meetings till late into the night to prevent all decisions being taken. With the prospect of another general election looming in 1974, Bob's former political agent Bryan Barnard was persuaded to come back and try to give some semblance of unity to the party. But it was an almost impossible task. Bob's opponents had really engineered the death of the Labor party in the constituency and they succeeded: to this day there has never been another Labor MP for North Bucks.

Despite all this unpleasantness, I was still going once a week to cook lunch for the elderly at the Wolverton Senior Citizens' club and regularly supervising the playgroup. I also attended every executive committee meeting, presiding whenever necessary. But my heart was no longer in it. As I wrote to Bob in 1973:

The nausea that this festering carbuncle gives me now is quite physical: it makes me feel wretched and physically sick. I dread going there so much that I have to watch my driving. I keep saying to myself that it would be the last straw if something was to happen to me on that bloody road when every fiber of my being tells me that it's a waste of time, a mistake, a nonsense and a fraud. Anybody who takes me away from you, the children and my own studies and then kicks me in the teeth is no friend of ours. We must be barmy to continue to waste our time like this. I've done my stint, let them find another sucker. That kind of fraudulent reality repulses me. When I believed in the new Jerusalem, I worked with all my heart, kidding myself that I was doing something worthwhile for my "neighbor." Now, I want to get out. What's more, I don't feel bad about it at all, I have not the slightest remorse. All I want is to achieve some success within the limited circle of those I love. I want you to disentangle me from all commitments. If you don't, I'll fall irremediably sick until you do so.

Yet in the last term before my final examinations at Oxford, I still had to find time to fight the general election of February 1974. We did our best to rally support, but the Liberal vote had soared throughout the country, and in our constituency, it favored the election of the Tory candidate. Bob lost by some three thousand votes, as he was to do once again in October that same year in an unprecedented second general election, when he faced the electorate of North Bucks for the sixth and last time.

For Bob and the family, though, there was to be a wonderful compensation. In early 1974, it seemed as if the impossible might really happen and that against all the odds, Bob might succeed in regaining control of Pergamon. On January 9, Bob announced that he was going to make a bid for Pergamon, pricing its shares at 11 pence each and valuing the company at £1.5 million. A few days later, he increased his bid to 12 pence per share. The irony was that most of the money for the bid was lent to Bob by Chemical Bank, the very bank Steinberg had attempted to buy in 1968, and further financial support came from Flemings, the merchant bank which had resigned as Bob's advisor back in the summer of 1969. Although the offer was judged "disappointing" in Sir Walter Coutts's circular to shareholders, the Pergamon board nevertheless recommended acceptance, and 90 percent of the shareholders, including Steinberg and the City institutions, accepted. By then Leasco itself was in financial trouble, with the computer leasing business beginning to decline as new technology and serious competition appeared. Its shares had plummeted from the price of $37 offered to Bob to a mere $7.

By the middle of February, just over four years after losing his company, Bob succeeded in regaining control. It was an amazing achievement and he owed a great deal to the staunch support of the friends, authors and editors who had battled on his behalf, and to Pergamon's staff, most of whom had remained loyal, keeping Bob informed of events and of the state of morale within the firm. I was full of admiration for his courage and determination. Congratulations came from many quarters and I remember Bob's joy as he read those letters and telegrams. He was back where he belonged and perhaps now, at long last, Pergamon would regain its former strength and rise to even greater achievements. The eminent lawyer David Freeman wrote that "Natural justice has been done" (although not by the DTI) and Professor Kurti found a telling image, "So at last the Prince of Denmark is back in the cast of Hamlet."

By April, Sir Walter Coutts had resigned as chairman of Pergamon and Bob had been reelected to the post. Bob was jubilant and looked forwards to reviving the fortunes of Pergamon after this disastrous period. Three months later, in July, Leasco and Bob settled all their outstanding litigation and Sir Walter Coutts was writing to thank Bob for a generous gift for loss of office, wishing him good luck and speaking nostalgically of his "soft spot" for Pergamon. The dark years were coming to an end, although the stigma of the DTI still rankled and the outcome of the subsequent police investigation was still a matter of serious concern.

My own priority in the summer of 1974 was to pass my degree and I gave my all to my studies in the last two months before "finals." My children were all abroad or still at school when I sat for a daunting thirty-three hours of written exams over a two-week period in June. But I was fortunate that a young American friend of Isabel's gave me moral support during this grueling experience. A postgraduate, Greg, was killing time in Oxford before taking up an appointment as dean of an American law faculty, and Isabel had entrusted him with the task of looking after me at this demanding time. He was thirty, dashingly good-looking, sensitive and cultured. I had invited him home to meet Bob one weekend and he had unfortunately witnessed one of Bob's disgraceful outbursts, accompanied by the usual humiliating comments about my character and intelligence. My new friend was greatly shocked, but had understood our whole drama: Bob battling the demons of the outside world to keep our ark afloat and jealous perhaps of my growing intellectual strength and inner freedom. Greg was constantly at my side for the next two weeks: he would come to my digs, sit in my only armchair, watch me feverishly revising or help by making endless cups of coffee. He would take me to Schools, the Oxford University examination building in High Street, then pick me up for lunch after my exam and persuade me to eat. If I wanted to revise my notes until I was literally outside the exam building, he would just remain silent, pocketing my notes as I left him. He would be there waiting for me as I came out, take me out for dinner and then back to my digs. I have no idea what he did in between—we never talked about anything but the subject of the next day's exam and my last-minute revision of vital points and quotations. His presence in my digs gave me confidence. His calmness forced me to concentrate, although I was exceedingly tired. When he arrived early in the morning, I would be feeling nervous at the prospect of the day ahead, but he would take me to the full length wardrobe mirror and say, "Just look at yourself! You look just like any other kid taking her exams, except that you're beautiful, knowledgeable and wise. It's going to be all right, I can see it in your eyes."

"You're just a flatterer."

"No. I'm not. Please look at me. You're going to make it. Why, I do believe you're blushing! You're so young in many ways, you can't even take a compliment and that's a sign of youth."

"It's time we left."

I was so struck by this unusual relationship that I was inspired to record my impressions in a "Prose Poem on Two Keys—Revision for Finals in an Oxford Digs:"

A man is a man is a man is a man . . .
 Linguistic paper IV: Modern French structure:
He came and sat in my big brown velvet armchair.
Nice lanky body, narrow hips, nonchalant walk,
 The difference between colloquial usage and
Tall, broad shoulders, casual sporty clothes,
 literary usage, although not clearly defined
Slender expressive hands drawing arabesques in the air,
 is nevertheless of primary importance, especially
Laughing generous mouth, sea green eyes,
 in the handling of conjunctions, prepositions and interrogation.
A shock of blond hair cut like a child's, yet a man.
 The everyday language tends to let go of
His composure, his loving warm heart and compassion;
 the complicated grammatical constructions involved

Feelings mixed up: mother's instincts, female desire
   in the usage of 'puisque' and 'car' and 'mais'
To rest her head against his heart and listen
   seeming to care little for logical sequence of 'pour' or 'de'
To the pang of young love pulsating, though restrained.
   and especially for the traditional question forms of
Why! so deeply natural the wish to hold her hand
   'Pourquoi,' 'comment' and the ordinary form of interrogation,
Too brief is the instant of stillness, enchantment,
   which it seems to avert by just making use of the tone of voice.
Silence, love flowing, nothing said, flutter of eyelids
   The simple affirmative turn is used with a provoking
Question not answered, pale spirals of smoke
   rise in the voice, thus replacing the interrogative inversion.
Soft, smooth, just a murmur, it is suddenly cold.
   Inversion is intensely disliked by ordinary users
She attends to the fire and sits down at his knees,
   who wish to revert to ordinary straight language.
He buries his face in her soft scented hair. A moment
   The omission of prepositions is explained by a need for brevity.
Detached from time as it rolls its torrent by her door.
   One finds reduction of expressions such as de crainte que
Soon he'll be on his way, enshrined in this, her vision.
   and omission of pendant *or de before* fin.
A wisp of fresh air, of love, of gentleness,
Gossamer threads beaded with dew on a July morning.

At the end of my marathon, Greg came to meet me outside Schools with a bottle of champagne, as is the Oxford custom at the end of exams. That night, the first time in four years, I agreed to go out and we went to see *2001*. I found it wholly appropriate that I should see my first science-fiction film with an American. Once my oral examination was over two weeks later, there followed an anxious period of waiting for the results. I went back to Headington to attend to all the motherly and wifely duties I had been neglecting so badly and Greg disappeared without telling me where he was going.

The day finally came when the Modern Languages results were due to appear on the green baize boards inside the examination building. My knight reappeared, collected me from home, and we walked into the building. I remember scanning the lists for my name, starting from the bottom with the Pass degrees, then going up to the Third and the Second classes. I was beginning to panic when I couldn't find my name at all, but Greg shouted, "You've passed." "Where? I can't see it." "Right there." My four years of hard work had been rewarded with a second-class honors degree. All of a sudden, I found myself being lifted off the ground and swung round and round in his arms. I was so overjoyed. I was crying, I was laughing, I was in seventh heaven. I turned and saw a friend of ours who was a rather staid Fellow of Balliol College and he promptly embraced me as well! I went back to my digs immediately to phone Bob, but he was not in the office and I had to be content with leaving a message.

Greg took me out that evening to The Trout, a well-known pub just outside Oxford. I felt guilty at not working, but he brushed aside my scruples telling me that it was my day and about time that I indulged in feeling free. For the first time we did not talk about exams and French authors, but about me, which was flattering if embarrassing. Greg was enormously considerate and a good listener. Although he was only thirty years old, the same age as my son Michael would have been, he was uncannily mature in his knowledge of the human heart. He understood that I wanted to keep my university life separate from the home front, that it was a lifeline that had to stay open for me. He never quizzed me about my relationship with Bob, but realized, perhaps from Isabel or from his own observations, that although I was deeply in love with Bob, I was struggling to assert my own personality.

He never called me by my real name: for him I was always Marguerite. That evening at The Trout, I was tempted into confidences I had never dared voice before. I soon found myself revealing some of my inner turmoils and feeling very embarrassed about it afterwards. When he asked me why I was so ashamed of venting my anger or expressing my sadness and bewilderment, I told him that for me it was a sign of weakness. "Nonsense, Marguerite," he replied. "There is a time that is absolutely right for words and deeds. Why shouldn't you let yourself go for a change? I'm not at all shocked by something that is honest and sincere. I love you as you are. I don't want you to be different. All I want is to see things as you see them." An echo ran through my mind of the words Bob had said to me some thirty years before. What was I doing there, flirting with another man after thirty years of a faithful marriage filled with stability, honesty and strength? Yet I had to admit that it was sweet music. Opposite me sat a man who had helped me to be myself for a short time. I was grateful and loved him dearly for liberating me from absurd conventions. I looked at him and said, "I may be your Marguerite, but you will not be my Faust. 'Vade retro Satana' [Get thee hence, Satan] and lead us not into temptation." He fully understood the implications of my remark.

I accompanied Greg that summer on a motoring holiday in France, introducing him to the country I loved as we drove from one set of my relations to another. We visited Versailles, Vézelay, Mérindol and all the glorious Cistercian abbeys of Provence, then made our way to Les Baux, Narbonne and Carcassonne before returning home via Les Landes, the Lot et Garonne, Chartres and Paris. I was able to put our relationship on a realistic footing by becoming more like a mother to him. He taught me about American music and literature and helped me to jettison many hang-ups that had hitherto restricted me. Above all, he persuaded me that I had to stop accepting bullying as normal behavior. I had to be assertive and stand my ground. He encouraged me to enroll for the research degree I so longed to undertake. Some time later, I was to introduce Greg to a sweet Lancashire girl who became his first wife, and I acted in loco parentis in preparing for his wedding in England. We corresponded irregularly for the next six years, after which we lost touch.

Towards the end of July, Bob and I gave a dinner for the tutors who had taught me as an undergraduate. Many were to remain good friends. Bob said a few words by way of a toast, but it was left to me to thank everyone present for contributing towards my success. I spoke in Franglais, which was easily understood by my largely bilingual guests. I gave special thanks to my children, who had had to be content with a sharply reduced quota of motherly love and attention and supported me with unflagging gallantry and encouragement. Above all, however, I thanked Bob for his support and steadfastness.

On November 2 I was formally admitted to the degree of Bachelor of Arts in an age-old ceremony in the Sheldonian Theatre, Oxford. Bob was present and told me how proud he felt of my achievement. Later that afternoon I sat down at my desk and wrote to him:

My darling,
We have been married thirty years and that is quite a while to have traveled together. At the end of this long and eventful trek, I realize that I love you deeply, irresistibly, fundamentally and for ever. I love you for the right reasons and for many others that I can't explain since, as Pascal said, "Le coeur a ses raisons que la raison ne connaît point."[4]
You were never so great, so human and so tragic as when you had your back to the wall, facing the firing squad and deflecting the bullets out of sheer willpower and determination. I felt totally weak at times, totally without courage and prepared to cave in. You never did. You are right that you alone know how much you went through. I accept that perhaps I never fully appreciated the stress you were subjected to, but in the same way you did not under-

---

4. The heart has its reasons which reason itself does not know.

stand the stresses of my life at other times. But I accept fully now that your hell was of a magnitude difficult to comprehend and I feel deeply sorry that I was unable to give you all the support you needed, although God knows how hard I worked to keep all balls in the air.

I loved you when you were a victorious conqueror, I love you even more when the world lets you down. I loved you less when you were arrogantly victorious because at that time you were less likable. But there is not time now for unrewarding delving into a part of the past which I cherish less. I love you basically for what I think are by far your best, permanent qualities, which so many who profess to know you well completely fail to appreciate. I love you for your quick and far-reaching intelligence, your immediate grasp of any subject, your instantaneous understanding of a problem, your endless compassion for those less fortunate than you, your unlimited generosity of spirit and infinite capacity to love me and our brood. You are the best companion any woman with courage and intelligence could dream of. "Non je ne regrette rien."[5]

You are all that I have ever wanted of life—and more. You are all that I ever dreamt that life could give me. You gave me love, intelligence, fun, excitement, achievement, fame and education. You made me a much better person, and if you were to leave me, the bottom would literally fall out of my world. When I look back at my life, I know that all I ever did was really for you, so that you would love me, recognize my efforts or have cause to admire or be proud of me. Even when I took up my studies again, I wanted to show you that I can still pull something out of my old hat, but I owe you my success because if you were not here to see it, I simply would not have done it. Within myself, I have never found sufficient reason for achieving anything. My greatest reward is your admiration and congratulations.

Perhaps it has been exacting to live with you at times, but it has been worth it. I am most grateful that you understood that my desire to pass that degree was not just a whim, but an absolutely necessary life belt. I think I would have gone nuts had I not been able to have a concrete aim with a concrete result as the end product. I have often had a nauseating feeling of tilting at windmills and this has certainly increased in the last three years. I am conscious of the fact that despite my best endeavors, I did per forza neglect the house and some of your comfort. Thank you for putting up with it.

That evening, we celebrated both my degree and Bob's return to the chairmanship of Pergamon with a private dinner and dance in the Hall for our friends and my favorite tutors. It was a memorable occasion for many reasons, not least of which was a hilarious episode that quite literally shattered the evening.

One of my guests was an Oxford don whose lectures on Proust I had taken as a special honors course and had found fascinating. He

---

5. "No, I Regret Nothing," is the title of one of Edith Piaf's best-known songs.

was, moreover, a good-looking man, which was an added bonus. His name was Dr. Pilkington. As he was introduced to my husband, Bob asked him the obvious question: was he connected in any way with the famous glass manufacturers of the same name? To which he replied that everyone asked that question, but regretfully the answer was no. When coffee was over, the dancing began and as I danced with Dr. Pilkington, he told me how Proustian my party was and how much he was enjoying it. I then changed partners and took to the floor again when, all of a sudden, I heard the most terrible noise rather like an explosion, followed by an almighty crash of broken glass. I caught sight of Dr. Pilkington emerging from the outer hall onto the dance floor straight through the plate-glass door that separated the outer and inner halls. What is more, he had left behind him the jagged, lacerated outline of his body, right in the center of my huge glass door, exactly as a magician would have done! I rushed towards him, unable to believe that he hadn't cut himself. Amazingly, he didn't have a single scratch. He was a little dazed but insisted that it was nothing and started apologizing profusely, whereupon my staff cleared up the debris, and I asked him if he would like to dance again. As I whirled him onto the dance floor, he started pondering what the famous hostesses of *A la Recherche du Temps Perdu* would have said on such an occasion: what would Madame Verdurin have said, what about Odette and the Countess of Guermantes? We went through half of Proust like that. It was an enchanted evening for me and a fitting celebration of my undergraduate years at Oxford. It remained an amusing conversation piece for our family. I am not so sure what it did for Dr. Pilkington, but he volunteered the comment that he could no longer claim to have no connection with glass.

Looking back today, there is no doubt that 1974 was a watershed year for us. It encompassed all the features of our chaotic lives of that period—the closeness of our relationship as we battled on all fronts, Bob's continual litigations, elections fought and lost, his triumph in regaining Pergamon Press, my success in gaining my degree and beginning to assert myself, some of the children growing to adulthood and leaving the nest and Bob's incessant traveling in his burning ambition to remake his fortune and clear his name.

Now that I was free of the restrictions of university life, I frequently traveled with Bob at a time when his efforts to rebuild Pergamon seemed to take him around the world almost continuously. Our first trip of the new era took us to Stockholm to launch the company's new Chess series; then we visited Rome, Paris and Abidjan, where I discovered the Western side of French-speaking Africa and met Noel Ebony, a very intelligent black writer who was reporting the conference we were attending. He later came to stay with us in Oxford and I learned a great deal from him about African psychology and politics. I, in turn, made him realize that France was not Paris alone, and the discovery of French provincial life helped him to understand French people and their literature better. I remember Bob saying of him, "He's so bright, that one, he'll either get to rule his country or be hanged!" He was very nearly right, for Noel died some years later at the wheel of his sabotaged car.

From Abidjan we flew to New York and then briefly to Beirut where Lebanon's civil war was still in progress, disfiguring that once beautiful city. We attended yet another scientific conference in Cairo and found ourselves staying in a former Khedive palace, sleeping in the apartment once occupied by Empress Eugenie when she opened the Suez Canal. The bedroom, furnished in rich rococo style, was about 10 meters long by 6 meters wide and had an exceedingly high ceiling. The drawing room, a gilded monstrosity of similar size, had a domed and painted ceiling supported by black marble columns, with a huge, four-tiered crystal chandelier hanging from the center. Persian carpets were strewn over the white marble floor and double glass doors opened onto a spacious balcony overlooking the Nile. I found it difficult, however, to equate our palatial comfort with the desperate poverty of Cairo and the country as a whole, which had suffered enormously from its defeats in the wars with Israel. Although there was little time for touring, I had a brief glimpse of the celebrated sights of Cairo, the pyramids, mosques and museum, enough to whet my appetite for later visits when I was able to tour extensively that country's rich cultural heritage.

All that traveling made Bob exceedingly tired and he was becoming more and more irritable as he waited to know whether the DTI inquiry would lead to a prosecution. At times I really despaired of our ever getting back on an even keel. We decided to do something special for the New Year and booked a cruise on the QE2. Our departure was delayed by a sailors' strike in Southampton, but the management placated its most irate customer with caviar and champagne and we finally set sail for Madeira and Senegal. I soon realized that we had made a disastrous decision. Once you have been on a yacht of your own, no public liner, however luxurious, can possibly compare. Bob quickly became bored, lacking stimulating company, and found being at sea for days on end both frustrating and claustrophobic. He discovered the casino and regularly played roulette from ten in the morning till four in the afternoon and every single night until three or four in the morning. On the whole he won, and fascinated those passengers in the gaming room by mounting huge piles of the larger-denomination chips in front of him, which most people only see happening in films. What was worse was that he insisted that I stay in the casino, too. He could see that I was bored so he would give me money to play the one-arm bandit machines, where I hit the jackpot over and over again, probably because I didn't care whether I won or lost. When I tried to intervene and persuade Bob to leave the gaming tables, he would say, "Go and dance, but not more than fifteen minutes." That was how I came to dance regularly with a good-looking stranger whose name I never knew, but who obviously liked dancing; whenever he saw me come into the ballroom, he would thank his partner and ask me to dance. I would have forgotten all about him had I not kept the poem I wrote in my extreme loneliness on that liner.

> Ocean deep dark, navy blue water,
> curling up in white foam
> Midnight sky with the Southern Cross
> soft music on the Queen of liners
> Midnight black Paris shiny sleek gown
> Curly auburn hair brushing against silver temples.
> Echoes of a good rhythm and soft husky voice
> Pink champagne sends you dreamily
> rolling across the dance floor
> swinging along, pitching forwards
> rocking backwards with the huge rollers
> held sideways in a strong pair of arms.
> No names exchanged, no questions asked,
> Just un homme et une femme
> seeking they know not what
> from they know not whom
> just dancing together, each one in his dream
> Alone on the dance floor
> alone at the bar
> alone on the empty windswept deck
> of a huge ocean liner plowing her course,
> a speck on the boundless waves
> under a dark blue sky studded with stars
> and the soft caressing light of the moon
> shining on a man and a woman
> who will never meet again.

The truth was that Bob and I had forgotten what it was like to be in each other's company for twenty-four hours a day. If we had been able to reflect more carefully before deciding on that cruise, perhaps we might have chosen to go somewhere quieter like Jamaica, where we could sit on a peaceful beach, talk things over and try to find each other again. I realize now that every time Bob could have faced up to our relationship in a mature way, he avoided it. He preferred to plunge back into the familiar domain of business with all the excitement and thrill of success it brought him, but my role in that world was strictly limited. Ever since the early days of our marriage, he had repeatedly promised to take me into his confidence on business matters, give me a seat on the board, entrust me with a responsible position where I could have really helped him. But he could never bring himself to fulfill those promises.

Bob's relationship with me became increasingly ambivalent: I had no doubt that he loved me dearly and wanted me to be happy. But for some reason he couldn't cope with me or my problems. One evening in September 1974 stands out in my memory as the nearest he ever came to putting this into words. We were having dinner alone together—a rare occurrence; he was relaxed and fetched a bottle of excellent white wine from the cellar. He started to tell me how grateful he was for all the help I was giving him in the election campaign and asked me what he could do afterwards to make me happy. Was there anything I particularly wanted or dreamt of that he could provide? It was a conversation we had had on several occasions before, and I had already explained that what I really wanted was to help him in the business so as to share his life. That evening, I decided to change my tune, so I told him I wanted to go to Valentino's in Rome for expert advice on makeup and hairstyles. "That's easy," he replied, "There's a conference in Rome after the election, I'll take you there. Anything else?" "Oh, yes, I'd like to buy my clothes in Paris from Givenchy, Yves St. Laurent and Ted Lapidus!" I thought Bob would understand that I was joking, but not at all. He really thought that these material goods alone could make me happy and promised to take me to Paris early the next year for the spring collections.

I asked him why he wanted all that for me, since he never seemed to notice what I wore or how I looked. "Your happiness," he said, "is vital to me. I want you to feel beautiful, to look beautiful, to attract people and be admired." I tried to explain that I needed much more than that from our relationship, that I was longing to do something constructive now that I had passed my degree. But he replied that he couldn't apply his brain to anything but business and politics at the time. He was getting up at five, going to bed at midnight and needed two more years and all his strength to rebuild his empire. As he told me that, I saw a new look in his eyes which gave me immense joy, a look of hope and enthusiasm for the years ahead. It was the first time I'd seen such a happy look for years. I just didn't have the heart to come between him and his plans for the future or add any personal problems to the ones he was already tackling. But he did promise to extricate me from all political involvement and have me properly trained for international conference work for Pergamon. He could see that my charm, looks and easy manner with people were tailor-made for that, and my degree was a further asset. For a time, I was pacified once again.

A few months later, on one of our many trips abroad, I told him again that I was frustrated with my intellectual inactivity and really couldn't go on following him around the world, packing and unpacking his bags and being useful in a menial way—it was extremely boring and gave me no satisfaction at all. Again there were promises. Then in 1975 when I went with him to Vancouver for the Habitat World Conference, all my hopes vanished. After manning Pergamon's exhibition stand and organizing a reception, I asked him one day if there was anything further I could do to help. "Just stand in line with me and look pretty" was his reply. I understood then that he would never seriously contemplate my closer involvement in his affairs. That was how I came to apply for a place at Oxford for a postgraduate degree in French. I was accepted as a research student by Dr. Mollie Gerard-Davis, a don at St. Hilda's College, who proved to be as exciting and interested a supervisor as I could have wished for. Taking a collection of unpublished family letters as the focal point of my research, I set out to study the art of letter writing for a doctoral thesis. It was to fulfill my urge for intellectual activity over the next five years.

For his part, Bob was working feverishly to rebuild Pergamon Press. When he had regained control earlier in 1974, the company was in financial difficulties and the staff's morale was extremely low. He showed himself as magnanimous in victory as he had been steadfast in defeat. One of his first actions was to address the staff. We walked up to the offices together and found them all gathered in the large open-plan office known as "the bowling green" because of its green carpet. In a moving speech, Bob made it plain that the past was over and done with and that he would welcome their continued support. He himself would bear no grudges, he went on, but would understand perfectly if any members of staff wanted to leave; he would accept their decision without question. What he wanted above all was to get on with the task of restoring Pergamon's fortunes after five years of losses. As Bob described in the Pergamon Annual Report for 1975, the interim years had caused the company enormous damage. Under inexperienced management and with its executives involved in endless investigation and costly litigation, Pergamon Press had suffered devastating losses, run up huge bank debts and come very close to bankruptcy. Assets had been drastically reduced in value and the company's 90 percent interest in the International Learning Systems Corporation (ILSC) was sold off for a mere £1 to the British Printing Corporation (BPC), followed nine months later by the remaining 10 percent for £200,000. Ironically, some four years later BPC sold 35 percent of ILSC Japan (a wholly owned subsidiary) to John Swire and Sons for £2,034,000, but unfortunately Pergamon had no share in that profit. Between 1969 and 1974, staff had been reduced and made to work under very difficult circumstances and Britain lost the benefit of substantial exports. Bob himself had suffered heavy financial losses and crushing legal expenses. The truth was, as he said, that nobody had gained and everyone had lost.

10

It grew so fast his life was overgrown,
And he forgot what once it had been made for,
And gathered into crowds, and was alone,
And lived expensively, and did without,
And could not find the earth which he had paid for,
Nor feel the love that he knew all about.

W. H. AUDEN, "IN TIME OF WAR"

By the end of 1975, a great deal of progress had been made in restoring Pergamon to its former prosperity. The bank overdraft was eliminated, dynamic expansion resumed, a profit-sharing scheme introduced, forty new journals' publication begun and modernization undertaken in all parts of the company. Bob could celebrate the twenty-fifth anniversary of the company in the October of that year, looking confidently towards the future. When the accounts for the year ending December 1976 were published, the company had fully recovered with a profit of £2 million. Financial journalist Patrick Hutber was perfectly correct when he wrote in April 1977, "This week, Robert Maxwell will be walking around with a grin like the Cheshire cat," although as Hutber went on to imply, there was still the matter of the DTI reports and whether any prosecution would ensue from the police enquiry. A month later, however, this was also to be resolved with the Solicitor General's statement in Parliament that no further action would be justified. Bob was in Peking at the time for talks about sales of educational and science books to China, but a cryptic telegram, "Doctor advises privately that George will be all right," gave him the news that he had been waiting to hear for so long. At last he was free of the anxiety that had continued to dog him. But he never abandoned the hope of removing the slur cast on him by the DTI, even though Lord Balogh wrote in April 1978 to say that his letter to the Lord Chancellor had been unsuccessful: "I was made to understand that no measure can now be taken to remedy the ill which has been caused to you. I am very sorry—I find it a scandal, but I fear not an unexpected one after my previous experiences."

Bob's conviction that he had suffered an injustice made him even more ferociously determined to succeed on a large scale and prove his detractors wrong. In later years it led him into endless litigation with journalists and biographers. For the moment, however, he concentrated all his efforts on Pergamon, consolidating, introducing a powerful new computer system and preparing major new reference works like the six volumes of *Comprehensive Organic Chemistry*. Pergamon's return to prosperity seemed assured, despite a series of devastating fires in 1973, 1976 and 1978 which the police finally concluded were the work of an arsonist. Every time, the fire broke out in the vicinity of the computer room, the nerve center of the company, but thankfully Pergamon's effective fire precautions ensured the safety of the computer, even though entire offices were destroyed in the blaze. Bob was always abroad when it happened and since the fires started during the night, the alarm was raised either by me or another member of the family. I have vivid memories of the July 1976 fire, which broke out about midnight. I was woken by a tremendous bang which sounded just like a bomb. Rushing to the window, I saw a huge column of fire shooting up from the middle of the new Pergamon building, soaring up into the darkness like an Apollo space rocket. I phoned the fire station immediately, dressed hurriedly and ran outside to find a group of local people already gathered. The fire engine arrived within minutes and I watched and waited anxiously as the firemen fought to extinguish the blaze, then finally went back to bed feeling totally dispirited. It was only next morning that I was able to assess the extent of the damage. The central area of the building had been totally gutted and the entire "bowling green" with its forty-six computer terminals was in ashes. It was an especially cruel blow at a time when we were just emerging from the gloom of the Leasco years. But the courage and loyalty of Pergamon's staff saved the day. I can still see them that morning, hundreds of them, like an army of ants in the black plastic rubbish bags they had adapted to protect their clothes. They worked tirelessly, carrying bundles of charred documents, only stopping briefly for the tea and sandwiches I provided. It was just like the spirit which had prevailed during wartime raids on London—business as usual. Bob arrived home the next day and directed the immediate measures necessary to rebuild the burned-out offices. His persuasiveness with builders and suppliers was amazing. Within a few days, we had a temporary switchboard with thirty telephone lines. Only four weeks later, the central part of the building had been rebuilt and forty-six new computer terminals installed.

Exactly the same kind of scenes resulted after Pergamon's other major fires, except that in 1978 fire broke out on the very day of the national firemen's strike. When, at the height of the fire with flames shooting as high as the tallest trees, I saw one small and lonely wartime "green goddess" fire engine arrive, manned by a volunteer, my heart sank and I really thought we had had it this time. But luck was with us: officers in the fire brigade were not on strike, and the fire officer who had directed operations the previous time was quickly on site. Knowing exactly where to find the hydrants, he organized us all using Pergamon's own equipment. I remember wielding an enormous canvas pipe, hitched to a hydrant drawing water from the swimming pool, although a longtime Pergamon employee soon came to my rescue saying "Oh no, Mrs. Maxwell, that's no job for a woman, let me handle it."

Although my studies brought me solace and solitude in my digs when I needed to collect my thoughts, the late seventies saw me desperately trying to keep my relationship with Bob on a reasonable footing. Athelstan Spilhaus, dean of Minnesota's Institute of Technology, came to stay with us once when he was over on business with Pergamon. He liked to sit in my office, sipping a cup of coffee and observing my life. In those days, my office was always rather like Piccadilly Circus and open to all comers; authors, staff, children and guests would wander in and out on any pretext, public or private. After watching my activities for a while, Athelstan turned to me and said with his heavy South African-American accent, "Betty, I know exactly what role you play in this company—you are the end basket!" It was a gem of a definition and it stuck. That was how I came to send Bob a series of memos from the "end basket," describing how my non-official position in Pergamon had developed into that of an exceedingly overworked administrator. The first one was addressed from "Mrs. Maxwell's desk to Robert Maxwell, Chairman" and read as follows,

THE END BASKET unLTD, acting for
Pergamon Press Ltd, Pergamon Press Inc,

The Oxford Guest House, Harmony Films Ltd,
The Maxwells, big and small

SPECIALIST in Public Relations,
Entertainment at Home and Overseas,
Guided Tours, Driving, Accountancy, First Aid
Cooking, French Translations, Shopping.
Packing, Playgroups, Foreign Schoolboys' mothering,
Students' Coaching, Senior Citizens' Welfare
General Dogsbodying.

EXPERT at dealing with disgruntled authors
and FEEDING any amount of people at short
notice whilst cramming for an Oxford Degree

Once Bob rashly agreed to publish a cookbook written by the
sister of one of our Pergamon authors. Gilbert Richards, a Pergamon
director, came into my office with an enormous manuscript and said,
"Betty, I am absolutely stuck with this one. Can you help review it?"
I was, as usual, dealing with three things at once, and said to him,
"Just leave it in my basket, but please put down on paper exactly
what you want me to do." In the next mail, I received Pergamon's
standard instructions to its professional readers. How many similar
publications were already on the market? How many copies should
we publish? What did I think of the recipes and illustrations and
how should the book be priced? When I eventually had time to look
at the manuscript entitled "Talking About Cakes," I realized immediately that the best way to judge the book would be to try out a certain percentage of the recipes. That is precisely what I did, and for
days on end, the Hall was transformed into a bakery-cum-tea shop.
Everyone available was asked to taste the cakes in the kitchen. I then
went to Blackwells bookshop in Oxford, scanned the cookbook
shelves for similar publications and, finding little more than five or
six books of the same ilk, went back home and wrote my report. The
illustrations, I remember, were amateurish and I suggested that good
professional photos should be taken. The book was duly printed,
sold well and went into a paperback edition. Several weeks later, I
received five guineas for my refereeing efforts. I had to laugh,
because it didn't even cover the cost of all the ingredients I had used
to try out the recipes. I promptly gave the money to the Pergamon
Social Club and put it down to experience. When, soon after, "Talking about Puddings" by the same author landed on my desk, I imme-

diately recommended we publish it and saved myself all the extra cooking.

Bob would often let himself in for publishing or printing unusual works. At a Printing Corporation dinner once, Earl Mountbatten cornered him and asked him whether he would do a facsimile reprint of a hand-printed book by his father, the Prince of Battenberg, called *Ein Besuch Beim Mikado* (A Visit to the Mikado). What he needed was twenty-five numbered copies to give as Christmas gifts to the Queen, Prince Charles and his closest relatives. Could Bob have it done discreetly? He agreed and managed to fulfill his mission, despite the difficulties in printing a watercolor background of delicate hues. He never told me anything about it until the following Christmas when he received a present of copy No. 25, kindly dedicated by Lord Mountbatten. Bob then told me that one difficulty in producing the book had proved insurmountable: he had not been able to find a printer willing to do less than a hundred copies. At this, he gave me the remaining seventy-five copies and told me that if ever anything happened to him, I was to send them straight away to Lord Mountbatten or his children so there was no chance they might fall into the public domain. After Bob's death, I followed his instructions to the letter and received a grateful acknowledgment from the present Lady Mountbatten. Now that both parties are dead, I feel free to tell the story; Bob never breathed a word.

By the second half of the seventies, Bob was starting to put on weight and was constantly trying to diet. Friends had told us about some health clinics in Germany and Bob suggested I should go first to see whether they were any good. So in 1976 I took myself to Bad Worishofen near Munich to try out the Kneipp establishment. You certainly needed courage! You were woken at five and rubbed down in cold water with a rough glove, then you got back into bed with a delicious sensation of warmth. This was followed by a series of hot and cold showers and herbal baths, after which you were allowed a scanty breakfast. The rest of the morning was occupied with long walks in the snowy, frozen countryside before a slightly more substantial lunch. Then it was time to have a rest, after which you swam energetically for an hour, went for more walks and had more baths. I was very slim in those days but managed to lose ten pounds and felt in excellent shape. From there, I went on to Tignes, where I went skiing and performed much better than usual. My ski instructor, who had known me for years, was convinced that they must have put a tiger in my tank! I wrote one of my usual long letters, which Bob loved to receive, telling him all about my experiences at the clinic. In reply, he sent me such a sweet and honest letter that it gave me hope for our future together.

I truly love you. This feeling has come over me in the plane to Glasgow on reading your last letter from Kneippland to the USA. I am glad that I married you and sorry that I have told you in times of great stress that this was not so. When next we are on our own and in the mood for a long, deep discussion, I will try to answer all the points you raise about our past and future life together. I hope that this will be soon.

I very much admire your courage and tenacity in trying to keep us together and working for a better and fuller life for us in our remaining years on this earth. I have some very practical and shortly realizable plans for us and I look forwards with excitement to revealing them to you, discussing and agreeing them with you and even more quickly implementing them together.
    With all my love,
    Your Bob

That autumn, however, a female American journalist came to interview Bob at home and he introduced her to me. As we were talking, she was constantly fingering a gold pendant which she was clearly trying to bring to Bob's attention. "Don't you know what this means?" she asked. When Bob replied in the negative, she insisted, "Don't you see, the letters G.B.? Can't you guess what they mean?" Bob again said no. "Well, it means 'Good in Bed,'" she laughed. Bob was very embarrassed, perhaps because this exchange took place right under my nose. After she left, Bob's reaction was, "What a brazen hussy," and after that we referred to her as "Good in Bed." Bob was still a handsome man in those days and always had an eye for a good-looking woman. I know that they did meet again in Geneva where she probably succeeded in proving how good in bed she was. After that, she pursued him all over the world, telephoning, trying to see him and leaving messages. Although they probably met a few times, the affair was not long-lasting. It is, of course, difficult to assess how much of what she went on to write after Bob's death was embellished. All I know for certain is that soon after the encounter, Bob gave instructions to his secretaries in New York and London that her calls were not to be put through to him. I am not by nature a jealous woman. My own upbringing and strong personal ethics always prevented me from indulging in affairs, but I did understand—perhaps because of my French background—that sexual desire can exist without love, that it is a natural instinct, especially for men, and of no importance unless the heart is involved. As far as I was concerned, it was a totally insignificant episode.

My reproaches to Bob at the time did not concern his possible peccadilloes, but his lack of consideration for me and his increasing selfishness. Yet I was still forgiving, knowing how much he had just gone through. I found it more and more difficult, however, to live with his sudden changes of mood, his dictatorial manner with the children, which was driving them away from home and his complete inability to recognize the enormous amount of work I was coping with in running Headington Hill Hall as our home, my office and Pergamon's hotel and restaurant. I was also distressed because he had started smoking again, cigars admittedly, but I knew it was very bad for his lungs. I eventually persuaded him to consult my nephew, Professor Polu, in Nancy, France. A trained cardiologist and specialist in pneumology, he was the ideal doctor to assess Bob's health and possibly help him to lose weight. We traveled to France together, Bob stayed in the hospital for two days and was given a complete checkup. Although he weighed 230 pounds at the time, his heart was examined closely and found to be normal. He was, however, suffering from respiratory insufficiency and hypoximia (a lowering of oxygen in the arterial bloodstream) and his exercise capacity was limited. Professor Polu encouraged him to lose weight and have some physiotherapy to increase the breathing capacity of the lung which had been operated on in 1955. Bob was enormously grateful that I had taken him to Nancy and that some good had come of it.

A trip to Russia in 1978 was also to bring us close together, but for a totally different reason. Back in 1956, Bob had asked permission to visit his native village, but Khrushchev had refused the request on the grounds that the area was too dangerous because of rebels. Bob had considered that a poor excuse and never asked again. In the late seventies, however, at the height of tough negotiations in Moscow with the minister of culture over the exchange of scientific literature, the minister had suddenly offered him an opportunity to go there, perhaps in an effort to facilitate the business deal. Uncertain how serious the offer really was, Bob replied that he would need to talk it over with his wife, who was also in Moscow, and would give them an answer next day. We decided that we could travel the following Monday, but when Bob suggested that to the Russians, they threw their arms in the air and told him it would take at least three months to organize the trip: the roads in that region were poor, all the relevant authorities would have to be informed and so on. We thought they were just procrastinating.

To our great surprise, we received a formal invitation to make the journey in September and left for Moscow immediately. From there, we flew to Lvov, then embarked on a bumpy and interminable car journey through the Carpathian mountains to Uzgorod, Mukachevo, Churst and finally Szlatina. Everywhere we went, we were treated like VIPs: as we approached the towns en route, dancers were out on the streets to welcome us and the best restaurant had been emptied of other customers, ready to receive us. Excellent food was accompanied by a plentiful supply of wine, cognac, and vodka, and gifts were showered upon us. Instead of taking us straight to the village, our hosts insisted first on taking us on a scenic tour where we were only too aware of Intourist's propaganda efforts. When we finally arrived in Szlatina, another splendid and lengthy reception had been arranged and we began to despair of ever seeing the village itself properly. It finally took Bob's commanding personality and strong voice to convince the flabbergasted mayor that we had not traveled all that way only to see the inside of the village hall. What we really wanted was to see the house where Bob had been born. With some reluctance, we were finally taken to the old Schulgasse, then to grandfather Yankel's house, which, although still standing, was much more dilapidated than in Bob's childhood. No wonder the Russians had been disinclined to take us there. In the last forty years, nothing had really changed, but the village had lost its soul—all the faces we saw were those of strangers: every single Jew had been killed, deported or had fled. Bob became very depressed. I was glad to have made that pilgrimage with him and in some small way helped him cope with the shock and relieve his suffering. That night we slept in a small inn in Churst and it was cold. I wrapped Bob in a sheep's wool blanket which he had received as a gift from Szlatina's *kolkhoz* and watched him fall asleep in its warmth, impregnated with the smells and tears of his native village.

It was as we made our way home, taking the Mezgorye mountain pass through the Carpathians, that Bob realized he had done Khrushchev an injustice: we came across a monument with an inscription recording how he had fought his way through those parts; and our guides told us that partisans had indeed taken a shot at him there in 1953.

But whilst incidents like this brought us close together for a short period, most of the time I was desperately trying to build bridges between us. In a strange repetition of past patterns, as Bob regained prestige, confidence, success and power, so he became more selfish and dictatorial. I noticed a definite change in his attitude to me after he received the "all clear" from the Solicitor General. It was such a relief for us all and yet it really came too late: the damage done had been horrifying and costly. Bob wasted no time in celebrations. He plunged back into work and set about leading Pergamon Press to greater heights. That sparkle I had seen in his eyes in 1974 had by now been transformed into a confident glint of victory with the amazing turn-around in the company's fortunes.

From time to time, we would still have a reasonable weekend when, over Sunday lunch or dinner Bob, in an expansive mood, enthralled us with his vision of the future. On those occasions, he was wonderful and immensely attractive. Long before it became reality, he would depict a futuristic world of satellite communications and information retrieval via remote computers. At other times, he would talk of international politics, and his views were sometimes quite prophetic. I greatly admired his originality of thought and skill in expressing his ideas, and we would sometimes be quite close and loving. But however exhilarating those moments were, they did not compensate for his vicious attacks on me and the children on so many other occasions. Our eldest daughter, Anne, by then an actress, was most frequently on the receiving end of his ill humor. He could not accept that she was neither Glenda Jackson nor Judi Dench and that she was not an overnight success despite being in a film starring Sean Connery. Nor could he understand her apparent inability to find herself a "decent husband." Like all of her brothers and sisters, she faced the difficulty that few partners ever matched up to Bob's expectations. There was a dichotomy in his attitude to the children: on the one hand he wanted to keep them all under his control, preferably with them working in the business, but on the other hand he made life at home or in his immediate vicinity absolutely unbearable for them.

Bob was especially hard on the two younger boys and drove them mercilessly. Barely eighteen months after Ian joined the business in 1978, Bob installed him as managing director of Pergamon's small, Paris-based bookselling operation. The business had performed badly for as long as I can remember, and restoring its fortunes would have been a daunting task for an experienced manager, let alone for a willing but inexperienced twenty-three-year-old. Within six months of Ian moving to Paris (the first of three such "tours of duty" in France), Bob discovered that a major fraud had occurred in Pergamon's Frankfurt office, whose managing director and chief accountant had vanished with several million marks of the company's money (they were eventually caught and prosecuted). He promptly made Ian managing director of the Frankfurt operation as well as the Paris one, so that he was commuting twice a week between Paris and Frankfurt before flying home for weekends to report to his father. Considering his limited professional experience, the need to conduct business in three languages whilst living out of a suitcase and being dressed down by his father almost every weekend, Ian did the best job he knew how. It was to end in tears in a now famous episode, frequently cited by Bob in press interviews over the years. Ian was fired by his father one weekend for failing to meet him at Charles de Gaulle airport in Paris. If he could not keep small commitments, he would never learn to keep big ones: that was Bob's justification.

It was a harsh lesson and in my view completely over the top. Ian was deeply hurt at the time and humiliated when his father told the story in public. It naturally made him wary of crossing his father in the future. He was to spend six months out of the business. When Bob and he patched things up, Ian asked to be given some formal publishing training and Bob appointed him assistant to the president of Pergamon's American operations in New York, where Ian was to remain for the next three years.

Sunday lunch continued to be a point of conflict and Bob would invariably become extremely bad-tempered if the children didn't come home, even when they were grown up, accusing them of selfishness and disloyalty. They wanted to come, but dreaded it at the same time: it was so emotionally draining for us all. We almost never had a conversation that was a real exchange of views: none of us was allowed to hold an opinion that differed significantly from his. I became almost paralyzed when he asked me questions, because as I tried to answer, he would quickly become impatient and interrupt me, saying, "I can't understand what you're trying to say." If I carried on talking, it would not be long before he butted in again with, "What you're really trying to say is . . ." Or if I asked a question, he would rephrase it completely and preface it with "What you meant to ask was . . ." and "Why on earth can't you put your questions in a normal way?" Such criticism would finally make me loath to ask or answer any more questions, whereupon I would promptly be accused of sulking. It was endless. Whenever any of us was enthusiastically trying to recount something exciting that had happened, he would repeatedly interrupt, insisting on careful rephrasing until all the joy had gone out of the telling. Yet if strangers were with us, he would be patience itself with them and put up with crushingly boring people by turning on his charm.

Another means of influence and control over me was Bob's conviction that he would not live long. After his operation in 1955, it became a recurrent theme of his letters and for years I believed it, too. In 1956 for instance, he was constantly writing about "the little time that life has still left for us," in 1960, of "the few years we still have to live together" and in 1969, "We have not very much time to live." The idea of his impending death was constantly in my mind and so I frequently gave in to him, especially when he was about to leave on his travels. I would never let him go without patching up our quarrels just in case we might never see each other again. I would also avoid provoking quarrels, partly for the sake of the children, whom I always tried to shield from our marital difficulties, but also because they always left me exhausted and enervated. He would persuade me that they were caused by my fundamental character defects and "lack of moral fiber and principles." I never accepted that judgment, though I know that I frequently caved in when I should have stood up to him. I am not aggressive by nature; I often prefer to seek a compromise solution rather than make an enemy or have an unnecessary quarrel over something relatively minor. As far as Bob was concerned, I was completely irredeemable.

For me, however, it was unthinkable to live in a state of tension with Bob: I wanted and needed his love and would frequently be reduced to tears and beg his forgiveness to bring an end to the argument. After a massive row, the air would be cleared and I would then make tremendous efforts to match up to his expectations. For a short time, he would be magnanimous and generous and the whole family would bask in a transient state of peace and euphoria. But every joyous reconciliation was followed by a new crisis, and as the years passed, the crises became ever more frequent.

Yet whenever we were separated, his rare and short letters were always complimentary and loving and I would take courage in reading them: "I love you, only you, I adore you for ever my untamed, wild but fascinating creature, I love you and desire nothing else but to make you feel safe and needed, so please live in this belief."

Throughout the late seventies and the eighties, I lived in a perpetual state of mental and physical exhaustion. There is no doubt that Bob had an idealized picture of me and that I fell short of his dream. He also had a rather Oriental view of women: he wanted me to love him, be loyal to him and unconditionally surrender my whole being to him, but whilst he valued my opinion on most things, he found it almost impossible to accept that I should have a life of my own. Our constant separations also added to our problems: we were so seldom together that when we did meet, it was extremely difficult to be on the same wavelength, and we were perpetually having to adjust to each other's new experiences or feelings. Yet the separations also helped our relationship to survive: as soon as we were apart, we would both forget reality and re-create in our minds the love we had first known.

Bob's success led him to believe that he was special. He would often say to me or the children, "Are you comparing yourself to me?" as if such a comparison was beyond the bounds of possibility. It was clear that he could not cope with competition, and this led to further difficulties for us in later life, especially when I was praised and honored in my own right as an international lecturer on the subject of the Holocaust. He had not been taught humility and certainly believed that he was above all petty rules. There is no doubt that in many ways he was emotionally immature. He found it extraordinarily difficult to accept his own faults and would often find a way of transferring the blame to someone else. Yet if he did recognize that he was at fault, then he would say quite readily, "I'm sorry, I was wrong." One has to remember that his childhood and youth were cut short, so that he was plunged into adult relationships when he was hardly more than a boy. My greatest rival was his mother, but his memory of her had inevitably been transformed by her martyrdom: in Bob's mind, she had become the saint I could never be.

This unending striving for perfection and tension at home was a tremendous strain and I often felt exceedingly tired and depressed. Rather than stay at home and fight, I took flight. I would regularly join my sister for skiing holidays, often taking one or two of the children with me. But most of my traveling was more directly connected with research for my doctoral thesis, which took me frequently to France and Switzerland to explore private family archives and major libraries. Bob would continue to telephone me regularly and I would receive bouquets of flowers accompanied by notes like: "My favorite truant: Welcome to Geneva! I love you. Bob."

Those four postgraduate years at Oxford gave me the best possible grounding for researching and writing to a scholarly standard. I learned how and where to check my sources, to verify the credentials of people who gave me information, never to be content with approximation nor make any statement I could not justify with authentic documents. If for any reason I was unable to satisfy those exacting standards, then I had to say so clearly. Everything that has happened since Bob's death has made me wish that journalists could be made to observe that same kind of rigor. Perhaps readers might then be treated to less fiction masquerading as truth, more accurate information and less assertion of "facts" culled from unchecked sources.

I also took a university course on the use of computers to analyze word frequency in literary research. It was a new field at the time and was only well developed in France and Canada, but it was opportune for the purposes of my research. I decided to study my letters from this point of view and was greatly helped by a French professor in Nice who had worked on the vast new French dictionary, *Le Trésor de La Langue Française* (*The Treasure of the French Language*).

To help me compare the language of my own letter writers with that of well-known French writers of the same period, Professor Etienne Brunet created a special data bank for me, based on the new Frequency Dictionary from the *Trésor*. It was a fascinating aspect of my research—and also one of the most frustrating as I struggled to come to terms with the eccentricities of "George," the university computer, and the inevitability of the dictum, "Garbage in, garbage out!" By 1980 my thesis was ready, but unfortunately my principal examiner, Dr. Robert Shackleton, fell seriously ill. He was interested in my work and reluctant to hand over my thesis to a colleague for examination, and in the end I was to wait a whole year before my doctorate viva—an oral examination—in February 1981.

Three months earlier, Philip and his wife, Nilda, whom he had married in 1975, had returned from Argentina where they had been living since 1974 and were later joined by Marcela, Nilda's daughter. It was so good to have them back. Philip joined Pergamon Press and became the managing editor of a complex, multi-volume work, *The Encyclopedia of Materials Science and Engineering*. He was then to remain with Pergamon until his resignation in 1989. His return also enabled him to take part in a unique family occasion when I was presented with my "D.Phil" on a Saturday in mid-June and our three sons joined me to receive their own degrees that day—Kevin and Ian their B.A.s and Philip his M.A. All the other children made a great effort to come, too, especially Christine from California and Ghislaine from Madrid, where she was studying Spanish. After the ceremony in the Sheldonian Theatre, Oxford, we took a memorable photo for the album, with Bob and me surrounded by our children, all wearing their university gowns. Afterwards, we gave a celebratory lunch, attended by members of my French family, some of the dons who had helped me in my research and Dr. Shackleton as the guest of honor. When Bob got up to speak after lunch he was full of praise for me. Dr. Shackleton then followed and again there were more compliments and congratulations. I found it all very embarrassing and was relieved when it was my turn to say a few words. I stressed the forbearance Bob and the children had shown during those years of research. I knew that I had neglected some of my family duties, although I reminded them that I had done all my most crucial work between nightfall and daybreak. Above all, I wanted to thank my friend, Dr. Wendy Whitworth.

As a young postgraduate, Wendy had found herself teaching me French literature at St. Hugh's. Elected a Fellow when she was only twenty-one, she was one of the youngest Fellows in Oxford—if not the youngest—and a gifted teacher. I was old enough to be her mother, but we soon developed a creative working relationship, much more than that of pupil-teacher, which gave us both great intellectual satisfaction. We inspired each other and sparked off ideas like fireworks. Wendy's help was invaluable throughout my years at Oxford, and I in turn was able to assist her when she took a teaching job at Aix en Provence University only a few weeks after her marriage. Luckily for us both, Aix is close to our old family home in Mérindol, where a great many of our archives were located, and we arranged for her to assist in organizing the papers to earn extra cash for flights home to England. After that, she taught for a while at college, but eventually decided it was not the life for her and resigned. We remained in close contact, however, and during my doctorate years, she was always there to encourage, act as sounding board and urge me over the last hurdle when I was exhausted and suffering from the effects of my worsening relationship with Bob. Since then, we have continued to work together on all kinds of projects—Bob's family tree and biography, Pergamon's international Holocaust conference, translations, lectures and exhibitions—and Wendy also worked as a legal researcher for Bob until Maxwell Communication Corporation's (MCC) collapse. Over the years, we have developed a close friendship as well as a rare writing partnership. At times, our minds are so in tune that she can finish the sentence I have started with almost the exact words I would have chosen. As I wrote to her in 1981, a few days before my doctorate party: "You were always there, calm, knowledgeable, experienced, understanding, reliable: in every sense the best possible friend." Wendy has also been my principal collaborator in the writing of this book.

I couldn't help comparing Bob's fulsome praise for me that day with the way he sometimes treated me in private and the terrible crisis we had gone through in 1980 and early 1981. By then, Pergamon was thriving and Bob was once again a very successful man, but he was beginning to champ at the bit. True to form, as he reached a particular summit in his achievements he would invariably try, although unconsciously I think, to free himself from me. He was becoming insufferable at home, rather like a caged lion. I was getting frequent headaches, I couldn't sleep and was physically and mentally exhausted. Nothing I said was right, nothing I did met with his approval. If I talked, it was too loud. If I asked a question, I hadn't phrased it correctly. If I ventured an opinion, it was incomprehensible. I used to dread his phone calls, wondering every day what kind of mood he would be in, and lived in constant apprehension of what I might have forgotten to do for him. I could no longer endure constantly having to apologize to him; in fact, I felt as if I had to say "sorry" simply for being alive. As I wrote to him:

> I truly cannot live any longer without kindness and friendship. I am too lonely, too sick in my heart. Away from you, I may try and remember the man you used to be and not the one you have become: harsh, cruel, uncompromising, dictatorial, exceedingly selfish and inconsiderate, totally unaware of the feelings of others, least of all those who are loyal and devoted to you, those you take a sadistic pleasure in crushing and humiliating. The demeaning way in which you treat me is unforgivable and your language has deteriorated to such an extent that I feel ashamed that you should permit yourself to hurl such vulgar expressions and swear words in my direction, especially as most of the time, the reasons for your monstrous anger are so trivial. You talk in millions of pounds, and at the same time blast me for the money I spent on Ghislaine's room or the kitchen floor or the new lift so that I don't have to climb 60 feet of stairs all day long. Yet at the very same time you throw away a million pounds on the gaming tables. This is so galling that I cannot reconcile it with a sane family life.

In early December 1980, I took myself to Los Angeles to see Christine, whose marriage was giving us all great cause for concern. A couple of years previously, she had fallen in love with a young, penniless film director. Although he certainly had intelligence, charm and talent, he turned out to be unfaithful and a typical product of the California of the sixties. The marriage was a disaster and after less than two years, he had left her to carry on an affair with another woman. Christine was deeply upset and I wanted to go and comfort her. At the same time, she had told me about the Pritikin center, a health clinic in Los Angeles where they helped you lose weight successfully by changing both your eating habits and lifestyle. Christine was convinced that it might work for her father, so with Bob's consent and encouragement, I set off for another slimming course. The results were spectacular. I lost fifteen pounds in four weeks and acquired wonderfully healthy eating and living habits, some of which I have kept to this day. I read a great deal and had ample time for quiet thought during my long walks on the seashore and hours on the treadmill. I wrote to Bob every day, trying to analyze the state of our relationship and force him to consider where we should go from there. I sent him a quotation from a book I had been reading which depicted perfectly my state of mind on arrival at Pritikin.

All my ties to my own good life had slipped their moorings and I found myself hopelessly adrift in a sort of limbo that is hard to describe. Fear and deep anxiety gripped me, and I fell easy prey to depression and even melancholia with the end result of frustration at every turn. I feared everything—everyone. I no longer controlled my destiny—my destiny controlled me.[1]

The same book recommended a regime based on six cardinal principles: daily exercise, positive thinking, proper nutrition, emotional serenity, mental balance and objectivity, spiritual control and direction—which I decided to adopt in order to rebuild my shattered confidence. It certainly helped me to see things more clearly. As I wrote:

I could only see a vortex in which I was being swallowed. I know now that I won't let it happen. Now that you are in charge of your future again, what is it to be? A few years ago, you told me, "If I get us out of this mess, I shall leave you." Is it still on? At the same time, I said, "If you get us out of this mess, I shall get out of your life so I don't plague you any longer." Is that still what you want? I know that if I could persuade you to come here, in fifteen days you would be a different man; and if you stayed a month, you would be changed completely. The ocean brings me its wonderfully pungent saline smell, the sun is shining, the sand is all around me and I think of you, of us, of our children in one all-embracing sweep, you are still my world.

Just after my doctorate was awarded in February 1981, I wrote Bob a momentous letter, congratulating him on his recent successes, admiring his flair for business, but spelling out my analysis of

---

1. Stan L. Zundel, *I Climb to Live: Health and Transcendency on the Mountain* (privately published).

aspects of his behavior which I considered unacceptable and which had become clearer since my stay in Pritikin:

It seems somehow appropriate that my first letter based on the conclusions of my thesis should be written to you. My doctorate viva has merely confirmed my impression that I am not and never will be able to respond quickly orally: I need more time for reflection. In other words, good ideas always come to me afterwards. . . . That is certainly why the letter is really my domain, whilst you excel in the realm of conversation. With me, however, you no longer have conversations but communications in which you consider it your duty, rather like a Roman magister, to analyze every word I utter, correcting its delivery, pronunciation, motivation, intention and value. The result is that my conversation is stilted and false because I am thinking more of not annoying you than of telling you what I really want you to know. . . . All my joy, spontaneity and enthusiasm, all that is fundamental to my warm, loving and observant nature, all that deep-seated part of me that needs to surface and used to give you pleasure in the past—all that I now have to suppress in your presence. . . .

Alas, what I want to write to you is about the most negative and destructive aspect of your life, the one you keep for your family, for your Jekyll and Hyde personality makes you reserve the worst of yourself for those you claim to love best. It's sometimes amazing to watch you talking and acting with strangers—polite, attentive, oozing charm—and to compare this with your shameful behavior with me. . . . I simply could not live through the past year again: I reached absolute rock bottom and don't intend to spend the rest of my days like that. Working nonstop as you do, you are bound to make yourself ill, and in your state of health and exhaustion, your judgment is clouded: everyone else is wrong and you alone are right. But I can no longer wait for you to suggest a solution; I want to enjoy a time of relative calm, which I have certainly earned.

I will be sixty on March 11. That is the deadline I have set for major decisions affecting the rest of my life on earth. You, it seems, have decided to reconquer your name, reputation and position in the City, seeking the approval of the very people who ten years ago would have thrown you to the dogs. . . . There was in principle nothing to stop my sharing that new rise to fame with you, except that your behavior with me has changed so radically that you have extinguished all the reasons why I followed you without question. . . . If I were to endure all the humiliations you subject me to, all your outbursts, continual preaching, constant reproaches and criticism, I would need to feel there is a depth of love within you which corresponds to my own. Just occasionally, you would need to keep one of your promises and make me feel useful to you. . . . At the end of the day, all that is left now between us is the tenuous thread of correspondence—as long as you still consent to read my letters and I still have patience and optimism enough to write them. . . .

I don't think you have ever really taken the time to get to know me properly: you only saw the practical advantages of the well-brought-up girl, the fertile mother, the competent hostess, the hardworking woman of action. . . . You have always refused to recognize my deeply creative instincts, the poet, dreamer, writer and storyteller within me. You have tried so obstinately to turn me into something I am not, to mold me into a kind of super-efficient secretary. . . . All my life, in order to please you, I have forced myself to take on the most burdensome material tasks . . . when by preference I would have liked to write, draw and make music under the warm Mediterranean sun, breathing in the scented fragrances of the garrigue and pinewoods. . . .

For years, I've accepted it all—a complete lack of love and consideration, derision, condescension. I've put up with your sermons, your unjustified reproaches, your sudden absurd anger, your murderous moods for the most trivial of reasons. Your latest mania is to dramatize everything: it's almost as if your anger can only be appeased by the weekly ritual of family catharsis. Like the Hydra of the ancients, you have to devour your victim, one of your own children, every week. You cannot live without your ration of Maxwellian drama, accompanied by exorcism, yelling, threats, tears, gnashing of teeth, repentance and contrition. What I can't understand is how you managed so long to make me play a role in these absurd dramas. When I think that I wanted to re-create your murdered family, you make me regret it now that I see each one in turn become the object of your fury. . . . But of course, all their faults are laid at my door. . . .

Why can't you try and accept me for what I am, not for what you would like me to be? Why can't you allow the children to grow to maturity in their own way? We may neither of us live much longer. Isn't it time you adjusted to the wife of your youth and the children we have created?

There remains a great deal to do if you and I are going to resume a tolerable life together in Oxford. I'll give you until 9th March to reflect on possible solutions. . . . I am ready for all eventualities but no longer prepared to tolerate the hypocrisy of our relationship or accept the uncertainty of my future. . . . At Pritikin I finally realized that I do have the moral and physical courage to refuse to be insulted. . . . I will not stop loving you. . . .

I went on to offer Bob a number of solutions to our problems. There could be a complete separation, a de facto separation or a partial separation; or I could stay at Headington Hill Hall in more tolerable conditions of work and private life. If I were to do so, however, radical changes would be needed to help me cope with a workload that was often insane. I reminded him of my many responsibilities:

1. Running of Headington Hill Hall as a hotel and three-star restaurant
2. Dealing with accommodation requests, control of maintenance costs, upkeep and unfinished renovation of the Hall and Oxford properties
3. Establishing the guest house in St. Margaret's Road as a going concern and maintaining the other guest houses in Woodstock Road and the Hall's Lodge House
4. Organizing domestic arrangements for in-house conferences
5. Arranging and supervising large business parties
6. Liaising with the Executive Dining Room
7. Supervising the upkeep of the gardens, walls, sheds, sauna and barbecue kitchen
8. Supervising the restoration of the Park Lane flat
9. Liaising with your Oxford staff over your constantly changing schedule

10. Liaising with your London staff and housekeeper
11. Liaising with security

And I didn't even include the children in my list! As I expected, Bob took the line of least resistance. He wanted me to stay at Headington; it was by far the easiest solution and he always had a tendency to evade our personal problems rather than face them head on. But he did listen to my pleas and we reached a compromise that made me willing to give it another chance. Bob was very overworked, virtually living in London and therefore spending much less time on Pergamon's affairs. He needed me, he said, to keep an eye on things there and take a more active role in the company by representing him at business functions at home and abroad. He also agreed that I needed more help at home and allowed me to employ two extra staff to cope with the massive increase in entertaining since the business had started expanding again. With these improvements, my hopes were restored and life resumed its normal hectic course, with frequent trips to far-flung places, often at short notice when Bob decided he was too busy to go himself. On one occasion, I was dispatched to an important international pharmacology congress in Tokyo. Ian, who speaks Japanese, was to go with me, but he was traveling from New York. I still smile at the memory of meeting him under the huge polar bear in the main hall of Anchorage Airport. After the congress, our dear friends Min Chien and Keiko Lu invited me to their country home in the mountains, and I was also entertained in Kyoto by the wealthy businessman Ryoichi Sasakawa. I was also able to give my personal thanks to Dr. Ishizuka, the surgeon who had saved Ian's life in Tokyo a few years earlier. Before going to Oxford, Ian had spent a year in Japan studying Japanese language and literature at Sophia University, and barely a week after his arrival was rushed to hospital suffering from peritonitis. He made a good recovery, but it gave Bob and me a terrible scare.

Another time, I found myself representing Bob in Rome when Pergamon's first journal, *Spectrochimica Acta,* which had originally been acquired from the Vatican, was celebrating its fiftieth anniversary with a special symposium at the Pontifical Academy of Sciences in the Vatican. Our host was Bishop Dardozzi, dean of the Academy, who preferred to be called by his title of Ingeniere Dardozzi. The meetings took place in the lecture theaters of a magnificent seventeenth-century "villa," bequeathed to the Academy by a Pope and subsequently transformed into a prestigious center of science and research. Bob really should have been there himself, but as usual I was called in at the last minute. I was one of the few ladies present amongst a contingent of forty men.

Spectrochimica Acta's early history was described at that meeting as intimately connected to two powerful and influential forces: the Roman Catholic Church on the one hand and Robert Maxwell and Pergamon Press on the other. One of the highlights of that visit was a private tour of the Vatican City and its museum. There was also a memorable tête à tête lunch with Ingeniere Dardozzi, served by nuns who tiptoed around as we discussed the definition of death. The next Academy symposium was to discuss exactly that subject and after hearing my views and experiences with my son Michael, Ingeniere Dardozzi invited me to attend the meeting. He intimated that he would like His Holiness to hear such opinions directly from someone who had experienced that death is not the death of the heart but of the brain. I had also taken with me a set of the "Remembering for the Future" conference proceedings published by Pergamon—an important series of papers on Holocaust studies—as a gift for the Vatican Library. Bishop Dardozzi accepted them on behalf of his library, but asked whether it would be possible to have another set for the Pope himself, bound in white leather with red lettering, as was the tradition. I had these volumes prepared when I returned to Pergamon but am still waiting for a suitable opportunity to deliver them to His Holiness.

Representing Bob often took me on exotic adventures like this and all went well for a while, although at home the workload seemed to have increased tenfold as Bob's activities multiplied. He didn't have full-time domestic staff in London at the time, and all his laundry and valeting was brought back to Oxford to be done. I was still buying all his clothes and even his shoes. I carried on doing this until 1988 when Bob's favorite valet, Simon Grigg, a competent and charming young man who had joined his staff in 1986, began to share the task with me. Simon was then to travel constantly with Bob until January 1990 when he decided he wanted to gain experience abroad and left to work in Italy and France. Bob never had a personal valet until 1986; until then I and my domestic staff at Headington managed everything. But my two dear Filipinos, who by then had been with me for close on twenty years, could not possibly work any longer hours than they already did, and even with casual labor and extra help, it was no longer a viable proposition. There were big dinners almost every Friday for the Annual General Meetings of Pergamon journals, lunches every Saturday for Bob and his senior managers and sometimes even on Sundays as well. Mid-week, we would have Pergamon authors and editors as guests and I would be asked to represent Bob. Our guest houses were often full, and although we had staff in "situ," I needed to make sure all ran smoothly. Whenever there was a medical or scientific conference in Oxford, the organizer would invariably ask us to invite the participants to the Hall for a special reception. It was killing. During the course of 1981, I began to get more and more exhausted and eventually wrote to Bob in desperation, asking him to appoint a major domo to take charge of all the entertaining. In reply, he sent me a curt note, telling me that I was quite mad to propose such an idea!

Betty,
In addition to 4 servants, you ask for a major domo as a way of ensuring what? By adding more staff to our home, will this enable you to convince me that you care to avoid quarrels or avoid my complaints over the material side?
Bob.

He had of course simply no idea what it entailed to run a hotel-restaurant twenty-four hours a day, seven days a week, although other people were well aware of it. The lawyer John Levy, for instance, wrote to me on the day before he left Lewis Silkin & Partners in May 1980:

I should like to thank you for all of the hospitality you have shown to me over the years, particularly last year when I was such a frequent overnight visitor, and for the way you and all the children made me feel welcome at all times: the Headington Hill Hall Hotel definitely achieves a 5-star rating in the *Levy Guide*, an exclusive publication with a print number lower (but standards higher) than the *Guide Michelin*.

As autumn 1981 approached, a tempting offer of adventure took me away briefly from this strenuous routine, giving me time to think and strengthening my resolve not to accept it any longer. On my trip to California in 1980, I had met Arlene Blum, a friend of Isabel's who was a professional mountaineer and had led the first all-women team which conquered Annapurna, one of the highest peaks in the Himalayas. At the time, she was organizing another expedition to the Himalayas with Hugh Swift, an experienced mountaineer who spoke several Himalayan dialects. She was going to trek across the entire mountain range from east to west at high altitude—"The Great Himalayan Traverse," as she called it—and was planning to finance her trip by leading small groups of people on parts of the journey. The first of these smaller treks was to take place in Bhutan, aiming for the base camp of the sacred mountain, Chomolhari. In those days, Bhutan was only just opening up to tourism, but Arlene was known there and able to obtain all the necessary permits. Isabel and Arlene were both keen for me to join them.

I had loved mountaineering in my youth and was sorely tempted, even though I was nearly sixty. I felt very fit after my stay at Pritikin and decided to talk it over with Bob, who was reassured when he heard that three of my coclimbers would be Isabel, her boyfriend Dale Djerassi and his father Carl, a distinguished chemist and Pergamon author whom I liked and knew well. Isabel and Dale, both film producers, had decided to make a film on Bhutan and had good introductions to the Bhutanese authorities through Isabel's friend Michael Aris, an Oxford don who had been tutor to the young King of Bhutan. It was an exciting prospect, an opportunity I felt I could not miss.

We left in late September, flying via Calcutta to Bagdogra and drove into Bhutan along a primitive road to the small town of Paro, 8,600 feet above sea level, ready to start the trek. That was where I first met my little pony Tsi Tsi, typical of those wiry mountain breeds, with their uncanny knack for picking a way over high mountain trails, across precariously balanced narrow bridges and down paths of old torrents strewn with boulders. The ponies used for trekking have a hard, wooden saddle with a long, pointed pommel which you cling on to as they climb the steep, rocky slopes. You barely need to use the reins since the ponies choose their own path with infallible instinct and you ride with long stirrups made of rope, allowing you to move in the saddle to maintain your balance. At the beginning, I would either find myself slipping perilously over the horse's neck or painfully flung backwards with my crotch squeezed up against the pommel, but I did eventually become quite an expert! Trekking at high altitudes, you cannot carry very much because of the rarefied oxygen in the air, so although Arlene's group was only fourteen people, we had quite a procession of Sherpa guides, horsemen, cooks and porters—some thirty people in total—accompanying us. It was all essential because for three weeks we would be up in remote areas with no access to lodging or food and medical supplies. Nem, our official leader, was a young well-educated Bhutanese who spoke good English and was the King's cousin. Over the next three weeks, we were to get to know him well and understand much more about the Bhutanese who are very different from the Nepalese and peoples of nearby India. Originally from Tibet, they are a strong and sturdy mountain race, generally quite tall and expert at their national sport of archery. As yet, their wise young monarch has protected them from excessive tourism and they are content with their traditional simple, healthy life.

Our trek towards the base camp of Chomolhari took us through high mountain passes with spectacular views of the East Himalayan chain and Mount Everest ever dominant in the distance. We would walk up to seven hours a day, but being the "grandmother" of the party, I would also ride part of the way. Our porters would go on ahead to set up camp, almost running along the mountain paths. As the paths twisted and turned, we would catch sight of them in the distance, their heavily laden ponies tinkling their little bells and easily recognizable by the red-and-blue flags which decorated their collars. Camp was always pitched around 12,000 feet and from there we would climb on to the next pass, most of them ranging between 15,000 and 17,000 feet. We journeyed through medieval villages with peasants using oxen and primitive wooden plows to till their land. Once on the other side of the passes, we came upon immense high plateaux where yak herders camped in their fabulous black tents made of yaks' hair. The yaks themselves seemed prehistoric-giant creatures, and their milk and cheese is greatly prized by the Bhutanese. I remember being invited inside one of those smoky tents, home to an entire family, and being offered tea which tasted like salty stock, with thick yak's cream floating on top. Lovely Mongolian-featured daughters prepared cheeses in huge copper cauldrons. They were wearing Bhutanese national costume—long woolen skirts and embroidered waistcoats over wide-sleeved blouses, with brightly colored silver and beaded jewelry. The men were clad in thick woolen robes, intricately pleated and held in position at the waist by a slim belt called the *kira*.

At times, riding was even more difficult than walking and I remember being frightened most of the time as we negotiated the screes and came so terrifyingly near the precipices that I had to look the other way! One day, we came close to losing one of the horses when he bolted off into the distance after Carl had dismounted. The horseman Kado immediately ran after him, shouting at me to follow on my pony. Soon all the Sherpas were running in all directions, trying to stop the runaway horse and yelling instructions in my direction. I shot off in hot pursuit down the steep rocky slopes, only too aware of the trouble we would be in if we found ourselves one horse short. After some confusion, Kado eventually managed to catch the runaway and headed back towards me at full speed. He grabbed my horse's reins as he drew alongside me, then we galloped back together at a furious pace, making a thunderous entrance into our camp.

That night, alone in my tent and muffled up against the cold, I wrote a graphic description of the whole episode in my diary, feeling thankful that I had survived the experience without injury. Those nights were freezing cold, and you needed the very best equipment and clothing to survive, although in the daytime when the sun was out, cotton shorts and a T-shirt were quite sufficient. In the morning, we were woken at five with a bowl of hot water for washing, but I would always wash again in the icy-cold water of the mountain stream. It was a habit I had acquired in "Kneippland" and I found it very invigorating. Then, after breakfast, we would start our trek at daybreak, climbing up towards the pass, crossing the high plateaux and descending to our next camp, which we usually reached around five or six in the evening.

Although we traveled as a group and met at lunch to exchange impressions, as we walked we were stretched out in a long line, going at our own pace, much too short of breath to talk, with Isabel and Dale filming along the way. Feeling at peace with myself, away from it all, I had ample time to reflect on my problems. During rest periods, I would read Peter Matthiessen's *The Snow Leopard,* which sustained me with inspiring Zen Buddhist quotations and its account of a difficult personal relationship. I felt greatly in sympathy with the author as I read, "Between clinging and letting go, I feel a terrible struggle. This is a fine chance to let go, to win my life by losing it."[2] This feeling of humility and of deeper enlightenment was enhanced by the silence all around. It is difficult for anyone who has never been at a high altitude to imagine the quality of the surrounding silence. It is quite unlike any silence you may experience anywhere else. It is thick and pure, disturbed only by the occasional cracking of the ice on a glacier a mile away. It may sound trite, but you really do feel nearer to heaven and the divine. The rarefied oxygen changes your normal perception of life, inducing a state of euphoria which eases the burden of your earthbound worries. Though we talked little on the trek, I was never lonely. I found myself thinking more clearly and with better perspective and could contemplate my future

---

2. Peter Matthiessen, *The Snow Leopard* (London: Chatto & Windus), p. 140.

with much greater objectivity. By my own choice, I was battling with extreme physical demands and at the same time reflecting on the meaning of my life. I was "returned into myself,"[3] seeking my destiny, my own particular laws for the internal way, the Tao of the Chinese. I thought about my past life, remembered my childhood full of mystery and promise. How was it that when I had attained what I thought I wanted in life, it had not brought me fulfillment?

My overriding memories of that unforgettable experience center on unbroken visions of snowcapped mountains, monasteries perched like eagles' nests in impregnable positions, traveling Buddhist monks in their red robes, high mountain passes with lilting names like Lathila, Thombala, Yalela and Yusela. Camps with equally quaint names—Lingshi, Shodug and Yusholawoma—whose little blue tents in the distance gave us the courage to continue. Dzongs or fortresses built four hundred years ago set high on ridges with commanding views of several valleys. Steep descents of 1,200 feet amidst sheer, huge rocks, plateau after plateau, lake after lake, torrent after torrent, endless herds of yaks and blue sheep, whole vistas of deep blue gentian, edelweiss and wild marijuana growing beside the mountain tracks, terraces of rice paddies, forests of rhododendrons, hibiscus and other luscious vegetation. White prayer banners flapping in the wind, sweet-natured yet tough Sherpas, sun-drenched valleys, crystal clear streams cascading their glitter down the mountainside and green rivers with stones like emeralds. Hair-raising rides through rocky hollows and stone screes. The feeling of exhaustion and elation on reaching Gepotengkha camp at the base of Chomolhari.

Before I flew back to London, I decided to go to Calcutta to visit Mother Teresa's mission there. I wanted to find out more about her great humanitarian work amongst orphans, lepers, the sick and dying. Whilst I had been literally on top of the world, I had come to the conclusion that if ever I parted from Bob, I would never be able to plunge straight away into an insipid, everyday life. I would need first to go and help those much worse off than myself, touching real human misery before I decided what to do with the rest of my life. Unfortunately Mother Teresa was not in Calcutta when I visited and it was to be Bob who met her some years later when he supported one of her fund-raising appeals. But I did have a frank discussion with the sister in charge of the main convent about what I might be

---

3. *Ibid.*, p. 213.

able to do to help. What worried me most was not the hard work they undertook, but the fact that I might not be able to adapt to their very rigorous and austere living conditions, nor be strong enough in health to cope without Western conditions of hygiene. I did not want to become a burden rather than a help, but I did seriously consider living in Calcutta for a couple of years, seeking to ease my own unhappiness by relieving the suffering of others.

Two years later, I was to join another trek, again with Arlene, Dale and Isabel, but this time to Nepal. It was a different, but similar experience, although my physical courage was even more severely tested. I had to cross handmade suspension bridges balanced hazardously over fast-flowing rivers and negotiate sheer rock faces from which all traces of paths had been washed away by the last monsoon. I could say with Peter Matthiessen that this was the best trip I had ever made, "tough enough so that we feel we have really accomplished something, but not so tough that it wiped us out entirely."[4]

My trekking expeditions in the Himalayas certainly changed me for ever. They distanced me from my problems, allowed me time to think and above all gave me confidence. I came back from them much stronger, both mentally and physically.

I returned from Bhutan in 1981 to find that nothing had really changed on the home front. I was almost immediately plunged back into Bob's hectic lifestyle of nonstop entertaining and traveling, but was even more determined than before to make him give me more help. He was doing far too much, was consequently overtired and lost his temper more and more frequently. I managed to convince him that in order to be sure of enjoying the great future he was carving out for himself, he needed to take major decisions about his health, beginning with losing some weight. I persuaded him that he should go to the Pritikin clinic to learn the essentials of a healthier attitude to food and therefore a healthier life. I booked us both into the Los Angeles clinic for three weeks in late December 1981, hoping that if I could only get him there and have him taken in hand by Nathan Pritikin himself, I might succeed in making him alter his eating habits. At the same time we decided to spend Christmas Day with the children in San Francisco before they all left to go skiing upstate.

---

4. *Ibid.*, p. 229.

I left England two days before Bob, intending to make sure that all was prepared for his arrival and that we had the best suite in the clinic. Unfortunately, when Bob arrived on Christmas Eve, Nathan was not there and Bob was not seen immediately by the clinic's medical team. He went to eat in the restaurant and of course hated it. Obviously, the health center was not the Ritz! Although Pritikin had recently moved into the premises of a once famed hotel, it was in need of some refurbishment. Bob started ranting and raving at me. How could I possibly have thought of taking him to that flea pit? Was I out of my mind? He ordered me to pack his bags, since he was leaving immediately. This developed into an almighty row, with Bob accusing me of being stupid, incompetent and incapable of following him in his newly successful career. It was so bad that day that we decided we really should part.

He did, however, agree to spend Christmas Day with the children, most of whom were in America. It was one of the most miserable Christmases we ever spent together. We were cooped up in the penthouse suite of a hotel whose best feature was its extensive view of San Francisco Bay and the Golden Gate Bridge. Bob was at his absolute worst and Ghislaine the scapegoat that time. We told the children openly that we had decided to separate, but they were not greatly shocked. They all thought it would be better than the tension and awful rows they were witnessing more and more frequently. Bob then decided to go and have a week's holiday with our friend Dolly Burns in Jamaica. Dolly was the daughter of Lord Duveen, the peer who gave his collection of French and English Impressionists to the National Gallery along with a huge donation which helped to finance the establishment of the Tate Gallery. She had a beautiful house in Montego Bay where we had previously stayed together and a home in Mayfair where she entertained politicians, earning herself the nickname of "the Gucci Socialist." It was the only house I have ever visited where a most exquisite painting (in this case a Marie Laurencin) had to be hung in the bathroom because all the other walls were crammed full of even better pictures by greater painters.

After Bob left for Jamaica, I went back to Pritikin, but I was dejected and my heart no longer in it. I went home to Oxford by myself. From Jamaica, Bob went immediately back to the States on business. I did not see him for several weeks although he did telephone me and we spoke amicably; but I heard no more about the separation. I was unhappy at being left in limbo and thought that the proposed manner of our parting was unworthy of two intelligent people who had been married for thirty-seven years. I decided to carry on as normal and see what happened on Bob's return. By the time we saw each other again in early February, there had been plenty of time to think things over and Bob had realized he still needed me. He wanted me to look after Pergamon and hold the fort in Oxford. I agreed, pending time to look honestly at where we were both going, and laid down some conditions, not least of which was the appointment of a trained and experienced major domo. Over the next month, I carried on doing all Bob's entertaining as usual, but inquired at regular intervals about my promised professional help. When nothing had materialized by March 1982, I decided to send him my resignation, effective April 5, from all responsibilities connected with running the Headington Hotel. I tried a humorous approach with the last of my "End-Basket" memos on my birthday, March 11:

To Robert Maxwell, Urgent attention from the local branch of the HFU: Home Front Union.

The Hall on the Hill administrative staff chapel sends greetings and congratulations to Brother Maxwell on his recent spectacular achievements and the Establishment's recognition of his genius, originality and effectiveness in carrying out immensely complex and difficult plans. They respectfully draw his attention to the worrying fate of the longest-serving employee with 36 years active service in the End-Basket department of the company. They suggest consultation with either Professor De Bono, a Russian specialist in brainwashing or member of the British Hypnotists' Society on how to reprogram brain of imaginative, poetic and artistic expert in Romantic written communication, with no training in hotel or office management, to mind-reader and numerate, logical, oral communicator to suit exacting, impatient, overworked boss. After sustained efforts over many years and honest desire to continue loyally to serve where recognized talents well suited, subject not unwilling, but unable to achieve desired transformation unaided. In our opinion needs expert advice and help on a regular basis until requested personality change accomplished. Please advise urgently how to proceed.
    Signed: Hotel manager, Restaurant Major Domo, First floor manager, Penthouse suites supervisor, Cellar stock clerk, Warehouse storekeeper, Office private secretary, Office typist, Office filing clerk, Hall receptionist, Hall translator, Hall accountant, Hall insurance clerk, Hall driver, Hall porter, Private lines day shift switchboard operator, Private lines night shift operator, Bell captain, Bell boy, Night watchman, and End-basket disposal unit.

This approach got me nowhere and I realized I would have to take more drastic action. I took my pen and wrote:

My darling,
Since you obviously think that I do nothing and that the house runs very well on its own, I am leaving for France. If and when you find out for yourself that I am right and you are wrong, and you hire extra servants and a major domo, I'll come back, not before. Good-bye, farewell,
Betty

I stayed away for two months. Soon after my departure in April, Bob phoned me to say that he would definitely find a major domo, but I insisted on my conditions and refused to return until he had actually short-listed several for interview. Whilst I was in France, Bob would phone me almost daily, asking me to come back, but I stood my ground. By mid-April, he decided to come and see me to talk things over and I planned to spend a few days with him in Tignes, staying in a tiny apartment I had inherited there. I met him in Geneva and we drove back to France together, stopping en route for a memorable dinner at Le Père Bise, a three-star restaurant on Lake Annecy. We drove to Tignes the next day. Bob liked the resort and had visited it before when we spent a very happy family Christmas there in 1972. That time, we had stayed in my sister's large apartment next door to mine. He felt cooped up in my small flat and decided that we ought to look for better accommodation. By sheer good fortune, we happened to find a really delightful, large apartment overlooking the lake which the former mayor of Tignes was selling. Bob loved it and decided there and then to buy it jointly with me. In later years, I was able to enlarge it further by purchasing adjoining properties myself. We were relaxed together in those few days in Tignes, and before he left for London, Bob promised to appoint a major domo as quickly as possible. He came back at the end of April to sign the contract to buy the flat and I returned to England at the end of May to meet my new major domo, Mike Day. At long last I was relieved of the material side of managing the entertaining and guest houses. I had to smile though, when soon after his arrival, he made Bob agree to double the staff immediately!

It was whilst I was in France, waiting for Bob to see sense, that I made an even more major decision, but this time without telling him anything about it. I had been wanting to buy a house in France for my retirement for many years, but whilst Bob had always been in agreement, he continually procrastinated. When I came across a partially reconstructed ruin near my sister's small farmhouse in the Lot et Garonne, I knew that I had found exactly what I was looking for. I sold some shares I owned to buy the house and its small holding of land. Meanwhile, my architect nephew, Patrick Vittoz, drew up plans to turn it into a family home to suit my taste and requirements. It became my secret dream, my refuge when things got too tough. Although I often felt guilty at hiding all this from Bob, I waited until my sixty-third birthday in 1984 before I breathed a word of my dream house to him. When I did eventually tell him, he was pleased for me and raised no objections, but never gave me any money for it. He only once came to the house and that was in late August 1991, barely two months before he died, for a party we gave to celebrate Ian's wedding. Knowing that he liked the warm climate of the south of France and might even be an invalid one day, I had had a special ground-floor suite built with him in mind which he used for just two nights. He was most impressed, amazed, I think, at what I had achieved, and said so to Kevin, although never personally to me.

It took Bob just five years to reestablish Pergamon to its former position as one of the world's leading scientific publishers and information providers. By then, he was on the lookout for new business opportunities, especially in the communications and printing sectors. In a dawn raid in July 1980, he bought a 29 percent stake in the ailing British Printing Corporation (BPC), then the largest printing company in Europe. Whilst he knew of its dire financial position, his previous dealings with the company had made him aware that it was badly managed but had great potential. This action provoked a wave of press profiles as he "bounced back" into the public arena, with prominence given to Jacob Rothschild's famous comment, "I've shot this man seventeen times and he's still alive." He was, as the papers said, a little more mellow, a little less vociferous, no longer courting the limelight, and at this stage issued a firm denial that he was interested in bidding for the company. By early 1981, however, BPC was fast heading towards bankruptcy and Bob was the company's last chance. The company's bankers, National Westminster, had confidence in him and discussions of a plan to patch up the giant company's tattered finances centered around Bob's involvement. With a cash injection from Pergamon of £10 million and a further advance from the bank, the deal was done and Bob became deputy chairman and chief executive, with Lord Kearton as chairman. But the rescue and reconstruction of BPC would be no easy task. As Lord Kearton told the *Financial Times* in February 1981, "I'm always interested in solving difficulties—and believe me this is going to be difficult. BPC is in a very desperate state. . . . But Robert Maxwell has this enormous dynamism. Just what will be needed for the most difficult job I've ever seen anybody take on."

Bob swiftly set about the radical surgery required. It meant heavy layoffs and the closure of several BPC plants, but the only alternative was for the whole company to go under, with the loss of 12,000 jobs. He immediately made a helicopter tour of BPC's many companies all over the country as he put together the details of his survival plan. He even moved his bed into the Covent Garden headquarters so as not to waste any time. There were ferocious battles with the unions, but Bob was tenacious and BPC was soon on the road to recovery. By the summer of 1981, Lord Kearton resigned, confident that the future of the company was assured, as indeed it was. On his last official day with BPC, he wrote to Bob: "Your courage in taking on the task of restoring and rehabilitating BPC was immense and your achievements to date have matched the challenge. . . . With your leadership, energy, imagination, panache and flair, BPC should do very well."

By the second half of 1981, the company was "out of the terminal ward," as Bob put it, and recovering strongly. It had undergone a complete restructuring and in early 1982 its name was changed to the British Printing and Communication Corporation (BPCC) to reflect an important new field of interest for the company. Bob's success in turning the group around brought him many congratulatory letters from leading politicians. Tory MP and former Minister Geoffrey Rippon considered it a splendid example of what teamwork can achieve and commented, "If everyone took your advice to heart, we would indeed all have something to be proud about," whilst Labor MP and former Minister Fred Mulley described the turn-round as "remarkable" and lamented that the same dramatic events were not happening in the Labor party. The MP Leo Abse's letter made Bob laugh: "You are as superb an entrepreneur as you are disastrous a politician."

With his success with BPCC, there seemed to be no stopping the rise of the phoenix. Bob was in an ebullient mood and when we discussed plans for Christmas 1983, he suggested his favorite type of holiday relaxation—a cruise. That year we chartered the yacht *Le Bonheur* for a Caribbean cruise to the enchanting islands of Guadaloupe and Martinique. As usual when he was on a boat, Bob was much more normal and relaxed. He liked having the children around, and conversation could be challenging and exhilarating. Yet even then, when the children were all adults, he found it difficult to abandon his pater familias attitude. That Caribbean cruise took place soon after Kevin and Bob had had a heated argument over

Kevin's girlfriend, Pandora. The two had been going out together for four years, but Bob thought Kevin was too young to get married—it would interfere with his business training. He sent Kevin to America for two years, but contrary to Bob's wishes, Pandora visited him there. As far as Bob was concerned, that constituted a breach of trust, and he relieved Kevin of his duties in the States on the spot. Although Kevin was invited on the cruise in the hopes of patching up their differences, Bob had not invited Pandora, and Kevin declined, wanting to spend Christmas with her in England. Bob was furious; for him it was a matter of principle. If Kevin could not be trusted to carry out his father's instructions, however painful, for a brief time, he could not be relied upon at all. For his part, Kevin had decided to draw the line at what he considered unjustified intrusion into his personal life. After four years with Pandora, he knew his own mind; she was the girl for him and she in no way impeded the performance of his professional duties. They went their separate ways that Christmas and I was caught in the middle, trying to convince Bob that he had to take a more understanding approach to his grown-up son. It was virtually a repeat performance of Bob's fallout with Ian three years previously.

As usual on our cruises and family holidays, Bob still insisted that we all take turns in writing the holiday log book. His own handwriting was almost illegible because as a child he had been naturally left-handed but was forced to write with his right hand, so he dictated his own contribution to me:

Regrettably, the case of Kevin and Pandora came up. For the umpteenth time, the whole of my family disregarded what they know to be true. If Kevin was not determined to force the issue of Pandora, he and I could start to rebuild our bridge of confidence. To a man, everybody shouts "You don't like Pandora." When I query, "What the hell has that got to do with the relationship between Kevin and me?" everybody looks as if they've seen the golden calf. I am not saying that he can't marry her in due course, let's say in two or three years from now. I repeat again the principle by which I live and will die. In return for my trust in members of my family and my total support of them, I am entitled to and look for total support and trust in return. Any member of the family, like Kevin, who arrogantly decides that he knows better than me what is best for him at the present stage of his life must take the consequences.

Sometimes, Bob's dictatorial behavior on cruises was directed at the captain of the ship, with whom he discussed the yacht's route. Although he had great respect for his captains and would usually bow to their superior knowledge of the sea, weather and coastline, there were occasions when Bob would insist on a particular itinerary. I remember one cruise on the *Southern Breeze* which we started in Athens, intending to head for the Turkish Coast. After visiting Rhodes, we set sail for Istanbul where I took the children to see all my favorite haunts. But we hardly had time to do justice to the city before Bob decided, quite suddenly, to take up an invitation he had been given by the Bulgarian president, Todor Zhivkov, to visit him in Varna, the finest Bulgarian resort on the Black Sea. When Bob instructed the captain to head for the iron gates of classical myth and forbidden territory, I really thought the skipper was going to faint. He had never in all his career been further than the Bosphorus and the mere idea of entering unfamiliar waters made him go pale with fright. Bob insisted, however, and off we sailed. As we cruised along, the waters got distinctly blacker and I began to wonder who on earth would choose to live in that forsaken part of the world. I could only think of Ovid's "Laments" and his description of his own exile there: "a place alas, no fortunate man should visit."

As we entered Bulgarian waters, the captain was becoming increasingly agitated, partly because he had no Bulgarian flag. I hastily sewed one together from a red tea cloth, white napkin and green hand towel (which became a conversation piece at ambassadorial dinners for months following). It was not long before naval police drew alongside and boarded the *Southern Breeze*. Bob answered their questions in his best Bulgarian, saying that he was a guest of the president, although Zhivkov, I am sure, had never imagined that Bob might arrive by sea. By the time we entered the huge harbor of Varna, the captain was practically a nervous wreck, with Bob standing alongside him directing operations. Seeing an enormous Russian destroyer, Bob said to him, "Lay anchor right alongside her." I shall never forget the entire crew of that enormous warship staring down at us whilst we gazed up at them, neither side knowing what to make of the other. After frantic phone calls, a police motor launch appeared to lead us to another part of the harbor: we had sailed, completely unaware, into a military zone that was totally forbidden to civilians!

Later that night, as we sat down to dinner, we were again boarded by naval police, who told us that the president was unfortunately detained in Sofia. He had, however, given instructions for us to be taken to his private "villa" a little further along the coast.

So after midnight, carrying some hastily packed luggage, we embarked on the presidential motorboat and soon found ourselves landing at the jetty of a huge palace. We were instantly surrounded by an army of servants who had probably been woken up to serve us dinner and look after us. The next day, we went for a swim in a secluded cove just below the terraces, having been told that the president's private beach was the only place on the Bulgarian coast that was regularly cleared of stinging jelly fish. Yet some of us stepped on sea urchins which had not been cleared from the sea bed. By the time we got back to the *Southern Breeze,* we heaved a sigh of relief and made for Istanbul and more familiar shores with great haste.

Kevin and Bob were to remain estranged for the best part of a year. Kevin went to work for an American-owned publishing company in the south of England, and Bob, who missed him greatly, refused to back down. Matters came to a head again over Kevin's decision to marry Pandora in May 1984. Up to the last minute, I was unsure whether Bob would even go to the wedding and he was threatening to stop me and the other children from going, too, as he had done with Philip's wedding in Latin America seven years earlier to which he had also been vehemently opposed. At that time, I had caved in, as had the grown-up children, when he had raised concerns about the civil war raging in Argentina and blackmailed us by threatening to cut off all financial support. I was also afraid that his anger would rebound on the younger children. This time, however, I decided I was going irrespective of the consequences, and all the other children took the same line. Bob had misjudged the strength of tribal feeling: we would instinctively give our support to the one who was in the doghouse. Of course, I was accused of leading the rebellion, but Bob did attend the wedding in the end. He stayed for a reasonable length of time, although he tore me away from the festivities as soon as it was decent for us to leave. It was to be some months before Kevin and Bob patched up their quarrel and Kevin rejoined the business. Although father and son were both deeply upset by the whole episode, it gave Kevin the chance to prove to himself and to Bob that he could make a living on his own. As a result of the shared painful experiences of having fallen out with their father, it also brought Kevin and Ian closer together than ever before, with Ian being his brother's best man at his wedding—a real show of fraternal solidarity in the face of paternal misgiving. By then Bob had plunged headlong into an acquisition that distracted him completely from family problems.

* * *

When in July 1984 an opportunity arose to acquire the Labor-supporting *Daily Mirror*, Bob was ready for fresh challenges. He had always harbored ambitions to own a newspaper but had been defeated in the past by Rupert Murdoch for the *News of the World*, the *Sun* and in 1981 for the *Times*. A newspaper co-operative venture in 1975 in Scotland, the *Scottish Daily News*, had been short-lived and provoked great controversy but had not cured Bob of his yearning to become a newspaper baron. The strategy he used to acquire the Mirror Group is by now well known: by negotiating to buy the *Observer* and subsequently increasing his stake in Express Newspapers, publishers of the *Daily Express* and *Sunday Express*, he put the hounds off the track, whilst coolly laying his hands on another of Fleet Street's jewels. By July 13, 1984, the ten-day battle was over and another lifelong dream had been realized: Bob agreed to pay Reed International £113.4 million for Mirror Group Newspapers.

He was jubilant and immensely touched by the flood of letters he received from friends and well-wishers. Lord Kearton echoed Bob's real reasons for wanting to buy a newspaper when he said, "I am absolutely delighted that you have brought it off; you will have a national platform. I hope your voice will pull the nation forwards. You can do it like no one else can. You are unique."

Bob's sister, Sylvia, was convinced that his determination to acquire a newspaper stemmed from his memory of his mother's avid reading and her recognition of newspapers as a force for political change. Michael Foot wrote to wish Bob the best of luck and commented, "If the Labor party can recover and win the next election, as I am sure we can, then one of the events which will have led to it will be your arrival at Mirror Newspapers. You seem to have got off to a flying start."

Vere Harmsworth, chairman of Associated Newspapers, recognized the problems Bob would be facing, "You will bring much needed energy and efficiency to that indulgent and Trotskyite organization. I have always had a soft spot for the *Mirror* because as you well know it was founded by my great uncle and for many years owned by my grandfather."

Hugh Cudlipp, a legend from the *Mirror*'s past, was absolutely right in his analysis: "The financial operation to acquire the citadel was devastatingly brilliant, but being personally responsible for the policy of the newspapers will give you greater enjoyment and fulfillment than anything else you have achieved so far. . . . I wish you good luck and good fortune."

Within days of receiving this letter, Bob was in touch with Cudlipp. Acknowledging his own inexperience in the world of newspapers, he persuaded him to become his personal consultant on the revitalization of the paper—"A brilliant stroke," according to the former editor of the *Times,* Harold Evans. This appointment was to be the start of a correspondence which traces those early days of Bob's *Mirror* ownership in fascinating detail. Reading these letters and memos today, I am struck by Cudlipp's frank and sensible advice—and even more so by the fact that Bob listened to most of it. It was Cudlipp, for instance, who suggested that the *Mirror* should hire a train to bring the paper to the British people, that Bob should use the title "Publisher" not "Proprietor," that he should launch a major "Forward with Britain" campaign and not delay the appointment of an independent ombudsman. His memos contained all kinds of advice on the paper's columns and on particular journalists, on "phony writing" that is an insult to the reader's intelligence, on the uselessness of vendettas against other newspaper publishers, the right formula for a gossip page, typographical overkill and so on. Cudlipp was well aware that "The standing of the British press in the eyes of the British public has never been lower than it is today. Outside Fleet Street, you will rarely hear a word of respect for newspapers." His general feeling was that Fleet Street was too preoccupied with producing newspapers to impress or irritate commercial rivals.

By October 1984, he was writing to congratulate Bob on immense and dramatic improvements to the paper: "Its confidence—and essential insolence, irreverence and enterprise—have been restored after ten years in the wilderness. It is now again the foremost campaigning newspaper," but he still complained that the *Mirror* was trying to shout its rivals off the newsstands with oversize headline type. More significantly, he advised Bob not to allow stories about himself to appear too frequently in the paper. As he wrote:

In 1984, it is true to say that anyone in the United Kingdom not aware that all the Mirror Group Newspapers are now published By Robert Maxwell must be deaf, dumb, blind or all three. . . . But from now on, I believe the Editors will be doing you an acute disservice if they mention the publisher's name too frequently in his own newspapers.

There was no doubt that Bob should have listened more closely to that piece of advice. There were, inevitably, some matters over which they agreed to differ. Bob, for instance, was very keen to appoint the first woman editor of a national newspaper (and did in fact appoint Eve Pollard editor of the *Sunday Mirror* in 1987), but Cudlipp's view was:

There is obviously no anti-feminine prejudice on my part. I appointed the first Fleet Street woman assistant editor, associate editor, director of promotions and publicity, and put the first woman on the board of a national newspaper. But to appoint a woman as Editor of a national daily or Sunday newspaper is a different matter. . . . To have any hope of being a successful Editor of a national newspaper requires far more experience than has come the way of a woman news reporter or woman writer of articles.

Cudlipp's consultancy agreement ended amicably in May 1986 and he wrote to Bob to say how much he had enjoyed their working relationship. In the same letter, he gave his impressions of the distance the *Mirror* had traveled in just under two years: "The paper is now being EDITED. It has cohesion: it is no longer a lot of different things slung together and called a newspaper. It has no longer got pop stars on every page and there is serious material that an intelligent person would not be ashamed to be caught reading."

On the family front, that first summer of Bob's ownership of the *Mirror* had been marked with the happiness of Isabel's marriage to Dale Djerassi, but near tragedy was soon to follow. I had gone to spend the summer holidays in France, where Isabel and Dale joined me on a delayed honeymoon trip. A few days after they arrived at my sister Vonnic's house in the Lot et Garonne, Isabel suddenly fell ill with a very high temperature. Sensing that this was no ordinary fever, Ian, who was also staying there, drove her straight to Paris where Vonnic had arranged to have her admitted to the same hospital where her life had been saved as a baby. The disagnosis of leptospirosis, a rare but often fatal disease, was all the more worrying because Isabel was pregnant and the illness endangered both her and her unborn child. Those were very anxious days at her bedside, but Isabel gradually pulled through. The miracle was that her son Alexander, our first grandchild, although born very prematurely, survived unscathed and has grown into a healthy and superactive youngster.

After Bob's acquisition of the *Mirror*, his business empire grew at an astonishing rate. I watched it all happening, but by now I was relegated more and more to the sidelines and learned more from the newspapers than I did from Bob himself. I would read the cuttings sent by his press officer, especially when it was time to write the preface for the annual scrapbook for our family records. I would also do some hasty homework when sent to a function for a firm I had never heard of. I would insist on receiving Bob's diary every week, but it rarely corresponded with reality. There were more and more business ventures that he didn't have time or did not want to share the details with me, although he still continually sent me to represent him at business social functions at home and abroad. He must have sensed my growing trepidation about this dramatic expansion. My instincts told me that he was taking on too much, that somewhere along the way he was bound to step into a mine field. I looked on in bewilderment as the group's operations became staggeringly diversified during the late eighties—newspapers, television, helicopters, football—and increasingly international. All of this happened so fast that I could hardly keep up with it or sort out what he was doing. He was like a tornado spiraling from one end of the world to the other.

Perhaps I should have insisted on being told more about what he was doing, but I found myself caught up in a constant swirl of engagements, frequently representing Bob on my own: lunches and business dinners, banquets, dances, private and public functions, in this country and abroad. He would agree to sit on numerous charity committees, but I was often the one dispatched to attend the meetings, arrange fund-raising receptions and contact potential donors. At other times, we would find ourselves sitting side by side at a table and use these rare moments together in a crowded room to exchange essential information on the next move of our crazy lives—and people would envy us our obvious happiness at being together!

Whatever the effects on his vanity, the truth is that he was courted by world leaders, powerful businessmen and financiers. He had easy access to Mikhail Gorbachev, François Mitterrand, Ronald Reagan, Margaret Thatcher, Deng Xiao-ping and Yitzhak Shamir. Even though they well knew that Bob reveled in and publicized his association with them, they also recognized that his was a brilliant mind, incisive, quick, inventive. They sought his advice and they got what they came for. His name was continually to the fore. And when, after a bitter eight-month takeover battle in 1988, he made the fateful acquisition of Macmillan, the great American publishing company which also owned the language-teaching company Berlitz for the massive sum of $2.7 billion, he was triumphant. At one swoop, he had achieved what had been his driving ambition for over a decade: the Maxwell Group had become one of the world's biggest communication companies. Yet the price of his victory—some $3 billion in loans at the start of an international recession and economic crisis—brought with it suffocating, inescapable financial pressures, which only got worse in the years to come. I see now that it was the beginning of the end.

Nineteen-eighty-eight was the culmination of an astonishing fourteen years in Bob's life: even his bitterest critics have to admit that his success since reacquiring control of Pergamon had been meteoric. He had rebuilt his fortune and reputation and was on good terms with the highest of the land in social, business, financial and political circles. The guest lists for his birthday parties in those years read like pages from *Who's Who*. Those celebrations were to provide a regular rhythm for my life in the eighties, making colossal demands on my time and energy, but some of them, like the receptions we gave for Christine and Isabel's weddings, were family occasions rather than exercises in public relations. These were the exceptions, however, and most of the time my life was filled with what my younger sons called "Mummy's professional socializing." BPCC and Pergamon vied for my presence at social functions if Bob was unavailable, and when the *Mirror* came into our lives, it brought with it a whole new dimension. I remember laughing with the children when the *Mirror* literally sent me to the dogs. One of my first official functions for the paper was to present the Mirror Cup at the Greyhound Derby. Back in the 1950s, I had been to the dog races with Isidore Kerman, Bob's then solicitor, but had never imagined myself as the center of attraction there, surrounded by panting greyhounds, posing for photographs as I gently patted the winning dog's head and presented a silver cup to its owner.

I would also be delegated to attend horse races at Ascot and The Derby. *Sporting Life,* the Mirror Group's racing title, had a box at Epsom race course, and Bob would send me to entertain suppliers, important advertisers, public relations agents and so on. I would often attend Ascot on Ladies' Day, climaxing in the running of the highly coveted Gold Cup trophy. I would fly by helicopter from the roof of the Maxwell Group's headquarters in London with some of the guests, having arranged three more shuttle trips to transport the others. Douglas Harrod, an impressive-looking and experienced butler with whom I got on well, had "done" many more Ascots than I had and took charge of all the catering. I would welcome my guests with champagne, then we would all rush to the balcony to see the Queen, her family and guests arrive in open landaus from nearby Windsor, to loud cheers from the happy crowd. It was a fine sight:

the ladies in their elegant afternoon dresses and glamorous hats, the men in top hats and morning suits and colorful family parties picnicking on the grass. At twelve o'clock, Douglas would serve a delicious and traditional Ascot lunch, accompanied with champagne and always ending with strawberries and cream. Mike Molloy, then editor of the *Daily Mirror,* would help me entertain the guests and guide me through the complexities of the betting system. We would of course consult the *Sporting Life* for its betting tips, but I always went by the name of the horse or jockey or the colors he was wearing. With beginner's luck, I would often win and those guests who had gallantly followed my hunches would share my delight.

I remember that Bob once went with me to the races, but after that he would say he didn't have time. The truth was that he was not a "season" man. Going a second time to any event he had already experienced bored him completely; it was the excitement of novelty and the first impression that he liked. That was how I came to do the regular rounds of London's June season, including Wimbledon, Henley regatta, the Chelsea flower show where the *Daily Mirror* exhibited an attractive small garden and Glyndebourne opera, either deputizing for Bob to entertain guests or being entertained in return. The only sports event Bob would regularly take me to was the Cup Final or one of those memorable Oxford United matches as, under Bob's ownership, the team moved up from the third division to the first and won the Milk Cup at Wembley, a triumph for a small club.

Many of the social functions I attended were charity fund-raising events. With the acquisition of BPC and the Mirror Group, our charity sponsorships increased enormously and I found myself sitting on numerous committees covering a wide spectrum of good causes—the Royal College of Nursing, Organization for Rehabilitation by Training (ORT), Mencap, Yad La Yeled (an Israeli Holocaust educational charity for children), the Philharmonia Orchestra, the Royal Opera House, to name but a few—either as chairman or supporting member. I took this work very much to heart and would beg shamelessly from all our friends and often wondered how anyone was still on speaking terms with me after my constant badgering for money! Only once in my career as a fund raiser did I get my comeuppance. It was at the opening of Spencer House, the beautiful seventeenth-century London home of the Princess of Wales's ancestors, which had been bought and restored to its former splendor at great cost by Jacob Rothschild. That evening, I met Lord Forte, a good friend of many years standing, whose generosity to many of my charitable causes was unsurpassed. As we got talking and I tried to interest him in my next project, he cut me short with, "Betty, this time the answer is no!" I was taken aback, although I did think his refusal was quite justified. But I was working on behalf of a good cause and determined to persuade him, so I said, "Charles, if you help me this one last time, I promise you I'll never ask again." I was being completely honest because I had by then decided to give up most of my charitable work to concentrate on other interests. "How much do you want?" he asked, and I proceeded to name what I thought would be a reasonable donation, coming from him. He pondered for a minute, then said, "That's it, then." We shook hands and Charles kept his word, as I did mine.

Shaking hands reminds me of another story, which took place at the prime minister's table in Downing Street at a lunch in honor of Hans Brunhart, Liechtenstein's head of state. It was a small affair by Downing Street standards, only six tables of eight people each. I was seated opposite Mrs. Thatcher with Sir Hugh Casson on my right and Jacob Rothschild on my left; Hans Brunhart was on the prime minister's right and the Swiss ambassador François Pictet, who is also my cousin, on her left. Sitting next to Jacob was very embarrassing for me since I had studiously avoided him for the previous fifteen years. I just could not forgive his actions at the time of the Leasco affair. We had hardly sat down when Jacob turned to me and said, "As you may know, Bob and I shook hands last year in Israel. We have laid our differences to rest and I would like to do the same with you." I knew I ought to be able to forgive him, but couldn't help reminding him of his statement that he had shot my husband seventeen times and he was still alive. How could I make peace with a man who had wished my husband dead? All this conversation was being conducted sotto voce, but every now and then, the prime minister would interrupt with a shrill "Is it not so, Betty Maxwell?" a phrase she had taken to saying whenever I was at hand, to which I would answer, as if by reflex, "Yes, Prime Minister." Those words about shooting Bob were a journalist's invention, Jacob said, but I retorted that he had never made any effort to deny them, and we argued about the rights and wrongs of those events of long ago. We were getting nowhere, so I turned resolutely towards Hugh and started to talk to him about the architecture of Maxwell House, a building which he had designed. By the time we had waded through fillet of sole with crab, fillet of lamb Marly and reached the chocolate and vanilla terrine, Jacob returned to our conversation, perhaps mellowed by a Johannisberger Klaus Riesling, a Château Beychevelle, followed by a Rémy Martin cognac. He reminded me that he had wanted to make his peace with me in Israel but had been unable to find me; in fact I had deliberately avoided him then. A lot of water had, however, passed under the bridge and I made up my mind it was really time for the quarrel to be ended. As I said good-bye to Jacob that day, we shook hands and I told him, "I shake hands with you today because my husband was able to do so. I shall never mention our conversation or this incident again, either to you or anyone else." A few days later, however, when I had lunch with a good friend of ours in the City, he greeted me with, "I hear that you shook hands with Jacob Rothschild last Friday!" I felt disappointed; Jacob was apparently so pleased by the whole episode that he had been dining out on it. There was another painful end to this new dawn in our relationship after Bob's death. When I was at my lowest ebb and went personally to Jacob to ask him for a short-term loan, he could not find it in his heart to assist me.

Glyndebourne, the renowned summer opera festival held in Sussex, was one of my favorite social events. In the Esher days, Bob and I would go every year with our family doctor, taking turns with him to provide the food and drinks. Later on, dinner would be on a grander scale in the restaurant there. The last time I went, in 1989, Bob and I were due to go by helicopter to have drinks at the home of Sir Robert and Lady Clark, then go on with them as our hosts to Glyndebourne. Well, the inevitable happened. At the last minute, I had the unpleasant task of phoning Robert to say that the other Robert would not be able to join me and hoped another escort for me might be found. Gallant Sir Robert did indeed manage to rope in a friend at the eleventh hour.

Another opera performance, this time at the Royal Opera House, stands out in my mind: the 1984 Christmas production of the Nutcracker ballet in aid of the National Society for the Prevention of Cruelty to Children (NSPCC) Centenary Year, sponsored by Bob and Gerald Ronson through BPCC and Heron. The sheer scale of that event, both in the amount of money raised and in the Christmas magic of its royal first night, surpassed any gala night I had witnessed at Covent Garden. Perhaps it was the spirit of Christmas that pervaded the opera house or the rare occurrence of the joint presence of the Queen, Prince Philip, the Queen Mother and Princess Margaret. Perhaps it was the continental decoration of the Christmas trees which greeted you in the foyer with their heady scent of spices and cinnamon or the surprise gift of the tiny Victorian program which Jocelyn Stevens had designed and published and Ian had arranged to have printed. Perhaps it was simply the audience's unbe-

lievable elegance in white tie and fabulous beaded ballgowns set off
with sparkling jewelry or the magic of the Nutcracker story itself. Or
perhaps it was the free-flowing champagne, a special gift from a generous champagne producer and guest. Whatever its special quality
was, no one present that night will ever forget it.

Bob and I were privileged to sit beside the royal party in the
Dress Circle. At first, Bob was next to Prince Philip, with whom he
exchanged a few words since they had met several times before, but
after the interval, when the royal party changed seats around the
Queen, he found himself beside the Queen Mother. We were both
extremely tired, but the sparkling performance of the ballet and
excitement of the surroundings kept me awake. Bob, however, fell
asleep almost as soon as the lights were dimmed and I was constantly poking him in the ribs to wake him up. I could not let him
commit the crime of lèse majesté by falling asleep next to a Queen!
As president of the NSPCC, Princess Margaret wrote to me afterwards through her Lady in Waiting to say how much she had
enjoyed the gala, and she later invited Bob and me and the Rousous
to a private dinner at her home in Kensington Palace.

The joy of attending such fabulous parties was most dearly paid
for, as far as I was concerned, by the extreme exertion involved
which almost left me too tired to enjoy them. Anyone who has done
charity work will know that all committees are made up of doers
and drones. Being a doer by nature, I would always inherit a great
deal of the work, not to mention sorting out the inevitable last-
minute minor tragedies. As Bob would often say, "If anything can go
wrong it will." Either too many of the best seats had already been
allocated and we couldn't find a pair for one of the most generous
sponsors, or tickets would go astray altogether. One irate and fussy
woman would threaten never to help again unless she were presented
to the Queen, another resented being right at the end of the presentation line. You could never afford to offend a donor!

There were, however, compensations in the invitations we received
to parties, where all I had to do was relax and enjoy myself. Two
fairly recent ones stand out as great events, planned to absolute perfection and with meticulous attention to detail. One was given by
Andrew Lloyd Webber at his country home, Sydmonton Court, after
his marriage to Madeleine Gurdon in 1991. It had a similar atmosphere to our own parties, especially in the way a huge marquee
adjoined the reception rooms of Andrew's great home, with its splendid collection of pre-Raphaelite paintings. The marquee was just like

another room of the house and we dined there by candlelight under a star-studded midnight blue ceiling, exquisitely entertained by Andrew's well-known cellist brother, Julian. Everything possible had been done to ensure the guests' comfort, enjoyment and happiness— right down to the lavish loos designed as intimate boudoirs.

Sadly, this was yet another occasion when Bob didn't turn up, but I was escorted by Ian and much appreciated the company of my table companion, Michael Grade, whom I like very much. Bob had been friendly with his father, Leslie, whom he always considered the brightest of those clever and talented brothers, Lew Grade and Bernard Delfont. Unlike them, Leslie was not an extrovert, but so modest that the public was largely unaware of his accomplishments.

The other extravaganza of that period was the fantabulous "Ali Dada's party" in 1989 which Malcolm Forbes's sons gave to celebrate his seventieth birthday in his own palace, the Palais Mendoub, in Tangier. The invitation read: "Our father is not in Heaven yet and, as he also pays our paychecks, we are anxious to make his 70th birthday party a memorable one. Sheherazade took a thousand and one nights to keep her old man happy—we're counting on one night in a thousand in a Moroccan palace to keep the Chairman smiling. Black tie, ball gowns, turbans and tiaras are all in order for an evening of exotic dancing, dining and fireworks."

Malcolm Forbes had invited Elizabeth Taylor as his guest of honor and had her flown to Tangier from her home in Los Angeles in his private jet, the *Capitalist Tool*. Other guests had been flown from New York in a fleet of specially chartered jets, including a Concorde and a Boeing 747, and the Solazur Hotel had been taken over to accommodate them. Other guests such as Rupert Murdoch and ourselves had private yachts anchored in the harbor. As the time of the party drew near, we left our yacht and made our way to the private palace, duly attired for the occasion. Bob had gone completely over the top and taken the invitation's reference to a turban to mean Oriental fancy dress. I must say that he looked totally splendid, if somewhat grotesque, wearing a fantastic gold embroidered djellaba, straight out of "The Thousand and One Nights," complete with pasha's turban and Turkish slippers! I was wearing a striking white dress with the bodice embroidered with blue and red beads, which Ian Thomas had designed for me for the bicentennial of the French Revolution earlier in the year, but the French tricolor was equally good for the red, white and blue of the American flag and it was considered quite appropriate. As we arrived at the palace, we were greeted by a mounted guard of Berbers with swords drawn, and a splendid detachment of Touaregs in their impressive, fierce-looking black attire, their faces partially hidden by black veils.

Malcolm and Liz were brilliantly radiant: Liz in a green gown wore a huge Gorgon-like dark wig, which gave her a distinct Cleopatra look; Malcolm in a Scottish kilt, which, to the great dismay of his former compatriots, he was wearing back to front.

Eight hundred guests, the Who's Who of the media, business and fashion worlds were gathered there to celebrate Malcolm, the billionaire publishing magnate and "fun guy of the Western world," as an American journalist described him. They milled around in the splendor of the palace, under the five Byzantine tents complete with onion domes erected in the palace gardens and fitted with more than 3,000 square yards of Moroccan carpet. Bob and I were privileged to be included in Malcolm's own large tent with Henry Kissinger, three members of the Rockefeller family, the Crown Prince of Morocco, former King Constantine of Greece, Oscar de la Renta, John Hennessy, Walter Cronkite and an "embarrassment of extraordinarily rich people," as one of the journalists reported, estimating that "Forbes's guests were 'so rich that a brace of them, on average, was worth $133 million'!"

We sat down to an exquisite Moroccan meal of méchoui (roast lamb on the spit), egg dishes, chicken, a variety of delicious vegetables, a galaxy of deserts, washed down with excellent Moroccan wine and French champagne and served by literally hundreds of waiters, all dressed in splendid new Moroccan uniforms. Then there was sumptuous entertainment with belly dancers, singers and hundreds of acrobats. There were orchestras everywhere inviting the guests to dance and later on we were all taken to a terrace overlooking the Mediterranean to watch an extravagant fireworks display across the bay. It was a night of pure opulence which seasoned partygoers judged to be even better than the late Shah of Iran's megaparty in Persepolis or President Mitterrand's bicentennial celebration in Paris. For me, it was like the wildest of Hollywood's film extravaganzas—except it was the real thing.

The next day, we were the guests of King Hassan of Morocco, who entertained us at the Tangier country club in tents arranged in a crescent shape around the polo ground. That day we shared a table with Jimmy Goldsmith and his friends for a memorable méchoui lunch. Even more unforgettable, however, was the Fantasia entertainment given by the King. I had seen a few before on films, but they certainly didn't do justice to what we saw that day. Wave upon wave of warriors riding the most splendidly harnessed horses galloped towards us, coming to a halt a mere three feet from the tent where we were eating. One thousand fierce-looking riders, firing their rifles in the air gave an incredible display of horsemanship to a bemused audience of mostly American businessmen and their ladies.

That evening we attended a friendly buffet dinner on Rupert Murdoch's yacht anchored next to the *Lady Ghislaine*, then sailed out during the night for the Spanish coast, en route for Cannes. I liked being at sea; it was quiet and peaceful and the *Lady Ghislaine* was a really beautiful and superbly designed yacht. Every time I sailed on her, I would think back to the weekend in Oxford in 1986, when we had celebrated Ian's thirtieth birthday on the Saturday and the next day Bob had suddenly announced he was taking us all on a mystery trip. His secret had been so well kept that we had absolutely no idea where we were going and were utterly amazed to find ourselves flying to Amsterdam. From there we drove to a small harbor half an hour away where an impressive yacht lay at the quayside. It was then that Bob let us into his secret: this was the yacht he had bought, and Ghislaine was to christen the ship with her own name. A small scaffolding had already been erected for the launch ceremony and the champagne bottle was in place. Ghislaine went up the few steps, cut the rope attached to the bottle which smashed into the side of the yacht as she pronounced its name. At the same time, a cover was removed to reveal a shiny, new nameplate, the *Lady Ghislaine*. We all clapped enthusiastically, then went aboard with the Dutch constructors from Amels shipyard. Bob loved that boat from the start. He walked around excitedly, proudly showing us her every feature, although on that first visit the interior was not yet complete. That was to be my job, working closely with the well-known yacht designer Jon Bannenberg.

The boat had been originally commissioned by Adnan Khashoggi's brother, but had never been completed and was left in an unfinished state. This was, I think, an advantage, since we were able to complete the interior decor to suit our own taste. It was a real treat working with Jon and his assistants and we became good friends as we worked on the project. Jon has excellent taste and an instinctive feel for design. The whole boat exuded extreme peace and elegance. There was nothing garish about it and subsequent charterers often commented how much they liked its simplicity of decor.

When we arrived in Cannes, Bob sent me back to London in his private plane, which was returning to base. He meanwhile was setting off on a cruise to Sicily where his personal assistant was to join him. I remember clearly my last vision of him that day as the plane circled the boat, as it always did when he was on board. He waved and I waved back as he stood there alone on the main deck. My heart was heavy, not so much with disappointment at not joining him on the cruise, but with sadness at his self-imposed loneliness and solitude.

Bob's high profile, high-speed lifestyle in the second half of the eighties prompted an enormous amount of press interest in his every move. By 1988, the sheer volume of press articles was such that my annual scrapbook overflowed into two volumes for the first time. At the same time, curiosity about Bob's past life, character, business style and success sparked off a "biography race," with authors competing to be first to the tape with their version of Bob's story. During the course of 1987, Bob became aware that two unauthorized biographies were being written about him. That prompted him to commission Joe Haines, political editor of the *Daily Mirror*, to write an authorized biography. Bob appreciated Joe's incisive writing style, along with his intelligence and grasp of world affairs, although I barely knew Joe at all. I shall never forget my dismay when Bob brought him to Headington and told me in his presence, without any preamble, that Joe was going to write his biography and I was to hand over all my precious archives to him, helping him in any way I could. For the whole of our married life, I had been carefully saving all kinds of personal and public documents, intending one day to write Bob's story for our children and grandchildren. I was furious, but ultimately agreed to let Joe use my archives to enable him to authenticate the facts he would be writing about. That evening, however, I took my pen and wrote to Bob:

> That you should have disposed of my lifetime's most intimate work without talking it over with me goes contrary to your often repeated promise that you would not decide on a biographer who would use my work without consulting me. It shows on your part a lack of sensitivity which leaves me wounded and with the feeling of having been publicly raped.
>
> I also wondered why you deemed it necessary to chide me in front of Joe and his wife by saying "and make sure not to lose any sheets of the family tree"? I have already worked for five years, and am still working, on what has become my sacred Kaddish, although secular, to your family murdered in the Holocaust. Every name on that tree has been a personal act of love and research. I have made sure that over 500 dead people would be remembered, prayed for, and loved for generations to come. What was that cutting remark in aid of?

I was quite frosty with Joe at first, although over the months I got to know him much better and came to like him and admire his writing ability. I can hardly believe that he was able to produce a 450-page biography in six months flat! With the time limitations imposed on him, he obviously had little time to research beyond the main body of information in our own archives, but his book was nevertheless valuable, the most accurate of the biographies produced at the time, certainly for all the periods and events that I knew well. As for the other biographies, one of them read more like fiction and was withdrawn from sale on grounds of libel and pulped by court order. The other became the object of an intense legal battle, both in France, where Bob won damages, and in England, where the case was never settled. When the book appeared, however, many people told Bob or wrote to him that their words had not been accurately reported or had been quoted out of context.

The author later wrote that he felt he understood Bob perfectly and that was why Bob disliked his book so much. It is difficult to see how that could possibly be true when, of his own admission, he had spent so little time with him, had no direct knowledge of our family bonds nor access to my personal archives. Judging his book by my own documents and a lifetime married to Bob, I feel that it is rather like the proverbial parson's egg, good in parts! Unfortunately, its value is undermined by a host of factual errors caused by insufficiently careful research, and by some serious distortions and exaggerations.

The year Macmillan was acquired, 1988, was highly significant for both of us. For Bob, that acquisition would mark both the crowning glory of his business career and sow the seeds of his and his Group's downfall. It was also the year he celebrated his sixty-fifth birthday and Pergamon its fortieth anniversary—quite a landmark considering the trials and tribulations it had survived. Bob and I had agreed that something special should be done to mark both occasions. The Pergamon party would provide an opportunity to thank our authors, editors and staff for the skill and loyalty they had given us over those years.

It was Bob's idea to combine a mammoth party celebrating the fortieth anniversary in style with a symposium, a forum on innovation where ideas could be exchanged, criticisms and suggestions voiced and plans for the future formulated. Pergamon would then be able to introduce the necessary editorial and technological changes for the last decade of the century and look forward with confidence to the new one.

At the same time, I suggested that authors and editors might like to contribute to a souvenir volume, recording how they came to be associated with Bob and Pergamon Press and retelling some of their favorite personal anecdotes. That was how I came to be involved in the festschrift volume, *Robert Maxwell and Pergamon Press: 40 Years' Service to Science, Technology and Education*. It was a massive task, and some Pergamon editors doubted whether I would be able to assemble the many contributions to complete the book in the relatively short time available.

As I embarked on this task in late 1987, my office was inundated with work. We were already helping with Bob's biography, organizing an international Holocaust studies conference, preparing a surprise private volume for Bob's birthday and dealing with the logistical problems involved in entertaining 3,000 people at five separate events over a long weekend. There were to be two formal dinner-dances for our friends, one enormous buffet lunch for 2,000 business contacts, a second lunch for participants at the Pergamon symposium and a final Sunday evening dinner for members of staff. I would never have been able to organize all that without the help of my executive assistant, Jay Miller. Jay was invaluable to me. She spoke several languages, had an excellent memory and good personal relations with her colleagues. Above all, she always kept her cool, even when constantly interrupted by telephone calls and visitors. She was at my side for ten years, offering me her constant and devoted support.

When the festschrift was finally produced, it contained some three hundred contributions from Pergamon editors, authors and staff. Prefaced with a brief history of Pergamon Press, it proved a fascinating source of information, especially on the early history of the company, adding many insights and anecdotes of which I had previously been unaware.

After months of feverish preparation, the great weekend of Pergamon's fortieth celebration was upon us. For such a major event, we had enlisted professional help with the organization and entertainment. That year, we opted for a much more rigid marquee which covered the entire front lawn and sat 600 for dinner. We even temporarily removed two huge floor-to-ceiling windows to improve access between the house and the marquee. A large stage was built at one end, and the dining area, set with small round tables, was built on two levels so that everyone would have a good view of the entertainment. That weekend we gave two gala dinner-dances: Friday night was white tie and decorations, Saturday black tie. Floral centerpieces and attractively wrapped gifts decorated every table. Speeches were kept to a minimum, the accent being on entertainment. On Friday night, the cast of *Me and My Girl* performed high-lights of the well-known musical, whilst on Saturday there was classical and modern ballet.

Bob and I made our entrance for that party to a grand fanfare of trumpets! I wasn't expecting it and thought it was really over the top, but managed to play my part. I was wearing one of Ian Thomas's beautiful creations of old-gold-embroidered tulle over yellow taffeta silk. Bob looked splendid with his distinguished bearing, seeming slimmer in his black tails, proudly displaying the attractive Order of the White Rose from Finland around his neck and his miniature medals on his black satin lapel.

Our guests came from near and far. It was a glittering gathering of politicians, ministers, ambassadors, businessmen, financiers, bankers, scientists, lawyers and media personalities. It was a balmy evening and our guests took romantic walks in the gardens. Dancing went on until well into the night. Yet for all its success, for me, it had lost the intimate quality that our previous parties had had; it was just too vast. As one of his friends put it, my husband had become a "Global Man."

Congratulatory telegrams and letters arrived in profusion from those who were unable to attend. Ronald Reagan wrote effusively, "As the 'Happy Birthdays' ring out, Nancy and I are delighted to join in the chorus of admiration." Other people expressed their admiration and appreciation in personal contributions to a souvenir birthday volume. The Labor leader Neil Kinnock, for instance, wrote expansively:

If Bob Maxwell didn't exist, no one could invent him. . . He thrives on knocks—which is just as well for someone who has faced hardship and war in youth and who, in adulthood, has known family tragedy, commercial failure and political defeat as well as sharing joy and triumph with his beloved Betty at home and in business. . . . The basic convictions of liberty and fairness have stayed with him. They inspire many of his actions still. Some are accompanied by a flamboyance that makes even dedicated exhibitionists blush. Others are delivered with a modesty that disarms the most practiced cynics.

And Prime Minister Margaret Thatcher wrote:

Robert Maxwell has never made any secret that officially he is politically opposed to me. He's always been straightforward about it and I appreciate that. But, to tell the truth, I rather think he likes my approach to politics and government—a sense of direction and decision. These are the very qualities that have taken him so far.

Bob was at a peak of fame and success and his personal fortune at the time was immense and solid. He had businesses and assets with a net worth of close to a billion pounds. His achievements were being increasingly recognized both in England and abroad. He had already been honored by the United States, Russia, Sweden, Bulgaria and Poland, but 1988 was also to bring him an honorary doctorate of law from Aberdeen University, honorary life membership of the Institute of Philosophy, the Order of the White Rose of Finland and news that Imperial College had awarded him an honorary fellowship. As the dean, Professor Eric Ash, wrote in December 1988, "This is the highest award which it is in the power of the College to bestow on persons of outstanding distinction. . . . My personal congratulations to you on this well-deserved mark of recognition of your contribution to scientific and technological publishing through the Pergamon Press." These marks of public recognition were to be followed in the years ahead by further honorary doctorates from universities in Great Britain, Poland, America, Israel and Canada, by the award of Officier de l'Ordre des Arts et des Lettres in France and B'nai B'rith's "World of Difference" Award in America. The day before he died, he had just heard that his name had been put forward for the French Légion d'Honneur.

Honors were also to come my way in 1988 and subsequent years, but for very different reasons. When my thesis was finished and Bob was living most of the time in London, I needed to find another project to help me survive my loneliness, having to all intents and purposes lost a fulfilling relationship with my natural companion and the company of my children, who by now had all left home. Even my super-active professional social life was no compensation for unrequited love. My doctoral research, however, had given me an idea. Whilst working on my thesis, I had to draw up my family tree in order to document the origins of the letter writers and show how the correspondents were interrelated. Fortunately, all the relevant papers, going back to the sixteenth century, had been preserved in family homes. I had had enormous fun delving into those archives, then linking my findings with other sources and as an end product had a family tree going back to the reign of Charlemagne on one side and prior to the French Revolution on the other.

Inspired by this success, I decided to try my hand at reconstructing Bob's family tree, so that our children would know something of both sets of ancestors. I hoped that my efforts would please Bob and show him how much I still cared for him. Tracking down his family, however, was an extremely difficult task. In Bob's home village, all the houses had been ransacked and not a single family member remained to pass on the family lore. The only way to do it was to locate survivors and distant cousins in England, America, Argentina, Switzerland, Belgium and Israel. So 1985 saw me traveling the world in search of Bob's roots, gathering together his relatives, school friends and contemporaries from Szlatina and slowly fitting together the pieces of the jigsaw puzzle as one person led me to another. It was an emotionally draining experience. I had taken my friend Wendy with me, and we would often feel immensely moved as we listened to those survivors' stories and lived the Holocaust vicariously through their memory of that appalling tragedy.

On a trip to meet relatives in Israel, Bob came with us; he was attending a meeting in Jerusalem of the editorial board of Pergamon's *Holocaust and Genocide Studies* and wanted us to be present to take the minutes. That time, the pain was of a different kind as he publicly humiliated me in front of a committee of eminent Jewish scholars and repeatedly in Wendy's presence. He seemed to take pleasure in deliberately belittling any suggestion I made and deriding my lack of expertise in publishing. Wendy was shocked at the way he treated me and found herself caught in the middle of an unpleasant row between Bob, her employer, and me, one of her closest friends. That episode was to cement our friendship. Whilst remaining loyal to Bob, I was able to discuss some of my problems, although never at that stage revealing their true extent, with her. That episode could not have demonstrated more clearly that Bob had not managed to reconcile himself with his grief or overcome his guilt complex at having married a Christian. Confronted by Israeli Jews, most of them survivors, and dealing with the subject of the Holocaust, he took his distress out on me.

As I discovered the links between families and heard their fate from survivors, I marked on my developing family tree all those murdered in the Holocaust with a small yellow star of David. Entire families had been wiped out, multiple generations, and when you unfold that concertina of a family tree, you are practically blinded by a shower of golden stars. I was numb. Nothing could ever convey so graphically and so cruelly what had happened in that small, ordinary, long-forgotten village at the foot of the Carpathian mountains, in the very heart of Europe, between 1940 and 1944. I understood then that we must never allow the world to forget the murder of those victims. I was determined to try and understand how such a catastrophe had happened and how six million Jews could have been exterminated in the middle of Christian Europe in the middle of the twentieth century.

My research led me first to survivors, then to Jewish and Christian historians and theologians. I was in my sixties; there was so little time and so much to learn. I read voraciously and acquired a smattering of Hebrew. My new field of studies became my overriding preoccupation—perhaps obsession would be a better word. I was having to digest some unpalatable truths, which shook my faith to its foundations. The Holocaust was the ultimate horror in perversion and degradation of the human mind, the worst crisis of our civilization. It would not have taken place if millions of Christians had not been bystanders, collaborators or perpetrators. Christianity bore a large responsibility in this catastrophe: as the distinguished French historian, Jules Isaac, so aptly put it, throughout centuries of anti-Semitic teaching, contempt had led to derision, derision to hatred, hatred to violence and violence to death in the crematoria.

I traveled my own road to Damascus and knew that I wanted to work towards Jewish-Christian reconciliation. I made a commitment never to remain a bystander, never to remain silent when I disagreed with an opinion or action directed against the Jews. I felt a need to bring awareness of the Holocaust to the public, and that was how I came to travel widely to research and lecture on the Holocaust, its causes and consequences. That was also how, with the help of many scholars, the international congress "Remembering for the Future" came into being.

Held in Oxford and London in July 1988, it was sponsored by Pergamon Press, with Bob's financial support, and attended by some 600 participants, both Christian and Jewish, from 24 countries. As chairman of the executive committee, I was closely involved in all aspects of its organization, both the academic side and the more public event with accompanying films, a commemorative concert and an art exhibition. I traveled to Poland with the artist and Holocaust survivor Roman Halter to seek permission from General Jaruzelski to exhibit in London drawings done by artists in Auschwitz. We also organized the first, very moving, gathering of survivors in Great Britain. On the academic side, the pioneers and scholars in the field honored us with their presence, along with Church dignitaries, rabbis, teachers and younger research students. It was an impressive meeting. Although ignored at first by the media, the conference subsequently became well known in Europe for its efforts to disseminate the truth about the Holocaust, its determination to face the difficulties of teaching its history and its role in persuading churches of the urgent need to revise their theology. It was, in the words of Holocaust writer and survivor Dr. Yaffa Eliach, a "landmark conference . . . the beginning of a new era." The conference proceedings were published in three volumes by Pergamon Press and have since become a valuable reference work. Such was the success of "Remembering for the Future" that a second conference was held in Berlin in March 1994, in which I again participated.

For me personally, those years of preparing the conference were amongst the most rewarding, although painful, of my life. Almost every day I found myself confronting heartrending stories of man's inhumanity to man. Bob had difficulty controlling his own emotions and once again the depth of his scars was only too clear. At the opening of the conference in Oxford Town Hall, he broke down in tears and was unable to finish his speech. I had to read it for him.

My work on the Holocaust had given me a much better understanding of Bob's trauma. In some ways it brought us closer together; in others, it widened the gulf between us as I gradually became more recognized in my own right. When journalists began talking of my coming out of Bob's shadow into a share of the spotlight, and I found myself given awards for my work, Bob was full of praise for me in public, but I think found it hard to cope with my success. I was often embarrassed by the praise. I did not feel I had achieved anything extraordinary, but was pleased to have helped in some small way in the field of Jewish-Christian dialogue. When in May 1988 I received the Sir Sigmund Sternberg award from Cardinal Hume in recognition of my work towards inter-religious understanding, I was of course delighted but knew there were many other people who had done much more than me and for a much longer period of time. As I said that day, "In honoring me, I feel that you have honored very many people who are working quietly towards peace, tolerance and understanding between people of different faiths." I was later able to enlarge the scope of my work when I became the first woman vice president of the International Council of Christians and Jews.

By the time the biography and the Pergamon festschrift were finished, Bob had come to realize how valuable my archives were and insisted that his staff send me significant letters from VIPs, press releases, newspaper articles and so on for inclusion. He was beginning to find that it was quicker to ask me to locate a piece of information or a date than it was to ask his own staff! The truth was that by the late 1980s, Bob's private office was in an appalling state of

chaos. Jean Baddeley, his loyal office director of many years standing, was by then working for the Mirror Group as Group Hospitality Director and his efficient Australian assistant Debbie Dines had
been posted to another Mirror Group subsidiary, Mirrorcolour Print
at Watford. In their place, Bob had appointed a bevy of young girls
with little experience and little initiative. There was, however, still a
semblance of civil-service type order as long as Peter Jay, Britain's
former ambassador to Washington, remained as chief of staff. He
had joined Bob's personal staff in 1986 and taken on the complex
job of coordinating Bob's multiple activities. As long as Peter could
count on Jean and Debbie's cooperation, Bob's office functioned
well; with the departure of these stalwarts and the advent of the new
private assistant, however, Peter had little support and found himself
considered an interloper. It is possible that this was largely due to
Bob's mania for compartmentalization. Yet Bob trusted Peter. Faced
with disorder and antagonism, Peter made efforts to bring discipline
into the office, but he already had his hands full with all his management responsibilities and the many diplomatic duties he undertook
on Bob's behalf. He was unfailingly courteous and gave the best of
his unquestionable knowledge and gifts, whilst certainly enjoying
Bob's intelligence and quixotic way of life. Charming, exquisitely
mannered Humphrey Mews, former private secretary to the Prince
of Wales, fared no better when he was appointed Bob's office director in 1988. When both these experienced members of staff left, the
situation deteriorated at an alarming rate, and Bob's personal office
became a law unto itself.

By then, Bob was relying largely on his private assistant who
became his de facto "office manager" and with whom he was
increasingly besotted, his infatuation blinding him as to her suitabil-
ity for the job. It was ludicrous to expect a girl in her mid-twenties
and with her lack of experience to be able to assume responsibility
almost single-handedly for an office as busy as Bob's, but he liked
her, partly because she followed his instructions, didn't answer back,
didn't nag him and had an even temper. However, her eagerness to
follow Bob's directions blindly resulted in serious blunders being
made in the "back office." It was not unusual, for instance, for multiple invitations to be accepted for Bob to attend functions on the
same evening—sometimes in different countries—with the result that
I or the boys were often frantically called upon at the last minute to
stand in for him. On one famous occasion Bob sent the helicopter to
rush me to London for a television show where he was to present a
donation of £100,000 raised by Mirror Group newspaper readers in

the Telethon Appeal. I didn't even have time to change and I took my dress and cosmetics with me in the helicopter and said to Dick, my favorite pilot, "Please, don't turn around, I'm changing," whereupon I peeled off my clothes in that tiny confined space and put on my makeup. We made it on time and I appeared in front of a large television audience, as if I had spent all day getting ready for the occasion.

Ian and I stood in for Bob on numerous occasions—at Kensington Palace for a reception hosted by the Prince of Wales; at 10 Downing Street where Mrs. Thatcher greeted us, asking me in her unmistakable voice, "Where is Robert?"; at the Lord Mayor's dinner at the Mansion House; and at countless private dinner-dances. Perhaps one of the worst of these incidents occurred at the French Embassy when Bob failed to put in an appearance twice in succession. I was friendly with the then ambassador, Luc de la Barre de Nanteuil, and his charming wife. On the first occasion, they excused Bob with, "It's just one of those things," but the second time, the ambassador was furious—and rightly so. Bob made his peace subsequently with the ambassador and continued to be invited to embassy functions, although I always wondered afterwards if they had a replacement in reserve, just in case!

Sometimes, Bob's office would even omit to send me the invitations to functions I was supposed to be attending on his behalf and I would find out in the nick of time—or miss them altogether and incur his wrath. When I phoned to complain, my calls would be taken by an office junior, not the person responsible. I really hit the roof on getting curt memos stating simply, "Mrs. M. to attend," or "Mrs. M. to deputize," without any consultation over dates. One day, I could stand it no longer and wrote Bob a letter:

> You must give orders to your secretaries that no invitations should be accepted on my behalf without having had the courtesy to send or fax me the invitation. I no longer want to stand in for you unless you deem my presence imperative.

Things improved for a while, but slipped back after a month or two. The secretaries' office was like a transit lounge with people passing through all day long. You never had the impression that it was a place of work. One girl who was employed there for a year told me what it was like to work there. The girls would chatter and giggle all day long. The minute Bob opened the door of his adjoining office, they would look busy, but resume their prattle as soon as he went away. Whenever a serious and hardworking girl joined the office staff, her life was made a misery until she asked for a transfer or resigned. If they didn't like the look of a new executive, his or her memos to Bob would be put at the bottom of the pile and their calls not put through; they would either resign or be sacked. Calls would be deliberately cut off, letters destroyed and Bob was often told lies. Piles of mail would lie unanswered on the desks and windowsills whilst the girls spent their time chatting, mostly about people's love lives and Bob's alleged affairs with his secretaries. The turnover of staff in the chairman's office was the highest in the whole company—and it was not only due to Bob's temper. Sometimes I would meet Jean Baddeley and we shared our dismay and frustration, remembering the "good old days" when she and I collaborated closely to run Bob's public and private lives smoothly, protecting him from his own excesses and exercising some control over him.

Bob could not fail to notice this lamentable state of affairs. On one occasion, after his anger had subsided, he told me of a terrible faux pas made by one of those girls. A personal phone call had come through for Bob on his ultra-private line from Monsieur Mitterrand. "Mr. Who?" said the hapless secretary. "President Mitterrand." "President of what?" she asked. "Monsieur Mitterrand, President of France!" Other important businessmen who called Bob on his private line were told that he was unavailable, irrespective of the urgency of their message or their closeness to Bob. They would then phone me in Oxford, voicing their fury and asking me how to bypass the ladies in his office. Things were no better when eminent people visited Bob at the office. His notoriously hectic day would be so overloaded with meetings, which never ran to schedule, that distinguished bankers, political figures and businessmen would be kept waiting in every available room on the office floor, overflowing into the corridor outside the elevators, for anything up to an hour or two, even if Bob had requested the appointment!

On occasions, Bob would ask Wendy and me to try and sort things out for him. We were reluctant to intrude, but Bob would insist. I shall never forget when Wendy found a check for £23,000, six months old, just lying there amongst a pile of miscellaneous papers in the outer office! It was impossible to believe that anyone could operate in such disorder. Bob's own office would be even worse: although the heaps of paper looked reasonably tidy, when we looked at them closely, some of them were years old and we found another check for £6,000, which had never been banked. The problem was that Bob's office staff rarely dealt with anything other than what was immediately vital. Every time Bob sent us on these rescue operations, he would ask Wendy to report our findings to him. On the second such occasion, he asked her to stay in his London office for a week, observing what was happening, talking to the managers and staff and finding out what was going wrong. At the end of the week, she gave Bob a confidential report, having first discussed it with me. She had decided to give him her honest opinion, knowing that in the past Bob had listened to and respected her views, but nevertheless she did so with some trepidation since she was inevitably criticizing his staff. What was needed was a strong, experienced office manager who would stand up to Bob and not be frightened by his bullying, someone who could take the junior secretaries in hand. Bob read the report in front of Wendy, folded it and placed it in his breast pocket, saying "I agree with you completely."

It was to be some months before Bob acted on those suggestions, but he did eventually reshuffle his office and turn his private assistant into his "program manager," a position which allowed her to travel with him without being missed in the office, where before long, chaos resumed. I have since read that the woman complained of Bob's attentions. If this were true and her complaints serious, she could easily have walked out. She obviously enjoyed the high salary and perks of the job—traveling in private jets, staying in deluxe hotels or on the *Lady Ghislaine*. She eventually left with a generous golden handshake. Much of the confusion in Bob's office in the last years can be laid at the door of his personal office. Bob himself should have known better, but in the end the infatuation of an aging man for a young girl appeared to take precedence over his duties as the chairman of a vast empire.

Bob's irritation with the muddle in his office and the emotional toll of his crush on his "program manager" inevitably rebounded on me and I was finally a victim of that chaos. I never ventured any remarks on his infatuation because I knew that it would soon be over, but I was extremely sad to see him in such a pathetic situation. I was also deeply hurt to discover that Bob was now deliberately ignoring some of my letters. On the rare occasions that I visited his apartment, I would find them in his bedroom, unopened, unread, cast aside. It was cruel of him, but the final humiliation was to come in late June 1990, when he had accepted an invitation for both of us from the Gourlay family to a party at their country house, not far from Oxford. The inevitable phone call came at the last minute, telling me that Bob would not be going and suggesting I should take Ian with me instead. Later that day, however, just as we were about to leave for the party, we heard the familiar noise of the helicopter overhead and Bob arrived, completely unannounced, saying that he had a headache and wanted to go to bed immediately. I rushed upstairs to turn down his bed, close the shutters and make sure he had everything he needed for his comfort. He then abruptly dismissed me and asked me to leave him alone. I hurriedly got ready for the party, but went again to his bedroom before I left to ask if there was anything else I could do. He was in an appalling mood and shouted at me, accusing me of complete callousness at leaving him in the hands of servants when he was ill. I was outraged. He was accusing me of abandoning him, when he had practically walked out of my life. I couldn't take any more of his ranting. I ordered hot soup and a light meal for his dinner, then left for the engagement with Ian. But we were only about ten minutes away from Oxford when the car phone rang and I knew immediately it would be Bob. "This time, you've really gone too far," he said. "You're heartless and stupid and I'm leaving you." I tried to reason with him on the phone, but it was useless. He was so angry and irrational that I asked the driver to make a U-turn and take me back home. Ian then went on to the party and gave apologies for both of us.

I went straight up to his bedroom and asked what on earth had possessed him, and he told me, "I've come to the conclusion that you're absolutely raving mad. After all I've done for you, you don't even have the decency to stay with me when I come home sick and tired; you prefer to go out dancing. I've decided irrevocably to leave you." I tried to argue with him and make him see the episode from my point of view, but he simply would not listen. I had never seen him so angry. I left him and went to my room.

The next morning, around eleven o'clock, he asked me to go to his office. Quietly, in bitter and uncompromising words, he told me that our relationship was at an end. He repeated his words of the previous night that I was mad and added that he would have nothing more to do with me. What he wanted was an immediate legal separation, advertised in the *Times* of July 1. I was stunned. I didn't argue with him, but just said, "Why do you want to make it such a public affair? What have I done to deserve that? If you want me to leave, I'll go. I've no wish to hurt you in any way. All I need is a financial settlement to ensure my security, which I am sure you'll make, and I'll go quietly." But Bob insisted on a public declaration. He didn't want any more joint invitations; he wanted people to know that we were separating and would no longer attend functions together. He added, "I don't want to see you again, I don't want you to phone me, I don't want to talk to you any more. I no longer love you. This is the end and I really mean THE END."

Once again I remonstrated that it was unnecessary to go to such lengths, but he was adamant, claiming that "everybody did it like that; people were separating from their wives all the time, nobody would think anything of it; such events were two a penny in the City." And he added with emphasis, "I don't want a divorce, just a legal separation." He asked me whether I had any particular requests concerning the wording of the announcement and I answered, "No, you're the communications man, you must do as you think best." "All right," he answered, "people will say it was all my fault in any case." I couldn't stop myself from retorting, "Yes, they're sure to say that—and they'll be right, too." At that, he told me I had until the next morning to give him my conditions—where I wanted to live, what kind of financial settlement I expected and any other wishes I might have. His last words as he boarded the helicopter for London really hurt me. "It's quite final. Our relationship is a complete sham and has been for years. I'm not prepared to put up with you or your heartlessness any longer." I was cold all over. In a few minutes, Bob had just severed forty-seven years of married life.

As soon as Bob left, I telephoned Kevin, told him what had happened and asked if he had any idea why his father was behaving like this. But my real reason for speaking to Kevin was to seek his help in assessing my financial needs. I needed to have enough money to ensure a decent standard of living, with a small place in London and my house in France. I wanted to continue my work on Jewish-Christian relations, write, visit my children, and grandchildren, family and friends in France, England, America and Israel. If Bob wanted a separation, that was fine by me, but I wanted to be independent financially and free to live my life as I wished. Kevin's reply comes back to me clearly, "Mother, don't do an Ivana Trump on him. Just ask him for what will amply cover your present and future needs." At the time, I felt unable to confide in anyone other than Kevin on these matters.

Around ten o'clock on Sunday morning, the helicopter brought Bob back. He had by then calmed down a great deal, but he was still determined to go through with a legal separation. We sat down at his desk and he asked me, "Have you thought it over?" I said yes, and handed him my list of conditions. I had written them down because I feared that he would not listen to me.

1. I wish to spend eight days alone with you on the yacht so that we can discuss the various aspects of our separation in a civilized manner, as two people who have loved each other very much and spent forty-seven years together.

Specifically, I need sufficient money to:
   complete the building of Fraytet (my French home)
   buy myself a pied-à-terre in London
   pay for the removal of all my personal furniture and chattels from Heading-
      ton and their installation in my new London base and in Fraytet
   settle such debts as I may have in England
   2. I wish to leave Headington Hill soon after March 11, 1991, my seventieth
birthday
   3. On my birthday, I would like you to give me a lump sum to ensure an adequate income for me for life.

He took my list, grunted, passed no comment, pocketed it and
said, "My answer is yes for the eight days on the boat, when would
you like it to be?" I told him that any time during the month of
August would be fine. Bob then left and I found myself alone,
reflecting what a ridiculous way this was to part and wondering
what on earth had happened to the man I had loved so dearly, protected and slaved for all my life.

July 1 came and went, no announcement appeared in the *Times*
and I heard nothing more from Bob. The next few months were
very painful for me. For close on forty-seven years, we had telephoned each other almost every day, even when we had our differences, but this had now stopped. We had agreed by memo on a date
I would join him on the boat in August. At first I was supposed to
join him in Athens, then it was to be Istanbul, but when I arrived
there, Bob had just left by private plane. With no further instructions, I asked the captain to head for Troy, opposite the Gallipoli
promontory. I had always wanted to go there after reading the
account of Schliemann's excavations and his discovery of the gold
of Troy. After this, I plucked up my courage and phoned Bob in
London, and he asked us to head for the island of Samos. We went
there, but he never turned up. I phoned again, this time he suggested meeting in Lesbos, but the same thing happened. I phoned
yet again and Bob asked me where my next port of call would be,
so I told him to come to Ephesus, the modern Ismir. I had a wonderful day visiting that stupendous ancient city so full of significance
for me, with its Greek and Roman past and association with Saint
Paul's preaching. Once again, there was no sign of Bob.

After I returned home there was no more contact between us
until one day in November 1990 when Bob's office summoned me to
join him at a dinner in honor of the president of Italy at the Victoria
and Albert Museum, at which the Queen would be present. I did as

requested. I traveled from Oxford, Bob from London. We were not sitting at the same table but met on the way out at the cloakroom as he collected his coat. He said, "It's nice to see you, we're still together then?" I replied, "Are we?" and he mumbled something to the effect that we were actually physically side by side. He asked me where I was going and I answered "Home," whereupon he left in his Rolls and I in mine.

Shortly before Christmas, he phoned me one day to say that he would spend Christmas with me in the Caribbean on the *Lady Ghislaine*. He would give me the eight days I had requested and make up for the missed opportunity of the summer. I duly flew to St. Thomas and Bob arrived the next day, Christmas Eve. Unfortunately, the captain by then had rammed the boat onto a sand bank, damaging the propellers, and the yacht could not sail. Although I had taken all the traditional homemade festive fare and superb decorations to enliven the "last parting," we had an indifferent Christmas. Bob was far too exhausted to talk and we watched videos together. I felt no particular rush to discuss things since we were going to spend a week together. But next day, Bob suddenly announced that he was leaving for New York since the spare part for the boat would obviously not arrive in time. I was to sail back to Florida on her and he would join me there. . . . The vital spare part never arrived and I flew back to London.

Looking back on those encounters now, perhaps I should have realized how much he needed me then, but I no longer had the strength to fight. He had cut the thread of my love irremediably. I did not see him again until January 5, when I made a last attempt at reconciliation. I wrote him a letter eighteen pages long, then went to his office and made him read it in front of me. I was suggesting a fresh start with a different approach to our life together and less expectations on either side. He annotated it as he read it, agreeing with some of my practical suggestions for a modus vivendi, but choosing not to comment on more emotional issues. Then he said he had urgent matters to attend to and I left with the letter. Every time I met him when we were no longer living together, he always showed pleasure at seeing me, and at times was even affectionate, but his attention span on our personal problems was short. In truth, he had no desire to deal with them, either positively or negatively, or take any action which would upset the status quo. The next time I saw Bob was on March 11, 1991, my seventieth birthday.

As my "special" birthday approached, it was largely my children who organized a celebratory dinner and dance for me at the Dorchester in London. Christine and Isabel compiled a beautiful birthday book with contributions from my relatives and closest friends over the years. It was a special publication, full of nostalgia and warmth, and touched me deeply. The other girls dealt with the party arrangements, and Ian and Kevin followed their sisters' instructions and badgered Bob to attend. In the early days of March, he was deep in negotiations to buy the New York *Daily News* and we were uncertain up to the last minute whether he would come at all. When he did eventually turn up, he demonstrated publicly his affection for me and kissed me warmly; but he stayed for the briefest time possible, spoke mostly in his speech about his whirlwind talks to buy the paper then flew back to America immediately. It was months since I had seen him and I was embarrassed by his perfunctory appearance, but I was surrounded by all those dearest to me, who helped me forget my sadness. It was a joyous occasion with a wonderfully intimate atmosphere, and I was so proud of my children that night—their tremendous care, their moving speeches and the way they supported me throughout.

One of my unexpected birthday presents was Ian's official announcement that he and his American girlfriend, Laura, had decided to marry the following June. We were all delighted for him, welcomed Laura into the tribe and plans were put in hand for a wedding from Laura's family's country home in Wyoming. For the European contingent, there would be a second reception at Fraytet in August.

As soon as my birthday festivities were over, I rushed to France to supervise the final construction work on my house. Building had started in February 1989 when I invested all my available savings in the project. Before our serious quarrels, Bob had repeatedly promised to help me financially, but all he ultimately did was guarantee a £1 million bank loan. After Bob told me so bluntly that he wanted nothing more to do with me, I arranged for a mortgage on the property and took over the loan in my name.

The construction was proceeding splendidly and I was becoming excited at the thought of celebrating Ian's wedding in my home. Furnishing the house kept me busy the whole summer, although I did go to Wyoming for a short interlude of five days for the wedding proper. To my surprise and delight, Bob also made the effort to come. We had rented a delightful house on the golf course near Laura's family's home with a spectacular view of the Teton mountains, and Bob flew in with his chef, Martin Cheeseman, who was going to run the house and organize the food. Nearly all our children were present and Bob was in exceptionally good humor.

The religious ceremony took place in a small log-cabin chapel high up in the mountains. It was austere and rather like a French Protestant church, with just a simple wooden cross. I was always nervous when Bob had to attend any church ceremony because it was really alien to him, but I need not have worried that day. The priest talked of the ecumenism of our family, knowing that Laura was a Roman Catholic, Ian, myself and all his brothers and sisters Protestants and Bob a Jew. Then with great sensitivity and knowledge, he spoke of Christian-Jewish rapprochement and the efforts being made by Christians to alter their attitudes to Jews, referring to the "Remembering for the Future" conference. It was only when I discovered he had been a student of John Pawlikowski, the courageous Catholic theologian from Chicago, that I realized how fortunate we were to have him conducting the ceremony. As we were leaving the church, Bob shook hands with him and said, "You are the first priest I have ever heard who has moved me. You are a good man and I am pleased to shake your hand."

The wedding festivities were beautifully organized by Laura's mother, Judy, and Bob enjoyed himself immensely and behaved impeccably. Ian and Laura left for their honeymoon that night, and the next day Bob took the rest of the family on a memorable picnic in Yellowstone National Park. That day is one of my last really happy memories of Bob, joking, relaxed and good company. After visiting the famous geyser Old Faithful, we found a place beside a broad, slow-flowing river and sat down to a picnic as good as any we had enjoyed at Glyndebourne in the past. I had almost forgotten how nice Bob could be and that day we probably all had our last glimpse of the Bob of old.

I did not see him again until August 24, the day of our reception in France to celebrate Ian's marriage, when he spent two nights in Fraytet. On his arrival, I was stunned by the deterioration in his appearance. All of a sudden, he looked very old; he was gasping for air and sweating profusely. At first I took it to be the heat, but I couldn't get over how much weight he had put on since I had seen him barely two months previously. Although our guests that weekend included many people whose company he enjoyed, Bob was far from his usual exuberant self. My doctor nephew Jean-Marie Polu was shocked when he saw him, and we discussed his health at some length after the party. He told me then that he was obviously suffering from increasing hypoxemia and hypercapnia (an excess of carbon dioxide in the blood) and that unless he went in for serious treatment, he was courting disaster.

I know that Bob was impressed both by the house and the wedding reception, but he could never bring himself to say it directly to me. After that party, I stayed in France until early October when I had to travel to New York, where Bob and I had been invited by Edmond Safra to attend the Elie Wiesel Foundation Humanitarian Award Annual dinner in honor of the King and Queen of Spain. I phoned the Helmsley Palace Hotel where Bob was staying, to let him know I had arrived. He asked me where I was staying and I told him I would either stay with friends or with my niece Helene, unless of course there was a spare room in his suite, which was in fact where I stayed for a week. We went together to the Elie Wiesel dinner and Bob also asked me to attend the party he was hosting at the United Nations on the launch of the North American edition of *The European* newspaper—his brainchild—of which he was inordinately proud. The event was admirably organized by Ian, the paper's deputy publisher, who had attended with him the ceremony to which we had been invited.

Towards the end of our stay in New York, Bob, who had been feeling unwell for several days, developed a dreadful cold, as he often did when he stayed in air-conditioned buildings; he was coughing heavily. Whenever he was staying in a hotel, Bob preferred to be looked after by his own staff, but for some reason, this time he had allowed his butler Nigel to return to England a couple of days before his own departure, with the result that he was not as well looked after as he might have been. Bob was also affected and deeply hurt by the false accusations in a recently published book that he was a Mossad agent and involved in arms-dealing. On the morning I was due to fly back home, I went into the kitchen of his suite to make a cup of coffee, but the place was in such a terrible mess, with every cup and plate dirty, that I couldn't even find the kettle, and we were in the presidential suite of one of the world's top hotels! Bob came down from his bedroom on the mezzanine floor to the vast drawing room and started ranting at me for not giving him a cup of coffee. I asked him why he had let Nigel go back ahead of him and suggested he call room service since I was rushing to catch my plane. I have a last vision of him on the settee that day, full of his cold, looking miserable and angry.

We were due to meet again three weeks later, on Monday, November 4, when Bob was to speak at the Anglo-Israel Association dinner in London. Still feeling unwell, he had flown directly from New York to the *Lady Ghislaine* in Palma in search of heat and sunshine to cure his cold. He was in touch with the boys over the weekend and reported that he was feeling a little better but was still bothered by an irritating cough. On Monday morning I phoned him myself, since I suspected I might well be asked to deputize at the dinner. Bob told me that he had decided to stay on board for an extra couple of days. I replied, "Don't worry, Ian and I will hold the fort. It's more important for you to get rid of your cold. We'll do our best." To which he replied, "Yes, I know you will." Those were his last words to me.

That evening I went with Ian to the Grosvenor Hotel. When the time came for Bob's speech, Ian and I walked together to the platform and I had the difficult task of explaining to a stunned audience that the guest speaker would not be speaking that night. Ian then delivered his father's speech with great confidence, so much so that people soon forgot that his father should have been there instead of him. It was an excellent speech and Ian made his father proud for the last time that night. He phoned Bob as soon as he was home to tell him that all had gone well. "So, you'll be home by Wednesday, Dad?" asked Ian, and Bob replied, "You bet I will." Those were to be his last words to his family.

EPILOGUE

Every strange effect has some strange cause. My sons and I have done nothing to deserve this. It is an inscrutable punishment, therefore I weep!

THOMAS MERTON, *THE WAY OF CHUANG TZU*

Yet he that can endure
To follow with allegiance a fallen lord,
Does conquer him that did his master conquer,
And earns a place in the story.

SHAKESPEARE, *ANTHONY AND CLEOPATRA*

I had left my husband's body in Jerusalem and felt at peace on my return to England. Just as I dream of being buried in Mérindol in Provence, where my ancestors fought and died for their faith, Bob was laid to rest, as he had wished, in that most hallowed ground for Jews. There, in the cemetery on the Mount of Olives, not far from the Dome of the Rock and the site of the holy temples, I knew his body would lie in the safekeeping of a people who have great respect for their dead, and the massive Jerusalem stone slab of his tomb, inscribed with the names of his parents and siblings who themselves had no grave, would forever seal the mystery of his death. His soul had returned to God, all-knowing and all-forgiving. I returned to the silence of my home where the loving care of my staff cushioned my loneliness. My primary concern, however, was for my children. Christine was still in Paris expecting her baby; Ian and Kevin were facing an ordeal far beyond their years and experience; Ghislaine was on her own in New York, uncertain of her future; the others were coping with the trauma as best they could. They all needed comfort and support. For myself, what I most needed in those early days was sleep to recover from my immense fatigue.

As an immediate consolation, I began reading some of the condolence letters I had received, which matched the mood of the many tributes published in the national and international press. Most of those letters and telegrams recognized Bob's undeniable qualities, some also gently pointed out his shortcomings. One of the most balanced assessments of Bob came from Chaim Bermant, a Jewish writer and journalist I had long admired, whose article for the *Jewish Chronicle* corrected the nonsense previously written about Bob's "sudden reconversion to Judaism." Chaim stated the simple truth as only a Jew could:

> The fact that he had fought in the War and been decorated for valor by Montgomery, that he had a stately home in Oxford, was a Member of Parliament and was married to a Christian woman who was every inch a lady, did not, however, make him an English gentleman. Here, as elsewhere, he was in too much of a hurry, for the process takes about 300 years and when it became clear that in spite of his wealth and prominence he would never become an establishment figure, he reverted to his origins and became a Jew again. . . .
>
> His re-conversion was not an overnight phenomenon and the process must have been helped by the adverse publicity he provoked, not a little of which had distinct anti-Semitic undertones. . . . Once he became a Jew again, it was inevitable that he should become a super-Jew, not in the religious sense, but the nationalist one.

What was striking about the nearly five thousand letters and messages I received was the recurrence of similar words to describe the impact Bob had made on people. From prime ministers and presidents to employees, journalists, heads of large corporations and banks, Labor party workers, scientists and ambassadors, the words were frequently repeated—"giant of a man with heroic qualities," "titan," "colossus," "towering figure," "larger than life," "the most fascinating man" they had met in their lives. Many commented on his "inexhaustible thirst for life," "the sheer force of his magnetic power," his "extraordinary perceptiveness" and "remarkable tenacity." His generosity, of which he did not boast, was mentioned by many. As his Israeli lawyer told me, Bob could be praised as a *matan baseter,* an anonymous benefactor, and I myself only discovered through those condolence letters just how many individuals and institutions he had helped financially or materially.

Mrs. Thatcher sent a three-page handwritten personal letter in which her admiration for Bob was clearly in evidence: "No one will ever replace the energy, vision and resolve personified in Mr. Maxwell. He was and will remain unique. Above all Mr. Maxwell showed the whole world that one person can move and influence events by using his own God-given talents and abilities." Neil Kinnock hailed Bob as "a true day star of his age" and added, "Many, like me, valued Bob's friendship and loyalty and admired his remarkable tenacity, intelligence and insights. We will all miss the infectious vitality of one of the few people that I have known who deserved to be called irreplaceable." John Major was even said to have delayed his weekly audience with the Queen so that he could release his tribute to the press: "No one should doubt his interest in peace and his loyalty to friends. During the attempted Soviet coup this August, he was able to give me valuable insights into the situation in the Soviet Union because of his many contacts. . . . [His was] a quite extraordinary life, lived to the full." Chancellor Helmut Kohl wrote, "I am very sad that such a good European, who did so much for our better understanding, has died." Israel's Prime Minister Yitzhak Shamir wrote, "God bless his memory. I knew him as a person who was greatly interested in the Israeli economy, invested money in Israel and offered to put his wide contacts on the international arena at Israel's service." President Bush wrote of Bob's "humanitarian endeavors and of his unwavering commitment to the fight against bigotry and oppression." I was particularly touched that people took the trouble to write at length and by hand, recounting personal anecdotes or recollections that were often new to me. There was the nurse who described how Bob had toiled through the night to locate and deliver expensive medical equipment needed in Bradford after the Valley Parade fire, the Armenians who would never forget how Bob had rushed to the aid of the victims of the 1988 earthquake or the Ethiopian commissioner of relief and rehabilitation who recalled that Bob was one of the first people to arrive in his country with food aid in 1984, at the time of the severest drought in living memory. There were the soldiers who remembered his escape from Hungary or his bravery at the Battle of the Orne in Normandy. It took me many nights to read all those messages, and they brought me great solace.

I also caught up with the newspapers. The first two weeks after Bob's death were to be the "honeymoon" period with the press, when, as the journalist Ivan Fallon stated in the *Sunday Times* on November 10, 1991, "Lifelong enemies suddenly became friends and bankers and investigative journalists who had traded vicious stories in his lifetime joined up to agree on how much they would miss him." Their columns echoed the sentiments expressed in the many letters I had received, and even gilded the lily further. They recalled Bob's tycoon's lifestyle as he held court at the World Economic Forum in Davos with secretary, butler and chauffeur in attendance, entertaining in his suite Hans-Dietrich Genscher, the German minister for foreign affairs; Karl-Otto Pöhl, president of the Bundesbank; Gianni de Michelis, Italy's foreign minister; Andrei Lukanov, prime minister of Bulgaria; and Franjo Tudjman, president of Croatia. Tam Dalyell, a respected MP and good friend since Bob's Parliament days, took it upon himself to distinguish fact from gossip in Bob's political record.

Bob's flagship newspaper, *The European*, launched by him with great fanfare sixteen months earlier, focused on his vision of Europe, explaining that while he was extraordinarily proud of being British, he saw it only as part of a greater identity that went "beyond the bounds of narrow nationalism in a Europe to which everyone can belong, from the Urals to the Atlantic." As for Bob's much criticized meetings with the ex-Communist leaders of Eastern Europe, the paper reminded its readers that he had viewed those contacts as helping to build a bridge of mutual understanding. The many who chided him after 1989 for such encounters often forgot that he had made precisely the same "error" as many Western politicians: Helmut Kohl and François Mitterrand had given Erich Honecker state welcomes; Jimmy Carter had embraced Nicolae Ceaucescu, Britain's Premier Jim Callaghan had invited him to England and the Queen accorded him a state visit. The people's revolutions of 1989 throughout Eastern Europe caught Maxwell and the rest of the world by surprise.

The press was not, however, unanimous in its views on Bob. In an editorial published on the day after his funeral, the *Times* concluded: "Robert Maxwell was abnormal. Even the abnormal are entitled to rest in peace, perhaps the only peace Mr. Maxwell has ever known." Peter McKay penned an article with anti-Semitic undertones in the *Evening Standard* asking, "If you are a British Jew, is Israel your true home?" and concluding, "So did he die an Englishman, or not? Probably not." His article was to prompt the riposte from a British Jew, "Since when did British nationality mean that one had to be buried in Britain? . . . I cannot believe Mr. McKay is trying to infer that one's religious beliefs make a difference to one's feelings of patriotism?" But the most wounding article appeared in the supposedly serious newspaper, *The Guardian*, suggesting that the body Philip and I had identified as my husband's was a substitute, and that I had refused to pass on dental records for formal identification purposes. The paper was wrong on both counts, as it later admitted.

Friends in Paris were so outraged that they advised me to accept an invitation to appear on television to refute such downright disinformation. That was how I came to appear on Elkabbach's program,[1] alongside the friendly figure of Cardinal Lustiger. My television interview was well received, and I felt better for it, but to my intense disappointment, it was to prevent me from being with Christine for the birth of Giselle, my eighth grandchild. Just as I was going into the studio, I received a message to say that the baby had been safely delivered, and I mentioned it in my interview. I was so pleased for Christine and her husband, Roger; she was still terribly upset about having missed her father's funeral and the prospect of rebuilding her home in California after its destruction in the disastrous Oakland fire two months earlier. But as always, Christine's twin sister, Isabel, and her second husband, David Hayden, would be there to help and support her.

I was subsequently approached by two Jewish organizations that had made plans to confer awards on Bob prior to his death and wanted me to receive them in his stead. One was the Zionist Organization of America, which had selected Bob for its prestigious Justice Louis D. Brandeis Award for exemplary service to Israel, the Jewish people and the community; the other was the YIVO Institute for Jewish Research, which wanted to pay tribute to Bob's commitment to Jewish history and culture. I left for New York towards the end of November and was away for three days.

By the time I returned, my fragile equilibrium was shattered by the devastating reports of serious defalcations involving the Maxwell Group. The collapse of Bob's empire was speedy, calamitous and complete. The event was as sudden as it was unexpected. I was dazed. Each day brought fresh allegations and accusations, and my sense of profound shock deepened into despair as I read with mounting disbelief of "missing monies" from the Group's pension funds. On December 3, the share quotations of the Group's two UK publicly quoted companies—Maxwell Communication Corporation (MCC) and Mirror Group Newspapers (MGN)—were suspended. That morning, Ian

---

1. Jean-Pierre Elkabbach, now a director of France's TF1 channel, hosted a popular television interview program at the time.

and Kevin had resigned from the board of directors of MCC on the grounds of potential conflict of interest and, by the late afternoon, both had also resigned from the board of MGN for the same reason. On December 5, administrators were appointed to Robert Maxwell Group, and on December 6, with Kevin in New York and Ian on his own in London, the Serious Fraud Office (SFO) raided Maxwell House, the Group's headquarters next door to the Mirror Building. Court actions against Ian and Kevin started almost immediately— their assets were frozen, their passports seized and the first of seemingly endless court orders issued. Within days they had received summonses to appear before the House of Commons Select Committee on Social Security in the new year. The SFO was subsequently to launch five separate investigations into the Maxwell Group's affairs, which are now the subject of court proceedings and which I do not propose to comment on in this book. Within three weeks of burying Bob, my world and that of my family had been shattered. The fragile process of grieving was replaced by a terrifying fight to survive.

The press was having a field day, producing a cascade of some of the most vicious reporting I can ever recall. The most grotesque, unsubstantiated and of course untrue stories began to appear daily in the press, with lurid details which the tabloids in particular thought would titillate the British public, ever hungry for scandal, especially of a sexual nature. Unscrupulous young women intent on cash rewards made preposterous claims of intimacy with my husband. Even self-proclaimed "serious" writers indulged in inventing madams whose charges had apparently been summoned to Bob's Maxwell House penthouse without any of the domestic or security staff being aware of it. With my knowledge of Bob's prudishness, his almost manic desire for personal cleanliness, and paranoia about AIDS, it made strange reading. Since I knew all such stories to be fiction, it did not affect me in my pride as his wife, but I was shattered to think that the reputation of a proud man like Bob could thus be dragged into the gutter by such worthless people. My respect for the press sank lower still when I saw decent journalists like John Jackson or Eve Pollard joining in the fray, or serious newspapers like the *Financial Times* taking their cue as to the value of my supposed assets from the magazine *Hello!*

Through all of this, I was sustained by my respect and love for the memory of Bob's mother, this woman I had never known but to whom I felt so close at the time. She and her family had gone through far worse, along with all their fellow Jews, who had been humiliated, vilified, degraded and finally murdered. How did I dare complain, even to myself? I felt supported by sharing vicariously, even in a small way, an appalling fate and being punished for alleged deeds I had neither committed nor been aware of. From the moment the media sluice gates opened, allowing the sewers of Fleet Street "to overflow into my drawing room,"[2] I decided that I had to survive, as many of my Jewish survivor friends had done in far worse circumstances, in order to bear witness. Nothing gives one more strength than the knowledge of one's innocence and the ingrained hope that justice must eventually prevail. I owed it to Bob to fight for his memory, for myself and for our children, and not to accept defeat—especially at the hands of such people, peddling their lies for cash and transient publicity.

Continual harassment by the press was to be our daily lot for the best part of a year. I was protected in Oxford, where the security guards at the entrance to Pergamon Press had become friends over the years and kept the journalists at bay. For the boys, however, who lived in London, it was an ordeal; reporters literally camped out on their doorsteps so that neither they nor their wives and children could carry on their normal lives without being followed everywhere. By the end of that first week in December, I really felt the need for a weekend of peace and sleep and I left by car for France with Isabel, my friend Wendy and Oping. Although I thought no one knew of our departure, the press was clearly tipped off and within hours of our arrival at Fraytet mounted a siege outside the gates of my home. I was fortunately shielded by a village farmer who had known me since my youth and patrolled the grounds with his retriever and shotgun! When an English journalist asked him if he would really use his weapon, my protector answered, pointing at the gate, "Behind there, no, inside here, yes!" This was the origin of the tale that I had surrounded myself with armed guards and rottweilers trained to attack poor innocent reporters.

Those journalists and photographers did not leave the gates for three days; they rang the doorbell at regular intervals all day long and left notes in the letterbox. Not content with these tactics, they even hired a microlight aircraft and "buzzed" the house and garden,

---

2. With apologies to Clarissa Eden, who first coined this expression in connection with the Suez Canal, at the time when her husband, Sir Anthony Eden, was prime minister.

taking photographs, preventing me from taking a stroll outside. I felt as if I had wandered onto a James Bond film set, except that 007 was not waiting in the wings to rescue me. We felt imprisoned in the house and began to wonder how on earth we would manage to leave without running the gauntlet of those insistent newsmen. Our prayers were answered when, over the weekend, a sudden bitter frost engulfed the countryside and the frozen journalists abandoned their siege. We left at three o'clock the next morning, a Sunday, and made for Bordeaux, where, with the help of friendly British Airways personnel, Isabel and I managed to catch a plane for Paris within ten minutes of our arrival, leaving our luggage with Wendy and Oping. They were to travel back from Bordeaux later that day, unrecognized and sitting alongside the very reporters who had been clamoring at my gates. From Paris, Isabel and I took a plane to Birmingham and from there a train to London's Euston Station. We had succeeded in losing our pursuers and I was able to travel back to Oxford undetected.

Immediately after that distressing weekend in Fraytet, I made a mistake I greatly regret. I had agreed to be interviewed by a freelance journalist, Edward Klein, for an article to appear in *Vanity Fair*. Those were early days in my exposure to the media after Bob's death; I was gullible and unaware of my right to impose conditions before I talked to the press. I know now that I should have insisted on seeing a draft of the article before it was published and asked for the scheduled date of publication. Had I done so, I would have avoided a situation which proved painful and highly embarrassing when the article was published two months later. In early December, MGN announced publicly in its papers and directly to all its pension fund contributors that their pensions were safe and not a single member would be affected by the shortfall discovered in the funds. So when I told Edward Klein on December 10 that I believed I was the only pensioner affected, I was presenting the situation as it was at the time, since my own pension had been stopped on December 1, without any prior notification either to me or my lawyer. By the time the article appeared in February 1992, however, these statements appeared callous in the extreme, when many other Maxwell Group pensioners were threatened with the loss of their pensions and had seen the security of their old age shattered. For these Group pensioners, alas, the financial situation has hardly improved since then and the outlook remains very bleak, although for Mirror Group pensioners the future is brighter. They have since continued to receive their payments regularly, with a 5 percent yearly increase put into effect since May 1992. As the chairman of the MGN Pension Trustees was to make clear in an open letter recently published in *The Independent on Sunday*, the Group has "agreed to refinance the pensions of all its current and former employees, no matter how much or how little of the missing funds are recovered."[3]

When Klein questioned me on the state of my finances, I told him the truth—that I was penniless and saddled with huge debts. Earlier that morning, I had talked at length with my newly appointed lawyer, David Freeman, who left me with no illusions as to the financial mess in which I found myself. He explained gently but clearly exactly what would happen to any money or chattels I might have inherited in Bob's will, or to any money, chattels or property of any kind I owned or to monies that Bob had given me over the last few years. The only positive note he sounded was that if property or chattels were mine and mine alone and had been for at least five years, and this could be proved to the satisfaction of the recently appointed receivers to Bob's estate, I would then be entitled to retain them. David advised me to make total disclosure of my financial affairs and I followed his advice.

After that interview with Klein, I was extremely wary of all reporters and deliberately avoided any contact with them. For the next two years, it became a private game to dodge the persistent attentions of the media. They finally concluded that I had ignominiously fled the country, taken refuge in my "castle" in France, full of eighteenth-century paintings and stained-glass windows (*sic*) and was living off the ill-gotten gains of the pots of gold hidden in Liechtenstein! This myth of my disappearance was to become so pervasive that it actually came to protect me; reporters eventually believed their own lies and even friends started sending their letters to France. I did, however, make a public appearance early in the new year, fulfilling a promise I had made many months earlier to open an exhibition of the paintings of Arnold Daghani, a Romanian Holocaust survivor who died in Britain. The hall was packed with reporters and photographers, and I told them in my opening remarks:

You may perhaps be a little surprised to see me here. Contrary to media lies about me, I have not had to return from anywhere because I have never fled

---

3. Letter from Colin Cornwall, *The Independent on Sunday*, 26 June 1994.

from this country. I am not the bolting type, nor a coward, nor have I ever fled from any of my responsibilities. I am a fighter, I am an action person and, as long as God gives me life, I shall fight for my beliefs irrespective of the price I have to pay.

As I faced the media that day, I was determined not to be cowed by their presence. But their intrusive reporting and endless speculation about Bob's death was soon to be further fueled by *Paris Match*'s publication of gruesome photographs of the second autopsy carried out in Israel just before Bob's funeral. The whole matter of the autopsies was exceedingly distressing for me. In mid-December, Judge Isabel Oliva had received the final Spanish autopsy report and ordered the case closed without giving any firm verdict on how Bob had died. This led the media to speculate even more wildly about the manner of his death. More significantly, it revived all those feelings of unease I had had on the boat. There were so many inconsistencies and unexplained details. In the shock of the early days, although I was bewildered by many aspects of Bob's death, my primary concern had been to ensure that he was buried in Jerusalem as he had requested. Only a few minutes after we had formally identified the body, the local doctors asked Philip in Spanish whether we wanted them to be solely responsible for the autopsy or did we want them to conduct it in the presence of a "British colleague" of our choice? Philip remembers that I was numb and in shock at the time. He thought the matter through briefly, translated for me what the Spanish doctors had asked then gave me his view: it was not essential to have a British specialist; it would only complicate matters. I was influenced by his opinion and decided—to their obvious relief—to let the Spanish doctors alone do the autopsy. My husband was dead; it was enough for me that the Spaniards could certify that fact. It was Bob's funeral that was uppermost in my mind. By the next day, however, a telephone call from my friend Sam Pisar, the international lawyer, had sown the first doubts in my mind as to the manner of Bob's death. Sam's subsequent fax with suggested questions to put to the crew and Spanish medical team alerted me to the importance of the autopsy. When, early that same morning, the Maxwell Group's insurance brokers also got in touch with me, I realized that the results of the autopsy would be crucial and asked the insurers via the brokers to send an English pathologist immediately. I was astonished when I was told that the pathologist they wanted to send would not be available until late afternoon on the Friday, three days after Bob had died, as he was working on another case. I explained that the weekend would be too late and asked that someone else be sent right away but I was told that they wanted Dr. West and no one else. They reassured me, however, that it did not matter, since the autopsy could be conducted in Tel Aviv where there were better forensic facilities, and I bowed to their professional advice.

The published results of the autopsy carried out in Spain were confusing. While the preliminary Spanish report releasing the body for burial had concluded that Bob had died of cardio-respiratory arrest and that there were no signs of violence, the external state of the body was not that normally found in corpses which have remained in contact with water for any length of time. The definitive Spanish report, however, pinpointed the time of death at 6 A.M. on November 5, give or take an hour, and concluded that the external signs from being in the water were just about compatible with the time between death and the recovery of the body. The final report also stated that there were no signs of external violence—no punctures, no injuries suggesting blockage of the respiratory canals, no wounds indicative of a criminal act. Taken together, all the evidence suggested an accidental death, a combination of a heart problem and drowning.

Yet the autopsy carried out on behalf of the insurers produced some troubling revelations. Conducted at the Tel Aviv Institute of Forensic Medicine on November 9, it had taken place with the collaboration of its director, Dr. Yehuda Hiss, and the British pathologists Dr. Iain Eric West and Dr. Vesna Djurovic (Mrs. West), along with other pathologists and technicians. I was subsequently contacted by both Dr. West and the insurance company's loss adjuster, Mr. Rich, who asked me to forward all Bob's available medical and dental records, which I did immediately. I know, however, that Dr. West experienced some difficulties with the Spanish authorities, specifically in obtaining a copy of their detailed final report to allow him to complete his own report. Both Dr. Hiss and Dr. West wrote separate accounts of their findings and a video and photographs were taken of the autopsy. Their reports revealed a disquieting range of injuries thus far unsuspected, and the pathologists' taped commentaries, which were later handed to my French lawyer, raised fresh questions in my mind about about the cause of death.

Dr. West's report, which finally appeared only in February 1992, gave precise details of a whole range of injuries which had been caused before death; there were significant hemorrhages in and around damaged tissues on the back, shoulders and arms. The right shoulder injuries appeared to have been caused by contact with a patterned surface, those to the legs were possibly caused by knocking against floating objects in the water but bruising under the right ear suggested a more substantial impact. The severe tearing and bleeding on the left shoulder was the result of sudden physical stress being applied to the muscle, suggesting that the deceased may at some point have been hanging by his left hand. The report reads:

> While the injuries on the back may, on the face of it, be more suggestive of accident, they can be explained in terms of suicide. . . . This group of injuries, therefore, should not be used as the sole indicator of suicide or accident; they must be considered with other factors.
>
> It is impossible to exclude homicide. There are no injuries on the deceased which indicate that he has been assaulted, but even a man of this size, particularly one who is unfit, could easily be pushed into the sea without leaving injuries which were characteristic of an assault.

As for the heart attack theory, Dr. West could find no evidence to indicate that Bob had suffered a thrombosis of the coronary circulation, nor any evidence of recent myo-cardiac infarction or heart attack, although he did regret the lack of a specific forensic test by the Spaniards, which could have determined this more precisely. By then, however, Bob's heart had been removed during the Spanish autopsy, sent to Madrid and dissected to such an extent "that it could not be anatomically reconstructed." Although Dr. West went to Madrid and returned to London with samples, it was clear that the Spanish "had retained the pertinent blocks of tissue" on the basis of which they had reached their conclusions. In fact, several organs, including the heart, much of the lungs, the brain, oesophagus, stomach and bladder, had been retained by the Spanish authorities for further forensic examination and dissection. This caused me considerable anguish, as had the embalming of Bob's body by the Spaniards, which I found distasteful, had not requested and which must have made the Tel Aviv autopsy much more difficult. The organs were later recovered from Madrid at my request and handed over to the Jerusalem Burial Society to be interred with Bob's body. Dr. West's final verdict, like Dr. Hiss's, was that the most likely cause of death was drowning, but he went on to suggest a variety of possible scenarios, apparently without any firsthand knowledge of the boat, some of which, in my opinion and experience of the *Lady Ghislaine*, are frankly implausible. According to press reports, West, possibly influenced by what he had read subsequently, speculated that suicide was the most probable cause of death, but it is impossible to know if he was correctly quoted.

The matter is by no means closed in my mind, nor in that of my family, and I bitterly regret that a full inquiry was not carried out by Scotland Yard at the time of Bob's death. It is easy to see things more clearly some three years after the event, but there were intense pressures on me at the time which prevented me from focusing clearly on the way the local investigation was being conducted and all the anomalies that subsequently emerged. In retrospect, notwithstanding my own insistence on their releasing Bob's body to me, the Spanish police, judges and forensic experts all seemed eager to get the body off their hands rather than become embroiled in an international investigation with potentially complicated overtones. The local police, in particular, appeared noticeably lax, attributable perhaps to the fact that we were on a remote island off the coast of Spain, an easygoing resort where "mañana" was very much the order of the day. I am not aware, for example, that any fingerprint investigations were carried out on significant areas of the boat, either on the day of Bob's death or in the days immediately following. I am surprised, too, that some unresolved matters were not investigated further. After I arrived home from the funeral, I was clearing out my handbag and realized that by mistake I had kept my key to the safe. I telephoned the captain immediately, asking him for a land address in Spain to which I could return the key by registered post. He said, "It's not necessary, Mrs. Maxwell, I have a key." I swallowed hard for a moment and asked, "Just out of interest, Captain, where did you find it?" He answered, "In one of Mr. Maxwell's suits in his cabin." From my thorough search of the cabin on the night of Bob's death, I could hardly believe that that was possible. A whole series of statements like this, which are at odds with the "official" facts surrounding my husband's death, have left me feeling very uneasy ever since.

I was shocked, too, that when the loss adjusters were preparing their report, they never sought to ask my opinion on Bob's death, nor did they ask me or my son Philip to comment on their findings nor even show me their report before it was released to the press. My other children should also have been interviewed, especially in light of the allegations of changes in Bob's behavior and personality in the days preceding his death. Some of the loss adjusters' conclusions seemed speculative and not based on the factual evidence I had seen or knew. They appear to have been reached principally on the strength of interviews of the crew conducted more than a week after the events, when wild press speculation may have influenced some crew members, several of whom had only recently been hired and barely knew Bob. I also remain puzzled as to why MGN and MCC, with their joint interest in the £20 million insurance claim and with the most to gain from challenging the loss adjusters' findings, have apparently chosen not to pursue the insurers through the courts on the basis of the pathologists' inconclusive reports as to the cause of death.

I said at the time—and will never alter my view—that Bob did not commit suicide. Even at this late stage, I would welcome a proper independent inquiry by competent authorities and I agree with the newspaper *Today,* which, on the day after Bob's burial, published an article headlined, LET YARD SOLVE MAXWELL RIDDLE. The article continued, "Almost a week after his death it is not even clear whether he died from natural causes, an accident, suicide or murder. The mystery of Mr. Maxwell's death needs to be cleared up, not just for the sake of his family, who should not have this additional burden of uncertainty to bear with their grief. Yet nothing that we have so far seen of the investigation into his death gives us any confidence that the Spanish authorities are remotely capable of even determining the cause of death."

I spent a very sad family Christmas at Kevin and Pandora's home in the country, the heavy atmosphere relieved only by the joy of their children, who were still too young to understand what had happened to us all as a result of "Granddad" Bob's death. Pandora is a great wife to Kevin, enormously loving and supportive, yet independent of spirit and quite prepared to speak her own mind. Even during the worst moments of crisis over the last two and a half years, she has managed to maintain a happy home life for her husband and family, ensuring their safety and well-being. I love her dearly and adore my grandchildren, and my only regret is that I have to work such long hours that I have little time to enjoy their company.

With no real break at Christmas, I plunged into 1992, the worst year of my life. From beginning to end, it was my own *annus horribilis.* Every day brought its share of bad news, and when I look back, I wonder how I survived it all. I was reliving 1969 to 1975 all over again, except this time the whole family was in the firing line and Bob was no longer there to provide material and moral support. I felt as if I were being publicly raped every day of the week. The only protection I had between me and the outside world was my lawyer, David Freeman, whom I had met once or twice some twenty years before and who had been recommended to me. My only previous contact with the legal profession had been with the American lawyer who had dealt quickly and effectively with Saul Steinberg's frivolous suit against me in 1969. Now suddenly I found myself having to talk to a man who wanted to know the most minute details about my personal and financial affairs and of my relationship with my husband and asked me to give him a full account of my life in the previous ten years. I had barely talked to anyone about my difficulties with Bob, let alone to a stranger; it was truly my very private and secret garden. But David left no stone unturned in getting at the facts and helping me to prove to the receivers my entitlement to my assets.

My relationship with David was difficult at first, but with hindsight I admire his patience with a woman who was intensely private by nature and also rebellious, angry, bewildered and resentful, a widow who had not been allowed to grieve for the husband she had loved. He coaxed me into accepting that from then on, for as long as any matters remained unresolved, I had to comply with the receivers' requests for documents, letters, accounts and bank statements. He was very protective but also very firm. Overnight, my life was transformed into that of a lawyer's assistant unraveling my own affairs. I had to look into documents going back five years, make sense of old bank correspondence, insurances, inventories, statements, contracts, expenses. The prying into my private life was endless. I was fortunate to have the help of my secretary, Jay Miller, who was to remain at my side during the first difficult months at a much reduced salary. When I wasn't at my desk dictating letters to lawyers or searching for answers in old documents, I was on my way to London in a small car belonging to Ghislaine which she had lent me, driven by a former Pergamon driver, Robert Ord, who had lost his job in the collapse of the Group and was helping me out of the goodness of his heart. Without this decent and caring friend, and others like him, I cannot imagine how I would have withstood the severe exhaustion caused by all the stress under which I was living.

As the year began, in what evolved into an almost daily ritual, I penned the first letter to my lawyer, who was to become something of a father confessor:

I find myself telling you my innermost thoughts, which I have never allowed to surface. I feel totally vulnerable and defenseless. My only protection against all these sharks is my business virginity, my innocence of alleged crimes, my physical and spiritual strength, my pugnacity and you, my own lawyer.

Sotheby's auction of the contents of Bob's London penthouse flat was one of the first ordeals of that year. The press turned it into a real circus, with "glamour" girls photographed on Bob's bed and former employees volunteering lurid details about his personal habits which they could not possibly have witnessed. It was a complete disgrace. I had rarely spent the night in the flat since Bob had moved there in the mid-eighties since I was not made to feel welcome. Nor was I sentimentally attached to its contents since hardly any of them belonged to me. Although the sale attracted a great many people, most were onlookers and it was not a great success. Serious buyers were frightened off by the press, who questioned both the origin and quality of the antique furniture. Everything had to be sold, by order of the receivers, and no reserve prices were set. A set of baseball caps worth a few dollars in America sold for over £1000, yet a most valuable mahogany period dining table, mirrors, chandeliers and expensive settees, as well as paintings by well-known artists, were all sold at bargain-basement prices. Such was the urge to dismantle the flat that even the beautiful specially woven carpets were taken up and remained unsold in a Sotheby's warehouse for months afterwards; whereas had they been left in place, they may well have enhanced the sale of the furniture.

On the legal front, predictably enough, 1992 started dreadfully with Kevin and Ian appearing before the House of Commons Select Committee to answer MPs' questions about the Maxwell Group's pension funds and the "missing monies." The hearing was to be public and televised. In a deeply hostile environment, they duly appeared, accompanied by separate teams of legal advisors. Both Kevin and Ian's barristers protested eloquently on their behalf at the wholly unjust and unprecedented nature of the event: the fact that it was to take place in public and be televised, although civil proceedings had already commenced on subjects the committee was likely to be asking them about, and there was a real prospect of criminal proceedings being brought against them; furthermore, their clients had had no indication beforehand of the questions that were to be put to them. It was to be of no avail. Despite offers by both Ian and Kevin to answer written questions in writing, provided that their answers would be kept confidential to the Select Committee, the committee chairman Frank Field, after consultation with his fellow MPs, decided against such a course of action and determined to go ahead with his questioning. His first question was to Ian, who answered through his barrister that for the reasons already stated he would not respond. Field then asked Kevin the same question and received an identical response from his barrister. This farce continued for a further ten minutes in an electric atmosphere; every attempt to elicit an answer was met politely but firmly with a rebuff. Field had had enough and the meeting broke up.

Kevin and Ian's refusal to answer the Select Committee's questions was the lead story in all the newspapers the following day. For once, the press grudgingly came out in almost unanimous support of the stance the boys had taken. The *Times* devoted several articles to the matter, one of which was headlined CHEERS FOR THE RIGHT TO SILENCE. In an editorial, the *Daily Mail* commented:

> If the Maxwell brothers had answered fully and frankly, their words could have been later used in evidence against them and so be held to have prejudiced their chance of a fair trial.
> That, the *Daily Mail* would have thought, is a good and sufficient reason why you may drag a potential defendant to the Commons, but you cannot make him speak.

Hardly had all the furore surrounding the hearing subsided when I found myself cited as corespondent in an action brought against Kevin by the liquidators of Bishopsgate Investment Management (BIM), erstwhile managers of the Common Investment Fund for the Group's pension schemes. BIM were attempting to recover their legal costs from me (as I had provided the funds for Kevin's defense to their action), but they eventually lost on this point and I was awarded costs.

I soon realized that I was engaged in a war and could only hope it would not turn out to be the Thirty Years' War! I found myself constantly dealing with the demands of Maxwell company administrators who, together with armies of lawyers, were engaged in carving up the Empire on behalf of its many creditors. Amongst the battles I was fighting, I had to disprove wholly untrue and offensive assertions that I was harboring my husband's business papers, that I had been seen late at night going to neighbors' houses to hide diskettes, microfiches and business accounts and that boxes of secret papers were lined up in the corridors of my home destined to be secreted overseas. There were indeed boxes at Headington—twenty-four to be precise—that were full of Bob's clothes ready to be dispatched to the World Jewish Relief Organization, and from there to war-torn Yugoslavia to help clothe refugees from Croatia and Bosnia. While in the Canary Islands, I was alleged to have convened a meeting of the "Maxwell Foundation" appointing Ian and Kevin as directors, which was a complete fiction. Every day there was another libel to contend with, endless lists of questions to be answered and sheet upon sheet of accounts to be gone through. After that, the charity commissioners froze Remembering for the Future's funds, even though Bob's signature had never been on the bank mandate. Once again, my lawyer came to the rescue and generously sorted out the problem without charging me or the charity any fees. Every time I won one battle, another front would open. I felt like Saint George fighting the dragon, but my beast was a multiheaded hydra. Ian and Kevin were under far more intense attack on multiple fronts, as were the twins and Ghislaine to a lesser extent, who were called upon to account for monies they had allegedly received from Bob or to defend and justify their so-called extravagant lifestyles. As in the early seventies, we made a conscious decision to pool what meager resources we had, giving each other moral strength and sharing our homes, friends, ideas and time. A battle won by one was a victory for us all, a battle lost meant reinforcements were immediately deployed.

My first "victory" was a financial one: at a time when not a single bank in England was prepared to lend me a penny, whatever security I could offer, a rescuer appeared on the other side of the Channel. I visited three of Bob's former friends in France to ask them to advance me money with Fraytet pledged as security. My first two visits resulted in refusals and I set out for the third expecting a similar response. I was shown into the office of a well-known head of an insurance and banking conglomerate. I had never met him before, but he received me courteously, telling me he would always remember my husband's extraordinary qualities and the sound business they had done together. He looked at me and asked, "And now, Madame, what can I do for you?" I simply told him the truth about my dismal financial situation and waited for the no I had become accustomed to hearing. But he picked up his telephone, called his bank director and said, "I'm sending Mrs. Maxwell to you, do the best you can for her." I felt faint and I shall never forget the way he dealt with my plight. It was his generous support that began to turn the tide for me and made me believe that I still had friends, even if I did not know them all personally. He was to be the first of four white knights who shall remain anonymous to protect them from the "Max Factor"—a journalistic expression referring to the stigma attached to Bob or anything or anybody associated with Maxwell. Thanks to this friend's intervention, within fifteen days of my visit the bank granted me a mortgage at a reasonable rate of interest on my home in France, which helped me to repay early a significant amount of my debts.

I had realized, more or less from the start of this terrible period, that I would have to find a way of earning a living since I had no capital to fall back on. For a man of his wealth, Bob had done little to ensure my security in old age. He had rarely given me gifts of money and had not invested in a nest egg for me; he just did not believe in tucking capital away like that. His approach to the children was similar, and having given them a good education, he expected them to make their own way. Ghislaine was perhaps in the most difficult position of us all: although rumor had it she was a wealthy young woman, she was in fact left to restart life on her own, with a bank overdraft and a huge mortgage in a falling property market. After sending three representatives to New York to interview her, the SFO was to discover that all the nonsense written about her "income from Gibraltar trust funds" was a complete fabrication.

As for me, at seventy years of age, the only practical skill I had was an ability to write. All my life I had written letters, poems, stories, speeches, lectures and finally a thesis. I decided that I would have to write my own story, even though I was reluctant to make my private life public. It was a matter of survival. I began working immediately on a book, which in England resulted in a publishing contract with Sidgwick & Jackson. Ironically, it was Rupert Murdoch, with whom Bob had had a far from cordial relationship, who ultimately helped me to secure a contract in America with his own publishing house, HarperCollins.

In June 1992 the family was to live through its worst crisis. In the preceding months, Ian and Kevin's solicitors had assured the SFO verbally and in writing that they would cooperate fully with the police investigations, and that in the event of any charges being made, they would present themselves on demand at a preselected police station to avoid the inevitable media circus and the prejudice they would certainly suffer resulting from a public arrest. Despite reaching what both sets of lawyers accepted as an understanding with the SFO, out of the blue on June 18, both Kevin and Ian were arrested at their homes at the crack of dawn in the glare of flash guns, with dozens of reporters witnessing the whole performance. The media, having clearly been tipped off the day before, had flocked to both boys' homes. In a now celebrated incident filmed by TV crews, Pandora, mistaking the police for journalists, shouted at them from her bedroom window to "piss off." In front of their wives and, in the case of Kevin, his children, both boys were bundled into waiting cars and driven off to Snow Hill Police Station near the Mirror building. Fingerprinted and photographed, they were then locked up in police cells prior to appearing in court later that morning.

Many people, whether they were friends of ours or not, wrote or phoned me to express their outrage at the press photos of those early-morning arrests and Ian and Kevin's subsequent transfer to court from the police station, ignominiously frog-marched in front of a massive crowd into a waiting Black Maria, each held tightly by a policeman for the few steps between the station and the vehicle. The director of the SFO later denied that his staff had tipped off the media, but I found it difficult to believe him. Looking back on those events, it seems to me that the timing of the arrest was primarily determined by mounting press criticism that no charges had yet been laid, some seven months after the launch of the police investigations, and by the SFO's need to be seen to take action. It was to be another thirteen months before Ian and Kevin were "transferred" to the jurisdiction of the Crown Court, where their case will be tried. A further sixteen months have since gone by, with their trial now likely to begin in the spring of 1995—forty months after the collapse of the Group.

I was spared the horror and pain of Ian's and Kevin's arrests since I was in Berlin that day, helping to rescue the second international Remembering for the Future conference, scheduled for 1994, which was in danger of collapsing for lack of funds. But I received desperate phone calls from Laura and Pandora, asking me to alert my friends to help the boys find bail, eventually set at £500,000 for Kevin and £250,000 for Ian, since I myself could not raise the required sums. I frantically began telephoning. It was Pandora's family who put up bail for her husband, and they also generously assisted with Ian's bail, together with a personal friend of his. Kevin's and Ian's arrests were given massive national and international coverage. One would be hard put to find a single person in Britain who had not read about or seen their arrest on TV and was not in some way negatively influenced by it, and by the mountain of prejudicial articles published before and after the event which virtually condemned them before their case could be tried in a court of law. From the date of their arrest, they were both granted Legal Aid.

In early September another ghastly event occurred. Following an action brought against Kevin in December the previous year by the liquidators of Bishopsgate Management, he was declared bankrupt for £406 million, making his the biggest personal bankruptcy in recorded history. I did wonder at the time, and still do, how it could be right to bankrupt one man for such a vast sum while so many others—directors and external professionals involved in running the Maxwell Group or advising it—were not themselves facing civil, let alone criminal charges. Personal bankruptcy is a terrible process and carries a real stigma. The immediate result was that Kevin's estate was put in the hands of a trustee in bankruptcy, his London home sold and his ability to earn any income beyond the bare minimum necessary to support a family of five children curtailed. Ian, meanwhile, against whom Bishopsgate had brought a virtually identical action, had been vigorously defending himself throughout the summer against their winding-up petition, but inexplicably, the judge presiding over the hearing was to reserve his judgment for nearly five months.

The family had barely come to terms with Kevin's bankruptcy when the news reached us that Laura's father, George, had died of a massive heart attack at the young age of fifty-six. I had not known him well, but remember him as an enormously kind man who bore a striking resemblance to George Bush. Laura was particularly close to her father and was quite devastated; Ian, who had come to know and love him, missed his wise counsel and constant support. I was so sad for them both. What a way to start their marriage, which we had all celebrated so joyously barely fifteen months previously.

Some happy events relieved the mood of all-pervading sadness. Back in March 1991, my children had offered me a special seventieth birthday present—a two-week cruise on the Nile with my sister, Vonnic, booked for November. Vonnic had originally suggested the idea to them, having taken up the study of hieroglyphics and Egyptian civilization in her retirement, after fifty years spent working as a gynecologist in the large clinic she founded. The trip of course had had to be postponed in 1991, but my children urged me to take it in the following November to give me a break from all the gloom. I had always dreamed of such a holiday and was finally persuaded to go. Vonnic and I flew from Paris to Cairo and I used my maiden name so that none of my traveling companions had the least idea who I was. It was a welcome diversion, and I came back to England revitalized and better able to face the final onslaughts of that miserable year.

The happiest event of 1992 was my eldest daughter Anne's wedding to her boyfriend, Laurens, whom Bob had only had time to meet once and liked. He was quickly adopted by the tribe and we all grew very fond of him. With good planning and a little luck they managed to marry quietly at Chelsea Registry Office in the late autumn, without any press intrusion, and their marriage was later blessed in Headington Hill Hall by the Reverend Donald Reeves of St. James's Piccadilly, where they both worship. The small wedding party was a sober but happy affair, despite the fact that it would be our last gathering as a family in the Hall and the last party I was to give there. A year later, Anne was to set a family record when she gave birth to Fleur, my tenth grandchild, at the age of forty-five.

A few days after the wedding celebration, a team from Sotheby's descended in force on Headington Hill Hall to catalog and clear its contents, which were to be sold by order of the receivers of Bob's estate. Under an agreement reached between them and my lawyer, half the proceeds would be theirs and half mine, except for a minimum amount of furniture and a few personal items I was allowed to keep. I had also received permission to buy back before the sale, at Sotheby's estimated medium value (which would be increased if the sale's overall value was higher than anticipated), some items I really could not part with: my piano, which I had purchased myself in 1950, and ancestral portraits and family heirlooms of great sentimental value. But the receivers did not allow me to buy back Bob's Military Cross. I was greatly saddened since it had meant so much to him, as it did to me and to our children. In a way, the enforced public sale of a decoration awarded for valor devalues the medal and what it stood for—commemorating the brave act of a young man who had risked his life for his country in 1945 and in so doing helped save the lives of others. Bob's medals in fact fetched over £14,000, although the man who bought them telephoned Sotheby's the next day to say that he had lost the MC and asked whether it had really been given to him! Sotheby's hardly dared tell me, although the buyer eventually found it. Other friends, concerned at my being forced to part with personal belongings, including most of my seventieth-birthday presents, attended the sale without my knowledge and bought back items they thought I would need or wish to keep. The following Christmas, I received a large parcel from some Italian friends of ours and, on opening it, found to my utter amazement some of the silver I thought had been lost to me for ever.

Not wishing to repeat the circus of the Maxwell House auction, I would have liked to put Christie's in charge of the Headington sale, but the receivers of Bob's estate insisted on Sotheby's, who entered into what became, in effect, a private auction between Christie's and themselves and were finally awarded the sale by the receivers at zero percent vendor's commission. To cap it all, Sotheby's then announced that since the auction of the Hall's contents was to take place in January, they needed to remove the furniture to their storage depot before Christmas and not, as I had hoped, early in the new year. It would take them two days and they wanted to start on December

22. That was what finally brought home to me that I would shortly have nowhere to live in England. It was out of the question for me to buy a house, and I hardly had enough money to rent one; above all I had no chance of finding anywhere a few days before Christmas. Although I could have gone to live in France, it was not practical and I wanted to be near the children. It was then that I went to see a friend to whom I explained the state of my finances and my immediate predicament—that I needed somewhere to stay in London for at least two years as from January to enable me to sort out my affairs, write my book and be of whatever help I could to the children, and particularly to Ian and Kevin. Although my friend had no particular reason to assist me, I was immensely moved by his response: "Don't say any more; I quite understand. I shall act and act quickly." He was as good as his word. Soon after Christmas, he generously offered me a two-bedroom house at a peppercorn rent, hidden away in the heart of the capital. Like my first benefactor in Paris, my second white knight acted decisively and with total elegance. I shall never forget it and I thanked God for supporting me through such generous friends.

Just before Christmas, the removers took over Headington Hill Hall and emptied my home of its contents of thirty-six years, leaving me with the few pieces of furniture I had repurchased from the estate or been allowed to keep by the receivers. That night was the saddest of all for me, and yet I was determined not to let myself go. As I wrote to a friend:

> I just sat at my piano, the only piece of furniture left at one end of the two long reception rooms and let the strings cry for me.
> They wept for the happy memories of this great house, for all the promises it held that will never be, for my scattered brood branded with the Maxwell stigma and fighting for survival, for my two handsome, valiant sons defending their reputations, trying to rebuild their shattered lives in a hostile climate and finally for the dispersal to the four winds of my most intimate possessions.
> In spite of its emptiness, the house remains a home, still infused with the love I lavished on it, and it will remain so until I and my soul leave it.

Late on Christmas Eve, in a state of exhaustion, Oping and I left for Kevin's home where we were once again to spend Christmas *en famille*. It had been a ghastly year, but we took comfort from the kindness and generosity of so many friends, as we read aloud the encouraging messages contained in the many Christmas cards and letters we had received. I remember sharing with them the following letter:

Do not refuse yourself a single tear—let them flow—their rivers washing away your anguish. Remember for your future the hell of Auschwitz, which Pisar, Primo Levi and other brave souls overcame. Have great pride in Kevin and Ian for their resilience, their courage, their love of you, the help they have given you unstintingly when they stand at the very gates of hell.

We returned to the Hall after Boxing Day and started to clear out the items which Sotheby's had determined were of little or no value and left behind. It was a question of disposing of all the accumulated possessions gathered over nearly fifty years of married life which might have "come in useful" one day. I decided to send most of them to Oxfam, only keeping a small amount of bric a brac for sentimental reasons. I was to stay in the Hall until New Year's Eve, when my own removers came to pack my personal belongings and take them to London.

But one last chore remained: to clean the house, a task which Oping and Robert Ord shared with me. It was a filthy job, but pride compelled me to leave everything impeccable. Shattered, we finally sat down to our "last supper" in the kitchen, sitting on borrowed office chairs at a small round table. The three of us shared two eggs, one tomato and a tin of sardines, and Oping managed to brew some tea, boiling water in a saucepan which had been left behind. We had a laugh when we remembered all the splendid meals of the past served from that very kitchen. Headington Hill Hall then stood empty. I couldn't help thinking back to my first visit there in 1959, when it had all looked so dilapidated and run-down. A great deal of love and energy had gone into its renovation; I was proud of the house I was leaving behind.

Whilst waiting to move into my new home, I planned to stay with Ian and Laura in London. Following the sale of their flat to pay Ian's mounting legal expenses, they had been fortunate enough to rent a house close to mine at a reasonable price. Just as I was preparing to leave the Hall for the last time, the telephone rang: it was a close friend inviting me to spend New Year with him and his wife in the country. Both of them had been unswerving in their friendship and had always kept up to date with events affecting me. With the perfect timing that only sensitive friendship can inspire, they knew instinctively that physically leaving the Hall would be the hardest day of all for me. Their invitation came at the moment I needed it most.

I arrived late on New Year's Eve at their welcoming Tudor house, comforted by their special friendship. I was tucked into bed almost like a child, being told, "You're very tired, have a good rest, sleep as long as you like in the morning." I had a severe cold and laryngitis and was so exhausted by all I had gone through recently that I didn't wake until eleven the next morning. My hosts had invited another couple, also good friends of mine, and this delightful reunion over lunch was followed by a bracing walk in the grounds of their home in the crisp New Year's weather. Later that day, my friend had a quiet talk with me about my affairs: not only did he give me sound advice, but he offered immediate practical help in the form of a loan and promised further assistance if necessary, a promise he has generously kept on a number of occasions since then. A third white knight had come to my rescue at a critical time, starting me off in the new year with renewed faith.

I left feeling refreshed and strengthened, my hopes for the future restored both by the kindness of my friends and by the news that Pandora had given birth safely to her fifth child, Madeleine. This tiny baby was to bring great comfort to both Kevin and Pandora; she was a sign of new life in all the decay that surrounded them. Tilly, their eldest, became a little mother overnight, helping Pandora to look after her.

In that first week of January 1993, I moved into my new home in London, with friends helping me to settle in and organize my belongings and even former Pergamon maintenance staff coming to lend a hand. It had been a long time since I had lived in a house on a city street and I felt terribly vulnerable at first, concerned about the reaction of my neighbors. They welcomed me with flowers and offers of help of all kinds and proved supportive and discreet. Late in life and battered, I discovered that I could still make friends; it was an enriching experience for me.

I settled down immediately to a strict work routine: I would get up at six, work till one o'clock, start again at two, carry on until late in the evening—or sometimes well into the night. In some ways, it was like working on my thesis all over again, but this time the pressures were far greater. I accepted few invitations, never read a newspaper or magazine unless it had a direct connection with my work and for weeks on end barely crossed the threshold of my house. The only outside commitments I kept were a series of lectures on the Holocaust and Christian-Jewish relations. Towards the end of the year, I was invited by Lehigh University in Pennsylvania to give an address on the occasion of the seventy-fifth birthday of Roy Eckardt, a Christian theologian who had been amongst the first to highlight Christianity's responsibility in the Holocaust. I was proud to honor his significant and courageous contribution to the post-Holocaust theological debate. I was also still involved on the fringes of preparations for the second Remembering for the Future conference in Berlin sponsored by the Group Relations Educational Trust (GRET) organization, which I attended in March 1994 accompanied by Ian's wife, Laura. With a strong American and German participation, it was a successful and well-organized gathering in the city where the infamous Wannsee Conference of 1942 had taken place, sanctioning the implementation of the Final Solution.

March 1993 was to prove another very tough month for the family. The judge presiding over Ian's court proceedings had finally passed judgment a few days before Christmas. Although he concluded that the case would have to go to a full trial as to 99.9 percent of Bishopsgate's claims, he made an interim order against Ian in the amount of £500,000. Ian had fought this judgment right up to the Court of Appeal but finally lost, and Bishopsgate petitioned for his bankruptcy. He could only pay such a sum if he was helped to raise the necessary funds, and so I became personally involved in this thankless task. During the week prior to the bankruptcy hearing, the £500,000 was raised via loans, many of them interest-free, from over fifty friends and family members from around the world who contributed individual sums to the fighting fund ranging from £750 to £50,000. Pergamon editors, former employees, friends of Bob's and of my children were amongst our supporters.

Borrowing funds from friends, however, is fraught with difficulty. I had naively believed that we would have no difficulty in borrowing such a sum. I could not recall anyone in trouble coming to Bob and going away empty-handed; his generosity was proverbial and it was not only financial. But I was now to discover a side of man's nature which Bob had never accustomed me to: meanness and cowardice. For every contributor, I faced countless put-downs. It is hard to bear immediate rejection from people one has considered to be longstanding friends. People who had been proud to be seen with me now argued that it would prejudice them commercially or socially if it became known they had lent me money: the Max Factor was again at work with devastating impact. Some rejections were as insensitive as those who proferred them: "You do not believe that I became a millionaire by giving money away?" Other wealthy friends to whom Bob had done signal favors, lending them money at difficult times, getting them out of trouble or saving their honor by putting his own on the line, sent me packing with the cowardly statement "I'll talk it over with my wife," or "I swore to Mary that I would never lend money again."

I was, however, received compassionately by many others, in particular by an American businessman who had got to know Bob during his brief ownership of the New York *Daily News* and admired his support for Israel. I had never met him before, but he was to become my fourth white knight, making the largest single contribution to the fighting fund. He has remained unfailingly generous to me ever since. That was perhaps the most surprising and uplifting aspect of this saga. I had learned from my work on the Holocaust that there is no set pattern for the courage to care. From my personal experience, I now know it to be true. Amazingly, we pulled it off and with five minutes to spare, a banker's draft for £500,000 was handed over on behalf of Ian to representatives of Bishopsgate's liquidators in the Bankruptcy Court. All the loans taken out at that time have since been repaid, in part from the proceeds of the sale of Headington Hill Hall to Oxford Brookes University.

Three years have passed since Bob died. Although I have had to cope with tremendous personal difficulties, not a day has gone by that I have not thought of how others have suffered in the aftermath of his death, a suffering made all the worse for being utterly unexpected and so undeserved. I find it enormously difficult to express adequately all I have felt and will feel for the rest of my days, in particular for the Group's pensioners and the appalling anxiety they have had to endure. One can only begin to imagine their sense of shock and bewilderment and their feelings of betrayal. The loss of financial security in old age is cruel indeed, destroying peace of mind so essential to the enjoyment of life and shattering dreams of a comfortable and well-deserved retirement. For the pensioners, only the restoration of their pension funds or, failing that, full compensation will alleviate their plight. Nothing short of this will do and nothing I can say or do now can possibly make up for the misery and heartache they have experienced and continue to suffer.

The fact that thousands of the Group's pensioners and former employees have been affected in this way puts my own very real difficulties into proper perspective. I knew all the long-serving staff in Oxford personally, having worked alongside them for many years, and was greatly moved by the dignity and fortitude they showed throughout the year I stayed in Oxford after the Group's collapse. Not one of them ever made an unkind remark to me. I cry for them; they were my friends and they have been so badly let down. Gilbert Richards, Pergamon's former deputy chairman and an employee of over thirty years standing, was two years away from retirement when the Group collapsed. He was left without employment, heavily in debt and with no guarantee of a pension. There were drivers like Eric Green, who was one year from retirement and had been with us in Oxford since we moved there; Brian Moss, the Group's fleet services director, who had come to us as a trainee; Malcolm Simmons, a skilled cabinet maker who had worked with complete loyalty for the firm for thirty years, all of them and their families—and countless others—found themselves faced with the severest financial difficulties. Many former colleagues have also suffered and still do—through no fault of their own—from the Max Factor backlash in their search for new employment, simply because of the opprobrium now attached to a man they had worked for, admired and respected. Even in America, where the Group companies' pension funds remained intact, many employees were made redundant and had great difficulty finding new jobs late in their careers. It is unbearable to think that Laszlo Straka, one of the longest-serving employees of the Group, who, back in 1970, along with Bob Miranda, Otto Rapp and Edward Gray, had mortgaged his own home to guarantee Bob's loan from Chemical Bank to buy back Pergamon Press, is now virtually bankrupt. How can I live with all these appalling realities? Where and when did it all start to go so terribly wrong? Did Bob's megalomania finally eclipse all common sense and suppress his extraordinary and well-honed instinct for survival?

People who worked for Bob were often asked, "What is he really like?" It was a question few of them could answer fully because he remained something of an enigma to all who knew or claimed to know him. He had an appealing aura of mystery, partly because he rarely talked about his past and partly because of his Protean character. Even for me, married to him for forty-six years, it is a difficult, if not impossible task, since I am naturally emotionally involved and lack the necessary distance and detachment to evaluate him dispassionately. The fact is that I loved him and a part of me still does. It is, moreover, a daunting task to attempt what might be seen by some as a definitive appraisal, when the controversies surrounding his life, particularly during the last years, are still so very much alive and remain unresolved.

There is no doubt that certain aspects of his character were already dominant in his youth, notably an unusual degree of self-reliance, to the extent that he trusted no one fully. The roots of this lack of trust can, I think, be traced a long way back in his life to the devastating events of the Holocaust; it is impossible to begin to understand the inner workings of Bob's character without a clear understanding of the legacy of that cataclysm for survivors. From an early age, he had to learn to rely entirely on himself, because the moment the Nazis' Final Solution was put into operation, Jews could no longer be sure of anyone or anything. You had to be brave and find your salvation within yourself, within the constraints of this lack of trust in others; you also had to take risks, more often than not gambling with your own life. Bob survived the war and overcame so many obstacles thereafter that he came to believe he was infallible and cleverer than any of those around him. This exaggerated opinion of his abilities was further enhanced by public recognition of his achievements, confirming the Chinese saying that "too much success is not an advantage because it blinds you to your own vulnerability," in Bob's case, hubris.

Beside this store of self-reliance, courage, early success and achievement, he harbored a deep sense of guilt and remorse. He was convinced that had he stayed at home, he could have saved the lives of his parents and younger siblings. Nothing he achieved in life would ever compensate for what he had not been able to accomplish—the rescue of his family. These feelings may have been largely unconscious, although he once told our son Philip, "Unlike you, I keep the door to my haunted inner chamber firmly closed." He was nevertheless driven by such a need to make amends and put right the wrongs of the world that his life was ever to be colored and affected by these ambitions. The outbreak of war gave him a mission to contribute to victory—thus avenging his people and eventually liberating them. It was to make him a brave and fanatical soldier, and his own self-confidence would help to save his life and the lives of the men under his command. After the war, his mission would be directed towards making his fortune as soon as possible, so as to be free to pursue his dreams through politics or, as it turned out, through communications and business. When you look back on his life, he was always driven by his "missions," which, although changing, were underpinned by a profound sense of guilt and the need to atone.

Once the war ended and civilian life resumed, Bob's salvation was the development of Pergamon Press. For as long as he remained personally and primarily involved with Pergamon, he was "contained" within a circle of learned senior academics who provided him with the security of wise and authoritative figures whom he admired and liked to emulate. The result was a highly successful enterprise with a mutually beneficial exchange for all parties. Although Bob was not conscious of it, this milieu may have contained similar elements to the scholarly and learned environment created by the rabbis of the yeshiva he attended in his youth. Those Pergamon years saw the best of Bob, admirably expressed by Thorne Shipley, professor of Vision Science and Theoretical Neuroscience at the University of Miami, in his condolence letter, written after the collapse of the Group:

Despite all that is being said widely in the press today, Bob Maxwell's greatest contribution remains wholly intact. It is . . . the absolutely extraordinary innovative way in which he expanded the publishing opportunities for innumerable modern scientists, in all nations and in all fields. . . . His genius in perceiving that science was growing exponentially after the war, and that scientists initially needed new and forthright and highly competent, indeed, uncompromisingly excellent means for expressing their ideas and presenting their findings to an ever-widening public, should not ever be lost sight of. He quite literally took field after field of modern science, and multiplied by several-fold the opportunities for private yet public communication within them in journal after journal after journal.

With all the adverse publicity being bruited about concerning Bob's newspaper activities, the world should not forget his absolutely fine, unimpeachable, and clearly immense contribution to modern science. Though he was not himself a scientist . . . he perceived our needs, anticipated our moves and contributed to the world's effort in the scientific advancement of knowledge in a manner absolutely unique in all of publishing history. . . . There are thousands of scientists around this world who owe a very, very special debt to him. Of that integrity and of that extraordinary achievement, nothing can ever deprive his memory.

Three years after Bob regained control of Pergamon, he relaunched it on a profitable path. It was then that he broke free from the confines of the stable and familiar world of scientific publishing to seize fresh business opportunities. This new direction was symbolized by the move of his headquarters from the sleepy academic atmosphere of Oxford to the cut-throat world of the City of London when he gained control of the British Printing Corporation. It was a decisive move away from the relatively human scale of the family business, Pergamon, based at Headington Hill Hall, into the demanding and impersonal world of the printing magnate, living in high-rise corporate headquarters, involved in intense struggles with trade unions and with responsibility for scores of factories and businesses in the UK and overseas, employing a huge workforce. The daily rhythm and overall scale of Bob's business life was drastically and irrevocably changed. His already busy schedule became insanely hectic as he traveled throughout his far-flung Group, making increased use of helicopters and private planes. Simultaneously, he ceased to live full time in Oxford and established a separate home base in London, thus diminishing the steadying influence I could still exert over him. Increasingly, his family life came to be entirely centered around the business and all of us contributed unconsciously to his personality cult. This radical change in Bob's business and personal lifestyle was further compounded when he acquired Mirror Group Newspapers and took an even bigger step away from the cocoon of Oxford and Pergamon. It is true that he remained as Pergamon's chairman, but by then he was running the company by telephone and sporadic visits. He had joined the big league of press tycoons.

Although Bob was fond of saying that "printing was a morning business and newspapers an evening business," the fact is, to quote a long-term employee, that "he drove himself harder than any man I have ever met." By the mid-1980s, he was undertaking a punishing work schedule for a man of his age. He still got up between 5 and 6 A.M. and worked right through the day till 8 P.M., then dined either alone or with business colleagues before working again till 11 P.M. or midnight. Despite his widely recognized achievements and successes, first with BPCC and then with the Mirror Group, Bob was still immensely impatient to take on more, perhaps in a desperate rush to make up for his "lost decade" of the seventies. His goal became even more ambitious: to build one of the world's top ten media companies before the turn of the century. In 1988 he tried to achieve it at a stroke when he purchased the giant American publishing group Macmillan.

By the end of the 1980s, the combination of his enormous financial muscle and political power through newspapers and latterly television resulted in his courting and being courted by the world's political and business leaders. It allowed him to launch many new enterprises and carry out a staggering number of business transactions. There were now many opportunities for his creativity as well as for his vanity—in 1987 he was to change the name of BPCC, his publicly quoted company, to Maxwell Communication Corporation. He became an ever greater world traveler and acquired publicity on a scale he had never known before. He enjoyed the adulation, the challenges, the excitement, and eventually became obsessed with power.

In strictly financial terms, 1987 saw Bob at the height of his career, an extremely wealthy man who had created a fortune in excess of £1 billion and who was respected and feared by his peers. Now, after the debacle, it would be easy—in fact too easy—to dismiss that measure of success and deny that there was any positive vision behind it. For Bob's vision was informed by noble ideals, which made the collapse of his Group all the more poignant. He had set himself three central "missions" during the last ten years of his life: to build a world-class multimedia communications company;

through this and his own diplomatic efforts, to contribute to world peace and, by the consolidation of Israel's international standing, to peace in the Middle East in particular; and through the Maxwell Foundation, a charity he established, to return to scientific and medical research the profits created by his businesses. Bob frequently referred to Armand Hammer's role in the 1920s and 1930s in developing economic and political relations between the former USSR and the West and believed that through communications, he would be in a similar position in the 1980s and 1990s to make a contribution to dissolving the legacy of the cold war.

Regarding Israel, many journalists have written that Bob was a late convert to Israel and the Jewish cause. This is not true. As early as 1957 he wrote to me:

As for my thoughts, I am dreaming about the help which I would like to give to the State of Israel to enable it to become one of the world leaders and a paradise on earth. My dreams very often revolve on this one line. This evening they were brought about by the big opening headline in the American journal, reading in red letters ISRAEL DESTINED TO LEAD MIDDLE EAST IN 10 YEARS, followed by a dispatch from the paper on Hearst, who is there on a visit justifying the headline.

By the mid-1980s, well on the way to fulfilling the first of his missions, Bob began actively to promote and carry through the remaining two. He became the largest private investor in Israel, and, more significant, he successfully influenced Mikhail Gorbachev's perception of that country, helping to convince him to allow Russian Jews to emigrate there, as he was also to help dissuade Russia from siding with the Arabs in the Gulf War. His crucial role in these matters demonstrated his talent for sophisticated diplomatic missions, and he would have been enormously gratified by the progress which has been made in bringing peace to certain parts of the Middle East over the last year.

Israel's former president Chaim Herzog told me recently that during his term of office, he gave a state dinner in honor of Gorbachev during the Russian leader's first visit to Israel a couple of years ago. During dinner, President Herzog asked his guest which of the many leaders he had met in the West had impressed him. Without any hesitation, Gorbachev answered that Robert Maxwell was one of the most impressive men he had ever met, despite all that had since been said and written about him. He added, "Your people owe a great deal to him." Gorbachev's change of attitude towards Israel was probably Bob's greatest diplomatic success.

Proud as I am of that achievement by Bob and of other lesser ones in the same diplomatic sphere, it is regrettable that these added extra fuel to Bob's already unbalanced opinion of himself. Perhaps he thought that his real and valuable contribution in such matters was sufficient reason to neglect his business. Flying like an eagle above the clouds in his own private jet and being received by the world's leaders made him feel even more superior to mere mortals and to the needs and constraints of ordinary family life. It was a dangerous drug for someone who was already on such a powerful stimulant as megalomania. In some ways, it was a miracle that he coped with everything and that everyone coped with him for so long. One way he channeled the terrifying stress of the last years of his life was by being still more demanding of his employees and family. Particularly in the last three years, he was even more obsessed and dictatorial, and less self-disciplined—in his use of foul language, for instance—than at any other time in his life. Food was another area in which his habits deteriorated from those of a gourmet to a combination of compulsion and greed. But his behavior—which almost constituted a caricature of the gross tycoon—needs to be understood against the background of his workaholic nature and incessant traveling.

For a while this disturbing lifestyle was accompanied by great business success, although Bob's physical health deteriorated alarmingly at the same time, with frequent bronchial infections aggravated by increasing hypoxemia, which was itself made worse by constant air travel. His obesity, which he failed to control despite repeated efforts, increased the strain imposed on his system. He was plagued by constant headaches and insomnia. All these clinical symptoms made him terribly irritable and also provoked bouts of sleepiness during the working day, which he had never suffered before. By the end of his life, he had lived for over five years in this dangerously unhealthy state, with the result that in his final months he was suffering from profound physical exhaustion. Yet he remained very much the captain on the bridge, in total control of the vessel, without an admiralty board to supervise his conduct.

With hindsight, and based on my detailed research into his medical history, I now understand that what I attributed to his consciously beastly behavior towards me was a consequence of the colossal stress he was constantly subjected to, which fueled his irritability and caused him to lose his self-control at the slightest provocation. In his final year, Bob's decline and wretched end coincided with tremendous pressures on the Maxwell Group, which was to survive its founder by a mere month.

For all of that, I can only reflect on the tragedy that his death represents. My primary feelings are ones of immense pity that a man of talent who had achieved so much should have unleashed such an avalanche of misery through his death, not only for his family and friends but for the many thousands of people who were dependent on the survival and prosperity of his businesses. For me personally, it was to precipitate a painful process of rethinking and analysis of our life together, to understand where and how things started to go wrong and whether I could have done anything to change the course of events. As long as I had allowed Bob to turn my love, that "most indecent of all obsessions,"[4] into a permanent act of duty which ruled my life, I had never been free. It took me years to achieve it, but I finally understood the need to establish a zone of personal freedom, which I did through my university studies and work on the Holocaust. Although I found contentment in my work, if I had really exercised my own mind and had the courage, I should have separated from him years before. The fact is, however, that I did love the man and felt sorry for him in later years; I decided that leaving him would amount to disloyalty and that my duty was to stand by him, come what may. In so doing, although I was unable to anticipate the final dramatic end, I had condemned myself to "keep on rowing, not until I reach port but until I reach my grave."[5]

I am fortunate indeed that God has endowed me with physical strength and the capacity to resist the fiercest blows. Fortunate, too, to be surrounded by seven loving children and their spouses, ten grandchildren and a large number of supportive friends. In spite of all that has happened and may still happen, good or ill, as Sören Kierkegaard said, "Life can only be understood backwards, but it must be lived forwards."

---

4. Colleen McCullough, *An Indecent Obsession* (London: Macdonald & Co., Ltd, 1981), p. 314.

5. Mme. de Staël.